Beginning SQL Server for Developers

Fourth Edition

bin Dewson

Apress®

Beginning SQL Server for Developers

ISBN-13 (pbk): 978-1-4842-0281-4

ISBN-13 (electronic): 978-1-4842-0280-7

Managing Director: Welmoed Spahr
Lead Editor: Jonathan Gennick
Technical Reviewer: Rodney Landrum
Editorial Board: Steve Anglin, Louise Corrigan, Jim DeWolf, Jonathan Gennick, Robert Hutchinson, Michelle Lowman, James Markham, Matthew Moodie, Jeff Olson, Jeffrey Pepper, Douglas Pundick, Ben Renow-Clarke, Gwenan Spearing, Steve Weiss
Coordinating Editor: Jill Balzano
Copy Editors: Ann Dickson and April Rondeau
Compositor: SPi Global
Indexer: SPi Global
Artist: SPi Global
Cover Designer: Anna Ishchenko

Distributed to the book trade worldwide by Springer Science+Business Media New York, 233 Spring Street, 6th Flo New York, NY 10013. Phone 1-800-SPRINGER, fax (201) 348-4505, e-mail orders-ny@springer-sbm.com, or visit www.springeronline.com. Apress Media, LLC is a California LLC and the sole member (owner) is Springer Science + Business Media Finance Inc (SSBM Finance Inc). SSBM Finance Inc is a Delaware corporation.

For information on translations, please e-mail rights@apress.com, or visit www.apress.com.

Apress and friends of ED books may be purchased in bulk for academic, corporate, or promotional use. eBook versions and licenses are also available for most titles. For more information, reference our Special Bulk Sales–e Licensing web page at www.apress.com/bulk-sales.

Any source code or other supplementary material referenced by the author in this text is available to readers www.apress.com/9781484202814. For detailed information about how to locate your book's source code, go www.apress.com/source-code/.

As always I dedicate this book to my wonderful family. To my three kids, Cameron, Ellen, and Scott, who have been brilliant and wonderful and whom I am very, VERY proud of in many ways. And they are such great kids because they have what can only be termed the best mother kids can have, right there, helping, loving, and, yes, screaming at them when needed. Julie, I love you more than I love my Irn-Bru, rugby, and lemon meringue pie . . . and you know how much that means to me! It is to them this book is wholly dedicated.

—Robin Dewson

Contents at a Glance

Contents

About the Author

Robin Dewson has been hooked on programming ever since he bought his first computer in 1980, a Sinclair ZX80. His first major application of his own was a Visual FoxPro program that could be used to run a Fantasy League system. It was at this point he met up with a great help in his PC development life, Jon Silver at Step One Technologies, where in return for training he helped Jon with some other Visual FoxPro applications. From there, realizing that the marketplace for Visual FoxPro was limited, he decided to learn Visual Basic and SQL Server.

Starting out with SQL Server 6.5, Robin soon moved to SQL Server 7 and Visual Basic 5, and became involved in developing several applications for clients both in the UK and in the United States. From there, he has moved through each version of SQL Server through to the current one. Robin now specializes in databases and C# in both client and server side coding. Robin can be contacted at robin@fat-belly.com or at www.fat-belly.com.

About the Technical Reviewer

Rodney Landrum went to school to be a poet and a writer. And then he graduated, so that dream was crushed. He followed another path, which was to become a professional in the fun filled world of Information Technology. He has worked as a systems engineer, UNIX and network admin, data analyst, client services director, and finally as a database administrator. The old hankering to put words on paper, while paper still existed, got the best of him, and in 2000, he began writing technical articles, some creative and humorous, some quite the opposite. In 2010 he wrote *The SQL Server Tacklebox*, a title his editor disdained, but a book closest to the true creative potential he sought; he wanted to do a full book without a single screen shot. He promises his next book will be fiction or a collection of poetry, but that has yet to transpire.

Acknowledgments

In every book there are so many people to thank either for helping with the book, or helping me in my role: Here, much like an Oscar-winning speech (without the tears), are my expressions of thanks to all those who helped: To Andrew and all at Host-It.co.uk, my ISP who give excellent support with the websites I run. Some great friends including Jane Harper and Mark Smith, Mark and Trudy Mather and the Harper family for making rugby on a Saturday so enjoyable. Many work colleagues including Anthony "Jock" Jawad, Aubrey Lomas, Harry Toland, Jason Oates, Steve Nicklin, James McVey, Andy Bennett, Richard Barclay, Ian Phillips, Guy Batey, Darren Skinner, the great Noel Morgala, Syed Yasir Shah, Yao Wu, and the rest of the team at Nomura; and Ian Howell and Nick Sharp for some great evenings out, Robert McMillan (Toad), a great mate from college with whom I got back in touch after many years—each in their own way have helped me over the months and years. Also thanks to Sams Species Reptile Sanctuary samsspecies.yolasite.com, especially to Sally Shapter for being a brilliant person with reptiles and their rescue and then safe keeping, Northampton Reptile Centre, especially Sam Shapter, Lois, and Ant Hook and Gary Rolfe for their time with my dragons and chameleon. Also thanks to "Guinness" John Mason and Richard Lowther for their help, input, and time with the www.rolling-maul.com and www.hospital-pass.com websites. Of course all the people at Apress and my long time friend Jonathan Gennick, and the others who have helped like Jill Balzano, a great person to keep me motivated and say the right things. And the book would be nothing without the brilliantly talented technical editor Rodney Landrum.

Then, of course, there are my mum and late dad who put up with not watching television while I commandeered it for my personal computer in 1980 and onward. I owe them so much and love them to bits. Without them I wouldn't be doing what I am doing today and I might be stuck in a job I didn't enjoy as much as I do this.

—Robin Dewson

Introduction

Beginning SQL Server for Developers is for those people who see themselves as becoming either developers, database administrators, or a mixture of both, but have yet to tread that path with SQL Server. This edition of my book is for readers who wish to learn and develop on either the free version of SQL Server, SQL Server Express, or with either the trial or licensed versions of SQL Server.

Whether you have no knowledge of databases, or have knowledge of desktop databases such as MS Access, or even come from a server-based background such as Oracle, DB2, Sybase, then this book will provide you with the insight to get up and running with SQL Server.

Right from the start, your basic knowledge will be expanded, and you will soon be moving from being a beginner through to a competent and professional developer. It is the aim of this book to cater to a wide range of developers, from those who prefer to use the graphical interface for as much work as possible, to those who want to become more adept at using SQL Server's programming language, T-SQL. Where practical, each method of using SQL Server is demonstrated, explained, and expanded so that you can evaluate what works best in your situation. You will also find a chapter on how to work with Excel, .NET and Java, and incorporate them with T-SQL into your programming.

There are plenty of examples within the book of every action, along with details about the security of your data. You will learn the best way to complete a task and even how to make the correct decision when there are two or more choices that can be made. And let us not forget that SQL Server can work with in-memory tables and natively compiled stored procedures.

Once you reach the end of this book, you will be able to design and create solid and reliable database solutions competently and proficiently.

CHAPTER 1

■ ■ ■

Overview and Installation

Welcome to *Beginning SQL Server for Developers*. This book has been written for those who are interested in learning how to create solutions with Microsoft SQL Server, but have no prior knowledge of SQL Server. You may well have had exposure to other database management systems (DBMSs), such as MySQL, Oracle, or Microsoft Access, but SQL Server uses different interfaces and has a different way of working compared to much of the competition. The aim of this book is to bring you quickly up to a level at which you are developing competently with SQL Server. This book is specifically dedicated to beginners and to those who at this stage wish to use only SQL Server. You may find this book useful for understanding the basics of other database management systems in the marketplace, especially when working with T-SQL within this book. Many DBMSs use an ANSI-standard SQL, so moving from SQL Server to Oracle, Sybase, and so on, will be a great deal easier after reading this book.

This chapter answers the following questions:

- Why should I use SQL Server?
- How do I know whether my hardware meets the requirements?
- Can I just confirm that I have the right operating system?
- What can I do with SQL Server?

We will also look at installing your chosen edition and cover the following topics:

- Installing SQL Server on a Windows platform
- Options not installed by default
- Where to install SQL Server physically
- Multiple installations on one computer
- How SQL Server runs on a machine
- How security is implemented
- Logon IDs for SQL Server, especially the sa (system administrator) logon

Why Should I Use SQL Server?

The following discussion is from my point of view, and although it no doubt differs from that of others, the basis of the discussion holds true. SQL Server faces competition from other database management systems, not only from other Microsoft products such as Microsoft Access, but also from competitors such as Oracle, Sybase, DB2, and Informix, to name a few.

You can find Microsoft Access on a large number of PCs. The fact that it is packaged with some editions of Office and has been around for a number of years in different versions of Office has helped make this DBMS ubiquitous; in fact, a great number of people actually do use the software. Unfortunately, it does have its limitations when it comes to scalability, speed, and flexibility, but for many small, in-house systems, these areas of concern are not an issue since such systems do not require major DBMS functionality. To this end, Microsoft Access can be the correct solution.

Now you come to the serious competition: Oracle and Sybase. Oracle is seen as perhaps the market leader in the DBMS community, and it has an extremely large user base. There is no denying it is a great product to work with, if somewhat more complex to install and administer than SQL Server; it fits well with large companies that require large solutions. It also forms the backbone of some major software packages. There are many parts to Oracle, which make it a powerful tool, including scalability and performance. It also provides flexibility in that you can add on tools as you need them, making Oracle more accommodating in that area than SQL Server. For example, SQL Server forces you to install the .NET Framework on your server regardless of whether you use the new .NET functionality. However, Oracle isn't as user-friendly from a developer's point of view in areas like its ad hoc SQL Query tool and its XML and web technology tools. It is also less straightforward in how to build up a complete database solution. Other drawbacks include its cost and the complexity involved in installing and running it effectively. However, you will find that it is used extensively by web search engines even though SQL Server could and does work just as effectively. SQL Server has always been a one-purchase solution, such that (providing you buy the correct version or license) tools that allow you to analyze your data or copy data from one data source such as Excel into SQL Server will all be "in the box." With Oracle, on the other hand, you have to purchase more options for every additional feature you want.

Then there is Sybase. It is very much like SQL Server with similar SQL commands and statements (this is the code used to work with the database and its data) although not as feature-rich. There is a GUI for Sybase although it is separate from the DBMS installation and a separate product. You will find that many Sybase developers use command-line commands or third-party tools.

Sybase is also mainly found on Unix/Linux although there is a Windows version. It is very fast and very robust, and it is rebooted only once, or maybe twice, a year. Being hosted on Unix, Linux, or Solaris also helps with the reduction in reboots because you don't have the monthly Windows patching. However, Sybase isn't as command-and feature-rich as SQL Server. SQL Server has a more extensive programming language and functionality that is more powerful than Sybase.

Each DBMS has its own SQL syntax although they all will have the same basic SQL syntax, known as the ANSI-92 standard. This means that the syntax for retrieving data and such is the same from one DBMS to another. However, each DBMS has its own special syntax to maintain it—trying to use a feature from this SQL syntax in one DBMS may not work, or may work differently, in another.

SQL Server for me is the best choice in the DBMS marketplace. There are versions of SQL Server that can be installed and be small enough for a handful of users and versions large enough for the largest corporations, and there is even a version for Cloud computing. There is also a specific Development Edition, which gives almost the full functionality of the most expensive version, the Enterprise Edition, but for a tiny fraction of the price. It has the ability to scale up and deal with terabytes of data without many concerns. As you will see, it is easy to install; it comes as one complete package for most of its functionality, with a simple install to be performed for the remaining areas if required.

Now that you know the reasons behind choosing SQL Server, you need to know which versions of SQL Server are available for purchase, what market each version is aimed at, and which version will be best for you, including which version can run on your machine.

SQL Server Editions

Before buying this book, you will have perhaps found the Microsoft SQL Server home page, taken a look at the different editions of SQL Server, and noticed that there are several choices to make. This book focuses on the Development Edition as this is the edition to work with prior to moving into industry. There are, however, many developers who will use the Express Edition because it is a free version that is ideal for smaller developments and,

where required, the change or non-existence of functionality is detailed. The differences between the two editions that this book will cover are the in-memory held data and options concerning backing up and restoring data. Other editions, where relevant, may be mentioned in passing.

The editions you have are as follows:

- Enterprise: the most powerful edition of SQL Server often used by corporations that will be running SQL Server on at least one powerful server; fully functional

- Developer: the same functionality as Enterprise but not licensed for production

- Business Intelligence (BI): tools and feature set orientated to building and browsing business intelligence based data; has a feature set that is reduced or not available where the feature is designed for transactional based data

- Standard: reduced functionality and memory allowed to be used is limited to 128GB; ideal for corporations that don't work with very large data sets due to the reduction useful functionality

- Web: ideal for web \-based corporations that work with smaller online-based data sets; also useful for ISPs to offer to clients to build their web sites off

- Azure: SQL Server is provided as a service in the cloud where you are supplied with a pre-installed SQL Server instance and you buy compute and memory

- Express: ideal for small companies and for those wishing to develop small database applications such as students, charity organizations, and small work-at-home developers. This edition is free to license.

If you are planning to read this book with an Express Edition of SQL Server, either the Express Edition with Tools or Express Edition with Advanced Services is required.

The Example

In order to demonstrate SQL Server fully, we will develop a system for a financial company that will have features such as banking, purchasing shares, and regular buying, including a unit trust savings plan. This is an application that could fit into a large organization or, with very minor modifications, could be used by a single person to record their own banking and financial transactions.

The book builds on this idea and develops the example, demonstrating how to take an idea and formulate it into a design with the correct architecture. It should be said, though, that the example will be the bare minimum to make it run, as I don't want to detract from SQL Server and why you have bought the book.

■ **Note** It would be possible to use the Microsoft standard example that can be downloaded; however, this detracts from many areas that, as a developer, you need to be aware of and be confident dealing with. Building an example from the very beginning is the only way to learn SQL Server.

If you are coming from another database, you may find that you can skip parts of the example building.

I also use a tool from Red Gate Software to generate some random test data. You do not need this tool for the book as the random data are available for download from the Apress web site and my own web site. But before you can get to this point, you need to install SQL Server.

Installation

This chapter will guide you through the installation process of the Developer Edition, although virtually all that you see will be in every edition. Reporting Services is only available within the Advanced Services Edition of the Express Edition, which is not covered within the book. Security is also different in the Express and Web Editions, as will be noted later. Microsoft offers a 180-day trial version at www.microsoft.com/sql, which you can use to follow along with the examples in this book if you don't already have SQL Server and are not ready to purchase. However, the Developer Edition is very cheap to purchase a license to use compared to other editions, and so, by selecting this version, it is not cost-prohibitive to continue past the trial period.

This book will cover many of the options and combinations of features that can be included within an installation. A number of different tools are supplied with SQL Server to be included with the installation. You will look at these tools so that a basic understanding of what they are will allow you to decide which to install.

Installation covers a great many different areas:

- Security issues

- Different types of installation—whether this is the first installation and instance of SQL Server or a subsequent instance, for development, test, or production

- Custom installations

- Installing only some of the products available

Most of these options will be covered so that by the end of the chapter, you can feel confident and knowledgeable enough to complete any subsequent installations that suit your needs.

As mentioned in the Editions section of the chapter, this book uses the Developer Edition because it is most likely the edition you will use as a developer since it doesn't have all the operating system requirements of the Enterprise Edition. I will denote in the installation when a feature is not available in other editions. Insert the CD or download and extract SQL Server from the web site for the Microsoft SQL Server edition of your choice or mount an ISO image as a virtual drive on your computer. The installation is based on a local computer with only a C: hard drive. I will also mention installation options concerning servers and network storage where appropriate.

Install

Ensure that you have logged on to the machine with administrative rights so that you are allowed to create files and folders on your machine, which is obviously required for installation to be successful. If you are using a CD-ROM and the installation process does not automatically start, open up Windows Explorer and double-click setup.exe, found at the root level of the CD-ROM. If you are not using a CD-ROM, double-click the installer executable that you downloaded. This may expand the downloaded single file to a folder with the setup.exe within it.

■ **Tip** For installation on multiple computers, it is possible to create an automatic build script to ensure all servers are built to the same company standard. I do not cover this topic, but it is an option to be aware of.

You are now presented with the installation screen for Microsoft .NET Framework if it is not already installed. .NET is a framework that Microsoft created that allows programs written in VB .NET, C#, and other programming languages to have a common compile set for computers. SQL Server uses .NET for some of its own internal work, but also, as a developer, you can write .NET code in any of Microsoft's .NET languages and include this within SQL Server databases. With SQL Server 2008 and later, there is also the ability to query the database using .NET and LINQ rather than native T-SQL, although for clarity the code would be converted to T-SQL.

You are then presented with the SQL Server Installation Center. This screen, shown in Figure 1-1, deals with all setup processes, including new installations, upgrades from previous versions of SQL Server, and many other options for maintaining SQL Server installations.

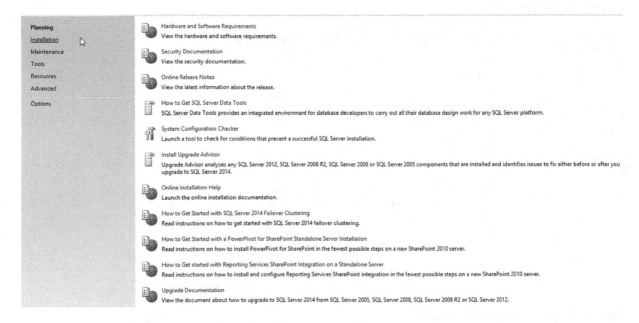

Figure 1-1. *Beginning the install with the Installation Center*

When you click Installation on the left-hand menu, the options within the main menu alter and you can now select the New SQL Server stand-alone installation or add features to an existing installation item (at the top of the Installation Center); then SQL Server installation starts. The first few screens may be different depending on the edition you are installing.

The first screen asks for an edition and product key. If you have a product key, such as that for the Developers Edition, you would enter it now. Whatever your selection you wish to use here, click Next. You will then be asked to accept the license terms. Then click Next. You then come to the system configuration check known as the Global Rules Check, as you see in Figure 1-2. This is my setup support rules screen, but your screen may slightly differ depending on operating systems and service packs. It will only be shown if you have action points; otherwise, the SQL Server installation process will continue automatically. Its main function is to check that the PC meets the hardware and software requirements, that there are no outstanding reboots, and that you are logged in as an administrator.

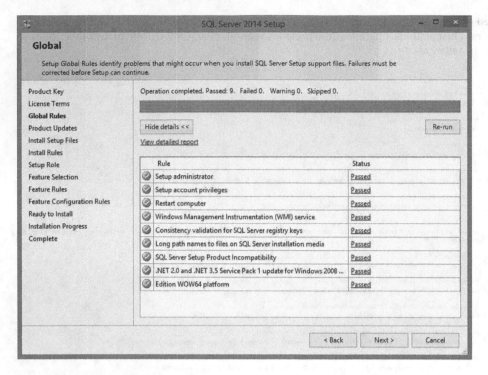

Figure 1-2. *System configuration check*

SQL Server will then attempt to connect to the Internet and check for any product updates and service packs. It is recommended that all updates and service packs should be installed; however, these should not be applied directly to a production install without an install on a development server and your code and application tested against any updates first. Occasionally, a service pack or product update can alter functionality. If there are no updates or Internet connection is not possible, the installation process will automatically move to the next stage, Install Rules.

After the setup, install files are installed. The second set of checks that are performed continues to ensure that the install will proceed without failures. These second checks are more to ensure that SQL Server itself will install and perform once installed, unlike the first set of checks, which was related to the computer and operating system requirements.

You will notice in Figure 1-3 that there is one warning triangle with a warning message in the screenshot; you may have more depending on your computer setup. SQL Server will still install. The warning at this point is unlikely to be of concern; however, if you are installing onto a machine that you will be accessing from a second machine either on a network or by the Internet, then the message is indicating that you have Windows Firewall enabled. If you want to connect using TCP/IP, then you need to have the correct ports open and enabled for use. Click Next.

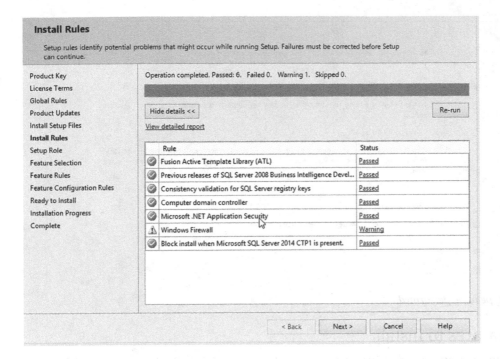

Figure 1-3. System configuration checks

Setup Role

You will now be presented with the Setup Role screen in Figure 1-4. There are three possible methods of installation that can be chosen. The first option allows you to select which specific features are to be installed on the computer. The second option allows Reporting Services to use powerful techniques and tools called PowerPivot to deal with data held in an Analysis Services database, or Business Intelligence database, in conjunction with SharePoint. SharePoint can be found in large organizations that use it to store generated reports that can be accessed in a secure and controlled method by users. The final option is instructing the setup process to install every feature, tool, SDK, and SQL Server service that is available. You will use the SQL Server Feature Installation option. Click Next.

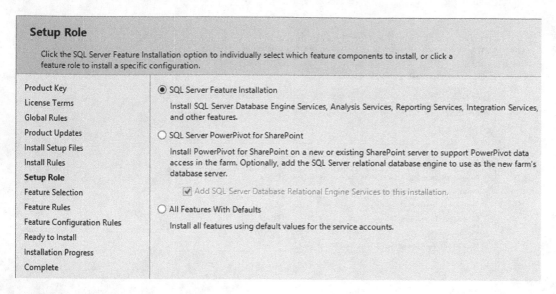

Figure 1-4. *Installation type to be performed*

Choosing the Features to Install

You now come to the Feature Selection screen, where you have to make some decisions. As shown in Figure 1-5, only certain options have been selected, and these are the options that will be discussed and demonstrated within this book. You can select all of the options so that you do not need to install features as you progress your SQL Server knowledge or if this will be your development instance where you'll be testing every aspect of SQL Server away from any development of projects taking place. No matter what you select, you can always run the installation process later and add features. I will go through all of the options in this chapter, but the options in Figure 1-5 are the ones I have used for this book.

Figure 1-5. *Selecting the features to install*

Let's briefly take a look at each of these components:

- *Database Engine Services*: This is the core for SQL Server, and this option installs the main engine, data files, and so forth, to make SQL Server run.

 - *SQL Server Replication*: When you want to send data changes not only on the database it is being executed on, but also on a similar database that has been built to duplicate those changes, you can use this option to replicate the changes to that database.

 - *Full-Text Search*: This option lets you allow searching of the text within your database. This is a very useful tool for searching documents or other large text-based data and could be used if you were building a search engine.

 - *Data Quality Services*: This tool allows you or users to inspect the data within your database for data quality. You can inspect your data for duplication and quality from a reference database using the client tool to inspect the results.

- *Analysis Services*: Using this tool, you can take a set of data, slice and dice, and analyze the information contained. Analysis Services has received a great deal of attention from Microsoft in the last few years as it improves and expands the ability to aggregate data and perform analysis functions. It is ideal for taking data such as sales figures and allowing you to see these by product, by sales region, by client, and by any other method that could be analyzed.

- *Reporting Services*: There are three different features for this service. One feature is installed for each SQL Server instance, and then two options are installed once and can be used by any installed instance on the server. Reporting Services allows reports to be produced from SQL Server instead of using third-party tools such as Crystal Reports. It is used by both SQL Server and Analysis Services.

- *Data Quality Client*: This is the client tool that allows you or users to inspect the data within your database for data quality. You can inspect your data for duplication and quality from a reference database using the client tool to inspect the results.

- *Client Tools Connectivity*: Some of these tools sit on the client machine and provide the graphical interface to SQL Server, while others sit on the client and work with SQL Server via tools such as Visual Studio, Excel, third-party tools and utilities such as iSQL, and a basic command prompt tool. Client Tools Connectivity is the option you would package up for rollout to developers to sit on their machines.

- *Integration Services*: This is a very powerful tool as it allows you to build packages of processes to complete actions, such as importing data from other data sources and manipulating the data. You will see Integration Services in action in Chapter 8 when you look at building a backup maintenance plan.

- *Client Tools Backwards Compatibility*: Previous versions of SQL Server used different tools and methods to access data from the client tools. This option will install these tools so that if you are accessing—as an example—Integration Services on a SQL Server 2005 database that was called DTS, then you will be able to do this.

- *Client Tools SDK*: This is a software development kit for client tools that Microsoft uses.

- *Documentation Components*: This is the help system. If you need more information, clarification, or extra detail on any area of SQL Server, this is the area to turn to.

- *Management Tools*: The basic option will install the components required for this book. There will be a graphical interface called Management Studio as well as the ability to write SQL at the command prompt. The complete option expands Management Studio to have the ability to interact with Reporting Services and Integration Services, as well as installing tools to help in performance monitoring of your SQL Server. You would tend to deploy the complete set to developers and the basic set to those dedicated to supporting a system, who need only to run queries against your data to solve production problems and to retrieve and execute ad hoc queries.

- *Distributed Replay Controller*: Distributed replay allows for workloads to be distributed over one or more clients to try to simulate a real-life workload on SQL Server. This option is the controller of the replay.

- *Distributed Replay Client*: This is the client software that would be used on one or more clients to send through a distributed replay of SQL Server actions to the controller. You would install this on each client that you want to partake in the replay.

- *SQL Client Connectivity SDK*: SQL Native Client provides the ability to connect to SQL Server with some limitation to the functionality available from development systems. In general, from .NET and other similar languages, you would connect to SQL Server using the SQL Server ADO.NET library. If you are accessing SQL Server from a COM-based language such as the C or C++ programming languages, you would look to install this option.

- *Master Data Services (MDS)*: If you have multiple servers used within your organization for different data repositories, for example, one database for clients, one database for orders, another database for delivery information, then by using MDS you can bring the data together in one master data hub. Each of the databases has a valid use in its own right and does belong as a separate entity; however, an organization's management or decision makers may need to see the whole picture to assess how the company is performing.

The locations shown in Figure 1-5 demonstrate the likely setup on a server although if you have a local machine with multiple drives, placing the data files away from the main system hard drive is preferable. The instance root directory folder in this example is named based on the next step in the setup process; however, I am using just the C: drive as this is the likely setup you will be using.

Of these components, Replication, Full-Text Searching, Analysis Services, SQL Server Data Tools, and Master Data Services fall outside the scope of this book, and I touch upon Integration Services only as mentioned.

■ **Note** At this point, SQL Server no longer has the option to install the sample databases. You can download the samples from www.codeplex.com/SqlServerSamples.

Naming the Instance

After a final check that nothing will block the installation via the Feature Rules check, you are ready to start defining the the options selected earlier.

It is possible to install SQL Server more than once on one computer. This could happen when you have a powerful server that has enough resources such as memory and processor to cope with two or three different applications running. ISPs will have this setup when you request SQL Server, as this is their and your cheapest option and allows SQL Server to be easily maintained by them. These different applications may be required to have their own SQL Server databases. Each install is called an *instance*. You are now at the stage that you can name the instance of the install. Each instance must have a unique name attached to it, although "no name," known as a *default instance*, is also classified as a unique name.

Naming instances is important as the first step to organizing your environments. For example, you may have an instance for development, another instance for system testing, and finally one for user testing. It is bad practice to share production server hardware with anything but production databases. If you share your hardware and if you have a rogue development action that occurs and crashes the server, you will stop production from running. Although you would have to make this decision at the start of the install process you are currently going through, it is a useful second reminder here when naming the instance to give some indication of what environment it is for. I tend to use DEV1, STG1, UAT1, and PRD1. The reason for the number is to cater for the scenario for replication, if you split audit, archiving, live data, and so on.

The default instance is available as an option, which is what is selected when you are not giving the install a specific name. You should avoid this, as it gives you an installation with no name and therefore no hint as to its use. Even if you believe this will be your only instance or that while you are learning and a name is not required, it is good practice to name the instance as shown in Figure 1-6. Choose the name you wish to use, and then click Next. Once you have instances installed on the server and you complete further installations, they will be listed here. You can also see the path detailed for each of the directories for the three services selected in the previous step if you chose them. Click Next. The next screen checks the amount of free space on the selected drive. Click Next.

Instance Configuration

Specify the name and instance ID for the instance of SQL Server. Instance ID becomes part of the installation path.

Product Key	○ Default instance
License Terms	◉ Named instance: APRESS_DEV1
Global Rules	
Product Updates	
Install Setup Files	
Install Rules	Instance ID: APRESS_DEV1
Setup Role	
Feature Selection	SQL Server directory: C:\APRESS_DEV1\MSSQL12.APRESS_DEV1
Feature Rules	Analysis Services directory: C:\APRESS_DEV1\MSAS12.APRESS_DEV1
Instance Configuration	Reporting Services directory: C:\APRESS_DEV1\MSRS12.APRESS_DEV1

Figure 1-6. *Naming the install instance*

Service Accounts

SQL Server and other services, as defined in the Feature Selection screen (shown in Figure 1-5), require you to log on to Windows before starting, just as you need to log on to Windows before using your system. SQL Server, Reporting Services, and so on can run without you or anyone being logged in to the computer the install took place on. They can run just so long as the computer has fired up successfully. This is normal when SQL Server is installed on a server that is held in a remote location like a server room.

When the computer boots up and loads Windows, not only will Windows be running but also there will be processes that run in the background before you or any other user has logged in to Windows. The ability to run services with no user-based account logged in to Windows is the behavior that is required for SQL Server. SQL Server needs to use a system-based Windows account.

Nothing can run on Windows without having some sort of login. If you do log in to the computer with your Windows account while working through this book, you can use this Windows user ID for SQL Server to also log in and start the required services manually. However, if you have your SQL Server running on a separate machine such as a server in a specialized server room, at your client's location, or at your ISP, you will not be around to log on to that machine every time SQL Server is required. In that situation, it is necessary to use a Windows service account, which is similar to how your virus checker runs without being logged in with your own account.

Each built-in service account, as shown in Figure 1-7, has special rights and privileges within Windows Therefore, choosing the correct service account for the correct SQL Server service is important. If you are on a network domain, not normally found in the home environment, it is possible for the domain administrator to create domain accounts that can be used as service accounts, and this is the option to choose when there is a network domain. For the moment, although not the best option within a production environment, you will use the built-in service accounts. In a networked environment, it is best to create new service accounts for SQL Server. It is better and more normal practice for each instance to have new, specific Windows system accounts so that if an account becomes locked, it does not affect every SQL Server instance installed.

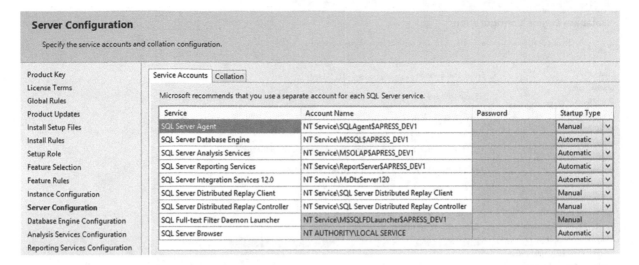

Figure 1-7. *Service account selection*

You will look at service accounts in more detail toward the end of the chapter. The options you see in Figure 1-7 will install SQL Server with a low-level set of privileges, and Figure 1-7 also shows more services than you would see if you chose the options in Figure 1-5. The extra services are included if you did choose more options to install.

You can always change which accounts are used to run SQL Server later. You may notice that SQL Server Browser service is disabled. If you install SQL Server on a remote computer such as a server, then you may opt to enable this service so that client computers can search and browse for your SQL Server installation rather than having to know the exact computer name and instance. ISPs are unlikely to switch this service on, as they will give any users the SQL Server server name; however, corporations are likely to have this service running so that you can find SQL Server instances within the network. For the book, switch this service to automatically start if it is not already defined as automatic.

Click Next to continue with the install.

Authentication Mode

You now come to how you want to enforce security on your SQL Server installation. As Figure 1-8 shows, there are two choices: Windows authentication mode and mixed mode. You will learn more about modes later in the chapter, but, very, very simply, Windows authentication mode denotes that you are going to use Windows security to maintain your SQL Server logins, whereas mixed mode uses either Windows security or a SQL Server–defined login ID and password. You also need to define a password for a special login ID, called sa, if you are working with mixed mode. Again, you will learn more about this in a moment, but for now you must enter a valid password. Use a meaningful and impossible-to-guess password, but not one that you will forget.

Database Engine Configuration

Specify Database Engine authentication security mode, administrators and data directories.

Product Key	**Server Configuration** \| Data Directories \| FILESTREAM
License Terms	
Global Rules	Specify the authentication mode and administrators for the Database Engine.
Product Updates	Authentication Mode
Install Setup Files	● Windows authentication mode
Install Rules	○ Mixed Mode (SQL Server authentication and Windows authentication)
Setup Role	
Feature Selection	Specify the password for the SQL Server system administrator (sa) account.
Feature Rules	Enter password:
Instance Configuration	Confirm password:
Server Configuration	
Database Engine Configuration	Specify SQL Server administrators
Analysis Services Configuration	FAT-BELLY-SONY\Robin (Robin)
Reporting Services Configuration	
Distributed Replay Controller	
Distributed Replay Client	
Feature Configuration Rules	
Ready to Install	Add Current User Add... Remove
Installation Progress	

Figure 1-8. *Authentication choices, including the SQL Server administrator account*

It is also necessary to define a SQL Server administrator account. This is a special account that you can use to log on in dire emergencies, such as when SQL Server refuses connections. This special account allows you to log on, debug the situation, and get SQL Server back up and running. Normally, this administrator account would be a DBA specific account ID so that any changes that had to be completed would leave an audit trail, but for now, use the account you have used to log on to your computer.

You will also see a similar screen for Analysis Services if you selected Analysis Services from the features list, and the settings are the same.

Defining the Data Directories

The Data Directories tab, as shown in Figure 1-9, is where you define where SQL Server stores its data, backup directories, and temporary database by default. It is normal practice to hold the data on a different disk drive to the Windows system drive, which is normally the C: drive. For each instance, you define where the relevant folders should reside. As stated earlier, you can have several installations on one physical or virtual server, and it is not uncommon for a physical or virtual server to hold more than one production installation of SQL Server. For example, there could be an installation for accounts, another for product control, and so on. Each instance would have its data held in a different data directory. This includes any temporary databases that are created and any log files that are generated, so although the physical server is shared, the installation is isolated. A virtual server is similar to a physical server, but it can be one large server that has been split, quite often using software, into multiple servers. This is the method used by many companies, including Microsoft on its Azure platform. The virtuality is dealt with by the Windows engineering teams rather than the DBMS engineering teams. As you are dealing with only one instance within this book, leave these settings as they are.

Server Configuration	Data Directories	FILESTREAM		
Data root directory:	C:\APRESS_DEV1			...
System database directory:	C:\APRESS_DEV1\MSSQL12.APRESS_DEV1\MSSQL\Data			
User database directory:	C:\APRESS_DEV1\MSSQL12.APRESS_DEV1\MSSQL\Data			...
User database log directory:	C:\APRESS_DEV1\MSSQL12.APRESS_DEV1\MSSQL\Data			...
Temp DB directory:	C:\APRESS_DEV1\MSSQL12.APRESS_DEV1\MSSQL\Data			...
Temp DB log directory:	C:\APRESS_DEV1\MSSQL12.APRESS_DEV1\MSSQL\Data			...
Backup directory:	C:\APRESS_DEV1\MSSQL12.APRESS_DEV1\MSSQL\Backup			...

Figure 1-9. *Defining the locations of SQL Server data directories*

You will see the same tabs shown in Figure 1-9 in the next step if you selected Analysis Services.

FILESTREAM Options

The FILESTREAM tab as shown in Figure 1-10 is another type of data directory that is used when dealing with large amounts of unstructured data. In the past, this data was held totally separate from SQL Server with a link to where the data was held, but FILESTREAM allows the data to be managed by SQL Server, and this tab informs SQL Server of where it resides. FILESTREAM data are also used for full-text searching. If you enable filestreaming, then you have the option to hold the data in FileTables. I think of this functionality as similar to SharePoint, which holds large unstructured data as do Word, Excel, and so on. SharePoint holds and manages the documents. By holding the data in FileTables, you can then access the documents from Windows and Windows applications, but SQL Server will also provide the ability to search the documents, similarly to a search engine. Leave this option disabled.

Figure 1-10. *FILESTREAM and FileTable options*

Creating the Reporting Services Database

If you selected Reporting Services to be installed (from the options in Figure 1-5), you need to create a database for the reporting server to use. There are three different possible installation options for Reporting Services: native, SharePoint, and installed but not configured. If you select the last option, SQL Server Reporting Services will be installed on the server but will not be configured. This is ideal if you're setting up a specific server just for the reporting options or if SQL Server is being installed in unattended mode and the reporting server will be configured after this completes. Once installed, you would then have to create a reporting database.

The native mode configuration, as shown in Figure 1-11, is the simplest and the option demonstrated here. It installs Reporting Services and also creates the necessary databases within your SQL Server. It will be available only if you are installing on a local instance rather than a remote instance and if Reporting Services is also on that local instance. Default values are used for the service account, the report server URL on the local instance (which will be localhost), the Report Manager URL, and the name of the Reporting Services.

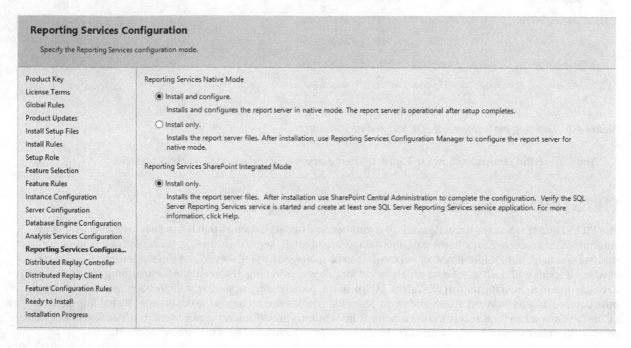

Figure 1-11. *Installing native mode configuration for Reporting Services*

If you have a SharePoint installation and you want Reporting Services to use that architecture, select the Reporting Services SharePoint install option, which allows you to use SharePoint's functionality and storage for reporting purposes.

Distributed Replay Options

Although not covered in the book, distributed replay allows for one or more client computers to connect to a SQL Server instance to send a workload to SQL Server for it to process. The controller will sit with the SQL Server installation and control the clients' connections through to the server. The client is used to mimic a user and the workload being sent through. Figure 1-12 shows the name of the controller for it to connect to.

Distributed Replay Client

Specify the corresponding controller and data directories for the Distributed Replay Client.

Product Key	Specify controller machine name and directory locations.
License Terms	
Global Rules	Controller Name: FAT-BELLY
Product Updates	Working Directory: C:\Program Files (x86)\Microsoft SQL Server\DReplayClient\WorkingDir\
Install Setup Files	Result Directory: C:\Program Files (x86)\Microsoft SQL Server\DReplayClient\ResultDir\
Install Rules	

Figure 1-12. *Controller computer for the Distributed Replay Client*

When you click Next, a final check is made to ensure that the install should be able to complete and, finally, by clicking Next, the final screen (see Figure 1-13) is displayed. The setup collection is complete, and you are ready to install. You can now install SQL Server, and you will be able to monitor the installation progress.

```
□ Summary
    ┆┈ Edition: Evaluation
    ┆┈ Action: Install (Product Update)
    □ Prerequisites
        □ Already installed:
            ┆┈ Windows PowerShell 2.0
            ┆┈ Microsoft .NET Framework 3.5
            ┆┈ Microsoft Visual Studio 2010 Redistributables
            ┆┈ Microsoft Visual Studio Tools for Applications 3.0
            └┈ Microsoft .NET Framework 4.0
        □ To be installed from media:
            └┈ Microsoft Visual Studio 2010 Shell
    □ General Configuration
        □ Features
            ┆┈ Database Engine Services
            ┆┈ Client Tools Connectivity
            ┆┈ Integration Services
            ┆┈ Documentation Components
            ┆┈ Management Tools - Basic
            └┈ Management Tools - Complete
        □ Instance configuration
            ┆┈ Instance Name: APRESS_DEV1
            ┆┈ Instance ID: APRESS_DEV1
            □ Instance IDs
                └┈ SQL Database Engine: MSSQL12.APRESS_DEV1
            └┈ Instance Directory: C:\APRESS_DEV1
```

Figure 1-13. *Complete setup details*

Security

To discuss further the Service Account dialog box that you came across in the installation properly, I need to delve into the area of Windows security.

In this section, I will first examine the concept of Windows services as opposed to programs, and then move on to discussing different types of authentication you can choose when installing SQL Server.

Services Accounts

SQL Server runs as a Windows service. So what is a service? A good example of a service is any antivirus software that runs continuously from when the user restarts a computer to the point that the computer shuts down. A program, on the other hand, is either loaded in memory and running, or not started. So what is the advantage of running a service? When you have a unit of work that can run as a service, Windows can control a great deal more concerning that process. A service can be set to start automatically before any user has even logged on; all other programs require a user to be logged in to Windows in order for the services to start.

A service also has absolutely no user interface. There will have no form to display and no user input to deal with at runtime. The only interaction with the process runs either through a separate user interface, which then links to the service but is a totally separate unit of work (for example, SQL Server Management Studio), or from Windows management of that service itself. Any output that comes from the service will usually go to the event log, which is a Windows area that stores any notification from the services that Windows runs.

Having no interface means that the whole process can be controlled without human intervention. Providing the service is designed well, Windows can take care of every eventuality itself, and it can also run the service before anyone has even logged in to the computer.

In most production environments, SQL Server will be running on a remote server, one probably locked away in a secure and controlled area, possibly where the only people allowed in are hardware engineers. There possibly isn't even a remote access program installed, as this could give unauthorized access to these computers. SQL Server will run quite happily and, with any luck, never give an error. But what if one day there is an error? If SQL Server is running as a program, you'll have to make some sort of decision. Even if SQL Server crashes, there at least has to be some sort of mechanism to restart it. This means another process needs to be run—a monitoring process, which in itself could result in a whole ream of problems. However, as a service, SQL Server is under Windows control. If a problem occurs, whether with SQL Server, Windows, or any outside influence, Windows is smart enough to deal with it through the services process and restart the SQL Server service.

If you do log in to the computer, as you likely will while working through this book, then you can use this Windows user ID for SQL Server to also log in and start its service. The Windows user ID that SQL Server uses is known as a *local system account*. However, if you followed the steps and used the accounts in Figure 1-7, there are other specific accounts created for some services that SQL Server services will use.

On the other hand, you can create a new Windows login that exists purely for SQL Server, and this is the correct behavior to implement in production. You avoid it in this book only to keep things simple while you are learning SQL Server.

Your personal Windows account should be set up so that the password expires after so many days, or so that it locks out after a number of incorrect password attempts. This is to protect your computer and the network, among many other things. SQL Server should follow a similar security process and use a separate account that locks the account after a number of unsuccessful attempts as well as some mechanism to force developers to change the password on a regular basis (this could be through company policy and a process to cross-check when passwords were last altered). Be aware that choosing a locking password account may affect a production running system if a lockout occurs. The account will also be set up to access only specific resources both on the local computer as well as network-related. This kind of non–user-specific, "generic" account removes the link between SQL Server and a person within an organization. If you are looking at the domain account option as shown earlier in Figure 1-7, this account is likely to be in a network environment or a production environment. There is an option to define a different account for each service. This ability is crucial when in a corporate environment because of the security implications that you must deal with.

SQL Server has several different processes that exist for different work. There is an executable named `sqlservr.exe` that is used to run SQL Server itself. You'll see that process listed in Task Manager as `MSSQL$instancename`. Including the instance name as part of the process name allows each instance to be unaffected if a different instance is stopped. Another executable named `sqlagent.exe` represents the SQL Server Agent, which runs processes such as batch jobs and is shown in Task Manager as `SQLAgent$Instancename`. Finally SQL Server Agent, because it runs batch processes and complex tasks including working with other servers, needs a more powerful domain account than the SQL Server process. Your network administrator may have created these accounts and will know which account is best to use or best to create for these tasks.

It's time to move on to the options you are given during installation regarding authentication mode.

Looking at the Authentication Mode

Probably the most crucial information in the whole setup process, and also the biggest decision that you have to make, concerns the authentication mode you wish to apply to your server. As you saw earlier in the setup process, there are two choices: *Windows authentication mode* and *mixed mode*.

Windows Authentication Mode

To log on to a Windows machine, the user must supply a username. There is no way around this. So, to log on to Windows, the username and password have to be validated within Windows. When this is done, Windows is actually verifying the user against username credentials held within the domain controller, or, if you are running Windows/SQL Server on a stand-alone machine at home, the credentials held locally. These credentials check the access group the user belongs to (the user rights). The user could be an administrator, who has the ability to alter anything within the computer, all the way down to a basic user, who has very restricted rights. This then gives you a trusted connection; in other words, applications that are started up after logging in to Windows can trust that Windows has verified that the account has passed the necessary security checks.

Once you have logged in to Windows, SQL Server uses a trusted connection when working with Windows authentication mode. This means SQL Server is trusting that the username and password have been validated as I just mentioned. If, however, the Windows username you give does not exist within SQL Server, you won't be able to log on to SQL Server. However, if the username isn't valid, SQL Server will check the Windows group that the user belongs to and check its security to see whether that group is set up to access SQL Server. If that user has administration rights to your computer, then the user may well be able to at least connect to SQL Server.

You are in a bit of a Catch-22 situation here. You need to know about security for your install process, but to demonstrate it fully means working with SQL Server Management Studio, which the next chapter covers. I will keep that area simple, so let's look at an example involving security now.

■ **Note** To follow Exercise 1-1, you will need the Professional version of Windows 7 or 8

EXERCISE 1-1. TRY IT OUT: WINDOWS AUTHENTICATION MODE

1. Ensure that you are logged on to your machine as an administrator. If you are on a local computer, chances are that your login is in fact an administrator ID. If this computer is on a network and you are unsure about your access rights, ask your PC support desk to help you out with the ID and password. On Windows 7, you may need to change your user control access to avoid many dialogs confirming that you wish to continue with each step.

2. From Control Panel, select User Accounts.

3. When the Users Accounts screen is displayed, click Manage Another Account, followed by Create New Account in Windows 7 or Add a new user in PC settings in Windows 8 followed by Add an account. If you are on Windows 8, then create the account without a Microsoft account. Once selected, click the Local Account button.

4. Once the Add a user dialog box comes up, enter the username MSmith, as shown in Figure 1-14.

Figure 1-14. Creating a new user account

5. Ensure that the account type specified is Standard on Windows 7. On Windows 8, by default, it will be added as a Standard user. This means that it will not have administrator privileges.

6. Repeat the process as you want to add a second username. Repeat the preceding process using the following details:

 • Username: NoelMorgala

 • Account type: Administrator (to create an administrator, first create the account, then select it, edit, and change the account type)

7. Log off from Windows, and then log on using the first ID that you created: MSmith.

8. Once logged in, start up SQL Server Management Studio by selecting Start ➤ All Programs ➤ Microsoft SQL Server ➤ SQL Server Management Studio or finding the app SQL Server Management Studio in Windows 8. You may need to populate the dialog with the server name of the install. Click Browse For More, select Database Engine, and select the install server and instance. We will go through this in more detail in Chapter 2. The dialog should look like Figure 1-15.

Figure 1-15. *Attempting to connect to SQL Server*

9. Examine the error message that appears, which should resemble what you see in Figure 1-16. MSmith as a login has not been defined within SQL Server specifically and does not belong to a group that allows access. The only group at the moment is a user who is in the Administrators Windows group. Recall that MSmith is a limited user.

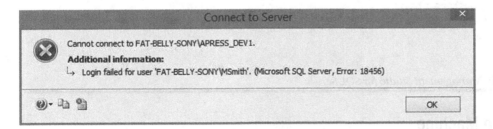

Figure 1-16. *Failed login to server*

10. You will now try out the other user you created. Close down SQL Server Management Studio, log off Windows, and log on using the second ID you created—NoelMorgala. Once logged in, start up SQL Server Management Studio and connect to your server. Similar to MSmith, the login will not work. Admin rights don't give you access to SQL Server unlike other programs with the exception of one specialized scenario covered at the end of this exercise.

11. Log off NoelMorgala and connect with your own login again. If you start up SQL Server Management Studio on your own login, then it should allow you to gain access within SQL Server. If you have followed the chapter, you will need to have as the server name the name of your computer, followed by a backslash (\) and the name of the instance, APRESS_DEV1. If you have installed SQL Server with no instance name, you need just your computer name or you need to enter (local), localhost, or a single dot. This is possible because during the installation you added your account in the Authentication Mode section.

You have created two usernames on top of the username you already have as your own account: one that has restricted access (MSmith) and one that has administration rights (NoelMorgala), as well as your own account that installed SQL Server. Neither of these specific usernames exists within SQL Server itself: after all, you haven't entered them and they haven't appeared as if by magic. Neither account is in any Windows group that has access to SQL Server as part of running any SQL Services. The Windows security model has ensured that both new IDs are valid as well as your own. If the ID or password were incorrect, there would be no way that you could be logged in to Windows. Therefore, when you try to connect to SQL Server, the only check that is performed is whether the user has access to SQL Server either via membership of a system group that has been defined within SQL Server or through the specific logged-in user account that has been defined to SQL Server. As you can see in Figure 1-17, neither MSmith nor NoelMorgala exists within SQL Server. You can see my login, and therefore I am entitled to connect. SQL Server in some previous versions added a group to the list of logins. The group is called BUILTIN\ Administrators, and NoelMorgala would have been a member of the group. If this group existed, then step 10 would have succeeded. BUILTIN\Administrators is a dangerous group to have within SQL Server, as many people can be administrators within a network domain and therefore could have access to your server and log in; it is a loophole in your security if you keep this as a login. In existing installations, if you see this group exists, investigate removing it and certainly do not add it for new installations. The same is true if you see a group called BUILTIN\Users. In Chapter 4, you will see how to build specific groups of users to allow individuals access to your server.

Figure 1-17. *Logins within Management Studio for SQL Server*

Administrators on a Machine

Any account defined as a member of the Administrators group can access SQL Server in one specific scenario. If at any point the accounts for System Administration are locked out, then as a System Administrator you will still need access to SQL Server to perform those tasks. Any account in the Administrators group can access SQL Server when SQL Server is placed in to a specific mode called Single User mode. This mode is where one user and one user only can access SQL Server. In this mode you can then connect with NoelMorgala as they are in the Administrators group.

■ **Note** There is a further way to access SQL Server when you need to troubleshoot a problem called Dedicated Administrator Connection (DAC), which will be used when SQL Server is unresponsive.

Mixed Mode

If you installed SQL Server with mixed mode, this means you could use either Windows authentication, as has just been covered, or SQL Server authentication.

How does mixed mode differ from Windows authentication mode? To start with, you need to supply a user ID and password to connect rather than SQL Server taking the Windows ID, or the group the user belongs to, of the logged-in account. There is no assumption that the username supplied is a valid Windows ID. SQL Server when authenticating a mixed-mode account will not verify any additional security from Windows. Using mixed mode is appropriate in many cases when working with ISPs. To clarify this, if you are working on your remote data at a local client machine, the remote machine would need to know the credentials of your login, and the easiest method is to use SQL Server authentication. Be clear that in this scenario, it is you connecting to your data from your machine. The web-site code used to access your data, if written in ASP.NET, may use a Windows account to log in, so although you may lock out your SQL Server mixed-mode account, it should not stop your web site from working.

I will demonstrate how to add usernames to SQL Server (as opposed to adding Windows users) when I talk about security in Chapter 4.

This leaves one area of security left that needs to be discussed here: the sa login.

The sa Login

The sa login is a default login that has full administration rights for SQL Server. If you selected mixed-mode authentication during the installation process, you would be forced to include a password for this account. This is because the sa user ID is such a powerful login. It also exists in every SQL Server installation; therefore, any hacker knows that this user ID exists and will try to connect to the server using it. Prior to SQL Server 2005, when creating a password became compulsory, many installations had the password blank, therefore allowing hackers instant access. If you log in to SQL Server as sa, you will have full control over any aspect of SQL Server. SQL Server inserts this ID no matter which authentication mode you install.

In a mixed-mode installation, sa will be a valid username and validated as such. As you can guess, if any user gets ahold of this username and the password, that user will have full access to view and amend or delete any item of data. At worst, the user could corrupt any database, as well as corrupt SQL Server itself. The user could even set up tasks that e-mail data to a remote location as it is being processed.

It is essential to set up a strong password on the sa account in the Authentication Mode screen if you choose mixed mode. It is a major improvement in SQL Server 2012 that you are now forced to enter a password, although it is possible to set up a very easily guessed password. Do not use passwords such as "password" or "adminpwd," for example. Always keep the password safe, but also make a note of it in a safe place. If you forget the sa password and this is the only administration ID that exists, you will need to reinstall SQL Server to get out of this problem. A good password is one that mixes numbers and letters, but doesn't include letters that can be made into numbers and numbers into letters in all cases. For example, pa55word is just as easy to guess as password. Or 4pr355 for Apress.

There is also another reason not to log on to SQL Server with the sa username. At times, it will be essential to know who is running a particular query on a SQL Server database. In a production database, someone may be running an update of the data, which is filling up the disk space or filling up the transaction log. You will need to contact that person to check whether he or she can stop the process. If that person logs in as sa, you will have no idea who he or she is. However, if that person logged on with an identifiable name, he or she would have an ID in SQL Server, which you could track. By restricting the sa login so that people have to use their own accounts, you can ensure a much higher degree of system monitoring and integrity.

There will be times that you want mixed-mode authentication; it is perfectly acceptable to want this. Internet providers use mixed mode because many applications may be on one web server. If this ISP is a reseller (in other words, many people around the globe use the one computer), you will not want these people to have the ability to see your data. You have also decided not to have sa as an administration logon at this point. So what do you do? Well, you create a logon ID that will have the access privileges you wish; in other words, it will have the ability to just see the data and work with the data you need, and no more. The ISP may require you to supply a user ID and password that it uses to create an account on its SQL Server instance. You will encounter more about this in Chapter 4.

■ **Note** Regardless of the authentication mode, it is important that you always supply a strong password.

Summary

By this point, you should understand the small differences between each version of SQL Server. You should also know how to check your computer to see whether it is suitable for a SQL Server installation.

By following the steps given earlier, you should have a successful installation of SQL Server on your computer. You may even have completed the installation twice so that you have a development server installation as well as a test server installation. This is a good idea and something to consider if you have only one installation so far. Whether you are working in a large corporation or are a "one-man band," keeping your production and development code separate leads to greatly reduced complications if, when developing, you need to make a production fix.

This chapter introduced you to security in SQL Server so that you can feel comfortable knowing which way you want to implement this and how to deal with different usernames. You may not have any data yet, but you want to ensure that when you do, only the right people get to look at it!

You are now ready to explore SQL Server. One of the best ways of managing SQL Server is by using SQL Server Management Studio, which will be discussed next.

CHAPTER 2

■ ■ ■

SQL Server Management Studio

Now that SQL Server is successfully installed on your machine, you can start exploring the various areas that make this an easy and effective product to use. With SQL Server, all the administration interfaces that reside in SQL Server can be accessed by graphical interfaces called *studios*, such as SQL Server Management Studio, which features tools for working with developing database solutions. This chapter concentrates on SQL Server Management Studio (SSMS), which you will use to develop and maintain your databases and the objects SSMS contains.

SSMS is the graphical user interface (GUI) you will use to build your database solutions. This is an easy-to-use and intuitive tool, and before long, you will feel confident using it to work with SQL Server quickly and efficiently. I will be discussing several aspects of SSMS in this chapter. You can then use this knowledge throughout the book. I'll discuss some aspects in more detail throughout the book. However, you can use other tools from third-party vendors or commands from the command prompt or within a file executed from the command prompt, and you can also use a command prompt tool called sqlcmd to work with your database. Finally, it is possible to use development tools such as C#, Java, PowerShell, and so on. No matter how you proceed, the work we will go through in SSMS can be completed in any of these choices. I will demonstrate sqlcmd within this chapter and you will see some development tools in Chapter 19. SSMS is crucial and the quickest tool to your success as a developer as it shows you how to build database solutions graphically. It also allows you to write and test lines of code to complete tasks that could then be placed into your programming language of choice. In Chapter 19, you will learn how you can transfer what you see demonstrated within SSMS to .NET, Excel, and Java. By the end of this chapter, you will have gained experience with it and be proficient in the following areas:

- The components of SSMS
- Working with the editor to enter queries
- SQLCMD and command line access

Let's start by having a look at SSMS and how it is used to work with SQL Server.

A Quick Overview of SSMS

SQL Server runs as a separate Windows process, as touched on in Chapter 1, whether on a stand-alone desktop machine, or on a server within a network. If you open Task Manager and move to the Processes tab, you will see, among other processes, sqlservr.exe. This process or service runs in its own process space and is isolated from other processes on the machine. SQL Server should not be affected by any other piece of software that does not talk to any SQL Server component. If you have to kill any other component's process, the SQL Server engine should continue to run.

SQL Server runs as a service that is controlled and monitored by Windows. SQL Server ensures that it is given the right amount of memory, processing power, and time from the operating system by instructing Windows on what it (SQL Server) needs within the confines defined at the database creation and what is available on the computer, although pressures on the server will mean that SQL Server will modify what it requests based on what is available.

Because SQL Server runs as a service and there is one service per database instance as well as main feature such as Reporting Services, Analysis Services and instance, it has no interface attached to it for a user to interact with. As a result, there needs to be at least one separate utility that can pass commands and functions from a user through to the SQL Server service, which then passes them through to the underlying database. The GUI tool that accomplishes the passing of SQL commands and functions is SSMS. You can use other tools, and you could even create your own GUI, but you'll concentrate only on SSMS within this book.

SSMS can be used to develop and work with several installations and instances of SQL Server in one application. These installations can be on one computer or on many computers connected through a local area network (LAN), a wide area network (WAN), or even the Internet and Cloud computing. Therefore, it is possible to deal with your development, system testing, user testing, and production instances of SQL Server from one instance of SSMS.

■ **Caution** It is highly recommended that you have at least two instances, one for production and at least one for development and testing.

SSMS helps you in the development of database solutions, including creating and modifying components of a database, amending the database itself, and dealing with security issues. Getting to know this tool well is crucial to becoming a successful professional SQL Server developer, as well as a database administrator.

One of the tools within SSMS that you will use for completing tasks is Query Editor. This tool allows program code to be written and executed, from objects to commands that manipulate data, and even complete tasks, such as backing up the data. This program code is called Transact SQL (T-SQL). T-SQL is a Microsoft proprietary language, although it is strongly linked to the ANSI-92 SQL standard of the American National Standards Institute (ANSI). The current specification Microsoft bases its code on is ANSI-92.

■ **Tip** Although Microsoft SQL is linked to ANSI-92, it can be more flexible and powerful than other databases. For example, there are scenarios that you can run as a stand-alone script in SQL Server that would require a stored procedure in DB2. There are also minor differences in implementation of some functionality.

Query Editor is a tool within SSMS that allows you to programmatically build the same actions as dragging and dropping or using wizards. However, using T-SQL within Query Editor can give you more control over certain aspects of certain commands. Although dragging and dropping and using wizards may be quick, as a developer knowing T-SQL allows you not only to put the T-SQL code into other languages and tools, but also to transfer your skills to many other databases. Do not underestimate the power you will gain by learning T-SQL. Note that the name "Query Editor" comes from the fact that it sends *queries* to the database using T-SQL. Don't worry if you don't quite grasp this—all will become clear very soon.

Spend some time taking a look at SSMS in more detail.

TRY IT OUT: TOURING SQL SERVER MANAGEMENT STUDIO

1. To start up SQL Server Management Studio, from Windows 8 you are looking for an app called SQL Server Management Studio or from Windows 7 select Start ➤ All Programs ➤ Microsoft SQL Server ➤ SQL Server Management Studio. If you are using Windows 8, I suggest pinning this app.

2. A Connect to Server dialog box similar to the one in Figure 2-1 should appear automatically. Note the following items in this dialog box:

Figure 2-1. *SQL Server Management Studio Connect to Server dialog box without expanded options*

- *Server type*: For the purposes of the examples in this book, leave the server type as Database Engine. The other options are other types of servers that are available for connection such as Analysis Services, Integration Services, and Reporting Services.

- *Server name*: The second combobox lists the SQL Server installations that the Connect to Server dialog box can find, or that it knows about. In the dialog box in Figure 2-1, you will see the name of the computer that the local install is on. If you open the Server name combobox, you can search for more servers locally or over a network connection using <Browse for more...>. The first time you connect to SQL Server, you may need to browse for or type in the details. You will have already found the server in Chapter 1.

- *Authentication*: The final combobox specifies which type of connection you want to use. You installed SQL Server with Windows authentication in Chapter 1; therefore, this is the option to use. If you had installed SQL Server with mixed mode or if in the future you wish to connect by this method, you could change this option to SQL Server authentication, which would enable the next two text boxes and allow you to enter a username and password.

3. Click Options, which will switch you to the Connection Properties tab. Here you will see specific properties for this connection, as shown in Figure 2-2.

Figure 2-2. *SQL Server Management Studio connection properties*

- *Connect to database*: This combobox provides a list of databases based on the server and login details in the Login tab. Clicking the down button for this combobox allows you to browse for and select a database on the server to which you want to connect. Only the databases that the Windows account or SQL Server login can connect to will populate this list. Also, any error in the login details will cause an error message to be displayed here instead of listing databases.

- *Network*: This area details how you want this connection to be made with SQL Server. At the moment, you don't need to change the current settings.

- *Connection*: This area deals with connection time-outs. The first item, Connection time-out, defines how long the connection should wait before returning an error. For local installs and even most network installs, a setting of 15 seconds should be more than enough. The only situation that may require you to increase this setting is if you were connecting over a WAN or to a SQL Server installation at an ISP and that connection was slow. A connection from New York to Moscow could exceed this value, for example. The second option, Execution tme-out, details the time-out value for any T-SQL code that you execute. A setting of 0 means that there is no time-out; there should be few, if any, occasions when you would want to change this setting.

■ **Note** Any subsequent connection parameters would appear in the third tab. This will be empty for this book.

4. Once you are happy with all of the items in the Connection Properties tab, click Connect. This brings you to SSMS itself. If you have ever used Visual Studio, you will notice that SSMS has a reasonably similar layout. This is deliberate on Microsoft's part, as the company is making SQL Server more integrated with Visual Studio. When you look at some of the options you can set and use in SQL Server, you will see functionality and options that exist in both software development tools. Your layout should look like the one in Figure 2-3, with only minor name changes based on the server you have connected to and the connection you have used. This figure shows I have connected to FAT-BELLY-Sony SQL Server using the Windows account FAT-BELLY-Sony\RobinDewson.

Figure 2-3. SQL Server Management Studio graphical interface for SQL Server

5. The first area of SSMS you will look at is the Registered Servers explorer. Access this explorer, shown in Figure 2-4, by selecting View ➤ Registered Servers or by pressing Ctrl+Alt+G. This area details all SQL Server servers that have been registered by you on this SSMS installation. Currently, there will be only the server just registered, but as time progresses and you develop more systems, this list will expand. This explorer will also show registered services for other services such as Analysis Services and Reporting Services.

Figure 2-4. A list of registered servers

6. The second node in the Registered Servers explorer, Central Management Servers, is where a SQL Server instance is used as a central management point from which you can perform actions against multiple other servers in your environment. This central point of management provides you with a lot of power. For example, you can run checks to ensure that all the servers have the same disk space, or the same values within rows of a specific table.

7. If you need to register another server, right-click the Local Server Groups node and select New Server Registration to bring up a dialog box very similar to the Connect to Server dialog box shown earlier. Go ahead and do this now to familiarize yourself with the New Server Registration dialog box, shown in Figure 2-5. You don't need to register servers to connect to them, but it will make it easier to find any regular servers. In Figure 2-5, you will see a demonstration of a registration to my ISP that uses SQL Server Authentication.

Figure 2-5. *The New Server Registration dialog box*

8. The differences from the Connect to Server dialog box are that the Server name combobox starts empty and there is a new section called Registered server. In this area, you can give a registration a different name, such as Development Server or User Testing Region, and on top of this give the registration a description. You don't have a server to register, so just click Cancel now. When bringing up the menu from the right-click within the Registered Servers explorer, you may have noticed an option to create a new server group. Along with using a different name, I suggest you also group your registrations so that you can instantly tell where a server resides, whether that is environment or locale.

9. Moving back to SSMS's explorer window below the registered servers, take a look at Object Explorer, which should have been present when you first opened SSMS; it normally sits below the Registered Servers explorer. If it isn't there or if it disappears, you can redisplay it by selecting View ➤ Object Explorer or by pressing F8. You will likely use this explorer the most, as it details every object, every security item, and many other areas concerning SQL Server. You can see that SSMS uses nodes (which you expand by clicking the + signs) to keep much of the layout of Object Explorer (the hierarchy) compact and hidden until needed. Let's go through each of the main nodes you see in Figure 2-6 now.

Figure 2-6. *Object Explorer nodes*

- *Databases*: Holds the system and user databases within the SQL Server you are connected to

- *Security*: Details the list of SQL Server logins that can connect to SQL Server; you will see more on this in Chapter 4.

- *Server Objects*: Details objects such as backup devices and provides a list of linked servers, where one server is connected to another remote server

- *Replication*: Shows the details involving data replication from a database on this server to another database (on this or another server) or vice versa

- *AlwaysOn High Availability:* Allows you to define groups of databases to failover to if the primary fails; provides a setup so that your database is always available

- *Management*: Details maintenance plans, policy management, data collection, and Database Mail setup, which you will learn more about in Chapter 8, and provides a log of informational and error messages that can be very useful when troubleshooting SQL Server *Integration Services Catalogs:* Created catalogs for working with SQL Server Integration Services (SSIS). SSIS is a servce that allows you to perform multiple tasks to achieve a goal. To give one example, you can have multiple tasks where a connection to a data source is made, data is loaded, the data is then transformed, enhanced, segregated and then placed in to a data location. A common example is to load data from files in to SQL Server.

- *SQL Server Agent*: Builds and runs tasks within SQL Server at certain times, with details of successes or failures that can be sent to pagers, e-mail, or operators defined within SQL Server; the running of these jobs and the notifications of these failures or successes are dealt with by SQL Server Agent, and the details are found in this node. You will look at this more in Chapter 8, where you will schedule backup jobs.

10. Select the topmost node, the server node, in the Object Explorer, and then from the menu select View ➤ Object Explorer Details, or press F7 to see a Summary Page similar to the one in Figure 2-7. This area is known as the documents area. You don't have to be on the top node for this page to be of use, as it will provide a summary of any node within this explorer. This works a bit like folders within Windows Explorer, where you can navigate through each item to get a summary of details of objects within the node. The left column matches the groupings below the node you have selected in Object Explorer, and the right column details how compliant your database is compared to a set of policies defined. You have no policies at this time, and therefore the column is blank. You will see policies detailed in Chapter 4.

Object Explorer Details ✕

Search

FAT-BELLY-SONY\APRESS_DEV1 (SQL Server 12.0.2000 - FAT-BELLY-SONY\RobinDewson)

Name	Policy Health State
📁 Databases	
📁 Security	
📁 Server Objects	
📁 Replication	
📁 AlwaysOn High Availability	
📁 Management	
📁 Integration Services Catalo...	
📖 SQL Server Agent (Agent X...	

FAT-BELLY-SONY\APRESS_DEV1 (SQL Server 12.0.2000 - FAT-BE...		Min Server Memory (MB):	16
8 Items		C2 Audit Mode Enabled:	0
Databases:	4	CLR Enabled:	0
Default Language:	0	Common Criteria Enabled:	0
MAX DOP:	0	Cross DB Ownership Enabled:	0
Max Server Memory (MB):	2147483647	Database Mail Enabled:	0
Max Worker Threads:	0		

Figure 2-7. Summary page

11. Moving to the menu bar of SSMS, the first item of interest is the View menu option. The first two options and the fourth and fifth options on the View menu, shown in Figure 2-8, open the two explorer windows, Object Explorer and the Registered Servers explorer, as well as the summary page you encountered previously. Therefore, if you ever need to close these items to give yourself more screen space, you can reopen them from the menu or with the shortcut keys you see defined. The other options on the View menu are as follows:

Figure 2-8. *The View menu options*

- *Utility Explorer*: Enables a central point for monitoring disparate servers; this is ideal for database administrators who monitor several servers within their organization that could be in one location, several locations, and even with external clients. From this one explorer, you can monitor how the servers are performing, if they have issues, and how the servers are performing against policies defined as part of the monitoring process.

- *Template Explorer*: Provides access to code templates; template functionality is similar to code snippets within Visual Studio.

- *Solution Explorer*: Displays *solutions*, which are convenient groupings of objects, T-SQL, or special programs called stored procedures, among other items. These are collected together to address a specific business or technical problem and can be collected for the whole system or collected to only contain scripts for a release. If you use Visual Studio, files are collected into projects, and one or more projects create the overall solution. I don't use the solution method of developing projects for SQL Server, as I find that good use of development and source control utilities such as SourceSafe or Team Foundation Server removes the need for that level of thought and complexity.

- *Bookmark Window*: Allows you to create *bookmarks*, which you place into various locations in your code to allow you to jump quickly to those locations.

- *Call Hierarchy*: As your application expands, you will find that you will have code that executes code in a different program and so on. This is a call hierarchy, and it is sometimes advantageous to see that hierarchy to debug a problem that you are experiencing.

- *Error List*: Shows errors found in the code you have entered in the editor; this can be compilation or syntax errors.

- *Output*: Unlike the Error List, this window is used to print output while debugging code or status messages from some commands. If output is being displayed from more than one location, you can filter the output to be displayed.

- *Task List*: If you need a method to keep a list of work items, or tasks, then you can use this area to keep a note and to track them. The task list is ideal if you are debugging your code and you want to take notes of areas that need working on, or if you wish to make a task list of items you need to complete to finish developing your application.

- *Toolbox*: holds a list of objects that are database maintenance tasks and details where these tasks can be altered.

- *Find Results*: If you need to search via a number of files for a particular phrase, then the results will be kept in the Find Results window.

- *Other Windows*: Allows you to access other windows generated when running T-SQL from Query Editor, which may hold error messages or results from queries

- *Toolbars*: Brings up toolbars: such as those for Query Editor, diagramming the database, and integration with Visual SourceSafe for source control, if they are not opened by default among many others

- *Full Screen*: Removes title bars and explorer windows, and then maximizes SSMS to show as much of the main pages as possible

- *Navigate Backward/Forward*: Allows you to navigate through the different Query Editor windows by either navigating forward or backward through the tabs

- *Next Task/Previous Task*: Once you have created tasks using the Task window described earlier, you can navigate through the list of tasks using this menu option. You may find using the arrow keys easier and quicker.

- *Properties Window*: Displays the set of properties for each object; you will see this from time to time throughout the chapters of the book.

12. As you develop complex code, the ability to test via debugging will have greater importance in your life. The next menu option, Debug, allows you to step through your code, pause at specific breakpoints, and perform checks on the code to see if it is performing as expected. You will see more of this in Chapter 17 when I take you through some advanced T-SQL. However, for the moment, it is useful to have a small flavor of what options are available, as shown in Figure 2-9.

Figure 2-9. *The Debug menu options*

- *Windows:* There are three window options possible from this menu option.

- *Start Debugging:* This starts the debugging process and will execute the first line of code.

- *Stop Debugging:* This allows you to stop debugging at the line of code you are on; it is not possible to restart from that point, and you would have to start over again.

- *Step Into:* When stepping through your code and reaching a stored procedure, you can step into that stored procedure and step through that code.

- *Step Over:* If you do not wish to step into the stored procedure, you can execute the whole code set and then step to the next line in your code.

- *Toggle Breakpoint*: It switches a breakpoint from being set to not being set, or vice versa.

- *New Breakpoint*: It creates a new breakpoint at the line of code; the cursor is on. A breakpoint is where the execution of the code will pause to allow you to complete other actions.

- *Delete All Breakpoints:* This selection is a good option if you are debugging code and you are happy with the code from the point you are at and do not wish to break any further. Deleting the breakpoints will allow this to happen.

- *Clear All DataTips:* A datatip is the ability to watch the contents of a variable as you debug your code. This menu option will remove all tips that you have stored.

- *Export DataTips:* Any datatips created can be saved and exported, allowing you to share datatips.

- *Import DataTips:* Any exported datatips can be imported.

13. SQL Server has two built-in tools, as well as the capability to include other tools when they are launched. These can be accessed through the Tools menu, shown in Figure 2-10, along with the means to customize keyboard commands, show or hide toolbar buttons, and so on, as is the case with other Microsoft products such as Word. The first two options are available outside of SSMS from the Performance Tools subprograms list from the Start menu. These programs are separate from SSMS. In particular, note the following options:

Figure 2-10. *The Tools menu options*

- *SQL Server Profiler*: There will come a time when you'll wish to monitor SQL Server's performance. This tool will monitor and log events, running code, and so on, that you have informed it to check when they happen within SQL Server.

- *Database Engine Tuning Advisor*: It is possible to take a workload of data and process it through your solution. This advisor can suggest ways to improve the performance of this process.

- *Code Snippets Manager*: It is possible to create useful short sections of code that will be used more than once. Unlike templates where a template of code for a whole action such as creating a new table, code snippets are at most a few lines of code and tend to be organizational or project-specific. An example of a code snippet would be a code snippet that performs logging of information as code executes. Another is for error logging where there is specific code to log any errors that occur. You will see how to test for errors in Chapters 16 and 17.

- *Options:* This option lets you access different options you can use to set up your SSMS as you like. I will take a look at each of these options in the next section.

14. The final part of SSMS that I will examine at this point is the main SSMS toolbar, as you can see in Figure 2-11. Some of the icons, such as the Save icon, will be instantly recognizable, but I will go through each button, from left to right, so that it is clear what they all do.

Figure 2-11. Main toolbar

- *New Project*: Creates a project within the solution. A project is a logical subset of scripts. A solution could be the whole script set for an application and a logical project set could be scripts for online ordering, scripts for batch processing, and so on.

- *Add item*: Allows you to add a script item to the project such as a stored procedure or a table but also non-script items such as a connection.

- *Open File/Save/Save All*: As standard throughout Microsoft products.

- *New Query*: In the next section, you will see how you can write code to add objects, work with data, and so on. Clicking the New Query button opens up a new query window, which allows you to do this using the connection already made with SQL Server.

- *Database Engine Query*: Similar to the New Query button, the New Database Engine Query button also creates a new query window. However, it gives you the option of having a different connection to SQL Server through which to run your code. This is a good way of testing code with a different connection to ensure that you cannot see data that should be secure, such as wages, via that connection. So to clarify if you have a connection pointing to DEV, you could use this option to create a connection to the UAT instance.

■ **Caution** The Database Engine Query also allows you to multitask with two different databases. This can be dangerous if your New Query is pointing to DEV but this new connection is pointing to Prod. However, with care and the right circumstances, it can be very useful since the only ways to know which connection a query is running against are by using the window bar of SSMS or by hovering over the particular tab. If you are working with different databases or instances, especially if you are connecting to a development and production instance of a similar database, then you should open another instance of SSMS for safety. Although the method of knowing which connection is the same via the toolbar or the tab, Object Explorer on the left is a quick reminder of which connection your SSMS is dealing with. By having different SSMSs, you should see which instance you are connected to.

- *Analysis Services MDX/DMX/XMLA Query*: Data within a specialized database known as an analysis database allow you to interrogate the data and analyze the information contained within. The three New Analysis Service Query buttons allow you to build different types of analysis queries. I include this information here only for your reference since analysis databases fall outside the scope of this book.

- *Cut/Copy/Paste/Undo/Redo*: Standard Windows actions as found in applications like Word and Excel.

- Navigate Backward/Forward: These two buttons allow you to move backward and forward through your query editors and to select the query editor you wish to use. As you work on your application, you will find that you have several query editors open achieving different tasks from querying the data multiple different ways, building T-SQL code. These buttons allow you to switch between the editors. The buttons work using Ctrl+Shift with either plus (+) or minus (-) and are very similar to using Ctrl+Tab when you switch between applications in Windows. These buttons work as the navigate menu options described in the View menu option.

■ **Note** A query editor is a tabbed document, sometimes known as a multiple document interface (MDI), and will be used extensively throughout the book to write code against SQL Server.

- *Activity Monitor*: This is a useful tool that allows you to monitor your SQL Server and investigate some performance issues within your server or your database. As a developer, optimizing your code so that it performs as efficiently as possible is crucial to a successful database application.

The main area of SQL Server Management Studio that you will be dealing with as a developer is Query Editor, which is covered next. It is a tabbed entry window where you have the ability to enter the code you want to execute.

Query Editor

As you progress through the book, the creation of objects, the manipulation of data, and the execution of code will be shown either by using the graphical interface and options that Object Explorer provides, or by showing code written using T-SQL. To write code, you need a free-form text editor so that you can type anything you need. Luckily, SSMS provides just such an editor as a tabbed screen within the document view on the right-hand side. This is known as Query Editor, and you can find it when you click New Query in the main toolbar or by selecting File ➤ New ➤ Database Engine Query.

There is not a great deal to say about the editor itself, as it really is a free-form method of entering commands and statements for SQL Server to execute, although it does have some good features that you will see as you work through the book. However, Query Editor has a toolbar that is worth covering at this point in time that is shown when you click New Query and a Query Editor window is displayed. Figure 2-12 shows this Query Editor toolbar, and Table 2-1 describes each of the toolbar options.

Figure 2-12. *Query Editor toolbar*

Table 2-1. *Query Editor Toolbar Options*

Tool	Tool Name	Description
	Connect	Requests a connection to the server if one doesn't currently exist
	Change Connection	Allows you to change the current connection by disconnecting and reconnecting the connection you are using
ApressFinancial	Available Databases	A combobox that lists all the databases in the server you are currently connected to; if you want to run a query against a different database, you can select the database here. The code will execute against the database displayed, provided that you have permission to run against it.
Execute	Execute	Executes the code in the query window, or if some of the code is highlighted, will execute only the highlighted code
Debug	Debug	Will debug and allow you to step through the code; you will see this in Chapter 17.
	Cancel Executing Query	Sends a cancel signal to the server to request the query that is executing to be stopped as soon as the server can; a cancel is not always immediate. There will be a delay in sending the command while SQL Server "pauses" to receive the command.
	Parse	Parses the query code looking for syntactical errors
	Display Estimated Execution Plan	Helps you to analyze your T-SQL query for optimization; displays the query plan SQL Server estimates would execute if you were to run the code
	Query Options	The connection options that will be used when executing the code
	IntelliSense Enabled	The ability to allow SSMS to help you write your code; when you start typing code, if IntelliSense is enabled, then SSMS will attempt to intelligently sense what you are wanting to achieve and suggest column names and syntax keywords and so forth to help you write your code more quickly than if you were to type it all out by hand.
	Include Actual Execution Plan	When your code is executed, you can also output the steps SQL Server executed between the start and end of your query. This will be placed in a separate tab to the results and any messages.
	Include Client Statistics	Displays statistics about the query; this will be placed in a separate tab to the results and any messages.

(continued)

Table 2-1. (*continued*)

Tool	Tool Name	Description
	Results To Text	Displays the results in text format
	Results To Grid	Displays the results in a grid format, the default
	Results To File	Places the results in an output file rather than in SQL Server Management Studio
	Comment out the selected lines	Takes the lines that are highlighted and comments them out so that they don't execute
	Uncomment out the selected lines	Takes the lines that are highlighted and uncomments them out so that they don't execute
	Decrease Indent	Decreases the indentation of the highlighted code
	Increase Indent	Increases the indentation of the highlighted code
	Specify Values for Template Parameters	SSMS has templates for many actions. You will see these used throughout the book. When a template is used, pressing this button will allow you to enter values in the template options.

You will see and use this toolbar quite extensively within this book and throughout your development career, so it will soon become very familiar to you.

sqlcmd

There is one final tool to demonstrate, which is called sqlcmd. This is a command prompt based tool that augments SSMS and is very useful for running scripts as a batch. You may also find DBAs who use multiple different databases such as Sybase and DB2. These databases are based on Linux and therefore are command-driven rather than GUI-driven. DBAs use the sqlcmd tool as they prefer more commonly use command prompt based methods of working. Finally, if you are using SQL Server Express without the tools addition, you are likely to use sqlcmd. Throughout the book, the scripts I use can be executed using sqlcmd.

To use sqlcmd, you need to open a command prompt. In Windows 7 this is from the Start ➤ Run ➤ cmd oρ finding the Command Prompt app in Windows 8. Once the command prompt window is open, you can navigate to where any script resides that you wish to execute or you can work in the default folder. You can also enter a T-SQL based script without a file.

Once a command prompt is open, to execute sqlcmd you type sqlcmd and then use a number of parameters to define some of the options you want to use. In Figure 2-13 the options, as defined with a hyphen and a letter, will connect to the server (-S) and instance of FAT-BELLY-SONY\APRESS_DEV1 to database (-d) APRESSFINANCIAL if it existed using Windows Authentication (-E). For SQL Server authentication, you would use parameters –U for user and –P for password. Parameters are case sensitive.

Figure 2-13. *Using sqlcmd within a command prompt*

At this point, there is no database within SQL Server to demonstrate sqlcmd, but I will demonstrate it further in Chapter 17.

In Chapter 1, I mentioned Single User Mode where you need to connect to SQL Server when the System Administrator account is locked out. By using SQL Server startup option –mSQLCMD, you can then use sqlcmd to access SQL Server and remedy the problem. You can set the startup option in the Services section on the SQL Server service as shown in Figure 2-14.

Figure 2-14. *Using sqlcmd within a command prompt*

Summary

SSMS is a tool for working with SQL Server that you will see in action throughout this book, whether you're working with the graphical interface or using Query Editor to write T-SQL code. As you learned in this chapter, the main areas of the tool are the Registered Servers explorer, Object Explorer, and the main documents window that will contain graphical representations of objects in the database.

You were also introduced to the sqlcmd utility, which is ideal for entering T-SQL code outside of SSMS when SSMS isn't available or unable to be used, such as when you need to connect in an emergency.

CHAPTER 3

■ ■ ■

Database Design and Creation

Now that you've installed SQL Server and examined the main tools you'll use as a SQL Server developer or administrator, it's almost time to start building the ApressFinancial database solution. However, you can't do this yet because you still don't know what the database will hold. At this point in time, all the information you have is that you'll be building a database to hold some financial transactions for a personal or corporate financial tool. You'll gear this database toward a financial tool that a corporation might use because SQL Server can be scaled from one user to thousands of users very easily. The next step is to gather more information about the requirements of the solution and about what data is required to be stored in the database. Once the information-gathering stage is complete, you'll then be able to create the database within SQL Server throughout the book. The book's main intent is to demonstrate to you how to build a database solution from the ground up.

The design of a database solution is not a simple task; it requires a great deal of work. This chapter will provide you with insight into the vast area that is database design for OLTP based databases, although there is an awesome book by Louis Davidson on this subject called *Pro SQL Server Relational Database Design and Implementation* (Apress). Armed with this information, you'll proceed through arranging the data so that retrieval is as efficient as possible (this is referred to as normalizing the data) and ensuring that data duplication is minimal or, ideally, that no data duplication exists. You'll also need to know how the system and the data within it will be used on a day-to-day basis. Finally, you'll need to know what type of system is being built—for instance, whether it will receive instant data updates or just be used to analyze already defined data. Once the design is complete, building a database solution will be a much smoother process. A good design ensures you've gathered all the information you need to build the correct tables with the correct information without duplication.

Although the methods and processes involved with the design may not meet the needs of every organization, this chapter presents an overview of the processes involved and also shows you how to build up information and ensure that the design is well thought out. This chapter will cover the following topics:

- What a database is, what it consists of, and where it is stored

- How to define the type of system: transactional or analytical

- How to collect data about the current system and seek out information about the new system

- How to create a database where the data is disk-based through SQL Server Management Studio, a wizard, or a Query Editor window, and how to set database options in a Query Editor window. The options for a database that also deals with in-memory will be covered in Chapter 7.

- How to review the database details

- How to remove a database using SQL Server Management Studio and a Query Editor window

■ **Note** No specific formal design techniques will be used in this chapter's exercise, as this is not a book specifically geared toward database design. However, the processes—both physical and logical—to get to the final design of the database will be the same.

Defining a Database

A *database* is a container for objects that not only store data, but also enable data storage and retrieval to operate in a secure and safe manner. A SQL Server database can hold the following objects (among others):

- Table definitions
- Columns within those tables, which make up rows of data
- Programs (either *stored procedures* or *triggers* written in T-SQL or *assemblies* that are written in .NET) used to access or manipulate the data
- Indexes, which are used to speed up the retrieval of data
- Views, which are specialized ways of looking at the actual data
- Functions, which are repetitive tasks that can be applied to rows of data

The preceding list contains a fair number of technical terms, so let's take a few moments to look at their definitions:

- *Tables*: Tables are where data are kept within the database. A database must contain at least one table to be of use, although you can have a database with no user tables and only system tables. *System tables* are special tables that SQL Server uses to help it work with the database. These tables contain information within rows and columns, much like in Excel, but they have a great deal more power than cells within Excel. *Temporary tables*—another type of database table—can take several different forms. These will be discussed at several points within the book. You can have tables that reside on disk or in memory.

- *Columns*: Columns provide a definition of each single item of information that builds up to a table definition. A column consists of cells that all hold data, much like a column in Excel. Unlike in Excel, though, where each cell can hold a different type of data, a column within a SQL Server table is restricted to what the data within it relates to, the type of data it will hold, and how much information can be stored in it. Each table must have at least one column, although the column doesn't need to contain any information.

- *Rows*: A row consists of one cell from every column defined for the table. There can be any number of rows in a table; you are limited only by your disk space or available memory, or the amount of disk space you defined as the maximum in your database creation definition or the amount of disk space on your server. A row will define a single unit of information, such as a user's bank account details or a product on an e-commerce site. *Stored procedures*: When it comes to requiring a program to manipulate or work with data, or perform the same data-intensive task repeatedly, it's often better to store this code in a stored procedure. Stored procedures contain one or more T-SQL statements, which are compiled and ready to be executed when required. Stored procedures are permanently stored in the database, ready for use at any time.

- *T-SQL statements*: A T-SQL statement is a program statement that SQL Server can use to work with your data.

- *Assemblies*: Assemblies are similar to stored procedures, in that they can be used to manipulate or work with data, but they are used more for procedural logic, as you might find in a .NET program. An assembly can be more than a replacement for a stored procedure and can take on many different guises—for example, you can also build data types using an assembly.

- *Indexes*: These can be regarded as predefined lists of information that can inform the database how the data is physically sorted and stored, or they can be used by SQL Server to find rows of data quickly using information supplied by a T-SQL query and matching this information to data within columns. An index consists of one or more columns from the table it is defined for, but it is not possible for an index to cover more than one table. A table with no index is called a heap. An index in SQL Server is very much like the index of a book, which is used to locate a piece of information faster than looking through the book page by page. An index is not mandatory for disk-based tables but is mandatory for memory-based tables.

- *Views*: Views can be thought of as virtual tables. Views can contain information combined from several tables and can present a more user-friendly interface to the data. Views can also add a great deal of security to an application, but they do give reduced functionality over the use of stored procedures or direct access to the tables. Views can also be indexed to speed processing of data within.

- *Functions*: A function is similar to a stored procedure, but it takes information one row at a time or produces information one row at a time as you work through the rows of data you re processing. For example, you would use a stored procedure to produce output to create a report, but you would use a function to go through each transaction to calculate interest on a daily basis.

Also within every database is a set of system tables that SQL Server uses to maintain that database. These tables hold information about every column, information about every user, and many other pieces of information (such as metadata). System table security in SQL Server is such that you cannot access these tables directly—only through views. You don't need to investigate system tables at this point because their data can't be modified and the information they produce is useful only for working with advanced functionality.

Prebuilt Databases Within SQL Server

Several databases are installed and displayed when SQL Server is first installed. A Microsoft pre-built example database can be downloaded and installed post installation. This section explores each of these databases so that you'll know what each does and feel comfortable when you come across them outside of this book.

Let's first look at the most important database in SQL Server: the `master` database. I will then cover the `tempdb`, `model`, `msdb`, and `AdventureWorks/AdventureWorksDW` sample databases.

■ **Note** The `AdventureWorksDW` database is used with Analysis Services, which will not be installed.

master

master is the most important database in SQL Server, so I must start off with a warning.

■ **Caution** Directly alter this database at your own peril!

There should be no reason to go into any of the system views within this database and alter the records or column information directly. There are system functions that allow a constructive alteration of any of the data in an orderly fashion, and these are the only approaches you should use to alter the master database.

The master database is at the heart of SQL Server, and if it should become corrupted, there is a very good chance that SQL Server will not work correctly. The master database contains the following crucial information used by SQL Server in its work:

- All logins, or roles, to which the user IDs belong

- Every system configuration setting (for example, data sorting information, security implementation, default language)

- The names of and information about the databases within the server

- The location of databases

- How SQL Server is initialized

- Specific system tables holding the following information (this list is not exhaustive):

 - How the cache is used

 - Which character sets are available

 - A list of the available languages

 - System error and warning messages

 - Special SQL Server objects called *assemblies* The master database is the security guard of SQL Server, and it uses the preceding information to ensure that everything is kept in check.

■ **Note** It is crucial that you regularly back up the master database. Make sure that doing so is part of your backup strategy. Backups are covered in more detail in Chapter 8.

tempdb

The tempdb database is—as its name suggests—a temporary database whose lifetime is the duration of a SQL Server session; once SQL Server stops, the tempdb database is lost. When SQL Server starts up again, the tempdb database is re-created, fresh and new, and ready for use. There is more to this process, but before I delve into that, you first need to know what the tempdb database is used for.

A database can hold data, and that data can be held in many tables. You use commands and functions to retrieve and manipulate that data. However, there may be times when you want to temporarily store a certain set of data for processing at a later time—for example, when you pass data from one stored procedure to another that is going to run right after the first one. One option is to store that data within a table within the tempdb database. Such a table could be thought of as a "permanent" temporary table, as it will exist until it is specifically deleted or until tempdb is re-created on a SQL Server restart. Another type of temporary table is one created within a stored procedure or query each time the stored procedure or query executes. This will also be placed within the tempdb database, although its lifetime will last only until all users of the table finish. You'll look at both of these types of tables in Chapter 16 when looking at essentials of coding T-SQL. Storing data in temporary tables is fine and something you will do in your lifetime as a developer, as long as the tempdb database is not refreshed. If it is, then your data will be gone, and you will need to rebuild them.

You may be thinking that this is not an ideal solution. After all, wouldn't it be wonderful if temporary information could be stored somewhere outside of the database? Well, that's not really where tempdb would be used. It really should be thought of only as transitional storage space.

Another reason tempdb is refreshed is that not only is it available for a developer to use, but also SQL Server itself uses tempdb. Actually, SQL Server uses tempdb all the time, and when you reinitialize SQL Server, it will want to know that any temporary work it was dealing with is cleaned out. After all, there could have been a problem with this temporary work that caused you to restart the service in the first place.

Being just like any other database, tempdb has size restrictions, and you must ensure that it is big enough to cope with your applications and any temporary information stored within it generated both by yourself and by SQL Server. An example of SQL Server using tempdb is when it has to hold data while it completes a sort of data for output. As you read through the next sections, you will see that a database has a minimum and a maximum size. tempdb is no exception to this, and you should ensure that its settings provide for expansion so it can grow as required.

■ **Caution** Because tempdb has a limited size, you must take care when you use it that it doesn't get filled with records in tables from rogue procedures that indefinitely create tables with too many records. If this were to happen, not only would your process stop working, but also the whole server could stop functioning and therefore impact everyone on that server!

As indicated in the first paragraph of this section, there's more to say about tempdb's refresh process,, which you'll examine in the next section.

model

Whenever you create a database, as you'll do shortly in this chapter, it has to be modeled on a predefined set of criteria. For example, if you want all your databases to have a specific initial size or to have a specific set of information, you would place this information into the model database, which acts as a template database for further databases. If you wanted all databases to have a specific table within them, for example, you would put this table in the model database.

The model database is used as the basis for creating the tempdb database as well as any other database created by you. Thus, you need to think ahead if you decide to alter the model database because any changes will be mirrored within the tempdb database. It is rare for the model database to be changed.

msdb

msdb is another crucial database within SQL Server because it provides the necessary information to run jobs to SQL Server Agent.

SQL Server Agent is a Windows service in SQL Server that runs any scheduled jobs that you set up (for example, jobs that contain backup processing). A *job* is a process defined in SQL Server that runs automatically without any manual intervention to start it but can be manually started if desired.

As with tempdb and model, you should not directly amend this database, and there is no real need to do so. Many other processes use msdb. For example, when you create a backup or perform a restore, msdb is used to store information about these tasks.

AdventureWorks/AdventureWorksDW

AdventureWorks and AdventureWorksDW are the example databases that can be downloaded and installed from Microsoft's CodePlex web site, www.codeplex.com. There is a link from the SQL Server install placed on your computer that can be used. Once these databases have been downloaded and installed on the computer, you have to attach these databases to SQL Server. Attaching databases will be demonstrated in Chapter 8. You will use the AdventureWorks database when looking at Advanced T-SQL in Chapter 17. These databases are based on a manufacturing company that produces bicycles. They exemplify the new features in SQL Server as well as demonstrate the features that already exist in earlier SQL Server versions, such as Reporting Services and CLR functionality, in a simple, easy-to-follow way.

The following excerpt from the Microsoft documentation provides a concise overview of what the AdventureWorks databases are about:

> *Adventure Works Cycles, the fictitious company on which the AdventureWorks sample databases are based, is a large, multinational manufacturing company. The company manufactures and sells metal and composite bicycles to North American, European, and Asian commercial markets. While its base operation is located in Bothell, Washington, with 290 employees, several regional sales teams are located throughout their market base.*

The example databases are not meant for novice SQL Server developers, although you'll have no problems with them after you learn the basics of SQL Server. They are also very good for practicing what you learn about SQL Server from this book with different data to check out what you're learning.

Now that you know what databases are in SQL Server, let's start building one! You'll start by deciding what type of database to create, depending on what it will be used for.

Choosing the Database System Type

Before you can design a database, you have to decide whether the system will be an Online Transaction Processing (OLTP) system or an Online Analytical Processing (OLAP) system, also known as a Business Intelligence (BI) system. You could find this out prior to your first meeting with the users, or even during the first meeting, but the choice of OLTP or OLAP will probably be indicated in the initial proposal.

Before you make a decision, you need to understand these two key types of systems.

OLTP

An OLTP system provides instant updates of data. There is a good chance that an OLTP database system has a separate user front end written in a .NET language such as Visual Basic .NET (VB .NET), C#, or ASP.NET. This user front end calls through to the database and instantly updates any changes a user has made to the underlying data.

OLTP systems require many considerations to ensure they're fast and reliable and can keep the data integrity intact. When you design an OLTP system, it's crucial that you get not only the database structure right, but also where the data physically resides. It's common to find that OLTP systems are normalized to third normal form (more on what this term means later in the chapter), although this may not happen in every case. By normalizing your data, you will aid the achievement of one of the main goals of an OLTP system: keeping data updates as short as possible. When you normalize your data by removing redundant or duplicate columns, you should ensure that the data to be written is as compact as possible. In many OLTP systems, normalization is critical.

Backups

Many OLTP systems are in use 24 hours a day, 7 days a week. The high frequency of changes in such a system's data means that backing up the database is a necessary and mandatory task.

It is possible to back up a database while SQL Server is in use, although it is best to perform a backup either when SQL Server is not in use or when there will be a small amount of activity updating the data taking place. The ideal time frame might be in the middle of the night or even during a break period.

Whenever you decide to perform a backup, it's crucial you constantly monitor and check the backup to ensure that the system is still performing as desired. You would not be the first person to find that what you thought was a valid backup that could be restored in a disaster situation was in fact corrupt, incomplete, or just not happening. Therefore, periodically take a backup from production and reload it into a secure development area just to confirm that it works. I have found the best solution to be a refresh of a non-production database to be completed on a Monday from a production backup taken over the weekend.

Indexes

Speed is essential to a successful OLTP system. You should see a higher number of indexes within an OLTP system as compared to an OLAP system, with these indexes used not only to help relate data from one table to another, but also to allow fast access to rows within tables.

■ **Note** Chapter 6 covers how to build indexes, how indexes work, and how to manage indexes within your solutions.

In-memory data

Staying on the subject of speed, working with high-access critical data as fast as possible is a major tennet of a successful OLTP system. Having data in memory reduces the need for any disk I/O, which is slower than having the data already loaded. SQL Server will attempt to keep the correct data loaded as best as possible, but you are limited by memory constraints so SQL Server can unload the data from memory requiring the data to be re-read from disk when next required. It is possible to define a table that is permanently held in memory and the data never unloaded therefore providing you with the fastest access. This decision and method of design should not be applied to all tables as you could exhaust the memory on the server as your application and data requirements increase. In-memory data is covered in great detail throughout the book so that you are fully aware of best practices and how to use it safely.

BI/OLAP

When considering an OLTP system, you must keep in mind that an update to the database could happen at any moment in time, and that update must be reflected within the database instantly. It is also crucial that the system performs many updates simultaneously and that it does not corrupt any data when it does so.

A BI system is designed with the premise that the data remains fairly static with infrequent updates. These updates could be nightly, weekly, monthly, or any other time variant as long as updates aren't happening on a frequent basis, like in an OLTP system. As the name "Business Intelligence" suggests, in this system a large amount of the processing involves analysis of existing data to provide intelligent, analytical, and informative data to the business. There should be little or no updating of that data—ostensibly only when the data within the analysis is found to be incorrect or, as mentioned previously, when more data are being applied for analysis. Backing up the data will probably take place only as a "final action," after the database has had changes applied to it. There is no need to make it a regular occurrence. Many BI systems can also be refreshed from empty from the host data source.

BI systems tend to have two databases involved in their overall architecture. The first database is a normal SQL Server database in which you would store the data to be used to build your BI database. This could be your main database, although you would need to take care with the processing time and resources that can be taken up when the BI database extracts that data. A BI database has a completely different database infrastructure and objects compared to OLTP, and what you are going to learn in this book and does not have tables and indexes. Instead it uses the data loaded from the SQL Server database and stores the data in files on the servers where the data has been aggregated with measures and dimensions. BI databases require a totally different mindset and use different SQL called MDX to extract the data.

Systems designed for BI sometimes do not follow any design standards or normalization techniques. You tend to see no normalization in an OLAP system, as it is easier to take data and to slice and dice it without having to bring in data from a normalized table.

Example System Choice

When you take into consideration all the information presented in the preceding sections, it becomes fairly obvious that although the data updates will be relatively infrequent in the example system (in other words, only when a financial transaction occurs or a statement is generated), there will be updates occurring online with instant results expected. Therefore, the system you will be building will be an OLTP system.

Gathering the Data

Among the first things you need to do before building a database is to find out what information the database system has to hold and then decide how that information should be stored (for example, numerical or text, length, and so on). To achieve this goal, you'll perform a data-gathering exercise, which could involve talking with those people who are the owners of the system and those who will be using the system.

For larger systems, you would hold several meetings, each of which would pinpoint one area of the system to discuss and research. Even then, several meetings may be spent going back and discussing each area. You could also conduct interviews, distribute questionnaires, or even just observe any existing processes in action, all in an effort to gather as much information as possible about the database and how it will be used.

The key indicator of whether a database solution is successful is not found so much in the building of the system, but rather in the information-gathering process before the first line of code is actually written. If you're working off an incorrect piece of information, or you're missing an element that might be crucial to the final solution, already the system is flawed. Involving the users as much as possible at the earliest stage and then including them as the design progresses should result in a significant reduction of errors and missing parts in the final product.

For the example financial program, the first people you would want to talk to are the owners of the data that will be displayed. These are the people in the banking department who handle checks, cash withdrawals, credit card transactions, and so forth, and also those people who handle the purchase and sale of stock shares, unit trusts, life insurance policies, and so on. These people will know what documentation or statements are sent to which customers, as well as the information those statements contain. In addition, these people will likely have a good idea about how customers may want to reconcile these statements, and also what data will be allowed to be downloaded and inserted into your SQL Server database.

At the first meeting, you examine all the documentation to see what information is stored in the current system. You find out at the meeting that the current system sends out different statements, one statement for the customer's current account and a separate statement for each financial product the customer owns. When you examine the statements, you focus on the information each contains that you need to capture to produce a similar statement. This could be not only customer-related information, but also regulatory statements.

With the information from all the documentation in hand, you can start discussions about what is required from the system you are to build. Obviously, a great deal of information will be discussed in these meetings; some of it is useful and some not. Make sure that the discussions are recorded in the order in which the people present make points and not in "logical" order. This simulates meetings where people "remember" items that have to be catered to, where one point raised may make someone remember a point elsewhere.

Out of the initial discussions, you note the following points:

1. The software must be able to handle working with more than one product. The main product is a current checking account that a bank or a single user might use to hold banking details. The system also must be able to manage by-products such as loans, life insurance policies, and car insurance policies, and it should be able to record any trading of shares on the stock market.

2. Statements are produced on a monthly basis or at any time the customer requests them from the system. If a customer requests a statement within the month, there will still be a statement produced for that month.

3. Interest accrues daily on accounts that are in credit and is subtracted daily from overdrawn accounts.

4. Annual, monthly, or single-premium products can be held for a customer or held by a customer in a stand-alone version of the system. You need to know when to start and stop collecting payments, and you also need to determine which products you send out a reminder for (for example, a notice to let a customer know her car insurance policy is up for renewal).

5. If a collection for a product failed, the system needs to recognize this so the amount can be collected the next time a collection is due.

6. Each product will have its own statement, but only banking statements will be produced on request.

7. Trading of stock shares is allowed, so the system needs to record and display the current value for a customer's specific share at any time.

Notice how the information in this list is in no set order because this is how information tends to come out. Also notice that there is a little bit of duplication of information in points 2 and 6; if this is not realized or understood, it could cause problems.

■ **Note** This is the only data-gathering exercise performed for the example database. The information gathered here should be cross-checked later in the design phase with the users, although this is beyond the scope of this book.

Determining the Information to Store in the Database

Using the notes you took in the previous section, you'll now try to find every area each point has an interest in. Looking at the list of areas that require information to be recorded and stored within the database, it's clear you need to arrange them in some sort of order. You're still looking at your solution from a logical viewpoint, and you're not ready to start building anything in SQL Server yet.

First off, let's scan through the points listed and try to group the information into specific, related areas. The list items are numbered, so I will be able to easily demonstrate the groupings. The following list shows some initial groupings and reasons for them:

- Financial products

 - 1: You are dealing with more than one product. You need to record each product.

 - 2: Statements will be produced for each product, and specific product information for those statements will be recorded here, such as the name of the product.

 - 4: You need to record what type of premium is associated with this product.

 - 5: This point deals with a financial product's premium collection.

 - 6: This point deals again with statement production.

- Customers

 - 2: Customers can request statements.

 - 3: You need to record the amount of interest for a customer.

 - 4: A list of the different products associated with each customer is required.

 - 7: For each share, you need to keep a current value.

- Customer addresses

 - 2: You need each customer's address in order to send a statement.

 - 6: As with point 2, you need the customer's address to send a statement.

- Shares

 - 1: You trade shares on the stock market; therefore, you need to record share information.

 - 7: You need to keep a given share's value.

- Transactions

 - 2: A list of transactions is required for statement production.

 - 3: Interest charges have to be calculated and recorded.

 - 4: Regular and ad hoc premiums have to be recorded.

 - 5: You need to record failed transaction collection.

 - 6: Statements will be produced for each product.

These five distinct groups could translate into five distinct tables within the proposed database. At this point in the logical design process, you would base your design on these five tables. From here, it is then possible to start examining the information that should go into these logical tables. There might be duplication of data with columns in the "wrong" table, and the potential for multiple columns to hold "similar" information or the same column in more than one table.

Let's look at the list points in turn in the following sections and examine what information should be stored in each "table." The information listed in the sections that follow is taken from the discussion with the users, and a list of the columns is supplied that may initially form the basis of the tables. Each column has a description, so when you go back to the users, they'll understand the purpose of the columns. Also at this stage, you will add columns to hold any identifiers for finding the records; in the following sections, these are denoted with (K). These are potentially the keys, which I'll cover in more detail later in the "Building Relationships" section of this chapter.

Financial Products

The aim of this table is to hold the different products the company sells. From bank accounts to life insurance, all products will be held here. This table will be used when producing statements and creating transactions when the user's balance changes—for example, when buying further shares:

- *Financial Product ID (K)*: This is a unique identifier.

- *Financial Product Name*: This is the name of the product, such as checking account, share, loan, and so forth.

- *Frequency of Payment*: For each product, this indicates how often payments are collected for those products that require it, such as a loan, a regular savings account, and so on.

Customers

This table will hold customer details, such as the customer's products and balances. To clarify and reiterate, there will be items currently within this table that will no longer reside within it once you normalize the data. For example, you will see an attribute for "Account Numbers for Each Product." When you proceed through normalization, you will see how attributes such as this are "moved":

- *Customer ID (K)*: This is a unique ID for each customer.

- *Financial Product Balance*: This is the current balance of each product.

- *Title*: This is the customer's title (Mr., Ms., and so on).

- *First Name*: This is the customer's first name.

- *Last Name*: This is the customer's last name.

- *Address*: This is the customer's address.

- *Account Numbers for Each Product*: This is the account number of each product the customer owns.

- *Financial Products Details*: These are the details of each financial product the customer owns.

Customer Addresses

As part of the analysis, you will not hold your own address information, and you will instead get this from a third-party system. This table will therefore not exist within your database.

Shares

This table holds the details of each stock share, such as its current price and its price history:

- *Share Price ID (K)*: This is a unique ID for each share.
- *Share Name*: This is the name of the share.
- *Current Price*: This is the current price of the share.
- *Previous Price*: This contains previous prices of the share.
- *Price Date*: This is the date the price was set at this level.
- *Stock Market Ticker ID*: This is the ID for this share on the stock market.

Transactions

This table holds the details of each financial transaction that takes place for each product.

- *Financial Transaction ID (K)*: This is a unique ID for each financial transaction.
- *Customer ID*: This is the customer's unique identifier, as defined in the "Customers" section earlier.
- *Date of the Transaction*: This is the date the transaction took place.
- *Financial Product*: This is a link to the financial products table.
- *Amount*: This is the amount the transaction is for.
- *Debit/Credit*: This flag denotes whether the transaction is a debit or a credit.

External and Ignored Information

At this point, you have a first draft of the logical tables and attributes, but there are still no relationships between these tables. There is one more piece of information that you need to know, which concerns information not recorded because it won't be included within this database.

The example database will not hold every item of information that is required to make the system complete. This is to keep the example simple and to avoid having extra tables that will not be used within the book's exercises. However, there may be other times when you may want to implement only some of the tables—for example, when performing a viability study (in other words, when you're building part of a system to prove the viability of an idea). Or perhaps a third-party tool can fill in the gaps.

For example, a system might use an external addressing system, and instead of holding all customer addresses within the system, it may use a cross-reference ID. A table could also exist to hold all of the financial transactions for products not covered where specialized tables are required, such as for company pension plans.

Next, let's move on to consider relationships between the tables in the database.

Building Relationships

Much like people, databases can be temperamental creatures and need a bit of TLC. Good relationships can provide this kind of care and attention.

At the moment, the tables in the example database are essentially single, unrelated items. Of course, they have columns with the same name in different tables, but there is nothing tying them together. This is where defining relationships between the tables comes in. Binding the tables together in this way ensures that changes in one table do not cause data in another table to become invalid.

Using Keys

A *key* is a way of identifying a record in a database table. You can use keys to build relationships between tables because a key refers to a whole record—a property you can exploit when working with columns that, for example, have the same name in different tables or even a different name in different tables but the columns hold the same information. Using a key as a shortcut, you can make the link between the two very easily. Keys can also uniquely identify a record in a table when that is an important part of the database's design.

A key can be defined on a single column if that's enough to identify the record, or it can be defined on more than one column if not. The sections that follow introduce the three kinds of keys you can use in a database: primary, foreign/referencing, and candidate/alternate. You will also look at using a SQL Server method called a constraint instead of a primary key.

Primary Key

The *primary key* is probably the most important key type. First and foremost, the column (or combination of columns) on which the primary key is defined must contain only unique values. A primary key cannot be defined on a column, or a sequence of columns, that does not return a single row. To this end, it is not possible to define a primary key for any columns that allow NULL values. A further restraint is that a table may have only one primary key.

A primary key can be used to link data from one table to data from another. For instance, in your example database, you have two tables: one holding customers and another holding customer banking transactions. You will define a primary key on the Customers table on the customer ID that is generated uniquely each time a new customer record is inserted. This is then used to link to the many records within the banking transactions table, to return all the transactions for that customer ID. The link between these two tables is the customer ID, which as previously mentioned is defined as a primary key in the Customers table.

Later in this chapter, you'll see how to join tables together and define a relationship between them. A join and a relationship are essentially the same thing: a logical link between two or more tables that can be defined through a specific column or set of columns between the tables.

Foreign/Referencing Key

There will be times when you have two or more tables linked together in a relationship, as demonstrated in the earlier example, where the link between the Customers and Transactions tables is the customer ID column. This column returns a unique row in the Customers table; hence, it is defined as the primary key of the Customers table. However, there has to be a corresponding *foreign* (or *referencing*) *key* in the Transactions table to link back to the Customers table, which is the customer ID column of the Customers table.

When it comes to creating relationships within your example database, you will later see how a foreign key is created that will create a link, or a relationship, between two columns. This link is created through a *constraint*, which is a method SQL Server uses to check the details built into the relationship. From the viewpoint of a foreign key, this constraint, or check, will ensure that the relationship follows the conditions set with it. You'll examine foreign keys in more depth in the "More on Foreign Keys" section.

Candidate/Alternate Key

As mentioned previously, a table can have only one primary key. However, there may be another key that could just as easily be defined as a primary key. This is known as a *candidate key* because it is a candidate for being the primary key.

There is no logical difference at all between the definition of a candidate key and a primary key. For example, if you have a table that holds spare parts for a General Motors (GM) vehicle, you could have an internal GM part number to use when ordering parts at the head office for various GM branches. This part number would be unique and would likely be used as the primary key. However, a part number is also created by each of the manufacturers, which is unique to them. This, too, could be a primary key if you include the supplier identifier in the database. You can't have two primary keys, and you've chosen the GM part number as the primary key, but you could create a candidate key using the manufacturer identifier and part number.

A Unique Constraint Instead of a Primary Key

This is where having a constraint defined will ensure that only unique values can be entered into columns defined within the constraint. This sounds very much like the previous primary key definition, but there are differences.

A *unique constraint* is not a primary key, but the column or columns defined within the constraint could be a primary key. Also, a unique constraint can contain NULL values, but recall that a primary key cannot. However, NULL is treated as any other value within a column; therefore, the columns used to make a unique constraint must remain unique, including the NULL value, when you're looking to insert or update data. Therefore, this means that there would only be one NULL value to keep the uniqueness. Finally, it is possible to have multiple unique constraints, but you can have only one primary key. An example of a table with a unique constraint could be a table that holds the dates and numbers that correspond to the weeks of the year. Week 1 could begin on January 4, Week 2 would then begin on January 11, and so on. The primary key would be the week number; however, a unique constraint could also be placed on the date column.

Creating Relationships

A *relationship* in a SQL Server database is a logical link between two tables. It is impossible to have a physical link, although, as you will see later, a physical line is drawn between two tables when designing the database. Having a physical link, such as having a table holding relationship data, would mean the actual data linking the two tables would be stored only once in a central location, and that information within the keys linking the tables would be stored more than once, which is just not the case.

When defining a logical relationship, you're informing SQL Server that you'll be linking a primary key from the master table to a foreign key in another table. So already there is a need for two keys: one on each table.

The following sections present specific details about relationships, starting with a look at how relationships work with the concept of referential integrity.

Relationships and Referential Integrity

A relationship can be used to enforce data integrity. In other words, if you are expecting data in one table because there is data in another, you can place a relationship between these two tables to ensure that no SQL command breaks this rule.

Referential integrity revolves around the idea that there are two tables in the database that contain the same information, and it requires that the duplicated data elements are kept consistent. For example, if you have a primary key in one table and a foreign key in another table that have data that match exactly, it is important that both pieces of data either change together or don't change at all. Relationships are not the only way referential integrity can be enforced; you can also use triggers to ensure that data remains valid (you will examine this further in Chapter 18). For instance, the example banking system includes the Customers and Transactions tables. It is not possible to record customer transactions without a customer record. As a result, you have to use referential integrity to enforce data integrity between these two tables so that a customer record can't be removed from the database while there are customer transaction records for that customer. Similarly, this rule should allow the removal of a customer record when there are no customer transaction records.

Another result of enforcing referential integrity is that it isn't possible for a customer transaction to be entered using a customer reference number that doesn't exist within the Customers table. Instead, to enter a customer transaction in this situation, you first have to create the customer record, and then you can carry out the transaction.

Finally, if you had a customer record and related customer transaction records, you couldn't alter the customer reference number in the customer record without first altering the customer transaction records and checking that the reference you're altering the customer transaction records to already exists.

■ **Note** Don't confuse referential integrity with other processes that are associated with maintaining data integrity, such as placing checks or default values on columns to ensure that values for a specific column are valid.

So, there are a number of rules to follow if you want to maintain the integrity of your data. If you so desired, you could use referential integrity to enforce data integrity. However, a flip side to all of this to be aware of is that you can keep data integrity within a system and not use referential integrity. Instead, you can create stored procedures or triggers, which are types of programs within SQL Server, to do this task. We will look at these topics in Chapters 15 and 19.

Using stored procedures and triggers is a possible but undesirable solution because it leaves the system open to instances where data integrity is not kept due to holes within the design of the system or the fact that perhaps a developer doesn't have the correct processing sequence to ensure that all data are always valid. Not only that, but if someone adds data directly to a table, the referential integrity could be lost. That said, having the data integrity checks in an application does lead to less traffic flow over the network and potentially less work on the server as the client application is performing the referential integrity checks instead. In most cases, I personally prefer the referential integrity to be performed within the database.

There is one more important point about referential integrity before I move on to discuss database relationship types: If you want to maintain referential integrity by creating a relationship between two tables, these two tables must be in the same database. It is not possible to have referential integrity between two databases.

Types of Relationships

Three main relationship types can exist in a database:

- One-to-one
- One-to-many
- Many-to-many

The sections that follow cover each type, so when it comes to creating a relationship, you'll know which one to create, when to create it, and why. We'll start off by looking at the one-to-one relationship, which is perhaps the easiest type of relationship to understand, although it is one of the least used.

One-to-One

This relationship type isn't very common within a working database. Typically, there is no real reason for one record in one table to match just one record in another. This scenario would exist, for example, only if you were splitting a very large table into two separate tables.

To illustrate the one-to-one relationship, imagine that in the example bank database there is a table that holds PINs for ATM cards, keeping them completely separate from the remainder of the customer records (see Figure 3-1). In most cases, there would be one PIN record for each customer record, but there may be exceptions—for instance, a high-interest deposit account may not have a card, and therefore there would be no associated PIN record.

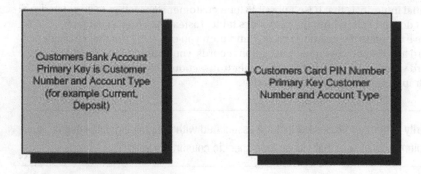

Figure 3-1. *One-to-one relationship*

One-to-Many

Perhaps the most common relationship found in a database is the one-to-many relationship. This is where one master record is linked with zero, one, or more records in a child table.

Using the banking example, say you have a customer master record along with any number of associated transaction records. The number of these transaction records could range from none, which corresponds to when a customer is new to the bank and hasn't made a deposit or performed a transaction, to one or more, which corresponds to when there has been an initial deposit in an account, and then further deposits or withdrawal transactions after that (see Figure 3-2).

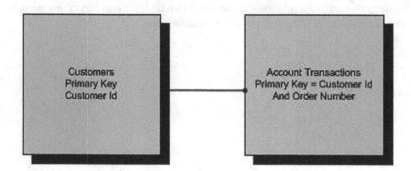

Figure 3-2. *One-to-many relationship*

You'll see this concept in action again in the customer-to-transactions relationship you will build for the solution.

Many-to-Many

Many-to-many is the final relationship type that can exist in a database. This relationship can happen relatively frequently where there are zero, one, or indeed many records in the master table related to zero, one, or many records in a child table.

An example of a many-to-many relationship might be where a company has several depots for dispatching goods, presented in the master table, which then dispatch goods to many stores, presented in the child table (see Figure 3-3). The depots could be located and organized so that different depots could all supply the same store, and they could be arranged in groups of produce, frozen, perishables, and bonded. In order for a store to be supplied with a full complement of goods, it would need to be supplied by a number of different depots, which would typically be in different locations.

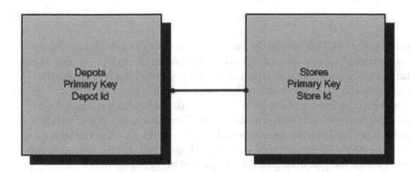

Figure 3-3. *Many-to-many relationship*

When building relationships within a database, it is necessary to have a foreign key whether that is logically defined in code where the relationship is checked or physically via keys. I covered foreign keys briefly earlier in the chapter; let's take a closer look at them in the next section.

More on Foreign Keys

A foreign key is any key on a child table where a column, or a set of columns, can be directly matched with exactly the same number and information from the master table. By using this foreign key, you can build up the data to return via a relationship.

However, a foreign key does not have to map to a primary key on a master table. Although it is common to see a foreign key mapped to a primary key, as long as the key in the master table that is being mapped to is a unique key (a candidate or alternate key), you can build a relationship between a master table and a child table.

The whole essence of a foreign key lies in its mapping process and the fact that it is on the child table. A foreign key will exist only when a relationship has been created from the child table to the parent table. But what exactly are the master table and the child tables? To demonstrate, let's refer to the relationship examples. Take the one-to-many relationship. The master table would be on the left side, or the "one" side of the relationship, and the child table would be on the right side, or the "many" side of the relationship (see Figure 3-4).

Figure 3-4. *Foreign key*

It is totally possible for the master table and the child table to be the same table, and for the foreign key and the unique key to both be defined within the same table. This is called a *self-join* or a *reflexive relationship*. You don't tend to see this much within a database because it is quite an unusual situation, although you could use it to ensure that the data in one column exactly match the information in another column, just as in any other join.

For example, say you have a table built around customers and you have two columns, one of which is a parent customer ID, which holds an ID for the head office and is used to link all the branches. If the head office is also seen as a valid branch of the conglomerate, the second column could be the specific branch ID. You could put a link between these two columns so that there is still a valid link for the head office as a branch as well (see Figure 3-5). Another example is in an employees table where all employees reside, with a self-join from an employee back to his or her manager.

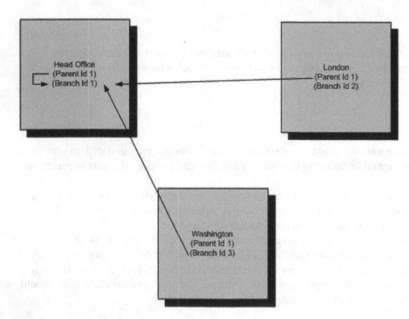

Figure 3-5. *Foreign keys in same table*

Now that we've looked at relationships, let's move on to see how to normalize the database.

Normalization

Normalizing a database means minimizing data redundancy to avoid update anomalies. Removing duplicate data leads to smaller, more compact databases. This avoids confusion over which column holds data and reduces the overhead of keeping data up to date.

■ **Note** Just a reminder that you're still in the logical phase of building the solution and you're not ready to start building your database within SQL Server.

A database designer should not normalize with impunity because this may negatively affect data retrieval. In good normalization, the removal of the duplication of data will provide faster sorting of data and queries that run faster, thereby improving performance. Although normalization can make a database more efficient, overnormalizing may create too many relationships and too many slim, small tables so that to retrieve one piece of information requires access to many tables and many joins between these tables. Database design is an art, and a knowledgeable designer knows when to stop normalizing. In fact, after normalizing a design, it's often wise to denormalize it by adding back some redundancy to make critical queries run faster (see "Denormalization" later in this chapter).

In this section of the chapter, you'll model your example in a method known as *logical modeling*. The purpose of the logical model is to show the data that the application must store to satisfy business requirements. It demonstrates how these data are related and explores any integration requirements with business areas outside the scope of the development project. It is created without any specific computer environment in mind, so no optimization for performance, data storage, and so forth is done.

In logical modeling, the term *entity* is used to mean a conceptual version of a table. As you're still in the logical modeling stage of designing your database, I'll use "entity" rather than "table" in this discussion, since it is less tied to implementation. Also within logical modeling, a column of data is referred to as an *attribute*. To build the logical model, you will take the information gathered previously in the chapter and implement attributes in the entities. From that, you'll see how you need to alter the design.

The question remains, what should be contained in an entity? Three principles should govern the contents of an entity:

- Assign each entity a unique identifier.

- Store only information that directly relates to that entity.

- Avoid repeating values or columns.

The sections that follow provide more detail about each principle.

Assign Each Entity a Unique Identifier

It must be possible to find a unique row in each entity. You can do this through the use of a unique identifying attribute or the combination of several attributes. However, no matter which method you use, it must be impossible for two rows to contain the same information within the unique identifying attribute(s).

Consider the possibility that there is no combination of attributes in an entity that can make a row unique, or perhaps you want to build a single value from a single attribute. SQL Server has a special data type, called *unique identifier*, that can do this, but a more common solution is to build a column attribute with an integer data type and then set this up as an *identity* column. You'll learn more about this technique when building the tables in Chapter 5.

Store Only Information That Directly Relates to That Entity

It can be very easy in certain situations to have too much information in one entity and, as a result, almost change the reason for the existence of the specific entity. Doing so could reduce efficiency in an OLTP system, where duplicate information has to be inserted. It could also lead to confusion when an entity that has been designed for one thing actually contains data for another.

Avoid Repeating Values or Columns

Having attributes of data where the information is an exact copy of another attribute within either the same entity or a related entity is a waste of space and resources. If you don't avoid repeating values or attributes within two or more tables, the information is duplicated and will require two modiciations to avoid the data becoming out of sync and confusing or duplicated data where there are subtle differences leading to uncertainty of which is correct. If you find repeating values or columns in your design, you should normalize this so that the information is only held once. You will see this expanded in the First Normal Form section in a moment.

Normal Forms

Now that you know what should be contained within an entity, how do you go about normalizing the data? The normal forms addressed within this chapter are as follows:

- First normal form (1NF)

- Second normal form (2NF)

- Third normal form (3NF)

There are other, "higher" normal forms, but they are mainly of theoretical significance, so they will not be covered here.

First Normal Form

To achieve 1NF within a database, it is required that you eliminate any repeating groups of information. Any groups of data found to be repeated will be moved to a new table. Looking at each table in turn, you find that you have two tables in the example database that potentially flout the first requirement of 1NF: customers and shares.

Customers

There are two columns with possible repeating values in this table:

- Title: A customer's title will be Mr., Miss, Ms., or Mrs., all of which you could put in to a reference table. Some corporations do this; others don't. It all depends on whether you want to restrict what users can enter.

- Address: The address should be split out into separate lines, one for each part of the address (for example, street, district, and so on.). It is probably well worth having a reference table for cities, states, and countries, for example.

Shares

There is one column that will possibly repeat: share name. This is really because the Shares table actually does two jobs: holds details about the share, such as its name and the market ticker, which really are unique; and holds a historical list of share prices. This table actually needs to be split into Share Details and Share Prices, which you'll see happening when we discuss the 3NF.

Second Normal Form

To achieve 2NF, each column within the table must depend on the whole primary key. This means that if you look at any single column within a table, you need to ask whether it is possible to get to this information using the whole key or just part of the key. If only part of the key is required, you must look to splitting the tables so that every column does match the whole key. To do this, you would look at each column within the table and ask, "Can I reach the information contained within this column just using part of the key?" All of the tables use an ID as the primary key, and only one column will define that ID. Therefore, to break 2NF with this is almost impossible. Where you are more likely to break 2NF is a scenario in which the primary key uses several columns.

If you look at all the tables within the example, every column within each table does require the whole key to find it.

Third Normal Form

To achieve 3NF, you must now have no column that is not part of the primary key be dependent on any other column within the table.

The Customers table does have data derived from another table, with account numbers for each product the customer has bought and financial product details. This means the account number plus details about the product such as the date opened, how much is paid with each payment, and the product type do not belong in the Customers table. If such information did remain in the table, Customers would have multiple rows for the same customer. Therefore, this table also now needs to be split into Customer details such as name and address, and CustomerProducts, such as a row for each product bought with the customer details about that product.

We have now reached full normalization to 3NF of the tables within the database. Let's take a moment to clarify where you are. Figure 3-6 shows that you're now moving from a logical model to a physical model, where you are physically defining what information is stored where.

TransactionTypes
- ⚿ TransactionTypeId
- TransactionDescription
- CreditType
- AffectCashBalance

Transactions
- ⚿ TransactionId
- CustomerId
- TransactionType
- DateEntered
- Amount
- ReferenceDetails
- Notes
- RelatedShareId
- RelatedProductId

FinancialProducts
- ⚿ ProductId
- ProductName

Customers
- ⚿ CustomerId
- CustomerTitleId
- CustomerFirstName
- CustomerOtherInitials
- CustomerLastName
- AddressId
- AccountNumber
- AccountTypeId
- ClearedBalance
- UnclearedBalance
- DateAdded

CustomerProducts
- ⚿ CustomerFinancialProductId
- CustomerId
- FinancialProductId
- AmountToCollect
- Frequency
- LastCollected
- LastCollection
- Renewable

Shares
- ⚿ ShareId
- ShareDesc
- ShareTickerId
- CurrentPrice

SharePrices
- ⚿ SharePriceId
- ShareId
- Price
- PriceDate

Figure 3-6. Physical database model

Denormalization

Despite having normalized your data to be more efficient, there will be times when denormalizing the data is a better option. *Denormalization* is the complete opposite of normalization: It is where you introduce data redundancy within a table to reduce the number of table joins and potentially speed up data access. Instances of denormalization can be found in production systems where the join to a table is slowing down queries, or perhaps where normalization is not required (for example, when working with a system in which the data are not regularly updated). You may also denormalize your data to make full use of data being held in-memory so that a small amount of data can be read optimally without the need to access disk-based data. If you consider this, I would add a word of caution not to let your application performance dicate bad practice. What is meant by this is that you shouldn't alter your design or create extra data to be held just to place a piece of information in memory.

Just because others say your data should be totally normalized, it is not necessarily true, so don't feel forced down that route. The drawback of denormalizing your data too far, though, is that you'll be holding duplicate and unnecessary information that could be normalized out to another table and then just joined during a query. This will, therefore, create performance issues as well as use a larger amount of data storage space. However, the costs of denormalization can be justified if queries run faster or the data is denormalized to improve performance of areas such as reporting. That said, data integrity is paramount in a system. It's no use having denormalized data in which there are duplications of data where one area is updated when there's a change, and the other area isn't updated.

Denormalization is not the route you want to take in the database example. Now that you have all the data to produce the system, it's time to look at how these tables will link together.

Creating the Sample Database

Let's now begin to create your example database. In this section, you will examine two different ways to create a database in SQL Server:

- Using the SQL Server Management Studio graphical interface

- Using T-SQL code

Both methods have their own merits and pitfalls for creating databases, as you'll discover, but these two methods are used whenever possible throughout the book; where you might find one method is good for one task, it may not be ideal for another. Neither method is right or wrong for every task, and your decision of which to use basically comes down to personal preference and what you're trying to achieve at the time. You may find that using T-SQL code for building objects provides the best results because you will see instantly the different possible selections. Using T-SQL also provides you with a greater base from which to work with other programming languages and databases, although some databases do differ considerably in the language used to work with them. However, if the syntax for the commands is not familiar to you, you may well choose to use a wizard or SQL Server Management Studio. Once you become more comfortable with the syntax, then a Query Editor pane should become your favored method. Finally, T-SQL code allows for deployment of your code in a repeatable fashion such as a deployment to production, or a re-deployment of development code after a restore from an earlier backup.

You'll also examine how to drop a database in SQL Server Management Studio.

Creating a Database in SQL Server Management Studio

The first method of creating a database you will look at is using SQL Server Management Studio,, which was introduced in Chapter 2. The databases being created will be defined to only hold disk-based data. In Chapter 7 when you are introduced to in-memory data, you will see how to alter the database to accommodate in-memory data.

TRY IT OUT: CREATING A DATABASE IN SQL SERVER MANAGEMENT STUDIO

1. Before creating the database, you'll need to start up SQL Server Management Studio. To do this, select Start ➤ All Programs ➤ Microsoft SQL Server ➤ SQL Server Management Studio or start the app SQL Server Management Studio from list of apps in Windows 8.

■ **Tip** I run all this book's examples from a server called FAT-BELLY-Sony using the named instance APRESS_DEV1. You will have your own name for your host computer and possibly even your own name for the installed instance. Therefore, throughout the book, when you see FAT-BELLY-Sony, you should substitute your own host computer name.

2. Ensure that you have registered and connected to your server. If the SQL Server service was not previously started, it will automatically start as you connect, which may take a few moments. If it still fails to start, then check the service is running from Control Panel ➤ Administrative Tools ➤ Sercices finding the service SQL Server (APRESS_DEV1). However, if you have not shut down your computer since the install of SQL Server, then everything should be up and running. SQL Server will stop only if you have shut down your computer

and indicated not to start the SQL Server service automatically or the Windows account used to start the service has a problem, such as being locked out. To start SQL Server, or conversely, if you want to set up SQL Server not to start automatically when Windows starts, set this either from Control Panel mentioned at the start of this point or from the SQL Server Configuration Manager found under Start ➤ All Programs ➤ Microsoft SQL Server ➤ Configuration Tools or from the App window.

3. In Object Explorer, expand the Databases node until you see either just the system database and database snapshot nodes that always exist. Ensure that the Databases folder is highlighted and ready for the next action, as shown in Figure 3-7.

Figure 3-7. The Databases node in Object Explorer

A minimum amount of information is required to create a database:

- The name the database will be given

- How the data will be sorted

- The size of the database

- Where the database will be located

- The name of the files used to store the information contained within the database

SQL Server Management Studio gathers this information using the New Database menu option.

4. Right-click the Databases node to bring up a pop-up menu with a number of different options. Select New Database, as shown in Figure 3-8.

Figure 3-8. *Selecting to create a new database*

5. You are now presented with the New Database dialog box set to the General tab. First, enter the name of the database you want to create—in this case, ApressFinancial. Notice as you type that the two file names in the Database Files list box also populate. This is simply an aid, and you can change the names (see Figure 3-9). However, you should have a very good reason to not accept the names that the screen is creating, as this is enforcing a standard.

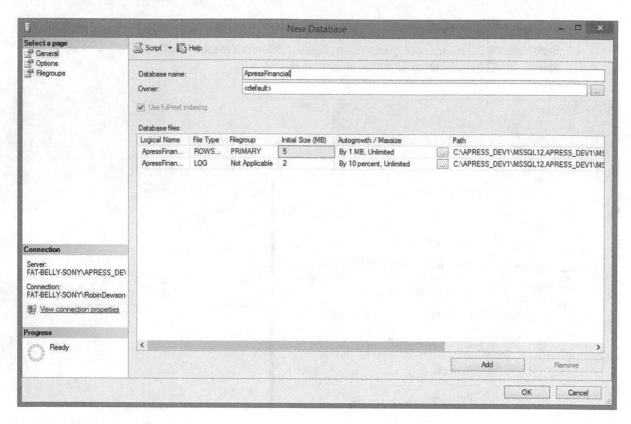

Figure 3-9. *General settings in the New Database dialog*

The General screen within this page collects the first two pieces of information. The first piece of information required is the database name. No checks are done at this point as to whether the database exists (this comes when you click OK); however, there is some validation in the field so that certain illegal characters will not be allowed when OK is clicked.

■ **Note** Characters to avoid for a database name are as follows: " ' */?:\<>

Keep to alphabetic, numeric, underscore, or dash characters. Also, you may want to keep the database name short (but meaningful), as the database name has to be entered manually in many parts of SQL Server. Below the database name is the owner of the database;in other words, the login defined as having the ability to do anything within the database as well as determine what other logins can do with the database. This can be any login that has the authority to create databases. A server in many—but not all—installations can hold databases that belong to different development groups. One example is an ISP who on one server will hold databases for multiple customers. Each group would have a login that was the database owner, and at this point, you would assign the specific owner. For the moment, let it default to the <default> account, which will be the account currently logged in to SQL Server; you'll learn how to change this later. If you're using Windows authentication, then your Windows account will be your user ID. If you're using SQL Server authentication, it will be the login ID you used at connection time.

The database owner, which is often shortened to dbo, initially has full administration rights on the database, from creating the database, to modifying it or its contents, to even deleting the database. Because a dbo account has such power, it is best to create either a user or a group specifically for administration rights. You will see groups discussed in Chapter 4.

■ **Caution** An account with such power needs to be carefully controlled and secure in a production environment.

Ignore the check box for Full-Text Indexing. You would select this option if you wanted your database to have columns that you could search for a particular word or phrase and Full-Text Indexing had been installed. As Full-Text was not installed, the check box is disabled. For example, search engines could have a column that holds a set of phrases from web pages, and full-text searching could be used to find which web pages contain the words being searched for.

The File Name entry (off-screen to the right in Figure 3-9) is the name of the physical file that will hold the data within the database you're working with. By default, SQL Server takes the name of the database and adds a suffix of _Data to create this name.

Just to the left of the File Name option is the physical path where the files will reside. The files will typically reside in a directory on a local drive and, if possible, on a different physical drive to the system files. Many larger companies attach network storage to the server, and the data will reside there, off the main computer. In this case, you would enter the network path or the mapped network drive letter. For an installation such as you are completing on a local machine, the path will normally be the path specified by default defined at installation of SQL Server. If you are working on a server, although you will be placing the files on a local or mapped drive, the path may be different to the SQL Server install option so that different teams' installations will be in different physical locations or even on different local drives.

The database files are stored on your drive with an extension of .MDF—for example, ApressFinancial_Data.MDF. In this case, .MDF is not something used by DIY enthusiasts, but it actually stands for Master Data File and is the name of the *primary data file*. Every database *must* have at least one primary data file. This file may hold not only the data for the database, but also the location of all the other files that make up the database, as well as startup information for the database catalog. An MDF is an allocation of space on the hard drive where SQL Server places the tables as well as the rows of information that are within the tables.

It is also possible to have *secondary data files*. These would have the suffix .NDF. Again, you could use whatever name you wished, and, in fact, you could have an entirely different name from the primary data file. However, if you did so, the confusion that would abound is not worth thinking about. So do use the same name, and if you need a third, fourth, and so on, then add on a numerical suffix.

Secondary data files allow you to spread your tables and indexes over two or more disks. The upside is that by spreading the data over several disks, you will get better performance. In a production environment, you may have several secondary data files to spread out your heavily used tables.

■ **Note** As the primary data file holds the database catalog information that will be accessed constantly during the operation of the server, it would be best, in a production environment at least, to place all your tables on a secondary data file.

Finally, there will be another file type, which is .LDF. This is the transaction log file that holds a record of certain actions you perform. This is covered in detail in Chapter 8 when we take a look at backup and restores. You would place the file name for a secondary data file in the row below the ApressFinancial_Data entry in the Data Files list box, after clicking the Add button. The File Type column shows whether the file is a data file or a log file, as in a file for holding the data or a file for holding a record of the actions done to the data.

The next column in the grid is titled Filegroup. This allows you to specify the PRIMARY disk-based filegroup and any SECONDARY data disk-based filegroups for your database. Memory-based filegroups are covered in a moment. Filegroups are for grouping logical data files together to manage them as a logical unit. You could place some of your tables in one filegroup, more tables in another filegroup, indexes in another, and so on. Dividing your tables and indexes into filegroups allows SQL Server to perform parallel disk operations and tasks if the filegroups are on different drives. You could also place tables that are not allowed to be modified as one in a filegroup and set the filegroup to Read-Only. If you want to have another filegroup file, you can click Add at the bottom of the General page. Figure 3-10 shows the dialog for creating a new disk-based filegroup, which is displayed if you click the combobox in the Filegroup column on any newly created database file. The top option allows you to create read-only filegroups. Finally, when creating a database object, the default filegroup is the PRIMARY filegroup. In a production environment—and therefore in a development environment as well, so that it is simpler to move from development through to production—you would create a secondary filegroup and set it as the default. In this book, you will just keep to the PRIMARY filegroup for simplicity. At this point, a third disk database filegroup is not required.

Figure 3-10. *New filegroup*

The logic behind secondary data files is relatively straightforward. A PRIMARY filegroup will always—and must always—contain the system tables that hold the information about the database, the tables, the columns, and so on. If you have the Autogrowth file option (covered shortly) switched off, the PRIMARY filegroup is likely to run out of space at some point. If this happens and no secondary data files are specified, the database will grind to a halt until some space is added. However, in most instances, especially when you're first starting out, you can leave the database with only a PRIMARY filegroup.

Don't misunderstand filegroups and space, though: filegroups are there to help you organize your files within your database storage, and the files that make up the filegroup may span several disks for a performance issue. You will move files around filegroups for speed, efficiency, security, backups, and a number of other reasons.

6. Click Cancel in the New Filegroup dialog box, and then click Remove in the New Database dialog box to remove the third line within the database files grid if you added a line while checking out the filegroup discussion for Figure 3-10.

■ **Note** Remember that the PRIMARY filegroup may hold not only data, but also the system tables, so the PRIMARY filegroup could fill up purely with information about tables, columns, and so forth used to run SQL Server.

The next item in the New Database dialog box is the Initial Size (MB) column. The initial size of the database is its size when empty. Don't forget that the database won't be totally empty and is created from the model system database, and some of the space will be initially taken up with the system tables. It is impossible to say, "I'm creating a database, and the initial size must be *nn*MB"—the database size depends on many factors, such as the number of tables, how much static information is stored, to what size you expect the database to grow, and so on. It would be during the investigation phase that you would try to determine the size that you expect the database to reach over a given period of time. If anything, estimate larger rather than smaller to avoid fragmentation. This size is the disk-based size for the files and will not include the size of memory-based tables.

Moving on to the next, and possibly most important, area: Autogrowth. This option indicates whether SQL Server will automatically handle the situation that arises if your database reaches the initial size limit. If you set this option for no automatic growth, you will have to monitor your database and expand its size manually, if and when required. While starting out, let your database grow automatically. However, do set a reasonable maximum size so that you have some emergency disk space available in case it is required.

■ **Note** In a production environment, or even when you're developing in the future, it will be more common to switch Autogrowth on and fix the maximum size. This prevents your hard drive from filling up and your server from being unable to continue. You would also define database size monitoring so that you could see when the database size was increasing toward the limit and an action plan can be put in place.

While SQL Server handles increasing the size of the database for you, it has to know by how much. This is where the Autogrowth option comes in. You can let SQL Server increase the database either by a set amount each time in megabytes or by a percentage. If you want to change the autogrowth options by selecting the autogrowth options button (the ellipsis) to the right of the current setting, you can disable autogrowth of your database in the dialog that appears.

In the Autogrowth dialog, the Maximum File Size option sets a limit on how large the database is allowed to grow. The default is "unrestricted growth"—in other words, the only limit is the spare space on the hard drive. This is not good. What if you have a rogue piece of code entering an infinite loop of data? This scenario is rare, but not unheard of. Also, many firms run many databases and you should divide up storage in a sensible manner, leaving room for new databases and for new file space to be attached to relevant databases. With a setting of unrestricted growth, it might take a long time to fill up the drive, but fill up the drive it will, and with a full drive, purging the data will prove troublesome. When it is time to start moving the database to a production environment, ensure the Restrict File Growth (MB) option is set to guard against such problems.

The final column that you will find in the New Database dialog box by scrolling to the right is Path. In this column, you define where the database files will reside on your drive. If SQL Server is installed on your C drive, no paths for the data were changed, and you are working on a default instance, then you will find that the default is C:\Program Files\Microsoft SQL Server\MSSQL.nn.MSSQLSERVER\MSSQL\Data. Figure 3-9 shows I'm working on a mapped drive that has been given the drive letter C. The command button with the ellipsis (. . .) to the right of the path brings up an explorer-style dialog that allows you to change the location of the database files. For example, if you move to a larger SQL Server installation, moving the location of these files to a server or network storage relevant to the needs of your database will probably be a necessity.

The line that has a File Type setting of Log includes the same information as a Data File Type setting, with one or two minor exceptions. The File Name places a suffix of _Log onto the database name, and there is no ability to change the Filegroup column, since the Transaction Log doesn't actually hold system tables and so would fill up only through the recording of actions. It is possible, however, to define multiple log file locations. Filling the transaction log and not being able to process any more information because the log is full will cause your SQL Server to stop processing. Specifying more than one log location means that you can avoid this problem. The use of a failover log file in larger production systems is advisable.

Let's now move on to discuss the Options page of the New Database dialog box (see Figure 3-11).

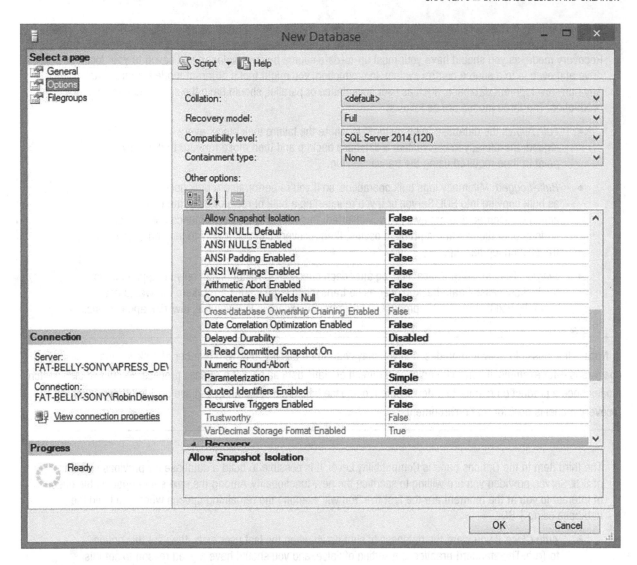

Figure 3-11. *Options page of the New Database dialog*

The first field in the Options page is labeled Collation—I discussed this option in Chapter 1 when installing SQL Server. If you need to alter a collation setting post installation on a database, you can do so, but care is required. Note that altering the collation sequence on a server should be undertaken only by the system administrator, who will be aware of the issues and have the authority to perform this task. Changing a collation setting can alter areas such as how data is searched and sorted, and how the queries work with upper- and lower-cased data.

The next setting is Recovery Model. You'll learn about backing up and restoring your database in Chapter 8, and this option forms part of that decision-making process. In development, the best option is to choose the Simple Recovery mode, as you should have your most up-to-date source being developed and saved to your local hard drive and even in to a source control system. In production, you might feel a different mode is more suitable. Any non-development database, such as user acceptance or parallel, should have the same recovery model as production. The three modes are as follows:

- *Full*: Allows the database to be restored to where the failure took place; every transaction is logged; therefore, you can restore a database backup and then move forward to the individual point in time required using the transaction log.

- *Bulk-Logged*: Minimally logs bulk operations, so if you're performing a bulk operation such as bulk copying into SQL Server, or if you're inserting a bulk of rows of data, then only the action is recorded and not every row is inserted; this will increase performance during these sorts of operations, but if a problem occurs, then recovery can occur only to the end of the last transaction log backup.

- *Simple*: Truncates the transaction log after each checkpoint; restores can only be applied up to the last successful data backup only, as no transaction log backups are taken. You would not normally use this mode in a production environment except in low-volume, low-risk applications.

■ **Note** It is possible to switch modes, and you may want to do this if you have a number of bulk-logged operations—for example, if you're completing a refresh of static data as part of a release process. You would also switch modes once a production restore to a development database has taken place and you have decided that a different recovery model is best for that environment.

The third item in the Options page is Compatibility Level. It is possible to build a database for previous versions of SQL Server, provided you are willing to sacrifice the new functionality. Among the next set of options, the ones of interest to you at the moment are the first five. You will examine the remaining options when you build the database using T-SQL.

- *Auto Close*: If you want the database to shut down when the last user exits, then set this option to True. The standard practice is a setting of False, and you should have a good reason to set this option to True, especially on a remote server.

- *Auto Create Statistics*: This option relates to the creation of statistics used when querying data. The standard practice is a setting of True; however, in a production environment, especially if you have a nightly or weekly process that generates statistics on your data, you would switch this to False. Creating and updating statistics while your system is being used does increase processing required on your server, and if your server is heavily used for inserting data, then you will find a performance degradation with this option set to True. To clarify, though, it is necessary to balance your choice with how much your system will have to query data.

- *Auto Shrink:* Database and transaction logs grow in size not only with increased data input, but also through other actions, which I'll discuss in more detail in Chapter 8. You can shrink the logical size of the log file through certain actions, some of which can be instigated by T-SQL and some as a by-product of actions being performed. Shrinking a database, whether automatically or manually, takes processing power and time. You should be in control of when shrinking takes place rather than leaving this to SQL Server, and therefore Auto Shrink should be set to False in a production environment. Even if the database is remote, alerts should be set up to warn you about database size reaching its limit rather than allowing SQL Server to perform this task unattended.

- *Auto Update Statistics and Auto Update Statistics Asynchronously:* These are more common options to have set to True, even on production servers, although there is still a performance degradation. These options will update statistics as data are inserted, modified, or deleted for tables for use in indexes, and they will also update statistics for columns within a table. I will discuss indexes further in Chapter 6. Statistics are used by SQL Server to find the best method to work with your data, and having good statistics will ensure the best method is normally chosen.

■ **Tip** You don't need to create the database at this point if you don't want to. There are several other options available to you to save the underlying T-SQL to a file, to the clipboard, or to the Query window. The first two options are very useful as methods of storing actions you're creating to keep in your source code repository, such as Visual SourceSafe. The first two options are also useful if you wish to keep T-SQL code to execute when deploying on several different computers at client sites. Clients may have SQL Server installed on a server but no SSMS installed locally from which to build a database graphically. They should have sqlcmd, which as shown as an introduction in Chapter 2 could also be used to deploy the scripts. Finally, by using T-SQL rather than dialog screens, you will achieve consistency and clarity when performing an action multiple times. The third option is ideal if you wish to add more options to your database than you have defined within the wizard setup. All of the options enable you to see the underlying code and understand what is required to create a database. You will look at the code in a moment.

7. Click the OK button at the bottom of the screen to create the database.

SQL Server will now perform several actions. First, it checks whether the database already exists; if so, you will have to choose another name. Second, once the database name is validated, SQL Server does a security check to make sure the user has permission to create the database. This is not a concern here since by following this book, you will always be logged on to SQL Server with the proper permissions. Now that you have security clearance, the data files are created and placed on the hard drive. Provided there is enough space, these files will be successfully created, and it is not until this point that SQL Server is updated with the new database details in the internal system tables.

Once this is done, the database is ready for use. As you can see, this whole process is relatively straightforward.

When you return to Object Explorer in SQL Server Management Studio, refresh the contents manually if the explorer hasn't auto-refreshed. You will see the new database listed, as shown in Figure 3-12.

Figure 3-12. The new database within Object Explorer

SQL Server Management Studio is simply a GUI front end to running T-SQL scripts in the background. As you progress through the book, you'll see the T-SQL generated for each object type you're using, and you'll create the objects graphically, as you've just seen.

Once the database has been created, you can right-click and, as shown in Figure 3-13, have the details sent to one of four locations.

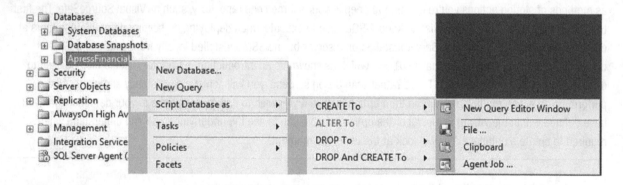

Figure 3-13. Scripting the database from SSMS

Whichever method you choose to use, the script will be the same, with the exception of a comment line when you create the script in the second option. The script for generating the database from this option is listed here, so you can go through what is happening. The fourth option allows you to schedule a re-create of the database at a certain point in time. This is ideal to use when building a database from scratch on a regular basis. For example, you might create a daily job for setting up a test area.

First of all, SQL Server points itself to a known database, as shown in the following snippet. master has to exist; otherwise, SQL Server will not work. The USE statement, which instructs SQL Server to alter its connection to default to the database after the USE statement, points further statements to the master database:

```
USE [master]

GO
```

Next, the script builds up the CREATE DATABASE T-SQL statement built on the options selected. (I'll walk you through the CREATE DATABASE syntax that could be used in the "Creating a Database in a Query Pane" section, as this statement doesn't cover all the possibilities.) Notice in the code that follows the next note that the name of the database is surrounded by square brackets: []. SQL Server does this as a way of defining that the information between the square brackets is to be used similarly to a literal and not as a variable. Also, it defines that the information is to be treated as one unit. To clarify, if you want to name the database Apress Financial (in other words, with a space between "Apress" and "Financial"), then you and SQL Server need to have a method of knowing where the name of the database starts and ends. This is where the identifier brackets come in to play.

■ **Note** There is an option that can be set for a SQL Server connection where instead of square brackes you can use quotation marks. This is called the Set Quoted Identifier option defined with the T-SQL command SET QUOTED_IDENTIFIER ON/OFF. Therefore, instead of using the square brackets around master as you see in the preceding text, you can define identifiers by surrounding them with double quotation marks using this command. Therefore, anything that has double quotation marks around it is seen as an identifier rather than a literal, if this option is set to ON. To get around this requirement, you can use single quotation marks, as shown in the example, but then if you do have to enter a single quotation mark—as in the word "don't"—you would have to use another single quotation mark. As you can see, this situation can get a bit messy. I prefer to have QUOTED_IDENTIFIER set to OFF to reduce confusion.

The following code is generated by the script for creating the ApressFinancial database:

```
CREATE DATABASE [ApressFinancial]
 CONTAINMENT = NONE
 ON  PRIMARY
( NAME = N'ApressFinancial',
FILENAME =
N'C:\APRESS_DEV1\MSSQL12.APRESS_DEV\MSSQL\DATA\
ApressFinancial.mdf',
 SIZE = 5120KB , MAXSIZE = UNLIMITED, FILEGROWTH = 1024KB )
 LOG ON
( NAME = N'ApressFinancial_log',
FILENAME =
N'C:\APRESS_DEV1\MSSQL12.APRESS_DEV\MSSQL\DATA\
ApressFinancial_log.ldf',
SIZE = 2048KB , MAXSIZE = 2048GB , FILEGROWTH = 10%)
GO
```

Most of the preceding code should be easy to understand and follow as it is taking the details entered in the database creation dialog screen and transforming those details into T-SQL. However, there is one item I would like to bring to your attention and that is the CONTAINMENT = NONE argument. With SQL Server, databases can be fully contained, partially contained, or non-contained. A fully contained database is one in which all of the objects, data, accounts, and metadata are contained within that database. You can then move databases between SQL Server instances and installations much more easily than is the case with partial or non-contained databases, as all of the information required to move a database is held by the database itself. Previous versions of SQL Server are seen as non-contained, and therefore porting databases have problems with database ownership and some of the metadata required to be rebuilt when placed on the new server. Partially contained databases have some of the information held within the database itself, although code can have dependence outside of its own database. One example would be when trying to retrieve customer information from the Customer database from within the Invoicing database.

Finally, non-contained databases, as created for ApressFinancial, are built similarly to previous versions of SQL Server, where to move a database from one server to another requires some work. At this point, I am building the database as a non-contained database for simplicity of discussion throughout the book and to ensure you have the basics of databases clear in your mind before introducing these complexities.

The CREATE DATABASE command is followed by a GO command. This signals to SQL Server—or any other SQL Server utility—that this is the end of a batch of T-SQL statements and the utility should send the batch of statements to SQL Server. Certain statements need to be in their own batch and cannot be combined with other statements in the same batch. To clarify, a GO statement determines that you have come to the end of a batch of statements and that SQL Server should process these statements before moving on to the next batch of statements.

■ **Note** GO statements are used only in ad hoc T-SQL, which is what I'm demonstrating here. Later in the book, you'll build T-SQL into programs called stored procedures. GO statements are not used in stored procedures.

Next, you define the new database's compatibility level. The following ALTER DATABASE statement sets the database's base level to SQL Server 2014. It is possible to define SQL Server to an earlier level, as far back as SQL Server 2005, by changing the version number. A base level of 110 actually means 11.0, as in version 11 (110), which equates to SQL Server 2012.

```
ALTER DATABASE [ApressFinancial] SET COMPATIBILITY_LEVEL = 120
GO
```

You then can define the remaining database options. The statements to set those options have GO statements separating them. But in this scenario, the GO statement is superfluous. So why are they included? When SQL Server is preparing the wizard, it is safer for it to place GO statements after each statement because it then doesn't have to predict what the next statement is and, therefore, whether the end of the batch of transactions has to be defined.

It is possible to initialize full-text indexing or remove all full-text catalogs from the current database. By default, all user-created databases in SQL Server 2012 are enabled for full-text indexing if the feature is installed.

There is an IF statement around the following code that enables or disables full-text searching. This code is testing whether full-text indexing has been installed as part of the current instance. If it has not been installed, then by default the option is not enabled.

```
IF (1 = FULLTEXTSERVICEPROPERTY('IsFullTextInstalled'))
begin
EXEC [ApressFinancial].[dbo].[sp_fulltext_database] @action = 'enable'
end
```

There will be times when columns have no data in them. When a column is empty, it is said to contain the special value of NULL. Setting ANSI_NULL_DEFAULT to OFF means that a column's default value is NOT NULL. You'll learn about NULL values in Chapter 5 during the table creation discussion. The following is the statement to define the default setting for a new column definition when defining a new column within a table in SQL Server. If you define a new column for a table without defining whether it can hold NULL values using the T-SQL ALTER TABLE command, then the column by default will not allow NULL values.

```
ALTER DATABASE [ApressFinancial] SET ANSI_NULL_DEFAULT OFF
GO
```

Still on the topic of NULL values, the ANSI standard states that if you are comparing two columns of data that have this special NULL value in them, then the comparison should fail and the two columns will not be considered equal. They also won't be considered not equal to each other. Setting ANSI NULLS to OFF alters that behavior, so that when you do compare two NULL values, they will be considered equal to each other. The following is the statement to use:

```
ALTER DATABASE [ApressFinancial] SET ANSI_NULLS OFF
GO
```

There are columns of characters that can store variable-length data. You'll come across these when you build your table in Chapter 5. If set to ON, this option makes every column of data contain the maximum number of characters, whether you sent through just one character or many more. It is common to have this set to OFF.

```
ALTER DATABASE [ApressFinancial] SET ANSI_PADDING OFF
GO
```

If an ANSI standard warning or error occurs, such as divide by zero, switching the ANSI_WARNINGS setting to OFF will suppress these. A value of NULL will be returned in any columns that have the error.

```
ALTER DATABASE [ApressFinancial] SET ANSI_WARNINGS OFF
GO
```

If the ANSI_WARNINGS setting were ON, and you performed a divide by zero, the query would terminate. To change this in combination with ANSI_WARNINGS set to ON, you tell SQL Server not to abort when there's an arithmetic error.

```
ALTER DATABASE [ApressFinancial] SET ARITHABORT OFF
GO
```

If you have a database that is "active" only when users are logged in, then switching the AUTO_CLOSE setting to ON would close down the database when the last user logged out. This is unusual, as databases tend to stay active 24/7, but closing unwanted databases frees up resources for other databases on the server to use if required. One example of when to switch this setting ON is for a database used for analyzing data by users through the day (for example, one in an actuarial department, where death rates would be analyzed).

```
ALTER DATABASE [ApressFinancial] SET AUTO_CLOSE OFF
GO
```

If the volume of data within your database grows smaller (for example, if you have a daily or weekly archive process), you can reduce the size of the database automatically by setting the following option ON. It is standard to have the option OFF because the database size will simply increase as data are re-added. It would be switched ON only if a reduction in the database is required—due to disk space requirements, for example—but it is never a good idea for this option to kick in when the database is in use, so really it is best to keep it off.

```
ALTER DATABASE [ApressFinancial] SET AUTO_SHRINK OFF
GO
```

■ **Note** It would be better to shrink the database manually by using the DBCC SHRINKDATABASE command if you do need to shrink it. Shrinking databases helps backups but SQL Server would need to re-allocate if it expands again. You will see this in Chapter 8.

When data are added or modified to SQL Server, statistics are created that are then used when querying the data. These statistics can be updated with every modification, or they can be completed via a T-SQL set of code at set times. There is a performance reduction as data are inserted, modified, or deleted, but this performance is gained back when you want to return data. Your application being a pure insertion, pure query, or a mix determines whether you'll want this option on. If you have a pure insertion application, you probably want this option switched off, for example, but this is an optimization decision.

```
ALTER DATABASE [ApressFinancial] SET AUTO_UPDATE_STATISTICS ON
GO
```

A *cursor* is an in-memory table built with T-SQL used for row-at-a-time processing. It's a temporary memory resident table, in essence. A cursor can exist for the lifetime of a program, but if you switch the following setting to ON, when a batch of data is committed or rolled back during a transaction, the cursor will be closed.

```
ALTER DATABASE [ApressFinancial] SET CURSOR_CLOSE_ON_COMMIT OFF
GO
```

A cursor can exist either locally or globally. This means that if GLOBAL is selected for this option, then any cursor created in a program is available to any subprogram that is called. LOCAL, the other option, indicates that the cursor exists only within that program that created it.

```
ALTER DATABASE [ApressFinancial] SET CURSOR_DEFAULT  GLOBAL
GO
```

If you're concatenating character fields and if the following option is ON, then if any of the columns has a NULL value, the result is a NULL.

```
ALTER DATABASE [ApressFinancial] SET CONCAT_NULL_YIELDS_NULL OFF
GO
```

When you're working with some numeric data types, it is possible to lose precision of the numerics. This can occur when you move a floating-point value to a specific numeric decimal point location, and the value you're passing has too many significant digits. If the following option is set to ON, then an error is generated. OFF means the value is truncated.

```
ALTER DATABASE [ApressFinancial] SET NUMERIC_ROUNDABORT OFF
GO
```

As mentioned earlier, when you're defining database names, if there is a space in the name or the name is a reserved word, it is possible to tell SQL Server to ignore that fact and treat the contents of the squared brackets as a literal. You are using *quoted identifiers* when you use the double quotation mark instead of square brackets. I'll delve into this topic further when showing how to insert data in Chapter 10, as there are a number of details to discuss with this option.

```
ALTER DATABASE [ApressFinancial] SET QUOTED_IDENTIFIER OFF
GO
```

The following option relates to a special type of program called a *trigger*. A trigger can run when data are modified, and one trigger can call another trigger. A setting of OFF means that an AFTER trigger is not allowed to recursively cause itself to be invoked. This is known as a direct recursion.

```
ALTER DATABASE [ApressFinancial] SET RECURSIVE_TRIGGERS OFF
GO
```

Service Broker provides developers with a raft of functionality, such as asynchronous processing or the ability to distribute processing over more than one computer. Such a scenario might be heavy overnight batch processing that needs to be completed within a certain time window. By distributing the processing, it could mean that a process that wouldn't have been distributed could finish within that time frame.

```
ALTER DATABASE [ApressFinancial] SET DISABLE_BROKER
GO
```

I mentioned statistics earlier with another option and how they can be updated as data are modified. The following option is similar to AUTO_UPDATE_STATISTICS. If this option is set to ON, the query that triggers an update of the statistics will not wait for the statistics to be created. The statistics update will start, but it will do so in the background asynchronously.

```
ALTER DATABASE [ApressFinancial] SET AUTO_UPDATE_STATISTICS_ASYNC OFF
GO
```

If there is a relationship between two tables via a foreign key, by setting this option to ON, SQL Server will correlate statistics for the two tables to try to improve query optimization. Unless you have this scenario, the setting should be switched to OFF, which is the default:

```
ALTER DATABASE [ApressFinancial] SET DATE_CORRELATION_OPTIMIZATION OFF
GO
```

This option defines whether this database is seen as trustworthy with what resources it can access. For example, the option defines whether SQL Server can trust the database not to crash the server. By setting the option to OFF, you ensure (among other things) that SQL Server will not allow any code developed to have access to external resources.

```
ALTER DATABASE [ApressFinancial] SET TRUSTWORTHY OFF
GO
```

If you build a database that is set for replication—in other words, where data changes are replicated to another server, which you sometimes see for distributed solutions—then this option details how SQL Server deals with data you are trying to process when it is involved in a transaction. This is an advanced topic outside the scope of this book.

```
ALTER DATABASE [ApressFinancial] SET ALLOW_SNAPSHOT_ISOLATION OFF
GO
```

The basis of the following option is to inform SQL Server how best to work with code that has parameters within it and to decide the best and fastest way to work with that query. To clarify, when you try to retrieve data from a table, you are likely to have some sort of filtering such as a specific value, a range of values, and so on. This is a query parameter. SQL Server can discard the value when trying to figure out the best way to get the data from the database based on previous queries. SQL Server uses previous query executions to try to calculate the fastest method of getting that data, known as a query plan. By keeping the parameterization simple, SQL Server will look at the query, and if

the query is a simple query with very few parameters, it will try to find a query plan that it has in memory to use. If the query is complex or SQL Server feels the number of parameters is too high to be deemed simple, then SQL Server will build a new query plan. If the query has only one possible execution such as an insert of data of pure values, then this is called a trivial plan and will be used immediately.

```
ALTER DATABASE [ApressFinancial] SET PARAMETERIZATION SIMPLE
GO
```

SQL Server has many features and techniques for ensuring that your data are correct, safe, and valid. In Chapter 10, you will see one way to keep your data correct when you look at transactions. There are two ways SQL Server can enforce data safety: either by locking data that are being updated in a transaction, or by keeping a version of the row prior to the modification in tempdb until it is committed via a transaction. This latter technique is known as row versioning. By setting READ_COMMITTED_SNAPSHOT to OFF as in the following example, you are indicating that you will be taking the approach that the data will be locked. You guarantee that the information being read contains the value currently committed to the database. If you set the option to ON, it is possible that you could be reading the data after it has been altered within T-SQL but before it has been committed to the database. There are pros and cons of both methods, and I will cover more about transactions in Chapter 10.

```
ALTER DATABASE [ApressFinancial] SET READ_COMMITTED_SNAPSHOT OFF
GO
```

The option HONOR_BROKER_PRIORITY, shown in the example to follow, is used with SQL Server Service Broker, which is used by SQL Server when XML messages are being passed from one SQL Server to another. One way of thinking about how Service Broker works would be to compare its use to having a chat conversation over the Internet in Facebook. The software accepts the message you type and sends it to the recipients, and the recipients send back an acknowledgment indicating that the message has been successfully received. A setting of ON indicates that if messages are given a priority, then SQL Server will process these in a priority order. A setting of OFF indicates that messages will be processed in order of generation.

```
ALTER DATABASE [ApressFinancial] SET HONOR_BROKER_PRIORITY OFF
GO
```

The next option determines how your data can be recovered when a failure such as a power outage happens. In other words, the following option defines the recovery model, as discussed earlier. You'll look at this in more detail when I discuss database maintenance in Chapter 8.

```
ALTER DATABASE [ApressFinancial] SET RECOVERY FULL
GO
```

The following option defines the user access to the database. MULTI_USER is the norm and allows more than one user into the database. The other settings are SINGLE_USER and RESTRICTED_USER, where only people who have powerful privileges can connect. You would set your database to RESTRICTED_USER after a media or power failure, for example, when a database administrator needs to connect to the database to ensure everything is okay. (The setting RESTRICTED_USER causes the database to allow only administrator logins.) Specify SINGLE_USER when you want to lock down the database so that no other person can connect—for example, when you are detaching the database from this instance and you are moving it to another instance. Specify MULTI_USE when you want to open the database up for general use, as in the following example:

```
ALTER DATABASE [ApressFinancial] SET  MULTI_USER
GO
```

When you have an I/O error (for example, a hard drive might be on its way to breaking down), then this option will report an error if checksums don't match:

```
ALTER DATABASE [ApressFinancial] SET PAGE_VERIFY CHECKSUM
GO
```

The following line is used for controlling whether permissions checks are required when referring to objects in another database:

```
ALTER DATABASE [ApressFinancial] SET DB_CHAINING OFF
```

If you are using your database to hold unstructured data such as Word documents, it is possible to work with that data within or outside of a transaction. The default is that working with files-treamed data it has to be within a transaction.

```
ALTER DATABASE [ApressFinancial] SET FILESTREAM( NON_TRANSACTED_ACCESS = OFF )
GO
```

When you write data to a database, the data is to a transaction log and in to memory; data is not instantly written to disk as writing to disk is slow. SQL Server will write data to disk at some point of its choosing based on a setting at the instance level (around one minute although this can and will vary and is an estimate) and, once it is completed, a checkpoint is issued. This process is automatic. If you want to reduce the number of checkpoints, this option can do this. If you extend the time, then fewer checkpoints will be issued. Large data modifications will be faster; however, if the database has a failure, it will take longer to recover. This option should be altered after extensive testing.

```
ALTER DATABASE [ApressFinancial] SET TARGET_RECOVERY_TIME = 0 SECONDS
GO
```

When you update a table, SQL Server will record the fact in the transaction log. The transaction log in simplest terms is how SQL Server records the updates to data so that if there is a server or database failure, or if you wish to revert your changes, the correct action to the underlying tables can be achieved correctly. Transactions and the transaction log are discussed more in Chapter 10. The following setting defines that data modifications are written to the transaction log before notification back to the client is sent to indicate that the work is complete. It is possible to change this so that writing to the transaction log is completed asynchronously, which has a performance improvement but you may get data loss if there is a sudden unexpected failure.

```
ALTER DATABASE [ApressFinancial] SET DELAYED_DURABILITY = DISABLED
GO
```

The final option defines how the filegroups are set: READ_WRITE or READ_ONLY. The use of READ_ONLY is ideal when you have a backup database that users can use to inspect data. The database is an exact mirror of a production database, for example, so it has the security on it set to allow updates to it, but by setting this option to READ_ONLY, you can be sure that no updates can occur.

```
ALTER DATABASE [ApressFinancial] SET READ_WRITE
GO
```

Dropping the Database in SQL Server Management Studio

To follow the next section properly and build the database using code, it is necessary to remove the database just created. It is also handy to know how to do this anyway, for those times when you have made an error or when you want to remove a database that is no longer in use. Deleting a database is also known as *dropping* a database.

TRY IT OUT: DROPPING A DATABASE IN SQL SERVER MANAGEMENT STUDIO

1. If SQL Server Management Studio should still be running from the previous example, expand the nodes until you see the database ApressFinancial.

2. Right-click ApressFinancial to bring up the context menu.

3. Click the Delete option, as shown in Figure 3-14.

Figure 3-14. *Deleting a database within SSMS*

4. The dialog shown in Figure 3-15 will display. Select Close Existing Connections and then click OK.

Figure 3-15. *Selecting to delete a database in the Delete Object dialog*

The first check box, Delete Backup and Restore History Information for Databases, gives you the option of keeping or removing the history information that was generated when completing backups or restores. If you want to keep this information for audit purposes, then uncheck the box.

The second check box is very important. If there is a program running against a database, or if you have any design windows or query panes open and pointing to the database you want to delete, then this option will close those connections. If you are deleting a database, there really should be no connections there. This is a good check and will prevent accidents from happening, and it also allows any rogue databases to be removed without having to track down who is connected to them.

5. Click OK. The database is now permanently removed. You will be re-creating the database in a moment, so it is okay for you to delete.

When you click the OK button, SQL Server actually performs several actions. First, a command is sent to SQL Server informing it of the name of the database to remove. SQL Server then checks that nobody is currently connected to that database. If someone is connected, through either SQL Server Query Editor or a data access method like ADO.NET, then SQL Server will refuse the deletion. Only if you select Close Existing Connections will this process be overridden.

For SQL Server to refuse the deletion, it does not matter whether anyone connected to the database is actually doing anything; all that is important is the existence of the connection. For example, if you selected ApressFinancial in Query Editor and then returned to SQL Server Management Studio and tried to drop the database, you would see an error in the Delete screen which, when you clicked the message, you would see the error shown in Figure 3-16.

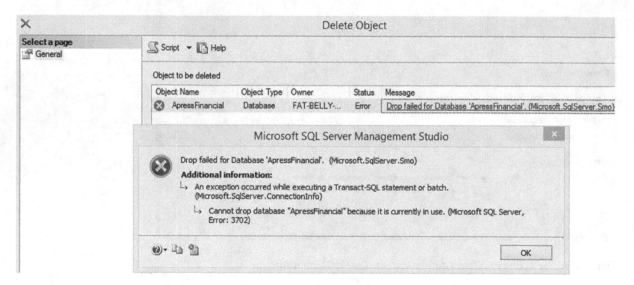

Figure 3-16. *Failed database deletion*

Errors like the one shown in Figure 3-16 on the screen in the background provide hyperlinks to documentation that can give you further help, as shown in the dialog box in the foreground. Figure 3-17 displays the information found when the button called Technical details is clicked, which is found at the bottom left of the error dialog

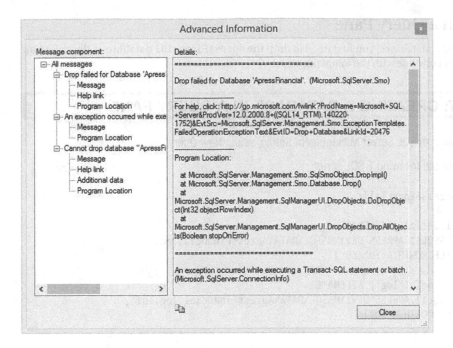

Figure 3-17. *Further technical details*

Once SQL Server has checked that nobody is connected to the database, it then checks that you have *permission* to remove the database. SQL Server will allow you to delete the database if it was your user ID that created it, in which case you own this database and SQL Server allows you to do what you want with it. However, you are not alone in owning the database.

If you recall from Chapter 1, there was mention of the sa account when installing SQL Server. Since it is the most powerful ID and has control over everything within SQL Server, there were warnings about leaving the sa account without any password and also about using the sa account as any sort of login ID in general. This section also mentioned that the sa account was in fact a member of the sysadmin server role. A *role* is a way of grouping together similar users who need similar access to sets of data. Anyone in the sysadmin role has full administrative privileges—and this includes rights to remove any database on the server.

So, regardless of whether you are logged in as yourself or as sysadmin, take care when using SQL Server Management Studio to drop a database. I cover different roles and their power in Chapter 4.

Creating a Database in a Query Pane

To use the second method of creating databases, you first need to drop the ApressFinancial database as described in the previous section. Then you can continue with the following steps.

TRY IT OUT: CREATING A DATABASE IN A QUERY PANE

1. From the standard toolbar of SQL Server Management Studio, select New Query.

2. In the query pane, enter the following T-SQL script:

```
CREATE DATABASE [ApressFinancial]
 ON  PRIMARY
( NAME = N'ApressFinancial', FILENAME =
 N'C:\APRESS_DEV1\MSSQL12.APRESS_DEV1\MSSQL\DATA\ApressFinancial.mdf',
 SIZE = 5120KB , FILEGROWTH = 1024KB )
 LOG ON
( NAME = N'ApressFinancial_log', FILENAME =
 N'C:\APRESS_DEV1\MSSQL12.APRESS_DEV1\MSSQL\DATA\ApressFinancial_log.ldf',
 SIZE = 2048KB , FILEGROWTH = 10%)
 GO
```

3. Execute this code by pressing F5 or by clicking the Execute Query toolbar button.

4. Once the code is executed, you should see the following result:

```
Command(s) completed successfully.
```

HOW IT WORKS: CREATING A DATABASE IN A QUERY

The main focus of this sidebar is the code listed in the previous exercise: the CREATE DATABASE command.

When placing code in the Query Editor, you're building up a set of instructions for SQL Server to act on. As you progress through the book, you will encounter many commands that you can place in Query Editor, all of which build up to provide powerful and useful utilities or methods for working with data. Before you actually look at the code itself, you need to inspect the syntax of the CREATE DATABASE command:

```
CREATE DATABASE <database name>
[CONTAINMENT = NONE | PARTIAL | FULL]
[ON
   ( [ NAME = logical_name, ]
       FILENAME = physical_file_name
     [, FILESIZE = size ]
     [, MAXSIZE = maxsize ]
     [, FILEGROWTH = growth_increment] ) ]
```

```
[LOG ON
    ( [ NAME = logical_name, ]
        FILENAME = physical_file_name
      [, FILESIZE = size ]
      [, MAXSIZE = maxsize ]
      [, FILEGROWTH = growth_increment] ) ]
[COLLATE collation_name ]
```

The parameters are as follows:

- `database name`: The name of the database that the CREATE DATABASE command will create within SQL Server

- `Containment`: Defines whether the database is fully contained or whether there is usage of metadata, logins, and so on, outside of the database

- `ON`: The ON keyword informs SQL Server that the command will specifically mention where the data files are to be placed, as well as their name, size, and file growth. With the ON keyword comes a further list of comma-separated options.

- `NAME`: The logical name of the data file that will be used as the reference within SQL Server

- `FILENAME`: The physical file name and full path where the data file will reside

- `SIZE`: The initial size, in megabytes by default, of the data file specified; this parameter is optional, and if omitted, it will take the size defined in the model database. You can suffix the size with KB, MB, GB, or TB (terabytes). The minimum size for a database will be the same size as the `model` system database, defined by default as 4MB. MAXSIZE indicates the maximum size the database can grow to.

- `FILEGROWTH`: The amount that the data file will grow each time it fills up; you can specify either a value that indicates by how many megabytes the data file will grow or a percentage, as discussed earlier when you created a database with SQL Server Management Studio.

- `LOG ON`: The use of the LOG ON keyword informs SQL Server that the command will specifically mention where the log files will be placed, and their name, size, and file growth.

- `NAME`: The name of the log file that will be used as the reference within SQL Server

- `FILENAME`: The physical file name and full path to where the log file will reside; you must include the suffix `.LDF`. This could be a different name from the `FILENAME` specified earlier.

- `SIZE`: The initial size, in megabytes by default, of the log file specified; this parameter is optional, and if omitted, it will take the size defined in the model database. You can suffix the size with KB, MB, GB, or TB.

- `FILEGROWTH`: The amount by which the log file will grow each time the data file fills up, which has the same values as for the data file's `FILEGROWTH`

- `COLLATE`: The collation used for the database; collation was discussed earlier in the chapter when you created a database with SQL Server Management Studio.

It's now time to inspect the code entered into Query Analyzer that will create the ApressFinancial database.

Commencing with CREATE DATABASE, you are informing SQL Server that the following statements are all parameters to be considered for building a new database within SQL Server. Some of the parameters are optional, and SQL Server will include default values when these parameters are not entered. But how does SQL Server know what values to supply? Recall that at the start of this chapter, I discussed the built-in SQL Server databases—specifically, the model database. SQL Server takes the default options for parameters from this database unless they are otherwise specified. Thus, it is important to consider carefully any modifications to the model database.

The database name is obviously essential, and in this case, ApressFinancial is the chosen name.

The ON parameter provides SQL Server with specifics about the data files to be created, rather than taking the defaults. Admittedly, in this instance, there is no need to specify these details, as by taking the defaults, SQL Server would supply the parameters as listed anyway.

This can also be said for the next set of parameters, which deal with the Transaction Log found with LOG ON. In this instance, there is no need to supply these parameters, as again the listed amounts are the SQL Server defaults.

Finally, the collation sequence you specify is actually the default for the server.

Taking all this on board, the command could actually be entered as follows, which would then take all the default settings from SQL Server to build the database:

```
CREATE DATABASE ApressFinancial
```

You can then set the database options as outlined during the discussion of the script earlier in the chapter.

Similarly, if you want to delete the database using T-SQL code, it's a simple case of ensuring that you are not connected within that particular query pane to ApressFinancial via the USE command. Then you use the command DROP followed by the object you want to drop, or delete, and then the name of the object.

```
USE Master
GO
DROP DATABASE ApressFinancial
```

You may be thinking that it is a lot of work to type in the CREATE DATABASE T-SQL statement when there is a quick and simple screen that can do the job for you. This is true; however, there are limitations to using the screen that sometimes make T-SQL the better option. I have mentioned before that by using T-SQL you can place code in programs. You will see how to do that in Chapter 20. Using T-SQL also enables you to store the code in a source repository such as Visual SourceSafe that then allows you to track any amendments to the database code as you release upgrades to your application. T-SQL can also be read by other developers to ensure the code is delivering what is expected. Finally, in some institutions, auditors will visit your premises to check code releases to ensure that the release code matches what was sought.

Summary

In this chapter, you looked at designing and creating the example database. Though just a sample database, it still required careful thought. The chapter discussed the different types of database and that the book will be working with an OLTP based database. You saw how some basic database designing was achieved. Although this is a much larger process in real life, enough was covered to talk about data gathering, normalization, and how the data will be stored.

You also saw a discussion on relationships and keys and what types of keys there are. Finally, a database was built and the possible options were discussed to give you a solid base of understanding of databases. In the next chapter, you will take a look at security and start investigating how to ensure your database is safe and secure from within and outside your organization.

CHAPTER 4

■ ■ ■

Security and Compliance

Security is important—more so, in fact, than design, creation, and performance. If your database had no security measures in place, absolutely anyone could come along and steal or corrupt the data, causing havoc to you and your company—and not in just one database, but in every database in every server.

Security can be enforced in many ways on SQL Server: by Windows itself through Windows authentication; by restricting users' access to sensitive data through views; by specifically creating users, logins, and roles that have explicit levels of access; or by encrypting your database, logs, and files.

This chapter covers some parts of security, although it is impossible to talk about every area of security, mainly because you haven't seen much of SQL Server's feature set yet! In Chapter 1, you looked at the difference between Windows authentication and SQL Server authentication, so already you know your options with regard to the type of security you might want to use. In this chapter, you'll go deeper. You will see security mentioned at some other points in the book, where relevant, to give you a good level of knowledge about securing your database solution. You will also see a section in Chapter 14 of the book once many of SQL Server's features have been covered.

You will also learn about Declarative Management Framework (DMF). In the past, a database administrator had to write tools and monitor systems to ensure that any new database created in production was created with the right options. The database administrator also had to monitor to ensure that items were not being created when they should not be. Now it is possible to create rules on databases, tables, views, and so on to check whether an object in question is compliant with standards defined by those rules. If an object isn't, then you will be notified and a simple click will allow changes to be made to bring the object back into alignment with the policy.

By the end of this chapter, you will have dealt with the following:

- Logins for individuals and groups

- Roles at the server, database, and application level

- Schemas

- Applying policies to your database to ensure compliance

- Encryption within the database

The first area of security and compliance you need to understand is what *roles* and *logins* are.

Logins

The only way anyone can connect to SQL Server is via a login. As discussed in Chapter 1, this doesn't necessarily mean that every user has to have a specific login within SQL Server itself. With Windows authentication, if a Windows user belongs to a specific Windows group, just by belonging to that group, provided that group is contained within SQL Server, the Windows account will have access to SQL Server.

■ **Note** All groups discussed within the book are created on the local computer. In organizations, you will find that groups will be created on the network domain and Windows users added to the necessary groups. Users can be added to multiple groups.

When a database is created, initially only the database owner and system administrator (sysadmin) has any rights to complete any task on that database, whether that be to add a table, insert any data, or view any data. This was the case when you first created your `ApressFinancial` database in Chapter 3. It is only when the database owner grants permissions to other users that they gain extra access to complete tasks.

It is common practice to create a Windows group and place Windows user accounts into that group. In a networked organization, you would create a domain group and place the specific user into that domain group. However, I am demonstrating on a local non-domain setup. In a network domain, the steps will be similar; the main difference is that you will have to complete the steps using utilities such as Microsoft Active Directory. Using Windows groups is not mandatory, though, and it is possible to add a login for individual Windows users. You can also have a mix of groups and individuals. However, as you proceed through the chapter, you will see the benefit of groups and the large amount of overhead you may have to incur when using individual logins.

Using Windows groups is how I wish to work with the `ApressFinancial` system, so I will create some Windows groups for it. I will group logins depending on which department the login relates to and what I want to allow each group to do. I will allow some groups to add new financial products and other groups to add customers, and, finally, I'll set up a group for batch processes to add interest and financial transactions. I will create a few of these groups so that later in the book you can see security in action.

On some versions of Windows, such as Windows 7 Home or Windows 8 (standard), creating groups is not possible. By not having the ability to create groups, each user who is required to access the database needs to be defined individually. I tend to find that developers who are building databases at home with SQL Server Express Edition fit this category.

■ **Note** The process you are about to go through would be the same if you were adding a single user.

TRY IT OUT: GROUPS, LOGINS, AND SQL SERVER ACCESS

1. Navigate to your Control Panel and then select Administrative Tools ➤ Computer Management.

2. This brings up a screen that shows different aspects of your computer management. I am interested in selecting Local Users and Groups. When you do so, you will see that there are already several groups within your computer, as shown in Figure 4-1. If you installed features more than the default required for the book, such as Full-Text Service or Analysis Services, you will see a larger number of groups already defined for the use of SQL Server. These groups differ from groups that we will be defining for accessing the data.

Figure 4-1. *List of groups on the computer*

3. MSmith is a product controller in the fictitious corporation and can add new corporate financial products. Right-click Groups and select New Group. This brings up the New Group screen, as shown in Figure 4-2, where you can add your grouping for the product controllers. `Apress_Product_Controllers` is the group you will use in this chapter.

Figure 4-2. Adding the first group for your application

4. By clicking Add, you can then add all the Windows user accounts that you need to be part of this group. You can either type MSmith or click Advanced, which brings up a selection dialog box. If you click Find Now, as I assume that there will be only a few accounts on your computer if you are working locally, you should find MSmith. Clicking the Check Names button adds the object names text box, as shown in Figure 4-3.

Figure 4-3. MSmith found, ready to add to the group

If MSmith were on your company network, you may have to prefix the name with the domain name, and you definitely would if the account were on a different domain. For example, if you had a network domain called Apress, and MSmith were on that domain (as opposed to your local computer and therefore your local domain, as is the case for this example), then you would type Apress\MSmith. Figure 4-3 shows MSmith is on the FAT-BELLY-SONY local domain.

5. Click OK and then click the Create button on the New Group screen. Once you have created the group, you should close the New Group dialog box, as you don't want to create any more groups at the moment. This brings you back to the Computer Management dialog box, where you see your new group added, as shown in Figure 4-4.

Figure 4-4. *New group added*

6. You now need to add this group to SQL Server as a login. Open SQL Server Management Studio and navigate to Security ➤ Logins within Object Explorer. Once there, right-click Logins, and then click New Login, which brings up the dialog box shown in Figure 4-5.

Figure 4-5. *Creating a new login*

7. Click Search to display the Select User or Group dialog box, where you will begin your search for the group. This is very similar to the previous search box you saw but has been defined to search for a user or built-in security principal. However, by default, the search will not search for groups. You need to click Object Types and ensure the Groups option is checked on the screen that comes up. You will then see Group added to the list of objects in the top text box, as shown in Figure 4-6.

Figure 4-6. *Searching for groups*

8. By clicking Advanced, you can refine the search for the group that is to be added rather than typing it in. After clicking Advanced, you can click Find Now, is a button about halfway down on the right, which will then list all of the group, user, and principal objects on your computer, and the selected domain. Highlight the following group—Apress_Product_Controllers, in this case—as shown in Figure 4-7, and click OK.

Figure 4-7. *Finding the* Apress_Product_Controllers *group*

9. This brings you back to the Select User or Group dialog box, where you will see your group has been added, as shown in Figure 4-8. You can then click OK.

Figure 4-8. *Group found, ready for adding*

■ **Note** You are now back at the new login screen where the group will be populated. If you clicked OK at this point, this would allow the group to connect only to SQL Server and nothing else. Members of this group would therefore not be able to do anything. While creating this login, I will not be demonstrating the Credentials section. This is used when a login has to access external SQL Server resources.

10. You need to give this group access to the databases you wish to allow its members to use. It is vital that you allow users or groups of users login access only to the resources they need and don't use the "allow everything, it's easier" approach that I have seen on my travels. You want your users to see only the ApressFinancial database. Click User Mapping in the left-hand list of items, and then, within the Users Mapped to This Login section of the screen shown in Figure 4-9, select ApressFinancial.

Figure 4-9. *Giving a login access to a database*

11. Before you click OK, click the Script button at the top of the screen and choose to place the script into a new query window. The SQL generated from Figure 4-9 follows. You will look at it in more detail in a moment when you more closely examine adding a login, but you can use this in the next section, as a basis of adding the next login. The code will be explained in that section.

```
USE [master]
GO
CREATE LOGIN [FAT-BELLY-SONY\Apress_Product_Controllers]
FROM WINDOWS WITH DEFAULT_DATABASE=[master]
GO
USE [ApressFinancial]
GO
CREATE USER [FAT-BELLY-SONY\Apress_Product_Controllers]
FOR LOGIN [FAT-BELLY-SONY\Apress_Product_Controllers]
GO
```

12. Returning to SQL Server Management Studio, you can see in Figure 4-10 that I have moved to the Status page. Here you can grant or deny access to SQL Server for a Windows account, SQL Server login, or, in your case, Windows group. The second set of options is for enabling or disabling SQL Server logins, which is ideal for when someone leaves the firm if you are creating a login for a single user. The final set of options, specific to SQL Server authentication, allows an account to be unlocked after it has been locked out either by too many incorrect passwords or by someone with the authority to lock it.

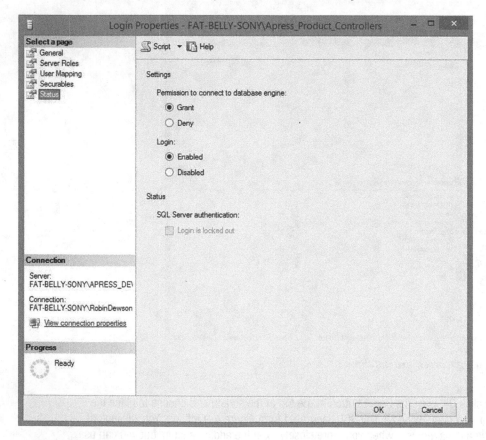

Figure 4-10. *Login status*

13. You can now click OK to add the login. This will complete the addition to SQL Server.

Now that you have created the new server login and placed it within SQL Server, you could within Windows now switch the user account to MSmith and successfully connect. However, as MSmith, you would be able to explore only the ApressFinancial database created in Chapter 3. As this is the ideal secure scenario, the task has succeeded in its objective.

■ **Note** As I mentioned at the start of this discussion, the process of creating a login would be the same if you wished to add a single user.

What has been described in the preceding exercise is Windows authentication. For SQL Server authentication, each user needs to be added separately. The process is very similar to that for adding users with Windows authentication, but you can specify a password expiration and enforce password complexity. This forces the Windows password policies for expiration and complexity that exist on the local computer or domain to apply to this login's password.

So now that you have added a server login graphically, the same can be achieved via a query pane using T-SQL code. You saw the code generated from my computer when I took this from the scripting option, and you will use it as the basis of your next login creation to demonstrate using T-SQL this time. This is a very straightforward process, so let's take a look at it next.

TRY IT OUT: PROGRAMMATICALLY WORKING WITH A LOGIN

1. From SQL Server Management Studio, select New Query. This brings up an empty query pane.

2. It is necessary to add a second login group for the book example. You have available two different methods to create the login via T-SQL, and which one you use depends on whether you are going to use Windows authentication or SQL Server authentication. The first example takes a look at the Windows authentication method. Locate the code from Steps 10 and 11 in the previous "Try It Out: Groups, Logins, and SQL Server Access" exercise (it is repeated here for ease of reference).

```
USE [master]
GO
CREATE LOGIN [FAT-BELLY-SONY\Apress_Product_Controllers] FROM WINDOWS
WITH DEFAULT_DATABASE=[master]
GO
USE [ApressFinancial]
GO
CREATE USER [FAT-BELLY-SONY\Apress_Product_Controllers]
FOR LOGIN [FAT-BELLY-SONY\Apress_Product_Controllers]
GO
```

3. You can now alter this code to create a group that will be defined for users wishing to view customers and their information that could be used in call centers, for example. Just to remind you that a group is being created so that you do not need to create a login for each person in that call center. Also, this time you are going to set the database that will be connected to by default by this login to the ApressFinancial database. This is so that user groups do not connect to a system database as they should have no reason for any user to connect to a system database. For developer groups, you can, and in some companies you will, make the login connect to a system database, such as the master database, by default. Then, if the default login user database is dropped or is offline, the logins can still log in without a problem. Developer accounts quite often are defined to connect to a system database, such as the master database, but user and system logins are not and are defined to log in to the user database. Before entering the following code, you will of course need to add the new group, Apress_Client_Information, within your Computer Management icon found in the Administrative tools of the Control Panel first (see the "Try It Out: GROUPS, LOGINS, AND SQL SERVER ACCESS" exercise earlier for more on this specifically—steps 1–5). Once you've done this, enter the following code in a new Query Editor window (don't execute it yet):

```
CREATE LOGIN [FAT-BELLY-SONY\Apress_Client_Information]
FROM WINDOWS
WITH DEFAULT_DATABASE=[ApressFinancial],
DEFAULT_LANGUAGE=[us_english]
GO
```

The format of this syntax is straightforward. In this case, CREATE LOGIN instructs SQL Server that you want to create a new login called FAT-BELLY\Apress_Client_Information, where FAT-BELLY-SONY is the name of the network domain in which the Apress_Client_Information group can be found. You should change the prefix to match your own setup. Here the definition appears surrounded with optional square brackets in case of spaces in the name.

Next, the keywords FROM WINDOWS inform SQL Server that you are creating a login with Windows authentication. After that, you define the name of the database that the login will connect to when a connection is made using WITH DEFAULT_DATABASE. Finally, the second option specifies the default language the connection will use, although it is possible at any time to alter the language using the Set Language option. This allows this group to connect to SQL Server. Defining the default language is optional and will take the server language.

4. Once you have placed the code in your query pane, you can execute it by pressing F5 or by clicking the Execute button on the toolbar. Once it finishes executing, you should see the new login in the Security node within Object Explorer on the left, as shown in Figure 4-11. If you right-click the new login and select Properties, you will see the same screen and details as you saw when you created the login graphically.

Figure 4-11. *Both logins created*

5. You can then enable the login's ability to access SQL Server or disable it by using the ALTER LOGIN command. It is also possible to alter the login's default database. In the graphical example, if you check back to Figure 4-5, you will see that the default database found near the foot of the graphic was called master. It would be better for the login to connect to the correct database as this is a user-based login rather than a developer login. The following code informs SQL Server that it should connect your login to the ApressFinancial database by default, rather than the master database as defined previously. Remember to change the prefix as appropriate:

```
ALTER LOGIN [FAT-BELLY-SONY\Apress_Product_Controllers]
WITH DEFAULT_DATABASE=ApressFinancial
```

6. The final piece in the jigsaw is to grant the Windows account access to the database, which will then allow the login to use the ApressFinancial database. To do this, you need to switch from the master database to the ApressFinancial database with the USE keyword followed by the name of the database.

Using CREATE USER, you can then specify the name of the user you want in your database. The standard procedure is to use the same name as the login, which makes life so much easier when maintaining the system in general. You then use FOR LOGIN to define which server login you want to map to this database user:

```
USE ApressFinancial
GO
CREATE USER [FAT-BELLY-SONY\Apress_Client_Information]
FOR LOGIN [FAT-BELLY-SONY\Apress_Client_Information]
GO
```

Server Logins and Database Users

As you now know, there are two steps to complete, whether you want to create a login based upon SQL Server authentication or Windows authentication. The first step is to create a server login, which was the first part of creating a login that you went through. A login is also quite different from a user, and the two may look the same, but this is not the case. With a login, you can connect to SQL Server, but a user is an account that is database-specific. The two may have exactly the same name, and this can cause confusion, but a login cannot connect to a database or perform database actions without an association with a valid user account. A server login is one that, when used, can connect only to the server itself. It cannot use any of the user databases within SQL Server. The second step is creating the database user; in the graphical section that you looked at first, this is when you selected the databases you wanted to use.

Within SQL Server, permissions can be granted at multiple levels, including the server and database levels. Examples of server-level permissions include creating new logins or managing server properties. Examples of database permissions include being able to read data from a table or being able to create new tables. One server login can be associated with multiple users in different databases. Generally, when using Windows authentication, a database username is the same as the login name, but this does not have to be the case. It does, however, simplify administration. In this book, I will mostly be dealing with database-level permissions, but I will briefly examine server roles in the following section.

Roles

Three different types of roles exist within SQL Server: fixed server roles, database roles (which are the general roles included during installation of SQL Server, component-specific roles such as those for Reporting Services that are added when the component is installed, and user-defined roles), and application roles.

Fixed Server Roles

Within SQL Server, specific predefined roles are set up to allow certain tasks and to restrict other tasks. Someone with the right permissions, such as a sysadmin, can assign these roles to any login ID within SQL Server.

■ **Note** These are server roles and therefore are assigned to logins.

If you look at the Server Roles node in Object Explorer, you will see a list of roles as shown in Figure 4-12. But what do they mean? You get a little hint within the Server Roles node within SQL Server Management Studio.

Figure 4-12. *Fixed server roles*

These roles, available for anyone to use across the server, can perform the following tasks:

- bulkadmin: Run BULK INSERT statements. These are statements that load large amounts of data in bulk with almost no transaction logging very quickly.

- dbcreator: Create, alter, or drop databases as well as restore them

- diskadmin: Administer disk files

- processadmin: Kill a process running T-SQL code

- public: Every login belongs to the public role. Has the ability to view database permissions but by default can perform no other tasks. If you add the public role to any task or object, be aware that every login will have the ability to perform what has been assigned and therefore could be a huge security risk.

- securityadmin: Manage logins including passwords for SQL logins and login permissions

- serveradmin: Administrate the server and carry out tasks such as changing options and even starting and shutting down the server

- setupadmin: Work with more than one server with which anyone in this role can add, remove, and manage linked servers

- sysadmin: Perform any activity. BUILTIN\Administrators, which is the Windows administrator account, is not added to this role automatically; however, if you want an administrator of the server to be able to connect to your SQL Server, then adding BUILTIN\Administrators is possible and is suggested by Microsoft. I personally would not add the BUILTIN\Administrators group, as I believe that it is a security risk that can be reduced by having a specific group.

Server roles are static objects. They contain groups of actions that operate at the server level rather than at the database level. When creating a new login, you could assign these server roles to it if you wanted the login to carry out server actions as well as any database-related actions, if required.

Database Roles

Database roles deal with actions that are performed at the database level. Actions within SQL Server can be grouped into different types.

The following bullet points list the existing database roles installed with SQL Server and what they can or cannot do:

- dbo/db_owner: Specifies the owner of the database

- db_accessadmin: Can manage access to a database for logins

- db_backupoperator: Can back up the database

- db_datareader: Can read data from all user-defined tables

- db_datawriter: Can perform any write actions to user tables

- db_ddladmin: Can perform Data Definition Language (DDL) actions such as creating tables

- db_denydatareader: Cannot read data from user tables

- db_denydatawriter: Cannot write data from user tables

- db_securityadmin: Can modify database role membership and manage permissions

- public: Can see any database objects that are created with public, or full rights, access (every user that you create will belong to the public database role)

Although you will put the existing database roles to use, you'll find it helpful to create new database roles—a common task in SQL Server—when you want to be very specific about permissions particular users have. You do this by creating a specific database role and then adding the database user IDs to your role. If you wanted to group several user IDs together, then you might create a new role.

Application Roles

Databases are written for applications. However, not all databases exist for just one application. Application roles allow you to define one role for accessing a database based on the application that is connecting, rather than having security via database roles for different groups of users or single users. Let's look at an example.

Consider a central database that holds client data. This database is in turn accessed from the sales order department, which has its own separate database. The client database is also accessed from the debt recovery department, which also has its own database.

As a database administrator, you may set up database roles for each application. Say you have a Debt Recovery database role and a Sales Order Processing database role. Debt Recovery would want to see information that was hidden from the Sales Order role, such as how in debt a customer is. But what if a user, such as MSmith, worked in both the debt recovery and sales order departments, in two different part-time jobs, for instance? While working as part of the Sales Order group of users, MSmith could see information that was not pertinent to that group.

You can set up an application role for the Sales Order application and another for the Debt Recovery application, thus removing the conflict of having two different sets of security settings for the one user login. Also, when users move departments, you are not wasting time revoking one set of database roles to give them a new set of database roles for their new department. The security is controlled via the application as it would log on to the database via an application role.

An application role overrides any user security settings and is created for giving an application access to SQL Server. Therefore, the Sales Order Processing application would define the access for anybody using it.

An application role has no users; it is used when you wish to define what an application can access within your database and what it cannot. You need to create an application role for examples shown later in this book, so let's do this now.

TRY IT OUT: CREATING A NEW APPLICATION ROLE

1. Navigate to the ApressFinancial database, expand the Security node, right-click Roles, select New, and then New Application Role. In the dialog box that appears, enter a useful role name and a password, as shown in Figure 4-13. This role will be for the banking application through which users will want to look at checks, cash withdrawals, and so on.

Figure 4-13. *Creating a new application role*

2. Click Securables in Object Explorer on the left-hand side, and then click Search. This is how you begin to define what objects you want to assign to this role.

3. In the Add Objects dialog box that appears, leave the options as they are shown in Figure 4-14 and click OK.

Figure 4-14. *Selecting the type of objects to add*

4. Select All Object of the types and click OK, which will bring up a list of objects that you can select from. Since you don't have much within your database that you can apply permissions to at this point in the book, select Databases, as shown in Figure 4-15, and click OK. You are going to give this application authority to access your database, but not the ability to do anything (mainly because you don't have anything it can do yet).

Figure 4-15. *Selecting the database*

5. By clicking OK once you have selected Databases, which brings you back to the Securables page, where you can allow or deny specific actions, as you see in Figure 4-16. Leave everything unchecked for the moment; you will come back to this later in the book when you look at stored procedures in Chapter 14.

Figure 4-16. *Application roles' explicit permission settings*

6. Click OK to finish creating your application role.

Schemas

In the following chapters, you will be creating SQL Server objects to hold and work with your data. You could create these objects so that each could be seen as its own small part of the overall solution. It would make for better organization, though, if objects that could be seen as subsets of the whole solution were grouped together. For instance, in your example, you could group share details and share prices together as share information, or group the financial transactions the customer makes using the transactions and transaction types tables together. These groupings could then be used as the basis of security to the underlying data for when a SQL Server connection tries to access the data. These groupings I have just talked about, called *schemas*, exist at the database level within SQL Server. Therefore, a schema is a method of creating a group and placing objects within that group, which can then be used to grant or revoke permissions as a group to SQL Server connections. You may find some applications where the database has only one schema for every table as the team found that their application security was such that it was simpler to have everything under one umbrella. Whatever the decision all database objects must reside in a schema. My advice to you on whether to break out objects to different schemas or to hold in one schema would be to use multiple schemas where you can place an object in to a specific logical scope. Try to avoid schemas that are named to cover multiple functional scopes.

Prior to SQL Server 2005, each object was owned by a user account. Whenever a user left, quite often it would mean moving the ownership of objects for that user's account to a new account. As you can imagine, in a very large system this could take hours or even days to complete. Now objects are owned by schemas, and the many objects that exist will be contained within one schema in a very large system. Although a schema will still be owned by a SQL Server account, as you will see when you take a look at the syntax in a moment, the number of schemas should be a fraction of the number of objects, even in very large systems, and therefore moving ownership will be easier and faster.

So by having a schema within your solution and assigning objects to that schema, not only are you improving security, but also you are grouping logical units of the database together, making your solution easier to understand and use.

Creating a schema is very simple, and the syntax is defined as follows:

```
CREATE SCHEMA schema_name AUTHORIZATION owner_name
```

You can now put this in action.

TRY IT OUT: CREATING SCHEMAS AND ADDING OBJECTS

1. Open up a Query Editor window so you can create your first schema. This schema will be used to keep all your transaction details together. Enter the following code:

   ```
   USE ApressFinancial
   GO
   CREATE SCHEMA TransactionDetails AUTHORIZATION dbo
   ```

2. When you execute this by pressing F5 or by clicking the Execute button, you should see it successfully complete. This will have created a new schema where the owner of the schema is the dbo user. This means that any login with sysadmin privileges will automatically have access to this schema because it maps to the dbo user in all databases. If you execute the code successfully, you'll see the following message:

   ```
   Command(s) completed successfully.
   ```

3. You can then create further schemas for other groupings, such as one for share details or customer details including products. Enter the following code:

   ```
   CREATE SCHEMA ShareDetails AUTHORIZATION dbo
   GO
   CREATE SCHEMA CustomerDetails AUTHORIZATION dbo
   ```

4. Execute this code, which adds the schemas to the database. If you execute the code successfully, you'll see the following message:

   ```
   Command(s) completed successfully.
   ```

5. If you move to Object Explorer, you can see your schemas in place, as shown in Figure 4-17.

Figure 4-17. Schemas applied

Before You Can Proceed with Your Solution

You have now created a database and gained an understanding of the different roles in SQL Server at both the server and database level. Before you can proceed and create objects such as tables, you need to clear a couple of obstacles. After the database, the next objects you will create are tables, which you will learn about in Chapters 5 and 7. So what security considerations do you need to check before you can do this?

First of all, you must be using a database user account that has the authority to add tables to the specific database you are required to—in this case, ApressFinancial. This is the next security issue you will tackle, and you should keep in mind what you have learned about accounts and roles in this and the previous chapter. You also need to have access to that specific database. Let's look at the issue of access to the database if you are using a user ID that did not create the database.

The database was re-created at the very end of the previous chapter under user ID FAT-BELLY-Sony\Robin. The user who created the database is the database owner, also known as dbo. So how can you check who created the database if you did not?

At the end of the previous chapter, I asked you to create the database under your own user ID, which, if you followed the instructions so far and you are a local administrator of the machine SQL Server is installed on, you should have the right privileges within SQL Server to do the check. In your organization, this is more likely to be a specific but generic Windows user account not linked to a physical person. For example, you might have a specific DBO user account used for DBO-based actions restricting who can perform DBO-based tasks.

The following exercise will demonstrate how you check the identity of the database owner.

TRY IT OUT: CHECKING THE DATABASE OWNER

1. Ensure that SQL Server Management Studio is open.

2. Navigate to the database that you wish to check on—in this case, ApressFinancial.

3. Click the ApressFinancial database node in Object Explorer on the left-hand side of the screen once, and then right-click.

4. Select Properties to bring up the Database Properties dialog box shown in Figure 4-18. On the General tab, you will see an item named Owner. This is the fully qualified account preceded by the domain or local machine name.

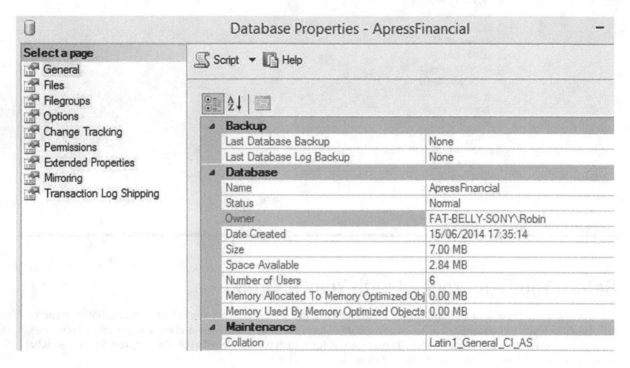

Figure 4-18. Database Properties window

5. Click Cancel to close this dialog box.

Ownership of tables and other database objects is just as important. If you create a table using the same user ID as that which you created the database with, or use a user ID that is a member of the sysadmin role that is also implicitly mapped to the dbo user in the database, the table will have a default schema of dbo. However, if you logged in with a different user ID that was not a dbo user but had sufficient privileges such as db_creator server role, the table would have that user's default schema as the prefix to the table name, replacing the dbo prefix.

Now that you know who the database owner is, it is up to that user, or another user who has system administration rights (in other words, a login that has the sysadmin server role or a user ID that has the db_owner database role), to allow any other specified user the ability to create tables within the database. You have a user called MSmith who is not a system administrator, but a developer. Recall you created this user as a Windows user in Chapter 1, and that this user could not log in to SQL Server.

The next section will go through a scenario where, as a developer, MSmith has no rights to create any new items. However, you will rectify this situation in the next exercise, where you will alter MSmith's user privileges so that he or she can connect to SQL Server and create a table.

TRY IT OUT: ALLOWING A USER TO CREATE A TABLE

1. Log on to SQL Server as a sysadmin if required. (However, you are probably already logged in as a sysadmin if you are following the book.) Create a new login by right-clicking the Logins node on the Server Security node and selecting New Login. This brings up the new login screen, which you can populate with the login name of the account by typing in the details of the login, as shown in Figure 4-19, or by searching for the object using the button to the right. You are also going to allow this user to connect to ApressFinancial by default when he or she logs in. Once you are ready, click OK.

Figure 4-19. *New login*

2. You are not going to assign this user any server roles, but you are going to assign this login to the db_owner database role, as you see in Figure 4-20 in the User Mapping section. This will allow the user to create tables as well as create and work with other objects and data. You could have selected db_ddladmin, but this would have allowed the user to create only objects and not data.

Figure 4-20. *New login with database access*

■ **Note** Recall in the introduction to this section in "Before You Can Proceed," I said that you would give a db owner to a system account for DBO work; what you are doing in this exercise is similar to that task.

3. Click OK, which will create not only a server login, but also a database user in ApressFinancial for MSmith, as shown in Figure 4-21.

```
☐ 🗍 ApressFinancial
    ⊞ 🗀 Database Diagrams
    ⊞ 🗀 Tables
    ⊞ 🗀 Views
    ⊞ 🗀 Synonyms
    ⊞ 🗀 Programmability
    ⊞ 🗀 Service Broker
    ⊞ 🗀 Storage
    ☐ 🗀 Security
        ☐ 🗀 Users
            🔓 dbo
            🔓 FAT-BELLY-SONY\Apress_Client_Information
            🔓 FAT-BELLY-SONY\Apress_Product_Controllers
            🔓 FAT-BELLY-SONY\MSmith
            🔓 guest
            🔓 INFORMATION_SCHEMA
            🔓 sys
```

Figure 4-21. *User login accounts*

MSmith is now in a position to log in to SQL Server and create tables in the ApressFinancial database.

Declarative Management Framework

The security of a database does not just involve ensuring that only the correct people can log in to the system and see only the data that they are authorized to see. Security also involves knowing that the basis of the data has met certain defined compliance criteria. This comes under the header of Declarative Management Framework (DMF). SQL Server's DMF allows policies to be defined to ensure that SQL Server objects follow a defined set of rules. These rules are not compulsory, but rather generate warnings showing that you are not in compliance. DMF also includes tools to rectify such problem situations. The logic behind DMF is for administrators to determine how an installation should be defined as part of its setup and to then have the ability to enforce the rules of their definition should they be violated.

There are three aspects to DMF, and you must understand all three before you can make DMF work for you:

> *Facets*: A facet is a grouping that exists to place conditions into. Facets are prebuilt within SQL Server and expose conditions that can be tested within a policy. Each facet group will contain logically combined conditions. One example is the Login facet, which contains conditions to test whether a login is locked, the default database, the last time the password was altered, whether password expiration is enabled, and so on.

> *Policies*: A policy defines one or more conditions to be applied to a server. Policies will be defined by database administrators, or even auditors, to ensure that specified conditions are met. Historically, one of the largest areas of contention with installations of SQL Server has been that it required the database administrators to write their own stored procedures and schedule them to ensure that every database complied with company policy. Now it is a simple method of defining a condition and letting Service Broker execute and report on the condition. The result is a greater degree of standardization, as well as ease of programming.

> *Conditions*: A condition within DMF is similar to any other condition and is a test on an attribute to make sure that it meets a certain criteria. A number of conditions for your installations will be built up over time, and it is even good practice to set up conditions to test the value of attributes that should be set by default. Such conditions could surround the checking of the ANSI NULL default, for example. Such a condition would then trap for any database where, even by accident, the tested value was altered as part of the setup. Conditions need to be part of a policy.

TRY IT OUT: BUILDING A CONDITION AND A POLICY

1. Ensure that SQL Server Management Studio is open. There are two ways to progress with this example. It is possible to create a condition and then the policy, or you can create the condition while building the policy. There is no right or wrong way. For this example, you will be building a condition while building the policy. From within Object Explorer, expand the Management node, followed by the Policy Management node, and then the Policies node. Right-click Policies and select New Policy, as demonstrated in Figure 4-22.

Figure 4-22. *Creating a new policy*

2. You are now presented with an empty Create New Policy screen. Enter a description of Database ANSI NULL Default in the name. Below this, you will see the Check Condition combo box, which holds the condition the policy is testing. When you click the down arrow, select New Condition, as shown in Figure 4-23.

Figure 4-23. *Creating a new condition*

3. Selecting New Condition takes you to the Create New Condition screen. It is then necessary to enter a name and select the type of facet you wish to select for your condition. As you are creating a database condition, select Database Options under the Facet option. You will be testing that the database has been set up with AnsiNullDefault set to False, so in the Expression section, which has been filtered to show only the Database Options facets, select the facet @AnsiNullDefault from the list of expressions (see Figure 4-24). Then in the Value column, select False from the list of available options. Give the condition a name—I gave it Database ANSI NuLL Default—and once complete, click OK.

Figure 4-24. The Create New Condition screen with the description and test expression

4. Clicking OK returns you to the New Policy screen, which should be like the one shown in Figure 4-25. The Enabled box is protected because the policy is to run On Demand. If you wanted to run the policy at set periods, then you would select a schedule option from the Evaluation Mode found toward the bottom of the dialog. The Check Condition combo box should be populated, and in the Against Targets list, the condition should check Every Database as the database server. You could also refine this condition to only databases that are over a certain size or to online databases.

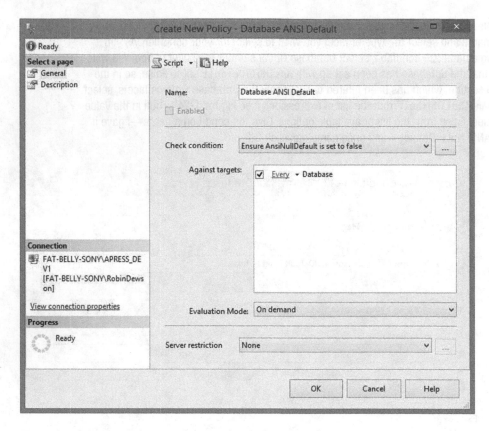

Figure 4-25. New Policy screen that sets the condition

5. Once you click OK, you should notice both the policy and the condition listed, as shown in Figure 4-26. At this point, nothing has been tested and no policy or condition has been checked against any database.

Figure 4-26. New policy in Object Browser

■ **Tip** Once a policy is built, you can export it to then import in to other servers by highlighting the specific policy, right-clicking and export. Apress has published a policy-based book called *Pro SQL Server 2008 Policy-Based Management*, which is still relevant today.

6. Now to test the policy and its condition. Find the `ApressFinancial` database, and select Properties, as shown in Figure 4-27. You are going to alter the `AnsiNullDefault` option on the database to break the policy. Select Options from the page list on the left.

Figure 4-27. *Opening the database properties*

7. In the Options page, scroll down to the Miscellaneous section and switch ANSI NULL Default to True, as shown in Figure 4-28. Click OK.

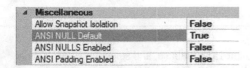

Miscellaneous	
Allow Snapshot Isolation	False
ANSI NULL Default	True
ANSI NULLS Enabled	False
ANSI Padding Enabled	False

Figure 4-28. *Altering the database property to break the condition*

8. Now that the database is no longer compliant, you need to run the policy and test it. Running the policy normally would be a task scheduled at periodic times, with the results sent to the relevant person. You can schedule the running of a policy by using a job to build the script. You will learn about the use of jobs in Chapter 9, when you see how to back up and restore a database. For the moment, as demonstrated in Figure 4-29, highlight the policy, right-click, and select Evaluate from the pop-up menu.

Figure 4-29. *Finding the policy and testing it*

9. You are now presented with the results of the evaluation, and you should see something similar to the results shown in Figure 4-30, which demonstrate that your database is out of policy with the red ball and white cross denoting an error. If you click View in the Target Details section in the lower half, you will be shown a set of more detailed results of the results of the conditions within the policies.

Figure 4-30. *The results of the test in the evaluation window*

10. It is not necessary to close this dialog and to correct every failure manually one by one. To clean up your database of all policies that you have set up that have failed, even if there is just one, as you have built in this example, ensure the check box for each failure is selected and click the Apply button, as shown toward the right in Figure 4-31. You are then presented with a confirmation dialog, and clicking Yes will apply the correction required to the database so that it conforms.

Figure 4-31. *All is well with your database*

Encryption

At this point, you are probably feeling your database is pretty secure, and it is. You have restricted who can log on to the server and who can connect to the database. However, if someone steals the media your database or backup is held on, then someone could take this and restore it to their own server. This isn't as impossible as it may sound as many large corporations hold their data in a separate location from their head office. Of course they will be very secure locations with tight controls in place, but if your data is of a highly sensitive nature, you should consider real-time data and transaction log encryption.

■ **Note** To achieve data encryption, a key and a certificate needs to be created on the database and a key applied. You must store the key safely away from the database on a separate media item so that if the media with the encrypted data is stolen, the chances of finding the key on a second media item is reduced. I will not encrypt the ApressFinancial database as it is a complication not needed for this database or while you are learning. There is an excellent book from Apress called Expert SQL Server 2008 Encryption by Michael Coles and Rodney Landrum, two great, authors which is still relevant today.

Summary

There is a great deal to cover concerning security and its different aspects. I would like to recap everything that we have seen just for one last time to ensure that you understand how everything fits together.

Before you can connect to SQL Server, an administrator of the SQL Server installation must give you permission to connect. In a Windows authentication setup, the administrator would either allow your Windows account or a group that contains your Windows account to connect to SQL Server. He or she can do this by either using the GUI and creating a login via the Security node or using the CREATE LOGIN ... FROM WINDOWS T-SQL statement. If you are in a SQL Server authentication setup, then a user ID and password would be created within SQL Server, again either via the Security/Logins node or by using the CREATE LOGIN ... PASSWORD = 'password' syntax.

Once a connection has been made, you can create a user login within the database using the CREATE USER ... syntax. This allows either the Windows account or the SQL Server login access to the database.

It is then possible to place the user into a role: either a predefined role or, more likely, a custom role that you create. This role can be used to determine what can and cannot be accessed within SQL Server tables, views, stored procedures, and any other object. Therefore, a role allows groups of users in one statement to be granted or revoked access to objects within SQL Server. Without roles, as new people join and as others leave, or as people move between departments, you would need to grant or revoke privileges as required—quite an onerous task.

Finally, when creating objects, as you will see in the next few chapters, these objects are owned by schemas. This allows for groups of objects to belong to a specific schema rather than a specific user login. This also reduces the overhead of granting privileges and allows the grouping of objects that belong together, making your application easier to understand.

This chapter continued your coverage of security within SQL Server. At this point in the book, you now know about SQL Server authentication and Windows authentication, and you have discovered how to control access to databases. The discussions on security are by no means finished because there are still several areas that we need to explore together, which we will do as we go through the book.

Security is the most important part of ensuring that your organization continues to have the ability to work. A security breach could result in lost income and will certainly mean that many people will be unable to do their work. It can also lead to unfulfilled orders, backlogs, or even fraudulent transactions. Regardless of whether you have the most well-designed database or the most poorly performing application ever, if you allow the wrong person into the wrong database, the result will be catastrophic.

The security of the database becomes a whole lot easier with the use of Declarative Management Framework (DMF). By setting up policies using DMF, it is possible to instantly see which databases meet the necessary criteria and which fail. It is then just a simple select-and-click to bring the database into alignment. Setting up correct policies in the development and staging environments is just as crucial as in production because this will allow the correct testing to take place before the database reaches production. Changing a setting in production on a failed condition within a policy could have serious ramifications.

CHAPTER 5

■ ■ ■

Defining Tables

Now that you have created the database, it needs to have the ability to store information. After all, without this, what is the point of a database? The first area that needs to be worked on is the table definitions.

To be functional, a database needs at least one table, but it can have many and, depending on the solution you are building, the number of tables can become quite large. Therefore, it is important that you as a developer know as much about tables, their structures, and their contents as possible. The aim of this chapter is to teach just that so that you have a sound base to work from regarding tables. From this base, you can then create other associated objects such as views, triggers, and so on.

The design of a table is crucial. Each table needs to contain the correct information for its collection of columns to allow the correct relationships to be established. One of the skills of a database developer or administrator is to ensure that the final design is the correct solution, hence avoiding painful alterations once further development of the system is in progress. For example, if you designed a system where the table definitions had some major problems and required columns to be moved around, you would have to revisit any applications using the tables. This can involve an enormous amount of work. You learned about database design in Chapter 3; in that chapter, you also created the database in which your tables will reside, so you know what tables you need and what data they will store.

So that we can successfully create a table, this chapter will cover the following topics:

- How to define a table—disk- and memory-based

- The different types of data that can be stored

- How and where a table is stored—disk and memory

- Creating a table using SQL Server Management Studio and Query Editor

- Dealing with more advanced areas of table creation, including the following:

 - How to make a row unique

 - Special data states

- Dealing with large text and binary data

What Is a Table?

A table is a repository for data, with items of data grouped in one or more columns. Tables contain zero or more rows of information. You can think of an Excel spreadsheet as a table, albeit a very simple table with few or no rules governing the data. If you look at Figure 5-1, you will see that the first three columns contain data that can be assumed to be first name, last name, and date of birth, but the fourth column is free-format and varies between a hotel room number, a house number, and a flat number. There is no consistency. In fact, in Excel, all the columns could in reality contain any data.

	A	B	C	D	E	F	G
1	Julie	Dewson	12/12/1971	Room 213	Grand Hotel	Regents Park	London
2	James	McVey	30/04/1982	Flat 2	Block 71		
3	Steve	Nicklin	21/07/1969	133	Park Avenue	Washington DC	
4	Chris	De Souza	12/01/1991	22			

Figure 5-1. *Excel showing partial address details*

What sets a table inside SQL Server apart from other kinds of tables is that a SQL Server table will have specific types of data held in each column. A predetermined type of data defined for a column can never change without affecting every row of data within that column for that table. If you use Excel, in a specific column you could have a character in one row, a number in the next row, a monetary value in the following row, and so on. That cannot happen in a database table. You can store all of these different values, but they would all have to be stored as a data type that holds strings, which defeats the purpose of using a database in the first place.

At the time a table is created, every column will have a specific data type. Therefore, very careful consideration has to be made when defining a table to ensure that the column data type is the most appropriate. There is no point in selecting a generic data type (a string, for example) to cover all eventualities because you would have to revisit the design later anyway. Leaving all data types as a string would cause problems with math functions, for example, when you needed to add taxes to a price or when you wanted to add a number of days to a date for delivery times after an order is placed.

A table's purpose is to hold specific information. The table requires a meaningful name and one or more columns, each given a meaningful name and a data type.

When it comes time to create a table, you do have to be connected to SQL Server with a login that belongs to the correct server and a database role that can create tables, such as sysadmin or db_ddladmin. When you create a table, it has to be owned within the database, and this is done by assigning the table to a schema. Recall that Chapter 4 discussed a schema for grouping objects to be used as a basis for object security. As a developer, grouping objects together into a schema gives your database a more logical feel and will also allow you to reduce development time as part of the natural order of objects.

Some data types have fixed storage specifications, whereas with other data types, you have to decide for yourself how many characters the maximum will be. If you had a column defined for holding surnames, it would hold character values. There would also be no sense in setting the maximum length of this column at 10 characters because many surnames are longer. Similarly, there would be little sense in saying the maximum should be 1,000 characters. You have to reach a sensible balance. Some of that balance will come from the data analysis, which you completed in Chapter 3; some of the size setting will come from data that already exist either in a database you are expanding or perhaps another database, as there will be similar data held. To expand on this point, if you were developing a sales database, the size of a part item number would be defined from the inventory database, as this would hold all of the part details including part number.

■ **Note** Even when working with variable-length data types for which you specify a maximum amount of characters to be stored, SQL Server still stores only the data you actually enter. Thus, you can create a surname column to hold up to 1,000 characters, and space is not wasted when most names are far shorter than that. However, you need to keep a sensible and valid balance. A surname of 1,000 characters does not meet that balance.

The rows of data that will be held in a table should be related logically to each other. If a table is defined to hold customer information, this is all it should hold. Under no circumstances should you consider putting information that is not about a customer in the table. It would be illogical to put, for example, details of a customer's orders within it. When you are defining columns, avoid the temptation to use one column for more than one piece of information. This is one of the easiest mistakes a developer can make. A column usage should be to hold one item type of data. For example, a column created to hold the date an order was received could also be used to hold the date an order was dispatched, but that would give you problems with knowing what the date being held actually was. Having separate columns for these dates would keep things completely clear.

■ **Note** There are two types of tables—system and user tables. System tables should never be accessed directly, although some information is available through a system view.

With SQL Server, a second type of user table is available to you as a developer called a FileTable. This is a specialized user table type that allows for files of unstructured data, such as Word documents and Excel spreadsheets, that can be held within SQL Server for unstructured access. It is then possible for SQL Server to search these documents using FILESTREAM technology. Within this book, I look only at traditional user tables.

Finally, there is third type of table called an in-memory table. I discuss this at length in Chapter 7 as there are a number of areas that an in-memory table differs from a traditional disk-based table. Differences include data types, mandatory requirements of the database and table that must be defined for you to be able to create an in-memory table as well as the performance aspect. For the moment, be aware that tables and their data can reside on disk or in-memory.

■ **Note** Although this chapter deals with disk-based tables, a great deal of the information does relate to both disk and in-memory.

SQL Server Data Types

You have learned a great deal about SQL Server in the prior chapters before you have even created your first table. However, it is essential to know all this information before creating a table and looking at the security of your database to avoid any ramifications of it all going horribly wrong. You also now know why you have to be careful with users to ensure that a user has enough security privileges to build tables. In this section, you will be introduced to the data types that exist within SQL Server. Some of these can be defined as data types for columns within tables, and others are used within T-SQL programs.

Defining a table can be completed either in SQL Server Management Studio, Query Editor, or in SQL Server's database designer tool. You can also create a table through a number of other means using SQLCMD, developer tools, and languages, but these first three methods are the ones on which this book will focus. You will create the first table with SQL Server Management Studio. This is the Customers table, which will hold details about each customer. But before you can do this, it is necessary to look at the different types of data that can be stored.

Table Data Types

SQL Server has many different data types that are available for each column of data. This section will explain the different data types and help choose the right type for each column. Data types described in this section are known as base data types. This book concentrates on base data types only. However, it is possible to create your own user data type, and there are advantages to doing so. If you want to have consistency over several tables, usually but not exclusively on the same server for a specific type of column, then it is possible to create a data type and give it a name. It can then be used when defining a table. An example is where you want all tax identifiers to be defined the same— you would create a user-data type using a base data type as its type definition and then name it accordingly. Then instead of using the base data type for any tax identifier columns, you would define the column with the user data type. Once I have covered these base data types, you will see a demonstration of this.

■ **Note** You can use .NET to build more complex data types that also perform extra functionality.

You will find that several data types may look similar, but keep in mind that each data type has a specific use. For example, unless you really need to define characters to be stored as Unicode, don't use the N prefix data types. Unicode characters use up more space than standard characters due to the potentially wide range of characters that SQL Server has to store. Also, when looking at numbers, if the largest value you will store in a column is 100, don't go for the data type that will allow the largest number to be stored. This would be a waste of disk space.

Let's take a look at the possible base data types you can use in a table. Afterward, you'll see data types you can use in a program, and throughout the book you will see several of these data types in use in the example.

Char/nchar

The char data type is fixed in length based on the length assigned at definition for the column and can hold a maximum of 256 characters. If you define a column to be 20 characters long, 20 characters will be stored. If the data entered is less than the number of characters defined, the remaining length will be space filled to the right. Therefore, if a column were defined as char (10), "aaa" would be stored as "aaa". Use this data type when the column data are to be of fixed length, which tends to be the case for customer IDs and bank account IDs. If you define the column with no length, a length of 1 will be defined. However, that is not good practice, and all lengths should be defined for clarity.

Varchar/nvarchar

The varchar data type holds alphanumeric data, just like char. The difference is that each row can hold a different number of characters up to the maximum length defined for the column. If a column is defined as varchar(50), this means that the data in the column can be up to a maximum of 50 characters long. However, if you store a string of only three characters, only three storage spaces are used up. This definition is perfect for scenarios in which there is no specific length of data—for example, people's names or descriptions where the length of the stored item does not matter. The maximum size of a varchar column is 8,000 characters. However, if you define the column with no size—that is, varchar()—the length will default to 1.

You can also use another setting that can exceed the 8,000-character limit, by defining the data type with the constant max. If you know you will exceed the 8,000-character limit in at least one row, use this option. Finally, you should use max for large blocks of text, because it will eventually supersede the text data type.

Text/ntext

The text data type holds data where the data are longer than 8,000 characters, but do not use this data type as it is deprecated and will be removed. Use varchar(max) instead.

image

image is very much like the text data type, except it is for any type of binary data. However, like text and ntext, this data type will also be removed and you should use varbinary(max) instead.

int

The int data type, or integer, is used for holding numeric values that do not have a decimal point (whole numbers). There is a range limit to the value of the numbers held: int will hold any number between the values of –2,147,483,648 and 2,147,483,647.

bigint

The bigint data type, or big integer, is similar to int, except that much larger numbers can be held. A range of –9,223,372,036,854,775,808 through 9,223,372,036,854,775,807 can be stored.

smallint

The smallint data type, or small integer, holds small integer numbers in the range of –32,768 through 32,767. Do take care when defining columns with this data type, and make sure there really is no possibility of exceeding these limits. There is always the danger when creating a column with this data type that you have to go back and change the data type; so if in doubt, select int.

tinyint

The tinyint data type, or tiny integer, is even smaller than smallint and holds numbers from 0 through 255. It could be used to hold a numeric value for each US or Canadian state or perhaps every county in the United Kingdom.

decimal/numeric

Both of these data types hold the same precision and ranges of data. The range is from –10 to the power 38 + 1 through 10 to the power 38 – 1. These are quite large ranges, from –0.00000000000000000000000000000000000001 through 10,000,000,000,000,000,000,000,000,000. However, do take care with this because you cannot store 38 digits to the right and left of the decimal point. You can store only up to and including 38 digits. So, the greater the precision required to the right of the decimal point, the fewer digits are left to represent the whole number.

float

For me, the float and real data types are the most dangerous of data types for a novice developer; they should be used in the correct circumstances and should be avoided if complete accuracy is necessary. The float data type is used for numbers where the decimal point is not fixed. float data types hold very large numbers in the range of −1.79E+308 through 1.79E+308. There is a warning with this data type: the values cannot always be seen as 100% accurate because they can be approximate. The approximation arises from the way the number is physically stored as binary code. You will have problems where a number ends in .3, .6, or .7. The value stored has to be approximated, or rounded, because some values can't be stored accurately since they may have more decimal places than can be catered to. A well-known example is the value of pi.

real

The real data type is very much like float, except that real can store only numbers in the range of −3.40E+38 through 3.40E+38. This data type also holds an approximate value. The real and float data types can look like the ideal data type for their flexibility on the numerics they can hold, but look at other numeric data types when you need accurate numbers.

money

The money data type is used for holding numeric values up to four decimal places. If you need to use more than four decimal places, you need to look to another data type, such as decimal. This data type doesn't actually store the currency symbol to signify the monetary type, so you should not use this data type for different currency values. The money data type has a range of −922,337,203,685,477.5808 through 922,337,203,685,477.5807. If you need to store the currency symbol of the currency that is held here ($ or USD for dollars, £ or GBP for British pounds, and so on), then you would need to store this separately because the money data type does not hold the currency symbol. A column defined as money will hold the money to 1/10,000 of a decimal unit.

smallmoney

This data type is similar to money, with the exception of the range, which lies between −214,748.3648 and 214,748.3647.

date

The date data type has been built to hold a date from January 1, AD 1 through December 31, 9999. The format is YYYY-MM-DD. Until SQL Server 2008, it was not possible to treat the date and time as two separate data types without having to build such types yourself using .NET. As a result, in the past you were storing unnecessary data. For example, it is common to see datetime columns holding only date values. This data type is a great advancement, as it reduces confusion and gives the correct refinement for the data that the column contains.

datetime

The datetime data type will hold any date and time from January 1, 1753 through December 31, 9999. However, it stores not only a date, but also a time alongside it. If you populate a column defined as datetime just with a date, a default time of 12:00:00 will be stored as well.

datetime2

Similar to datetime, datetime2 is used to hold a date and a time. The main difference is that, with datetime2, the fractions of a second can be held with greater precision. In addition, this type can also store a date from January 1, AD 1 through December 31, 9999. The format is YYYY-MM-DD hh:mm:ss[.nnnnnnn].

smalldatetime

This data type is very much like datetime, except the date range is January 1, 1900 through to June 6, 2079. The reason for the strange date at the end of the range lies in the binary storage representation of this datetime.

datetimeoffset

If you need to store a time relative to a specific date and time zone, you should define your column with this type. The date and time are stored in this data type in Coordinated Universal Time (UTC). You define the amount of time to add or subtract depending on the time zone to which the value should relate. For example, if you want to store 6 p.m. on March 24, 2014 in US Eastern Standard Time, the value would be stored as 2014-03-24 13:00:00 +05:00. The +05:00 relates to the fact that US Eastern Standard Time is five hours ahead of UTC. The format for this data type is YYYY-MM-DD hh:mm:ss[.nnnnnnn] [+|-]hh:mm.

time

If you just want to hold a time based on the 24-hour clock, you can define a column in this data type. The format is hh:mm:ss[.nnnnnnn]. Similar to the date data type, this has been introduced to provide a column storing just the time of day. As you can see from the format, a time column can hold up to a precision of 100 nanoseconds. This is greater precision than is supported by the datetime data type.

hierarchyid

Prior to SQL Server 2008, producing a hierarchy of data could prove complex and usually had to involve a self-join of the data. An example of a hierarchy of data would be the structure of employees in a company from the lowest-level employee up through the management structure to the CEO. Now, however, it is possible to define a column of the hierarchyid data type that will allow you to say how a given row sits in an overall hierarchy of rows. This data type is a system variable length data type to a maximum of 892 bytes.

geometry

The geometry data type is a planar CLR data type that allows you to store geographical information in a "flat Earth" way. Data within this data type can be one of eleven different geometry measurements including a point, curve, and polygon, among others. It is possible to store only one type of measurement in each column defined, and part of the data stored will be the definition of the type of data.

geography

This CLR data type stores "round Earth" data. Therefore, data are stored as degrees of latitude and longitude but use the same type of measurement as the geometry data type.

> ■ **Note** The geometry and geography data types require a chapter, if not a whole book, to understand and deal with fully. They won't be covered within this book, but they can be found in *Beginning Spatial with SQL Server 2008*, by Alastair Aitchison (Apress, 2009).

rowversion

This is an unusual data type as it is used for a column for which you would not be expected to supply a value. The rowversion data type holds a binary number generated by SQL Server, which will be unique for each row within a database. Every time a record is modified, the column with this data type in the record will be modified to reflect the time of modification. Therefore, you can use columns with this data type in more advanced techniques where you want to keep a version history of what has been changed.

> ■ **Note** rowversion used to be called timestamp, and you may come across timestamp in databases created in older versions of SQL Server.

uniqueidentifier

The uniqueidentifier data type holds a globally unique identifier (GUID). This is similar to the timestamp data type, in that the identifier is created by a SQL Server command when a record is inserted or modified. The identifier is generated from information from the network card on a machine, the processor ID, and the date and time. If you have no network card, uniqueidentifier is generated from information from your own machine information only. These IDs should be unique throughout the world.

binary

Data held in this data type is in binary format. This data type is mainly used for data held as flags or combinations of flags. For example, perhaps you wanted to hold flags about a customer. You need to know whether the customer is active (value = 1), ordered within the last month (value = 2), placed the last order for more than $1,000 (value = 4), or meets loyalty criteria (value = 8). This would add up to four columns of data within a database. However, by using binary values, if a client had a value of 13 in binary, then he would have values 1 + 4 + 8, which means he is active, his last order was more than $1,000, and he meets the loyalty criteria. When you define the column of a set size in binary, all data will be of that size.

varbinary

The varbinary data type is very much like binary, except the physical column size per row will differ depending on the value stored. varbinary(max) can hold values more than 8,000 characters in length and should be used for holding data such as images.

bit

The bit data type holds a value of 0 or 1. Usually, bit is used to determine true (1) or false (0) values.

xml

XML data can be held in its own special data type rather than in a varchar(max) column. There are special query commands that can then be used to query and work with this data. Prior to SQL Server 2005, XML data was almost an afterthought with no data type, and earlier versions of SQL Server had extremely limited functionality to work with the XML data that did exist.

Program Data Types

There are three more data types that can be used within a program, which we will take a look at now.

cursor

Data can be held in a memory-resident state called a cursor. It is like a table because it has rows and columns of data, but that's where the similarity ends. There are no indexes, for example. A cursor is used to build up a set of data for processing one row at a time.

table

A table data type has similarities to both a cursor and a table. It holds rows and columns of data, but the data cannot be indexed. In this case, you deal with the data a "set at a time," like a normal table. You'll learn about both the cursor and table data types later in the book, in Chapter 17, because they are more advanced topics.

sql_variant

It is possible to have a data type that can hold a few different data types. I will be honest—I don't recommend using this data type because it shows you are unsure of your data and what type of data to expect. Before putting data into a data type, you need to be sure what type of data you are getting. You can use sql_variant as a program data type or a column data type, but the same argument applies in both cases. I won't discuss this data type any further within this book.

Columns As More Than Simple Data Repositories

Assigning a data type to a column defines what you expect the column to hold. But column definitions have more power than just this. It is possible to fill the column with a seed value, or even with no value whatsoever.

Default Values

As a row is added to a table, rather than requiring developers to add values to columns that could be populated by SQL Server, such as a column that details using a date and time when a row of data was added, it is possible to place a default value there instead. The default value can be any valid value for that data type. A default value can be overwritten and is not "set in stone".

Generating IDENTITY Values

When adding a new row to a SQL Server table, you may want to give this row a unique but easily identifiable ID number that can be used to link a row in one table with a row in another. Within the ApressFinancial database, there will be a table holding a list of transactions that needs to be linked to the customer table. Rather than trying to link on values that cannot guarantee a unique link (first name and surname, for example), a unique numeric ID value gives that possibility, provided it is used in conjunction with a unique index. If you have a customer with an ID of 100 in the Customers table and you have linked to the Transaction table via the ID, you could retrieve all the financial transactions for that customer where the foreign key is 100. However, this could mean that when you want to insert a new customer, you have to figure out which ID is next via some T-SQL code or using a table that just holds "next number" identities. But fear not, this is where the IDENTITY option within a column definition is invaluable.

■ **Note** For those readers who have used Microsoft Access, the IDENTITY keyword option is similar to AutoNumber.

By defining a column using the IDENTITY option, you are informing SQL Server of the following:

- The column will have a value generated by SQL Server.

- There will be a start point (seed).

- An increment value is given, informing SQL Server by how much each new ID should increase.

- SQL server will manage the allocation of IDs.

You would have to perform all of these tasks if SQL Server did not do so. Therefore, by using this option in a column definition, you can use the value generated to create a solid, reliable, and unique link from one table to another, rather than relying on more imprecise selection criteria. However, you have to realize that the numbers generated are not guaranteed to be in ascending sequential order, as gaps can occur, as you will see in an example later in this chapter.

Uniqueidentifiers for an Identity

Using IDENTITY is ideal if you wish to create a column within your table with unique numbers. There is an alternative, which is to use the unique identifier data type with a default value of a system function called NEWID(). There are a few drawbacks to using this data type as it will always use 16 bytes of data (bigint is only 8 bytes); if you want to know the value of an inserted row, you need to generate the value before the row is inserted (IDENTITY values can be retrieved via a system variable), and the value generated would be awkward to use in any reporting outside of the database. Finally, if the column holding the value was used within a unique index, there will be a performance overhead.

Normally, a user would not insert the value; instead, SQL Server would create it automatically. However, you can enter explicit values if you use the SET IDENTITY_INSERT option to alter the database setting to ON for the specific table. This is not a regular occurrence, but you will come across scenarios when you will find this a useful feature. I have used this option in the past when archiving data from the production system, and then when I wanted to un-archive the data back into the production system with the initial identity values.

Sequences Instead of IDENTITY

IDENTITY-defined columns are ideal for small, low-frequency row insertions, but there is a small performance overhead each time a value is created. It has been requested for some time from developers that Microsoft look at this problem and find a way to improve performance, and so for this problem, Microsoft has developed *sequences*. An identity column is defined for a single table, whereas a sequence is defined for generating a sequence of numbers bound to a schema, therefore having the ability to generate a sequence of numbers for multiple tables.

The first benefit of sequences is that it is possible for SQL Server not only to retrieve the next values one at a time from the underlying sequence table (like IDENTITY), but also to cache a range of numbers in memory for faster access and retrieval. A cached set of numbers will work faster than using the IDENTITY property, which is generated with each insertion.

You can also define a sequence so that the sequence can loop around when a maximum value is reached. This allows you to reuse numbers.

It is also possible to retrieve the next sequence value and place it into a local variable before the row is inserted. This will give you the flexibility of knowing the "identity" column value for any child tables' insertions. With IDENTITY, you can retrieve the value assigned to a row only after the row is inserted. By having the ability to assign the value to a variable with sequence, you can avoid gaps through insertions failing by reusing the value if, for example, a rollback occurs. Gaps will still form, though, if the server is rebooted or the SQL Server Windows service stopped, so using a local variable is not a complete solution to the gapping issue.

Sequences can deal with generating a value for multiple tables and potentially different columns all from the single sequencing object, unlike the IDENTITY keyword, which is bound to one column in one table. The ability to split sequencing across multiple tables allows you to keep the sequence of data intact if, for example, you have a table holding incoming records but two tables for processed data—one for accepted records and one for rejected records. By inspecting the sequence column value on both these tables, you would be able to see the order in which the rows had been processed.

■ **Caution**　If you use sequences within a transaction and the transaction is rolled back, then the sequence is *not* rolled back and the values retrieved will look as if they have been used.

Using sequences, you can assign a value to a column programmatically. This functionality removes the problems that can occur when using IDENTITY because IDENTITY column values are awkward to alter within a column after they are assigned. When completing a bulk insertion or even modifying the value within a column, an incorrectly inserted value can be modified when using sequences, as you will see in the Alter Sequence section of the exercise in Chapter 17 The downside, however, is that developers have to be aware that a column is logically linked to a sequence and use the sequence functionality rather than enter values manually. You can apply a sequence as a default value to the relevant column, as will be demonstrated shortly in the sequence exercise. This will still allow you to insert the sequence value like IDENTITY. However, when I use a sequence in the exercises in this section, I will not use it as a default value so that you can see explicitly what is happening.

The Use of NULL Values

Columns can be defined as NULL or NOT NULL within your T-SQL code, or, if using the Table Designer, you can check or uncheck the Allow Nulls option. These two different constraints define whether data must be entered into the column. A NULL value means there is absolutely nothing entered in that column—no data at all. A NULL value is in a special data state, with special meaning. It means that data value within the column is unknown.

If a value is a NULL value, no data has been inserted into the column or the data that did exist has been eradicated. This also means that you have to perform special function statements within any T-SQL code to test for this value. Take the example of a column defined to hold characters, but where one of the rows has a NULL value within it. If you executed a query that carries out string manipulation, the row with the NULL value might cause an error. The use of NULLs is covered in Chapter 10.

Creating a Table in SQL Server Management Studio

It is now time for you to create the first table in your example application. Every organization has to have a set of customers and will need to store these details. Within this table, it will hold information such as each customer's name and an ID to an external system where addresses are held. The only product that your company has where a customer can have an ongoing cash balance with funds that aren't cleared is a bank account. This means your table will also hold the bank account ID, the current balance, and any amount clearing.

TRY IT OUT: CREATING A TABLE

1. Ensure that SQL Server Management Studio is running.

2. Expand Object Explorer so that you can see the ApressFinancial database, created in Chapter 3.

3. Expand the ApressFinancial database so that you can see the Tables node, as shown in Figure 5-2.

Figure 5-2. *ApressFinancial with no user tables defined in the Tables node*

4. Right-click the Tables node and select New Table. This will take you into the Table Designer. Figure 5-3 shows how the Table Designer looks when you first enter it.

Figure 5-3. *Creating your first table with no columns as yet*

5. From this screen, you need to enter the details for each column within the table. Enter the first column, CustomerId, in the Column Name column.

■ **Tip** When naming columns, try to avoid using spaces. Either keep the column names without spaces, like I have done with CustomerId, or use an underscore (_) instead of a space. It is perfectly valid to have column names with spaces. However, to use these columns in SQL code, you have to surround the names with a quoted identifier, such as square brackets ([]), which is very cumbersome.

6. At the moment, notice that Column Properties in the middle of Figure 5-3 is empty. This will fill up when you start entering a data type after entering the column name. The Column Properties section is just as crucial as the top half of the screen where you enter the column name and data type.

7. The drop-down combo box that lists the data types is one of the first areas provided by SQL Server to help you with table creation. This way, you don't have to remember every data type there is within SQL Server. By having all the necessary values listed, it is simple enough to just select the most suitable one. In this instance, you want to select int, as shown in Figure 5-4.

Figure 5-4. *Selecting the data type*

8. The final major item when creating a column within a table is the Allow Nulls check box option. If you don't check the box, some sort of data must be placed in this column. Leaving the check box in the default state, which alters to checked when you start typing the column name, will allow NULL values in the column, which is not recommended if the data are required (name, order number, and so on) or the column(s) are going to be used as the main method to find data within your queries, relationships, or indexes. You can also allow NULLs for numeric columns, so instead of needing to enter a zero, you can just skip over that column when it comes to entering the data. In this instance, you want data to be populated within every row as it will be used within a relationship, so remove the check mark that has appeared automatically.

9. The Column Properties section for the column will now look like the screen shown in Figure 5-5. Take a moment to peruse this section. You can see the name, whether NULLs are allowed, and the type of data you are storing. There will be changes to what is displayed depending on the data type chosen.

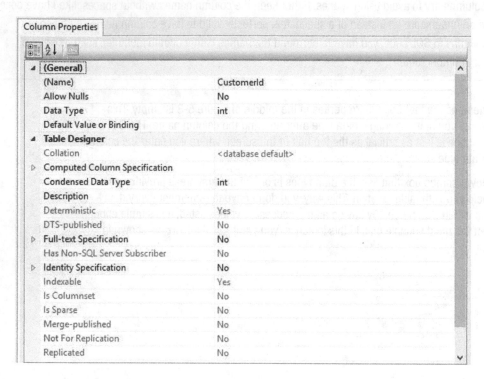

Figure 5-5. *More in-depth properties for columns*

10. You want this column to be an identity column as it will be used to link with other tables. If you have not already done so, within the Column Properties area, expand the Identity Specification node, as you need to set the Is Identity property to Yes, as shown in Figure 5-6. This will set the Identity Increment to 1 and the Identity Seed to 1 as well. You can alter the increment and seed values if you wish, but generally the default settings are used.

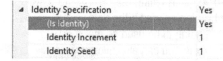

Figure 5-6. *Defining a column as having an identity*

11. It is now possible to add in a few more columns to the table, as shown in Figure 5-7. Go ahead and add the columns now. Title is an integer data type as this will reference a table of titles such as *Mr, Mrs, Miss, Dr*, and so on. This will avoid storing free text that could result in values such as Mr, Mr., mr., mister, mR, and so on which is not ideal. Not everybody will have more than a first name and last name, although some people may have initials. Therefore, allow NULL values for any initials they may have. Leave the box checked on the OtherInitials column, as shown in Figure 5-7. Alter the length of this column to ten characters, which should be more than enough. The list of columns is provided for ease of use:

- Title: tinyint

- FirstName: varchar(50)

- OtherInitials: varchar(10) and also allow NULL values

- LastName: varchar(50)

Column Name	Data Type	Allow Nulls
CustomerId	int	☐
Title	tinyint	☐
FirstName	varchar(50)	☐
OtherInitials	varchar(10)	☑
LastName	varchar(50)	☐

FAT-BELLY-SONY\AP...ial - dbo.Table_1* ✕

Figure 5-7. *A column that will allow NULL values*

12. You can now define your final columns, which you see in Figure 5-8. I suggest that you allow AccountType and CustomerBalance to allow NULL values, as this would be a good indicator of when a customer has no account, such as when the customer is in the process of creating an account. This is a good demonstration of where a NULL value removes confusion. If a value were forced into these two columns, you would need a row in the account types table to indicate "No accounts." Similarly a NULL value in UnclearedBalance can indicate there are no funds pending clearance, but a value of zero could indicate that funds were processing and all amounts have been dealt with or perhaps the incoming and outgoing uncleared transactions totaled zero. The last two columns will record when the account was opened and closed. By setting the default value of the DateAdded column using a SQL Server function that returns the current date and time, GETDATE(), every time a row is added, it is not necessary for a value to be entered for this column, as SQL Server will put the date (there will be no time as it is a date only based column) in for you. A default value can be a constant value, the value from a function, or a value bound to a formula. The DateClosed column allows NULL values, and this is the perfect indicator to demonstrate when the account is fully closed when DateClosed has a value contained within it. The full table layout is shown in Figure 5-8, and the columns are defined here.

Figure 5-8. *The table column definition is now complete*

■ **Caution** Defining columns with default values with a constant can be time-saving in one respect, for every row added it will have a performance degradation while SQL Server builds and then sets the value. Performance degrades further the more complex the method for defining the value. If speed of insertion is a priority, consider looking at alternative methods.

- AddressLine1: varchar(100)

- AddressLine2: varchar(100) and allow NULL values

- AddressLine3: varchar(100) and allow NULL values

- TownOrCity: int

- ZipCode: varchar(20) and allow NULL values

- USState: tinyint

- AccountType: tinyint and allow NULL values

- ClearedBalance: money and allow NULL values

- UnclearedBalance: money and allow NULL values

- DateOpened: date and have a default value defined as GETDATE()

- DateClosed: date and allow NULL values

■ **Note** In Chapter 3, when discussing normalization, I also covered when data should be denormalized. The `Customers` table is the one place a small amount of denormalization for speed of access is required. To speed up the process when a client goes to a cash point, there is a column that holds the account number so that a single row of data to the cash point can be sent. The system can therefore cross-check with the client's card as well as the cleared and uncleared balance for display. This data will also be held within the `CustomerProducts` and `Transactions` tables, which will be defined later. If the account number was stored in the `CustomerProducts` table only, you would have to access two rows of data before you could send the data to the cash machine: one with the account number and one with the balances. With the number of actions that happen at peak times from cash machines, point of sale terminals, and so on, speed is critical and small design considerations such as this can make a huge difference. As a developer, it is vital that you build an optimized database.

13. Before you save the table, you need to define some properties for it, such as the schema owner. On the right, you should see the Table Properties dialog window, as shown in Figure 5-9. If this is not displayed, you can press F4 or, from the menu, select View ➤ Properties Window. First of all, give the table a name, `Customers`, and give the table some sort of description. Then move to the schema owner details. When you click the Schema combo box, it presents you with a list of possible schemas the table can belong to. In Chapter 4, you built the schema to use for this table, `CustomerDetails`.

Column Name	Data Type	Allow Nulls
CustomerId	int	☐
Title	tinyint	☐
FirstName	varchar(50)	☐
OtherInitials	varchar(10)	☑
LastName	varchar(50)	☐
AddressLine1	varchar(100)	☐
AddressLine2	varchar(100)	☑
AddressLine3	varchar(300)	☑
TownOrCity	int	☐
ZipCode	varchar(20)	☐
USState	tinyint	☐
AccountType	tinyint	☑
ClearedBalance	money	☑
UnclearedBalanace	money	☑
DateOpened	date	☐
DateClosed	date	☑

Properties

[Tbl] CustomerDetails.Customers

▲ (Identity)	
(Name)	Customers
Database Name	ApressFinancial
Description	Apress Customers
Schema	CustomerDetails
Server Name	fat-belly-sony\apress_dev1
▲ Table Designer	
Identity Column	CustomerId
Indexable	Yes
Lock Escalation	Table
▷ Regular Data Space Spe	PRIMARY
Replicated	No
Row GUID Column	
Text/Image Filegroup	PRIMARY

Figure 5-9. *Table properties*

14. Now that you are finished, you can save the table either by clicking the Save toolbar button, which sports a floppy disk icon, or by clicking the X (close) button on the Table Designer to close the window, which should bring up the Save dialog box, asking if you want to save the changes. By clicking Yes, you get a second box asking for the name of the table if you didn't enter a table name in the Table Properties dialog window, as shown in Figure 5-10, or if you did enter a table name, then the table is saved using the name specified and you are returned to SQL Server Management Studio.

Figure 5-10. *Saving a table that was not given a name*

15. Object Explorer in SQL Server Management Studio may not automatically refresh the Tables node and show your new table. If it does not, highlight Object Explorer and refresh either via F5 or by clicking the refresh icon. If you now right-click the table and select Properties, you can see important details about the table, as shown in Figure 5-11. The first section details who is currently connected. Then you see the date the table was created, its name, and the schema name of the owner of the table.

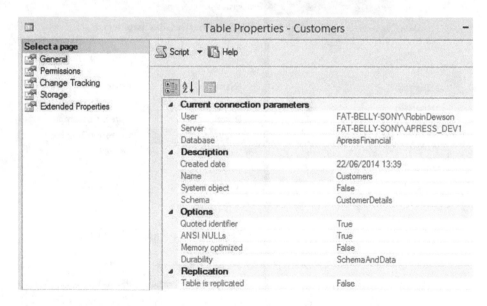

Figure 5-11. *Table properties*

- The menu that opened when you right-clicked the table included various other options (see Figure 5-12).

Figure 5-12. Table properties

Although many of these options are discussed elsewhere in the book, let's take a look at them briefly before moving on:

- New Table: Builds a new table as has just been demonstrated

- *Design*: Takes you into the design mode (Figure 5-8) to let you alter a table definition; it will also allow you to access other attributes of a table such as indexes and relationships.

- *Select TOP 1000 Rows*: Displays up to the first 1,000 rows of data; the number of rows returned can be altered via the Tools ➤ Options ➤ SQL Server Object Explorer.

- *Edit Top 200 Rows*: Allows the first 200 rows to be displayed and can be edited; this can also be altered via Tools ➤ Options ➤ SQL Server Object Explorer; however, increasing this number can have issues, especially over a slow connection from the client to the server. There are ways you can work with this option so that 200 rows or even fewer can be used to update the data. However, I strongly recommend that you do not use this option in a production environment. When I discuss the use of transactions in Chapter 10, you will see how this option could cause problems.

- *Script Table As*: Displays several different scripting options, including scripting the table as a CREATE or a DROP, as well as options for SELECT-ing rows, DELETE-ing rows, UPDATE-ing rows, and INSERT-ing rows; if you do use the designer to build a table, then building a script for the table that is then placed in source control along with all your other code is very useful. It's also ideal if you deploy changes via scripting to your production databases. You will see this later in the chapter.

- *View Dependencies*: Lists out any other stored procedures, views, and objects that use the table; this is a good option when you want to alter the properties of a table including adding columns. As a developer, your system will constantly be improved with new functionality, and finding the dependencies of your table will help you understand and realize the scope of related objects that require investigation and also potentially need to be altered.

■ **Caution** Don't rely on View Dependencies being 100% accuarate. There are times when creating a stored procedure, the dependent stored procedure doesn't exist. Therefore, when it is added, the dependency may not be created. However, this isn't a regular occurrence for many systems, and this issue should be known.

- *Memory Optimization Adviso*r: A wizard used to look at the highlighted table and advise on what is required to migrate the table from disk-based to memory-based. This wizard is demonstrated and discussed in Chapter 7.

- *Full-Text Index*: Displays a special type of indexing for text data; data can be stored so that keywords within the data are indexed. One example system I have worked on stored Word documents of publications that were then indexed so that keywords could be searched for. You could also store web pages and use full-text indexing to build a search engine, for example.

- *Storage*: An advanced feature of SQL Server is the ability to split, known as *partition*, the data within tables. Partitioning can be used to speed up performance on tables with a very large number of rows. If a table has millions of rows, then a range of rows can be placed in one partition, a second range in a second partition, and so on. This is outside the scope of this book for implementation because it is an area that requires a great deal of thought. However, it is briefly covered later in the chapter.

- *Policies/Facets*: Lets you view and run policies for the table; this was demonstrated in Chapter 4 when you saw how to enforce ANSI NULLs on a database.

- *Start Powershell*: Opens a command prompt window that allows you to create PowerShell scripts using the PowerShell scripting language

- Reports: Executes a prebuilt custom report

- *Rename*: Renames a table to a new table; renaming a table in early development can be acceptable, but renaming a table after this point should be avoided unless absolutely necessary. If you do have to rename a table, use the View Dependencies option to see what else requires altering, and don't forget your .NET, Java, and so on code that could also work with the table by name.

- *Delete*: Drops the table from the database; before dropping a table, I strongly suggest you click the Show Dependencies button, equivalent to the View Dependencies menu option that is displayed on the screen, but I will go through deleting a table toward the end of this chapter.

- *Refresh*: Refreshes the list of tables; sometimes SQL Server does not automatically or quickly update the list of tables. There are triggers that will cause a refresh, such as collapsing and expanding the tables node, but selecting this menu option, clicking the refresh button at the top of Object Explorer, or pressing F5 will refresh the node you are on. If you are at the database level, then pressing F5 or the refresh button will refresh the objects within the database at all levels.

- *Properties*: Produces a dialog with a number of properties about the table; this is shown in Figure 5-11.

Now that a table has been created in SQL Server Management Studio, let's look at creating a table within Query Editor.

Creating a Table Through Query Editor

The next table that needs to be created is the one that will hold the details of the financial transactions that each customer has. These transactions will not be just simple money-in and money-out transactions, but will also be those financial transactions involving shares when a dividend is received or a tax credit if the shares are held in a product that is tax-free. You know from the design that details of which product the transaction relates to will be held in a separate table, so you need to create a link between the transaction table and one holding some sort of reference data. It is also necessary to have a link between this table and the `CustomerDetails.Customers` table. Notice the slight name change in the discussion of the `Customers` table to allow for the inclusion of the schema name. This should mean that your naming convention should be `schemaname.tablename`. Using `schemaname.tablename` avoids confusion. Finally, moving back to the financial transactions table, if the transaction relates to shares and is not recording the finances involved, you need to record that this is the case. To clarify this last point, when a client buys some shares, there will be two records: one for the money leaving the account to buy the shares and another showing the physical number of shares purchased.

Now, let's create this table using Query Editor instead of SQL Server Management Studio.

TRY IT OUT: DEFINING A TABLE THROUGH QUERY EDITOR

1. Ensure that you are pointing to the `ApressFinancial` database in Query Editor. If you're not, you'll find that you may be creating the table in the wrong database. If you are creating code to be placed in .NET, Java, and so on, then there are advantages to prefixing the code with the following T-SQL syntax. This will then point the connection to the correct database. You will see this on occasion within the book as a reminder.

```
USE ApressFinancial
GO
```

2. In Query Editor, enter the following code:

```
CREATE TABLE TransactionDetails.Transactions
    (TransactionId int IDENTITY(1,1) NOT NULL,
    CustomerId int NOT NULL,
    TransactionType smallint NOT NULL,
    DateEntered datetime NOT NULL,
    Amount numeric(18, 5) NOT NULL,
    ReferenceDetails nvarchar(50) NULL,
    Notes nvarchar(max)  NULL,
    RelatedShareId int NULL,
    RelatedProductId int NOT NULL)
```

■ **Note** Notice that when you type this code into Query Editor, the keywords are colored. For example, CREATE TABLE is in blue, NOT NULL is in gray. This helps you to avoid typing mistakes. The colors are defined in the options Tools ➤ options ➤ Environment ➤ Fonts and Colors.

3. Execute the code by either pressing F5 or clicking the toolbar's Execute button.

4. You should now see the following message in the Results pane:

```
The command(s) completed successfully.
```

5. However, you may have received an error message instead. This could be for a number of reasons, from a typing mistake to not having the authority to create tables. I could list every message that you could receive at this point, but I would be doing so for many pages. Taking one example here, as you can see, the error messages generated are usually self-explanatory. This is informing me that I have a typing error on line 5:

```
Msg 102, Level 15, State 1, Line 5
Incorrect syntax near 'NUL'.
```

6. Now move to Object Explorer. If it is already open, you will have to refresh the Table details tree nodes (by right-clicking the Tables node and selecting Refresh). You should then see the TransactionDetails.Transactions table alongside the CustomerDetails.Customers table created previously.

HOW IT WORKS: DEFINING A TABLE THROUGH QUERY EDITOR

Using Query Editor to define a table works very much like SQL Server Management Studio without the graphical aids. All of the code will be discussed in a moment. Recall that SQL Server Management Studio has prompts for column name, data type, and so on, but here you have to type in every detail. However, many people prefer to create a table this way.

By keying the T-SQL code, you are improving your T-SQL skills that make you more marketable as a developer. When you have a job interview, you will be asked T-SQL questions rather than about creating a table in Management Studio. You can also store the T-SQL code into a source control system. This not only allows all code to be securely held but also provides an audit trail when you are upgrading your system. By knowing T-SQL code, you can also write code for other databases such as Sybase and complete many actions in Oracle. The query can be saved to a file until it is time to run it and build the table in the database. And, finally, as I have mentioned before, but it is important to reiterate, you can execute T-SQL code in any programming language, something that is not possible to perform graphically. As a developer, knowing T-SQL is mandatory if you want to succeed.

Let's now take a look at the T-SQL code that was used to create the table. This code does not include all the options available for creating a table, as there are a large number not used within this book. The basic syntax for creating a table is as follows:

```
CREATE TABLE [database_name].[schema_name].table_name
    (column_name data_type [length] [IDENTITY(seed, increment)] [NULL/NOT NULL])
```

There are a greater number of possible options, and I show only the basic syntax. You should be able to create most tables using this syntax. You will still come across options not listed here within the book, as some of these can be added separately, such as indexes and keys. Other options not listed are for areas that I don't cover, such as full-text searching and also for areas such as data locking, which is very advanced and if you don't have experience, it can be dangerous if incorrectly set.

The items listed in square brackets in the CREATE TABLE syntax are optional; however, there are times when you will require them. Let me explain. Take the first option, database_name: if you are in the master database and you wish to create a table in the ApressFinancial database, you would have to either switch to that database with the USE command as mentioned in the first point of this exercise, or use the database_name option. Usually, you will be in the database where you want to create the table, but this option is ideal when creating code that will be executed unattended. It will ensure that the table is built for the correct database rather than trusting that you are in the right area.

The schema_name option allows you to assign the table to the correct and relevant schema rather than in the default schema of the user connected.

Next you define the columns. Column name and data type are mandatory. However, depending on the data type, the length is optional. You must prefix the first column with an opening parenthesis (and once you have defined the last column, close the list with a closing parenthesis). Each column should be separated from the previous column by a comma. There is a limit of 1,024 columns for a table. If you get anywhere close to that number, you should sit back and reevaluate your table design because chances are the design needs to be revised.

Now that you've created a table in SQL Server Management Studio and another using Query Editor, let's create one using SQLCMD.

Creating a Table: Using SQLCMD

SQL Server has a third method of creating tables via a method called sqlcmd. This is a command prompt tool used to execute scripts from a file against a SQL Server instance, as mentioned in Chapter 2. The tool has several uses including an easy method for accessing SQL Server in single user mode. DBAs who look afer many databases, especially from different venders, use sqlcmd as a command line prompt that gives the DBA the consistency of interface look and feel. One of the more significant uses is where the tool is used for script deployment. Once you start working on larger databases, you will have hundreds of stored procedures, tables, functions, and other areas, and for each regular deployment to production there will be a number of changes. Also during testing you will have at some point a refresh of a non-production database from a production backup where you can then test the deployment of your release scripts. To perform the execution of these scripts, loading them one at a time in to SQL Server Management Studio where they are then executed is cumbersome at the very least. Through the use of a command line tool it is possible to build up a process to perform the release in one action. The sqlcmd tool performs more than T-SQL commands and statements but can also execute some commands such as retrieving the files in a directory.

It is also possible to select SQLCMD mode within a query editor within SQL Server Management Studio. Once a query editor pane is open, from the menu you can select Query ➤ SQLCMD mode. This will allow you to either execute or write scripts written for SQLCMD mode within SQL Server Management Studio.

In this example, you will just be releasing one file using the sqlcmd tool and there will be no need to use any of the command options available.

TRY IT OUT: CREATING A TABLE USING SQLCMD

1. Either start a plain text editor like notepad or create a new empty query editor.

2. Within the editor of choice, you will be creating a table to hold the types of transactions that are held within the TransactionDetails.Transactions table. In this script, there will be a USE command pointing the script to the ApressFinancial database even although the sqlcmd connection will be connecting to the ApressFinancial database. Having the USE command ensures the script is being deployed to the correct database because detailing the database at connection is optional and, therefore, the connection may be pointing to the default database for the login, which may be the master database for example.

 The code for the TransactionDetails.TransactionTypes table follows. There is a fourth column that should be held within this table, but you are not going to place that column in at this time. It will be added when you take a look at how to alter a table in the section "The ALTER TABLE Statement" later in this chapter.

```
USE ApressFinancial
GO

CREATE TABLE TransactionDetails.TransactionTypes
(
    TransactionTypeId smallint IDENTITY(1,1) NOT NULL,
    Description varchar(50) NOT NULL,
    CreditType bit NOT NULL
)
GO
```

3. Once the code is in the editor, save the file to a central, well-named location. For this example, I will save the file in the following location:

   ```
   C:\Development\ApressFinancial\Releases\Dec2014
   ```

4. Now start a command prompt found in the Apps list for Windows 8 or if you are using Windows 7 by selecting Start ➤ Run ➤ cmd and pressing enter.

5. Navigate to where the script is to make it easier to release the script. You then execute the sqlcmd tool passing in the relevant parameters. In this case, the parameters in use are the following:

 - -S—Where you define the name of the server including the instance name

 - -E—Indicates that you are using a trusted connection (Windows authentication)

 - -i—the name of the script to run

     ```
     sqlcmd -S FAT-BELLY-SONY\APRESS_DEV1 -E -i TransactionTypes.sql
     ```

 Figure 5-13 shows the command in the command prompt post execution.

Figure 5-13. *Creating a table using SQLCMD tool*

6. If you move back to SQL Server Management Studio and refresh the Tables node for the ApressFinancial database, you should see the `TransactionDetails.TransactionTypes` table.

Now that you have your third table, I can take you through the steps of altering a table.

The ALTER TABLE Statement

When using the table `TransactionDetails.TransactionTypes`, you had created the table with only three columns; however, the table requires a fourth column. One solution is to delete the table with `DROP TABLE` and then recreate it. However, if you had placed some test data in the table before you realized you had missed the column, this would not be ideal, and of course once the table is in a production environment, dropping the table would not be possible without losing the data. There is an alternative: the `ALTER TABLE` statement, which allows restrictive alterations to a table layout but keeps the contents. SQL Server Management Studio uses this statement when altering a table graphically, but here I will show you how to use it to add the missing fourth column for the `TransactionDetails.TransactionTypes` table.

Columns can be added, removed, or modified using the `ALTER TABLE` statement. Removing a column will remove the data only within that column and not any other column, but careful thought has to take place before adding or altering a column.

There are two scenarios when adding a new column to a table: Should it contain `NULL` values for all the existing rows, or should there be a default value instead? Any new columns created using the `ALTER TABLE` statement where a value is expected and therefore defined as `NOT NULL` will take time to implement. This is because any existing data will have `NULL` values for the new column or will be defined with a default value; after all, SQL Server has no way of knowing what value to automatically enter if you want specific values without the business logic there. To clarify, in the `CustomerDetails.Customers` table, if you were adding the `DateOpened` column after the table was created, SQL Server has no method of working out the date each individual customer's account was opened as it is unable to read the customer agreement that would have been signed.

■ **Note** It is common practice when creating columns to allow `NULL` values, as the default value may not be valid in some rows.

In the following exercise, you will be adding a new column to a table without a default value, and it can contain `NULL` values. You will then alter the table so that it cannot contain `NULL` values.

TRY IT OUT: ADDING A COLUMN

1. First of all, open up Query Editor and ensure that you are pointing to the ApressFinancial database in the Query Editor connection. Then write the code to alter the TransactionDetails.TransactionTypes table to add the new column. The format is very simple. You specify the table prefixed by the schema name you want to alter after the ALTER TABLE statement. Next, you use a comma-delimited list of the columns you wish to add, though in this case you are adding a single column. You define the name, the data type, the length if required, and finally whether you allow NULLs. As you don't want the existing data to have any default values, you will have to define the column to allow NULL values.

   ```
   ALTER TABLE TransactionDetails.TransactionTypes
   ADD AffectCashBalance bit NULL
   GO
   ```

2. If your table had data within it, you could update the existing data for each row to hold the value that is correct. Once this has been achieved, you may then want to remove the ability for further rows of data to have a NULL value. In the case of the TransactionDetails. TransactionTypes table, a NULL value for AlterCashBalance is not valid, so the NULL option for the table needs to be switched. This new column will take a value of 0 or 1, denoting false or true. Again, you would use the ALTER TABLE statement, but this time you will add the ALTER COLUMN statement with the name of the column you wish to alter. After this statement, you would define the alterations you wish to make. Although you are not altering the data type assigned to the column, it is a mandatory requirement to redefine the data type and data length. After this, you can inform SQL Server that the column will not allow NULL values.

   ```
   ALTER TABLE TransactionDetails.TransactionTypes
   ALTER COLUMN AffectCashBalance bit NOT NULL
   GO
   ```

■ **Note** If there was data in the Transactiondetails.TransactionTypes table, you would need to update all the rows to have a value of 0 or 1 before you SQL Server would allow you to successfully alter the column.

3. Execute the preceding code to make the TransactionDetails.TransactionTypes table correct.

Defining the Remaining Tables

Now that three of the tables have been created, you need to create the remaining three tables. You will do this as code placed in Query Editor. There is nothing specifically new to cover in this next section; therefore, only the code is listed. Enter the following code and then execute it as before. You can then move into SQL Server Management Studio and refresh it, after which you should be able to see the new tables. Note that the CustomerDetails.CustomerProducts and CustomerDetails.FinancialProducts tables have no IDENTITY columns. These two tables will be used in Chapter 17 to demonstrate how the SEQUENCE object works as an alternative to IDENTITY.

```
USE ApressFinancial
GO
CREATE TABLE CustomerDetails.CustomerProducts(
        CustomerFinancialProductId int NOT NULL,
        CustomerId int NOT NULL,
        FinancialProductId int NOT NULL,
        AmountToCollect money NOT NULL,
        Frequency smallint NOT NULL,
        LastCollected datetime NOT NULL,
        LastCollection datetime NOT NULL,
        Renewable bit NOT NULL
)
ON [PRIMARY]
GO
CREATE TABLE CustomerDetails.FinancialProducts(
        ProductId int NOT NULL,
        ProductName nvarchar(50) NOT NULL
) ON [PRIMARY]

GO
CREATE TABLE ShareDetails.Shares
(
    ShareId int IDENTITY (1,1) NOT NULL,
    Description varchar(50) NOT NULL,
    StockExchangeTicker varchar(50) NULL,
    CurrentPrice numeric(18,5) NOT NULL
)
GO
CREATE TABLE ShareDetails.SharePrices(
        SharePriceId bigint IDENTITY(1,1) NOT NULL,
        ShareId int NOT NULL,
        Price numeric(18, 5) NOT NULL,
        PriceDate datetime NOT NULL
) ON [PRIMARY]

GO
```

Setting a Primary Key

Setting a primary key constraint can be completed in SQL Server Management Studio with just a couple of mouse clicks. This section will demonstrate how easy this actually is. In Chapter 3, I discussed how primary keys are used for referencing other tables as well as aiding data integrity, and I will discuss the difference between a primary key constraint and an index in Chapter 6.

TRY IT OUT: SETTING A PRIMARY KEY

1. Ensure that SQL Server Management Studio is running and that you have navigated to the ApressFinancial database. Find the ShareDetails.Shares table, right-click it, and select Design.

2. Once in the Table Designer, select the ShareId column. This will be the column to set the primary key for. Right-click to bring up the pop-up menu shown in Figure 5-14.

Figure 5-14. *Defining a primary key*

3. Select the Set Primary Key option from the pop-up menu. This will then change the display to place a small key in the leftmost column details. Only one column has been defined as the primary key, as you see in Figure 5-15.

	Column Name	Data Type	Allow Nulls
▶🔑	ShareId	int	☐
	Description	varchar(50)	☐
	StockExchangeTicker	varchar(50)	☑
	CurrentPrice	numeric(18, 5)	☐
			☐

FAT-BELLY-SONY\AP...areDetails.Shares* ✕

Figure 5-15. *Primary key defined*

4. However, this is not all that happens, as you will see. Save the table modifications by clicking the Save button or pressing Ctrl+S. Click the Manage Indexes/Keys button on the toolbar, which is the fourth button from the left on the Table Designer toolbar, which should be visible as you are in design mode. This brings up the dialog box shown in Figure 5-16. Look at the Type, the third option down in the General section. It says Primary Key. Notice that a key definition has been created for you, with a name and the selected column, informing you that the index is unique and clustered (more on indexes and their relation to primary keys in Chapter 6).

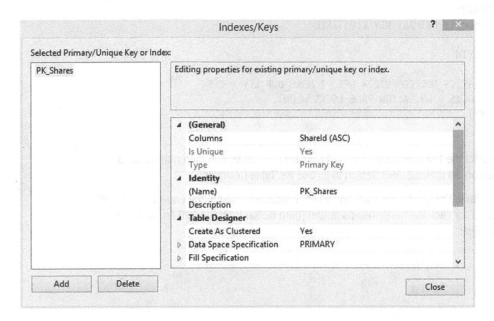

Figure 5-16. *Indexes/Keys dialog box*

That's all there is to creating and setting a primary key. A primary key has now been set up on the `ShareDetails.Shares` table. In this instance, any record added to this table will ensure that the data will be kept in `ShareId` ascending order (this has to do with the index, which you will see in Chapter 6), and it is impossible to insert a duplicate row of data. This key can then be used to link to other tables within the database at a later stage.

Creating a Relationship

I covered relationships in Chapter 3, but no relationships have been created yet. The first relationship that you create will be between the customer and customer transactions tables. This will be a one-to-many relationship, in which there is one customer record to many transaction records. Keep in mind that although a customer may have several customer records—one for each product he or she has bought—the relationship is a combination of customer and product to transactions because a new `CustomerId` will be generated for each product the customer buys. You will now build that first relationship.

TRY IT OUT: BUILDING A RELATIONSHIP

1. Ensure that SQL Server Management Studio is running and that the `ApressFinancial` database is selected and expanded. You need to add a primary key constraint to `CustomerDetails.Customers` first of all so that the relationship can be built. Enter the code that follows and then execute it:

```
ALTER TABLE CustomerDetails.Customers
ADD CONSTRAINT
    PK_Customers PRIMARY KEY CLUSTERED
    (
    CustomerId
    )
WITH( STATISTICS_NORECOMPUTE = OFF, IGNORE_DUP_KEY = OFF,
ALLOW_ROW_LOCKS = ON, ALLOW_PAGE_LOCKS = ON)
ON [PRIMARY]
GO
```

2. Find and select the `TransactionDetails.Transactions` table, and then right-click to display the pop-up menu. Select Design to invoke the Table Designer.

3. Once in the Table Designer, right-click and select Relationships from the pop-up menu shown in Figure 5-17, or click the Relationships button (third button from the left) on the Table Designer toolbar.

Figure 5-17. Building a relationship

4. This brings up the Relationship Designer. As it's empty, you need to click Add. This will then populate the screen, as shown in Figure 5-18.

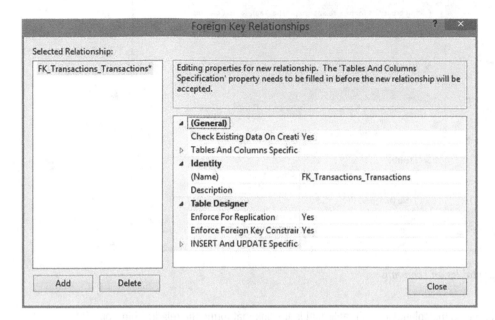

Figure 5-18. Foreign Key Relationships dialog box

5. The first requirement is to change the name to make it more meaningful. Quite often, you will find that naming the key FK_ParentTable_ChildTable (or a shortened best derivative of) is the best method, so, in this case, change it to FK_Cust_Trans, as the CustomerDetails. Customers table will be the master table for this foreign key. Next expand the Tables And Columns Specification node, which will allow the relationship to be built. Notice that there is now an ellipsis button on the right, as shown in Figure 5-19. To create the relationship, click the ellipsis.

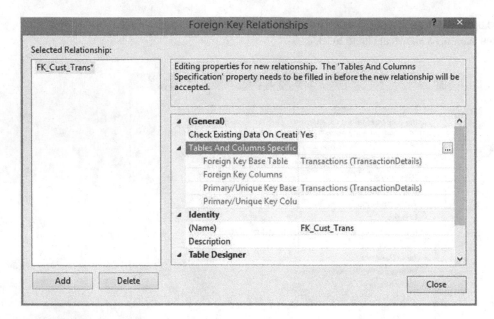

Figure 5-19. *Adding tables and columns*

6. You need to define the column in each table that is the link that forms the relationship. You are linking each customer record to many transaction records, and you can do so via the CustomerId. Select that column for both tables, as shown in Figure 5-20. Now click OK.

Figure 5-20. *Columns selection*

■ **Note** In this instance, both columns have the same name, but this is not mandatory. The only requirement is that the information in the two columns be the same.

7. This brings you back to the Foreign Key Relationships definition screen, shown in Figure 5-21. Notice that at the top of the list items in the grayed-out area, you can see the details of the foreign key you just defined. Within the Identity section, there is now also a description of the foreign key.

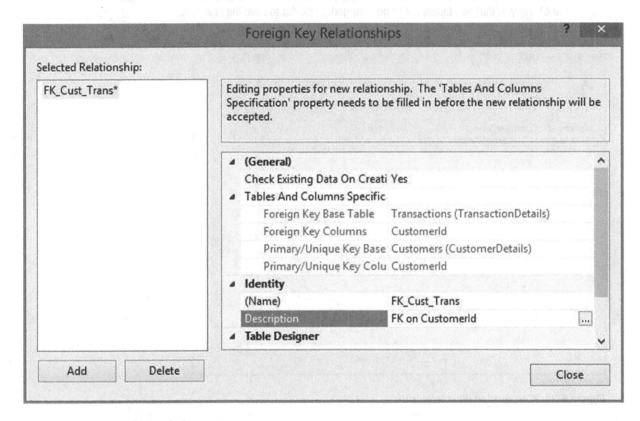

Figure 5-21. *Foreign key with description*

8. Ignore the option Enforce for Replication found if you scroll the window displayed. Replication is when data that is inserted in one database is then replicated to a different database. You can enforce that the foreign key is checked when data has come from the source database to be inserted in to the recipient table (this table).

9. There are two other options that are displayed at the bottom of the dialog box, as shown in Figure 5-22. Leave the options as the defaults, and I will explain them in a moment.

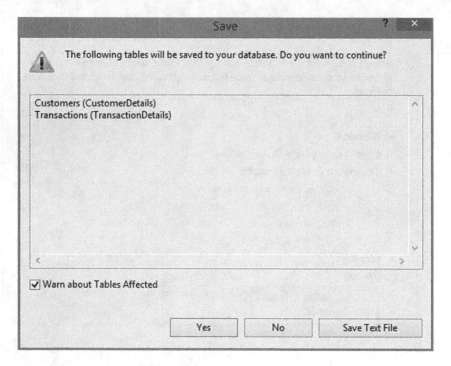

Figure 5-22. *INSERT And UPDATE Specification*

10. Closing this dialog box does not save the changes. Even when you save the changes using the Save button, the relationship is not added. Not until you save or close the Table Designer will the changes be applied. When you do so, you should see the dialog box in Figure 5-23 notifying you that two tables are to be changed. Click Yes to save the changes.

Figure 5-23. *Committing the relationship*

The relationship is now built, but what about those options you left alone? Let's go through those now.

Check Existing Data on Creation

If there is data within either of the tables, by setting this option found at the top of the relationship design window to Yes, you are instructing SQL Server that when the time comes to physically add the relationship at the point of saving the table, the data within the tables is to be checked. If the data meets the definition of the relationship, then the relationship is successfully inserted into the database. However, if any data fails the relationship test, then the relationship is not applied to the database. An example of this would be when it is necessary to ensure that there is a customer record for all transactions, but if there are transaction records that don't have a corresponding customer record, the relationship creation would fail and would not be applied. Obviously, if you come across this, you have a decision to make. Either correct the data by adding master records in the customers table or altering the transactions table, and then reapply the relationship, or revisit the relationship to ensure it is what you want.

By creating the relationship, you want the data within the relationship to work; therefore, you would select No if you were going to go back and fix the data after the additions. What if you still miss rows? Would this be a problem? In the preceding scenario, there should be no transaction records without customer records. But you may still wish to add the relationship to stop further anomalies going forward.

Enforce Foreign Key Constraints

Once the relationship has been created and placed in the database, it is possible to prevent the relationship from being broken. If you set Check Existing Data on Creation to Yes as I have just discussed, then you are more than likely hoping to keep the integrity of the data intact. That option will check only the existing data. It does nothing for further additions, deletions, and updates on the data. However, by setting the Enforce Foreign Key Constraints option to Yes, which is found toward the bottom of the relationship designer window, you ensure that any addition, modification, or deletion of the data will not break the relationship. It doesn't stop changing or removing data, provided that the integrity of the database is kept in sync. For example, it would be possible to change the customer number of transactions, provided that the new customer number also exists with the `CustomerDetails.Customers` table. If an application does try to add data that will break the relationship, an error is generated and the change is not committed to the table.

Choosing Delete and Update Rules

The final section to discuss is found as the last area of the relationship designer under INSERT And UPDATE Specification. This area deals with when a deletion or an update of a row is performed on the parent table, in this case the `CustomerDetails.Customers` table. It is possible for one of four actions to then occur on the related data, based on the following options:

- *No Action*: If a customer is deleted, then no further actions occur and could potentially leave the database with transactions for `CustomerIds` that no longer exist. However, a positive for this action is that as a developer, you would write code to complete the deletion of transactions for this customer and so as a developer you would be in control. This is ideal if you were archiving the data from one database to another.

- *Cascade*: If you delete a customer, then all of the transaction rows for that customer will also be deleted.

- *Set Null*: If you delete a customer, then if the CustomerId column in the TransactionDetails. Transactions table could accept NULL as a value, the value would be set to NULL. In the customers/transactions scenario, we have specified the column cannot accept NULL values, and therefore the value will remain. In this scenario, this action would be the same as No Action. The danger with this option is that you are leaving "unlinked" rows behind—a scenario that can be valid, but do take care.

- *Set Default*: When defining the table, the column could be defined so that a default value is placed in it. On setting the option to this value, you are saying that the column will revert to this default value—again, a dangerous setting, but potentially a less dangerous option than SET NULL, as at least there is a meaningful value within the column.

■ **Note** If at any point you do decide to implement cascade deletion, then please do take the greatest of care, as it can result in deletions that you may regret. If you implemented this on the CustomerDetails.Customers table, all the transactions will be gone when you delete a customer. This is ideal for use if you have an archive database to which all rows are archived but not ideal if you are auditing the transactions table for financial information. To keep your current and online system lean and fast, you could use delete cascades to quickly and cleanly remove customers who have closed their accounts.

Building a Relationship via T-SQL

It is also possible to build a relationship, or constraint, through a T-SQL statement. This would be done using an ALTER TABLE SQL statement. In the following example, a relationship will be created between the TransactionDetails.Transactions table and the ShareDetails.Shares table. This will ensure that there is a relationship between the transactions table and the shares table when the transaction relates to a share. This will be a zero- or one-to-one relationship. Let's now take a few moments to check the syntax for building a constraint within T-SQL code:

```
ALTER TABLE child_table_name
WITH NOCHECK|CHECK
ADD CONSTRAINT [Constraint_Name]
FOREIGN KEY (child_column_name, ...,)
REFERENCES [master_table_name]([master_column_name, ...,])
```

You have to use an ALTER TABLE statement to achieve the goal of inserting a constraint to build the relationship. After naming the child table in the ALTER TABLE statement, you then need to decide whether you want the foreign key to check the existing data when it is being created. This is similar to the Check Existing Data on Creation option you saw earlier.

Now we move on to building the constraint. To do this, you must first of all instruct SQL Server that this is what you are intending to complete, so you will need the ADD CONSTRAINT command.

Next, you name the constraint you are building. Again, I tend to use underscores instead of spaces. However, if you do wish to use spaces, which I wholeheartedly discourage, then you'll have to surround the name of the key using the square brackets ([]). I know I mentioned this before, but it's crucial to realize the impact of having spaces in a column, table, or constraint name. Every time you wish to deal with an object that has a name separated by spaces, you will also need to surround it with square brackets. Why make extra work for yourself?

Finally, you will instruct SQL Server whether you wish to check or not check the existing data to ensure that the new foreign key relationship is valid. It is common practice to use the WITH CHECK option to ensure that the data is valid. It is possible not to check the data, but you have to be aware that you will have existing data that may break your application.

Now that the name of the constraint has been defined, the next stage is to inform SQL Server that a FOREIGN KEY is being defined next. Recall that a constraint can also be used for other functionality, such as creating a default value to be inserted into a column.

When defining the foreign key, ensure that all column names are separated by a comma and surrounded by parentheses. The final stage of building a relationship in code is to specify the master table of the constraint and the columns involved.

The rule here is that there must be a one-to-one match on columns on the child table and the master table, and that all corresponding columns must match on data type.

It is as simple as that. When building relationships, you may wish to use SQL Server Management Studio, as there is a lot less typing involved, and you can also instantly see the exact correspondence between the columns and whether they match in the same order. However, with T-SQL, you can save the code, and it will be ready for deployment to production servers when required. You can also keep a copy for storage in your code repository, such as Visual SourceSafe.

TRY IT OUT: USING T-SQL TO BUILD A RELATIONSHIP

1. In a Query Editor pane, enter the following T-SQL command and execute it by pressing F5 or clicking the Execute button:

```
USE ApressFinancial
GO
ALTER TABLE TransactionDetails.Transactions
WITH NOCHECK
ADD CONSTRAINT FK_Transactions_Shares
FOREIGN KEY(RelatedShareId)
REFERENCES ShareDetails.Shares(ShareId)
```

2. You should then see that the command has been executed successfully:

```
The command(s) completed successfully.
```

That's it. The relationship is created in the second batch of T-SQL code, the first batch ensuring that you are pointing to the right database. Once the index is built, it is possible to alter the table to add the relationship.

With your code, although you are executing an ALTER TABLE statement, no columns are being altered, but a constraint is being added. A relationship is a special type of constraint, and it is through a constraint that a relationship is built.

A constraint is, in essence, a logical checking mechanism, checking data modifications within SQL Server and the table(s) that it is associated with.

Relationships: Database or Application

Here is one last, quick discussion before you reach the end of the chapter. You have seen a relationship between two tables built. There are positives to this approach as it will enforce referential integrity via SQL Server. If referential integrity breaks, then SQL Server will return an error code from the T-SQL that is executed.

However, there is an alternative approach, and that is to enforce referential integrity via code. This can be achieved with several different methods, including extra T-SQL code that is written when a data modification is to be executed, the building of a trigger that executes automatically when a modification occurs, or within your application code written in Java, Excel, .NET, and so on. Further thought and design away from the database are required to accomplish this task, and strong control is required on the coding techniques within your application or elsewhere within the database. You may be wondering why you should put yourself through the extra work and hardship: By keeping the referential integrity through code, it does provide for flexibility if data are loaded correctly but out of sequence. For example, if you loaded customer transactions before you inserted customers, or you wanted to be in full control of archiving your data, the integrity checks would not interfere.

It can be a hard choice, but I believe that using physical relationships is the best option in the large majority of cases; however, you have to be aware that, as a developer and as you progress through your career, you will find applications that use the logical implementation, and you should be aware that it exists. However, when given the choice, I strongly believe that relationships should be held within the database rather than the application code.

Finally, enforcing a relationship within SQL Server is a process that takes time to perform at each insertion. Not a great deal of time but time nonetheless. For high-frequency, high-volume, rapid-responding applications, you may find that a logical relationship where the relationship is within your code may be the correct option.

Partitioning

The final area on tables I would like to bring to your attention is a methodology called partitioning. There may come a time that you are working on some very large volumes of data—millions of rows, maybe even hundreds of millions of rows—that take up gigabytes of space. To search this amount of data takes time for SQL Server to process. Even if you are finding a single specific row that can be accessed via an index, there is a cost to seek and return a row. One method to improve performance is to section data into segments of logical "chunks." This, at a very high level, is what partitioning is. Take, for example, the TransactionDetails.Transactions table. Over time, this table could hold a vast amount of data as your financial firm becomes successful. Some of the transaction records could be months and even years old and rarely or even ever referenced. You could archive them to a different table, of course, but there may be a reason they need to stay in the current table. It could even be that the firm is so successful that it generates a million rows a day. Whatever the background, you know you need to improve the performance of some queries.

To give the discussion some meaning, imagine the TransactionDetails.Transactions table has 10 million rows of data and 10,000 rows of new data is added daily. The table is required to only hold three years of data, after that it can be deleted. Most of the queries are looking at the current financial month of data, which starts on the first of the month based on the column DateEntered.

Without partitioning and without getting too involved in detail of how the database works, SQL Server takes data in a tables index (indexes are discussed in Chapter 6) and creates a tree-based structure called a B-Tree where the data is split in such a way that SQL Server follows a path through the B-Tree structure to get to the row or rows of data it requires for the query. If you look at Figure 5-24 this is a basic B-Tree (if you look at it upside down, it is similar to a tree where you have the trunk [the IAM page], then the branches [the non-leaf pages] with the last level being the leafs. SQL Server keeps the B-Tree balanced such that the root node [the top] is in the middle of the tree structure, which is how it gets its name of a B-Tree). SQL Server will look at the top of the structure and navigate through searching down each level to the bottom row (leaf level) for the query. You can see in Figure 5-24 that this only deals with a small number of rows of data. Notice that the data is being shown in CustomerId order as this has been deemed as the best order for the data.

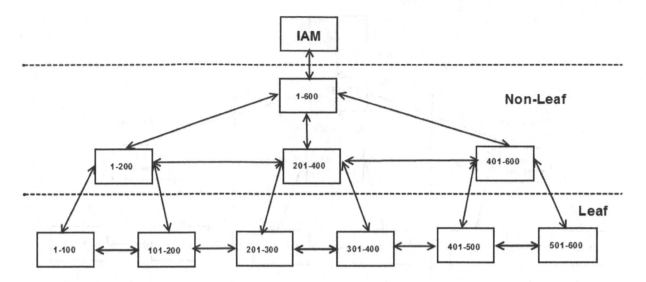

Figure 5-24. *A small B-Tree*

When there are millions of rows SQL Server will not create a very tall tree splitting the data downward to accommodate the splitting of data equally down the middle each time. There is a limit on the number of levels the B-Tree will have and therefore with large volumes of data the B-Tree will become wider rather than taller. SQL Server widens the tree creating more branches. Put this in to the scenario I set of 10 million rows and expanding daily and you can see how much work SQL Server would have to do. The data is still in CustomerId order.

By dividing, or partitioning your data by the DateEntered column in to calendar months when looking at transactions—whether that is for overall transaction reporting or customer query-based transaction queries—SQL Server can use the partitioning to know that there are a number of branches it can ignore completely and concentrate its search efforts in the partitions that meet the date entered. Figure 5-25 shows a potential B-Tree structure in such a partitioned state for the TransactionDetails.Transactions table. The table is partitioned on a year's worth of data and has a clustered index on the CustomerId. SQL Server, if given a query to look for rows in 2014, will know to ignore the first two partitions and only look at the data in the third partition.

Figure 5-25. *A "partitioned B-Tree"*

■ **Note** This is not a accurate representation of the actual B-Tree as SQL Server also performs some additional identification work to improve scanning performance. Also, the layout is difference, but it demonstrates how a smaller subset of data is scanned.

The final point I wish to make is that to delete a month's worth of data once the three-year holding requirement is met will take time to process as SQL Server has to delete 300,000 rows potentially. With partitioning it is possible to delete the partition, which is much faster as SQL Server deletes pages of data rather than rows.

To be clear, this is very high-level, simple, low-volume data example with no walkthrough Try It Out example quite deliberately. Partitioning has much more functionality, risks, checks, design, and monitoring considerations to take in to account, and it is quite an advanced topic. However, it is important to be aware of such technology for when you are presented with very large amounts of data.

Summary

So, now you know how to create a table. This chapter has covered several options for doing so, but there is one point that you should keep in mind when building a table, whether you are creating or modifying it. When creating a table in SQL Server Management Studio, you should always save the table first by clicking the Save toolbar button. If you have made a mistake when defining the table, when you close the table designer which will close the designer and save the changes in one action, you will get an error message informing you that an error has occurred, and all your changes will be lost. You will then have to go back into the Table Designer and reapply any changes made.

Try also to get used to using both SQL Server Management Studio and Query Editor, as you may find that Query Editor gives you a more comfortable feel to the way you want to work. Also, you will find that in Query Editor, you can save your work to a file on your hard drive as you go along. You can also do this within SQL Server Management Studio; however, the changes are saved to a text file as a set of SQL commands, which then need to be run through Query Editor anyway.

CHAPTER 6

■ ■ ■

Creating Indexes and Database Diagramming

Now that you have created the tables, you could stop at this point and just work with the data from here. However, this would not be a good decision. As soon as any table contained a reasonable amount of information and you wished to find a particular record, it would take SQL Server a fair amount of time to locate it. Performance would suffer, and your users would soon get annoyed with the slowdown in speed.

In this scenario, the database is like a large filing cabinet in which you have to find one piece of paper, but there's no clear filing system or form of indexing. If there were some sort of cross-reference facility, then it would likely be easier to find the information that is needed. And if that cross-reference facility were in fact an index, this would be even better, as you might be able to find the piece of paper in your filing cabinet almost instantly. It is this theory that you need to put into practice in your SQL Server database tables. Generally, indexing is a conscious decision by a developer who favors faster conditional selection of records over modification or insertion of records.

In this chapter, you'll learn the basics of indexing and how you can start implementing an indexing solution. This chapter will cover the following topics:

- What an index is

- Different types of indexes

- Size restrictions on indexes

- Qualities of a good index and a bad index

- How to build an index in code as well as graphically

- How to alter an index

Let's begin by looking at what an index is and how it stores data.

What Is an Index?

In Chapter 5, you learned about tables, which are, in essence, repositories that hold data and information about data—what it looks like and where it is held. However, a table definition is not a great deal of use in getting to the data quickly. For this, some sort of cross-reference facility is required, where for certain columns of information within a table it should be possible to get to the whole record of information quickly.

If you think of this book, for example, as a table, the cross-reference you would use to find information quickly is the index at the back of the book. You look in the book index for a piece of information, or key. When you find the listing for that information in the index, you'll find it's associated with a page number, or a pointer, which directs you to where you can find the data you're looking for. This is where an index within your SQL Server database comes in.

You define an index in SQL Server so that it can locate the rows it requires to satisfy database queries faster. If an index does not exist to help find the necessary rows, SQL Server has no other option but to look at every row in a table to see if it contains the information data required by the query. This is called a table scan, which by its very nature adds considerable overhead to data-retrieval operations.

■ **Note** There will be times when a table scan is preferable to using an index. For example, if SQL Server needs to process a reasonable proportion of rows within a table (as a rule of thumb, 10% or more of rows), a table scan is likely to be better than using an index. Decisions such as this one are made by SQL Server based on costs, like the cost of accessing the hard drive a row at a time as opposed to retrieving large chunks of data and holding the data in memory. SQL Server uses a cost-based optimizer. There are other costs, but this is one example of why table scans may occur. This is all to say that a table scan isn't wholly a bad thing, but on large tables, it could take some time to process.

When searching a table using the index, SQL Server does not go through all the data stored in the table; rather, it focuses on a much smaller subset of that data, as it will be looking at the columns defined within the index, which is faster. Once the record is found in the index, a pointer states where the data for that row can be found in the relevant table.

There are different types of indexes you can build onto a table. The circumstances of the column or columns you select and the data that will be held within these columns determine which type of index you use.

Types of Indexes

Although SQL Server has three types of indexes—clustered, nonclustered, and primary and secondary XML indexes—I will concentrate only on clustered and nonclustered in this book, as XML and XML indexes are quite an advanced topic.

The index type refers to the way the index and the physical rows of data are stored internally by SQL Server. The differences between the index types are important to understand, so I will delve into them in the sections that follow.

Clustered

A clustered index defines the order of the data in the table. If you have more than one column defined in a clustered index, the data will be stored in sequential order according to columns: the first column, then the next column, and so on. Only one clustered index can be defined per table, and the clustered index has to generate unique values. It would be impossible to store the data in two different orders.

Going back to the earlier book analogy, if you examine a telephone book, you'll see that the data are presented in alphabetical order with surnames appearing first, then first names, and then any middle-name initial(s). Therefore, when you search the index and find the key, you are already at the point in the data from which you want to retrieve the information, such as the telephone number. In other words, you don't have to turn to another page as indicated by the key because the data are right there. This is a clustered index of surname, first name, and initials. The clustered index not only defines the order of the data but also holds the data of the columns not defined as the index.

As data are inserted, SQL Server will take the data within the index key values you have passed in and insert the row at the appropriate point if possible. It will then move the data along so that it remains in the same order. You can think of this data as being like books on a bookshelf. Let me take you through a simple analogy, and I will put the relevant technical terms in brackets where appropriate. In the analogy there is an assumption that one book = one kilobyte of data and a shelf can hold eight kilobytes (8KB page).

When a librarian gets a new book, he will find the correct alphabetical point and try to insert the book at that point (searching the B-Tree). All the books will then be moved within the shelf. If there is no room as the books are moved, half the books approximately at the end of the shelf will be moved to the next shelf down, and so on, until a shelf with enough room is found (page splitting). However, if there were no shelves left, the librarian would build a

new shelf (page) at the relevant point (new page allocation). With all the shuffling around of books, he may find that there are shelves only partially filled and maybe shelves with only one or two books on them because of the way the shuffling has taken place (fragmentation). The librarian would do only so much shuffling before he decided it would be easier to insert a new shelf, as he doesn't want to be spending all day shuffling books around. It's not effective to shuffle and modify at the same time (optimization), so he would build the shelf and place the book on that shelf. All of the actions taken would also occur for updates. However, the librarian does know that there is a limit to the number of shelves they can add as the bookcase has a definite height. It's the same with the B-Tree—there are only so many levels created before no more levels are created.

Also, librarians take pride in their shelves and how quickly they can find a piece of information (index scan). They don't particularly wish to scan every book on every shelf for a specific book (table scan), although their first main task is to ensure every book that they have is held on the shelves (consistency). So the head librarian finds a quiet time, such as breaktime, lunchime, nighttime, or weekends, to allow the library staff to take all the books off the shelves, replace them on the shelves in the right order (reindexing) with a set amount of spare space on each shelf for future insertions, and leave enough space at the end for expansion. Then, if any shelves are left over, they will remove them and reclaim the space (fill factor).

I hope this analogy shows how important it is that the correct columns are chosen for a clustered index. You want to avoid shuffling as much as possible; data are always added at the end so that the librarian does not need to shuffle the data around. Although this analogy puts the process in simple terms, this is exactly what SQL Server does. A clustered index should also be as narrow as possible. Any table with a clustered index has the index key used as part of any nonclustered index, as the nonclustered index would retrieve its data from the clustered index. Also, if you have a column that is varchar, try to place that at the end of the list of columns selected for the index, which is why numerically based columns are best.

As a clustered index contains the table data itself, SQL Server would perform fewer I/O operations to retrieve the data using the clustered index than it would using a nonclustered index. Therefore, if you have only one index on a table, try to make sure it is a clustered index. If a table has no clustered index defined, it is known as a heap table and the data in the table is stored in no particular order.

Nonclustered

Unlike a clustered index, a nonclustered index does not store the table data itself. Instead, a nonclustered index stores pointers to the table data or clustered index as part of the index keys; therefore, many nonclustered indexes can exist on a single table at one time.

As a nonclustered index is stored in a separate structure—in fact, the index data is really held as a table with a clustered index hidden from your view—from the base table, it is possible to create the nonclustered index on a different filegroup from the base table. If the filegroups are located on separate disks, data retrieval can be enhanced for your queries as SQL Server can use parallel I/O operations to retrieve the data from the index and base tables concurrently.

When you are retrieving information data from a table that has a nonclustered index, SQL Server finds the relevant row in the nonclustered index. If the information you want doesn't form part of the data in the index, SQL Server will then use information in the index to retrieve a key pointer to the relevant row and retrieve the row (fetch) in the data or clustered index if the table is defined with one. As you can see, this involves at least two I/O actions— and possibly more, depending on the optimization of the index. A nonclustered index also uses the B-Tree structure and therefore the analogy of page splits and fragmentation described for a clustered index also exists; however, a nonclustered index holds just the number of bytes for the columns defined for the nonclustered index and not the number of bytes for the whole row. This means that although the data will be page split, it will usually occur less often.

When a nonclustered index is created, the information used to build the index is placed in a separate location from the table and therefore can be stored on a different physical disk if required.

■ **Caution** The more indexes you have, the more times SQL Server has to perform index modifications when inserting or updating data in columns that are within an index.

■ **Note** If you wish to index XML data, which I cover only briefly later in the book, you should read "SQL Server Books Online," as this topic is beyond the scope of this book.

Uniqueness

An index can be defined as either *unique* or *nonunique*. A unique index ensures that the values contained within the unique index columns will appear only once within the table, including a value of NULL.

SQL Server automatically enforces the uniqueness of the columns contained within a unique index. If an attempt is made to insert a value that already exists in the table, an error will be generated and the attempt to insert or modify the data will fail.

A nonunique index is perfectly valid. However, as there can be duplicated values, a nonunique index has more overhead than a unique index when retrieving data. SQL Server needs to check if there are multiple entries to return, compared with a unique index, where SQL Server knows to stop searching after finding the first row (although in reality SQL Server will return internally the whole 8KB page of data as it makes a performance assumption that there is a possibility you will need other data from the ordered page).

Unique indexes are commonly implemented to support constraints such as the primary key and clustered indexes. Nonunique indexes are commonly implemented to support locating rows using a nonkey column.

Determining What Makes a Good Index

To create an index on a table, you have to specify which columns are contained within the index. Columns in an index do not have to all be of the same data type. You should be aware that there is a limit of 16 columns on an index, and the total amount of data for the index columns within a row cannot be more than 900 bytes. To be honest, if you get to an index that contains more than four or five columns, you should stand back and reevaluate the index definition. Sometimes you'll have more than five columns, but you really should double-check.

It is possible to get around this restriction and have an index that does include columns that are not part of the key: the columns are tagged onto the end of the index known as included columns. Included columns are also useful if you have a small amount of data not to index but that is very commonly retrieved during searches on the table. This means that the index takes up more space, but if it means that SQL Server can retrieve all of the data from an index search, then it will be faster and potentially remove the need for a row fetch. However, to reiterate, if you are going down this route for indexes, then perhaps you need to look at your design.

In the sections that follow, you will examine some of the factors that can determine if an index is good:

- Using "low-maintenance" columns
- Using primary and foreign keys
- Being able to find a specific record
- Using covering indexes
- Looking for a range of information
- Keeping the data in order

Using Low-Maintenance Columns

As I've indicated, for nonclustered indexes, the actual index data is separate from the table data, although both can be stored in the same area or in different areas (e.g., on different hard drives). To reiterate, this means that when you insert a record into a table, the information from the columns included in the index is copied and inserted into the index area for nonclustered indexes. So, if you alter data in a column within a table and that column has been defined as making up an index, SQL Server also has to alter the data in the index. Instead of only one update being completed, two will be completed. If the table has more than one index and in more than one of those indexes is a column that is to be updated a great deal, then there may be several disk writes to perform when updating just one record. While this will result in a performance reduction for data-modification operations, appropriate indexing will balance this out by greatly increasing the performance of data-retrieval operations.

Concerning a clustered index if the altering of data in the columns that define the index, this could mean SQL Server having to move rows of data around within the BTree.

Therefore, data that are *low maintenance*—namely, columns that are never or not heavily updated—could become an index and would make a good index. The fewer disk writes or maintenance tasks that SQL Server has to do, the faster the database will be, as well as every other database within that SQL Server instance. Don't let this statement put you off. If you feel that data within a table is retrieved more often than it is modified or if the performance of the retrieval is more critical than the performance of the modification, then do look at including the column within the index.

In the example application you are building, each month you need to update a customer's bank balance with any interest gained or charged. However, there is a nightly job that wants to check for clients who have between $10,000 and $50,000, as the bank can get a higher rate of deposit with the Federal Reserve on those sorts of amounts. A client's bank balance will be constantly updated, but an index on this sort of column could speed up the overnight deposit check program. Before the index in this example is created, you need to determine if the slight performance degradation in the updating of the balances is justified by the improvement of performance of the deposit check program.

Using Primary and Foreign Keys

A primary key is a constraint and therefore can be enforced logically. However, SQL Server enforces a primary key uniqueness by creating an index. You can see this in the ApressFinancial database by looking at the CustomerDetails.Customers table, and you will see the index PK_Customers. The index created will be a clustered index if the table has no clustered index already defined. If the table has a clustered index, you can have only one clustered index per table, and therefore SQL Server will create a nonclustered unique index instead. Personally, I prefer to use a primary key constraint rather than a unique clustered index because—although SQL Server will generate a clustered index for the primary key—you may feel that a different set of columns would be a better clustered index even though there is a slight performance degradation of a constraint over an index.

One important use of indexes is on referential constraints within a table. A referential constraint is where you've indicated that through the use of a key certain actions are constrained depending on what data exists. To give a quick example of a referential constraint, say you have a customer who owns banking products. A referential constraint would prevent the customer's record from being deleted while those products existed.

SQL Server does not automatically create indexes on your foreign keys, although it is likely that an index is created when you build a primary key. However, as the foreign key column values need to be identified by SQL Server when joining to the parent table, it is almost always recommended that an index be created on the columns of the foreign key.

Finding Specific Records

Ideal candidates for indexes are columns that allow SQL Server to quickly identify the appropriate rows. In Chapters 10–13, you will meet the WHERE clause of a query. This clause lists certain columns in your table and is used to limit the number of rows returned from a query. The columns used in the WHERE clause of your most common queries make excellent choices for an index. So, for example, if you wanted to find a customer's order for a specific order number, an index based on customer_id and order_number would be perfect, as all the information needed to locate a requested row in the table would be contained in the index.

If finding specific records is going to make up part of the way the application works, then do look at columns that will reduce significantly the rows that would be returned from a search as an area for an index to be created, especially if the column or columns would return one row.

Using Covering Indexes

As mentioned earlier, when you insert or update a record, any data in a column that is included in an index are stored not only in the table/clustered index, but also in the indexes for nonclustered indexes. From finding an entry in an index, SQL Server then moves to the table to locate and retrieve the record. However, if the necessary information is held within the index, then there is no need to go to the table and retrieve the record, providing much speedier data access.

For example, consider the ShareDetails.Shares table in the ApressFinancial database. Suppose that you wanted to find out the description, current price, and ticker ID of a share. If an index was placed on the ShareId column, knowing that this is an identifier column and therefore unique, you would ask SQL Server to find a record using the ID supplied. It would then take the details from the index of where the data are located and move to that data area. If, however, there was an index with all of the columns defined, then SQL Server would be able to retrieve the description ticker and price details in the index action. It would not be necessary to move to the data area. This is called a *covered index* since the index covers every column in the table for data retrieval. However, as the current price could be altering a great deal, you might find that the index was not ideal because too many updates to both the data and the index would be occurring.

Looking for a Range of Information

An index can be just as useful for searching for a range of records as it can be useful for finding one record. For example, say you wish to find a list of towns in Florida with names between Orlando and St. Petersburg in alphabetical order. You could put an index on the town name, and SQL Server would go to the index location of Orlando and then read forward from there an index row at a time, until it reached the item after St. Petersburg, where it would then stop. Because SQL Server knows that an index is on this column and that the data will be sorted by town name, this makes it ideal for building an index on a town name column.

It should be noted that SQL Server indexes are not useful when attempting to search for characters embedded in a body of text. For example, suppose you want to find every author in a publisher's database whose last name contains the letters "ab." This type of query does not provide a means of determining where in the index tree to start and stop searching for appropriate values. The only way SQL Server can determine which rows are valid for this query is to examine every row within the table. Depending on the amount of data within the table, this can be a slow process. If you have a requirement to perform this sort of wildcard text searching, you should take a look at the SQL Server full-text feature as this will provide better performance for such queries.

Keeping the Data in Order

As previously stated, a clustered index actually keeps the data in the table in a specific order. When you specify a column (or multiple columns) as a clustered index, upon inserting a record, SQL Server will place that record in a physical position to keep the records in the correct ascending or descending order that corresponds to the order defined in the index. To explain this a bit further, if you have a clustered index on customer numbers and the data

currently have customer numbers 10, 6, 4, 7, 2, and 5, then SQL Server will physically store the data in the following order: 2, 4, 5, 6, 7, 10. If a process then adds in a customer number 9, it will be physically inserted between 7 and 10, which may mean that the record for customer number 10 needs to move physically. This was discussed in the book analogy when clustered indexes were introduced earlier in this chapter. Therefore, if you have defined a clustered index on a column or a set of columns where data insertions cause the clustered index to be reordered, this will greatly affect your insert performance. SQL Server does provide a way to reduce the reordering impact by allowing a fill factor to be specified when an index is created. I will discuss the fill factor shortly; however, this option allows you to define how much of an index leaf will be filled before a new leaf is created. Think of an index leaf as your index card for each cabinet. You know that more items are going to come in, and you'll need to add some of them to existing index cards. You try to estimate how many items you'll need to add to each card, so you can leave space for them and avoid creating any new cards unnecessarily.

Determining What Makes a Bad Index

Now that you know what makes a good index, let's investigate what makes a bad index. There are several "gotchas" to be aware of:

- Using unsuitable columns
- Choosing unsuitable data
- Including too many columns
- Including too few records in the table

Using Unsuitable Columns

If a column isn't used by a query to locate a row within a table, then there is a good chance that the column won't need to be indexed, unless it is combined with another column to create a covering index, as described earlier. If this is the case, the index will still add overhead to the data-modification operations but will not produce any performance benefit to the data-retrieval operations.

With clustered indexes, as I have mentioned before, columns that are modified frequently are not ideal candidates for forming the index.

Choosing Unsuitable Data

Indexes work best when the data contained in the index columns are highly selective between rows. The optimal index is one created on a column that has a unique value for every row within a table, such as a primary key. If a query requests a row based on a value within this column, SQL Server can quickly navigate the index structure and identify the single row that matches the query predicate.

However, if the selectivity of the data in the index columns is poor, the effectiveness of the index will be reduced. For example, if an index is created on a column that contains only three distinct values, the index will be able to reduce the number of rows to just a third of the total before applying other methods to identify the exact row. In this instance, SQL Server would probably ignore the index anyway and find that reading the data table instead would be faster. Therefore, when deciding on appropriate index columns, you should examine the data selectivity to estimate the effectiveness of the index and keep the index highly selective.

Including Too Many Columns

The more columns there are in an index, the more data writing has to take place when a process completes an update or an insertion of data. Although these updates to the index data take a very short amount of time in SQL Server, they can add up. Therefore, each index that is added to a table will incur extra processing overhead, so it is recommended that you create the minimum number of indexes needed to give your data-retrieval operations acceptable performance. Recall that a page of data in the B-Tree is 8KB and the more bytes in the index, the less data can be held within the 8KB page.

When There Are Too Few Records in the Table

From a data-performance viewpoint, there is absolutely no need to place an index on a table that has only one row. SQL Server will find the record at the first request, without the need of an index, because it will use a table scan. That said, you may wish to include a primary key that can then be used to enforce data integrity.

This statement also holds true when a table has only a handful of records. Again, there is no reason to place an index on these tables. The reason for this is that SQL Server would go to the index, use its engine to make several reads of the data to find the correct record, and then move directly to that record using the record pointer from the index to retrieve the information. Several actions are involved in this process as well as passing data between different components within SQL Server. When you execute a query, SQL Server will determine whether it's more costly (recall SQL Server is a cost-based database and performing disk I/O is costly) to use the indexes defined for the table to locate the necessary rows or to simply perform a table scan and look at every row within the table.

Reviewing Your Indexes for Performance

Every so often, it's necessary for you as a developer to review the indexes built on your table to ensure that yesterday's good index is not today's bad index. When a solution is built, what is perceived to be a good index in development may not be so good in production—for example, the users may be performing one task more times than expected. Therefore, it is highly advisable that you set up tasks that constantly review your indexes and how they are performing. This can be completed within SQL Server via its index-tuning tool, the Database Engine Tuning Advisor (DTA).

The DTA looks at your database and a workload file holding a representative amount of information that will be processed. It uses the information it gleans from these to figure out what indexes to place within the database and where improvements can be made. At this point in the book, I haven't actually covered working with data, so going through the use of this tool will just lead to confusion. This powerful and advanced tool should be used only by experienced SQL Server developers or database administrators. However, it is useful to know that a tool exists that can aid you in keeping your database tuned well.

Getting the indexes right is crucial to your SQL Server database running in an optimal fashion. Spend time thinking about the indexes, try to get them right, and then review them at regular intervals. Review clustering, uniqueness, and especially the columns contained within indexes so that you ensure the data are retrieved as quickly as possible. Finally, also ensure that the order of the columns within the index will reduce the number of reads that SQL Server has to do to find the data. An index where the columns are defined as `FirstName`, `LastName`, and `Department` might be better defined as `Department`, `FirstName`, and `LastName` if the greatest number of queries is based on finding someone within a specific department or listing employees of a department. The difference between these two indexes is that in the first, SQL Server would probably need to perform a table scan to find the relevant records. Compare that with the second example, where SQL Server would search the index until it found the right department and then just continue to return rows from the index until the department changed. As you can see, the second involves much less work.

Creating an Index

Now that you know what an index is and you have an understanding of the various types of indexes, let's proceed to create some in SQL Server. There are many different ways to create indexes within SQL Server, as you might expect. Those various methods are the focus of this section of the chapter, starting with how to use the table designer in SQL Server Management Studio.

The first index you will place into the database will be on the LastName and the ZipCode fields within the CustomerDetails.Customers table.

Creating an Index with the Table Designer

In this section, you will be creating an index using SQL Server Management Studio via the Design option against the CustomerDetails.Customers table. There is already an index on the CustomerId, which is a good column to have an index on once you have retrieved a customer, but is not a good index to find a customer by their name.

The index created will be used to find the record to update with a customer's information. An application will usually have to find a specific customer using a combination of name and address rather than a customer ID. It is possible to have multiple records with the same details. For example, you may have John J. Doe and his son, John J. Doe, who are both living at the same address; however, a search of LastName and ZipCode would return a very small set of records to display for the operator to choose from. Once you have sufficient details displayed on the screen of all the possible customers based on the search criteria, the user can ask a few more questions such as date of birth or when the account was opened. The user can then select the specific customer from the list. However, how will the computer program know which John J. Doe to use when it comes to completing an update?

Instead of looking for the customer by first name, last name, and address for each modification, the application will know the CustomerId and use this to find the record within SQL Server. When completing the initial search, the CustomerId will be returned as part of the set of values, so when the user selects the appropriate John J. Doe, the application will know the appropriate CustomerId. SQL Server will use this value to specifically locate the record to update. In the following exercise, we'll add an index to the CustomerDetails.Customers table to perform the search on LastName and ZipCode.

TRY IT OUT: CREATING AN INDEX GRAPHICALLY

1. Ensure that SQL Server Management Studio is running and that you have expanded the nodes in the tree view so that you can see the Tables node within the ApressFinancial database.

2. Find the CustomerDetails.Customers table where the index is to be added. Right-click and select Design. This will bring you into the Table Designer. Either right-click and from the pop-up menu select Manage Indexes and Keys or from the toolbar select the Manage Indexes and Keys icon (see Figure 6-1).

Figure 6-1. *The Manage Indexes and Keys button*

3. The Indexes/Keys dialog box will appear and look similar to Figure 6-2. Notice that there is a Primary Key already defined. You created this in Chapter 5.

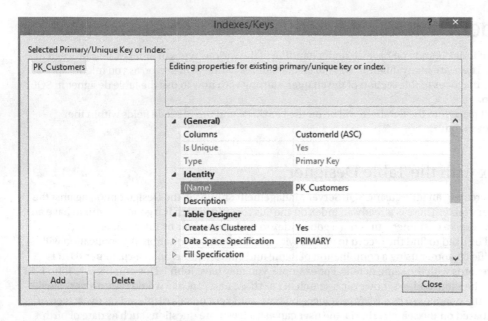

Figure 6-2. The Indexes/Keys dialog box

4. Click Add to create a new index or key. The first area to change is the name of the index. Notice that in the (Name) text box, SQL Server has created a possible value for you. The name is prefixed with IX_, which is a good naming system to use. It is also good to keep the name of the table and then a useful suffix, such as the name of the column or a shortened version of this. In this case, the index will be called IX_Customers_LastNameZip. It might also be good to place something in the description. However, index names should be self-explanatory, so there really shouldn't be a need for a description.

5. SQL Server has, in this instance, incorrectly selected CustomerId as the column that will make up the index. Click the CustomerId text box, which should then highlight an ellipsis, as you can see in Figure 6-3.

Figure 6-3. *Selecting the columns to index*

6. Clicking the ellipsis will display the Index Columns dialog box, where you can select the correct columns. Choose LastName and ZipCode, as shown in Figure 6-4, and then click OK.

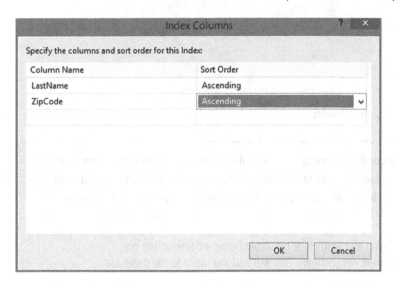

Figure 6-4. *Choosing the correct columns for this index*

7. The sort order of the index column is useful when creating an index on the columns that will be used in an ORDER BY clause of a query when there are multiple columns with differing sort orders. If the sort order of the columns within the index matches the sort order of those columns specified in the ORDER BY clause, SQL Server may be able to avoid performing an internal sort, resulting in improved query performance.

■ **Tip** If an index is only one column, SQL Server can read the index just as fast in a forward direction as it can in a backward direction.

8. Move to the Fill Specification area within the Indexes/Keys dialog box, and you will see two options: Fill Factor and Pad Index. For the moment, set Fill Factor to 90 and Pad Index to Yes, as shown in Figure 6-5. Both these options will be described in detail outside of the exercise in just a moment.

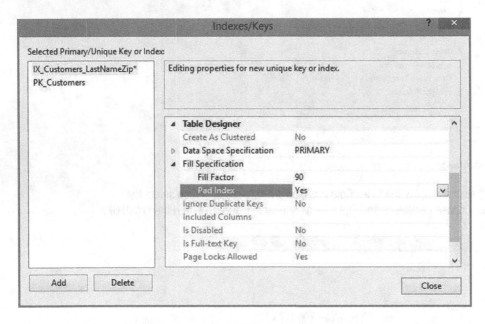

Figure 6-5. *Choosing the fill factor and padding for an index*

■ **Note** If this were a production environment or if you were creating a system in a development environment to move to a production environment, you would need to take a couple of other considerations into account. You would need to alter the Filegroup or Partition scheme so that indexes were placed on a different filegroup, as I discussed earlier.

9. Click Close on the Indexes/Keys dialog and then close the Table Designer, answering Yes when you are asked if you wish to save the changes. This will add the index to the database.

Building an index in Management Studio is a straightforward procedure, as you have just seen. Although this is the first index that you have created yourself, it took only a few moments, and there were just a couple of areas where you had to do any reasonable amount of decision making. I will cover those areas now.

Choosing the name of the index and the columns to include is easy and is not worth dwelling on. You should know which columns to include from the discussions at the start of the chapter, where I examined the basics of building indexes.

The first major decision you need to make is determining whether a column carries unique or almost unique values. The columns chosen for this index would not necessarily give a unique row, as there could be two people with the same last name in the same ZIP code as mentioned earlier; however, it would give a very small list from a potentially large table. Therefore this makes last name and ZIP code a good choice. The same could be said with last name or phone number.

Fill Factor, found in the Fill Specification area, tells SQL Server how much of a page should be filled with index data before SQL Server starts a new page of data to continue with the index. In an index such as this, some space should be set aside for new data to be inserted to avoid page splits when the page becomes full. I mentioned page splits in Chapter 5 when introducing partitioning. You will never get the perfect value as you never know at what point new customers will be joining, but you can make a good estimate. A page of data in SQL Server is 8KB. The size of the index in the example that has been built is a maximum of varchar(70) (LastName is varchar(50) and ZipCode is varchar(20)), so you have hit your first problem in reaching an accurate estimate as the data will be variable in length; one method is to take an average of the data in the table, either at creation if you know the data that will be used to populate the table, or make an estimate based on a good set of random data. For the moment, an assumption is made based on a set of random LastNames and ZipCodes you know will be entered that the average index width is 35 bytes. You then also have to add a further 2 bytes for each index value for SQL Server to use. As well as each index length, an index page has information at the start of each page for SQL Server's internal use of 96 bytes. A full index page would be (8192 − 96) / 37, which works out as just over 218 index rows. A fill factor of 60, or 60% full, would mean 130 index rows on each page at the time the index was created or rebuilt using the existing data. This would mean that between index rebuilds you are expecting 88 new rows of data to be inserted. That's quite a lot of data and therefore too low a value. A fill factor value of 90 might be a better setting, as this would allow 22 new index rows before SQL Server had to split the page (shuffle the books in the librarian scenario).

Pad Index is similar to Fill Factor but indicates whether the same amount of space is reserved in the index tree structure. To expand a little on this, indexes are held in a top-down tree structure, a bit like a family tree, where you have the head of the family at the top, then the next two people in the hierarchy, and so on. This was also mentioned in the partitioning section in Chapter 5. This is known as a B-Tree structure. At the top level in SQL Server are links to the next level in the tree that allow SQL Server to get to the index row quickly. Setting Pad Index to Yes will mean that each page on each level will also have a 90% fill rate before the pages are split.

Finally, an option that can be found at the bottom of the Indexes/Keys dialog is the Re-compute Statistics option, which determines whether SQL Server automatically recomputes the statistics on the index when data are modified. Recomputing statistics will increase the use of SQL Server resources as each modification updates the statistics, but having good statistics also means good performance. Depending on how often you rebuild your statistics, and whether your system is a high-insertion/low-retrieval system and also if the profile of you data alters such that the statistics would need re-computing, you could switch this option off. By default the option is set to recompute statistics.

Indexes and Statistics

When retrieving data, SQL Server obviously has to make some decisions as to the best way to get to that data and return it to the query requesting it. Even if an index has been created on a set of columns, SQL Server may determine that it is better and faster to use another method to retrieve the data—through a table scan, perhaps. Or maybe there are a couple of indexes that could be chosen to retrieve the same data. No matter what the scenario, SQL Server has to have some basis of information on which to make sensible and accurate choices. This is where statistics come in.

SQL Server keeps statistics on each column contained within an index if you have Auto Create Statistics set to True. This is set at the database level. These statistics are updated over a period of time and over a number of inserts or modifications. The specifics of how all of this works in the background and how SQL Server keeps the statistics up to date are an advanced topic. What you need to know is that if you alter or build an index on a table that has data in it, and you don't let SQL Server update the statistics on the table, then SQL Server could be using inaccurate information when it is trying to decide how to retrieve the data. It could even mean that the index change you thought would improve performance has in fact made the performance much slower.

That said, it is not always prudent to let SQL Server recompute statistics automatically. SQL Server will do the updates when it feels they are required. This may happen at a busy time of processing; you have no control over when it will happen. However, if SQL Server does update the statistics, the query that caused the update to start will not be impacted, as the statistics will be updated asynchronously if the AUTO_UPDATE_STATISTICS_ASYNC option is switched on.

It may be more efficient to manually update the statistics via a scheduled job and keep all statistics building off. This is what you quite often see within production environments that have a number of inserts and modifications to the data.

The main point about SQL Server and statistics is that statistics are what SQL Server uses as its method of cost-based calculations for finding the right query plan. If the statistics are out of date or if SQL Server feels the statistics may be out of date, it may ignore them. Therefore, whether you allow statistics to be updated automatically by SQL Server or you wish to update the statistics manually, they have to be recalculated regularly so that they are not seen as stale.

The CREATE INDEX Syntax

Creating an index using T-SQL is a lot easier than creating a table. In this section, we will look only at indexes on tables, although there is an object within SQL Server called a *view* that can also be indexed.

The full syntax for creating an index is not listed here, although you can find it within "SQL Server Books Online" once you progress in your SQL Server knowledge. A reduced version will be sufficient while you are learning SQL Server. Most of your indexes will use the following version:

```
CREATE [UNIQUE] [CLUSTERED|NONCLUSTERED]
INDEX index_name
ON table (column [ASC|DESC] [ ,...n ] )
[WITH {IGNORE_DUP_KEY|DROP_EXISTING|SORT_IN_TEMPDB}]
[ON filegroup ]
```

Let's go through each point so that the options in this cut-down version are clear:

- CREATE: Required; this keyword informs SQL Server that you will be building a new object.

- UNIQUE: Optional; if used, this option will inform SQL Server that the columns listed in the index will bring back a single unique row. This is enforced by SQL Server when attempting to insert a duplicate row, as an error message will be returned.

- CLUSTERED *or* NONCLUSTERED: Optional; if neither CLUSTERED nor NONCLUSTERED is explicitly listed, the index will be created as NONCLUSTERED.

- INDEX: Required; this informs SQL Server that the new object will be an index.

- index_name: Required; this is the name of the index being built. This name must be unique for the table, and it is advisable to keep this name unique for the database, using the naming method of IX_table_column discussed earlier.

- ON table: Required; this is the name of the table with which the index is associated. Only one table can be named.

- `column`: Required; this is the name of the column(s) in the table that we wish to include in the index. This is a comma-separated list.

- `ASC`: Optional (default); if neither ASC nor DESC is mentioned, then ASC is assumed. ASC informs SQL Server that it should store the column named in ascending sequence.

- `DESC`: Optional; this informs SQL Server that the column is to be stored in descending order.

- `WITH`: Optional; it is, however, required if any of the following options have to be used:

 - `IGNORE_DUP_KEY`: This option is available only when the index is defined as UNIQUE. If this option has not been used earlier, then it is not available to you. I'll explain this further in a moment.

 - `DROP_EXISTING`: This option is used if there is an existing index of the same name within the database. It will then drop the index before re-creating it. This is useful for performance if you are not actually changing any columns within the index. More on this in a moment.

 - `SORT_IN_TEMPDB`: When building an index where there is already data within the table, it may be advisable, if the table is a large table, to get the data sorted for the index within the temporary database, `tempdb`, as mentioned in Chapter 3. Use this option if you have a large table, or if `tempdb` is on a different hard disk from your database. This option may speed up the building of the index, as SQL Server can simultaneously read from the disk device where the table is located and write to the disk device where `tempdb` is located.

- `ON`: Optional; this option is, however, required if you are going to specify a filegroup. It is not required if you wish the index to be built on the PRIMARY filegroup.

- `filegroup`: This is the name of the filegroup on which the index should be stored. At the moment, there is only one filegroup set up: `PRIMARY`. `PRIMARY` is a reserved word and is required to be surrounded by square brackets, [], if used.

Two options need further clarification: `IGNORE_DUP_KEY` and `DROP_EXISTING`. We'll look at both in the sections that follow.

IGNORE_DUP_KEY

If you have an index defined as `UNIQUE`, then no matter how hard you try, you cannot add a new row whose values in the index columns match the values of any current row. However, there are two actions that you can perform, depending on this setting within an index.

When performing multirow inserts, if the `IGNORE_DUP_KEY` option is specified, then no error will be generated within SQL Server if some of the rows being inserted violate the unique index. Only a warning message will be issued. The rows that violated the unique index are not inserted, although all other rows are inserted successfully.

■ **Caution** The system variable called `@@ERROR` can be tested after every SQL Server action to see if there has been an error in any item of work or through another error-handling command called `Try/Catch`. If there has been an error, some sort of error handling within the batch will usually be performed. If you have `IGNORE_DUP_KEY`, then no error will be produced when there is an attempt to insert a duplicate row, and the batch will run as if everything had been inserted. So, be warned: it may look like everything has worked, but in fact some rows were not inserted! You will see `@@ERROR` and `Try/Catch` used in Chapter 17.

DROP_EXISTING

When data are being inserted and modified, there will be times when an index bloats to a less than ideal state. Just as an Access database may need to be compacted, indexes within SQL Server also need to be compacted sometimes. Compacting the index will speed up performance and reclaim disk space by defragmentating the index. To compact an index, you re-create the index without actually modifying the columns or, in fact, starting from scratch and having to rebuild the whole index and visit every row within the table.

The DROP_EXISTING clause provides enhanced performance when rebuilding a clustered index compared to a DROP INDEX command followed by a CREATE INDEX command. Nonclustered indexes will be rebuilt every time the clustered index for a table is rebuilt if the columns are included in the clustered index. The name of the clustered index must also remain the same, as must the sort order and the partition the index is built on. Finally, the uniqueness attribute must not change. So, if you drop a clustered index and then re-create it, the existing nonclustered indexes will be rebuilt twice (if they are to be rebuilt): once from the drop and once from the creation. With the DROP_EXISTING clause, an index would be built only once. Keep this in mind as it is crucial if you are working in a time-critical batch window. With the size of table and indexes created, it may be possible to re-create a clustered index only on a weekend.

DROP_EXISTING can allow an existing index to be rebuilt by explicitly dropping and re-creating the index. This is particularly useful for rebuilding primary key indexes. As other tables may reference a primary key, it may be necessary to drop all foreign keys in these other tables prior to dropping the primary key. By specifying the DROP_EXISTING clause, SQL Server will rebuild the index without affecting the primary key constraint.

Creating an Index in Query Editor

In the following exercise, you will create two indexes and a primary key within a Query Editor pane. This will allow you in the next section to build a foreign key between the two tables, TransactionDetails.Transactions and TransactionDetails.TransactionTypes. The code will also demonstrate how to build T-SQL defining the options for the index presented during the CREATE INDEX syntax discussion earlier.

TRY IT OUT: CREATING AN INDEX WITH QUERY EDITOR

1. Enter the following code into an empty pane of Query Editor. The first index you will be creating in this section is a uniquely clustered index on the TransactionDetails.TransactionTypes table.

```
USE ApressFinancial
GO
CREATE UNIQUE CLUSTERED INDEX IX_TransactionTypes
ON TransactionDetails.TransactionTypes
(
    TransactionTypeId ASC )
WITH (STATISTICS_NORECOMPUTE = ON, SORT_IN_TEMPDB = ON,
 DROP_EXISTING = OFF, IGNORE_DUP_KEY = OFF, ONLINE = ON,
 ALLOW_ROW_LOCKS  = ON, ALLOW_PAGE_LOCKS  = ON)
ON [PRIMARY]
GO
```

2. The second index you'll create is a nonclustered index on the `TransactionDetails.`
 `Transactions` table based on the `TransactionType` column. You won't make this index
 clustered, as it would be better to consider either `CustomerId` or `DateEntered` as clustered
 columns.

```
CREATE NONCLUSTERED INDEX IX_Transactions_TType
ON TransactionDetails.Transactions
(
    TransactionType ASC)
WITH (STATISTICS_NORECOMPUTE = OFF, SORT_IN_TEMPDB = ON,
DROP_EXISTING = OFF, IGNORE_DUP_KEY = OFF, ONLINE = ON,
ALLOW_ROW_LOCKS = ON, ALLOW_PAGE_LOCKS = ON)
ON [PRIMARY]
GO
```

3. The final action is to add a primary key to the `TransactionDetails.TransactionTypes`
 table. You do this through an `ALTER TABLE` statement:

```
ALTER TABLE TransactionDetails.TransactionTypes
ADD CONSTRAINT
    PK_TransactionTypes PRIMARY KEY NONCLUSTERED
    (
    TransactionTypeId
    )
WITH (STATISTICS_NORECOMPUTE = OFF, IGNORE_DUP_KEY = OFF,
ALLOW_ROW_LOCKS = ON, ALLOW_PAGE_LOCKS = ON)
ON [PRIMARY]
GO
```

4. You can now execute the preceding code by pressing F5, Ctrl+E or clicking the Execute
 toolbar button. You should then see the following success message:

```
The command(s) completed successfully.
```

As noted, two different indexes are created in this example. The first one is a unique clustered index, based on
the identity column of the `TransactionDetails.TransactionTypes` table. The second index's column was
chosen because you will be linking to this table using the `TransactionType` column. Rarely, if ever, will you link
on any other column within this table, so the two indexes would be sufficient. The overhead of the second index
is microscopic, though, due to the few records you will be entering, and it is therefore not really a concern, but it
does need to exist for the foreign key that you will be building shortly. It also allows you to see where to place the
keyword within the example.

The second index, built on the `TransactionDetails.Transactions` table, cannot be a unique index; there will
be multiple entries of the same value because there are multiple transactions for the same type. However, it is
still possible to make this index clustered. Changing the transaction type on a transaction will be rare, or, if you
had a full audit trail built within your system, you may "ban" such an action. The only way to change a transaction
type around this ban would be to cancel the entry, record the cancel action, and create a new entry. However, a
clustered index on transaction types will not give us much of a gain in performance, as there will be few queries
of data based on transaction type alone. As mentioned earlier, there are better choices for clustering. It should

be noted that this second index is probably a poor choice of index for finding specific single rows and is unlikely to be used as an index. It exists for creation of a foreign key. Uniqueness, known as cardinality, will be low as there will be a large number of rows with the same value. However, as an index, it may be useful for queries that request data as a range where you want transactions of all the same transaction type.

What is interesting about this example is that two indexes are created in one execution—albeit in two batch transactions—whereas in the previous examples, only one index was created at a time. Notice the keyword GO between the two CREATE statements creating the index; each index creation has to be completed on its own, without any other SQL statements included. If you need to create more than one index, but you would prefer to build them at the same time, then this may be the solution you need. (Please see Chapter 10 for details on transactions.)

An area I have not yet covered is what happens if you try to create an index twice using the same index name. The preceding indexes have already been created, but if you run the query again, SQL Server will produce error messages informing you that the index already exists. You should see messages like the following:

```
Msg 1913, Level 16, State 1, Line 1
The operation failed because an index or statistics with name
'IX_TransactionTypes'
already exists on table 'TransactionDetails.TransactionTypes'.
Msg 1913, Level 16, State 1, Line 1
The operation failed because an index or statistics with name
'IX_Transactions_TType' already exists on table
'TransactionDetails.Transactions'.
Msg 1779, Level 16, State 0, Line 1
Table 'TransactionDetails.TransactionTypes' already has a primary key
defined on it.
Msg 1750, Level 16, State 0, Line 1
Could not create constraint. See previous errors.
```

Even if you alter the contents of the index and include different columns but still use the same name, it is not possible to create another index with the same name as an existing one.

In the last part of the example, you altered the table so that you could add a primary key. There are different types of constraints that can be defined for a table: column constraints are used for default values, as you saw in the previous chapter, but constraints are also used for primary and foreign keys.

Once again, a couple of new areas were covered in this section, but you now have the information you need to be able to create the most common indexes. Indexes need a lot less coding than tables and can be created quickly and easily. However, if you are adding a new index to an existing table that has a substantial amount of information, adding this new index could take a few minutes to complete, depending on the scenario. It is possible to add indexes while the system is being used and the table or clustered indexes are being updated. This is available only in SQL Server Enterprise Edition, by specifying the index action with the REBUILD WITH (ONLINE = ON) option. Take care when using this option. If anybody tries to access the relevant table while the index is being built, SQL Server will not recognize the index until it has been built, and when working out the best way to access the data, it will ignore this index.

If you are creating the index after removing it for rebuilding statistics, for example, problems may arise if you don't use the ONLINE = ON option. With this option ON, SQL Server will allow access to the table to add or modify data. However, if it is set to OFF, then all actions against the table will have to wait until the index is re-created. This will mean that any part of your system that requires access to the table that the index is being built on will pause while the index is being generated. Therefore, if you are rebuilding an index with the database available, you have to decide which of the two problems that may arise is acceptable.

Dropping an Index

There will be times when an index is redundant and should be removed (that is, dropped) from a table. Dropping an index is simply a case of executing the DROP INDEX statement, followed by the table name and the index name. Keep in mind that for every index that exists, processing time is required to keep that index up-to-date for every data modification. Therefore, when you create a new index that uses the same columns as an existing index, you should drop the old one; or when an index is no longer providing speedy data access and is therefore being ignored by SQL Server, it should be dropped.

■ **Note** If the index is used by a primary key or unique constraint, you cannot drop it directly. In this case, you must use the DROP CONSTRAINT command. The removal of this constraint will also remove the index from the table.

```
┌──────────────────────────────────────────────────────────────────┐
│         TRY IT OUT: DROPPING AN INDEX IN QUERY EDITOR             │
└──────────────────────────────────────────────────────────────────┘
```

1. If you want to drop the clustered index created in the last section, all you need to do is execute the following code. This will remove the index from SQL Server and also remove any statistics associated with it.

```
USE ApressFinancial
GO
DROP INDEX IX_TransactionTypes ON TransactionDetails.TransactionTypes
```

2. After execution, you should see that everything executed correctly:

```
Command(s) completed successfully.
```

3. Don't forget to re-create the index by running the following code. This code is the same as in step 1 of the last "Try It Out" exercise. If you still have that Query Editor open, highlight just that part of the query code and execute it.

```
USE ApressFinancial
GO
CREATE UNIQUE CLUSTERED INDEX IX_TransactionTypes
ON TransactionDetails.TransactionTypes
(
    TransactionTypeId ASC )
WITH (STATISTICS_NORECOMPUTE = ON, SORT_IN_TEMPDB = ON,
 DROP_EXISTING = OFF, IGNORE_DUP_KEY = OFF, ONLINE = ON,
 ALLOW_ROW_LOCKS  = ON, ALLOW_PAGE_LOCKS  = ON)
ON [PRIMARY]
GO
```

In the next section, we'll examine what's needed to alter an index.

Altering an Index

Unlike a table, it is not possible to use an ALTER command to change the columns contained in an index. To do this, you first have to drop the index and then re-create it. The DROP command will physically remove the index from the table; therefore, you should ensure that you know what the contents of the index are before you drop the index if you want to re-create a similar index.

■ **Tip** One method that should allow you to re-create the index is storing all your database code in a source control system such as Visual SourceSafe.

Re-creating an index can take a large amount of time, depending on the index, the columns, and the volume of data. It could take hours, so you have to take this into account and definitely complete a "dry run" on a development instance of an index build where there are hundreds of thousands or millions of rows involved. Don't be caught out with unexpected rebuild times in a production environment.

■ **Note** In Management Studio, you can add and remove columns from an index's definition without dropping and re-creating the index, as this is all done for you behind the scenes, although the actions will be the same.

This next exercise demonstrates the steps you need to take to alter an index.

TRY IT OUT: ALTERING AN INDEX IN QUERY EDITOR

1. First, you want to create an index to retrieve the transactions for a customer at a set point in time or for a range in time. The following index will do just that, as you are querying the data using the customer ID and the date or date range you want the transactions for. Since this could become a large table, notice that the index is built using tempdb, but also that the code locks the table while the index is being built, as this is simulating a build on the weekend during scheduled downtime. If you were doing the alter when the bank was open, you would perform this as an online alteration. Execute this code to create the index, which you will then correct in step 2:

```
USE ApressFinancial
GO
CREATE UNIQUE CLUSTERED INDEX IX_CustTransDate
ON TransactionDetails.Transactions
(
    CustomerId ASC,
    DateEntered ASC
) WITH (STATISTICS_NORECOMPUTE = OFF, SORT_IN_TEMPDB = ON,
DROP_EXISTING = OFF, IGNORE_DUP_KEY = OFF, ONLINE = OFF,
ALLOW_ROW_LOCKS  = ON, ALLOW_PAGE_LOCKS  = OFF)
ON [PRIMARY]GO
```

2. However, it would be better to have the DateEntered descending, so that the latest transactions are at the top:

```
CREATE UNIQUE CLUSTERED INDEX IX_CustTransDate
ON TransactionDetails.Transactions
(
    CustomerId ASC,
    DateEntered DESC
) WITH (STATISTICS_NORECOMPUTE = OFF, SORT_IN_TEMPDB = ON,
DROP_EXISTING = ON, IGNORE_DUP_KEY = OFF, ONLINE = OFF,
ALLOW_ROW_LOCKS  = ON, ALLOW_PAGE_LOCKS  = ON)
ON [PRIMARY]
```

3. Now execute the code using your chosen method, and you should see the following results. The index created in the first step is dropped, and then the new index is created:

```
The command(s) completed successfully.
```

By using the optional DROP_EXISTING clause of the CREATE INDEX command in the second step, this will drop the existing index and re-create it.

■ **Caution** Take care when building indexes. It is possible to use the same columns in the same order, thus creating the same index twice, but under two different index names. This is a waste of time and will place unnecessary overhead on SQL Server. It is unusual, but I have seen it happen. However, when including key column(s) from a clustered index in a nonclustered index, because the row pointer is actually the clustered index key, SQL is smart enough not to store the underlying information twice—once in the clustered index and once in the nonclustered index Instead, it will be the clustered index pointer instead of the data that is stored in the nonclustered index, and you can explicitly define the order of the clustered index keys or key columns as they are used in the nonclustered index.

There are more indexes to build and this index to improve further, which you will see next, but you will take a look at these later.

Included Columns

Indexes are very useful database objects for finding data. With the right columns you can find the information quickly, but there will be many times that you will require further information from the table. In the first example, which created an index on the CustomerDetails.Customers table with LastName and ZipCode, this would allow you to find customers rapidly. But that is all it does, although that is pretty useful. If you needed to also retrieve the cleared balance attached to the customer (for example, this is what most people are contacting their account for), it would be useful to also retrieve that column of information at the same time. The ClearedBalance column is not a logical column for the index; you are unlikely to look for a a customer for a specific amount. In this situation, SQL Server has functionality called included columns that allow you to add extra columns to the end of an index. A word of caution though—don't add every column, only add low-maintenance columns (columns with changes in values mean that SQL Server has to update the index as well as the table) and only add columns that are logical to be added to reduce

any table access. Included columns are a fine balancing act and although it is not rare to have an index with included columns, it certainly is not the norm. Keep in mind that any additional column will have a knock-on effect on index performance and space used. Keep in mind that included columns are not part of the index and, therefore, will not count toward the 16-column restriction that exists for indexes. Finally, included columns only exist for nonclustered indexes as a clustered index is the table and, therefore, having included columns doesn't make sense.

In the following example, the index IX_Customers_LastNameZip will be altered to add the ClearedBalance to the index.

TRY IT OUT: ALTERING AN INDEX TO HAVE INCLUDED COLUMNS

1. In a Query Editor window, enter the following T-SQL code. This code will drop the existing index and re-create the IX_Customers_LastNameZip with the included column of ClearedBalance.

```
DROP INDEX IX_Customers_LastNameZip ON CustomerDetails.Customers
GO
CREATE NONCLUSTERED INDEX IX_Customers_LastNameZip
ON CustomerDetails.Customers
(
        LastName ASC,
        ZipCode ASC
)
INCLUDE (ClearedBalance)
WITH (PAD_INDEX = ON, STATISTICS_NORECOMPUTE = OFF,
SORT_IN_TEMPDB = OFF, DROP_EXISTING = OFF, ONLINE = OFF,
ALLOW_ROW_LOCKS = ON, ALLOW_PAGE_LOCKS = ON,
FILLFACTOR = 90)
GO
```

2. Once entered, execute the code (F5, CTRL+E or press the Green arrow in the tool bar).

It is not possible to alter an index to add an included column; the index has to be dropped and re-created.

When an Index Does Not Exist

As the amount of data in your database expands, expansion may occur in areas that are unexpected. The application originally built with your database could have been extended, so your original database design and index decisions may not still be 100% correct.

When SQL Server accesses data, it uses its query optimizer to generate what is termed a *query plan*. A query plan is a plan of actions that SQL Server uses to perform the query you have built against the data. The query plan could consist of several steps that SQL Server performs to execute your query and produce the results you require. The query plan could show that a table scan is being performed, which is an action where the data in the table is read from start to finish. There could also be a step that performs an intermediate sort. SQL Server also attempts to identify missing indexes and record this within the system.

■ **Note** These can be seen by accessing a view of the system table using a Dynamic Management View (DMV). DMV's are special views in to system-held information.

Diagramming the Database

Now that the database has been built, the tables have been created, a number of the indexes have been inserted, and relationships link some of the tables, it's time to start documenting. To help with this, SQL Server offers you Database Diagram Designer, which is the topic of this section. This is an excellent tool as it can give developers a great deal of information about a database and a good start to documentation with little effort (and documentation is always the last piece of work to be completed). It can also help build relationships between tables and, therefore, can be more than just a simple diagramming tool.

One of the most tedious aspects of creating documentation is often the task of documenting tables and showing how they relate to one another in a diagram. Done manually, such work is tedious indeed, and the results are difficult to keep up-to-date. A database diagram tool, however, can do the work very quickly and simply, with one caveat: if more than one person is using the database diagram tool on the same database and there are two sets of changes to be applied to the same table, such as rearranging tables or something more substantial such as applying a relationship, the person who saves his or her changes last will be the person who creates the final table layout. In other words, the people who save before the last person will lose their changes. Therefore, I advise that you develop a database solution using the diagramming tool only on single-developer applications. At all other times, use it as a tool for understanding and documenting the database.

As you developed tables within your database, hopefully you will have commented the columns and tables as you go along to say what each column and table is. This is a major part of documentation anyway, although a database-naming convention should make your solution self-documenting to an extent. Providing that you comment columns and tables at the start, it will be less of a chore to add in further comments when you add new columns. If you do have comments on each of your columns within a table, this will help overall with the documentation shown within the diagram.

That said, SQL Server's database diagram feature is more than just a documentation aid. This tool provides developers with the ability to build and maintain database solutions. It is perhaps not always the quickest method of building a solution, and it is not the most flexible or best method, but it is one that allows the entire solution to be completed in one place. Alternatively, you can use it to build up sections of a database into separate diagrams, breaking the whole solution into more manageable parts, rather than switching between nodes in Management Studio. You will see this later in this section.

Database Diagramming Basics

In the book so far, with the creation of databases, tables, indexes, and relationships, as much documentation as SQL Server will allow should have so far been maintained, although it should be noted that databases should be self-documenting, just as your source code for your application should be self-documenting. However, there is no documentation demonstrating how the tables relate to one another within the database. This is where the database diagram comes to the forefront.

A database diagram is a useful and easy tool to build simple but effective documentation on these aspects. You build the diagram yourself, and you control what you want to see within the diagram. When you get to a large database solution, you may want diagrams for sections of the database that deal with specific aspects of the system, or perhaps you want to build a diagram showing information about process flows. Although there are other external tools to do this, none is built into SQL Server that can allow diagrams to be kept instantly up-to-date.

A diagram will show only tables, columns within those tables, and the relationships between tables in a bare form. You will also see a yellow "key," which denotes a primary key on the table where one has been defined, but that is all the information displayed. It is possible to define the information that is to be displayed about the columns in the table, whether it is just the column name or more in-depth information, such as a column's data type and length, comments, and so on. However, to display more than just the bare essentials, a little bit of work is required.

Although the diagram shows the physical and logical attributes of the database that is being built or has been built, it also allows developers and administrators to see exactly what is included with the database at a glance and how the database fits together.

In the next section, you will delve a bit deeper into what the SQL Server database diagram is all about.

The SQL Server Database Diagram Designer

Management Studio's database diagram tool aids in the building of diagrams that detail aspects of the database that a developer wishes to see. Although it is a simple and straightforward tool and it's not as powerful as some other tools on the market for building database diagrams, it is suitably sufficient for SQL Server.

The biggest restriction of any diagram-based database tool comes down to the amount of screen space available to view the diagram. As soon as your database solution consists of more than a handful of tables, you will find yourself scrolling around the diagram, trying to find the table you are looking for or reducing the zoom to a percentage that may be too small to read well.

Second, you cannot add stored procedures, schemas, users, views, or any object that is not a table. Other products allow you to include these objects, or they may even build some of them for you.

Finally, for the moment, when altering any of the information you can change within this tool, you are usually using the same dialogs and screens as you would in Management Studio.

As you will see as you go through the chapter, the database diagram tool is quite powerful in what it can achieve, but there are some areas of concern that you have to be aware of when working with diagrams. Keep in mind that the database diagram tool is holding all the changes in memory until you actually save the diagram.

For example, if you have a database diagram open and a table within that diagram is deleted outside of the diagram, perhaps in Query Editor or Management Studio by yourself or another valid user ID, then one of two things can happen. First, if you have unsaved changes to the deleted table, saving your diagram will re-create the table, but don't forget that through the earlier deletion, all the data will be removed. If, however, you have no changes pending to that table, then the table will not be re-created. When you come to reopen the diagram, the table will have been removed.

With several developers working on the database at once, any changes made from the diagramming tool of your Management Studio will not be reflected in any other developer's diagram until his changes are saved and his diagrams are refreshed. If you have multiple diagrams open and you alter a table and insert or remove a column, then this will reflect immediately in all the open diagrams within your own Management Studio only. Don't forget this is an in-memory process, so this process can't reflect on anyone else's diagrams until the changes are saved and the diagrams are refreshed.

Also, if you remove an object in your diagram, when you then save the diagram, the object will be removed and any changes completed by others will be lost. Effectively, the last person who closes his or her diagram wins!

To summarize, if you use the database diagram tool, use it with care and use it only to diagram. Because the diagram is held in in-memory, you could inadvertently cause problems.

The Default Database Diagram

Although it's not mandatory, I do feel every SQL Server database solution should have a default database diagram built into it so that any developer—new or experienced—can instantly see how the database being inspected fits together.

A default database diagram should include every table and every relationship that are held for that database. Unlike other diagrams that may take a more sectionalized view of things, the default database diagram should be all-encompassing.

As mentioned earlier, it is imperative that you keep this diagram up-to-date. You will notice this statement repeated a few times in this chapter. Don't use the default diagram as the source of development for your database solution. The default diagram includes all the tables, which means that if you're using the database diagram tool for development, you are potentially logically locking out all other users from touching any other table as part of their development, in case their changes are lost. Update the diagram with tables and relationships only once they have been inserted in the database. We'll look at this in more detail later when we discuss the dangers of using the database diagram tool as a source of development.

Now that you know what diagrams are and what the tool is, it's time to create the first diagram for this database.

TRY IT OUT: CREATING A DATABASE DIAGRAM

1. To create a diagram, the database needs to be owned by the sa account. In versions prior to SQL Server 2014, a login with the sysadmin server role was sufficient. To change the owner from your account for the ApressFinancial database, enter the following code in to a Query Editor and execute:

 ALTER AUTHORIZATION ON DATABASE::ApressFinancial TO "sa"

2. Move to the Object Explorer and expand the ApressFinancial database Database Diagrams node. Select the Database Diagrams node and then right-click. Choose New Database Diagram (see Figure 6-6).

Figure 6-6. *Creating a new database diagram*

3. If this is the first diagram you are creating for the database, you'll need to install support objects. Without them, you cannot create the diagram, so click Yes at the next dialog prompt (see Figure 6-7).

Figure 6-7. *Installing diagramming support*

■ **Note** You can also install diagramming support from the menu.

4. The first screen you'll see when creating the diagram is the Add Table dialog (see Figure 6-8). Select all of the tables listed, as you want to use all the tables in your diagram, and then click Add. This will "empty" the screen. Click Close.

Figure 6-8. *Selecting tables*

5. After a few moments, you will be returned to Management Studio, but with the database diagram now built. The diagram will not show all the tables at this point and will be very large. You can reduce the size through the Size combo box in the diagramming toolbar, as shown in Figure 6-9. Select the size To Fit.

Figure 6-9. *The Size combo box*

6. You'll then see a diagram similar to that shown in Figure 6-10. (Don't be surprised if the layout is different, though.)

Figure 6-10. *Tables with relationships built so far*

That's all there is to building a basic diagram.

The Database Diagram Toolbar

Let's next take a look at the toolbar and how each of the buttons works within the diagram. The whole toolbar is shown in Figure 6-11, and each button is described in Table 6-1.

Figure 6-11. *Database diagram toolbar*

Table 6-1. *Toolbar Buttons and Descriptions*

Toolbar Button	Description
	This button will create a new table within the database designer, which is a similar process to that shown in Chapter 5. The difference is that you need to use the Properties window for each column rather than have the properties at the bottom of the table designer.
	When building the diagram, you selected every table. If you hadn't done so and you wanted to add a table, this button displays the Add Table dialog shown earlier to add in any missing tables.
	This button adds tables related to the selected table into the designer. Any table that has a relationship to the table selected, and then any tables related to those tables, and so on will be added.
	This button deletes the highlighted table from the database.
	This button removes the highlighted table from the designer only.
	Any changes made to the database within the designer can be saved as a script rather than applied immediately.
	If you wish to set a column to be the primary key, select the relevant column within a table and click this button.
a\|b	This button is used to create a place within the diagram to put ad hoc text.
Standard Column Names Keys Name Only Custom Modify Custom ...	Each table displayed is set to a standard layout. It is possible to change this to a different predefined layout or to create your own custom view. You can use this to alter the diagram to display enough information to modify the underlying tables. You will see this in a few moments.
	Relationships that exist between tables will, by default, show as a line. However, it is possible to show the name of the relationship as a label. This button toggles the relationship text to show or be hidden.
	Diagrams are ideal methods of documenting the database. Diagrams can be printed for meetings, discussions about future development, and so on. This button shows the page breaks.
	Page breaks in diagrams remain as they were first set up until they are recalculated. You are able to view the page breaks and arrange your tables accordingly. This button will recalculate the page breaks based on the new layout.

(*continued*)

Table 6-1. (*continued*)

Toolbar Button	Description
	Tables can be expanded or shrunk singly and manually, but when you select one or more tables using the Ctrl button, clicking the relevant tables and then clicking this button will resize the tables to a uniform size.
	This will rearrange the tables that have been selected only where SQL Server will make the arrangement choices.
	SQL Server will do its best to get the best layout for all the tables and relationships in the diagram when you click this button.
50%	This is the zoom option on the diagram and will allow you to zoom in or out to see less or more of the diagram.
	This button will display the relationships dialog, as you saw in Chapter 5.
	This button manages indexes and keys, as you saw in Chapter 5.
	This button will display the dialog that would allow you to manage full-text indexes. This was mentioned in Chapter 5.
	If you wanted XML indexes for the XML data, then you would click this button to display the XML indexes dialog.
	To manage any constraints as covered in Chapter 5, clicking this button will display the Manage Constraints dialog.
	This button will display the spatial indexes dialog for indexes pertaining to geographical spatial data.

Modifying Your Database Using Database Diagram Designer

Although Database Diagram Designer will be used mainly for documentation, it can also be used to perform a few database functions, including adding, altering, and removing columns, setting primary keys, and creating a relationship between two tables. There are other tools that can perform these functions as well as many more. For example, one of the market leaders in database design tools is a product called SQL Power Architect. SQL Power Architect is a powerful database utility that not only builds diagrams of databases, but also provides data dictionary language output, which can be used to build database solutions. Through links such as OLE DB data providers, these tools can interact directly with databases and so they can be used as a front end for creating databases. They can also, at the same time, keep the created source in alignment and under control from a change control perspective, not only ensuring that the code exists within the database, but also issuing a command to create a new database quickly, if necessary. An example of where this might be useful is when you're creating a new test database.

From my perspective, this is not an ideal scenario as your code should be backed up, held within Visual SourceSafe, and deployment strategies should be created. In some projects, I have used a tool from Red Gate called SQL Compare to deploy from development to production. It allows you to compare two databases and detail the changes between them, and you can then decide and detail what has to be deployed.

Summary

We've covered yet another major building block in creating a SQL Server solution. The last few chapters have shown you how to store data, and in this chapter, you've learned about indexes and how to use them to quickly and efficiently retrieve the data stored in the table.

There are many types of indexes, and choosing the right one at the right time to complete the right job is quite an art. This chapter has taken you through the steps to decide which columns will make an efficient index, and then build those columns in the right type of index to make the most of the information.

This chapter also covered database diagramming. Database diagrams should initially be thought of as a form of documentation. Keep in mind, though, that the database diagram tool may expand in future versions of SQL Server to become much more sophisticated and powerful than it is now—although even now it is quite a powerful utility.

■ **Tip** Remember, those who save last save the changes.

Don't be caught off guard by the fact that changes in the diagram are not applied until the diagram is saved, and that your changes could overwrite another's changes. If you're using the database diagram tool for development in any sort of multiuser environment, take the greatest of care when completing updates (in fact, try to avoid them altogether). Unless you split your database solution into multiple diagrams, with any table being found in at most one diagram, don't use the database designer as a development tool.

CHAPTER 7

■ ■ ■

In-Memory Tables

Chapter 5 introduced you to disk-based tables and how they are defined within a database. As I have mentioned in previous chapters, SQL Server tries to be as fast as possible in completing the given unit of work. The slowest component of completing the unit of work will be accessing data in tables on a disk, physical I/O. To try to reduce physical I/O and instead use logical I/O, SQL Server will try to hold data in memory based on its own calculations on what data should be held and how recently the data was last accessed. It would be better for you to be able to define to SQL Server which tables are so important that the data they hold should be permanently held in memory. This is where in-memory tables come in to their own. Up to and including SQL Server 2012, the only way to achieve holding data permanently within memory was to pin a table to being held in memory. SQL Server used disk-based optimizations as the table was on disk, but from SQL Server 2014 it is possible to define a table to permanently reside in-memory, and it now also has its own database optimized engine to fully utilize in-memory held data.

In-memory tables are restricted on the SQL Server versions that can implement them to 64 bit Enterprise or Developer Editions. There are also some requirements to be met on the server for instruction sets and, of course, the amount of memory required can be larger than disk-based for the same data so that the data can be held. You will find out why this might within the chapter through row versions.

In this chapter, you will see the following:

- How SQL Server prepares your T-SQL, builds a plan and determines the costs

- What an in-memory table is

- The differences with disk-based tables

- Creating in-memory tables

- Migration of a disk-based table to in-memory

Cost-Based Processing

Every action that is performed by SQL Server has a logical cost. Accessing data to read, processing that data such as sorting the data, fetching further data, and writing data to tables uses resources either on the server such as its memory and processor or on disks to either read or write information. There are also costs in preparing your code that works with the data as well as the execution of the code. In Figure 7-1 you will see a query plan for a simple query, which is coded just above the figure. A query plan is how SQL Server takes the T-SQL you write and builds a set of steps on actions it has to perform to achieve the results you require in the most cost effective way.

```
SELECT FirstName As 'First Name',LastName AS 'Surname',
ClearedBalance Balance, p.LastCollected, fp.ProductName
FROM CustomerDetails.Customers c
join CustomerDetails.CustomerProducts p
    ON p.CustomerId = c.CustomerId
left outer join CustomerDetails.FinancialProducts fp
    ON fp.ProductId = p.FinancialProductId
```

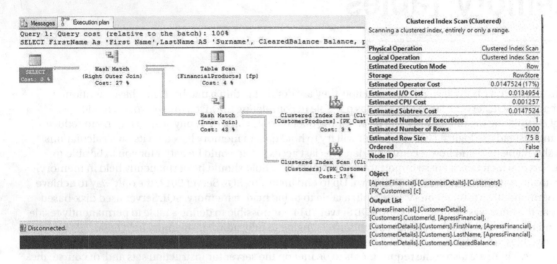

***Figure 7-1.** Query plan for a random query*

Understanding query plans is a whole book in itself, but let's take a very quick high-level look at what is presented in Figure 7-1. Query plans are read from right to left, with the resulting action the left-most icon. In Figure 7-1, I have hovered over the Clustered Index Scan, which generates a pop-up Windows in the very right of the figure. (I will come back to the figure in a moment—this window is only shown when you hover over a query plan step). The query I built has three tables involved in the query, as shown just above Figure 7-1. Don't worry too much about understanding the query, as you will see how queries like this are created as you progress through the book. The main point to note is that each step has a cost percentage of the overall cost of the plan. The Hash Match step, second from the left, has a cost of 27%, for example. You can therefore see which steps take the greatest percentage of cost, and from this you can start to identify where you might be able to improve a query that is not performing as well as you hoped. Keep in the forefront of your mind, though, that the query will always reach 100% cost and, therefore, tuning may not be possible as it runs as optimally as it can. Also, if a query takes a long time, it could be other factors and not the query that is the issue. Figure 7-1 is an estimated query plan costing, which means SQL Server has not run the query against any data and, therefore, has not given details of the actual cost of the query.

Move back to the pop-up window on the right of Figure 7-1, as this is where the interesting information about cost-based processing is that I want to cover. The window shows a breakdown of the estimated cost of that particular step as well as useful information about what the step is doing. Concentrating on the costs, notice that in this window there are four costs listed and notice how much more the cost is with IO over CPU. The main point I want to make, though, is how SQL Server allocates costs to each step and each processing area within that step. As memory processing involves no physical IO, the cost of any step involving an in-memory table will be less and, therefore, should mean a more efficient query.

Cost isn't everything, as I mentioned earlier. To expand on this, you may have a query that has a very high cost value but runs as efficiently as possible. A high cost could be the result of several reasons from the number of rows processed by the query but it could also be that your query finds the necessary data in an index but then has to access the underlying table to retrieve further column values which means a high I/O cost. However using cost is a good starting point for performance.

What Is an In-Memory Table?

An in-memory table is where all the data for the table is held in the memory allocated on the server for SQL Server installation with an aim of being as fast and as efficient as possible. To help achieve this, an in-memory table will hold as few locks as possible when working with data modifications reducing contention on the data.

SQL Server can be installed multiple times on the same computer/server. For each installation, it is normal practice for a DBA to allocate a certain amount of maximum memory slice for each instance, leaving memory for normal server operations and also quite often "spare" memory that can be allocated to a server if required. An in-memory table would reside in the memory allocated for the instance of SQL Server it resides within.

As I mentioned in the introduction, SQL Server, like all databases, has an aim of working with data to complete its given task in the most efficient and quickest way possible. As a database designer, you have a responsibility to help SQL Server achieve this through the design of your database and the objects within the database as well as code programs that work with this data in the most efficient manner. SQL Server also tries to ensure it works effectively through its own internal processes and tools.

One technique that SQL Server employs to work with its data efficiently is to retain disk-based data in-memory. SQL Server is unlikely to be able to retain all of your data from every disk-based table in-memory unless you have a data in a database that is less than the available memory on your server. If your database is greater than the memory available, data is removed from memory and, when required by SQL Server, to free up space for required data for the queries being executed. It is possible that some or all of the data in a highly accessed table is residing on disk and not in memory due to SQL Server deciding at some point that this highly accessed data has not been used for a while and has therefore "aged out" of memory. If a SQL Server process requires that data, then it will need to be reread from disk. As a developer, you know that from a performance view that it would be better to hold the data in this highly accessed data in memory permanently, which is where in-memory tables come in to the picture.

There are two types of in-memory tables that you can use. The first is where the data will remain in memory until a SQL Server recycles. When SQL Server is stopped and started, the schema definition of the table will remain, but all the data will be lost. This is ideal for data that can be easily re-created when SQL Server restarts and a process you build is executed to repopulate the data. When creating a table with this type of in-memory table, you define it as SCHEMA_ONLY. The second type is where the data will be kept not only in-memory but also stored on disk. This is ideal for when you need speed of access to the data but also require the durability of recording the data for future use. The table creation would be defined as SCHEMA_AND_DATA. Both types of in-memory tables are fully durable while SQL Server is running and therefore any data modifications will remain.

Differences to Disk-Based Tables

The most beneficial difference between in-memory and disk-based tables is speed of access to the data in both reading and writing. This has been touched on already, but the main driver of in-memory tables is that in-memory is faster than disk and every consideration Microsoft has taken about in-memory tables is "will this slow down data access and if it does is the speed reduction adding sufficient value?". This section of the chapter will cover some of the main differences between disk-based and in-memory-based tables and also cover areas that have already been discussed in previous chapters.

Disk-based tables only hold within their table one row for each row of data. This may be an obvious statement to make as why would you expect there to be multiple rows of data for each actual row of data. However, to achieve this single row requires there to be a reasonable amount of locking and "potential" locking, called latches, to ensure that the row of data you are reading is the correct row of data within a transaction (transactions are covered in

Chapters 10 and 12), that the data being written is being safely written. Locks are where SQL Server places a logical "do not touch" indicator on rows, pages, or even the whole table of data. To achieve the same requirements where you need to know the data you are working with is the correct definition SQL Server uses, a technique called row-versioning for storing data. Quite simply, whenever SQL Server has to modify a row of data, the previous version or versions of data remain and a new version is written to the table, therefore making multiple versions of the same uniquely defined primary key row. By having many versions of rows, it does increase the amount of space required. However, this is offset by the less need for latches and locks, which will have a performance impact.

You can use the T-SQL you learn throughout the book to access in-memory tables with very few exceptions. If you use T-SQL in an ad-hoc fashion, as you will see in Chapter 12, then this is known as interpreted SQL. When you have defined T-SQL and then send the T-SQL to SQL Server to execute, there are several steps involved. These steps are:

- the query is first parsed where the T-SQL is parsed for accuracy and for any errors

- a logical tree of steps is produced

- it is then passed to the query optimizer which looks at the logical tree and either uses an existing execution plan to execute the code or generates a new execution plan

- the plan is then executed as the final step.

Even as stored procedures, which are SQL Server resident modules of code, these steps are still performed. To improve performance, in-memory tables can use a process called natively compiled stored procedures. This is where the stored procedure is compiled to native code, which is much faster upon first execution. You will see natively compiled stored procedures in Chapter 15.

Another difference is that every table has to have at least one nonclustered index defined at the same time the table is defined. It is not possible to create a table without an index also defined, and any index on an in-memory table has to be created at the same time the table is created. The data within the columns defined for a primary key cannot be altered and would require a deletion and insertion of the row if an alteration was required. Also this would cause problems with how row-versioning would work, and you would lose the performance gains that row-versioning gives.

Once a table or an index is defined, you cannot alter the definitions without dropping and re-creating the table. You cannot execute the DROP INDEX or ALTER INDEX commands, and you cannot execute an ALTER TABLE command.

There are other differences that have been covered in the book prior to this point and, therefore, cannot be applied to in-memory based tables. These are the following:

- Cannot have IDENTITY columns

- Cannot have foreign keys

- Can be no check or unique constraints

- Three datatypes are not supported: datetimeoffset, hierarchyid, and sql_variant. Char and varchar datatypes also need to be defined as code page 1252 or defined as Unicode.

In-Memory Indexes and the Hash Index

When creating a table, an index has to be created at the same time as mentioned earlier in the chapter. The index can either be a nonclustered or hash nonclustered index. A nonclustered index can be defined either as a standard nonclustered index, as demonstrated in Chapter 6, or as a hash nonclustered index. First of all, let me detail what a hash nonclustered index is, and then I will detail when to choose which index to use.

If you have worked with languages such as C#, you may have come across a hash value. This is a value calculated with a function based on the data passed to the function. This is no different in SQL Server. When building a query to access the data, you will have a query that has a filter (known as a predicate) defining what data you want to return from a table. This predicate is what is used to pass to the hash function to create the hash value.

Hash indexes are perfect when you have a query that is looking for a specific value from a query in a table and then scanning from that point onward. A hash index is not good when you are looking for a range of values or when

you are looking for data that is not an "equality" request. To clarify this point just one step further, if you know a specific customer id but you are looking for transactions for a customer between the 1st and 24th of March, a standard nonclustered index is the best index. The difference here is that you are using the index to seek where the key values are not a specific value but a range. Another example of where a hash index is not appropriate is where you want to find all customer transactions that were not equal to withdrawal of funds. You can have both a nonclustered and a hash nonclustered index on a table.

You also have to define all the columns defined in the index for the predicate for a hash index to work. To give an example of this, if you know a specific customer number and you are looking for that customer's transactions in no particular order and there is a hash index that is defined as `CustomerId + DateEntered`, then you need to pass in both of these columns as the predicate. By passing in `CustomerId` only, the hash index could not be used and the query would scan the whole table. To explain why a hash index could not be used, behind the scenes SQL Server takes the values from the predicate and passes it through a function to create a hash value. As there is "insufficient" data, the hash value will match zero rows and therefore SQL Server knows this and so will discard using a hash index and either use a nonclustered index or scan the whole table.

Hash Buckets

When you insert data into a table that has a hash index, the values for the columns will have their hash value calculated, which points to a collection of indexes values in the hash index called a hash bucket. A hash bucket can be thought of as being like a leaf in a B-Tree in that both hold a collection of index values except that a hash bucket is a single dimension array of values and is, therefore, all on one level. The index values in the hash bucket have pointers to the rows of data in the in-memory table so you can retrieve the data. Just to complete the picture, in the in-memory table, each data row has a pointer to the next row for the hash index so SQL Server can retrieve all data for that hash index without having to constantly return to the hash bucket to retrieve the next value. To clarify this process, taking the example earlier of `CustomerId` and `DateEntered`, if you have a customer id of 12345678 and a date entered of 12th August 2015, this would generate a hash value. This hash value is used as a pointer to a specific hash bucket. The hash bucket will have the index values for the customer id 12345678 and the date entered of 12th August 2015. It may have other index values (like customer id 1238254 and 24th July 2012). Let's assume that the hash value for customer 12345678 points to bucket number 1. The hash bucket will then have a pointer to the row of data similar to any other index.

When defining the hash index when creating the table, you have to define the number of buckets you want to have. Too few will mean that when querying the data, a higher number of index searches may generate a hash value to point to the same hash bucket causing a collision and therefore a performance impact. Conversely, an index with too many buckets will have memory space reserved that is empty. To estimate the number of buckets, you look at the table data and count the number of unique rows of data for the index columns. If the number of unique values is not likely to increase, multiply the number of unique rows by 2. If there will be some additions, multiply the number of unique rows by 4.

However the number of unique rows is also important in the decision of whether to have a hash index on the columns or whether you should define the index as nonclustered. There should be a low ratio of number of unique values to number of rows in the table. The closer to a ratio of 1, the better. Anything above a ratio of 4 might have a performance impact with hash index collisions. So if you have a table with 100,000 rows, you would expect no fewer than 25,000 unique values. A unique index would give a ratio of 1:1 and therefore the perfect candidate for a hash index.

To summarize the discussion in this section, each index entry is defined as a hash value based on the data in the index, and several hashes are stored together in a hash bucket. Each hash value in the hash bucket relates to a row in the in-memory table. There is also no direct correlation of one hash value in a hash bucket with another hash value, although multiple hash values of the same hash value will reside together in the same bucket. A hash index is perfect in the following situations:

- You are searching on all the columns in the index.

- You are looking for exact values.

- You are happy for rows to be returned in a non-sorted order.

- There is a low ratio of number of rows in the table to number of unique values.

You will see a hash nonclustered index created in the first example below. When defining a hash index, you have to determine how many hash buckets the index will have, known as the BUCKET_COUNT.

General Index Points

Moving back to indexes in general, for SCHEMA_AND_DATA tables, where the data is durable even after a server restart, the table needs to be defined with a PRIMARY KEY. A primary key definition will create an index on the table; therefore, no further index creation would be required. Indexes are not persisted to disk even if the table is defined as SCHEMA_AND_DATA.

An in-memory table has a limit of 8 indexes that can be defined. Keep in mind that every index will have a performance degradation on row insertions and deletions and possibly updates as well.

■ **Note** A nonclustered index, as discussed in Chapter 6, used as the overhead of keeping a clustered index would slow performance. And remember that it is all about performance with in-memory tables.

Operating System and Hardware Requirements

As mentioned in the introduction, in-memory tables can only be created on 64 bit Enterprise or Developers Editions. The Evaluation Edition is Enterprise so it can also be implemented in this edition. The processor in the server or Virtual Machine must be new enough to be able to support **cmpxchg16b** instruction. A cmpxchng16b is a machine instruction that will compare in a transactional multithreaded way used for modifying data in memory, which is what in-memory data is all about. You also require a lot of memory that can't be definitely defined at the start even during use as there will be fluctuations, albeit not of a large magnitude. The rule of thumb to apply is to attempt to estimate how much data will be held in the tables and the indexes, and double it. This is the amount of memory required for the in-memory table and indexes only and not the data from other tables and processes. As you have probably deduced, this can mean a reasonable amount of memory allocated for one table.

Database Requirements Prior to Table Creation

Before you can create an in-memory table in a database, the database has to be defined to allow for in-memory tables to exist. The first requirement is to create a filegroup to hold the in-memory tables and related system objects. In Chapter 3 when the ApressFinancial database was created, you saw the PRIMARY filegroup defined. To recap, a filegroup is a method of grouping the data files in a logical manner. Data files hold database startup information as well as the database objects. When the database was created, it was defined with just one filegroup called the Primary file group, as shown in Figure 7-2.

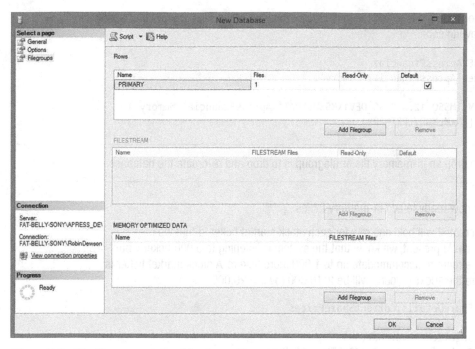

Figure 7-2. *The filegroups defined for ApressFinancial*

In-memory tables as mentioned throughout this chapter are similar to disk-based tables but are optimized for memory and, as such, need to be placed in a filegroup that can cope with the functionality. Once an in-memory filegroup is defined, it is then necessary to define the physical file location the filegroup will reside on. Unlike disk-based filegroups, only one filegroup is defined per database.

Creating an In-memory Table Using SQL

The following example will build a table in-memory after defining the filegroups and files for the database for the in-memory tables. The table will use a hash nonclustered index for the table.

TRY IT OUT: CREATING AN IN-MEMORY TABLE

1. Open a query window in Management Studio and enter the following code to create the filegroup for the database. Once entered, execute the code:

```
ALTER DATABASE ApressFinancial
ADD FILEGROUP [IN-MEMORY-PRIMARY]
CONTAINS MEMORY_OPTIMIZED_DATA
```

2. The second action required is to add the in-memory container to the filegroup. Enter and execute the following code:

```
ALTER DATABASE ApressFinancial
ADD FILE (name='ApressFinancial-Memory',
filename=
'C:\APRESS_DEV1\MSSQL12.APRESS_DEV1\MSSQL\DATA\ApressFinancial-Memory')
TO FILEGROUP [IN-MEMORY-PRIMARY]
```

■ **Caution** The only way to drop an in-memory file or filegroup is to drop and re-create the database.

3. The database is now ready to add in-memory tables.

4. The table to be created will hold one row for each stock market ticker id that we are receiving prices on. At present, we know that the system is listening to 9,000 tickers, but there needs to be room to accommodate up to 1,000 more tickers. A stock market ticker is unique. Therefore the BUCKET_COUNT will be 2*10,000 rows = 20,000.

```
CREATE TABLE ShareDetails.CurrentSharePrices
(
    StockExchangeTicker varchar(50)
        COLLATE Latin1_General_100_BIN2 NOT NULL
        PRIMARY KEY NONCLUSTERED HASH
        WITH (BUCKET_COUNT = 20000),
    CurrentPrice numeric(18,5) NOT NULL,
    LastTickTime smalldatetime NOT NULL
)
WITH (MEMORY_OPTIMIZED = ON,
DURABILITY = SCHEMA_AND_DATA)
GO
```

■ **Note** Because the hash index is on a VARCHAR column, the column needs to be defined with a BIN2 collation.

Migrating to an In-Memory Table

The following example will use the Migration Optimization Advisor to inspect the TransactionDetails. Transactions table and advise on the issues found, which will then be fixed. The exercise will then continue to migrate the table across from disk-based to in-memory based.

TRY IT OUT: CREATING AN IN-MEMORY TABLE

1. Highlight in the Object Explorer the `TransactionDetails.Transactions` table, right-click and select Memory Optimization Advisor, as shown in Figure 7-3.

Figure 7-3. Migration Optimizer Advisor

2. This will start the Memory Optimization Advisor and you will be presented with the Welcome screen. Click OK. The Migration Optimization Advisor will now inspect the table and validate it for migration. As you can see in Figure 7-4, there are three issues that require fixing.

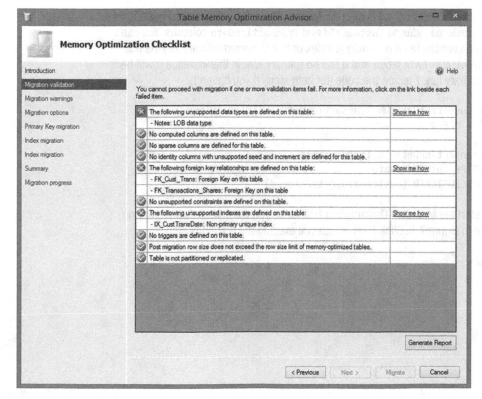

Figure 7-4. Migration Optimizer Advisor indicating issues

3. The first error concerns LOB data type. This is in relation to the NVARCHAR(MAX) on the NOTES column. This value will need to be reduced to 4000 bytes. The easiest method to achieve this is to use the Designer as demonstrated in Chapter 6. Open the Designer for the TransactionDetails.Transactions table, find the Notes column and alter the width from MAX to 4000 bytes while altering to VARCHAR, and then save. (See Figure 7-5).

ReferenceDetails	nvarchar(50)	☑
▶ Notes	varchar(4000)	☑
RelatedShareId	int	☑
RelatedProductId	int	☐

Figure 7-5. *Altering the table in the Designer*

4. The second error relates to foreign keys. In-memory tables cannot have foreign keys and, therefore, the two foreign keys will need to be dropped. By removing these if it is necessary to ensure referential integrity, this will need to be enforced logically.

```
ALTER TABLE TransactionDetails.Transactions
DROP CONSTRAINT FK_Transactions_Shares
GO
```

5. The final issue surrounds the index IX_CustTransDate. This index was created in Chapter 6. This is a unique clustered index on CustomerId and TransactionDate columns. You can alter this to either a nonclustered non-unique index or to a clustered primary key. As this is a durable (SCHEMA_AND_DATA table) and it has no primary key, in this instance it will be converted to a primary key. Execute the code (for both steps if you haven't).

```
DROP INDEX IX_CustTransDate ON TransactionDetails.Transactions
WITH ( ONLINE = OFF )
GO
ALTER TABLE TransactionDetails.Transactions
ADD CONSTRAINT PK_CustTransDate
PRIMARY KEY NONCLUSTERED (CustomerId,DateEntered)
```

6. Now when you start the Migration Optimization Advisor as you did in step 1, there are no errors, as shown in Figure 7-6. Click Next, which will execute the Warnings step.

✓	No unsupported data types are defined on this table.
✓	No computed columns are defined on this table.
✓	No sparse columns are defined for this table.
✓	No identity columns with unsupported seed and increment are defined for this table.
✓	No foreign key relationships are defined on this table.
✓	No unsupported constraints are defined on this table.
✓	No unsupported indexes are defined on this table.
✓	No triggers are defined on this table.
✓	Post migration row size does not exceed the row size limit of memory-optimized tables.
✓	Table is not partitioned or replicated.

Figure 7-6. Altering the table in the Designer

7. The next screen will let you know of any warnings that you may have. It does also list general in-memory table points to reiterate the areas you need to keep in mind. Click Next to move on within the wizard. (See Figure 7-7).

ⓘ	A user transaction that accesses memory-optimized tables cannot access more than one user database.	More information
ⓘ	The following table hints are not supported on memory-optimized tables: HOLDLOCK, NOLOCK, PAGLOCK, READCOMMITTED, READPAST, READUNCOMMITTED, ROWLOCK, TABLOCK, TABLOCKX, UPDLOCK, XLOCK, KEEPIDENTITY, KEEPDEFAULTS, NOWAIT.	More information
ⓘ	TRUNCATE TABLE and MERGE statements cannot target a memory-optimized table.	More information
ⓘ	Dynamic and Keyset cursors are automatically downgraded to a static cursor when pointing to a memory-optimized table.	More information
ⓘ	Some database-level features are not supported for use with memory-optimized tables. For details on these features, please refer to the help link.	More information

Figure 7-7. Altering the table in the Designer

8. You are now presented with the options for the migration of the table as well as informing you of some of the setup for in-memory tables. You are automatically given a suggestion of what to call the new name of the existing disk-based table. This table will remain post migration. It is also possible to copy the data from the dis-based table and altering the in-memory table to be SCHEMA_ONLY. For this exercise, keep the options as defaulted and click Next. (See Figure 7-8).

	ⓘ Help
Specify options for memory optimization:	
Memory-optimized filegroup:	IN-MEMORY-PRIMARY
Logical file name:	ApressFinancial-Memory
File path:	C:\APRESS_DEV1\MSSQL12.APRESS_DEV1\MSSQL\DATA
Rename the original table as:	Transactions_old
Estimated current memory cost (MB):	3.96

☑ Also copy table data to the new memory optimized table.

By default, this table will be migrated to a memory-optimized table with both schema and data durability.

☐ Check this box to migrate this table to a memory-optimized table with no data durability.

Figure 7-8. Options for the migration

9. The next step is how you would like the primary key to be defined. In this instance, the primary key will be a "standard" nonclustered index rather than a hash index as the data access is likely to be range based queries. If there was a varchar column, you would also be able to define the collation for the index if required. Click Next. (See Figure 7-9).

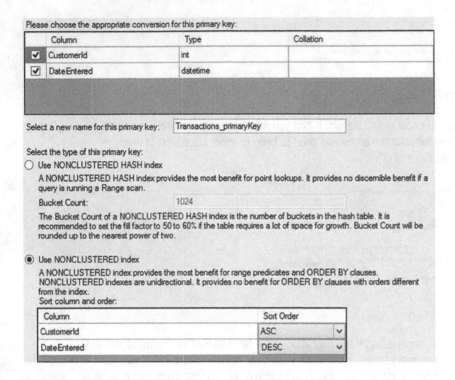

Figure 7-9. Primary key options defining the nonclustered index

10. The disk-based table also had an index defined for the foreign key access to the TransactionDetails.TransactionTypes index. The index will also be a standard nonclustered index. Click Next. (See Figure 7-10).

Please choose the appropriate conversion for this index:

	Column	Type	Collation
☑	TransactionType	smallint	

Select the type of this index:

○ Use NONCLUSTERED HASH index

A NONCLUSTERED HASH index provides the most benefit for point lookups. It provides no discernible benefit if a query is running a Range scan.

Bucket Count: `4`

The Bucket Count of a NONCLUSTERED HASH index is the number of buckets in the hash table. It is recommended to set the fill factor to 50 to 60% if the table requires a lot of space for growth. Bucket Count will be rounded up to the nearest power of two.

◉ Use NONCLUSTERED index

A NONCLUSTERED index provides the most benefit for range predicates and ORDER BY clauses. NONCLUSTERED indexes are unidirectional. It provides no benefit for ORDER BY clauses with orders different from the index.
Sort column and order:

Column	Sort Order
TransactionType	ASC

Figure 7-10. *Converting the IX_Transactions_Type index*

11. You will then be presented with a summary screen of all the points defined within the wizard. Click the button to migrate, which will start the migration progress.

12. As the migration progresses, a progress screen will populate details of the steps and show any errors. This completes the migration. (See Figure 7-11).

	Action	Result
✓	Renaming the original table.	Passed
	New name:Transactions_old	
✓	Creating the memory-optimized table in the database.	Passed
	Adding index:IX_Transactions_TType	
	Adding index:Transactions_primaryKey	
✓	Copying data from the original table to the new memory-optimized table.	Passed

Figure 7-11. *Post completed work with actions completed*

13. If you move to Object Explorer and refresh, you will see the disk-based table renamed as detailed within the wizard and then the new in-memory based table, as shown in Figure 7-12. Keep the disk-based table, as it will be used within the book.

Figure 7-12. *New and old table in Object Explorer*

Migration is as simple as this. You can achieve the same using T-SQL based commands. However, migration should be a rare occurrence and, therefore, a wizard is a quick and straightforward step-by-step process.

Summary

In-memory tables can generate a high-performance benefit to a system, especially for "hot" tables. They are not perfect for every situation, but where you have enough memory to hold the whole table and its expansion, where the data has performance degradation due to lock contention especially on high insertion or read-based tables, or where you need a fast "staging" table where data is inserted for fast insertion in-memory to be later placed in to slower disk-based tables, an in-memory table may be the ideal choice.

Everything in SQL Server has a cost, and in-memory tables are designed to look at areas to reduce the costs to make performance improvements. Not only by removing lock contention and having the data in-memory, further improvements can also come from natively compiled stored procedures.

How indexes are used within in-memory also differs from those for disk-based tables, and a new type of index called a nonclustered hash index for certain queries will provide further performance improvements. The choice of indexes should be a clear-cut one during design, although generating the correct hash bucket count for a nonclustered hash index will require some pre-analysis of the expected data volumes to create an accurate level.

You now have in-memory tables that will be used within the book for the in-memory chapters.

CHAPTER 8

■ ■ ■

Database Backups and Recovery

Before inserting and manipulating the data in the database you have created in the previous chapters, it is a good idea to back it up so that if things go wrong, it will be possible to recover the data back to a stable point.

What is abundantly clear when working with any sort of system where data are held is that there must be a comprehensible and workable backup and recovery strategy in place for when things go wrong. The recovery may also be required to cater to problems from a hardware failure due to an act of God. In any of these instances, we may move to an *offsite location*, which is a building a safe distance away from our current building housing the computing equipment. That is quite a dramatic step and is a decision that would be taken at a higher level of authority than you probably have; however, you must create a backup of your system and store it according to the recommendations of the board of directors, whether they are for in-house or offsite storage. Companies have gone bust because a good and secure backup storage plan wasn't in place when their building burned down, for example. This is, of course, a worst-case scenario, and there are times that moving out of the current building to a second secure location is not necessary.

This chapter looks at different backup strategies that can be implemented by you as a developer or an administrator and shows you how to implement them. I will also show you scenarios where the database is in use 24 hours a day, 7 days a week, and how you need to form a backup strategy around such scenarios. From there, I will show you how to perform an ad hoc backup of the database as well as scheduled transaction log backups. I make it clear in this chapter when you would perform both of these types of backups and when they would be useful. Of course, after the backup, you have to test that the backup can be restored. Generally, this backup is restored onto a nonproduction system. Some companies have complete environments established to test their disaster-recovery scenarios.

What you have to realize, and what will be demonstrated, is that there are different methods of taking backups depending on what you are trying to achieve. The most common scenarios are discussed and demonstrated in this chapter, but you will also to look at database maintenance plans. It is imperative that you get the correct backup strategy in place and that it works. This point will be repeated throughout the chapter.

So, in this chapter, you will learn about the following:

- Backup strategies

- When a problem might occur during the backup and restore process

- How to take a database offline and then bring it back online

- How to create a backup

- Different media for building a backup and what needs to be considered

- The transaction log and how to back it up

- When to back up the data and when to back up the transaction log

- Scheduling backups and what happens if the server isn't running at the scheduled time

- Restoring a database

211

- Detaching and attaching a database

- Working with users still attached to the database when you need them not to be connected

- Building SQL statements for backing up the database structure and when it is useful
 to have them

Backup Strategies

Backing up a database, no matter how large or small, should form part of your database solution. Even if a backup is taken only once a week or even once a month, it is crucial that you sit down and decide which backup strategy is right for you. Much of this decision lies in the hands of the system and business owners for your company since they must weigh the risk they're willing to take against the cost of minimizing that risk. Many different strategies can be adopted within your overall main backup strategy, depending on days of the week or perhaps a period within the month. In this section of the chapter, I will cover areas of backups to help you make the correct decision.

Recovery Models

When backing up a database, the information that is backed up is partially decided by the recovery model of the database as well as what type of database backup is being performed. In this section, I discuss these models, but you may find you return to this section once you have looked at the exercises within this chapter as well as after discussing transactions in Chapter 10. It is necessary to discuss models at this point, as they are something you need to be aware of for the rest of the chapter.

The first model to discuss is the Full Recovery model. This is the most comprehensive model available and is the most robust for data recovery from backups. This model allows recovery of a corrupt database from a backup to the granularity of a specific point in time. This is achieved by performing a backup on the database as well as the transaction log of the database. Transaction logs are discussed shortly. The ApressFinancial database is set to Full Recovery, and you will see how a backup and restore are performed in this model in this chapter and in Chapter 8. The main point about Full Recovery is that this mode provides the lowest level of recording of changes within your tables. This means that there are space and performance issues to consider compared to the recovery of the database.

The next model to discuss is the Bulk-Logged Recovery model. Similar to the Full Recovery model, both the database and the transaction logs are required to be backed up for a full model to be implemented. The difference is that less information is recorded in the transaction log on what work has been completed against your tables for bulk actions. A bulk action is an action that covers a large amount of data, such as a bulk load of data or creating an index. In Full Recovery, each row would be logged; in Bulk-Logged, only the action details are logged. However, in both of these models, any failure is recoverable using both the database backup and transaction log backups.

The last model is the Simple Recovery model. In this model, only the database is backed up; the transaction log is not. What this means is that the data in the tables ,once committed to the database, will be backed up. Any restore from a Simple Recovery model means that only data that were backed up can be restored. Therefore, if you completed a backup using the Simple Recovery model on Saturday and your database was corrupted on Tuesday, any changes to the database since the backup on Saturday would be lost. With the other two models, you could restore the data back to the point of failure. This model is available in all editions.

Types of Backups

Based on the strategy that you choose, you have to decide what type of backup you need. *Full database backups* take a complete snapshot of a database at any given point. A *differential backup* backs up only the data that has changed since the last full backup. Finally, a *transaction log backup* backs up only the data in the transaction log, which consists of transactions that were recently committed to the database. All of these types of backups can be done while your SQL Server is online and while users are actively hitting your database. To be able to restore a database to any point in time, you have to use a combination of these backup types.

Backup Strategy Decisions

When determining your backup strategy, first look at your application and ask yourself the following questions:

- How much of the data can be lost, if any, at any point of failure? In other words, how crucial is it that no data are lost?

- How often are the data updated? Do you need regular backups from a performance viewpoint as well as a recovery viewpoint? For historical databases that have their data modified only periodically, you would, at most, complete a backup post-population.

- Do you need to back up all the data all of the time, or can you do this periodically and then back up only the data that have altered in the meanwhile?

- How much of the data needs to be backed up and how long do you need to keep the copies of the backups?

- In the event of catastrophic failure, how long will it take to completely rebuild the database, if it's even possible?

Many more questions can be asked, but for the moment, these are the most crucial questions that need answers. If you can afford to allow data updates to be lost, then you need a straightforward periodic database backup—for example, you need to back up the whole database once a week. This is simple and easy to complete and requires little thought. However, this scenario is rare and is usually found in data-warehousing systems or those with a large amount of static data that can be rebuilt.

Transaction Log Backups

For every data modification, a record is kept in the transaction log file (discussed in more detail in the section "Transaction Logs"), which has a limited amount of space. This amount of space was defined when you set up the database as a fixed maximum size or, if you are allowing it to grow with or without restrictions, equals the amount set or the amount within the hard drive. If you back up and clear the transaction log file, initially this will free up the space logically and also aid performance. This is known as *logical log truncation*. The smaller the active part of the transaction log file, the better. The more transactions there are in the transaction log file, the longer it will take to recover from a corrupt database. This is due to the fact that a restore will have to restore the data and then every transaction log backup to the point of failure, and finally, depending on the failure and how you want to restore, you may have to restore any completed transactions that were in the transaction log but not yet physically committed to the tables. That is, each transaction log will have to be restored to update the database, not just the latest log file. If there are transactions in the transaction log that have been committed since the last transaction log backup and you want to restore these, you will need to back up the transaction log, called a tail backup, and restore that as well. This is a great deal to consider and may seem a lot to take in and decide upon, but as you will see throughout the chapter, it is not quite as daunting as this section may read. If you have multiple small files and they are held on media that has to be mounted each time, such as a tape, then you will have to take mounting time into consideration as well.

Frequency of a Backup

The real crux of a backup strategy is how frequently you want to take a backup. If you need to back up all the data each time, how often will that need to take place? This could well be every night, and many production systems do just this. By completing a full data backup every night, you are allowing yourself to be in a state where only one or two restores may need to occur to get back to a working state in a disaster scenario. This would be the data backup, followed by the single transaction log backup, if one was taken in the meantime. This is much better than having one data backup to be restored, and then a log file for every day since the data file backup. What happens if the failure is on a Friday at lunchtime and you completed your last whole database backup on a Saturday evening? That would take one data file and six transaction log file restores to complete.

Sit down and take stock. As often as you can, take a full database backup, then a differential backup, followed by transaction log backups. However, you have to weigh the time that a full backup takes against a differential backup or a transaction log; how much processing time you have to complete these backups; and the risk level of having to complete, for example, six transaction log restores.

The problem is that there is no universally right answer. Each situation is different and it is only through experience, which comes from testing your solution thoroughly, that you find out what is best for your situation. However, if in doubt, back up as frequently as you can and take a full backup each time.

Transaction Logs

Data within the database is stored, of course, on your hard drive, on a hard drive on a server, or within in-memory tables. Imagine the work involved on the disk controller for disk-based tables and imagine the work SQL Server has to do every time data are added, amended, or removed. Writing data is a slow process compared to other memory-based processes, so inevitably, SQL Server slows down every time data are written. A good comparison is to think how long it takes you to find a point in a document where you want to amend, insert, modify, or erase a sentence, even using MS Word, compared to how long it takes you to read a sentence. What if part of the way through writing the data, a power outage occurred and you had no uninterruptible power supply (UPS) in place? What a mess you would be in, not knowing what had been written to disk and, therefore, your tables within your database, and what hadn't!

It is also possible in SQL Server to update several tables at once. How would you work around the fact that some of the tables had been updated, but when it came to updating a specific table, the update failed? Well, this is where transaction logs come into play. Transactions themselves are covered in Chapter 10, but very simply, a *transaction* is a single unit of work that can contain one or more table modifications that are all successful and committed to the database or, if some are unsuccessful, the modifications are discarded. It is also possible to roll back a transaction so that no changes are made to the database, which can either be invoked by SQL Server or by issuing a specific T-SQL command. But you must be wondering what all this has to do with a transaction log, and you're probably even wondering what a transaction log is. Before moving on, there is one last area of background information we need to discuss first.

The *log file* is a complex item that consists of virtual, logical, and physical logs, but to keep it simple, the transaction log has a physical size—in other words, it is like any other file on the hard drive. Virtual log files are files of no fixed size and are built internally by SQL Server as part of the physical creation of the transaction log.

The transaction log increases in size as necessary to accommodate the transactions. It is a wraparound file. This means that when SQL Server reaches the end of the file as defined by the size when it was set up, it will wrap around to the beginning again, looking for free space to use. SQL Server can wrap around without increasing the physical log file size when there is free virtual transaction space. Virtual transaction log space becomes free when SQL Server can write the data from the transaction log into the underlying tables within the database.

Every database within a SQL Server instance has its own transaction log. Every time SQL Server is requested to do any data modifications—whether these are additions, deletions, or modifications—a record is kept of the action. There are several reasons for this.

First of all, a piece of code could in fact do several different updates at once, either to different rows of data or to rows of data in different tables or even databases. If one of the updates fails, for example, when you are attempting to place ASCII characters into a column that allows only numerics, then you may wish to return the values in all the updated fields to their original value. This is called *rolling back* a transaction. SQL Server achieves this, in part, by looking at the data held in the transaction log. However, any successful action where all the updates are valid could be permanently stored on file—a process called *committing* a transaction.

As more and more actions are placed in the transaction log, it will become full. Some of these actions will still be within a transaction, and others may form part of a completed transaction ready to be committed to the database. At certain points, SQL Server will want to remove all the actions it can by committing completed transactions to the underlying tables to relieve some space in the transaction log for further actions. One point could be when the transaction log reaches 70% full. SQL Server would then issue a *checkpoint*. The use of a checkpoint ensures that any data modifications are actually committed to the database and not held in any buffers or the transaction log so

that if a problem occurs, such as a power failure, there is a specific point that you can start from. Therefore, at the end of a checkpoint transaction, you know the database is in a consistent and valid state. As SQL Server knows that at a checkpoint all is well within the database, there is no need to keep the completed transactions recorded in the transaction log stored up to the checkpoint and, therefore, it will remove the transactions stored in the virtual logs. As a result, SQL Server issues a truncation of the transaction log to remove these records, minimizing the size of the log on the computer. This is known as *truncating* the transaction log. It is thus necessary to ensure that you have a large enough transaction log defined to hold the largest valid uncommitted transaction, as these transactions obviously will not be truncated. A transaction log can become full with a rogue query as well—that is, one that is coded incorrectly and keeps adding more and more uncommitted transactions. When the transaction log reaches 70%, there is nothing to checkpoint; eventually the transaction log will fill up, and your SQL Server will stop. This is where you will need the help of an experienced database administrator.

If you have a power failure, you might have to "replay" all the work completed since the last backup, and in certain scenarios, you could use the transaction log to do this. When a data modification is completed via a T-SQL command, the details are recorded first in the transaction log. These changes are flushed to disk and, therefore, no longer in memory before SQL Server starts to make changes to the tables that you are affecting. SQL Server doesn't write data immediately to disk. It is kept in a *buffer cache* until this cache is full or until SQL Server issues a checkpoint, and then the data are written out. If a power failure occurs while the cache is still filling up, then that data are lost. Once the power comes back, though, SQL Server would start from its last checkpoint state, and any updates after the last checkpoint that were logged as successful transactions will be performed from the transaction log.

Transaction logs are best kept, if at all possible, on a hard drive separate from that holding the data. The reason for this is that data are written serially when they are written to a transaction log. Therefore, if nothing else is on the hard drive except the transaction log, the disk heads will be in the right place to continue writing each time. This is a minor overhead, but if performance is an issue, this is worth considering.

When Problems May Occur

Obviously, when taking a backup, it must work; otherwise, you have wasted your time, but crucially, you are leaving your database and organization in a vulnerable position if the backup fails. If you have time within your backup window to verify that a backup has been successful, then you must do it. As you will see, SQL Server gives you different options for doing this. It cannot be stressed strongly enough that verifying a backup is just as crucial as taking the backup in the first place. There have been situations where a backup has been taken every night; however, no one has noticed that the backup has failed, and then when a hardware failure occurs, there's no backup to use as a restore on a new machine. In one case I know of, almost a week's worth of data was lost. Luckily, the weekend backups had succeeded; otherwise, the company would have been in a major data loss situation. The cause of the failed backups was that the tapes being inserted for the backup were not large enough to hold the backup being performed. Therefore, the tapes became full, and the backup failed. Obviously, this company failed not only to verify the backup, but also to have processes in place to check that its backup strategy was still working after a period of implementation.

The only sure and positive way of ensuring a backup has succeeded is to restore the database to a specific restore test location and check the data. Although you will see SQL Server does have a method of checking a backup, this still isn't a guarantee that the backup worked. Do take time to complete regular restores to a location to test that everything is okay. I believe for several reasons that restoring a backup to a test region after each backup should be mandatory for all installations. Not only are you checking that the backup has worked, but also you can use this restore to inspect production quality data as part of any problem solving or user requests without endangering your production system.

You should always review your backup strategy on a regular basis. Even better, put in place jobs that run each day that give some sort of space report so that it is possible to instantly see that a potential problem is looming. SQL Server Reporting Services is a new tool that would be ideal for producing and distributing space reports to database administrators and system owners alike. It is also possible to build an automated job to run that checks the space and e-mails the results. This is achievable via SQL Server Integration Services.

In-Memory Table Backup and Restore

Backing up and restoring a database with in-memory tables does not require any special actions within the backup or restore process. However, you have to be aware that once a database restore is complete, SQL Server needs to load the data from in-memory tables into memory, and that process takes some time.

Backups: Taking a Database Offline

SQL Server does not have to be offline to perform a backup, as you will see as you go through this book and work through creating SQL Server–defined backups using wizards and T-SQL. In most environments, you will not have the luxury of taking a database offline before backing it up because users are constantly making data changes. Backing up a database can take a long time, and the longer it takes, the longer users cannot be working with the data while it is offline. However, by taking your database offline, you do not have to use SQL Server to perform the backup. This strategy is one in which you take a disk backup, which means the hard drive is backed up, rather than a specific database within a server. However, don't forget that by taking your database offline, you will have to take a backup of the directory using some sort of drive backup.

If you have your database on a server, no doubt some sort of server backup strategy is in place, so your database will be backed up fully and successfully through this method. If you can take your database "out of service" in time for those backups, you should do so if you are using this option to back up your database. This does allow you to think about your SQL Server deployment strategy. If you have several databases that can be taken offline as part of the backup, it is worth considering whether they can all reside on the same physical server, and you can set your server backup times accordingly. However, this is a rare scenario, and even rarer within a production environment. Taking the database offline means taking your database out of service. Nobody can update or access the data, modify table structures, and so on. In this next section, you will take ApressFinancial offline, allowing a physical backup to be taken. Just to reiterate and clarify: This is being demonstrated only to complete your knowledge of backups, and it is rare that you will perform this action in a live scenario.

TRY IT OUT: TAKING A DATABASE OFFLINE

1. Open SQL Server Management Studio and open a Query Editor pane. Enter and execute the following code:

```
USE master
GO
ALTER DATABASE ApressFinancial
SET OFFLINE
```

2. Notice the first command is a USE command and then the master database is listed. This will move the connection away from the database that it is currently pointing at and point the connection to the master database. If you still had a connection, this code would fail, which is demonstrated in later examples in this chapter.

3. Try to click some of the nodes for the ApressFinancial database—for example, the Tables node if it is available. If you do not see the Tables node, try expanding the ApressFinancial database node. As shown in Figure 8-1, you are reminded that the database is offline by the change in icon and it therefore cannot be viewed or modified. You are also not able to access the database through any application such as Query Editor.

```
☐ 🐷 FAT-BELLY-SONY\APRESS_DEV1 (SQL Server
   ☐ 📁 Databases
      ⊞ 📁 System Databases
      ⊞ 📁 Database Snapshots
      ⊞ 🔵 ApressFinancial (Offline)
```

Figure 8-1. *The database is offline and therefore unable to be opened*

To take a database offline, SQL Server must be able to gain exclusive access to the database. This means that no user can be in the database when you issue the command. If users are connected, then the OFFLINE query will continue to execute and wait until all users are disconnected. You can force the query to take the database offline by rolling back any transactions that are running. To do this, you can execute the SET OFFLINE WITH ROLLBACK IMMEDIATE or SET OFFLINE WITH ROLLBACK AFTER nn SECONDS. Transactions are covered in Chapter 10. However, in essence what both of these options indicate to SQL Server is that any changes in progress to any data within the tables in the database should be discarded. I am not keen on either of these two options, unless the database needs to be taken offline for an emergency or you are aware at the time of the command of what the ramifications are of rolling back any changes.

As said earlier, that's all there is to it. The database is now no longer available for any updates or modifications, so you can back it up using any backup utility that takes files from a hard drive.

If you have to restore from a backup completed this way, don't forget to take the database offline first, then restore from the backup, and finally bring the database back online, ready for use:

```
USE master
go
ALTER DATABASE ApressFinancial
SET ONLINE
```

There is one area to note when using backup strategies that employ these methods. If you have a server backup that runs, for example, at 0200 hours, do you fancy getting up every night, just before 2:00 a.m., taking the database offline, and then bringing the server back up once the backup is complete? No—not many people would. Of course, there are installations where people are working through the night, so this is less of a problem, but what if they are busy? Or forget? Then your whole backup will fail because the files are in use and, therefore, the server will not back up these files. It is possible to create jobs that take your database offline and bring it online again so this method is still possible, but you are adding more steps to the process. This is not the most ideal method and better methods are discussed throughout the chapter.

So let's now look at a more friendly method of backing up the data by using SQL Server instead.

Backing Up the Data

You will probably use SQL Server to back up the database rather than a Windows backup utility with an offline database. As you will see in the coming exercises, it is a simple process with different methods of achieving the goal of backing up the data. By using SQL Server, you are keeping the backup of the database under the control of an automated process that can control its own destiny, and as you will find out later, it can also control the system when things go wrong. There are two types of backups that can be taken on the database and one backup option available for the transaction log providing the recovery model is Full or Bulk-Logged. Backing up in-memory tables are backed up just as disk-based tables and at the same time.

Backup Considerations

The first possibility, a full backup, is straightforward. Selecting the Full option ensures that the whole database will be backed up. The ApressFinancial database was built with Full Recovery mode, the default mode for databases built with SQL Server Enterprise and Developer Edition. In this mode, you only back up the database and not the full transaction log as this is completed separately. This database backup would be seen as any starting point for a restore from a database failure.

The second possibility is the differential backup, also known as an incremental backup. Use the Differential backup option when the circumstances are such that a full backup is either not required or not possible, but there has been at least one full backup completed at some point on the database and the full backup media has not expired. When a backup is taken, it is possible that the media has an expiration date, at which point the media is free and available to be used for any future backups. A differential backup performs a backup on data changed since the last backup. For example, you may take a full backup on the weekend and then a differential backup every night. When it comes to restoring, you would restore the weekend full backup and then add to that the latest differential backup taken from that point. A word of warning here: If you do take a week's worth of differential backups and you back up to magnetic tape rather than a hard drive, keep at least enough different tapes for each differential backup. Therefore, use a complete backup when necessary, and then in the interim, use a differential backup.

The last possibility, the transaction log backup, could be used as the most frequent method of backup in a production environment when using the Full or Bulk-Logged recovery models. As data are modified, details of the modifications are stored in the transaction log. These remain in place until an action "truncates" the transaction log, as I have discussed earlier in this chapter, which means that the transaction log will increase constantly in size if not in Simple Recovery. When you issue a transaction log backup, you are just backing up the transaction log, which issues a checkpoint, and all committed transactions are stored onto the backup. This means that if a system failure occurs, you will restore from a full backup, then from your differential backups for the week, and finally from any transaction log backups after that point.

You are probably wondering why you can't just use differential backups. Transaction logs can fill up during the working day, or perhaps you have set differential backups to happen weekly because there is so little data modification. However, you do need to account for when a transaction log may fill up before you reach the next differential backup. By taking a backup of the transaction log, this is a great deal faster than the other two methods. Certainly in heavily used databases, you may have several transaction log backups in the day. You see how to do this using T-SQL after you take your first full backup. To remind you, at least one valid and non-expired backup must exist before you can take a transaction log backup, as you need a point from which the transaction log can roll committed transactions forward.

Before moving on, there are a couple more points concerning backups that you must keep in mind, and it is recommended strongly that these directions be followed. The most important point is to keep a regular and up-to-date backup of the master and msdb system databases. SQL Server very rarely becomes corrupted, but it can happen for any number of reasons, from a hard drive failure to a developer altering the database in error. It doesn't really matter what the cause of the database failure is, but if you don't have a backup of the master database, you could find yourself in trouble. However, be warned. Restoring the master database should not be performed unless you really have to, and only if you are experienced with SQL Server. Restoring the master database is not like restoring other databases, and it has to be completed outside SQL Server Management Studio. This book quite deliberately does not cover having to restore the master database since it is a very advanced topic. If you wish to know more, take a look at "SQL Server Books Online" for more details.

When it comes to the msdb database and when to back it up, it could be that a daily backup is required. If you recall, this database holds job schedules and other information pertinent to SQL Server Agent for scheduling. If you have jobs that run each day and you need to keep information about when jobs were run, a daily backup may be required. However, if you wish only to keep a backup of jobs that are set up and there is no need to know when certain jobs ran and whether they were successful, then perhaps look at backing up this database weekly.

The model database should be backed up if any details within the model database have been altered. This should be fairly infrequent, and therefore backing up this database need not be as regular as any other database; once a week is probably frequent enough.

Backing up tempdb is not necessary because this should be seen as a transient database, which has no set state. Therefore, it would be very unusual to back up this database.

■ **Note** When SQL Server is restarted, tempdb is dropped and is re-created as part of the startup process.

As you can see, it is not just your own databases that need to be considered and remembered when it comes to dealing with your backup strategy. A database within SQL Server is not an insular arrangement and affects the system databases just as much. If in doubt, back it up more frequently than is required!

The backup coverage will be split into two parts. The first part will perform the backup manually. Obviously, this means we have to be available to perform the backup, but this can be rectified quite easily. Once this has been covered, the next section will show you how to schedule a backup to run at a specific time, which relieves us of needing to be available to complete a backup at the specified time.

Performing a Manual SQL Server Backup

Let's start by looking at the manual backup. As already mentioned, you have to be on hand to do this, but it is useful to understand all the steps even if you plan to set up automatic backups in your production environment. The aim of this first exercise is to perform a full backup on media that will never expire and therefore will exist until physically deleted. The backup will be placed in the SQL Server default location. You will also see how to cater for second and subsequent backups and the options available. You will at times have to take a manual backup.

It is possible to alter the expiry date of the backup. Different types of backups will have different expiry dates. This means that after the defined date, the media you have stored your backup on will allow the data to be overwritten if using SQL Server (you can't delete the file manually!). For example, you might have a weekly full backup that you want to keep three instances of, and then the first full backup of the month you may wish to keep for six months, or even longer if it is a database that you must keep for government legislation. In this option, you can retain the backup for a set number of days (for example, 21 days) or for a set period of time (a specific date covers for uneven days in a month, or a year, for example).

A default destination is defined automatically by SQL Server, which might be acceptable. In the example, it will be on your hard drive, in a location below where your data are. It is best to have a directory set aside for backups so that they are easy to find, perhaps with a name such as SQL Server Backups. However, it is not recommended in production to store your backups in a subfolder of where your database resides. What if the hard drive fails? You can gain a substantial performance improvement by backing up the database to a separate disk or to a RAID 1 drive if one is available. This is because data are written to the backup file in a sequential manner. Some installations will back up the database to the hard drive for speed but will then initiate a second automatic job that will copy to tape the backup file generated. This then allows for the speed of hard drive backup and the security of tape.

In this exercise, you will see the Options page discussed, but all the options will be left as a default; however, on the main page, you will alter the destination of the backup to be a folder that is more in keeping with a better strategy.

TRY IT OUT: BACKING UP THE DATA

1. Ensure SQL Server Management Studio is running. If you did not bring your database back online from the previous section, find the ApressFinancial database, right-click, select Tasks, and the select Bring Online. After the successful message, close the dialog, right-click again, select Tasks, and then click Back Up.

2. This brings up the SQL Server Back Up Database dialog box. Take a moment to peruse this dialog box, as shown in Figure 8-2. It is possible to back up not only to disk, but also to a URL, which allows for network backups where the drive is not mapped.

Figure 8-2. Backing up a database (Full Recovery mode)

3. Although you have chosen your own database to back up, you could alter which database by changing the value in the combo box. Next is the backup type, and you have up to three options to choose from: Full, Differential, and Transaction Log. The options depend on the recovery model you have in place. During the creation of the database, you specified Full recovery mode, which means that all the options are available. If you are developing with SQL Server Express, then the Simple recovery mode is chosen as the default.

■ **Note** If you were backing up the master database, then the only option that would be available to you would be a complete database backup via the Full option.

4. It is better to alter the destination folder away from the SQL Server folders. Windows protects these folders and permissions can alter. Click Remove, which will remove the single folder defined and will leave the list destinations empty.

5. Click Add, which will display a SQL Server Select Backup Destination dialog box, as shown in Figure 8-3.

Figure 8-3. Database backup destination file name selection dialog

6. You can either type in a folder location and file name for the backup or click the ellipsis to navigate and select a folder. You will also need to type in a file name and file suffix. I have a folder on my hard drive for my SQL Server backups, and I have named the backup file `ApressFinancialFirstFullBackup.bak`. Once you are happy, click OK.

7. Move to the Media Options tab, as shown in Figure 8-4, where you can define what options you want to happen as part of this backup.

Figure 8-4. Database backup options for the media

8. The first section of this dialog box deals with what you want to happen on second and subsequent backups. The first time the backup is run, it creates the backup files, but when you run subsequent backups, do you want to append to the current data or overwrite it? If this is a full backup, then you may overwrite, as you should be placing this full backup over an old, nonrequired backup. (Keep in mind not to overwrite the last full backup, though, just in case this full backup fails as you would then have no recent full backup to work with). To ensure that the correct media set has been loaded and that you do not overwrite a valid media set, ensure you check the media set name and expiry option found below the Overwrite option. However, if this is a differential backup, where it is perhaps the second or third of the week, then you will append to the existing backup set. This will be after the previous differential backups, and it means that if you need to do a restore, all the backups will be one after another and, therefore, will provide the fastest retrieval.

9. The Check Media Set Name option forces the backup to check that where the data are going to be backed up to is still a valid name and, if appending, that the data set has not expired. This is, of course, a backup point of failure that I mentioned before, which can mean a backup is not taken.

10. You use the Back Up to a New Media Set, and Erase All Existing Backup Sets option when any previous backups are no longer required. This is ideal when moving the database from development to either user testing or even production and you don't want to be able to restore from an incorrect backup. There is no point in wishing to restore a production server from a development backup, after all.

11. The second section deals with the reliability of the backup. It is possible to simply back up the data and trust that everything worked perfectly, meaning no data transmission errors occurred between your SQL Server and the backup device, or that no errors occurred when writing the data. A situation such as this is unusual, but there will be times when it does happen. Do you trust that those times will occur when you will not need a backup? I suggest this is something you cannot and should not rely on. Therefore, although it will increase the amount of time the backup takes, it is good to choose one of the two options in this section. The first option allows a verification of the backup where SQL Server compares what has been backed up with what it expects to have been backed up. The second option allows for checksum processing, whereby SQL Server performs a mathematical calculation on the data to back up, which generates a checksum that can then be compared once the data has been transmitted from SQL Server to the backup device. If you select the second option, you can also specify whether to continue if you get a checksum error.

12. If you are doing a transaction log backup, the next area of the dialog box will be enabled. You can logically shrink the transaction log by removing all entries that have just been backed up by selecting the first option, Truncate the Transaction Log. To save processing time, the physical transaction log is not shrunk and just the transactions are deleted. Recall from the Transaction Log section earlier how SQL Server will use a virtual log. The second option, Back Up the Tail of the Log, is used when there has been some sort of database corruption. If you want to back up transaction log records that have not been backed up prior to performing a restore to correct the corruption, you would use this option. To clarify, a database becomes corrupt, and you need to be able to restore up to the last backup and then add all the transactions that have occurred since the last backup. By executing a backup of the tail of the log, you can restore the database and then use this tail-log backup to add the missing transactions.

13. The penultimate area of the dialog box is available if you are using tapes as your backup medium. You can eject the tape once the backup has finished. This is a useful option, as the computer operators would know to remove the tape for dispatch to the safe backup area. The second option, which specifies a rewind, is useful for full backups. On differential backups, however, SQL Server would be halted when running the next backup while the tape device got to the right place on the tape to continue the backup. Therefore, rewinding the tape is not desirable.

14. Finally, move to the Backup Options page, as shown in Figure 8-5.

Figure 8-5. *Database backup options with expiry, compression, and encryption*

15. The first section of note after the media set name is the expiry options for the backup. At present, the backup is set to zero days, which means it will never expire. This doesn't mean it cannot be physically deleted if it is on a disk, but it does mean that when SQL Server is in control of the media, it will not be overwritten. In a production environment, you usually set up a system where backups are kept for a reasonable amount of time, a minimum of one month and often longer. You may be required, for legal reasons, to keep backups for many years.

16. It is possible to set the compression level for the backup. This is ideal if you need to keep space taken for each backup to a minimum. This may occur if you are then sending the backup over the Internet or your intranet for it to be used as a restore to a remote data server. Notice that, by default, it takes the compression level set for the server, but it's possible to overwrite this with a new setting. If your database server is set to no compression, you can change the backup to being compressed. If you do use compressed backups, then you will save on I/O and the backup operation will complete in less time, but completing the compression will increase the amount of processing SQL Server is using. It is possible to reduce the priority of completing a compressed backup so that it doesn't affect SQL Server by using the resource governor. This is an advanced topic and not covered in this book.

17. Finally, it is possible to encrypt your backup if you are backing up to a new media set using one of four encryption algorithms or a key. Perfect if you are exposing any backup to the outside world where theft or loss can take place.

18. Once you are happy and have everything set up, clicking OK starts the backup. Once the backup is finished, you should see the dialog box shown in Figure 8-6.

Figure 8-6. *A successful backup*

The first backup of the ApressFinancial database has now taken place and should have been successful. If you now move to the directory on the hard drive where the backup took place, you will see the ApressFinancial backup file.

Recall that it was mentioned earlier that a company lost a week's worth of data. It had set up the option to append to media, the tape had become full, and the administrator had not set up the proper scenario to alert someone when a problem occurred. So there was not just one failure in the system, but two; however, it still highlights that if you are using the option to append to the existing backup set, you must check that enough room is available on the medium that you are appending to for the backup to succeed.

Creating a backup of your database and the data is the most crucial action in building a database solution. Get it wrong, and you may as well go home. Well, not quite, but if (or when) things go wrong and you don't have a valid or recent enough backup that is acceptable to the users of your database, it will take a long time for you as a developer to recover from that situation and get back to the excellent working relationship you had beforehand.

The backup taken in the preceding example is the simplest backup to perform. It is a complete backup of the particular SQL Server database, and it happens while you are watching. If it goes wrong, you will instantly see and be able to deal with it. However, most backups, in a production system especially, do not happen when you are there; instead, they usually happen throughout the night. Creating a database backup with a schedule to run at the optimal time is the ideal solution and certainly an area to consider. You will see this in Chapter 8, although if you are using SQL Server Express Edition, the ability to schedule jobs is not available.

Backing Up the Database Using T-SQL

Now that you have backed up the database using the dialog within Management Studio, it is useful to see how to perform a backup with T-SQL. These commands and statements can be used within a stored procedure that can be scheduled to run at required intervals as part of an overnight task. If you are using SQL Server Express, there are third-party tools that you can purchase that will run a schedule and not just tasks for databases so scheduling a backup is still possible. As a developer, you can also write your own scheduling software using the development language of your choice, and it is not something that is too difficult to create.

There are two different types of backups. It is possible to back up either the database or specific filegroups or files that are part of the database. The code for the database backup follows. The highlighted code demonstrates which of the two possible options is the optional default used when neither option is specified and the option COMPRESSION/NO COMPRESSION is not available within SQL Server Express Edition:

```
BACKUP DATABASE { database_name | @database_name_var }
TO < backup_device > [ ,...n ]
[ [ MIRROR TO < backup_device > [ ,...n ] ] [ ...next-mirror ] ]
[ WITH
      [ BLOCKSIZE = { blocksize | @blocksize_variable } ]
      [ [ , ] { CHECKSUM | NO_CHECKSUM } ]
      [ [ , ] { STOP_ON_ERROR | CONTINUE_AFTER_ERROR } ]
      [ [ , ] DESCRIPTION = { 'text' | @text_variable } ]
      [ [ , ] DIFFERENTIAL ]
      [ [ , ] EXPIREDATE = { date | @date_var }
      | RETAINDAYS = { days | @days_var } ]
      | { COMPRESSION | NO_COMPRESSION }
      [ [ , ] PASSWORD = { password | @password_variable } ]
      [ [ , ] { FORMAT | NOFORMAT } ]
      [ [ , ] { INIT | NOINIT } ]
      [ [ , ] { NOSKIP | SKIP } ]
      [ [ , ] MEDIADESCRIPTION = { 'text' | @text_variable } ]
      [ [ , ] MEDIANAME = { media_name | @media_name_variable } ]
      [ [ , ] MEDIAPASSWORD = { mediapassword | @mediapassword_variable } ]
      [ [ , ] NAME = { backup_set_name | @backup_set_name_var } ]
      [ [ , ] { NOREWIND | REWIND } ]
      [ [ , ] { NOUNLOAD | UNLOAD } ]
      [ [ , ] STATS [ = percentage ] ]
      [ [ , ] COPY_ONLY ]
]
```

If instead you wish just to back up specific filegroups, the difference in the code is highlighted in bold in the BACKUP DATABASE statement shown here:

```
BACKUP DATABASE { database_name | @database_name_var }
      <file_or_filegroup> [ ,...f ]
TO <backup_device> [ ,...n ]
[ [ MIRROR TO <backup_device> [ ,...n ] ] [ ...next-mirror ] ]
[ WITH
      [ BLOCKSIZE = { blocksize | @blocksize_variable } ]
      [ [ , ] { CHECKSUM | NO_CHECKSUM } ]
      [ [ , ] { STOP_ON_ERROR | CONTINUE_AFTER_ERROR } ]
      [ [ , ] DESCRIPTION = { 'text' | @text_variable } ]
      [ [ , ] DIFFERENTIAL ]
      [ [ , ] EXPIREDATE = { date | @date_var }
```

```
| RETAINDAYS = { days | @days_var } ]
| { COMPRESSION | NO_COMPRESSION }
[ [ , ] PASSWORD = { password | @password_variable } ]
[ [ , ] { FORMAT | NOFORMAT } ]
[ [ , ] { INIT | NOINIT } ]
[ [ , ] { NOSKIP | SKIP } ]
[ [ , ] MEDIADESCRIPTION = { 'text' | @text_variable } ]
[ [ , ] MEDIANAME = { media_name | @media_name_variable } ]
[ [ , ] MEDIAPASSWORD = { mediapassword | @mediapassword_variable } ]
[ [ , ] NAME = { backup_set_name | @backup_set_name_var } ]
[ [ , ] { NOREWIND | REWIND } ]
[ [ , ] { NOUNLOAD | UNLOAD } ]
[ [ , ] STATS [ = percentage ] ]
[ [ , ] COPY_ONLY ]
```

I can now give a brief description of all the options that are available. You looked at some of these options previously with the Back Up Database dialog box. Seeing these descriptions allows you to compare options within T-SQL and within the backup dialog boxes:

- database_name | @database_name_var: Either the name of a database or a local variable that gives the name of the database to back up

- file_or_filegroup: The name of the file or filegroup to back up

- backup_device: The name of the logical or physical backup device to use

- MIRROR TO: The backup file is mirrored to two to four different file locations.

- BLOCKSIZE: The block size to use; for example, if backing up to CD-ROM, then you would set a block size of 2048.

- CHECKSUM | NO_CHECKSUM: Specifies whether to perform checksum calculations to ensure the transmission of data

- STOP_ON_ERROR | CONTINUE_AFTER_ERROR: Specifies whether to stop on a checksum error

- DESCRIPTION: A description of the backup

- DIFFERENTIAL: If this is a differential backup, then specify this option. Without this option, a full backup is taken.

- EXPIREDATE: The date the backup expires and is therefore available to be overwritten

- RETAINDAYS: The number of days the backup will be kept before the system will allow it to be overwritten

- COMPRESSION: Lets you compress your backup and reduce the amount of space taken

■ **Note** Compression backups are available only on the Developer and Enterprise Editions of SQL Server. If you don't define this option, then the server instance setting will be used. You can change it at the server level via the sp_configure system stored procedure.

- PASSWORD: The password associated with the backup; this must be supplied when interrogating the backup for any restore operation. There is no strong encryption on this option, so there is the potential that it could be broken easily.

- FORMAT | NOFORMAT: Specifies whether to format the storage medium

- INIT | NOINIT: INIT Keeps the media header created with the format but erases the contents provided that the expiredate and retaindays have expired. If you want to initialize the media without checking these options, define the next option; SKIP. NOINIT will not initialize the media.

- NOSKIP | SKIP: If you want to skip the checking of expiredate or retaindays when using the media set, then select the SKIP option. Otherwise, expiredate and retaindays will be checked.

■ **Note** A *media set* is an ordered set of backups on the same disk or tape.

- MEDIADESCRIPTION: Gives a description to the media set

- MEDIANAME: Names the media set

- MEDIAPASSWORD: Gives the media set its password

- NAME: Names the backup set

- NOREWIND | REWIND: Specifies whether to rewind a tape once the backup has completed

- NOUNLOAD | UNLOAD: Specifies whether the tape is unloaded or kept on the tape drive once the backup is completed

- STATS [= percentage]: SQL Server provides a message at this percentage interval telling you how much of the approximate backup has completed. It's useful for gauging the progress of long-running backups.

- COPY_ONLY: Tells SQL Server that this is a copy of the data; it cannot be used as a full backup point for differential backups, as the differential backups will be in line with the last "pure" full backup. This option is ideal if you take weekly backups for dumping the data to a user test region, as it will not affect the production backup process. The only remaining option is for files or filegroups where you can name the file or filegroup that the backup is for. The preceding options do not change for files or filegroups.

> ## TRY IT OUT: BACKING UP THE DATABASE USING T-SQL FOR A FULL BACKUP
>
> 1. Open up a fresh Query Editor window. It doesn't matter which database it is pointing to, as the BACKUP DATABASE statement defines the database the query will be backing up.
>
> 2. The T-SQL that is needed for the full backup follows. Enter the code (keeping the name of where the backup is located via the TO DISK option and the WITH NAME option all on one line). Notice that several of the options are not defined, as the query is accepting the default. The backup file generated within Management Studio in the previous exercise will be overwritten as the T-SQL uses the SKIP option.
>
> ```
> BACKUP DATABASE ApressFinancial
> TO DISK = 'C:\APRESS_DEV1\MSSQL12.APRESS_DEV1\MSSQL\Backup\
> ApressFinancialFirstFullBackup.bak'
> WITH NAME = 'ApressFinancial-Full Database Backup',
> SKIP,
> NOUNLOAD,
> STATS = 10
> ```
>
> 3. Execute the code and you will see results similar to those that follow. The main points to notice are the stats messages that come out in approximations of 10 percentage points. It then lists the number of data pages backed up and the number of log pages backed up. The *on file* part of the message details which file within the media set the backup now is. In this case, this is the second backup. You will possibly see *on file 2* if you had taken a subsequent backup since the previous exercise. The final message is the one of greatest interest, as it shows that the backup was successful and it displays the amount of time taken.

```
Processed 328 pages for database 'ApressFinancial',
file 'ApressFinancial' on file 1.
Processed 0 pages for database 'ApressFinancial',
file 'ApressFinancial-Memory' on file 1.
Processed 22 pages for database 'ApressFinancial',
file 'ApressFinancial_log' on file 1.
100 percent processed.
BACKUP DATABASE successfully processed 350 pages
in 1.515 seconds (1.802 MB/sec).
```

> You now have a full backup of the database, which could be used as the starting point of any recovery of a corrupt database. However, over time, changes will have been made to the database. Whether it is a few hours, days, or weeks later, you now want to perform a backup of those changes that have occurred. In the next section, you will see a differential backup where the options are shown within Management Studio, and from these the T-SQL will be generated for the backup.

TRY IT OUT: BACKING UP THE DATABASE WITH A DIFFERENTIAL BACKUP

1. From Management Studio, select from Object Explorer the ApressFinancial database, right-click, and from the menu that appears select Tasks and then Backup. You will then see the same screen as you saw in the "Backing Up the Data" exercise. The next backup of the database to be taken is a differential backup, so alter the Backup type to this option. This backup will be adding this differential backup to the full backup that was taken in the previous exercise. Notice that the Destination list box already has the correct location and file name, as shown in Figure 8-7.

Figure 8-7. *Backing up a database (differential)*

■ **Note** At the end of the screenshots, don't back up, but rather click the Generate Script button, which will place the T-SQL equivalent code in a new query window, where you will then be asked to run it.

2. Moving to the Media Options page, you will be appending the differential backup to the same media set as the full backup. This time you will include some reliability checking by clicking the "Verify backup when finished" option. Make sure your version of the window matches Figure 8-8.

Figure 8-8. *Options for backing up a database (differential)*

3. Rather than clicking OK, you will see at the top of the window a menu with the option Script. Click this menu drop-down and from the options displayed, select Script Action to New Query Window. Then click Cancel. This will generate code based on your options and place it in a new query window.

4. The first part of the generated code deals with the differential backup. I have put this code in bold. Again, ensure that the TO DISK and NAME options are all on the same line of the Query Editor windowpane.

```
BACKUP DATABASE [ApressFinancial]
TO  DISK = N'C:\APRESS_DEV1\MSSQL12.APRESS_DEV1\MSSQL\
BackupApressFinancialFirstFullBackup.bak'
WITH  DIFFERENTIAL,
NOFORMAT, NOINIT,
NAME = N'ApressFinancial-Full Database Backup',
SKIP, NOREWIND, NOUNLOAD,  STATS = 10
GO
declare @backupSetId as int
select @backupSetId = position
from msdb..backupset
where database_name=N'ApressFinancial'
and backup_set_id=(select max(backup_set_id)
                   from msdb..backupset
                 where database_name=N'ApressFinancial')
```

```
if @backupSetId is null
begin
    raiserror(N'Verify failed. Backup information for database
        ''ApressFinancial'' not found.', 16, 1)
end
RESTORE VERIFYONLY
FROM  DISK = N'C:\APRESS_DEV1\MSSQL12.APRESS_DEV1\MSSQL\
BackupApressFinancialFirstFullBackup.bak'
WITH  FILE = @backupSetId,
NOUNLOAD,  NOREWIND
GO
```

5. The second part of the query is where the reliability checking takes place. This is more complex T-SQL than I have covered, so for the moment just trust that it works and that it does what it is supposed to. You will encounter this code once more when looking at more complex T-SQL later in the book in Chapter 16. However, the basis of the code is that a check is made in the msdb database to retrieve the last backup set that was taken, that the query will perform a "restore" of the database as verification only without actually restoring any data, and that the restore can complete successfully. If it can't verify the backup set or that the restore is okay, then you will get an error message.

```
BACKUP DATABASE [ApressFinancial]
TO  DISK = N'C:\APRESS_DEV1\MSSQL12.APRESS_DEV1\MSSQL\
BackupApressFinancialFirstFullBackup.bak'
WITH  DIFFERENTIAL ,
NOFORMAT, NOINIT,
NAME = N'ApressFinancial-Full Database Backup',
SKIP, NOREWIND, NOUNLOAD,   STATS = 10
GO
declare @backupSetId as int
select @backupSetId = position
from msdb..backupset
where database_name=N'ApressFinancial'
and backup_set_id=(select max(backup_set_id)
                        from msdb..backupset
                        where database_name=N'ApressFinancial' )
if @backupSetId is null
begin
    raiserror(N'Verify failed. Backup information for database
        ''ApressFinancial'' not found.', 16, 1)
end
RESTORE VERIFYONLY
FROM  DISK = N'C:\APRESS_DEV1\MSSQL12.APRESS_DEV1\MSSQL\
BackupApressFinancialFirstFullBackup.bak'
WITH  FILE = @backupSetId,
NOUNLOAD,  NOREWIND
GO
```

6. When the code is executed, which you should do now, you will see something like the results that follow. Again, they contain details of the amount of data backed up as well as which file number on the media set the backup is.

```
10 percent processed.
Processed 40 pages for database 'ApressFinancial',
file 'ApressFinancial' on file 1.
Processed 0 pages for database 'ApressFinancial',
file 'ApressFinancial-Memory' on file 1.
23 percent processed.
Processed 30 pages for database 'ApressFinancial',
file 'ApressFinancial_log' on file 1.
100 percent processed.
BACKUP DATABASE WITH DIFFERENTIAL successfully
processed 70 pages in 0.291 seconds (1.865 MB/sec).
The backup set on file 1 is valid.
```

Transaction Log Backup Using T-SQL

You can back up not only the data, but also, and just as importantly, the transaction log for the database. Just to recap, the transaction log is a file used by databases to log every transaction, including data modification actions such as rebuilding indexes. In other words, every data modification that has taken place on any table within the database will be recorded within the transaction log. (There is one major exception, but I will cover this when looking at deleting data later in the book.) The transaction log is then used in many different scenarios within a database solution, but where it is most useful, from a database recovery point of view, is when a database crashes. In this case, the transaction log can be used to move forward from the last data backup, using the transactions listed within the transaction log.

If a database .crash occurs, then the full and differential backups will take you only to the last valid backup. For data entered since that point, the only way to restore the information is to then "replay" the transactions that were committed and recorded as committed in the transaction log via a tail-log backup. Any actions that were in progress at the time of the failure that were within a transaction that was still in progress would have to be rerun from the start.

So, to clarify, if you were in the process of deleting data within a table and the power was switched off, you would use your full and differential backups to restore the data. You would then use the information within the transaction log to replay all successful transactions, but because the delete had not been successful, the table would have all the data still within it.

Backing up the transaction log is a good strategy to employ when a large number of updates occur to the data through the day. A transaction log backup should take place at set times throughout the day, depending on how large the transaction log has grown and how crucial it was to get your system back up and running after any unexpected outage. When a transaction log is backed up, the transaction log itself is logically shrunk in size so that it is kept small. It also gives you point-in-time recoverability; this means that you can quickly restore to any time in the past at which the transaction was backed up.

Backing up a transaction log is similar to backing up a database. The full syntax is as follows and differs from a database backup only by using the LOG keyword instead of DATABASE and the options NO_TRUNCATE and NORECOVERY/STANDBY:

```
BACKUP LOG { database_name | @database_name_var }
{
    TO <backup_device> [ ,...n ]
[ [ MIRROR TO <backup_device> [ ,...n ] ] [ ...next-mirror ] ]
    [ WITH
    [ BLOCKSIZE = { blocksize | @blocksize_variable } ]
    [ [ , ] { CHECKSUM | NO_CHECKSUM } ]
    [ [ , ] { STOP_ON_ERROR | CONTINUE_AFTER_ERROR } ]
    [ [ , ] DESCRIPTION = { 'text' | @text_variable } ]
    [ [ , ] EXPIREDATE = { date | @date_var }
    | RETAINDAYS = { days | @days_var } ]
    | { COMPRESSION | NO_COMPRESSION }
    [ [ , ] PASSWORD = { password | @password_variable } ]
    [ [ , ] { FORMAT | NOFORMAT } ]
    [ [ , ] { INIT | NOINIT } ]
    [ [ , ] { NOSKIP | SKIP } ]
    [ [ , ] MEDIADESCRIPTION = { 'text' | @text_variable } ]
    [ [ , ] MEDIANAME = { media_name | @media_name_variable } ]
    [ [ , ] MEDIAPASSWORD = { mediapassword | @mediapassword_variable } ]
    [ [ , ] NAME = { backup_set_name | @backup_set_name_var } ]
    [ [ , ] NO_TRUNCATE ]
    [ [ , ] { NORECOVERY | STANDBY = undo_file_name } ]
    [ [ , ] { NOREWIND | REWIND } ]
    [ [ , ] { NOUNLOAD | UNLOAD } ]
    [ [ , ] STATS [ = percentage ] ]
    [ [ , ] COPY_ONLY ]
    ]
}
```

As with the database backup, if you are using SQL Server Express, the compression option is not available. Now let's look at the options not covered earlier when looking at backing up the database:

- LOG: Determines that you wish to produce a backup of the transaction log rather than a backup of a database or files/filegroups

- NO_TRUNCATE: Doesn't truncate the log after the backup; if the database is corrupt, using this option will allow the backup to be attempted at least. Without this option, you will get an error message.

- NORECOVERY | STANDBY: After the backup, the database will be in a state whereby it looks to anyone trying to connect as if it is still being restored and is not available.

■ **Note** The LOG options NO_TRUNCATE and NORECOVER | STANDBY are used when the database is corrupt and you wish to back up the transaction log prior to performing a restore.

In the following exercise, a transaction log will be backed up using T-SQL. As the ApressFinancial database is using a Full Recovery model, this action will back up all the transactions recorded since the last differential backup and then remove these transactions from the log itself. A transaction log backup is not available for Simple Recovery models.

TRY IT OUT: BACKING UP THE TRANSACTION LOG USING T-SQL

1. In a Query Editor pane, enter the following T-SQL code.

■ **Note** If you are in Simple Recovery mode, backing up the transaction log will fail.

```
BACKUP LOG [ApressFinancial]
TO  DISK = N'C:\APRESS_DEV1\MSSQL12.APRESS_DEV1\MSSQL\
BackupApressFinancialFirstFullBackup.bak'
 WITH NOFORMAT, NOINIT,
 NAME = N'ApressFinancial-Transaction Log Backup',
 SKIP, NOREWIND, NOUNLOAD,
 STATS = 10GO
```

2. This backs up the transaction log to the same media set as the full and differential backups. While you are developing and learning SQL Server, this is a valid scenario, and in some production setups you may want to back up to the same place as your daily full backup. However, the downside is that if you take several transaction log backups between each differential backup and full backup, then SQL Server will have to "skip" these if they were not required as part of the restore operation. On a tape drive, this could cause significant overhead. In this scenario, you would be better off saving the transaction log files to a different media set.

3. Execute the code to back up the transaction log, and you should see output similar to the following, where the transaction log has been successfully backed up and placed on file 2:

```
100 percent processed.
Processed 56 pages for database 'ApressFinancial', file
'ApressFinancial_log' on file 2.
BACKUP LOG successfully processed 56 pages in 0.232 seconds (1.885 MB/sec).
```

You can back up the transaction log from Management Studio similar to how you have performed the database backup earlier in the chapter. The only real difference is contained within the Options page, which is shown in Figure 8-9. Toward the bottom of the page, you will see the Transaction Log section, where you can either truncate the transaction log or back up the tail of the log. In this instance, you are performing only a backup of the transaction log. This will back up all the transactions completed since the last backup. The second option, backing up the tail of the log, is demonstrated and discussed later in the chapter when you will see how to restore a database to a point in time after the last backup was taken.

Figure 8-9. *Backing up a transaction log*

Restoring a Database

Now that the data has been backed up, what if you needed to complete a restore? As I have mentioned, there are two scenarios in which a restore could be required: either you are restoring to another system as a check that the database backup worked or as part of restoring the database to a different server, or you are recovering from a failure on your database. The second type of restore, in which a failure has occurred, is not one you wish to perform but will happen; it could be set up by creating a long-running transaction and then simply switching your computer off—not one of life's greatest ideas to do deliberately! This book, therefore, will not be demonstrating this option, and it is not really for a beginner to attempt. However, I will discuss the concept within this section of the chapter. The first option, a simple restore, is easy to replicate and perform, and this will be the option I will cover.

You can choose between two means to restore the database: SQL Server Management Studio and T-SQL. If you need a restore within the development environment to remove test data and get back to a stable, predefined set of data to complete the testing, this next section should help you. It might also be that you do a weekly refresh of your user test region from a production backup. The bottom line is that you are performing a "regular" restore.

Before completing the restore, you will first modify the `ApressFinancial` database to prove that the restore works, as there is no data within the database yet to prove the restore has worked by that method. Keep in mind, however, that a restore will restore not only the data structures, but also the data, the permissions, and other areas of the database not yet covered in the book—for example, views, stored procedures, and so on.

Restoring Using SQL Server Management Studio

The restore demonstrated in the following example will be a complete database restore of the `ApressFinancial` database. In other words, it will restore all the full and differential backups taken.

It is also possible to restore to a point in time, which is used if you are restoring the database as well as rolling forward changes recorded in the transaction log. This situation is similar to the scenario mentioned earlier about a power failure or hard drive failure. In the first restore, you will be restoring only from existing backups. You need to be aware of the point in time that you want to restore to; it is not possible to investigate the transaction log and make a decision based on information contained within it. The decision has to be time-based. On the General page, you will see a Timeline button, which would allow you to perform a restore to a point in time. This option will be discussed further later in the chapter.

When taking a backup, details are stored in `msdb`, but it is possible to restore a database from a backup that is not in `msdb`. For example, if you are rebuilding a server due to corruption and `msdb` was one of the databases corrupted, it is necessary to have the option of finding a backup file and restoring from that instead. Or perhaps the last full backup taken is not the backup you wish to restore. This might occur in a development scenario, in which you wish to restore to a backup before major changes were done that you wish to remove. There would be no transaction log involved or required to be involved; therefore, restoring to a point in time would not be a valid scenario. This is where you could use the From Device option. By selecting this option and clicking the ellipsis to the right, you can navigate to any old backup files.

Finally, on the General page, you can click which of the items in the backup you wish to restore. The default is all backups to be selected; however, if you want to restore to a point in an earlier backup and not to restore a later backup, you can unselect the late backups.

It is also possible to restore the database to a completely new location as well as a new name. This is ideal for a hardware failure or to restore to a copy location.

When restoring, there are a number of options concerning how the restore should be applied to the database. These are as follows:

- *Overwrite the Existing Database*: Although a potentially dangerous option to select, this is the most likely option to be enabled for a restore to a point in time contained within the latest backup. A restore to a point in the latest backup can be required when data modifications have taken place in error, such as deleting financial transactions in error and a backup of the transaction log had been taken. If the log backup was taken, financial transactions were added correctly. Then the error occurred and you wanted to keep the financial transactions added correctly. Now you have a small, but not insurmountable problem. The first action to complete would be a new transaction log backup, sometimes called a tail-log backup, by issuing a `BACKUP LOG` with the `WITH NORECOVERY` option. This backs up the database but then indicates that you want to restore the database. As a result, the database will not allow any new data modifications. You would then select restore but disable the Overwrite the Existing Database option, as this is the safer option.

- *Preserve the Replication Settings*: A more advanced option for when a database is sending changes to another database; for the time being, leave this option disabled.

- *Restrict Access to the Restored Database*: You may wish to check out the database after a restore to ensure the restore is what you wish, or in a production environment to run further checks on the database integrity.

- Recovery State has one of three options:

 - `RESTORE WITH RECOVERY`: This option defines whether users can immediately connect and work with the data after the restore.

- RESTORE WITH NORECOVERY: With this option, you can indicate that the database has been partially restored and you are unsure if you need to perform additional actions such as further restores. If a transaction is in progress, such as deleting a table, then whatever has been deleted will still be deleted and will not be rolled back.

- RESTORE WITH STANDBY: A combination of the first two options; if a transaction is in progress, such as deleting rows in a table, then the connection could occur once the deletion has been rolled back. However, the changes are also kept in a separate file, so that any of these actions that have been rolled back can be reapplied. This might happen if there are several actions within a transaction and some can be reapplied.

- *Prompt Before Restoring Each Backup*: If you would like a prompt message before each restore file is activated, then select this. This is ideal if you need to swap media over.

If you wanted to restore to a point in time, you would need to take a tail-log backup. I cover this later in the chapter when discussing restoring to a point in time. You can also force-close any connections that are currently connected to the database, and, finally, you can restore the database a file at a time with a prompt between each file restore.

You have had a lot of options and points thrown at you, so let's take a look at restoring a database.

TRY IT OUT: RESTORING A DATABASE

1. Add a new column to the ShareDetails.Shares table, using the following code in a Query Editor pane, and execute:

```
USE ApressFinancial
GO
ALTER TABLE ShareDetails.Shares
ADD DummyColumn varchar(30)
```

2. Once you have confirmed that the column has been added by looking in Object Explorer, you can now use the backup you created earlier to restore the database, which will remove the changes you have just completed. From the Object Explorer window, select the ApressFinancial database, right-click, and select Tasks ➤ Restore ➤ Database. This brings up the dialog box shown in Figure 8-10. You will be restoring from all of the existing backups, which will remove the column created in the previous step.

Figure 8-10. *Restoring a database: General tab*

3. It is possible to change the database you wish to restore by changing the name in the Destination Database combo box or by simply overwriting the name that is there.

4. If you switch to the Files page, you have the option of restoring the database to a new folder location as well as a new database name. This is ideal in scenarios such as taking a production backup of a database and restoring it to a production copy or if you need to restore a database to a new server. You would do this by selecting the "Relocate all files to folder" check box, as shown in Figure 8-11. As you will be restoring to the same location and name, leave the box unselected.

Figure 8-11. *Restoring a database: Altering the location of the database*

5. On the Options page, there are a number of points to consider as discussed prior to the exercise. You should select Overwrite the Existing Database and deselect the "Take tail-log backup before restore" check box, shown in Figure 8-12, as the database changes are not being replicated to another database. You also have no need to keep the database to a single user post-backup, as no further work may be required on a power failure, or to check that the correct restore has been completed.

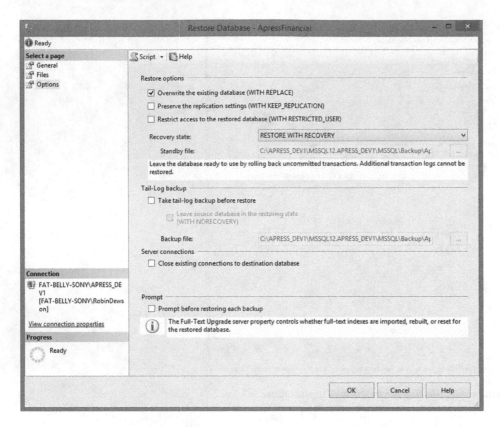

Figure 8-12. Restoring a database: Options tab

6. Once you have the option settings you require or use the settings suggested and there are no query editor panes open (no connections), a quick click of OK performs the restore. You should see the message in Figure 8-13. If you then move back to the database after clicking OK, you will see that the column you just added has been removed when you look in Object Explorer for the ApressFinancial ShareDetails.Shares table.

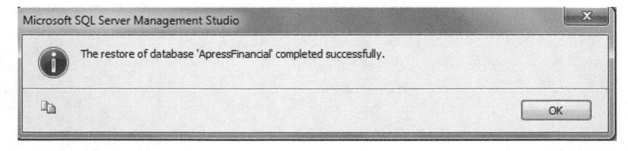

Figure 8-13. Restore successful

Restoring Using T-SQL

Using Management Studio is a pretty fast way to restore a database, and when under pressure, it may even be the best way forward. However, it is not the most flexible way of performing a restore, as some options that are available via T-SQL are not in this wizard. Some of these options were covered when you performed a backup, such as performing checksums when transferring data from the media device back to the database or unloading media at the end of the restore. If there is also a password on the backup medium, this option is not available within the screen in the example you have just completed, but you can use passwords with T-SQL. Being comfortable building a restore via T-SQL is important in becoming a more proficient and professional developer or administrator. Also by knowing how to restore via T-SQL, you can use the code in a scheduled script such as a nightly restore to a development server of your production data.

Restoring a Database

The syntax for restoring a database is similar to that for database backups. After looking at the syntax, I will then go through the options you will not be familiar with. The items in bold are the default values.

```
RESTORE DATABASE { database_name | @database_name_var }
[ FROM <backup_device> [ ,...n ] ]
[ WITH
  [ { CHECKSUM | NO_CHECKSUM } ]
  [ [ , ] { CONTINUE_AFTER_ERROR | STOP_ON_ERROR } ]
  [ [ , ] FILE = { file_number | @file_number } ]
  [ [ , ] KEEP_REPLICATION ]
  [ [ , ] MEDIANAME = { media_name | @media_name_variable } ]
  [ [ , ] MEDIAPASSWORD = { mediapassword |
                      @mediapassword_variable } ]
  [ [ , ] MOVE 'logical_file_name' TO 'operating_system_file_name' ]
            [ ,...n ]
  [ [ , ] PASSWORD = { password | @password_variable } ]
  [ [ , ] { RECOVERY | NORECOVERY | STANDBY =
         {standby_file_name | @standby_file_name_var }
  } ]
  [ [ , ] REPLACE ]
  [ [ , ] RESTART ]
  [ [ , ] RESTRICTED_USER ]
  [ [ , ] { REWIND | NOREWIND } ]
  [ [ , ] STATS [ = percentage ] ]
  [ [ , ] { STOPAT = { date_time | @date_time_var }
  | STOPATMARK = { 'mark_name' | 'lsn:lsn_number' }
           [ AFTER datetime ]
  | STOPBEFOREMARK = { 'mark_name' | 'lsn:lsn_number' }
           [ AFTER datetime ]
  } ]
  [ [ , ] { UNLOAD | NOUNLOAD } ]
]
```

The options I have not yet covered are as follows:

- KEEP_REPLICATION: When working with replication, consider using this option. Replication is when changes completed in one database are automatically sent to another database. The most common scenario is when you have a central database replicating changes to satellite databases, and possibly vice versa.

- MOVE: When completing a restore, the MDF and LDF files that are being restored have to be placed where they were backed up from. However, by using this option, you can change that location.

- RECOVERY | NORECOVERY | STANDBY: These three options are the same, and in the same order, as their counterparts (in parentheses) in the Management Studio screen:

 - RECOVERY (Leave the Database Ready to Use): This option defines that after the restore is finished, users can immediately connect to and work with the data. If a transaction is in progress, such as updating rows in a table, then not until the updates have been rolled back and therefore the table is back in its "original" state will connections to the database be allowed.

 - NORECOVERY (Leave the Database Non-operational): With this option, you are indicating that the database has been partially restored, and you are unsure whether you need to perform additional actions. If a transaction is in progress, such as inserting rows in a table, then the insertions will *not* be rolled back. This allows additional restores to get to a specific point in time. You will see how to then alter the database so that it is operational in the following exercises.

 - STANDBY (Leave the Database in Read-Only Mode): A combination of the first two options; if a transaction is in progress, such as deleting rows in a table, then the deletion will be rolled back. However, the changes are also in a separate file so that any of these actions that have been rolled back can be reapplied. This might happen if several actions occurred within a transaction and some can be reapplied.

- REPLACE: This works the same as the screen option Overwrite the Existing Database.

- RESTART: If a restore is stopped partway through, using this option will restart the restore at the point it was stopped.

- RESTRICTED_USER: Use this with the RECOVERY option to allow only users in specific restricted groups to access the database. Use this to allow further checking by a database owner, or by the dbowner, dbcreator, or sysadmin roles.

- STOPAT | STOPATMARK | STOPBEFOREMARK: Use this to specify a specific date and time at which to stop the restore.

Restoring a Transaction Log

The syntax for restoring the transaction log is exactly the same, with the only difference being the definition—you are completing a LOG rather than a DATABASE restore:

```
RESTORE LOG { database_name | @database_name_var }
    <file_or_filegroup_or_pages> [ ,...f ]
[ FROM <backup_device> [ ,...n ] ]
[ WITH
```

```
[ { CHECKSUM | NO_CHECKSUM } ]
[ [ , ] { CONTINUE_AFTER_ERROR | STOP_ON_ERROR } ]
[ [ , ] FILE = { file_number | @file_number } ]
[ [ , ] KEEP_REPLICATION ]
[ [ , ] MEDIANAME = { media_name | @media_name_variable } ]
[ [ , ] MEDIAPASSWORD = { mediapassword | @mediapassword_variable }        ]
[ [ , ] MOVE 'logical_file_name' TO 'operating_system_file_name' ]
            [ ,...n ]
[ [ , ] PASSWORD = { password | @password_variable } ]
[ [ , ] { RECOVERY | NORECOVERY | STANDBY =
       {standby_file_name | @standby_file_name_var } } }
]
[ [ , ] REPLACE ]
[ [ , ] RESTART ]
[ [ , ] RESTRICTED_USER ]
[ [ , ] { REWIND | NOREWIND } ]
[ [ , ] STATS [=percentage ] ]
[ [ , ] { STOPAT = { date_time | @date_time_var }
 | STOPATMARK = { 'mark_name' | 'lsn:lsn_number' }
            [ AFTER datetime ]
 | STOPBEFOREMARK = { 'mark_name' | 'lsn:lsn_number' }
            [ AFTER datetime ]
} ]
[ [ , ] { UNLOAD | NOUNLOAD } ]
]
```

TRY IT OUT: RESTORING USING T-SQL

1. Open up an empty Query Editor pane and enter the following code. This will add the column that you want to see "removed" after a restore.

```
USE ApressFinancial
GO
ALTER TABLE ShareDetails.Shares
ADD DummyColumn varchar(30)
```

2. Now replace this code with the restore code that follows. Don't execute any of the code just yet, as this piece of code is the first part only. Recall that when performing the backups, FILE 1 was the FULL backup taken. This is what the first restore will do.

■ **Note** Ensure that the FROM DISK option is all on one line. Also recall that FILE = 1 may be FILE = 2 or any other number, depending on the backups taken, and this may be the case with different file numbers as you progress.

```
USE [master]
GO
RESTORE DATABASE [ApressFinancial] FROM  DISK =
N'C:\APRESS_DEV1\MSSQL12.APRESS_DEV1\MSSQL\
BackupApressFinancialFirstFullBackup.bak'WITH FILE = 1, NORECOVERY, NOUNLOAD, REPLACE,
STATS = 5
GO
```

3. The next part of the restore operation is to restore the transaction log file. Once all this code
 is in, you can run it all.

```
RESTORE LOG [ApressFinancial] FROM  DISK =
N'C:\APRESS_DEV1\MSSQL12.APRESS_DEV1\MSSQL\
BackupApressFinancialFirstFullBackup.bak'
WITH  FILE = 2,  RECOVERY, NOUNLOAD,  STATS = 5
```

4. Once the code has fully executed, you should see results similar to those listed here:

```
100 percent processed.
Processed 42 pages for database 'ApressFinancial',
file 'ApressFinancial' on file 1.
Processed 2 pages for database 'ApressFinancial',
file 'ApressFinancial_log' on file 1.

RESTORE LOG successfully processed 6 pages
in 0.044 seconds (0.998 MB/sec).
```

You can now move back to the ShareDetails.Shares table and check that the column
added has now been removed. You may have to perform a refresh within Object Explorer first
to see the changes.

Restoring a database in production will, in most instances, take place under pressure, as the database will have
become corrupt or been inadvertently damaged. The production system is obviously down and not working, and you
have irate users wanting to know how long before the system will be up. This is hopefully the worst-case scenario,
but it is that sort of level of pressure that you will be working under when you have to restore the database. Therefore,
having the correct backup strategy for your organization based on full, differential, and transaction log backups
is crucial. Also having scripts in place ready for restores will help speed up getting the database back online. Full
database backups for a system that requires high availability so that the restore takes the least amount of time may be
what you need.

Restoring to a Point in Time

As mentioned a few times, there may come a time when you have taken a transaction log backup and before the next
transaction log backup is taken, a problem occurs—caused either by a developer or your system. This is when there
are actions that have occurred that you wish to keep, but there are subsequent actions that should not be restored.
What is required is a tail-log backup followed by a restore to a specific point in time.

In a real-life scenario on a production database, this can be tricky and dangerous to get the exact point in time if you have data modifications happening at the time of the failure. You may have to make a hard decision of where to restore to and realize that some data may be lost. If it is during an overnight batch, it may be easier, depending on your failure, as batches can be easier to track to where to restore to. You should be aware of what was running at any specific point in time to find the right point and then rerun any batches run post restore.

To restore to a point in time requires a number of actions to be performed successfully before the restore is complete.

First of all, you are required to back up the transaction log changes from the last successful backup to the current point in time. This is called taking a tail-log backup. You also need to put the database in NORECOVERY mode, which means that nobody will be able to connect. This will avoid database changes being applied that will be lost during the restore.

Once the backup is complete, the restore can commence. You would apply the last full backup, followed by all differential backups, and then the transaction log backups that have been taken. You are then left with the restore to the point in time from the tail-log backup. This uses the same syntax as the other transaction log restores but with the STOPAT option defined, which determines the date and time at which to stop restoring.

It is possible, if required, to then open the database to a single user, who can then check the tables that are required to be checked in case a different time would be better. You will see this option when detaching a database in the next section.

You have seen the process of performing a backup and restore of your database in the examples you have just performed, so in this section I will demonstrate how to restore up to a point in time with specific transactions restored and other actions after that point discarded.

To demonstrate this, the following exercise will apply two changes to the database, one of which will remain in place and the other will be rolled back as it will be after the point in time.

TRY IT OUT: RESTORE TO A POINT IN TIME

1. The first change will remain after the restore. Enter the following code, execute it, and take a note of the time of execution:

```
CREATE TABLE TransactionDetails.TransactionHistory
(Column1 varchar(200) NULL,
 Column2 int NULL)
 GO
```

2. Now wait a period of time. You will have to be able to distinguish between the times of the two actions, so pick something easy. I am going to wait five minutes.

3. Once a period has passed, enter the following code and execute it:

```
ALTER TABLE ShareDetails.Shares
ADD DummyColumn varchar(30)
```

4. Now you have two changes to the database; the first will be kept and the second will be rolled back. There is no backup taken at this point that you can restore to that would keep the TransactionDetails.TransactionHistory table and remove the DummyColumn column. Therefore, you need to take a tail-log backup first and then restore to a point in time. It is possible to do this in one action. Highlight the ApressFinancial database and right-click. From the pop-up menu, select Tasks ➤ Restore ➤ Database. The Restore Database window opens, as shown in Figure 8-14.

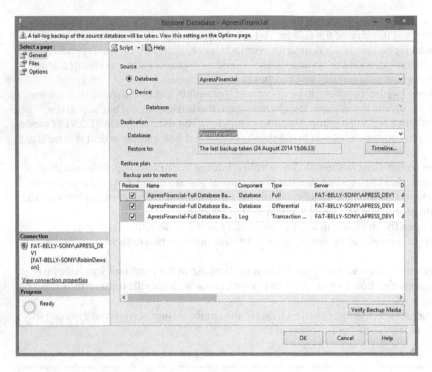

Figure 8-14. *Restore Database window*

5. Click the Timeline button, which should bring up a dialog similar to Figure 8-15. The date and times will differ but show the last backup that was taken. This is so that a regular restore will be to the last backup, which is a more regular scenario and therefore makes sense to be the default.

Figure 8-15. *The Backup Timeline dialog, wh*

6. To restore some of the modifications since the last backup, you need to select the option "Specific date and time". You would then select the date and time that the first modification was taken. The screen will look something like Figure 8-16 with a notification that a tail-log backup will be taken. Once you are happy, click OK.

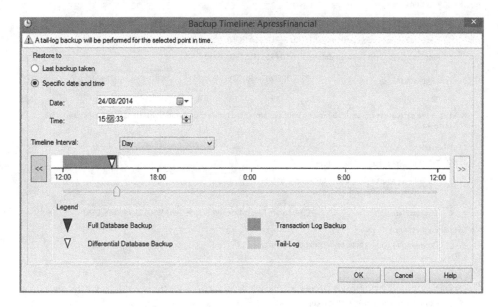

Figure 8-16. *The Backup Timeline dialog with the date and time set, wh*

7. Move to the Options page and select the options to overwrite the existing database. However, you need to leave the database in a NORECOVERY state after the tail-log backup so that the restore can be successfully completed (see Figure 8-17).

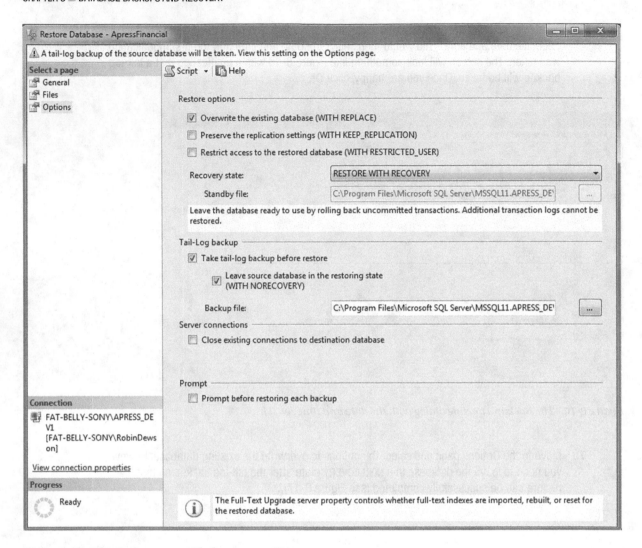

Figure 8-17. *The Options page with the proper settings*

8. Once you are happy, from the menu select Script ➤ New Query Editor window, which will generate the T-SQL that will achieve the restore. The code is split over the next three steps. The first section will back up the tail of the transaction log.

```
USE [master]
BACKUP LOG [ApressFinancial] TO  DISK =
N'C:\APRESS_DEV1\MSSQL12.APRESS_DEV1\MSSQL\Backup\
ApressFinancial_LogBackup_2014-08-24_15-26-04.bak'
WITH NOFORMAT, NOINIT,
NAME = N'ApressFinancial_LogBackup_2014-08-24_15-26-04',
NOSKIP, NOREWIND, NOUNLOAD,  NORECOVERY ,  STATS = 5
```

9. The next step is a restore of the full backup and the transaction log backup taken so far.

```
RESTORE DATABASE [ApressFinancial] FROM  DISK =
N'C:\APRESS_DEV1\MSSQL12.APRESS_DEV1\MSSQL\Backup\
ApressFinancial_LogBackup_2014-08-24_15-26-04.bak'
WITH  FILE = 1,
NORECOVERY,  NOUNLOAD,  REPLACE,  STATS = 5
RESTORE LOG [ApressFinancial] FROM  DISK =
N'C:\APRESS_DEV1\MSSQL12.APRESS_DEV1\MSSQL\Backup\
ApressFinancial_LogBackup_2014-08-24_15-26-04.bak'
WITH  FILE = 2,  NORECOVERY,  NOUNLOAD,  STATS = 5
```

10. The final step is where you can stop the restore of the transaction log at a specific point of time by using the STOPAT option.

```
RESTORE LOG [ApressFinancial] FROM  DISK =
N'C:\APRESS_DEV1\MSSQL12.APRESS_DEV1\MSSQL\Backup\
ApressFinancialFirstFullBackup.bak'
WITH  NOUNLOAD,  STATS = 5,  STOPAT = N'2014-08-24T15:22:33'
GO
```

11. Finally, I will drop the TransactionDetails.TransactionsHistory table, as it is not required for the book. I entered the following code and executed it. There is no harm in keeping this table if you want, but you will not see it in any figures within the book going forward.

```
DROP TABLE TransactionDetails.TransactionHistory
```

Detaching and Attaching a Database

Now that you can back up and restore a database, you have other methods available for dealing with the database. There may be a time in the life of your SQL Server database when you have to move it from one server to another or, in fact, just from one hard drive to another. For example, perhaps you currently have ApressFinancial on the C drive and this is getting full, so you would like to move the database to another hard drive. Or perhaps you are moving from an old, slower server to a new, faster server or a server on a better network. By detaching and reattaching the database, you can do this simply and easily.

I would like to make a few points here; they may seem straightforward and really obvious, but better to mention them than cause problems at a later stage. First of all, no updates can be occurring, no jobs can be running, and no users can be attached. Secondly, just in case, take a full backup before moving the database. This may add time to the process, but it is better to be safe than sorry. Also, ensure that where you are moving the database to has enough disk space, not only for the move, but also for expected future growth; otherwise, you will be moving your database twice. You should not attach your database to a server without immediately completing a backup on the new server afterward; this way, you can ensure that the databases are protected in their new state.

Detaching a database physically removes the details from the SQL Server master and msdb databases, but does not remove the files from the disk that it resides on. However, detaching the database from SQL Server then allows you to safely move, copy, or delete the files that make up the database, if you so desire within Windows. This is the only way that a database should be physically removed from a server for moving it.

Detaching and Attaching Using SQL Server Management Studio

Let's start by using SSMS to detach and attach a database.

TRY IT OUT: DETACHING A DATABASE

1. First of all, it is necessary to ensure that nobody is logged in to the database, and even if someone is, that the user is not doing any updates. However, to demonstrate what happens when a user is connected to the database, ensure that SQL Server Management Studio is running and that there is a Query Editor pane with a connection to the ApressFinancial database. You may already have a connection via a query pane still open from the previous examples.

2. Find the ApressFinancial database in Object Explorer and ensure that it is selected. Right-click and select Tasks ➤ Detach. This brings up the Detach Database dialog box for the ApressFinancial database, as shown in Figure 8-18.

Figure 8-18. *Detaching a database*

3. To remove all the connected users, select the Drop Connections check box. The second option, Update Statistics, means that the SQL Server statistics for indexes and so on will be updated before the database is detached. The information is stored separately from the other data files in SQL Server. Consequently, selecting this option ensures that when the database is detached the files are not lost and, therefore, don't need re-creating. The status is Not Ready due to the message indicating that there is still "1 Active connection(s)."

■ **Note** In this example, select the Drop Connections box. However, in a production environment, this could be very dangerous. There is a system stored procedure called sp_who that can tell you what connections exist within the server. The stored procedure sp_who will list the information from the whole data server and cannot be refined to the database you are interested in. You will see how to execute stored procedures in Chapter 14.

4. Once you are happy, you can click OK to finish detaching the database.

 That's it. The database is detached, is no longer part of SQL Server, and is ready to be moved or even deleted. If you check Object Explorer in SQL Server Management Studio, you will see that the database is no longer listed.

 Detaching a database, although seemingly a simple and innocuous operation, has the potential to be fraught with problems and worries. As the example demonstrated, ensuring that there are no users attached to the database at the time of detaching is not as easy as it first may seem. Setting up the database options to eliminate connections or to stop updates is possible only once everyone has been removed from connections to the database. There is no easy way of removing connections safely, as you never know what an application with a connection to the database is doing. You could remove a connection that is in the middle of processing. If you are going down the route of detaching the database, though, there is an obvious reason to do this, such as moving servers and removing the database, so you would have a plan of action, which would include reaching agreement with application owners that any connections found at the time of work will be removed. Users would have been notified days or weeks in advance, and the database owner would have coordinated a date and time when nobody should be connected. Also, the database owner would be around if there were any problems, and he or she could make the decision to kill any connections left hanging around.

To reiterate, detaching the database is a process that removes entries within the SQL Server system tables to inform SQL Server that this database is no longer within this instance of SQL Server and therefore cannot be used. It is as simple as that. If you are removing the database completely, then you will need to delete the files from the directory they were created in.

■ **Note** It is possible to detach the database using a system stored procedure, although this does not let you kill the connections. This has to be done via the T-SQL command sp_detach_db, which you will see shortly in the chapter.

You need to reattach the database before being able to demonstrate detaching via T-SQL, so let's do that now. This would occur on new SQL Server instances after physically moving the files.

TRY IT OUT: ATTACHING A DATABASE

1. Within Object Explorer, highlight the Databases node, right-click, and select Attach.

2. This brings up the Attach Databases dialog box, shown in Figure 8-19. To add a database, click Add.

Figure 8-19. Options for attaching a database

3. This brings up the Locate Database Files dialog box, shown in Figure 8-20. You can use this like other Windows explorers to locate where your database MDF files are. Once you find the database you want to reattach, highlight it and then click OK.

Figure 8-20. *Locating the database to attach*

4. This brings you back to the Attach Databases dialog box with the details filled in, as you see in Figure 8-21. Take a moment to look over the information in this dialog box. Any problems SQL Server finds will be detailed in the Messages column. It is also possible to attach more than one database, but it is best to do databases one at a time.

Figure 8-21. *Database located, preparing to attach*

5. This then leaves you to click OK to reattach the database. Moving to Object Explorer, you should see your database at the bottom of the list, where it will remain until the explorer is refreshed.

Attaching a database involves informing SQL Server of the name and the location of the data files and the transaction log files. The files can be placed anywhere on a computer, but it is recommended you place the data in a sensible location. For example, the folders `tempfiles` or `tobedeleted` sport extreme names, but do demonstrate the unsuitability that should be avoided.

When moving the data from one physical server to another, the data does not need to be in a subdirectory of Microsoft SQL Server installation found under Program Files. In fact, in production environments, this is the last place you would locate the data. In a production environment, you may have multiple drives or drive partitions; certainly many organizations have this set up. You would generally want to keep these files away from any program files or the `pagefile.sys` file because SQL Server's performance can be maximized when these files are separated; if a second drive is available, it is best to place the files on a different drive than system files. However, for the purpose of this book, placing the data in the DATA directory under the instance of SQL Server is perfectly valid and acceptable.

Once the two data files have been copied, it is a simple process of using a couple of mouse clicks to attach these files into the instance. What happens in the background, very basically, is that SQL Server takes the name of the database and the location of the data files and places them into internal tables that are used to store information about databases. It then scans the data files to retrieve information, such as the names of the tables, to populate the system tables where necessary.

The main point to keep in mind is the database owner (see Chapters 1, 2, and 5). It is just as important to use a valid database owner and not the `sa` login when attaching a database as it is when creating a database. The database, when it is attached, will be given the owner of the login attaching the database.

Detaching and Attaching Using T-SQL

Detaching and attaching a database is an ideal way to move a database from one server to another as part of an overall solution. It's clean, simple, and ideal if you are rolling out a "base" database to many client sites, but it's not the only way of doing it. Detaching a database is simply removing it logically from a server, but keeping the physical files. This then allows these files to be moved to anywhere, from another hard drive to a DVD, for further copying to a client computer if need be, and then reattaching the database at the other end.

Detaching a database removes entries from the master and `msdb` databases. The physical backup files will still be there, so if you do need to complete a restore after a detach and reattach, then you can use the From Device option in the Restore Wizard to define the full location in the RESTORE T-SQL command to get to those files.

■ **Note** Detaching a database can be done only by a member of the db_owner role.

```
sp_detach_db [ @dbname= ] 'dbname'
    [ , [ @skipchecks= ] 'skipchecks' ]
    [ , [ @KeepFulltextIndexFile= ] 'KeepFulltextIndexFile' ]
```

The options are straightforward, with each being optional. If they are not supplied, then the default value is mentioned within the following bulleted list:

- dbname: The name of the database to detach; if this option is missed, then no database will be detached.

- skipchecks: NULL (the default) will update statistics. true will skip the updating of statistics.

- KeepFulltextIndexFile: true (the default) will keep all the full-text index files that have been generated with this database.

■ **Note** *Full-text index files* are special files that hold information about data set up for full-text searching, which is an area outside the scope of this book. Basically, full-text searching gives the ability to search on all text in a column or multiple columns of data, and it is also functionality used by search engines.

You might be expecting that you would use a stored procedure called sp_attach_db to reattach the database. This command does exist, but it will be made obsolete in future versions of SQL Server. The correct syntax is a "specialized" CREATE DATABASE command:

```
CREATE DATABASE database_name
    ON <filespec> [ ,...n ]
    FOR { ATTACH [ WITH <service_broker_option> ]
        | ATTACH_REBUILD_LOG }
```

The syntax is easy to follow. The first option, ON, specifies the name of the primary database file to attach, which has the MDF suffix. We will ignore the second option, <service_broker_option>, as this is for a more advanced database.

The third option, ATTACH_REBUILD_LOG, is for situations where you wish to attach a database but at least one transaction log file is missing. Specifying this option rebuilds the transaction log. No database can be attached when SQL Server believes that there are missing files. If you do use this option, you will lose the full, differential, and transaction log backup chains that exist on SQL Server, so complete a full backup after attaching to reestablish the backup baseline. This option tends to be used when you deliberately wish to lose the transaction log file, such as a read-only version of the database for reporting purposes.

■ **Note** If you receive any error messages, reattach *all* files associated with the database, not just the main primary file, if you had more than one file, which can happen in large systems.

Now let's go through the steps for detaching and reattaching the ApressFinancial database using T-SQL.

TRY IT OUT: DETACHING AND REATTACHING A DATABASE USING T-SQL

1. The first test you will do is to check if there are any active connections before you try to detach. There is a system-stored procedure called `sp_who`, which you can execute that lists out the connections that are on the server and what database the connections are connected to. Figure 8-22 shows the stored procedure in Query Editor and a list of most of the connections on my server at the time of running. Notice that the last connection is connected to the `ApressFinancial` database.

Figure 8-22. *Server connections with* `ApressFinancial` *at the bottom*

2. The connection in Figure 8-22 is from Query Editor, which ran `sp_who`. The connection was pointing to the `ApressFinancial` database. If I alter the database to `master`, then there will be no `ApressFinancial` connections. You should be able to achieve the same goal and remove all connections yourself as only you are using the database and should know where the connections are.

3. You can achieve removing all connections by placing the database in single-user mode using T-SQL without needing to close your panes that have active connections. Open up a second tab with a connection to ApressFinancial and enter some random characters, any characters. You should now have two, or more, connections to the ApressFinancial database. You can now remove these connections and place the database into a single connection mode. Enter the following code and execute it:

```
ALTER DATABASE ApressFinancial
SET SINGLE_USER WITH ROLLBACK IMMEDIATE
```

4. As there should be only one connection at this point, you can proceed to detaching the database. Using the same Query Editor pane as the SET SINGLE_USER command, enter the sp_detach_db code as follows. Once you have done so, execute the code. Take note that you are simulating explicitly moving this connection to a "safe" system database, away from the database you wish to detach.

```
USE master
GO
sp_detach_db 'ApressFinancial'
```

5. The results you will see will be similar to the following:

```
Command(s) completed successfully.
```

6. Now that the database has been detached, you need to reattach it, simulating a move to a new server. Enter the following code in a Query Editor pane. Replace the FILENAME parameters with the path to where your database is located and ensure that the path is all on one line.

```
CREATE DATABASE ApressFinancial
ON (FILENAME=N'C:\Program Files\Microsoft SQL Server\MSSQL12.APRESS_DEV1\
MSSQL\DATA\ApressFinancial.MDF')
FOR ATTACH
```

7. After executing the code, you should see the following message:

```
Command(s) completed successfully.
```

8. To change the database from SINGLE_USER to MULTI_USER, enter the following code:

```
ALTER DATABASE ApressFinancial
SET MULTI_USER
```

You have now successfully detached and reattached the database.

Producing SQL Script for the Database

This section demonstrates a different method of backing up the structure of the database and the tables and indexes contained within it by using T-SQL commands to complete this.

■ **Note** Only the structure will be generated as T-SQL commands; no data will be backed up—only the schema that is needed to re-create the actual database can be scripted here.

The usefulness of this procedure is limited and is really helpful only for keeping structure backups or producing an empty database. However, it is useful to know rather than going through the process of copying the database with all the data when the data are not required.

This method tends to be used to keep the structure within a source repository such as Visual SourceSafe. It is also useful for setting up empty databases when moving from development to testing or into production.

TRY IT OUT: PRODUCING THE DATABASE SQL

1. Ensure that SQL Server Management Studio is running and that you have expanded the server so that you can see the ApressFinancial database. Right-click and select Tasks ➤ Generate Scripts. After the initial wizard introduction screen, click Next to see the Choose Objects screen shown in Figure 8-23 that allows the database to be scripted. There are two options for scripting: either the entire database, the default, and the option desired; or the ability to script just part of the database. Click Next.

Figure 8-23. *Scripting: Selecting the database*

2. On the Set Scripting Options screen, there are a number of options about the scripting. It is possible to script the database and save it to a file, or you can publish the script to a web service. Figure 8-24 shows the default settings for saving the scripts to a file. You will see an Advanced button on the right, which lets you alter some scripting options. I will go through this at the end of the exercise, but for purposes of this exercise, just accept the default settings. Click Next.

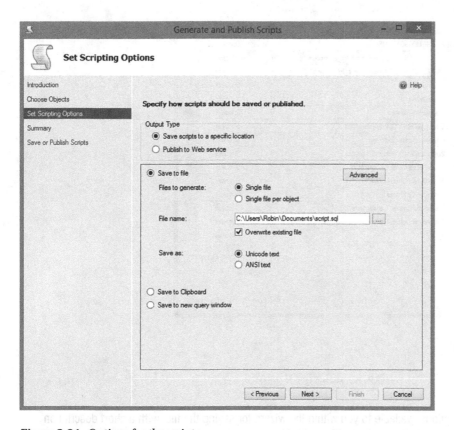

Figure 8-24. *Options for the script*

───

■ **Note** The ability to publish to a web service allows for a database script to be sent to a remote server.

───

3. You are now presented with a Summary screen, so simply click Next.

4. The scripts are then prepared as shown in Figure 8-25, with any problems or errors listed prior to saving the file. Clicking Finish closes the final wizard screen.

Figure 8-25. *Generating the script*

Advanced Script Options

Figure 8-26 shows the list of options available to you within the wizard for saving the file, with a short description of each detailed here. Several of the options will exist for publishing to a web service, but of course the web service option will have its own set of settings.

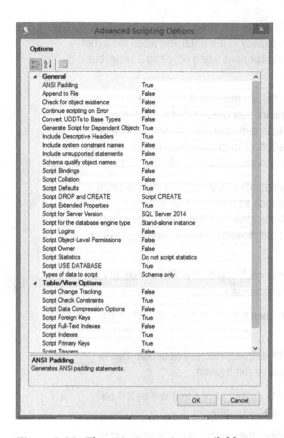

Figure 8-26. *The scripting options available*

- *ANSI Padding:* ANSI padding details how data are held when it doesn't fill the size defined for the data type.

- *Append to File:* If you set this to `true`, then SQL Server will append the script to the file selected instead of overwriting it.

- Continue Scripting on Error: If there are any problems in producing the script, you can decide if you wish to continue scripting.

- Convert UDDTs to Base Types: As part of SQL Server, you can change the base data types, such as `int`, to your own named type, so you could name a "copy" of `int` as `myint`. This is a bit more advanced, but if you do this, then selecting `true` will convert `myint` back to `int`.

- Generate Script for Dependent Objects: A very useful option; if there are any dependencies on what you are wanting to script and you haven't selected that object to script, then there will be problems rebuilding the object later. Selecting `true` means that these dependent objects will also be scripted.

- Include Descriptive Headers: This includes a date-time stamp as well as a short descriptive header of each object as it is reached within the script.

- Include If NOT EXISTS: If you select all the objects to be scripted and set this to `true`, SQL Server will put a test around each object so that if that object is already in the database when the script is run, it won't be created. There will be no test for specific columns when scripting a table, but there will be a test for the table itself.

- Include system constraint names: There are constraints that are generated by SQL Server automatically as part of Declarative Management Framework. You will see this functionality in Chapter 12. If you wish to keep the same names rather than generate new names, a value of `true` will keep the name the same. This is ideal for transferring an exact replica of the database from one location to another. It is not necessarily always needed to keep the same name.

- Include unsupported statements: If you want to keep statements that are no longer supported, then set this value to `true`. The unsupported statements such as those that have been deprecated will be kept, but there will be a comment. This is ideal for when you are scripting up or down a SQL Server version so that you know what functionality you will need to consider fixing before running on the target server.

- Schema qualify object names: Include the schema name in each object; it would be rare to have this set to `false`, as you would normally want to keep the schema names.

- Script Bindings: If a default value is defined for a column, then a value of `true` will define the column binding.

- *Script Collation*: If you wish the SQL Server collation to be scripted, enable this option. This is useful if you are unsure of the collation the script will then be run against.

- *Script Defaults*: In `ApressFinancial` tables, we have some default values that will be set on columns when rows are added. Setting this to `true` will set these defaults.

- *Script* `DROP` *and* `CREATE`: If you are generating a script where the objects may already exist in the target server, then it might be better to drop the object before creating. A value of `true` will generate within the T-SQL the `DROP` and then the `CREATE`.

- Script Extended Properties: Extra properties can be placed on every SQL Server object. These will be scripted if you select `true`.

- Script for Server Version: A setting of `true` will not script objects that are not supported on the SQL Server version you are generating the script for.

- Script for the database engine type: If you have objects in your database that are not available on the target engine type, such as targeting SQL Server Express from a script built on SQL Server Enterprise, then these objects will not be scripted.

- Script Logins: This scripts all Windows and SQL Server authentication logins.

- Script Object-Level Permissions: Each object will have permissions on who can do what. For example, on a table, you can set up permissions on who can add, delete, or select the data. This option includes these options.

- Script Owner: This scripts the owner of the database if specified.

- Script Statistics: This specifies whether to script the SQL Server column and index statistics. It avoids rebuilding them when re-creating the database using the script; however, it increases the time taken to build the script as well as the size of the script.

- Script USE DATABASE: Between each object, this specifies whether to script a USE database statement. It's ideal if used with scripting-dependent objects.

- Types of data to script: The default for this option is Schema, which means that the script will detail only the objects columns. You can just script the data within the database objects selected where INSERT statements are generated, or you can generate both the schema and the data. For large tables, this is not an ideal way to port database objects from a source to a target, but it does give the ability if required.

- Script Change Tracking: Change tracking allows for data modifications to be tracked within SQL Server where the data that existed before the change are kept. This allows you to see what information has been altered. This is ideal for any tables that you need to audit changes or if you want to know when and what changes have happened. This can also be achieved by creating a trigger that writes the before image to your own built-in audit table.

- Script Check Constraints: This script checks constraints.

- Script Data Compression Options: If you are using data compression, then setting this to true will also script the options that you have in effect.

- Script Foreign Keys: Any foreign keys are scripted.

- Script Full-Text Indexes: If you have any full-text indexes, this indicates whether you want to script them.

- Script Indexes: This specifies whether to script table and view indexes.

- Script Primary Keys: This dictates whether to script primary keys.

- Script Triggers: For any trigger, this specifies whether you wish these to be within the script.

- Script Unique Keys: Any unique keys are scripted.

Summary

You have seen a great deal in this chapter that is crucial to ensuring that your database is always secure. As a manager drummed into me, the unexpected will always happen, but you must always be able to recover from it, no matter what. Therefore, regular backups that are known to work and even the occasional "disaster recovery test" should be done to ensure that you can restore when something unexpected and bad happens. No matter what your managing director says, the data of a company are its most important asset, not the people. Without the data, a company cannot function. If you cannot ensure that the data will be there, then the company will be in a very dangerous position.

You should now be comfortable in taking different backups and restores and knowing what is required to keep your database secure.

This concludes your look at the different methods of backing up, restoring, moving, and scripting databases. While this covers every way of ensuring your database structure and data will never be lost, you still need to maintain the database on a regular basis. This is what you will take a look at in the next chapter.

CHAPTER 9

■ ■ ■

Database Maintenance

At this point, you have now created a backup and performed a restore of the example database. You have also covered the different methods to back up and restore the database. However, there is no real plan for regular maintenance and detection and reporting of problems in the database strategy. Any jobs for backup of the database or transaction log that I have demonstrated so far are held as single units of work called *steps*. Not only that, but also there is nothing in place that will look after the data and indexes held within the database to ensure that they are still functioning correctly and that the data are still stored in the optimal fashion. Without a process that runs regularly, you would need to perform all of this by hand regularly and check the results each time. What a waste of time, and boring to boot!

This chapter will demonstrate building an automatic maintenance plan and then checking on the plan after it has run to ensure that all has gone well with it. This plan will perform regular backups and checks on the database and keep it in optimum health. This chapter will then show you how to set up the ability to e-mail results.

To do this, you will use the Database Maintenance Plan Wizard, which will help you build an automated job to monitor corruption within the database, optimize how the data are stored, and back up both the database and the transaction logs. Finally, the wizard will generate a schedule for the job to process at regular intervals. You will also see how to set up and configure SQL Server Database Mail so that errors can be mailed to a team monitoring the servers.

Some areas of this chapter, like the backup screens, are straightforward, as they were covered earlier in Chapter 8; however, this now brings the whole maintenance of the database into one job.

Creating a Database Maintenance Plan

Now that the database is up and built and the tables are there, it really is time to start considering a whole database maintenance plan before data are entered. This will cover securing your data, ensuring performance, and rectifying database corruption through to ensuring that your database is performing as you expect it to be. Even though corruption is rare in SQL Server, it can be caused when SQL Server loses power abruptly, for example, or through hardware issues such as a motherboard failure or someone removing the network cable.

There are many areas of building a maintenance plan, and this section covers a lot of them. One or two areas are only touched on, as they are quite advanced and will not be covered in this book. You will still need a little background so that you can see how crucial this area is, and you can move on to those more advanced areas a bit later on.

A single maintenance plan can be built for one database or several databases, but I recommend one plan per database. A single plan can be set up for system databases and all user databases by selecting those options at the start of the Database Maintenance Plan Wizard. I also recommend one plan for each system database as well. The logic behind these recommendations is that each user database will have its own needs, its own overnight routines, and even its own people for callout when things go wrong, even if there is some sort of logical link between databases. Even if you are a one-man band, each user database should still have a maintenance plan. Therefore, in keeping with this, only the ApressFinancial database will be selected.

Once the plan has been built, it will be stored within SQL Server, but will have been built as a SQL Server Integration Services (SSIS) job. This is a technique within SQL Server for running several tasks in sequence with conditions, which also has the ability to work with errors that occur. SSIS could (and does) take up a whole book in itself, but building the plan and seeing what is generated will demonstrate the very basics of what it can achieve.

Maintenance plans use extended stored procedures, which are disabled by default. This means that until extended stored procedures arc enabled, it is not possible to build a maintenance plan. To demonstrate how you can enable this option via T-SQL, you will use a system-stored procedure in the first step to do this.

There are two methods to building a database maintenance plan: you can either use a wizard or select options from a multi-tabbed screen.

There are a number of tasks that can be included in a maintenance plan:

- *Check Database Integrity*: This executes SQL Server database integrity checks on the data and structure of the database, both physical and logical.

- *Shrink Database*: The transaction log is truncated and logically shrunk. The database is also shrunk.

- *Reorganize Index*: As data are inserted and deleted, fragmentation of indexes can take place. This reorganizes the index a bit like completing a disk defrag.

- *Rebuild Index*: Instead of just reorganizing the indexes, it is possible to drop and re-create them.

- *Update Statistics*: Statistics are kept to aid the execution of queries. These can get out-of-date if you don't have the option set to keep these up-to-date, and this option can update them at this point.

- *Clean Up History*: This removes historical information such as job history for a set period of time.

- *Execute SQL Server Agent Job*: This executes a predefined SQL Server Agent job. At present, there are no jobs in the database, so this option cannot be selected.

- *Back Up Database (Full)*: As discussed earlier, this backs up the full database.

- *Back Up Database (Differential)*: As discussed earlier, this backs up the changes since the last full backup.

- *Back Up Database (Transaction Log)*: As discussed earlier, this backs up just the transaction log.

- *Maintenance Cleanup Task*: This cleans up any transient files left over after the task has completed.

Let's take a moment to look at options that are likely to be the most useful aside from the backups—the reorganization and rebuild index options. If fragmentation is low—below 30%, typically—then you should perform a reorganization. If fragmentation is greater, then it is best to reindex. Indexes exist on tables and views and become more fragmented than whole pages of data on a high-data modification system. Like rebuilding indexes, reorganization of indexes should be completed on a regular basis, probably weekly; however, if your batch window allows you to perform this more frequently, then consider doing so. When rebuilding indexes, you can define with a certain amount of free space to allow for increases and mid-index insertions on each index page. This is a bit like inserting lines of text in a book. If you think you are going to do this, then leaving gaps at the end of the page allows for these rows to be added. Failure to leave enough means shuffling data from that page through to the end of the book.

A maintenance plan can run within a SQL Server Agent job either as an ad hoc process or on a scheduled basis. Depending on your overall application design, or even on your company standards, it may be that you have dependencies on when a database maintenance plan can run. To clarify my point, it could be that you have processes in the overall application that load data into your database. In `ApressFinancial`, this could be further details about shares, such as details of new stocks or stock actions. In corporations, it could be data from other systems, such as the orders system informing the inventory system a delivery of raw materials has been made. These processes would generate some sort of triggering action to indicate that they were complete and the database could start its maintenance. Over the years, I have used software called AutoSys, owned by Computer Associates, which schedules

these jobs. When a specific process completes, I use this completion to start my maintenance task. Therefore, depending on how the whole application has been designed, a scheduled maintenance plan may be the correct method or an ad hoc/on-demand plan should be generated. It is also very easy to switch between these two, so it is not a decision that you are stuck with.

If a plan is scheduled, it should be timed for an appropriate time for the application. This could be at a quiet time of your application or at specific times within any batch processing, but, depending on what you select, a maintenance plan can be quite labor-intensive, such as rebuilding indexes and reorganizing your data. You could set up a plan to run before batch processing, at the end, or even at both ends of the schedule. Depending on the actions in the plan, it is also possible to alter the scheduling to occur when the CPU is idle. This option is ideal for heavily used, large-volume, high-performance databases where no fixed time can be defined to run the schedule, or even if you wish the process to run multiple times in a day when the server can execute the plan. One scheduling option that can be very useful is to run when SQL Server Agent starts. If a server automatically reboots, as part of a scheduled weekly reboot, or if the reboot occurs due to a Microsoft patching installation, then you may want to have a plan that takes a backup of the database or a plan that verifies the integrity of the database post-reboot. You would create a maintenance plan to complete those tasks and use the SQL Server Agent schedule option to accomplish this.

The main option of interest when rebuilding indexes is Sort Results in tempdb. You could be low on disk space because when you built your database, you set it to grow no larger than a specific size. Couple this with a situation in which your indexes are so fragmented that they take up more space than they will post-defragmentation. This could be because you have a large number of gaps due to deletions of rows within the index or modifications on a clustered index causing rows to be moved. When rebuilding indexes, this would, by default, be completed within the database the rebuild is for. The "old" indexes are kept until the new indexes are built. If there is not enough space to store them, it would not be possible to rebuild the index, unless you physically increased the size of the database. This is not a simple process. Therefore, by using the option to rebuild the new indexes within tempdb, you do not need to increase your database size. Also, tempdb will not be used as intensively. Therefore, it might also be faster to rebuild your indexes within that database. This is an option you may use a great deal.

A maintenance task can also be synchronous or asynchronous where you have different tasks running at the same time. This has the potential to make the maintenance plan complete in less time, but you have to be careful that the right tasks run in the right sequence.

In the following exercise, I am going to demonstrate building a scheduled maintenance plan via a wizard.

TRY IT OUT: CREATING A DATABASE MAINTENANCE PLAN

1. This is a potentially two-stage process. First, configure the server to show advanced options. Then reconfigure the server and set it to true, as detailed by the number 1, the option Agent XPs. Enter and execute the following code:

```
sp_configure 'show advanced options', 1
GO
RECONFIGURE
GO
sp_configure 'Agent XPs', 1
GO
RECONFIGURE
GO
```

2. You should now see the following output, which is generated from the `sp_configure` statements:

```
Configuration option 'show advanced options' changed from 0 to 1.
Run the RECONFIGURE statement to install.
Configuration option 'Agent XPs' changed from 0 to 1.
Run the RECONFIGURE statement to install.
```

3. From Object Explorer, find the Management Node and expand it. You should find Maintenance Plans. Right-click and select the second option, Maintenance Plan Wizard, as shown in Figure 9-1. This starts the wizard. Once you have read the initial screen, click Next.

Figure 9-1. Generating a maintenance plan via the wizard

4. Enter a suitable name and description for the maintenance plan. It is possible to run tasks under either separate schedules or one schedule. Choose separate schedules when you want to space the tasks out or run them simultaneously. Choose a single schedule for the entire plan when you want to run the tasks synchronously. The single schedule is the option you want to take at this time as it is possible to break out certain tasks, and I will show how this can be achieved later in the chapter. You will notice at the bottom of the screen, as shown in Figure 9-2, that you can define a schedule for the plan. The default is for it to run On Demand; however, it can run at specified times and days, and this is the option that you want. Click the Change button found at the bottom right of the screen.

Figure 9-2. *Selecting the schedule for the maintenance plan*

5. You will now see the screen shown in Figure 9-3, which is where you can define the schedule times for the maintenance plan. The schedule type can be one of the options discussed prior to the exercise. This plan will keep the default options, for the moment, of running weekly on a Sunday at midnight. Once the database development has progressed, this can always be changed. Once done, click OK, and then click Next when you return to the screen shown in Figure 9-2.

Figure 9-3. Defining the schedule

6. The next screen brings you to a set of choices of actions that you wish the plan to perform. In your plan, you will be performing almost every action, with the exceptions of cleaning up the history of the database and the differential backup option. You will add the option of cleaning up the history later when showing how to modify a plan. Select the options as shown in Figure 9-4, and click Next.

Figure 9-4. *Options for the maintenance plan*

7. This then brings you to a summary of the options that have been selected. It is now possible to move the options to a different order if you wish. As you can see in Figure 9-5, the Back Up Database (Full) option has been moved up to the start and the transaction log backup second. This is in case any of the following options fail and cause corruption. You may wish to move these options to the end if you have a good backup scheduled before this maintenance work. This is a decision that you have to make as any restore may require a rerun of the commands after the full backup. There is no recommended order. Once you have the order you want, click Next.

Figure 9-5. *Options order for the maintenance plan*

8. The wizard then moves on and takes each task one at a time and gives you a screen containing options available for that task. The first option you have is a full backup, as shown in Figure 9-6, as this was the first option in the order defined. Most of this is very similar to the backup you completed earlier. However, it is possible to select specific databases or all databases as part of this plan. Select the Specific Databases option to be taken to a second screen, where you can define which ones to back up.

Figure 9-6. *Defining the database backup*

9. When you choose to back up specific databases, Figure 9-7 appears. Here you can select—only for this task within the plan—which database or set of databases you want to work with. It is best to have separate maintenance plans for each user database and one separate maintenance plan for the system databases, as I mentioned earlier. This splits up the workload not only into sizable, useful, and easy-to-understand units of work, but also into logical components as each database may have a different maintenance plan. You will also have different requirements for the system databases from the user-defined databases as mentioned in Chapter 8. It is preferable not to select the All User Databases option because SQL Server will automatically begin running the maintenance plan on databases that may have been added without your knowledge, and may not be under your "ownership." For your example, select the ApressFinancial database after clicking the "These databases" radio button. Click OK. This will return you to the full backup screen, where you can click Next. The full list of choices is as follows:

- All Databases: Specifies all system and user databases

- System Databases: Ignores all user databases, such as *ApressFinancial*

- All User Databases: Ignores any system-defined database, such as *master*, *model*, and so on

- These Databases: Allows you to select which system and user databases you wish to use

Figure 9-7. Selecting the database to use

10. The next option for the wizard is a transaction log backup. Select the specific databases option again and then ApressFinancial to back up its transaction log. Click Next to move on to the third item.

11. In the subsequent screen, which you see in Figure 9-8, you progress to the next task in the ordered list, which is the check integrity task. This task instructs SQL Server to perform a special SQL Server command that checks the integrity of the database to see that everything is in a stable and noncorrupt state. It does this by running a SQL Server command, DBCC CHECKDB. Once you have selected ApressFinancial, the "Include indexes" option is automatically checked. Click Next.

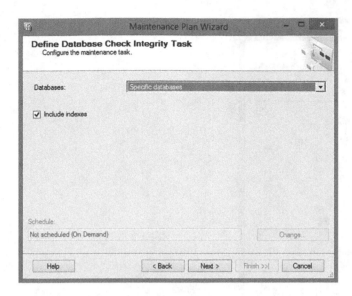

Figure 9-8. *Database integrity check*

12. DBCC is short for database console commands. The CHECKDB command runs three sub-DBCC commands to simplify the process so that you don't have to run the three commands yourself. The first is DBCC CHECKALLOC, and this checks the space allocation of the database. The second command is DBCC CHECKTABLE. This command will check that the pages of each table are valid and not corrupt. The final command is DBCC CHECKCATALOG, and this checks the consistency of the system metatables.

13. Moving on, you can define when to reduce the logical or physical size of your database through the screen shown in Figure 9-9. The "Return freed space to operating system" option will shrink the database if it has space it is not fully using, and return that space back to the server. This means that if you need the space again at some later stage, it has to be re-allocated. Also, if the server is shared, space you release may be allocated to another system.

Figure 9-9. Shrinking the database

14. Reducing the amount of physical space as described in the prior step will aid backup times. Be aware, though, that shrinking the database takes a fair amount of your server resources, and it may be better to keep the space within the database unless you had a one-off expansion. You don't want to shrink the database for it to have to be expanded very soon after shrinking the size. The shrinking of a database I have found not to be a common exercise, but it exists in this example so you are aware of the option. After you select this option, you will be given the opportunity to still leave a given percentage of space free for database growth. Do not fully shrink the database to 0% of free space or your performance will be worse, as the database will have to grow automatically.

15. Click Next to bring up the Define Reorganize Index Tag screen, shown in Figure 9-10. As data are added, modified, and deleted, indexes, like tables, can also require reorganizing, which you can do through this screen. Again, this is like a hard drive defrag where there are gaps or data out of order, and by reorganizing indexes you can ensure that SQL Server is able to access the data as fast as possible. This option, which should be completed at least weekly for a high-data modification system, moves only index pages. There is also an option to compact large objects. This option will compact any index that has a column that contains large binary object data.

Figure 9-10. *Reorganizing the indexes*

16. Click Next to bring up the screen shown in Figure 9-11. This next screen deals with individual rows of indexes. Before you go on, note that there is no real point to reorganizing and reindexing in the same maintenance plan. You should do only one or the other. Which option you should choose comes down to the amount of fragmentation within an index. Fragmentation and reorganization were discussed earlier. Select the ApressFinancial database in the Databases drop-down and the "Sort results in tempdb" option.

Figure 9-11. *The options for rebuilding an index*

17. Move on to the Define Update Statistics Task screen, shown in Figure 9-12, by clicking Next. As has been mentioned before, as data are created, modified, and deleted, SQL Server keeps statistics on that data to aid data retrieval. These can become out-of-date either because you have set up your database not to keep statistics updated automatically or because the statistics naturally become out-of-date. Therefore, you can re-create those statistics with the plan. Statistics are kept not only for indexes but also for data within individual columns.

Figure 9-12. *Updating the database statistics*

■ **Tip** The Auto Update Statistics database option is normally on; although this does mean more processing for SQL Server, the increase is minimal and you'll rarely notice any impact. Some installations will have this switched off so that statistics are updated via a scheduled task. This is sometimes the case when every nanosecond of response time is required from the server, so it is worth checking the setting if you are unsure.

18. Clicking Next will move you to the SQL Server Agent screen. Sometimes there will be a separate job or process to run that is outside of the possible actions within the wizard. This could be to check that the database still meets the standards defined as you saw when you checked whether the database met the ANSI NULLS test. The jobs that are currently defined within SQL Server Agent are listed in this dialog, as shown in Figure 9-13. Select any jobs you wish to run. There is a job within SQL Server that removes the history of checking policies already existing, and as you selected as one of the options that you wanted to define a job to execute, you do have to select at least one job to proceed to the next screen. Click Next.

Figure 9-13. *Defining a process to run inside a SQL Server Agent job*

19. The Define Maintenance Cleanup Task screen, shown in Figure 9-14, defines the cleanup actions of the maintenance task when it runs. This is ideal to ensure that your maintenance plans don't take up unwanted and unnecessary space and are easy to view and monitor. Click Next.

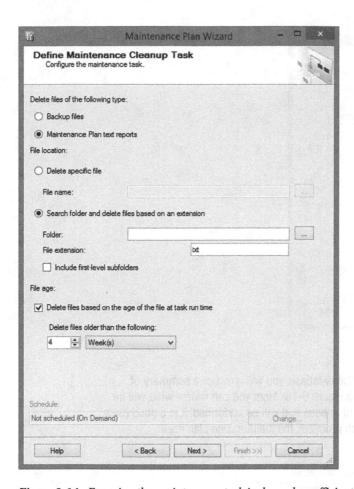

Figure 9-14. *Ensuring the maintenance task is cleaned up efficiently*

20. The next task, illustrated in Figure 9-15, involves choosing where to write out the details of the maintenance plan and each step's success or failure. For the moment, place the output in a report. Later in the chapter, you will see how to mail that report from SQL Server. Click Next.

Figure 9-15. *How to report the maintenance plan*

21. Similar to when you produced a script for the database, you will now see a summary of what will be performed within the plan (see Figure 9-16). Here you can review what will be completed, and with the number of different options that will be performed, it is a good place to complete a double-check. Clicking Finish produces the maintenance plan itself.

Figure 9-16. *Completing the plan*

22. Once the plan is within msdb database, you should see the completed screen shown in Figure 9-17.

Figure 9-17. *Maintenance plan created successfully*

You now have successfully built a maintenance plan. You may have several plans, one for a weekend, one for pre-batch, and so on, all dependent on how you want to maintain your database. The important point is that you back up your database.

The next step is to execute the plan.

Executing the Plan

Now that a plan has been built, the next step will be to execute the plan. For a maintenance plan to execute, SQL Server Agent needs to be running. It is likely at this point in the book that it is not, as it will be defined to start manually rather than automatically. This default exists for security reasons so that jobs cannot be built, deployed, and then executed on your server without your prior knowledge. You may find that some corporations keep SQL Server Agent stopped until required. It is possible to start SQL Server Agent within Management Studio for ad hoc starts of the process, or you can start the service from Administrative Tools within the Control Panel. It is also possible to start SQL Server Agent via a command prompt, therefore allowing you to put the start and stop into scheduling software.

In the following exercise, you will see how to start SQL Server Agent and then execute a maintenance plan manually.

TRY IT OUT: EXECUTING A DATABASE MAINTENANCE PLAN

1. You can start the SQL Server Agent service with one of two methods. The first and likely the most common method will be to start the service within Windows rather than Management Studio by selecting Control Panel app ➤ Administrative Tools ➤ Services, as shown in Figure 9-18.

Figure 9-18. *Finding the Services option within the Control Panel*

2. Double-click Services, which displays Figure 9-19. Scroll down until you see SQL Server Agent and the instance name you want to define the SQL Server Agent starting action. In your case, it will be APRESS_DEV1, but there will be one entry per SQL Server instance on a box. Notice in Figure 9-19 that the status is blank and the Startup Type is set to manual. This denotes that the service has not started and it will not start automatically.

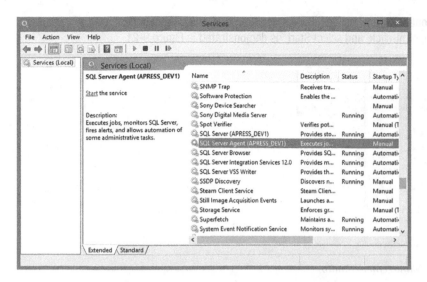

Figure 9-19. *Locating SQL Server Agent for the required SQL Server instance*

3. Highlight SQL Server Agent, right-click, and select Properties. This will display a screen similar to Figure 9-20. This screen is very similar to what you would see for any service listed within the Services window. The first tab indicates the service name, how the service starts, and the current running state of the service. It is advisable to keep the startup type as manual. You will return to this tab in a moment to start SQL Server Agent, but click the Log On tab.

Figure 9-20. *The properties of SQL Server Agent*

4. To start the SQL Server Agent service within SQL Server, find the SQL Server Agent node within Management Studio, right-click, and select Start, as demonstrated in Figure 9-21.

Figure 9-21. *How to start from within Management Studio*

5. When you were installing SQL Server in Chapter 1, you had to make a decision on what accounts should be used for certain processes. One of those processes was SQL Server Agent, and you will see the account chosen. Here you can alter which account you wish to use. Some companies wish you to use a separate Windows account rather than a Windows-system-based account as was chosen during installation and shown in Figure 9-22. Keep the account defined in Chapter 1 as this is the best option for the current setup. If you did not start SQL Server Agent from within Management Studio, move back to the General tab and click Start. Click OK to close the screen.

Figure 9-22. *The account for SQL Server Agent*

6. Now that SQL Server Agent is running, you can execute the plan. If the plan had a scheduled start date and time, it is possible to execute the plan outside of the maintenance plan schedule rather than having to wait on the chosen time. Move back to Management Studio, where the maintenance plan created previously can now be found under the Management/ Maintenance Plan nodes in Object Explorer. Right-click the nodes to bring up the pop-up menu shown in Figure 9-23. Selecting Execute starts the plan immediately. Do so now.

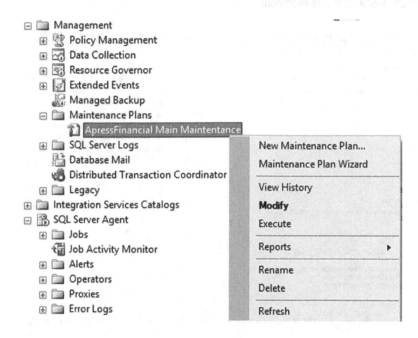

Figure 9-23. *Maintenance plan pop-up menu*

7. While the plan is executing, the dialog box shown in Figure 9-24 is displayed.

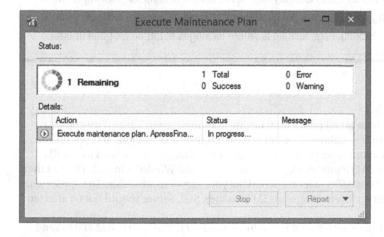

Figure 9-24. *Maintenance plan executing*

8. In Figure 9-25, you can see the log that has been created for the maintenance plan once that plan has been completed. You can view this log by selecting View ➤ History from the same pop-up menu used to execute the plan. On the left, you can view other logs that are generated within SQL Server. Notice in the figure that I have selected one of the steps that has an error detailed in the Selected row details section at the bottom of the screen. The error is indicating that during an index re-org, the index required page level locking, which is not enabled. You can also view the T-SQL that was executed.

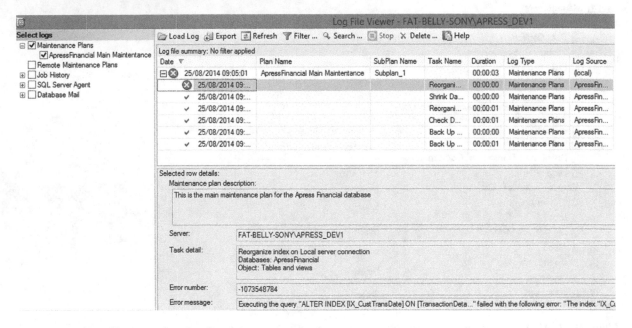

Figure 9-25. *Log file viewer showing the maintenance plan has run*

■ **Note** SQL Server uses different levels of locking on data. As a very high-level, simple description, locking is where SQL Server stops other processes from performing an action on a set of data that is in use. There are different levels of locking, from row locking to page locking to table locking. Page locking is where locking is set at an 8K page of data.

Setting Up Database Mail

It would be better to be notified about jobs that have failed rather than having to monitor each job as it processes manually. One of the ways to do this would be for the maintenance job to mail out results of its work. It is possible in SQL Server to use SMTP mail to send out notifications from your server. This means that you don't need to install a MAPI client, such as Microsoft Outlook, because SMTP processing is contained within a Windows install. The fact that you don't need another product on the server has benefits in terms of making your server more stable. To supplement stability, SMTP runs in a process outside SQL Server. Even if there are SMTP issues, SQL Server should not be affected if the SMTP process stops for any reason.

On top of this, SQL Server comes with built-in system-stored procedures and functionality to use SMTP to send out mail. These features are collectively called *Database Mail*.

The use of Database Mail has many positives for error notification, but it is not the total solution for monitoring SQL Server or even the underlying server. The most extreme problem is that the server crashes, reboots, uses 100% processing power, and runs out of memory, among other server-specific problems, all of which would stop an e-mail being sent. Other tools need to be deployed on the server that are either third-party-based or where you can write your own using .NET, Java, and so on. The very basic premise of these tools is that they "heartbeat" at regular intervals—in other words, transmit at regular intervals notifications to a central separate server that the Windows server is alive and performing well. The tool will have performed the necessary health checks about the server and notify via the heartbeat if it notices an issue arising to the central server. The central server looks out for problems and then it notifies the necessary person, who can then react to the issue. This tool is generally standardized company-wide and not on a per-server basis.

This section will cover only how to set up and test Database Mail and will not cover the monitoring of the Windows server. You will see how to implement Database Mail within the maintenance task created in the preceding section.

TRY IT OUT: SETTING UP DATABASE MAIL

1. To configure Database Mail, you need to create a mail profile for SQL Server to use. SQL Server Agent must be running to be able to create a mail profile. If SQL Server Agent is not running (although from the maintenance plan example it is likely that it is running), as denoted by a red circle with white cross or white circle with a red arrow, then highlight it, right-click, and select Start, as shown in Figure 9-26.

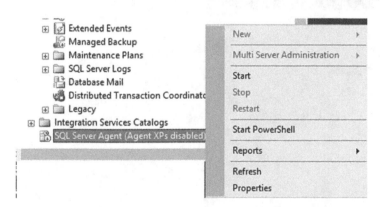

Figure 9-26. *The Configure Database Mail pop-up menu option*

2. Find the Database Mail node under the Management node. Right-click and select Configure Database Mail, as shown in Figure 9-27. By selecting Configure Database Mail, you start the Database Mail Configuration Wizard. The first screen is a welcome screen. Click Next to take you past the welcome screen within the wizard.

Figure 9-27. *Configure the database mailer*

3. Figure 9-28 shows the first screen of the configuration. This screen allows you to complete one of three tasks. As there are no existing mail accounts set up via either SQL Server or the Windows Control Panel's Mail option, you require the first Configuration Task option. If you already have on your server a mail account you wish to use, then select the second option. The third option lets you change the options if you already have Database Mail set up. Click Next.

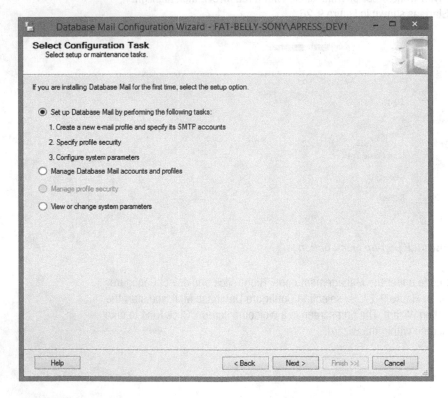

Figure 9-28. Create or manage a new profile and system parameters

4. Database Mail would normally be enabled via a system stored procedure, sp_configure 'Database Mail XPs'. If it is not enabled, then a helpful message is shown. If you see this dialog, click Yes.

5. You should now be at the start of setting up a new profile, as shown in Figure 9-29, where the profile name and description have been entered. Once you're happy with your description, click Add to create a new SMTP account.

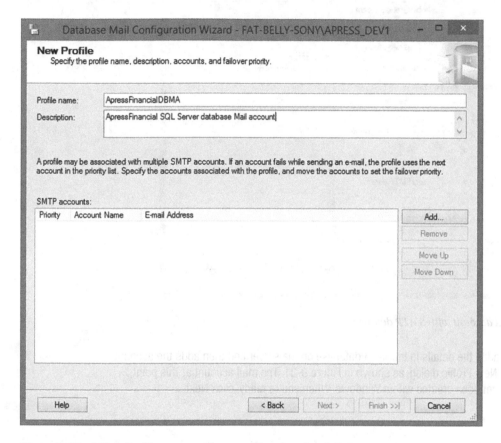

Figure 9-29. *A New Profile screen with no profiles already existing*

6. This brings you to the dialog shown in Figure 9-30, in which you need to specify your SMTP details. The settings are similar to what you would use when setting up your mail account within Outlook, Outlook Express, or any other SMTP (or MAPI) e-mail client. Recall, though, that SQL Server is using SMTP, so you don't need Outlook or any other MAPI mail client installed, and you need only the details you would use to connect to your SMTP server. If you're uncertain about any of the details that you need, contact your ISP or your mail administrator.

Figure 9-30. *A new mail account with SMTP details*

7. Clicking OK adds the details to the msdb database on the server and then adds the account
 name in the New Profile dialog, as shown in Figure 9-31. The mail account at this point,
 though, has not been created within Windows. When you're ready, click Next.

Figure 9-31. SMTP account added to the profile

8. You are now at the screen for the public and private profiles. A public profile is one that has been created for any login to use in sending an e-mail from within SQL Server. You will use that option for simplicity, as shown in Figure 9-32. However, you should use a private profile when you have decided on your SQL Server implementation strategy, as its use is restricted to specific roles within the database. Private profiles are the more secure option and would prevent someone from deliberately or inadvertently sending out a mass e-mail from your server. The final action would be to make the profile the default, also known as global, mail profile so that you don't have to define the specific profile each time. If you do decide on a public profile as part of your setup, then you could be opening your organization up to mass mailings via a rogue piece of code if you define the profile as the default. Select the public profiles option with care.

Figure 9-32. Private profile screen detailing private mail access only

9. The last screen, shown in Figure 9-33, details the system parameters for mailing. These are the same system parameters that you can alter through the third option that you saw in Figure 9-28. The parameters include the following:

- Account Retry Attempts: Determines the number of times to attempt to send a mail before marking the mail as failed to deliver

- Account Retry Delay (Seconds): Determines how long to wait before trying to send a mail again

- Maximum File Size (Bytes): Limits the size of mail that can be delivered to prevent large files being sent out; if you're sending out reports as well as job notifications, you may want to set up two profiles—one with a larger maximum file size than the other.

- Prohibited Attachment File Extensions: Defines which file extensions are prohibited; obviously, you don't wish your database to send out dangerous e-mails or even e-mails containing executables that are protected.

- Database Mail Executable Minimum Lifetime (Seconds): It's always best to shut down processes that are not required on a server to free up as many resources as possible. This option defines the number of seconds that Database Mail will continue to run while waiting on any new mails to process before shutting down. If the number's too low, resources will be used to start and stop frequently, so don't reduce this figure too much.

- Logging Level: When an e-mail is sent, fails to send, or is queued to send, these actions can be logged within the msdb database. Three possible logging levels for Database Mail can be used to track these and other scenarios:

 - Normal: Logs only any errors regarding sending your mail

 - Extended: Logs errors, warnings, and information about your mail

 - Verbose: Logs everything Database Mail does; this is the best setting to use when setting up Database Mail for the first time so that any errors generated from this wizard or your first executions are logged. However, the logging at this level is severe and not recommended to remain in force for extended periods, as it creates a large msdb.

Figure 9-33. *System parameters for Database Mail*

10. When you're done, click Next.

11. You will now see a summary screen indicating the options selected, as shown in Figure 9-34. When you click Finish, SQL Server processes the wizard and adds the profile and the mail account to SQL Server.

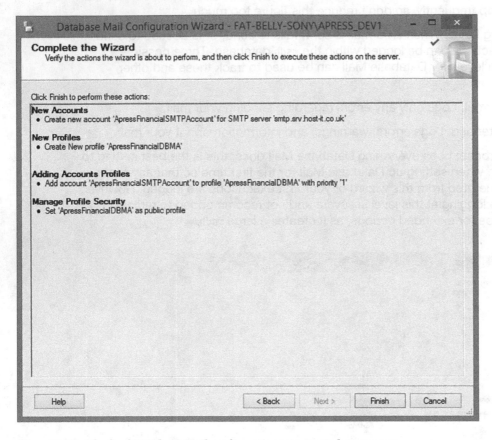

Figure 9-34. *The final Database Mail configuration screen, ready to process*

12. Providing everything has been created correctly, you should see a dialog similar to Figure 9-35. No mail testing is completed at this point, so to do that part of the setup, click Close. The next action will be to test out your setup.

Figure 9-35. *The account profile and details created successfully*

13. Now that your Database Mail is set up, send a test e-mail to check out your SMTP settings, connection, and so on. From the Database Mail node, right-click, and select Send Test E-Mail from the pop-up menu, as shown in Figure 9-36.

Figure 9-36. *The pop-up dialog to check for sending a test e-mail*

14. This then shows you a dialog similar to the one in Figure 9-37, which has been populated with the details of the test e-mail to send. If you have more than one profile, select each profile in turn to test them out and ensure they're working. Once completed, click Close.

Send Test E-Mail from FAT-BELLY-SONY\APRESS_...		
Database Mail Profile:	ApressFinancialDBMA	
To:	robin@fat-belly.com	
Subject:	Database Mail Test	
Body:	This is a test e-mail sent from Database Mail on FAT-BELLY-SONY\APRESS_DEV1.	
	Send Test E-Mail	
	Close	

Figure 9-37. *Sending a test e-mail to check that everything is all okay*

Modifying a Maintenance Plan

At this point, you have created a plan using the wizard, and you now have a working Database Mail account. In this section, you will apply the account to the maintenance plan and send the mail when the plan runs.

It is possible to modify the plan and add or remove steps, change the description, or add further subplans. The maintenance plan uses SQL Server Integration Services, which is commonly known as SSIS, to perform its duties. SSIS uses steps shown in a flowchart to demonstrate which items are being dealt with. SSIS is outside the scope of this book, so you won't be looking any further at modifying the plan by drilling into it to see the steps. Instead, you will alter only the reporting method. However, SSIS is an interesting area, especially if you want to move to the analysis of data via Business Intelligence and working with data in cubes. SSIS is used heavily in this area to load the initial data into a SQL Server database, which is then used to build a cube of data that is then "sliced and diced" to look at the data in many different ways. But if you are interested in using SSIS to work with your data, then I recommend the following books:

- *Pro SQL Server 2012 Integration Services*, by Francis Rodrigues and Michael Coles (Apress, 2012)

- *SSIS Design Patterns*, by Matt Masson et al. (Apress, 2012)

TRY IT OUT: SETTING UP DATABASE MAIL

1. The first step is to provide a specific operator within SQL Server Agent for the maintenance plan. From Object Explorer, select SQL Server Agent and highlight Operators. Right-click and from the menu select New Operator, as shown in Figure 9-38.

Figure 9-38. *Creating an operator from SQL Server Agent*

2. The New Operator screen is then shown, where you can enter how this operator will operate. You are required to give a name and then one of three methods of notification. The operator is for the maintenance plan, and the operator will have a "To" e-mail name. I have entered my own e-mail address, as shown in Figure 9-39. Once you have entered your own e-mail address, click OK to add the operator.

Figure 9-39. *New Operator screen defining notifications*

3. Now find the plan generated earlier in the Maintenance Plans node under the Management node in your SQL Server Object Explorer. It may well be highlighted from your execution earlier. Right-click and select Modify, as demonstrated in Figure 9-40.

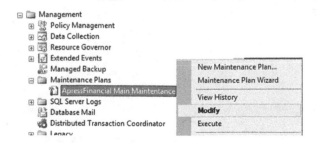

Figure 9-40. *Modifying the existing plan*

4. As partially shown in Figure 9-41, you are now presented with a new tab in SQL Server Management Studio that shows a graphical representation of the maintenance plan. What you will see is a simplistic SSIS project.

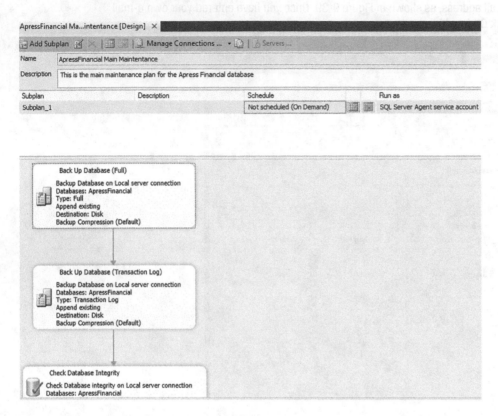

Figure 9-41. *The maintenance plan in graphical format*

■ **Note** In the bottom right of the screen, you will see a very faint graphic. This is a slider that will allow for zooming in and out of the maintenance plan. You can also drag the steps around the screen to get a different layout.

5. As shown in Figure 9-42, to the right of the Manage Connections button on the plan toolbar is a button to alter the reporting and logging options.

Figure 9-42. *Managing the Maintenance Plan connections*

6. You are now presented with the Reporting and Logging dialog, as you can see in Figure 9-43. It is possible to produce both a text and an e-mail version of the report. Select the "Send report to an email recipient" option to use the SQL Server Agent operator created in the previous section. Once complete, select OK.

Figure 9-43. *Reporting and logging*

7. Once you close and save the maintenance plan, you can now execute it. You should receive an e-mail detailing either a success or a failure of the job and the steps within the job.

Summary

Having a positive, regularly run maintenance plan is required to ensure your database is working correctly and performing as well as it has been designed to do. Ensuring that errors are found and dealt with by checking the database integrity, that statistics are as up-to-date as possible, making sure that indexes are reorganized, and ensuring that errors are logged and correctly reported will avoid problems occurring, as errors may occur at the worst possible time in the life of the corporation.

As part of this maintenance plan, you will be notified of problems so that you can deal with them quickly and efficiently. A database mail account is perfect for this, as it can notify you of problems in a process out of SQL Server.

CHAPTER 10

■ ■ ■

Data Insertion, Deletion, and Transactions—Disk-Based

The database is now defined, has a backup and recovery plan in place, and logins to the server and users to the database are defined, but you have not yet had to work with any data at this point. Within this chapter, you will learn about data insertion and deletion. In Chapter 12, this will progress to retrieving and removing data.

Inserting data can be straightforward when data is simply placed into each column of a table, but in some columns you may not want to add data, such as IDENTITY-based columns and those columns with a default value. This chapter will cover these areas for disk-based tables although there is also relevance to in-memory based tables. This chapter will also show how to work with IDENTITY values and some of the situations that can occur. Chapter 11 covers the differences and provides further information about in-memory based data actions.

We will then move on to see how to surround any data modifications with a transaction. A transaction will allow you to complete one or more data modification actions so that they are either all applied or all rejected if there has been a problem. Transactions have a danger element to them in that you can lock some data, which then stops other code from executing. You will see this in action and the dangers associated with it. You will also read about best practices with transactions.

The final section in the chapter covers removing data by deleting one or more rows, all the rows in the table, or even the whole table itself. Transactions will also be covered within this section and we will discuss how a transaction works when you remove all the rows in a table via a truncation. You will also see how to drop a table.

In this chapter, you will therefore see the following:

- How to insert data

- When a default value for a column is useful

- What happens when you try to insert invalid data

- Looking at when a value is not required in a column

- IDENTITY columns and the data generated

- Transaction basics

- Different methods of removing data

The first area you will look at is how to insert data into your tables.

Inserting Data

You have now built your tables, set up the relationships, and backed up your solution, so you are ready to start inserting your data. Not all the tables will be populated with data at this point. You will insert data in other tables later on in the book when different functionality of SQL Server is being demonstrated. Although data are being inserted, the database is still at the stage of being set up, as you are inserting static information at this point in the examples you are building together. To clarify, static data are data that will not change once set up, although there may be further additions to this data at periodic intervals, such as when a new share is created.

Not everyone who is allowed to access your database may, or should, be allowed to insert data directly into all of the tables. Therefore, you need to know how to set up the security to grant permission to specific user logins for inserting the data. The only people who really ought to be adding data directly to tables rather than using controlled methods such as stored procedures in production, for example, are special accounts like dbo accounts or specific accounts set up for production issues. In development, any developer should be able to insert data, but any login that would be testing out the application should not have that authority. You will see the reasons for this when you look at the security of adding data later in this chapter, and you will learn about alternative and more secure methods when you look at stored procedures and views.

Once you have set up users correctly, it is time to demonstrate inserting data into SQL Server. It is possible to insert data using SQL commands with T-SQL or through SQL Server Management Studio. Although both of these tools will have the same final effect on the database, each works in its own unique way.

When inserting data, you don't necessarily have to populate every column. You take a look at when it is mandatory and when it is not. There are many different ways to avoid inserting data into every column. This chapter will demonstrate the various different methods you can use to avoid having to use NULL values and default values. By using these methods, you are reducing the amount of information necessary to include with a record insertion. This method of inserting data uses special commands within SQL Server called *constraints*. You will see how to build a column constraint through T-SQL in Query Editor as well as in SQL Server Management Studio.

The T-SQL INSERT Statement Syntax

Before it is possible to insert data using T-SQL code, you need to be familiar with the INSERT statement and its structure. The INSERT statement is very simple and straightforward in its most minimal form, which is all that is required to insert a record.

```
INSERT [INTO]
   {table_name|view_name}
   [{(column_name,column_name,...)}]
   {VALUES (expression, expression, ...)}
```

You are required to start all data-based statements with the type of action you are trying to perform, which for the moment is the statement INSERT. The next part of the statement, INTO, is optional. It serves no purpose, but you will find some developers do use it to ensure their statement is more readable. The next part of the statement deals with naming the table or the view that the insertion has to place the data into. If the name of the table or view is the same as that of a reserved word or contains spaces, you have to surround that name with square brackets or double quotation marks, although, as mentioned earlier in the book, it is best to try to avoid names with spaces. However, if you do need to, it is better to use square brackets because there will be times you wish to set a value such as Acme's Rockets to column data, which can be added easily by surrounding it with double quotation marks.

I cannot stress enough that, really, there is nothing to be gained by using reserved words for table, view, or column names. Deciding on easy-to-use and unambiguous object names is part of a good design.

Column names are optional, but it is best practice to list them to help to have reliable code, as this ensures that data are inserted only into the columns into which you want it to be inserted. Therefore, it will be necessary to place the column names in a comma-delimited list. The list of column names must be surrounded by parentheses: (). The only time that column names are not required is when the INSERT statement is inserting data into every column

that is within the table in the same order as the column names are laid out in the table. However, this is a potentially dangerous scenario. If you build an INSERT statement that you then save and use later, you expect the columns to be in a specific order because that is the way they have always been. If someone then comes along and adds a new column, or perhaps alters the order, your query or stored procedure will either not work or give erroneous results, as values will be added to the wrong columns. Therefore, I recommend that you always name every column in anything but a query, which is built, run once, and thrown away.

The VALUES keyword, which precedes the actual values to be entered, is mandatory when you are inserting values. SQL Server needs to know that the following list is a list of values, not a list of columns. Therefore, you have to use the VALUES keyword, especially if you omit the list of columns as explained previously. Later in the chapter, I demonstrate when the VALUES keyword is not mandatory, and that is when you are building a query to define the values you are going to insert into your table. For the moment, though, I will be demonstrating only when you are inserting data with values.

You will have a comma-separated list surrounded by parentheses covering the values of data to insert. There has to be a column name for every value to be entered. To clarify, if there are ten columns listed for data to be entered, then there must be ten values to enter.

Finally, it is possible to insert multiple rows of data from the one INSERT statement. You can do this by surrounding each row you want to add with its own separate parentheses: (). You will see this in action later in the chapter. As with a single-row addition, it is necessary to have the same number of columns either as the table you are inserting into, if you are not defining the columns in the INSERT statement, or as the INSERT statement if you are defining the list. Now that the INSERT statement is clear, it's time to move on and use it.

INSERT SQL Statement

The first method of inserting data is to use the INSERT SQL statement as described previously. This example will insert one record into the ShareDetails.Shares table using Query Editor. When inserting the data, the record will be inserted immediately without any opportunity to roll back changes, as this statement does not use any transaction processing. You will also see with this example how Query Editor can aid you as a developer in building the SQL statement for inserting a row. Let's dive straight in and create the row.

TRY IT OUT: INSERTING DATA USING T-SQL

1. Ensure that you have a Query Editor window open, connected to your ApressFinancial database, and that you are logged in with an account that has insert permissions on the ShareDetails.Shares table. This will be any member of the administrator's or database owner's role including FAT-BELLY-Sony\MSmith, who we gave dbo rights to in Chapter 4.

2. Right-click against the ShareDetails.Shares table and select Script Table As ➤ INSERT To ➤ New Query Editor Window.

3. This will bring up the following code. SQL Server covers itself concerning the use of reserved words, spaces in names, and so on, by surrounding every object name with square brackets. It also fully qualifies the table name with the database name and schema owner—in this case, ShareDetails. Moving to the values, you can see the column name repeated so that when altering the VALUES section, if the table has a large number of columns, you know which column you are working with. The final part in the jigsaw is an indication of the data type and length to aid you as well.

```
USE [ApressFinancial]
GO
INSERT INTO [ShareDetails].[Shares]
        ([Description]
        ,[StockExchangeTicker]
        ,[CurrentPrice])
    VALUES
        (<Description, varchar(50),>
        ,<StockExchangeTicker, varchar(50),>
        ,<CurrentPrice, numeric(18,5),>)
GO
```

4. You need to insert a command at the top of this code, just to ensure that Query Editor has a setting to allow double quotes to be used to surround strings. This was covered in Chapter 5 when discussing database options. To cover yourself, though, you can always place the following code at the start of queries where quotation marks will be used. There is one hidden downfall that will be covered at the end. Notice as well that a GO command is included at the end of the SET command. This is because you want this command to take place in its own batch. Some commands need their own batch, while others don't. Some that do need their own batch are transaction-based commands, as you will see later in the book. Insert these two lines as the first two lines of your code.

```
SET QUOTED_IDENTIFIER OFF
GO
```

5. By altering the code within the Query Editor pane, you will see that the next section of code actually inserts the data into the ShareDetails.Shares table. Notice that no GO command is included at the end of this code. It is not necessary because there is only one INSERT statement and no other statements that need to form part of this same batch. The GO command is implicit.

```
SET QUOTED_IDENTIFIER OFF
GO
USE [ApressFinancial]
GO
INSERT INTO [ShareDetails].[Shares]
        ([Description]
        ,[StockExchangeTicker]
        ,[CurrentPrice])
    VALUES
        ("ACME'S HOMEBAKE COOKIES INC",
         'AHCI',
         2.34125)
```

6. Now that all the information has been entered into the Query Editor pane, it is time to execute the code. Press F5, or click the execute button on the toolbar. You should then see the following result, which indicates that there has been one row of data inserted into the table:

```
(1 row(s) affected)
```

After executing the code, the first record of information is placed into the database in the ShareDetails.Shares table. It is simple and straightforward. All the columns have been listed, and a value has been inserted. Because the name had a single quotation mark within it, it is simpler to surround the name with double quotation marks. However, to make sure that this string was not seen as an identifier, you have to switch that option off.

SQL Server Management Studio has the ability to create template scripts for several T-SQL statements. Templates, which you saw earlier in the book, hold parameter placeholders that require modification to build up the whole statement. Template scripts differ from actual templates, as the information created within Query Editor for these templates is for one statement only. Therefore, what you are actually seeing is the template for a one-line script.

When using the scripting options within Query Editor, it is possible to build the script as you have just seen for inserting a record into the ShareDetails.Shares table and save the T-SQL within a new Query Editor pane, to a file, or even to the clipboard. This would then allow the data to be reinserted instantaneously should the table be deleted. To an extent, scripting to files or a clipboard is not as useful as scripting to a Query Editor pane. By scripting to files or a clipboard, you would need to move back into these files to make the necessary changes for data insertion. As you saw, when the script is placed in the Query Editor pane, the table and the columns are listed, but obviously the values need to be altered. This would have to be completed in a file or a clipboard by reopening these contents and making modifications after the event.

The scripting template does build the whole INSERT statement and lists all the columns as well as—in the VALUES section of the statement—the name of the column and its data type definition. From there, it is easier to know what value is expected within the INSERT statement line.

The example mentions that using SET QUOTED_IDENTIFIER OFF does have one hidden downfall: in many cases, when using T-SQL statements, it is possible to surround reserved words with double quotation marks, rather than square brackets; however, with the QUOTED_IDENTIFIER set to OFF, you will be able to surround reserved words only with square brackets. If you had QUOTED_IDENTIFIER set to ON, then you could not have put ACME'S in the name; the code would have to have been written with two single quotation marks. Therefore, the code would have had to look like the following:

```
INSERT INTO [ApressFinancial].[ShareDetails].[Shares]
        ([ShareDesc]
        ,[ShareTickerId]
        ,[CurrentPrice])
    VALUES
        ('ACME''S HOMEBAKE COOKIES INC',
         'AHCI',
         2.34125)
```

I tend to run with SET QUOTED_IDENTIFIER set to OFF. Now that you know how to construct an INSERT statement, it is time to look at how you need not define all the columns within a table.

As you have just seen in your first example, you specified every column in the table within the INSERT statement. You are now probably wondering whether you have to specify every column every time a record is inserted into a table. The answer is not necessarily, and it depends on how your table columns are defined. The following sections look at two methods for inserting rows of data without specifying a value for each column: using default values and allowing a NULL value.

Default Values

One way to avoid entering a value for each column is to set a column or a set of columns with a default value. You set up the CustomerDetails.Customers table to have a default value when creating the tables in Chapter 5. Default values are used when a large number of INSERTs for a column would have the same value entered each time. Why have the overhead of passing this information, which would be the column name plus the value, through to SQL Server, when SQL Server can perform the task quickly and simply for you? Network traffic would be reduced and accuracy ensured as the column information would be completed directly by SQL Server. Do note, though, that a default value is not a mandatory value that will always be stored in a column. It is just a value that you think is the best value to use in the event that no other value is supplied. If you do pass a value, then the default value will be overridden, as you would expect.

Although it has been indicated that default values are best for a large number of INSERTs, it can also be argued that this need not be the case. Some people feel that all that is required is a significant number of rows to be altered from a default value setting for the use of default values to be a disadvantage. It does come down to personal preference as to when you think setting a default value will be of benefit. However, if there are times when you wish a column to have an initial value when a row is inserted with a specific value, then it is best to use a default value.

In the next section's example, where you'll build up your next set of INSERT statements, I will demonstrate how a default value will populate specific columns. When creating the CustomerDetails.Customers table, you created a column that is set up to be populated with a default value: the DateOpened column. In this column, you call a SQL Server reserved function, GETDATE(). This function gets the date and time from the operating system and returns it to SQL Server. By having this within a column default value, it is then inserted into a record when a row is added.

Using NULL Values

Another way to avoid filling in data for every column is to allow NULL values in the columns. You did this for some columns when defining the tables. Ensuring that each column's Allow Nulls option is checked can ensure this is true for all your columns. If you take a look at Figure 10-1, you'll see that one of the columns in the ShareDetails.Shares table, StockExchangeTicker, does allow a NULL value to be entered into the column.

FAT-BELLY-SONY\AP...areDetails.Shares ✕		
Column Name	Data Type	Allow Nulls
🔑 ShareId	int	☐
Description	varchar(50)	☐
▶ StockExchangeTicker	varchar(50)	☑
CurrentPrice	numeric(18, 5)	☐
		☐

Figure 10-1. NULLs selected on a column

Therefore, the previous example could have placed data only in the Description and CurrentPrice fields if you had wanted, as ShareId is an IDENTITY column and is auto-filled. If the ShareDetails.Shares record had been inserted only with those two columns, the statement would have looked like the following T-SQL:

```
SET QUOTED_IDENTIFIER OFF
GO
INSERT INTO [ApressFinancial].[ShareDetails].[Shares]
        ([Description]
        ,[CurrentPrice])
    VALUES
        ("ACME'S HOMEBAKE COOKIES INC",
         2.34125)
```

Figure 10-2 shows what the data would have looked like had you used the preceding T-SQL instead of the code in the previous example.

	ShareId	Description	StockExchangeTicker	CurrentPrice
1	1	ACME'S HOMEBAKE COOKIES INC	AHCI	2.34125
2	2	ACME'S HOMEBAKE COOKIES INC	NULL	2.34125

Figure 10-2. *Insert with NULL shown in SQL Server Management Studio*

As you can see in Figure 10-2, the column that had no data entered has a setting of allowing a NULL. A NULL setting is a special setting for a column. The value of NULL requires special handling within SQL Server or applications that will be viewing this data. What this value actually means is that the information within the column is unknown; it is not a numeric or an alphanumeric value. Therefore, because you don't know if it is numeric or alphanumeric, you cannot compare the value of a column that has a setting of NULL to the value of any other column, and this includes if that other also had a NULL value.

■ **Note**　One major rule involving NULL values: A primary key cannot contain any NULL values.

In the following exercise, you will use SQL Server Management Studio to see the effects of not populating a field defined as NOT NULL. The exercise also demonstrates how to edit rows of data using SSMS and how there can be dangers in this approach. You will see what happens to the IDENTITY values when an insertion has a problem and is not inserted. It is important to see these effects, so you need to see errors being generated.

When using SQL Server Management Studio, it is not always immediately apparent what data are valid in each column or if a column is NULL or NOT NULL. If you enter invalid data or leave a column empty, when in fact it should have data (in other words, it isn't set to accept NULL values), you will receive an error message. An IDENTITY column is protected.

Editing data within SSMS can be quick and easy but has the potential of some trouble when entering data, as demonstrated in the next example. SQL Server provides the ability to edit data by displaying an editable grid, not dissimilar to basic Excel. A new toolbar will be displayed, providing you with the options to let you work with the data. You will see this in the following exercise and how you can use this toolbar to access the underlying T-SQL that is used to provide the data for the grid. Once the toolbar is visible, by individually clicking the first four buttons, you can see your Management Studio display alter to show more and different information. You will be able to toggle the visibility of a pane diagramming the tables and relationships, the selection criteria, the SQL, and finally the results. This toolbar comes into its own when working with data, as you are seeing, but also when building views; you will see the toolbar again in Chapter 11. When you use the grid for working with data, as you will do when developing a system, then you may find these buttons useful, especially the SQL button.

TRY IT OUT: NULL VALUES AND SQL SERVER MANAGEMENT STUDIO

1. Ensure that SQL Server Management Studio is running and that you are logged in with an account that allows the insertion of records. Any of your users can do this.

2. Expand the ApressFinancial node in Object Explorer so you can see the CustomerDetails. Customers table. Right-click this table and select Edit Top 200 Rows.

3. In the main pane on the right, you should now see a grid similar to Figure 10-3. This grid would usually show all the rows of data that are within the table, but as this table contains no data, the grid is empty and ready for the first record to be entered. Notice that a star appears on the far left-hand side. The star is the record marker and denotes which record the grid is actually pointing to and working with for insertion. It will change to an arrow shortly. The arrow denotes which record you are viewing. When the marker changes to a pencil, it denotes that you are writing data in that row, ready for updating the table—perhaps not so relevant in this instance, but very useful when several records are displayed.

	CustomerId	Title	FirstName	OtherInitials	LastName	AddressLine1	AddressLine2
*	NULL	NULL	NULL	NULL	NULL	NULL	NULL

Figure 10-3. *No data held within the table*

4. It is a simple process to enter the information into the necessary columns as required. The first column, CustomerId, is protected, as this is an IDENTITY column. Try entering **Mr** into the CustomerTitleId column. When you try moving to another cell, you will see something similar to the message shown in Figure 10-4 that informs you that Title is expecting a tinyint data type, which is stored as a byte, hence the message showing as it does.

Figure 10-4. *Invalid data type error message*

5. Change the value in Title to 1, which is of the correct data type, a tinyint.

6. Although the data have not been entered, I want to demonstrate what happens when all of the data that are mandatory have not been filled into the row. Press the down arrow to indicate that you have finished creating this customer and wish to create the next. You will see a new error message indicating that some columns that have to be populated aren't, as shown in Figure 10-5. I wanted to create a row that was full of NULL values, but I can't. The error message indicates that CustomerFirstName has not been set up to allow a NULL value, and you need to put some data in there. You will be notified of only one column at a time, as the error message does not list out every column. If every column were listed, SQL Server would be exposing some of your table structure, which could be a security risk.

■ **Note** You will see that this error message says INSERT fails. This is important to note and will be clarified in step 9.

Figure 10-5. *Trying to insert a row with NULL when NULLs are not allowed*

7. Clicking OK allows you back into the grid where the whole row can be populated with the correct information. Notice that you can miss out placing any data in OtherInitials, AddressLine2, and AddressLine3, as well as a few other columns, as these columns allow NULL values.

8. Now populate your grid, completing all the required columns (see Figure 10-6), and click the down arrow. Your grid should resemble Figure 10-6. The red circle with the white exclamation mark denotes that although the record is in the database, SQL Server has not refreshed the grid. This is important as the CustomerId number has been generated by SQL Server and is therefore not displayed in the grid. So let's fix this so you can see the value.

	CustomerId	Title	FirstName	OtherInitials	LastName	AddressLine1	AddressLine2	AddressLine3	TownOrCity
❶	NULL	1	Noel	NULL	Morgala	87 Winnie Way	NULL	NULL	75
▶*	NULL	NULL	NULL	NULL	NULL	NULL	NULL	NULL	NULL

FAT-BELLY-SONY\A...Details.Customers ✕

Figure 10-6. *The populated grid*

9. Figure 10-7 shows the toolbar that is displayed when you edit or display data within SSMS. If you do not see the menu, then from the SSMS menu, you can select View ➤ Toolbars ➤ Query Designer.

Figure 10-7. *The Query Designer toolbar displayed when using the grid*

10. Let me go through each button with a short description of each one before you progress:

 - Show Details: Shows the tables and any relationships.

 - Show Criteria: Details the columns used in the SQL to produce the results grid; you can select or deselect columns as required.

 - Show SQL: Displays the underlying SQL that was created to produce the results grid.

 - Show Results: This is the grid that is displayed when the SQL is executed.

 - Change Type: It is possible to change a query from an INSERT to a DELETE or one of other several options.

 - Execute: Runs the underlying SQL.

 - Verify SQL: Checks that the SQL is valid; if you alter the SQL, then click this button prior to executing to ensure that any changes are correct.

 - Add Group By: This is a method to allow you to group results.

 - Add Table: If you would like your query to deal with more than one table, then you do this via this button.

 - Add New Derived Table: It is possible to build a table of data temporarily within a query and use the results from that table within the main query. The table of data that temporarily exists is a derived table.

11. Click the Execute button (red exclamation mark) on the Query Designer toolbar to refresh the grid. The point to notice is that this is the first record entered and that the CustomerId is set to 2, as you can see in Figure 10-8. It is not 1 because of the "insert fails" message from step 5. SQL Server has attempted to insert a row, and therefore an IDENTITY value has been generated and then discarded when the insertion failed. You may also notice how valuable using defaults as initial values for columns can be. If you scroll to the right, you will see where the DateOpened column has the date the record was inserted. Where the real benefit of using default values comes in is in ensuring that specific columns are populated with the correct default values. As soon as you move off from the new row, the default values are inserted and ready to be modified. There is now a record of when the record was added, ideal for auditing. Once you are happy, close the editor.

CustomerId	Title	FirstName	OtherInitials	LastName	AddressLine1	AddressLine2	AddressLine3	TownOrCity	ZipCo...	USState	AccountType	ClearedBalance	UnclearedBala...	DateOpened	DateClosed
▶ 8	1	Noel	NULL	Mergala	87 Winnie Way	NULL	NULL	75	52	1	1	NULL	NULL	2014-08-25	NULL
✻ NULL	NULL	NULL	NULL	NULL	NULL	NULL	NULL	NULL	NULL	NULL	NULL	NULL	NULL	NULL	NULL

Figure 10-8. *Data post refresh showing identity value*

■ **Note** By having an IDENTITY column, every time a record is entered or an attempt is made to enter a record and all the *data entered* are of valid data types—whether this is through SQL Server Management Studio or an INSERT statement—the column value within the table will be incremented by the Identity Increment amount that you defined when the table was created.

Now that you have seen how SSMS deals with NULL values and invalid data and how it is possible to modify the data in a table, the next exercise will demonstrate how the same set of problems works using T-SQL in Query Editor.

TRY IT OUT: NULL VALUES AND T-SQL

1. Open up a Query Editor window and enter the following code. This code will replicate the first part of the previous example in which you entered the wrong data type.

   ```
   USE ApressFinancial
   GO
   INSERT INTO CustomerDetails.Customers (Title) VALUES ('Mr')
   ```

2. Now execute this by pressing F5 or clicking the Execute button on the toolbar. This code will generate an error because, once again, this is the wrong data type. (Note that this error message specifies the expected data type tinyint.)

```
Msg 245, Level 16, State 1, Line 3
Conversion failed when converting the varchar value 'Mr' to data type tinyint.
```

3. Change the code to replicate your second attempt at entering a row where the data type for the title is now correct, but you are still missing other values.

   ```
   USE ApressFinancial
   GO
   INSERT INTO CustomerDetails.Customers (Title) VALUES (1)
   ```

4. Now execute this by pressing F5 or clicking the Execute button on the toolbar. This code will generate a different error, informing you this time that you didn't allow a NULL into the CustomerFirstName column, and therefore you have to supply a value.

```
Msg 515, Level 16, State 2, Line 3
Cannot insert the value NULL into column 'FirstName', table
'ApressFinancial.CustomerDetails.Customers'; column does not allow nulls.
INSERT fails.
The statement has been terminated.
```

5. This final example will work successfully. However, note that the LastName is before that of the FirstName column. This demonstrates that it is not necessary to name the columns within the insertion in the same order as they are defined within the table. You can place the columns in any order you desire.

```
INSERT INTO CustomerDetails.Customers
(Title,LastName,FirstName,
OtherInitials,AddressLine1,TownOrCity,USState,ZipCode,
AccountType,ClearedBalance,UnclearedBalance)
VALUES (3,'Lomas','Aubrey',NULL,'11c Clerkenwell',
4,8,0,2,437.97,-10.56)
```

6. Execute the code. This time you should see the following results, indicating the record has been inserted successfully:

```
(1 row(s) affected)
```

7. Now let's go back and view the data to see what has been entered. Find the CustomerDetails.Customers table in Object Explorer again. Right-click the table and select Select Top 1000 Rows. The table now has two rows with a gap in what you want the ideal ascending sequence to be, as you see in Figure 10-9.

Figure 10-9. *Second customer inserted*

■ **Note** There is a different gap because, using T-SQL, you have attempted to insert a row. When using SSMS, it is validating the data first. Depending on the number of attempts you have made, you may have a different gap.

That is all there is to it. It's just as simple as using SQL Server Management Studio, but you did get more informative error messages. You now have a slight problem in that already there are two gaps in the table, which may be acceptable and once you go live may be the norm; however, it would be useful at this early stage to have no gaps. This can be remedied easily within Query Editor, which you will do in the next section.

DBCC CHECKIDENT

The DBCC commands can be used for many different operations, from checking the integrity of the database, as you saw in Chapter 8 when building a database maintenance plan, to working with data and tables, such as working with IDENTITY columns.

If you find that when testing out IDENTITY columns, you receive a number of errors and the identity number has jumped up further than you wished, it is possible to reset the seed of the IDENTITY column so that Query Editor starts again from a known point. The syntax for this command is very simple:

```
DBCC CHECKIDENT ('table_name'[,{NORESEED |{RESEED[,new_reseed_value]}}])
```

The following elaborates on the three areas of the syntax that may need explanation:

- The name of the table that you wish to reset the identity value for is placed in single quotation marks.

- You can then use NORESEED to display what SQL Server believes the current identity value should be—in other words, what the current maximum identity value is within the IDENTITY column. Although rare, SQL Server can jump and skip a very large range of values with the potential of generating a gap. A smaller jump as you have just seen is more common when you have an issue. It is unusual for this to be a problem for you, but if it is, then don't use IDENTITY and generate the value yourself.

- The final option is the one you are interested in. You can reseed a table automatically by simply specifying the RESEED option with no value. This will look at the table defined and will reset the value to the current maximum value within the table. Or, optionally, you can set the column of the table to a specific value by separating the value and the option RESEED by a comma.

Resetting the seed for an IDENTITY column, though, does have a danger, which you need to be aware of. If you reset the point to start inserting values for the IDENTITY column prior to the greatest number on the given table, you will find that there is the potential of an error being produced. To clarify this point, when a value that already exists is generated from an INSERT after resetting the IDENTITY column value, you will receive an error message informing you that the value already exists. To give an example, you have a table with the values 1, 2, 5, 6, 7, and 8, and you reset the IDENTITY value back to 2. You insert the next record, which will correctly get the value 3, and the insertion will work. This will still work the same with the next insertion, which will receive the value 4. However, come to the next record and there will be an attempt to insert the value 5, but that value already exists; therefore, an error will be produced. However, if you had reset the value to 8—the last value successfully entered—then everything would have been okay.

As you do not have the value 1 for the first row in the CustomerDetails.Customers table, it would be nice to correct this. It also gives a good excuse to demonstrate CHECKIDENT in action. The code that follows will remove the erroneous record entry and reset the seed of the IDENTITY column back to 0, to a value indicating that no records have been entered. You will then reenter the customer information via T-SQL. Enter the following code into Query Editor and execute it. The first line removes the record from CustomerDetails.Customers, and the second line resets the identity. For now, don't worry about the record deletion part, as deleting records is covered in detail later in the chapter in the "Deleting Data" section. When inserting the first customer, Noel Morgala, I have demonstrated how through the use of the keyword NULL it is possible to place a NULL value into a field via T-SQL. In this example, it is superfluous as the two columns defined with a value of NULL did not need to be mentioned in the columns listed, and therefore a value would remain undefined such as the DateClosed column. SQL Server has inserted a NULL value for DateClosed.

```
DELETE FROM CustomerDetails.Customers
DBCC CHECKIDENT('CustomerDetails.Customers',RESEED,0)
INSERT INTO CustomerDetails.Customers
(Title,LastName,FirstName,
OtherInitials,AddressLine1,TownOrCity,USState,ZipCode
AccountType,ClearedBalance,UnclearedBalance)
VALUES (1,'Morgala','Noel',NULL,'87 Winnie Way',4,8,112,,0,NULL,NULL)
INSERT INTO CustomerDetails.Customers
(Title,LastName,FirstName,
OtherInitials,AddressLine1,TownOrCity,USState,ZipCode,
AccountType,ClearedBalance,UnclearedBalance)
VALUES (2,'Lomas','Aubrey',NULL,'11c Clerkenwell',2654,0,0,2,437.97,-10.56)
```

When the code is run, you should see the following information output to the Query Results pane:

```
(2 row(s) affected)

Checking identity information: current identity value '4', current column value '0'.

DBCC execution completed. If DBCC printed error messages, contact your system administrator.

(1 row(s) affected)

(1 row(s) affected)
```

Column Constraints

A constraint is essentially a check that SQL Server places on a column to ensure that the data to be entered in the column meet specific conditions. You first saw a constraint when creating a primary key in Chapter 6. This can keep out data that are erroneous, and therefore avoid data inconsistencies. Constraints are used to keep database integrity by ensuring that a column receives data only within certain parameters.

You have already built a non-key-based constraint on the CustomerDetails.Customers table for the default value for the column DateAdded. If you go to Object Explorer, right-click, select Script Table As ➤ Create To, and put the output in a new query window, you will see the following line from that output. So a constraint is used for setting a default value.

```
ADD CONSTRAINT [DF_Customers_DateOpened]
DEFAULT (getdate()) FOR [DateOpened]
```

Constraints are used to not only insert default values, but also validate data as well as primary keys. However, when using constraints within SQL Server, you do have to look at the whole picture, which is the user graphical system with the SQL Server database in the background. If you are using a constraint for data validation, some people will argue that perhaps it is better to check the values inserted within the user front-end application rather than in SQL Server. This has some merit, but what also has to be kept in mind is that you may have several points of entry to your database. This could be from the user application, a web-based solution, or other applications if you are building a central database. Many people will say that all validation, no matter what the overall picture is, should always be placed in one central place, which is the SQL Server database. Then there is only one set of code to alter if anything changes. It is a difficult choice and one that you need to look at carefully.

You have two ways to add a constraint to a table. You saw the first when creating a default value as you built a table via SQL Server Management Studio in Chapter 5.

To build a constraint via code, you need to use the ALTER TABLE command, no matter what type of constraint this is. The ALTER TABLE command can cover many different alterations to a table, but in this instance, the example concentrates on just adding a constraint. This makes the ALTER TABLE statement easy, as the only real meat to the clause comes with the ADD CONSTRAINT syntax. The next example will work with the CustomerDetails. CustomerProducts table, and you will see three different types of constraints added, all of which will affect insertion of records. It is worth reiterating the adding of a default value constraint again, as this will differ from the DateAdded column on the CustomerDetails.Customers table. Once the constraints have been added, you will see them all in action and how errors are generated from erroneous data input.

TRY IT OUT: ALTERING A TABLE FOR A DEFAULT VALUE IN QUERY EDITOR

Although all the examples deal with the CustomerDetails.CustomerProducts table, each constraint being added to the table will be created one at a time, followed by a discussion of each point.

1. Ensure that Query Editor is running. In the Query Editor pane, enter the following code, which will add a primary key to the CustomerDetails.CustomerProducts table. This will place the CustomerFinancialProductId column as the key, which will be clustered.

    ```
    USE ApressFinancial
    GO
    ALTER TABLE CustomerDetails.CustomerProducts
    ADD CONSTRAINT PK_CustomerProducts
    PRIMARY KEY CLUSTERED
    (CustomerFinancialProductId) ON [PRIMARY]
    GO
    ```

2. Next you add a CHECK constraint on the AmountToCollect column.

    ```
    ALTER TABLE CustomerDetails.CustomerProducts
    WITH NOCHECK
    ADD CONSTRAINT CK_CustProds_AmtCheck
    CHECK (AmountToCollect > 0)
    GO
    ```

3. The CustomerDetails.CustomerProducts table is once again altered, and a new constraint called CK_CustProds_AmtCheck is added. This constraint will ensure that for all records inserted into the CustomerDetails.CustomerProducts table from this point on, the amount to collect must be greater than 0. Notice as well that the NOCHECK option is included. This indicates that any records already inserted will not be checked for this constraint. At this point of your example, this table is empty, but if there were invalid data and invalid data existed, then the constraint would ignore those rows and apply the constraint from the point of implementation onward.

4. For the third constraint, add a DEFAULT value constraint as shown in the following code. This will insert a value of 0 in the Renewable column if no value is entered specifically into this column. This signifies that the premium collected is a one-off collection as a 0 indicates a false.

```
ALTER TABLE CustomerDetails.CustomerProducts WITH NOCHECK
    ADD CONSTRAINT DF_CustProd_Renewable
    DEFAULT (0)
    FOR Renewable
```

5. Execute the three batches of work by pressing F5 or clicking the Execute button on the toolbar. You should then see the following result:

```
The command(s) completed successfully.
```

6. There are two methods to check that the code has worked before adding in any data.

 - Move to Object Explorer in Query Editor. This isn't refreshed automatically, so you do need to refresh it. You should then see the three new constraints added—two under the Constraints node and one under the Keys node—as well as a display change in the Columns node, as shown in Figure 10-10.

```
CustomerDetails.CustomerProducts
    Columns
    Keys
        PK_CustomerProducts
    Constraints
        CK_CustProds_AmtCheck
        DF_CustProd_Renewable
    Triggers
    Indexes
    Statistics
```

Figure 10-10. CustomerDetails.CustomerProducts table details

 - Another method is to move to SQL Server Management Studio, find the CustomerDetails.CustomerProducts table, right-click it, and select Design. This brings you into the Table Designer, where you can navigate to the necessary column to check out the default value—in this case, Renewable. Also notice the yellow key against the CustomerFinancialProductId signifying that this is now a primary key, as shown in Figure 10-11.

	Column Name	Data Type	Allow Nulls
🔑	CustomerFinancialProdu...	int	☐
	CustomerId	int	☐
	FinancialProductId	int	☐
	AmountToCollect	money	☐
	Frequency	smallint	☐
	LastCollected	datetime	☐
	LastCollection	datetime	☐
▶	Renewable	bit	☐
			☐

Column Properties

(General)	
(Name)	Renewable
Allow Nulls	No
Data Type	bit
Default Value or Binding	((0))
Table Designer	
Collation	<database default>
▷ Computed Column Specification	
Condensed Data Type	bit
Description	

Figure 10-11. *Default value constraint on column Renewable*

 7. Move to the Table Designer toolbar, and click the Manage Check Constraints button, shown in Figure 10-12.

Figure 10-12. *Table Designer toolbar with Manage Check Constraints button*

8. This will display the Check Constraints dialog box, shown in Figure 10-13, where you will see the AmountToCollect column constraint displayed. You can add a further constraint by clicking the Add button. Do so now.

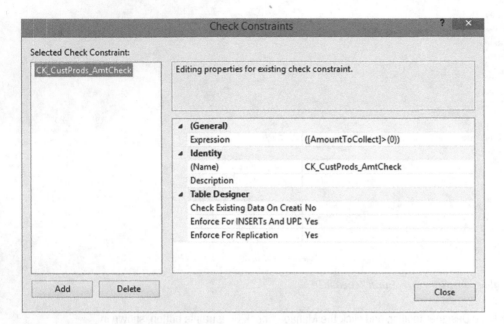

Figure 10-13. *Check Constraints screen with current constraint*

9. This check will ensure that the LastCollection date is greater than the value entered in another column. Here you want to ensure that the LastCollection date is equal to or after the LastCollected date. Recall that LastCollection defines when you last took the payment, and LastCollected defines when the last payment should be taken.

10. The expression you want to add, which is the test the constraint is to perform, is not a value or a system function like GETDATE(), but rather a test between two columns from a table, albeit the same table you are working with. This is as simple as naming the columns and the test you wish to perform. Also, at the same time, change the name of the constraint to something meaningful. Your check constraint should look something like what appears in Figure 10-14.

Figure 10-14. *LastCollection constraint in the Check Constraints dialog box*

11. Click Close. This adds the constraint to the list, although it has not yet been added to the table. It is not until the table is closed that this will happen, so do that now. Click Yes on the screen that is displayed, which is asking you if you wish to save.

12. Now it's time to test the constraints to ensure that they work. First of all, you want to check the AmountToCollect constraint. Enter the following code, which will fail, because the amount to collect is a negative amount:

```
INSERT INTO CustomerDetails.CustomerProducts
(CustomerFinancialProductId,CustomerId,FinancialProductId,AmountToCollect,
Frequency,LastCollected,LastCollection,Renewable)
VALUES (1,1,1,-100,0,'24 Aug 2014','24 Aug 2017',0)
```

13. Execute the code in Query Editor. You will see the following result. Instantly, you can see that the constraint check (CK_CustProds_AmtCheck) has cut in and the record has not been inserted.

```
Msg 547, Level 16, State 0, Line 1
The INSERT statement conflicted with the CHECK constraint
"CK_CustProds_AmtCheck". The conflict occurred in database
"ApressFinancial", table "CustomerDetails.CustomerProducts",
column 'AmountToCollect'.
The statement has been terminated.
```

14. You alter this now to have a positive amount, but change the LastCollection so that you break the CK_CustProd_LastColl constraint. By removing the Renewable column and value, you can also check that the default value is entered. Enter the following code:

```
INSERT INTO CustomerDetails.CustomerProducts
(CustomerFinancialProductId,CustomerId,FinancialProductId,AmountToCollect,
Frequency,LastCollected,LastCollection)
VALUES (1,1,1,100,0,'24 Aug 2014','23 Aug 2014')
```

15. Execute the preceding code. You will see the following error message:

```
Msg 547, Level 16, State 0, Line 1

The INSERT statement conflicted with the CHECK constraint

" CK_CustProdsStillToCollect". The conflict occurred in database

"ApressFinancial", table "CustomerDetails.CustomerProducts".

The statement has been terminated.
```

Adding a constraint occurs through the ALTER TABLE statement as you have just done. However, the ADD CONSTRAINT command is quite a flexible command and can achieve a number of different goals.

The preceding example uses ADD CONSTRAINT to add a primary key, which can be made up of one or more columns (none of which can contain a NULL value), and also to insert a validity check and a set of default values. The only option not covered in the example is the addition of a foreign key, but this is very similar to the addition of a primary key.

The first constraint added is the primary key, which you saw in Chapter 5. The second constraint definition builds a column check to ensure that the data entered is valid for INSERT and UPDATE statements.

```
ADD CONSTRAINT constraint_name CHECK (constraint_check_syntax)
```

The syntax for a CHECK constraint is a simple true or false test. When adding in a constraint for checking the data, the information to be inserted is valid (true) or invalid (false) when the test is applied. As you will see, using mathematical operators to test a column against a single value or a range of values will determine whether the data can be inserted.

Notice in the example that the ADD CONSTRAINT command is preceded with a WITH NOCHECK option on the ALTER TABLE statement. As mentioned in step 2 of the exercise, this informs SQL Server that any existing data in the table will not be validated when it adds the table alteration with the constraint, and that only data modified or inserted after the addition of the constraint will be checked. If you do wish the existing rows to be checked, then you would use the WITH CHECK option. The advantage of this is that the existing data are validated against that constraint, and if the constraint was added to the table successfully, then you know your data are valid. If any error was generated, then you know that there were erroneous data and that you need to fix that data before being able to add the constraint. This is just another method of ensuring that your data are valid.

Finally, for adding a default value, the ADD CONSTRAINT syntax is very simple.

```
ADD CONSTRAINT constraint_name
DEFAULT default_value
FOR column_to_receive_the_value
```

The only part of the preceding syntax that requires further explanation is the default_value area. default_value can be a string, a numeric, NULL, or a system function (for example, GETDATE(), which would insert the current date and time). So the default value does not have to be fixed; it can be dynamic.

Inserting Several Records at Once

It is now necessary to enter a few more customers so that a reasonable amount of data is contained within the CustomerDetails.Customers table to work with later in the book. You need to do the same with several other tables as well, such as TransactionDetails.TransactionTypes, CustomerDetails.CustomerTransactions, and so on. This section will prove that no extra or specialized processing is required when inserting several records. When working with data, there may be many times that several records of data are inserted at the same time. This could be when initially populating a table or when testing. In this sort of situation, where you are repopulating a table, it is possible to save your query to a text file, which can then be reopened in Query Editor and executed without having to reenter the code. This is demonstrated at the end of the upcoming example.

In the next example, you will learn how to insert several rows. The work will be completed in batches. There is no transaction processing surrounding these INSERTs, and therefore each insertion will be treated as a single unit of work, which either completes or fails.

■ **Note** A transaction allows a number of INSERTs or modifications to be treated as one unit, and if any insertion fails within the transaction, all the units will be returned to their original value and no insertions will take place. Transactions will be discussed in more detail in the upcoming "Transactions" section.

TRY IT OUT: INSERT SEVERAL RECORDS AT ONCE

1. Ensure that SQL Server Query Editor is up and running. In the Query Editor window, enter the following code. In this example, several customers will be added through only one INSERT statement.

```
INSERT INTO CustomerDetails.Customers
(Title,FirstName,OtherInitials,
LastName,AddressLine1,AddressLine2,TownOrCity,USState,ZipCode,
ClearedBalance,UnclearedBalance)
VALUES (1,'Bernie','I','McGee','35 Baldrick Ave','West Hampstead',
18651,0,0,6653.11,0.00),
(3,'Jane','L','Harper','122 West Drive','Tuala',
185111,14,111,53.11,27.50),
(12,'Mark',NULL,'Vernon-Smith','4155b Fredericks Street','London',
157,0,97,-751,900.00)
```

2. Now just execute the code in the usual way, pressing F5 or clicking the Execute button. You will see the following output in the results pane. This indicates that three rows of information have been inserted into the database, one at a time.

```
(3 row(s) affected)
```

Inserting data using named-value pairs of the column in the table with a corresponding value in the VALUES expression is straightforward and the simplest method of data insertion. Excluding columns where a value is not mandatory has benefits of reducing the columns required but also creating the ability to insert a NULL value, which denotes a special condition that is useful when interrogating the data at a later stage. You will use the methods shown in this section of the book on many occasions, but also take time to see the section on "Inserting Data" section later on where you will see how to use data in one or more tables to insert into the required table.

It is also possible to attempt to insert data and, if there is a problem, for the insertion not to occur and the attempt to be rolled back. This can be achieved via a transaction.

Transactions

A *transaction* is a method through which developers can define a unit of work logically or physically that, when it completes, leaves the database in a consistent state. A transaction forms a single unit of work, which must pass the ACID test before it can be classified as a transaction. The ACID test is an acronym for atomicity, consistency, isolation, and durability:

- *Atomicity*: In its simplest form, all data modifications within the transaction must be both accepted and inserted successfully into the database, or none of the modifications will be performed.

- *Consistency*: Once the data has been successfully applied, or rolled back to the original state, all the data must remain in a consistent state, and the data must still maintain its integrity.

- *Isolation*: Any modification in one transaction must be isolated from any modifications in any other transaction. Any transaction should see data from any other transaction either in its original state or once the second transaction has completed. It is impossible to see the data in an intermediate state.

- *Durability*: Once a transaction has finished, all data modifications are in place and can be modified only by another transaction or unit of work. Any system failure (hardware or software) will not remove any changes applied.

Transactions within a database are a very important topic, but also one that requires a great deal of understanding. This chapter covers the basics of transactions only. To really do justice to this area, you would have to deal with some very complex and in-depth scenarios, covering all manner of areas such as triggers, nesting transactions, and transaction logging, which are beyond the scope of this book. However, you will see more on transactions in Chapter 12.

Transaction Basics

A transaction can be placed around any data manipulation, whether it is an update, insertion, or deletion, and can cater to one row or many rows, and also many different commands. A transaction is required only when data manipulation occurs such that changes will be either committed to the table or discarded. A transaction could cover several UPDATE, DELETE, or INSERT commands, or indeed a mixture of all three. However, there is one very large warning that goes with using transactions (see the "Caution" note).

■ **Caution** Be aware that when creating a transaction, you will be keeping a hold on the whole table, pages of data, or specific rows of information in question. Depending on how your SQL Server database solution is set up to lock data during updates, you could be stopping others from updating any information, and you could even cause a *deadlock*, also known as a *deadly embrace*. If a deadlock occurs, SQL Server will choose one of the deadlocks and kill the process; there is no way of knowing which process SQL Server will select. Keep your transactions short and, when dealing with multiple tables within a transaction, keep the same order of table access as you would find in other transactions.

A deadlock is where two separate data manipulations, in different transactions, are being performed at the same time. However, each transaction is waiting for the other to finish the update before it can complete its update. Neither manipulation can be completed because each is waiting for the other to finish. Then a deadlock occurs, and it can (and will) lock the tables and database in question. So, for example, transaction 1 is updating the customers table followed by the customer transactions table. Transaction 2 is updating the customer transactions table followed by the customers table. A lock would be placed on the customers table while those updates were being done by transaction 1. A lock would be placed on the customer transactions table by transaction 2. Transaction 1 could not proceed because of the lock by transaction 2, and transaction 2 could not proceed due to the lock created by transaction 1. Both transactions are "stuck." So it is crucial to keep the order of table updates the same, especially where both could be running at the same time.

It is also advisable to keep transactions as small and as short as possible and, under no circumstances, hold onto a lock for more than a few seconds. You can do this by keeping the processing within a transaction to as few lines of code as possible, and then either roll back (that is, cancel) or commit the transaction to the database as quickly as possible within code. With every second that you hold a lock through a transaction, you are increasing the potential of trouble happening. In a production environment, with every passing millisecond that you hold onto a piece of information through a lock, you are increasing the chances of someone else trying to modify the same piece of information at the same time and the possibility of the problems that would then arise.

There are two parts that make up a transaction: the start of the transaction and the end of the transaction, where you decide if you want to commit the changes or revert to the original state. You will now look at the definition of the start of the transaction, and then the T-SQL commands required to commit or roll back the transaction. The basis of this section is that only one transaction is in place and that you have no nested transactions. Nested transactions are much more complex and should be dealt with only once you are proficient with SQL Server. The statements you are going through in the upcoming text assume a single transaction; the COMMIT TRAN section changes slightly when the transaction is nested.

Transaction Commands

A transaction, as I just mentioned, has two parts: the command that denotes the start of the transaction and the command that denotes the end. The end can be to commit the data or to roll back the changes, just as I have discussed. Let's take a quick look at these commands.

BEGIN TRAN

The T-SQL command, BEGIN TRAN, denotes the start of the transaction processing. From this point on, until the transaction is ended with either COMMIT TRAN or ROLLBACK TRAN, any data modification statements will form part of the transaction.

It is also possible to suffix the BEGIN TRAN command with a name of up to 32 characters in length. If you name your transaction, it is not necessary to use the name when issuing a ROLLBACK TRAN or a COMMIT TRAN command. The name is there for clarity of the code only.

COMMIT TRAN

The COMMIT TRAN command commits the data modifications to the database permanently, and there is no going back once this command is executed. This function should be executed only when all changes to the database are ready to be committed.

ROLLBACK TRAN

If you wish to remove all the database changes that have been completed since the beginning of the transaction—say, for example, because an error had occurred—then you could issue a ROLLBACK TRAN command.

So, if you were to start a transaction with BEGIN TRAN and then issue an INSERT that succeeds, and then perhaps an UPDATE that fails, you could issue a ROLLBACK TRAN to roll back the transaction as a whole. As a result, you roll back not only the UPDATE changes, but also, because they form part of the same transaction, the changes made by the INSERT, even though that particular operation was successful.

To reiterate, keep transactions small and short. Never leave a session with an open transaction by having a BEGIN TRAN with no COMMIT TRAN or ROLLBACK TRAN. Ensure that you do not cause a deadly embrace.

If you issue a BEGIN TRAN, then you *must* issue a COMMIT TRAN or ROLLBACK TRAN transaction as quickly as possible; otherwise, the transaction will stay around until the connection is terminated.

Locking Data

The whole area of locking data—how locks are held and how to avoid problems with them—is a very large, complex area and not for the fainthearted. However, it is necessary to be aware of locks and at least have a small amount of background knowledge about them so that when you design your queries, you stand a chance of avoiding problems.

The basis of locking is to allow one transaction to update data, knowing that if it has to roll back any changes, no other transaction has modified the data since the first transaction did.

To explain this with an example, let's say you have a transaction that updates the CustomerDetails.Customers table and then moves on to update the TransactionDetails.Transactions table, but hits a problem when updating the latter. The transaction must be safe in the knowledge that it is rolling back only the changes it made and not changes made by another transaction. Therefore, until all the table updates within the transaction are either successfully completed or have been rolled back, the transaction will keep hold of any data inserted, modified, or deleted.

However, one problem with this approach is that SQL Server may not just hold the data that the transaction has modified. Keeping a lock on the data that has just been modified is called *row-level locking*. On the other hand, SQL Server may be set up to lock the database, which is known as *database-level locking*, found in areas such as backups and restores. The other levels in between are row, page, and table locking, so you could lock a large resource, depending on the task being performed.

This is about as deep as I will take this discussion on locks so as not to add any confusion or create a problematic situation. SQL Server handles locks automatically, but it is possible to make locking more efficient by developing an effective understanding of the subject and then customizing the locks within your transactions.

Deleting Data

Deleting data can be considered very straightforward. As you read this next section, you will see how easy it can be. However, mistakes made when deleting data are very hard to recover from. Therefore, you must treat deleting data with the greatest of care and attention to detail, and especially test any joins and filtering via a SELECT statement before running the delete operation.

Deleting data without the use of a transaction is almost a final act: the only way to get the data back is to reenter it, restore it from a backup, or retrieve the data from any audit tables that had the data stored in them when the data was created. Deleting data is not like using the recycle bin on a Windows machine: unless the data are within a transaction, they are lost. Keep in mind that even if you use a transaction, the data will be lost once the transaction is committed. That's why it's very important to back up your database before running any major data modifications or have audit tables that record the actions and data on the overlying table.

This section of the chapter will demonstrate the DELETE T-SQL syntax and then show how to use this within Query Editor. It is also possible to delete records from the results pane within SQL Server Management Studio, which will also be demonstrated.

However, what about when you want to remove all the records within a table, especially when there could be thousands of records to remove? You will find that the DELETE statement takes a very long time to run, as each row to delete is logged in the transaction log, thus allowing transactions to be rolled back. Luckily, there is a command for this scenario, called TRUNCATE, which is covered in the section "Truncating a Table" later in the chapter. However, caution should be exercised when using this command, and you'll see why later.

First of all, it is necessary to learn the simple syntax for the DELETE statement for deleting records from a table. Really, things don't come much simpler than this.

DELETE Syntax

The DELETE statement is very short and sweet. To run the command, simply state the table you wish to delete records from, as shown here:

```
DELETE
[FROM] tablename
WHERE where_condition
```

The FROM condition is optional, so your syntax could easily read as follows:

```
DELETE tablename
WHERE where_condition
```

The only area that really needs to be mentioned is that records can be deleted from only one table at a time, although when looking for rows to delete, you can join to several tables, as you can with SELECT and UPDATE and will see demonstrated in Chapter 12. If you are joining to other tables, then you do need to name the table you are deleting from. I realize that we have not yet covered how to join two tables, but, for reference, the syntax when you are deleting from one table but using at least one other table to join as part of the filtering would be as follows:

```
DELETE
[FROM] tablename
JOIN tablename2 ON (join condition would be placed here)
... (for further joins if required)
[WHERE where_condition]
```

The WHERE clause can become optional as the filtering could be done by joining two tables. You will see why this can work in Chapter 12.

Before Demonstrating the DELETE Statement

At the moment, there is very little data in your database and to demonstrate deleting data in the following section could mean that you have no data left for the remainder of the book. This is a minor inconvenience as it would be possible to reinsert the data that has already been generated after you have completed the data selection. However, deleting the data that currently exist is not ideal. Having a much larger set of data would be much better. Finally, having a larger set of data will be useful for the remainder of the book.

One method to insert data is to write INSERT statements one row at a time. You can also use SQL Server Management Studio in both methods demonstrated earlier. However, an easier method is to use a tool to generate data. I use a tool from a company called Red Gate, which has a random data generator called SQL Data Generator, which is one of many useful database tools by Red Gate (www.red-gate.com). By using this tool, I have generated SQL statements for the tables within ApressFinancial, and this script can be found along with the other code from the book at www.apress.com. The code will also be available from my web site, www.fat-belly.com. Please run in this code before proceeding further in the book. The SQL will be marked as "BulkInsert" for Chapter 10.

Using the DELETE Statement

Imagine that you're at the ATM and you are transferring money from your savings account to your checking account. During that process, a transaction built up of many actions is used to make sure that your money doesn't credit one system and debit the other. If an error occurs, the entire transaction will roll back, and no money will move between the accounts.

Let's take a look at what happens if you were to run this statement:

```
BEGIN TRAN
    DELETE CustomerDetails.Customers
```

When this code runs, SQL Server opens a transaction and then tentatively deletes all the records from the CustomerDetails.Customers table. The records are not actually deleted until a COMMIT TRAN statement is issued. In the interim, though, SQL Server will place a lock on the rows of the table, or if this was a much larger table, SQL Server may decide that a table lock (locking the whole table to prevent other modifications) is better. Because of this lock, all users trying to modify data from this table will have to wait until a COMMIT TRAN or ROLLBACK TRAN statement has been issued and completed. If one is never issued, users will be blocked until SQL Server decides to give up and chooses one of the processes as the "deadlock victim," kills their data modification attempt, and rolls back their transaction. This problem is one of a number of issues frequently encountered in applications when analyzing performance issues. Therefore, never have a BEGIN TRAN without a COMMIT TRAN or ROLLBACK TRAN.

So, time to start deleting records while using a transaction. In the following exercise, it is a series of three short steps, in which you will see how to delete records with a rollback, when leaving the transaction incomplete and open, and finally a deadlock scenario.

TRY IT OUT: DELETING RECORDS

1. Enter the following commands in an empty Query Editor pane. They remove all the records from your table within a transaction, prove the point by trying to list the rows, and then roll back the changes so that the records are put back into the table. The SELECT is retrieving data, and the COUNT(*) is just counting the rows.

```
BEGIN TRAN
    SELECT COUNT(*) FROM TransactionDetails.Transactions
    DELETE TransactionDetails.Transactions
    SELECT COUNT(*) FROM TransactionDetails.Transactions
ROLLBACK TRAN
SELECT COUNT(*) FROM TransactionDetails.Transactions
```

2. Execute the code. You should see the results displayed in Figure 10-15. Notice that the number of records in the TransactionDetails.Transactions table before the delete is 1,000, and then after the delete the record count is tentatively set to zero. Finally, after the rollback, it's set back to 1,000.

Figure 10-15. *Deletion of all rows that were then rolled back*

You will see more on the DELETE statement in Chapter 12 when the WHERE clause is introduced to filter results.

It is useful to demonstrate transactions further by looking at an "open transaction" where you have started a transaction but neither committed nor rolled back the transaction. This can be achieved by using two Query Editors within SQL Server Management Studio, by keeping a transaction open by not committing or rolling back in one Query Editor and retrieving data in the second Query Editor. From the previous example, you saw that there are 1,000 transactions in the TransactionDetails.Transactions table, as shown in Figure 10-15.

3. In one query window, enter and execute the following code. This will start a transaction, show the number of records in the table, and then delete the rows. You will see the number of rows for each action in Figure 10-16.

```
BEGIN TRAN
    SELECT COUNT(*) FROM TransactionDetails.Transactions
    DELETE TransactionDetails.Transactions
```

```
(1 row(s) affected)

(1000 row(s) affected)
```

Figure 10-16. *Deleting the rows but the transaction is still open*

4. Now open up a second query pane, enter the following code, and then execute it:

```
USE ApressFinancial
go
SELECT COUNT(*) FROM TransactionDetails.Transactions
```

5. You will not see a record count displayed immediately. In fact, you will not see a record count of the TransactionDetails.Transactions table for quite some time. The query will continue to run as shown in Figure 10-17 until you close the transaction in the first Query Editor. In a production environment, by keeping an open transaction, you can prevent any other T-SQL code from executing while the transaction is open. This is because in the first query pane you have an open transaction that is keeping a lock on the table until you decide whether to roll back the transaction or to commit the transaction. Keep the transaction open and the second query running for the moment.

⟨⟩ Executing query... FAT-BELLY-SONY\APRESS_DEV1 ... FAT-BELLY-SONY\RobinDe... ApressFinancial 00:00:47 0 rows

Figure 10-17. *Transaction still running due to lock*

6. When a database stops responding to queries such as the scenario you currently have, there are tools available that can help track and monitor problems. As a developer, the quickest method is to run a system-stored procedure (a stored procedure is simply a program stored in SQL Server) called sp_who. sp_who lists the current connections to the database and what each connection is performing. It can also display where there is a block in progress. If you open a third query pane, type **sp_who**, and execute it, you will see something similar to Figure 10-18.

35	51	0	sleeping	FAT-BELLY-SONY\RobinDewson	FAT-BELLY-SONY	0	Apres...	AWAITING COMMA...	0
36	52	0	sleeping	FAT-BELLY-SONY\RobinDewson	FAT-BELLY-SONY	0	Apres...	AWAITING COMMA...	0
37	53	0	sleeping	FAT-BELLY-SONY\RobinDewson	FAT-BELLY-SONY	0	master	AWAITING COMMA...	0
38	54	0	sleeping	FAT-BELLY-SONY\RobinDewson	FAT-BELLY-SONY	0	Apres...	AWAITING COMMA...	0
39	55	0	suspended	FAT-BELLY-SONY\RobinDewson	FAT-BELLY-SONY	52	Apres...	SELECT	0
40	56	0	runnable	FAT-BELLY-SONY\RobinDewson	FAT-BELLY-SONY	0	Apres...	SELECT	0

Figure 10-18. *A list of processes including the "suspended" AWAITING COMMAND*

7. Line 36 denotes the open transaction query pane. There are two SELECT statements running against ApressFinancial by connection FAT-BELLY-SONY\RobinDewson in my Management Studio, and they are the two rows 39 and 40. Row 40 showing as runnable is from the execution of sp_who. Row 39 showing as "suspended" will be the code in the open transaction. The second SELECT in row 39 cannot complete until the first query has completed; therefore, row 39 is blocked until that time. Notice the seventh column (the blk column) of row 39 in Figure 10-18. This is the numerical process ID, known as the SPID, of the process that is stopping SPID 52 (line 36) from completing. The name blk is short for block.

■ **Note** In the scenario just discussed, the second column is the process SPID, and it is the process SPID that you would need to know if you get to the position of needing to "kill" a process.

8. Return to the first query pane and roll back the transaction using the following command. Execute only the following command, not the whole text in that query; you have to execute the code in the same Query Editor that you ran the BEGIN TRAN. You will then see that the command completed successfully in the first query pane, and a record count of 1,000 is shown in the second query pane. If you look at Figure 10-19, you will see how I have placed the code in Query Editor and highlighted the rollback tran code **only**, which I can then execute.

```
rollback tran
```

```
BEGIN TRAN
    SELECT COUNT(*) FROM TransactionDetails.Transactions
    DELETE TransactionDetails.Transactions
    rollback tran
100 %   ▼
Messages
Command(s) completed successfully.
```

Figure 10-19. rollback tran *highlighted to execute the code only with result of execution*

■ **Tip** If you highlight code such as Figure 10-19, you are indicating the only section of code you want to run. SQL Server will not run un-highlighted code. Do take care as you can highlight too much code and you won't get the results expected; however, it is very useful.

This third section will show a deadlock. To demonstrate a deadlock is not as easy as a real-life running example. A deadlock in a section of code can happen once and then not happen again for a number of attempts. It can occur every time, but the majority of incidences will be down to timing of code execution. However, the following steps will show a deadlock and how SQL Server can deal with a deadlock. You will need two query panes again.

9. In the first query pane, enter and execute the following code:

```
BEGIN TRAN
    SELECT COUNT(*) FROM TransactionDetails.Transactions
    DELETE ShareDetails.SharePrices
```

10. In the second query pane, enter and execute the following code. The first statement is setting a lock timeout of three seconds. This means that SQL Server will wait on a deadlock within this connection for three seconds. If the deadlock is not resolved in that time, then SQL Server will terminate this transaction.

```
SET LOCK_TIMEOUT  3000
BEGIN TRAN
    DELETE TransactionDetails.Transactions
    DELETE ShareDetails.SharePrices
rollback tran
```

11. Three seconds is a very short period of time and much shorter than you would see in a production environment. The amount of time to set in a production environment could vary. If you move to the code within the transaction, the deletion of the TransactionDetails. Transactions table can proceed as there will be no lock on that table from the first query; however, when SQL Server tries to delete the rows from ShareDetails.SharePrices, it cannot proceed as the first transaction has a lock. SQL Server will wait three seconds and then kill the transaction of the code in the second query pane.

12. When the transaction is killed, SQL Server produces an error message along with any information messages. The information message shows that it did delete the rows from the TransactionDetails.Transactions table, as you will see the informational message that 1,000 rows had been affected. You will then see the details concerning the lock timeout and that the code had been terminated. The transaction will be rolled back.

```
(1000 row(s) affected)
Msg 1222, Level 16, State 51, Line 4
Lock request time out period exceeded.
The statement has been terminated.
```

13. Rollback the transaction in the first query pane.

```
rollback tran
```

Although you have touched only on deleting rows from tables, you have seen how incorrect coding where a transaction is left open can cause an application to look as if it has stopped responding.

Truncating a Table

All delete actions caused by DELETE statements are recorded in the transaction log. Each time a record is deleted, a record is made of that fact. If you are deleting millions of records before committing your transaction, your transaction log can grow quickly. Recall from earlier in the chapter the discussions about transactions; now think about this a bit more. What if the table you are deleting from has thousands of records? That is a great deal of logging going on within the transaction log. But what if the deletion of these thousands of records is, in fact, cleaning out all the data from the table to start afresh? Or perhaps this is some sort of transient table? Performing a DELETE would seem to have a lot of overhead when you don't really need to keep a log of the data deletions anyway. If the action failed for whatever reason, you would simply retry removing the records a second time. This is where the TRUNCATE TABLE command comes into its own.

By issuing a TRUNCATE TABLE statement, you are instructing SQL Server to delete every record within a table, without any logging or transaction processing taking place. In reality, minimal data are logged about what data pages have been deallocated and therefore removed from the database. This is in contrast to a DELETE statement, which will deallocate and remove the pages from the table only if it can get sufficient locks on the table to do this. The deletion of the records with TRUNCATE TABLE can be almost instantaneous and a great deal faster than using the DELETE command. This occurs not only because of the differences with what happens with the transaction log, but also because of how the data are locked at the time of deletion. Let's clarify this point before progressing.

When a DELETE statement is issued, SQL Server will lock each row that is to be deleted so that no modifications or other DELETE statements can attempt to work with that row. Deleting hundreds or thousands of rows is a large number of actions for SQL Server to perform, and it will take time to locate each row and place a lock against it. However, a TRUNCATE TABLE statement locks the whole table. This is one action that will prevent any data insertion, modification, or deletion from taking place.

■ **Note** A TRUNCATE TABLE statement will delete data from a table with millions of records in only a few seconds, whereas using DELETE to remove all the records on the same table would take several minutes.

The syntax for truncating a table is simple:

```
TRUNCATE TABLE [{database.schema_name.}]table
```

■ **Caution** Use the TRUNCATE TABLE statement with extreme caution. There is no going back after the transaction is committed outside of a transaction; you cannot change your mind. Also, every record is removed: you cannot use this command to selectively remove some of the records. If you are within a transaction, you can still use the ROLLBACK command.

One "side effect" to the TRUNCATE TABLE clause is that it reseeds any identity columns. For example, say that you have a table with an identity column that is currently at 2,000,000. After truncating the table, the first inserted piece of data will produce the value 1 (if the seed is set to 0). If you issue a DELETE command to delete the records from the table, the first piece of data inserted after the table contents have been deleted will produce a value of 2,000,001, even though this newly inserted piece of data may be the only record in the table!

One of the limitations with the TRUNCATE TABLE command is that you cannot issue it against tables that have foreign keys referencing them. For example, the Customers table has a foreign key referencing the Transactions table. If you try to issue the following command, you will receive the following error message:

```
TRUNCATE TABLE CustomerDetails.Customers
```

```
Msg 4712, Level 16, State 1, Line 1
Cannot truncate table 'CustomerDetails.Customers' because it is being referenced
by a FOREIGN KEY constraint.
```

Dropping a Table

Another way to quickly delete the data in a table is to just delete the table and re-create it. Don't forget that if you do this, you will need to also re-create any constraints, indexes, and foreign keys; therefore you don't tend to drop main tables but ancillary tables and even temporary tables. When you drop a table, SQL Server will deallocate the table, which is minimally logged. To drop a table in SQL Server, issue the following command:

```
DROP TABLE table_name
```

As with TRUNCATE TABLE, DROP TABLE cannot be issued against a table that has a foreign key referencing it. In this situation, either the foreign key constraint referencing the table or the referencing table itself must first be dropped before it is possible to drop the original table.

Summary

This chapter has demonstrated how to add and remove data by looking at the INSERT and DELETE statements.

There are different ways the INSERT statement can be executed. An INSERT can be flexible in the data you need to insert into a table, such as the order of columns, when there are default values, and even inserting multiple rows. How tables are defined can aid insertions through the use of NULLs and constraints, so table design does form part of data manipulation.

The use of transactions for inserting and deleting data should be part of a large proportion of your coding so that you ensure consistency of your data. A transaction is not always required, but when one is used, ensure that you process your data against the tables in the same order to avoid deadlocks.

How to delete all the rows within a table using the DELETE statement was demonstrated.Finally, the removal of every record within a table was also shown, along with dire warnings if you get it wrong. Really, use the TRUNCATE TABLE command only in development or with the utmost, extreme care within production.

■ ■ ■

Selecting and Updating Data from Disk-Based Tables

In this chapter, you will see details on how to retrieve data correctly and professionally in a production environment, and this chapter will lay the foundation for the more advanced T-SQL found in the forthcoming chapters. This chapter also sets the stage for selecting and updating data in in-memory tables. There are a great many similarities between disk-based and in-memory tables. You'll learn more about in-memory tables in Chapter 13.

Up until now, you have witnessed a "lazy" method in that you have returned data from every column and every row in whatever tables you have been querying. This chapter will detail why that is not ideal, and it will demonstrate the correct methods. You will also see how to change column headings so that they provide more meaningful names for non-IT people. Then you will see how to reduce the data brought back by filtering for only the rows you want. The final sections in this chapter on retrieving data will introduce you to how to use some basic string functions, how to order the data, and how to find data when you are not quite sure of all the information.

It is also possible to create a table by selecting data from another table. You'll learn how to do that as well. Creating one table from another is ideal if you need to keep a temporary copy of certain data.

As I have mentioned many times throughout this book, securing your data is just as crucial, if not more so, as the design and creation of your database. You will see how to tighten up security so that a user can select data from only one specific table.

You will then move on to updating and deleting your data. You will see how transactions are involved in each of these processes, and you'll learn how to delete an entire table of data quickly, without using the traditional DELETE statement.

To summarize, in this chapter, you will see the following:

- How to retrieve data

- How to specify and limit the data returned

- How to retrieve the data in a specific order

- How to create a new table

- How to update the data

- How to update only specific data

- A bit more on transactions with updates

- How to update data with more than one table involved in the search

Retrieving Data

Although you have seen how to retrieve data a few times prior to this section, those examples have been at a basic level and contained limited details. In this first part of the chapter, I will detail good practice as well as different and more professional methods of retrieving and displaying data from your database. Many ways of achieving this are available, from using SQL Server Management Studio to using T-SQL statements, and as you would expect, they will all be covered here.

The aim of retrieving data is to get the data back from SQL Server using the fastest retrieval manner possible. You can retrieve data from one or more tables through joining tables together within the query syntax; all of these methods will be demonstrated.

The simplest method of retrieving data is using SQL Server Management Studio, and you will look at this method first. With this method, you don't need to know any query syntax: it is all done for you. However, this leaves you with a limited scope for further work.

You can alter the query built up within SQL Server Management Studio to cater to work that is more complex, but you would then need to know the SELECT T-SQL syntax; again, this will be explained and demonstrated. This can become very powerful very quickly, especially when it comes to selecting specific rows to return.

The results of the data can also be displayed and even stored in different media, such as a file. It is possible to store results from a query and send these to a set of users, if so desired.

Initially, the data returned will be in the arbitrary order stored within SQL Server. This is not always suitable, so another aim of this chapter is to demonstrate how to return data in the order that you desire. Ordering the data is an important part of retrieving meaningful results, and this alone can aid the understanding of query results from raw data.

Starting with the simplest of methods, let's look at SQL Server Management Studio and how easy it is to retrieve rows. I partially covered this earlier in Chapter 10 when inserting rows and when looking at transactions when deleting rows.

Using SQL Server Management Studio to Retrieve Data

The first area that we'll go over is the simplest form of data retrieval, but it is also the most limited. Retrieving data using SQL Server Management Studio is a very straightforward process, as no knowledge of SQL is required in the initial stages. You saw this for the first time in Chapter 10. Regardless of whether you want to return all rows or just specific rows, using SQL Server Management Studio makes this whole task very easy. This first example will demonstrate how flexible SQL Server Management Studio is in retrieving all the data from the CustomerDetails.Customers table. I will be using the data generated from Red Gate's SQL Data Generator that was used in Chapter 10. You can download the INSERTs from www.apress.com or from www.fat-belly.com.

TRY IT OUT: RETRIEVING DATA WITHIN SQL SERVER MANAGEMENT STUDIO

1. Ensure that SQL Server Management Studio is running. Navigate to the ApressFinancial database and click the Tables node to expand and list the tables within your database. Find the CustomerDetails.Customers table, right-click it to bring up the pop-up menu, and select Select Top 1000 Rows. The value of 1,000 is arbitrary and is set in the Options menu. This instantly opens up a new Query Editor window pane like the one shown in Figure 11-1, which shows all the rows that are in the CustomerDetails.Customers table. But how did SQL Server get this data? Let's find out (the secret may already be there, depending on the options set for SQL Server).

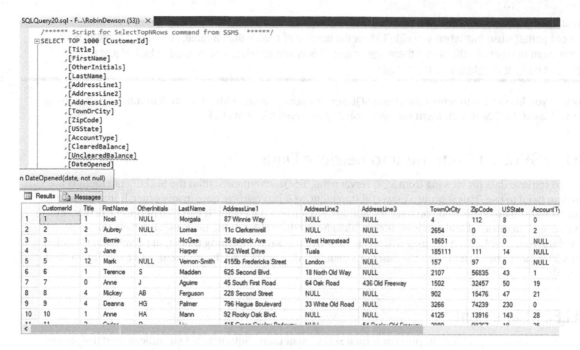

Figure 11-1. *CustomerDetails.Customers table retrieving data*

2. Above the results, you will see the SELECT T-SQL statement used to return the data. The SELECT statement is returning the top 1,000 rows and then defining the columns to display.

3. You can alter the number next to the top clause if you want to return a smaller or a greater number of rows, and then re-execute the query. For this first time, alter this number to 3, and you should see something similar to Figure 11-2. This will return a maximum of three rows.

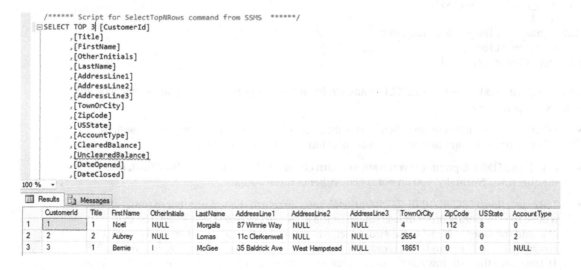

Figure 11-2. *Three rows are returned*

If you entered a value of 100 and you had only 20 rows in your table, you would get only 20 rows returned. You would perhaps use this when you didn't know the number of rows within a table, but were interested only in a maximum number of 100 even if there were more. This would be when you wanted to look at just a small selection of content in columns within a table.

Now that you know how to return data from SQL Server Management Studio, let's look in more detail at using T-SQL, as well as at the T-SQL statement you will probably use most often: SELECT.

Using the SELECT Statement to Retrieve Data

If you wish to retrieve data for viewing from SQL Server using T-SQL statements, then the SELECT statement is the statement you need to use. This is quite a powerful statement, as it can retrieve data in any order, from any number of columns, and from any table that you have the authority to retrieve data from. It can also perform calculations on that data during data retrieval and can even include data from other tables! If the user does not have the authority to retrieve data from a table, then the user will receive an error message informing them that permission is denied. SELECT has a lot more power than even the functions mentioned so far, but for the moment, let's concentrate on the fundamentals.

The SELECT Statement

Let's take some time to inspect the simple syntax for a SELECT statement. Square brackets indicate that the phrases are optional, and curly brackets show that at least one of the items must be selected, but there are choices available.

```
SELECT [ ALL | DISTINCT ]
[ TOP expression [ PERCENT ] [ WITH TIES ] ]
    {
                *
      | { table_name | view_name | alias_name }.*
      | { column_name | [ ] expression | $IDENTITY | $ROWGUID }
      [ [ AS ] column_alias ]
      | column_alias = expression
    } [ ,...n ]
[ FROM table_name | view_name alias_name ]
[ WHERE filter_condition ]
[ ORDER BY ordering_criteria ]
```

The following list breaks down the SELECT syntax, explaining each option. More explanation will be given throughout the chapter as well.

- SELECT: Required; this informs SQL Server that a SELECT instruction is being performed. In other words, you want to return just a set of columns and rows to view.

- ALL | DISTINCT: Optional; if you want to return either all of the rows or only distinct, or unique, rows. Normally, you do not specify either of these options.

- TOP *expression*/PERCENT/WITH TIES: Optional; you can return the top number of rows, which will be in an arbitrary order unless you order the rows with an ORDER BY clause. You can also add the word PERCENT to the end, which will mean that the top *n* percent of rows will be returned. WITH TIES can be used only with an ORDER BY. If you specify you want to return TOP 10 rows, and the 11th row has the same value as the 10th row on those columns that have been defined in the ORDER BY, then the 11th row will also be returned. It's the same for subsequent rows, until you get to the point that the values differ.

- *: Optional; by using the asterisk, you are instructing SQL Server to return all the columns from all the tables included in the query. This is not an option that should be used on large amounts of data or over a network. Particularly if the network is busy or there are a large number of columns, you really should not use this against production data. By using this, you are bringing back more information than is required. In essence, by using *, you are not in control of the column data you are returning. Wherever possible, you should name the columns instead.

- table_name.* | view_name.* | alias_name.*: Optional; similar to *, but you are defining which table, if the SELECT is working on more than one table, that all the columns will display from. When working with more than one table, this is known as a JOIN, and this option will be demonstrated in Chapter 11 when you take a look at joins, as well as at the end of this chapter.

- column_name: Optional but recommended; this option is where you name the columns that you wish to return from a table. When naming the columns, it is always a good idea to prefix the column names with their corresponding table names or table aliases (more on table aliases shortly). This becomes mandatory when you are using more than one table in your SELECT statement and in instances where there may be columns within different tables that share the same name (preferred to using the alternative *, as discussed previously).

- expression: Optional; you don't have to return columns of rows within a SELECT. You can return a value, a variable, or an expression. If you are using SELECT for an expression, then you won't require the FROM keyword.

- $IDENTITY: Optional; will return the value from the IDENTITY column.

- $ROWGUID: Optional; will return the value from the ROWGUID column.

- AS: Optional; you can change the column header name when displaying the results by using the AS option.

- Column_alias: Optional; you can give a column name an alias. This is ideal when a column name will form output that is sent to a user. You will see this in Chapter 13 when looking at views.

- FROM table_name | view_name: Required when selecting data from a data source, optional if you are using SELECT with an expression; you will see SELECT with expressions in Chapter 11.

- WHERE filter_condition: Optional; if you want to retrieve rows that meet specific criteria, you need to have a WHERE condition specifying the criteria to use to return the data. The WHERE condition tends to contain the name of a column on the left-hand side of a comparison operator, such as =, <, >, and either another column within the same table, or another table, a variable, or a static value on the other side. There are other options that the WHERE condition can contain, where more advanced searching is required, but on the whole, these comparison operators will be the main constituents of the condition.

- ORDER BY ordering_criteria: Optional; the data will be returned arbitrarily from the table if no ORDER BY expression is specified. Ascending (ASC) or descending (DESC) is defined for each column, not defined just once for all the columns within the ORDER BY. Sorting is completed once the data has been retrieved from SQL Server but before any statement such as TOP. You can also use this expression to return a specific number of rows and subsequent rows after that to enable you to paginate your data and reduce the amount of data returned from a query. You will see this in action later in this chapter.

Keep in mind that when building a SELECT statement, you do not have to name all the columns. In fact, you should retrieve only the columns that you do wish to see; this will reduce the amount of information sent over the network. There is no need to return information that will not be used.

Naming the Columns

When building a SELECT statement, it is not necessary to name every column if you don't want to see every column. You should return only the columns you need. It is very easy to slip into using * to return every column, even when running one-off queries. Try to avoid doing this at all costs; typing out every column name takes time, but when you start dealing with more complex queries and a larger number of rows, the few extra seconds are worth it.

Now that you know not to name every column unless required, and to avoid using *, what other areas do you need to be aware of? First of all, it is not necessary to name columns in the same order in which they appear in the table—it is quite acceptable to name columns in any order that you wish. There is no performance hit or gain from altering the order of the columns, but you may find that a different column order might be better for any future processing of the data.

When building a SELECT statement and including the columns, and if the final output is to be sent to a set of users, the column names within the database may not be acceptable. For example, if you are sending the output to the users via a file, then they will see the raw result set. Or if you are using a tool such as Crystal Reports to display data from a SELECT statement within a SQL Server–stored procedure, then naming the columns would help. The column names are less user-friendly, and some column names will also be confusing for users; therefore, it would be ideal to alter the names of the column headings. Replacing the SQL Server column headings with the new desired alias column headings, in either quotation marks or in square bracket delimiters, is easily accomplished with the AS keyword. There is more on this in the next section.

Now that you know about naming the columns, let's take a look at how the SQL statement can return data.

The First Searches

This example will revolve around the CustomerDetails.Customers table, making it possible to demonstrate how all of the different areas mentioned previously can affect the results displayed.

TRY IT OUT: THE FIRST SET OF SEARCHES

1. Ensure that Query Editor is running and that you are within the ApressFinancial database. In the Query Editor pane, enter the following SQL code:

```
SELECT * From CustomerDetails.Customers
```

2. Execute the code using F5 or the Execute button on the toolbar. You should then see something like the results shown in Figure 11-3.

	CustomerId	Title	FirstName	OtherInitials	LastName	AddressLine1	AddressLine2	AddressLine3	TownOrCity	ZipCode
1	1	1	Noel	NULL	Morgala	87 Winnie Way	NULL	NULL	4	112
2	2	2	Aubrey	NULL	Lomas	11c Clerkenwell	NULL	NULL	2654	0
3	3	1	Bernie	I	McGee	35 Baldrick Ave	West Hampstead	NULL	18651	0
4	4	3	Jane	L	Harper	122 West Drive	Tuala	NULL	185111	111
5	5	12	Mark	NULL	Vernon-Smith	4155b Fredericks Street	London	NULL	157	97
6	6	1	Terence	S	Madden	625 Second Blvd.	18 North Old Way	NULL	2107	56835
7	7	0	Anne	J	Aguirre	45 South First Road	64 Oak Road	436 Old Freeway	1502	32457
8	8	4	Mickey	AB	Ferguson	228 Second Street	NULL	NULL	902	15476
9	9	4	Deanna	HG	Palmer	796 Hague Boulevard	33 White Old Road	NULL	3266	74239
10	10	1	Anne	HA	Mann	92 Rocky Oak Blvd.	NULL	NULL	4125	13916

Figure 11-3. Customers table listing all columns (some not shown)

3. This is a simple `SELECT` statement returning all the columns and all the rows from the `CustomerDetails.Customers` table, as you have just seen. Let's now take it to the next stage, where specific column names will be defined in the query, which is a much cleaner solution that results in less traffic over a network.

4. In this instance, you would like to return a customer's first name, last name, and the current account balances from the `CustomerDetails.Customers` table. This would mean naming `FirstName`, `LastName`, and `ClearedBalance` as the column names in the query. The code will read as follows:

    ```
    SELECT firstname,lastname,clearedbalance
    FROM CustomerDetails.Customers
    ```

5. Now execute this code, which will return the results shown in Figure 11-4. As you can see, not every column is returned.

	firstname	lastname	clearedbalance
1	Noel	Morgala	NULL
2	Aubrey	Lomas	437.97
3	Bernie	McGee	6653.11
4	Jane	Harper	53.11
5	Mark	Vernon-Smith	-751.00
6	Terence	Madden	917.0126
7	Anne	Aguirre	NULL
8	Mickey	Ferguson	187.2192
9	Deanna	Palmer	148.0513
10	Anne	Mann	299.8416
11	Carlos	Liu	544.7332

Figure 11-4. *Specific columns returned*

6. As you have seen from the examples so far, the column names, although well named from a design viewpoint, are not exactly suitable if you had to give this data to a set of users.

7. Using the same query as before, a couple of minor modifications are required to give the columns aliases. The first alias is in quotes, as it contains a space. Notice the last column also does not have `AS` specified, because this keyword is optional.

    ```
    SELECT FirstName As 'First Name',LastName AS 'Surname',
    ClearedBalance Balance
    FROM CustomerDetails.Customers
    ```

8. Execute this code and the displayed output changes—it has much friendlier column names, as you see in Figure 11-5.

	First Name	Surname	Balance
1	Noel	Morgala	NULL
2	Aubrey	Lomas	437.97
3	Bernie	McGee	6653.11
4	Jane	Harper	53.11
5	Mark	Vernon-Smith	-751.00
6	Terence	Madden	917.0126
7	Anne	Aguirre	NULL
8	Mickey	Ferguson	187.2192
9	Deanna	Palmer	148.0513
10	Anne	Mann	299.8416
11	Carlos	Liu	544.7332

***Figure 11-5.** Friendly column names*

The first SELECT statement demonstrates the fact that in most SQL Server instances, your choice of using upper- or lowercase doesn't matter to your queries; however, some language installations are case-sensitive. When installing SQL Server, if you chose a SQL collation sequence that was case-sensitive, as denoted by CS within the suffix of the collation name—SQL_Latin1_General_Cp437_CS_AS, for instance—then the first SELECT query would generate an error. The collation sequence for SQL Server was chosen in Chapter 1 when you installed the application. Changing a collation sequence within SQL Server is a very difficult task that requires rebuilding parts of SQL Server, so this book won't move into that area.

■ **Tip** It is strongly recommended, and considered best practice, that you use the correct casing when using queries. Not only does this avoid confusion, but it also means that if you do switch to a case-sensitive installation, it will not be necessary to alter the query.

Let's return to the first query in step 1. This query will select all columns and all rows from the CustomerDetails. Customers table, ordered according to how the database sees it. As you can see in Figure 11-3, it has quite plainly done this.

In the second and third query examples, the results have been reduced to just three columns: the customer's first and last names and the cleared balance amounts. All the rows are still being returned. Notice in the previous example that after two of the three columns, there is an AS keyword. This signifies that the following literal is to be used as the column heading; note that if you wish to use two words separated by spaces, you must surround these words by identifiers, whether they be quotation marks, as in your example, or square brackets.

Now that the basics of the SELECT statement have been covered, we will next look at how to display output in different manners within Query Editor.

Varying the Output from a SELECT Query

There are different ways of displaying the output: as a grid, as you have seen; as a straight text file; still within a Query Editor results pane; or as pure text within a results pane. You may have found the results in the previous exercise laid out in a different format than you've seen previously, depending on how you initially set up Query Editor. In the results of the examples so far, you have seen the data as a grid. This next section will demonstrate tabular text output, otherwise known as Results in Text, as well as outputting the data to a text file. Let's get going with the first option, Results in Text.

TRY IT OUT: PUTTING THE RESULTS IN TEXT AND A FILE

1. You should still be in Query Editor. From the Query menu option, select Results To ➤ Results in Text, or press Ctrl+T. Figure 11-6 shows the other options available from the Results To menu.

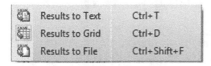

Results to Text	Ctrl+T	
Results to Grid	Ctrl+D	
Results to File	Ctrl+Shift+F	

Figure 11-6. *Sending the results to different places*

2. If you run the same query as that in step 5 of the preceding example (the code is detailed again here), you will be able to see the difference. Once the code is entered, execute it.

```
SELECT FirstName As 'First Name',LastName AS 'Surname',
ClearedBalance Balance
FROM CustomerDetails.Customers
```

3. Examine the output, which should resemble Figure 11-7. As you can see, the output has changed a great deal. No longer is the output shown in a nice grid in which the columns have been shrunk to a more manageable size, but rather each column's data take up, and are displayed to, the maximum number of characters that each column can contain. This obviously stretches out the display, but from here you can see easily how large each column is supposed to be.

```
 Results
Dion                                Ruiz                           153.6941
Jeremiah                            Dillon                         926.3311
Patrice                             Hanna                          510.5281
Annie                               Riggs                          323.1041
Gena                                Mckenzie                       881.1809
Miriam                              Hoffman                        501.7326
Allyson                             Esparza                        302.3074
Katina                              Thomas                         NULL
Teddy                               Fischer                        317.0485
Stacey                              Yates                          331.6614
Latoya                              Morris                         553.0335

(1000 row(s) affected)
```

Figure 11-7. *Results as text*

4. There will be times, though, when users require output to be sent to them. For example, they may wish to know specific details from a set of rows, and so you would build a query and save the results to a file to send to them. Or perhaps they want output to perform some analysis of data within a Microsoft Excel spreadsheet.

5. To send output to a file, go to the Query menu and select Results To ➤ Results to File, or press Ctrl+Shift+F. Specify sending results to a file and rerun the code. Once the code has been executed, a Save Results dialog box like the one shown in Figure 11-8 will appear: this could show any folder location—in this case, it shows the folder for results I have set up on my computer.

Figure 11-8. Locating where to save the results

6. So now that you know how to save to different locations, move back to displaying the output to a grid by pressing Ctrl+D.

■ **Note** Before you move on, a question: Have you noticed that when you type a query, SQL Server tries to provide you with options about what you may want to use next in your query? This is known as IntelliSense. SQL Server intelligently tries to sense what you may want to include next. You will find that IntelliSense is a very useful tool when building queries, especially, I find, with `SELECT` queries. If you find it annoying, you can turn it off from `Options` ➤ `Text Editor` ➤ `Transact-SQL/` ➤ `IntelliSense`.

You now know how to return data, but what happens if you don't want every row, and you want to select which rows to display? We'll look at that next.

Limiting a Search: The Use of WHERE

You have a number of different ways to limit the search of rows within a query. Some of the most basic revolve around the three basic relational operators: <, >, and = (less than, greater than, and equal to). There is also the keyword NOT, which could be included with these three operators. However, NOT does not work as in other programming languages that you may have come across, and this will be demonstrated within the example in this section so you know how to use the NOT operator successfully.

All of these operators can be found in the SELECT statement's WHERE condition, which is used to reduce the number of rows returned within a query.

■ **Note** You may come across some legacy code in which you will find that the WHERE condition is used to join two tables together to make the results look as if they came from one table. For some databases, this is the "standard" way to join two tables; however, with SQL Server, the WHERE condition should be used purely as a filter method.

The first exercise will look at how to filter information from your queries so as to reduce the output to records that you are interested in.

TRY IT OUT: THE WHERE STATEMENT

1. The requirement for this section is to find the current share price for Toland's Irish Whisky. This stock has a single quotation mark in its name, which would cause issues in the WHERE condition if you surrounded the description in single quotation marks. To circumvent this problem, set QUOTED_IDENTIFIER to OFF and then use double quotation marks. Then restrict the SELECT statement so that only the specific record comes back by using the WHERE condition, as can be seen in the following code:

```
SET QUOTED_IDENTIFIER OFF
SELECT Description,CurrentPrice
  FROM ShareDetails.Shares
 WHERE Description = "Toland's Irish Whisky"
```

2. Execute this code, and you will see that the single record for the share is returned, as shown in Figure 11-9.

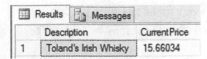

	Description	Current Price
1	Toland's Irish Whisky	15.66034

Figure 11-9. The results of limiting the search

3. You have seen WHERE in action using the equals sign; it is also possible to use the other relational operations in the WHERE statement. The next query demonstrates how SQL Server takes the WHERE condition and starts returning rows after the given point. This query provides an interesting set of results. Enter the code as detailed here:

```
SET QUOTED_IDENTIFIER OFF
SELECT Description,CurrentPrice
  FROM ShareDetails.Shares
 WHERE Description >= 'Mackrel Fisheries'
AND Description <= "Toland's Irish"
```

4. Once done, execute the code and check the results, which should resemble Figure 11-10. Notice that Toland's Irish Whisky was within the results in step 2, but the value in the "less than or equal to" condition is not listed. There is no row with that exact value within the ShareDetails.Shares table. There is a row with most of the text, but not an exact match, and therefore the row is not included. You will come back to this scenario shortly.

	Description	Current Price
1	Nicklins Nickle Ore	22.63715
2	Rolling Maulers	16.66973
3	MVS Inc	28.77407
4	Shiny Shoes Shone	5.11006
5	Old Time Movies	16.80973
6	Squirrels Servers	31.07362
7	Mackrel Fisheries	15.88709

Figure 11-10. Shares output using the WHERE condition to filter

5. The same results can be achieved by using the BETWEEN conditional operator rather than the mathematical operators. The following code will achieve the same results as above. The BETWEEN operator indicates to SQL Server to take the two values and find any values including and between them.

```
SET QUOTED_IDENTIFIER OFF
SELECT Description,CurrentPrice
  FROM ShareDetails.Shares
WHERE Description BETWEEN 'Mackrel Fisheries'
AND "Toland's Irish"
```

6. Let's now bring another option into the WHERE statement that allows you to avoid returning specific rows. This can be achieved in one of two ways: the first is by using the less than and greater than signs; the second is by using the NOT operator. Enter the following code, which will return all rows except Lomas Ambulances. Run both sets of code at once. This will return two sets of output, known as multiple result sets. I realize there are a lot of rows returned; you will see one method of reducing this in the next section.

```
SET QUOTED_IDENTIFIER OFF
SELECT Description,CurrentPrice
  FROM ShareDetails.Shares
 WHERE Description <> "Lomas Ambulances"

SELECT Description,CurrentPrice
  FROM ShareDetails.Shares
 WHERE NOT Description = "Lomas Ambulances"
```

7. Executing this code will produce the output shown in Figure 11-11.

	Description	Current Price
12	Old Time Movies	16.80973
13	Kinga Roys	33.84931
14	Apress	5.67051
15	Frying Tonight	32.00230
16	Squirrels Servers	31.07362
17	Downtown Donuts	12.66429
18	Fishy Friars	21.70924
19	Mackrel Fisheries	15.88709

	Description	Current Price
12	Old Time Movies	16.80973
13	Kinga Roys	33.84931
14	Apress	5.67051
15	Frying Tonight	32.00230
16	Squirrels Servers	31.07362
17	Downtown Donuts	12.66429
18	Fishy Friars	21.70924
19	Mackrel Fisheries	15.88709

Figure 11-11. Multiple output and the use of exclusion

8. I mentioned in Chapter 10 that you would return to the WHERE condition for DELETE statements. Filtering for deletions is the same as filtering for SELECT statements. Before executing a DELETE, I tend to build a SELECT statement, check that the data to delete is correct, and then switch the SELECT to a DELETE. The DELETE code here has two WHERE conditions to limit the number of deletions to one year of data and to where the price is greater than 6 trillion.

```
DELETE
FROM ShareDetails.SharePrices
WHERE PriceDate BETWEEN '1 Jan 2012' and '3 Jan 2012'
AND Price > 23.00
```

As you have seen, it is possible to limit the number of rows to be returned via the WHERE condition; you can return rows up to a certain point, after a certain point, or even between two points with the use of an AND or BETWEEN expression. It is also possible to exclude rows that are not equal to a specific value or range of values by using the NOT expression or the <> operator.

When the SQL Server data engine executes the T-SQL SELECT statement, it is the WHERE condition that is dealt with before any ordering of the data, or before any limitation placed on it concerning the number of rows to return. The data are inspected, where possible using an index, to determine whether a row stored in the relevant table matches the selection criteria within the WHERE condition and, if it does, to return it. If an index cannot be used, then a full table scan will be performed to find the relevant information.

Table scans can present a large performance problem within your system, although sometimes they are the fastest way to read the data, and you will find that if a query has to perform a table scan, then data retrieval could be very slow, depending on the size of the table being scanned. If the table is small with only a small number of rows, then a table scan is likely to retrieve data more quickly than the use of an index will. However, table scanning and the speed of data retrieval will be the biggest challenge you face as a SQL Server developer. With data retrieval, it is important to bear in mind that whenever possible, if you are using a WHERE condition to limit the rows returned, you should try to specify the columns from an index definition. By doing this, you will be giving the query the best chance for optimum performance.

As discussed in Chapter 6, getting the index right is crucial to fast data manipulation and retrieval. If you find you are forever placing the same columns in a WHERE condition, but those columns do not form part of an index, perhaps this is something that should be revisited to see whether any gain can come from having the columns be part of an index.

For any table, ensuring that the WHERE condition is correct is important. As has been indicated previously, from a speed perspective using an index will ensure a fast return of data. This gains greater importance with each table added, and even more importance as the size of each table grows.

Finally, by ensuring the WHERE condition filters out the correct rows, you will ensure that the required data are returned, the right results are displayed, and smaller amounts of data are sent across the network, as the processing is done on the server and not on the client. Having the appropriate indexing strategy helps with this as well.

It is also possible to return a specific number of rows, or a specific percentage of the number of rows, as you saw when displaying rows in SQL Server Management Studio. These statements are discussed next, with a short code example demonstrating each in action.

TOP (n)

This option, found within the SELECT statement itself, will return a specific number of rows from the SELECT statement, and is very much like the SET ROWCOUNT function that you will see shortly. In fact, the TOP (n) option is the preferred option to use when returning a set number of rows, as opposed to SET ROWCOUNT. The reason behind this is that TOP (n) applies only to the query statement that includes it; however, by using SET ROWCOUNT n, you are altering all executions until you reset SQL Server to act on all rows through SET ROWCOUNT 0.

Although it is possible to use TOP (n) without any ORDER BY statement, it is common to combine TOP with ORDER BY. When no order is specified, the rows returned are arbitrary, and if you want consistent results, ordering will provide this. If you are not concerned about which rows are returned, then you can bypass using ORDER BY. TOP (n) will still return and display the top n rows in an arbitrary order. You will see that the n for number of rows is surrounded by parenthesis, which for a SELECT statement are optional, but become mandatory for other statements, so I like to always use them for the sake of consistency.

Any WHERE statements and ORDER BY statements within the SELECT statement are dealt with first, and then from the resultant rows the TOP (n) function comes into effect. This then allows the correct number of rows to be displayed, as opposed to finding the number of rows from the TOP (n) function first, then filtering the rows using the WHERE statement, as the filter could make the number of rows remaining from the ones initially selected to be zero. Thus, it's best to save TOP (n) for last.

The use of WHERE and ORDER BY will be demonstrated with the following example.

TRY IT OUT: TOP (N)

1. In Query Editor, enter the following code into a new Query Editor pane:

```
SELECT TOP (3) *
FROM ShareDetails.Shares
WHERE CurrentPrice > 20
ORDER BY Description
```

2. Once entered, execute the code. It returns a result set, as shown in Figure 11-12, with three rows of data. SQL Server looked for rows where the CurrentPrice was greater than 20, then ordered the results, and finally displayed the top three of the result set.

	ShareId	Description	StockExchangeTicker	CurrentPrice
1	12	Airing Cadets	ACads	20.93191
2	5	Brownies	Browns	28.75828
3	19	Fishy Friars	FF	21.70924

Figure 11-12. Top three rows after filter and sort

You could run the code in step 1 without the ORDER BY, which will show you a different three rows returned.

TOP (n) PERCENT

TOP (n) PERCENT is very similar to the TOP (n) clause, with the exception that instead of working with a precise number of rows, a percentage of the number of possible result rows will be returned. Keep this in mind, as it is not a percentage of the total number of rows within the table. Also, the number of rows is rounded up; therefore, as soon as the percentage moves over to include another row, SQL Server will include this extra row.

You will see more of this option in Chapter 13, which discusses the building of views.

SET ROWCOUNT n

SET ROWCOUNT n is a totally separate statement from the SELECT statement and can be used with other statements within T-SQL. This statement will limit or reset the number of rows that will be processed for the session in which the statement is executed. It is better to use TOP. The reason is that in future releases, SET ROWCOUNT will not affect the number of rows inserted, deleted, or updated in a T-SQL statement.

■ **Note** Caution should be exercised if you have any statements that also use a TOP statement, which is described next.

The SET ROWCOUNT n statement stops the processing of the SELECT statement once the number of rows defined has been reached. The difference between SET ROWCOUNT n and SELECT TOP (n) is that the latter will perform one more internal instruction than the former. Processing halts immediately when the number of rows processed through SET ROWCOUNT is reached. However, by using the TOP statement, all the rows are returned internally, the TOP (n) rows are selected from that group internally, and these are then passed for display. Returning a limited number of rows is useful when you want to look at a handful of data to see what values could be included, or perhaps you wish to return a few rows for data sampling.

You can set the number of rows to be affected by altering the number, n, at the end of the SET ROWCOUNT statement. This setting will remain in force only within the query window in which the statement is executed, or within the stored procedure in which the statement is executed. It will also remain in force in that query window until you alter the value again. This is not a temporary setting per se.

To reset the session so that all rows are taken into consideration, you would set the ROWCOUNT number to 0.

TRY IT OUT: SET ROWCOUNT

1. In Query Editor, enter the following code into a new Query Editor pane:

```
SET ROWCOUNT 3
SELECT * FROM ShareDetails.Shares
SET ROWCOUNT 0
SELECT * FROM ShareDetails.Shares
```

2. Once it is entered, execute it. You should see two result sets, as shown in Figure 11-13. The first will return three rows from the ShareDetails.Shares table. The second result set will return all rows from ShareDetails.Shares.

	ShareId	Description	StockExchangeTicker	CurrentPrice
1	1	ACME'S HOMEBAKE COOKIES INC	AHCI	2.34125
2	2	ACME'S HOMEBAKE COOKIES INC	NULL	2.34125
3	3	Lomas Ambulances	LAMB	31.26386

	ShareId	Description	StockExchangeTicker	CurrentPrice
1	1	ACME'S HOMEBAKE COOKIES INC	AHCI	2.34125
2	2	ACME'S HOMEBAKE COOKIES INC	NULL	2.34125
3	3	Lomas Ambulances	LAMB	31.26386
4	4	Toland's Irish Whisky	TIW	15.66034
5	5	Brownies	Browns	28.75828
6	6	Nicklins Nickle Ore	NNO	22.63715
7	7	Rolling Maulers	RM	16.66973
8	8	MVS Inc	MVS	28.77407
9	9	Ding Dong Bells	DDB	3.13743
10	10	Julies Pantry	JP	26.66358
11	11	Shiny Shoes Shone	TripleS	5.11006

Figure 11-13. Limiting the output via ROWCOUNT

3. The final example will combine ROWCOUNT and TOP (n) in an example showing how these two statements can alter your results. Enter the following code:

```
SET ROWCOUNT 3
SELECT TOP (2) *
FROM ShareDetails.Shares
WHERE CurrentPrice > 20
ORDER BY Description

SET ROWCOUNT 2
SELECT TOP (3) *
FROM ShareDetails.Shares
WHERE CurrentPrice > 20
ORDER BY Description

SET ROWCOUNT 0
SELECT TOP (3) *
FROM ShareDetails.Shares
WHERE CurrentPrice > 20
ORDER BY Description
```

4. When you execute the code, you should see three result sets, as shown in Figure 11-14.

	ShareId	Description	StockExchangeTicker	CurrentPrice
1	12	Airing Cadets	ACads	20.93191
2	5	Brownies	Browns	28.75828

	ShareId	Description	StockExchangeTicker	CurrentPrice
1	12	Airing Cadets	ACads	20.93191
2	5	Brownies	Browns	28.75828

	ShareId	Description	StockExchangeTicker	CurrentPrice
1	12	Airing Cadets	ACads	20.93191
2	5	Brownies	Browns	28.75828
3	19	Fishy Friars	FF	21.70924

Figure 11-14. *Three results sets demonstrating ROWCOUNT and TOP (N)*

5. The first result set is limited by the TOP (2) expression within the SELECT. As long as the ROWCOUNT statement has a value that is the same as or greater than the TOP expression, two rows will be returned. Looking at the second result set, you can see that the ROWCOUNT statement is in control of the number of rows returned this time. Finally, the third result set returns the number of rows from the TOP expression.

String Functions

A large number of system functions are available for manipulating data. This section looks purely at the string functions available for use within a T-SQL statement; later in the book, you will look at some more functions that are available. Following are the functions that are used in the next example:

- LTRIM/RTRIM: These have similar functionality. If you have a string with leading spaces, and you wish to remove those leading spaces, you would use LTRIM so that the returned varchar value would have a nonspace character as its first value. If you have trailing spaces, you would use RTRIM. You can use this function only with a data type of varchar or nvarchar, or with a data type that can be implicitly converted to these two data types, or with a data type that can be converted to varchar or nvarchar using the CAST SQL Server function.

- CAST: This specialized function converts one data type to another data type. This is not specifically a string function, as you can cast from a string to a numeric; however, casting into a string is more common as it can be used to cast a number into a string, which is then concatenated into several strings.

- LEFT/RIGHT: This function returns the leftmost or rightmost characters from a string. Passing in a second parameter to the function will determine the number of characters to return from whichever side of the string. The LEFT and RIGHT functions accept any data type except text or ntext expressions to perform the string manipulation, implicitly converting any noncharacter data type or varchar or nvarchar and returning a varchar or nvarchar data type as a result.

It is possible to do more than just return columns. Columns can have further functionality applied to them. In the following example, some basic string functions will be shown.

TRY IT OUT: STRING FUNCTIONS

1. Enter the code that follows into an empty Query Editor window. Alter the output to text format by pressing Ctrl+T. Notice the use of the + operator within the SELECT query. This will concatenate the strings defined within the query into one single string value.

■ **Note** Unlike with some programming languages, you cannot use the & character, as this has a totally different meaning in SQL Server. It is used for bitwise operations.

```
SELECT FirstName + ' ' + LastName +
' has a cleared balance of $' +
CAST (ClearedBalance AS varchar(40))
FROM CustomerDetails.Customers
WHERE FirstName = 'Aubrey'
```

2. Execute this code, which produces the output shown in Figure 11-15.

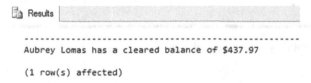

```
🗎 Results

----------------------------------------------------
Aubrey Lomas has a cleared balance of $437.97

(1 row(s) affected)
```

Figure 11-15. *Concatenating results*

3. As you can see, it's a bit unwieldy. The Name column heading goes far wider than is required, as denoted by the width of the hyphens. There is a complex way of getting this right, but a much simpler method is to use the LEFT statement. The sum of the width of the three columns gives this column width that is displayed in the output; by using the LEFT statement, it is possible to achieve something better. Clear the Query Editor pane and enter the following code:

```
SELECT LEFT(FirstName + ' ' + LastName +
' has a cleared balance of $' +
CAST (ClearedBalance AS varchar(40)),50)
FROM CustomerDetails.Customers
WHERE FirstName = 'Aubrey'
```

4. Execute the preceding code. This produces the results shown in Figure 11-16. What the preceding query has done is to reduce the output to the first 50 characters, starting from the left.

```
Results
------------------------------------------------
Aubrey Lomas has a cleared balance of $437.97

(1 row(s) affected)
```

Figure 11-16. Concatenating results and reducing the width

5. The best way to adjust the column width is to remove all trailing spaces rather than guesstimating how wide to make the string; this can be achieved via the RTRIM statement. The following code does this, although the output in the text layout doesn't. This is because SQL Server still doesn't know what the maximum size of the concatenation will be, and it has to believe that the maximum number of characters of the sum of the two columns could still be displayed. However, in truth, the amount of data returned will be minimal. Therefore, this is a great method of reducing the amount of data passed over a network.

```
SELECT RTRIM(FirstName + ' ' + LastName +
' has a cleared balance of $' +
CAST (ClearedBalance AS varchar(40)))
FROM CustomerDetails.Customers
WHERE FirstName = 'Aubrey'
```

In all of the examples thus far, rows are returned in an arbitrary order. You look now at how this can be changed.

Order! Order!

Of course, retrieving the rows in any order SQL Server desires may not always be what you want. It is possible to change the order in which rows are returned, however. This is achieved through the ORDER BY clause, which is part of the SELECT statement. The ORDER BY clause can have multiple columns, with some in ascending order and others in descending order if you wish.

If you should find that you are repeatedly using the same columns within an ORDER BY clause, or that the query is taking some time to run, you should consider setting the columns within the query as an index. (Indexes were covered in Chapter 6.)

Ordering the data will of course increase processing time, but it is a necessity if you want to display the data in the correct order. Ordering on varchar columns also takes longer than on numeric columns.

The ORDER BY clause also has the option to allow you to paginate your data, which is ideal if you are creating a SELECT statement to return rows to display on a screen. There are two options that are required: OFFSET and FETCH NEXT. The first option determines the number of rows to skip before returning data, and the latter option determines the number of rows to return. You will see a demonstration of this in the following section, and it will be demonstrated in action in Chapter 17 as well.

■ **Note** Ordering takes place after the filtering of rows but before the TOP statement, so you could still be ordering a large set of rows before returning the top few you may need.

Let's now take a look at building a query that uses an ORDER BY clause.

TRY IT OUT: ALTERING THE ORDER

1. Clear the query window in Query Editor and set the display option back to showing a grid by selecting, from the Query menu, Results To ➤ Results to Grid. Once complete, enter the following code into the Query Editor pane. This will return the data in the ascending (the default) order of the cleared balance of your customers for those customers who have a cleared balance value.

```
SELECT LEFT(FirstName + ' ' + LastName,50) AS 'Name',
ClearedBalance Balance
FROM CustomerDetails.Customers
WHERE ClearedBalance IS NOT NULL
ORDER BY Balance
```

2. Execute the code; this will produce the results shown in Figure 11-17.

	Name	Balance
1	Mark Vernon-Smith	-751.00
2	Shanda Friedman	1.9671
3	Grant Hutchinson	5.4008
4	Bobbi Chen	5.741
5	Trenton Barry	5.7874
6	Jeanine Best	5.8842
7	Alberto Pierce	6.0136
8	Jody Bailey	8.0958
9	Susan Ibarra	10.8675
10	Margaret Villarreal	10.9341
11	Rosemary Evans	12.3903
12	Myron Boyle	12.7317

Figure 11-17. Altering the order by balance and ignoring NULL values

3. You can also complete the same query, but with the cleared balance in descending order rather than ascending order. This is simply done by placing DESC after the column name. Change your code as detailed here:

```
SELECT LEFT(FirstName + ' ' + LastName,50) AS 'Name',
ClearedBalance Balance
FROM CustomerDetails.Customers
WHERE ClearedBalance IS NOT NULL
ORDER BY Balance DESC
```

4. Execute the code; this will produce the results shown in Figure 11-18.

	Name	Balance
1	Bernie McGee	6653.11
2	Teresa House	998.2392
3	Dennis Simpson	997.7163
4	Stuart Robles	993.0787
5	Omar Estes	992.5347
6	Tania Avery	992.0263
7	Ernesto Jensen	990.9479
8	Raymond Esparza	990.1083
9	Darcy Mc Neil	989.8681
10	Demetrius Farley	989.8569
11	Jeannette Richardson	985.8271
12	Latoya Henry	985.6434

Figure 11-18. Making the order in descending sequence

5. To paginate your data, there are three elements that have to be included in your SELECT statement.

 - The first element is the ORDER BY clause. This is so that SQL Server will know that the order in which the data will be returned will be as constant as possible. The caveat of "as possible" is because data may be added to the table between calls to display the paginated data.

 - The second element is the OFFSET clause, which determines the number of rows to skip before returning the data.

 - The final element is the number of rows to return.

6. To return the first four rows from `CustomerDetails.Customers`, the `OFFSET` would be 0 and `FETCH NEXT` would have a value of 4. Enter this code:

```
SELECT LEFT(FirstName + ' ' + LastName,50) AS 'Name',
ClearedBalance Balance
FROM CustomerDetails.Customers
WHERE ClearedBalance IS NOT NULL
ORDER BY Balance
OFFSET 0 ROWS
FETCH NEXT 4 ROWS ONLY
```

7. Now execute the code. Figure 11-19 shows the first four rows returned.

	Name	Balance
1	Mark Vernon-Smith	-751.00
2	Shanda Friedman	1.9671
3	Grant Hutchinson	5.4008
4	Bobbi Chen	5.741

Figure 11-19. Using OFFSET and FETCH NEXT to return rows

8. To return the next set of four rows, enter the following code. You may think that hard-coding the number for the starting position is not the correct method because the OFFSET will increase with each call. You would thus use a locally defined variable.

```
SELECT LEFT(FirstName + ' ' + LastName,50) AS 'Name',
ClearedBalance Balance
FROM CustomerDetails.Customers
WHERE ClearedBalance IS NOT NULL
ORDER BY Balance
OFFSET 4 ROWS
FETCH NEXT 4 ROWS ONLY
```

9. When you execute the foregoing code, you will see results similar to those in Figure 11-20.

	Name	Balance
1	Trenton Barry	5.7874
2	Jeanine Best	5.8842
3	Alberto Pierce	6.0136
4	Jody Bailey	8.0958

Figure 11-20. *Using OFFSET and FETCH NEXT to return subsequent rows*

The LIKE Operator

It is possible to use more advanced techniques for finding rows when a mathematical operation doesn't quite fit. For example, say someone is trying to track down a customer, but doesn't know the customer's full name, or does know the first part of the surname but doesn't know how to spell the full name.

Suppose you know that the surname ends in "Smith" but you cannot recall the first part of the surname. So how would this be put into a query? There is a keyword that you can use as part of the WHERE statement, called LIKE. This will use pattern matching to find the relevant rows within a SQL Server table using the information provided.

The LIKE operator can come with one of four operators, which are used alongside string values that you want to find. Each of the four specifiers is detailed in the following list. They can be used together, and using one does not exclude using any others.

- %: This would be placed at the end and/or the beginning of a string. The best way to describe this is through an example; if you were searching the customers who had the letter "a" within their surname, you would search for "%a%", which would look for the letter "a," ignoring any letters before and after the letter "a", and just checking for that letter within the surname column.

- _: This looks at a string, but only for a single character before or after the position of the underscore. Therefore, looking in the first name column for "_a" would return any customer who has two letters in his or her first name where the second letter is an "a." In the example, no rows would be returned. However, if you combined this with the % sign and searched for "_a%," then you would get back Jason Atkins, Ian McMahon, and Ian Prentice. You would not get back Vic McGlynn, because "a" is not the second letter.

- []: This lets you specify a number of values or a range of values to look for. For example, if you were looking in the customer's first name for the letters "c-f," you would use LIKE "%[c-f]%".

- [^...]: Similar to the preceding option, this one lists those items that do not have values within the range specified.

■ **Note** LIKE is *not* case-sensitive unless you have the SQL Server instance set to a collation that is case-sensitive.

The best way to learn how to use LIKE is to see an example.

TRY IT OUT: THE LIKE OPERATOR

1. We are going to try to find Mark Vernon-Smith via the LastName column. You know the name ends with Smith and the surname is hyphenated. The code that follows will search all of the customer rows looking for anything prefixing -Smith.

```
SELECT FirstName + ' ' + LastName
FROM CustomerDetails.Customers
WHERE LastName LIKE '%-Smith'
```

2. Execute the code; this will give the results shown in Figure 11-21.

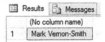

Figure 11-21. *Using the LIKE operator*

3. You can also go to extremes using the LIKE operator—for example, seeing which customers have the letter "q" anywhere in their name. The code for this is shown here:

```
SELECT FirstName + ' ' + LastName AS [Name]
FROM CustomerDetails.Customers
WHERE FirstName + ' ' + LastName LIKE '%q%'
```

4. When you execute this, you should get the results shown in Figure 11-22: 13 customers are returned, as they have a "q" somewhere in their name.

	Name
1	Quentin Schaefer
2	Norman Velazquez
3	Richard Vasquez
4	Alma Vazquez
5	Jacquelyn Burgess
6	Kurt Velazquez
7	Rita Vazquez
8	Angelique Erickson
9	Harold Quinn
10	Damion Vazquez
11	Angelique Huynh
12	Quincy Beasley
13	Angelique Quinn

Figure 11-22. Using LIKE to search for customers with "q" in their name

5. Why would you want to go to such lengths of concatenating the names? Would it not have been possible to use the Name alias, which is a combination of the first name and last name columns? Well, unfortunately not—the code you might expect to use would look something like the following. Enter this code:

```
SELECT FirstName + ' ' + LastName AS [Name]
FROM CustomerDetails.Customers
WHERE [Name] LIKE '%q%'
```

6. Execute this code. Instead of the success messages that you have become used to, an error message will be returned. You can search only on real column names, not on aliases.

```
Msg 207, Level 16, State 1, Line 3
Invalid column name 'Name'.
```

■ **Note** There may be times when you'll want to take data from a table in one database on one server and insert it into another table in another database on another server. A typical scenario might be when data have been inadvertantly deleted, but you have a backup on another database. By using a SELECT statement and many string actions, it is possible to build up a result set of INSERT statements. You can then store these to a text file, which you can use to run against in another database. A short code example would be:

```
SELECT "INSERT (Column1) VALUES ("'+column1+"'") FROM Table1
```

Creating Data: SELECT INTO

It's time now to start getting into a more advanced area of SELECT. It is possible to create a new table within a database by using the INTO keyword, like that found in INSERT INTO, within a SELECT statement, provided, of course, you have the right database permissions to create tables in the first place.

First, it is necessary to clarify the syntax of how the SELECT INTO statement is laid out; you simply add the INTO clause after the column names, but before the FROM keyword. Although the following section of code shows just one table name, it is possible to create a new table from data from one or more tables.

```
SELECT *|column1,column2,...
INTO new_tablename
FROM tablename
```

The INTO clause is crucial to the success of the creation of the new table. The SELECT statement will fail if there is a table already in existence with the same name for the same table owner. This will be demonstrated within the example in this section. You tend to use the SELECT INTO statement to create a temporary table in tempdb, although you can use it to build a table in your database.

The table generated will consist of the columns returned from the built SELECT statement, whether that is all the columns from the table mentioned within the FROM statement or just a subset. The new table will also contain only the rows returned from the SELECT statement. To clarify, this statement is creating a new table using the structure within the SELECT statement. There will be no keys, constraints, relationships, or in fact any other facet of SQL Server, except a new table. Hence, creating tables using SELECT INTO should be done with care.

Two tables can exist with the same name within a database, providing that they have different schemas. The tables in ApressFinancial all have the database owner as their owner, but it is possible for a CustomerDetails. Customers table to exist for an owner like MSmith.

■ **Note** Although possible, having two tables of the same name but with different owners is *not* recommended, as it causes confusion.

Let's look at the INTO statement in action.

TRY IT OUT: SELECT INTO

1. In an empty Query Editor window, enter the following code:

```
SELECT FirstName + ' ' + LastName AS [Name],
ClearedBalance,UnclearedBalance
INTO CustTemp
FROM CustomerDetails.Customers
```

2. Execute the code. This will return the following message in the results pane:

```
(1000 row(s) affected)
```

3. If you now move to Object Explorer on the left-hand side (if Object Explorer is no longer there, press F8) and complete a refresh, you should see a new table in the expanded Tables node, called dbo.CustTemp, as shown in Figure 11-23.

Figure 11-23. *New table created with SELECT INTO*

You should use the INTO clause with care. For instance, in this example, security has not been set up for the table, and you are also creating tables within your database that have not been through any normalization or development life cycle. It is also very easy to fill up a database with these tables if you are not careful. However, it is a useful and handy method for taking a backup of a table and then working on that backup while testing out any queries that might modify the data. Do ensure, though, that there is enough space within the database before building the table if you do use this technique.

■ **Note** It is best to avoid using SELECT INTO in a production environment unless you really do need to keep the table permanently. Also take note that the table in the previous "Try It Out" exercise was placed in the CustomerDetails schema. You may want to create a special schema for tables created using SELECT INTO if they are not permanent additions to your database. You may find, though, that it is better to use the temporary database, tempdb, as a place to put tables created using SELECT INTO, especially if they are going to exist for only a short period of time. The "Try It Out" code would then read as follows:

```
SELECT CustomerFirstName + ' ' + CustomerLastName AS [Name],
ClearedBalance,UnclearedBalance
INTO CustomerDetails.CustTemp
FROM CustomerDetails.Customers
```

Updating Data

Now that data has been inserted into your database, and you have seen how to retrieve this information, it is time to look at how to modify the data, referred to as *updating the data*.

Ensuring that you update the right data at the right time is crucial to maintaining data integrity. You will find that when updating data, and also when removing or inserting data, it is best to group this work as a single, logical unit within a *transaction*, thereby ensuring that if an error does occur, it is still possible to return the data back to its original state. You were first introduced to transactions in Chapter 10, and I will be building on this knowledge to cover nesting of transactions.

First of all, let's take a look at the syntax for the UPDATE statement.

The UPDATE Statement

The UPDATE statement will update columns of information on rows within a single table that are returned from a query that can include selection and join criteria. The syntax of the UPDATE statement has similarities to the SELECT statement, which makes sense, as it has to look for specific rows to update, just as the SELECT statement looks for rows to retrieve. You will also find that before doing updates, especially more complex updates, you will need to first build up a SELECT statement and then transfer the JOIN and WHERE details into the UPDATE statement. The syntax that follows is in its simplest form. Once you become more experienced, the UPDATE statement can made just as complex and versatile as the SELECT statement.

```
UPDATE
    [ TOP ( expression ) [ PERCENT ] ]
    [[ server_name . database_name . schema_name .
    | database_name .[ schema_name ] .
    | schema_name .]
table_or_viewname
    SET
        { column_name = { expression | DEFAULT | NULL }
        | column_name { .WRITE ( expression , @Offset , @Length ) }
        | @variable = expression
        | @variable = column = expression [ ,...n ]
    } [ ,...n ]
    [FROM { <table_source> } [ ,...n ] ]
    [ WHERE { <search_condition>]
```

The first set of options you know from the SELECT statement. The tablename clause is simply the name of the table on which to perform the UPDATE. Moving on to the next line of the syntax, you reach the SET clause. It is in this clause that any updates to a column take place. One or more columns can be updated at any one time, but each column to be updated must be separated by a comma.

When updating data in a column, there are four choices that can be made. Updates can be achieved through the following:

- A direct value setting

- A section of a value setting provided that the recipient column is varchar, nvarchar, or varbinary

- The value from a variable

- A value from another column, even from another table

You can even have mathematical functions or variable manipulations included in the right-hand clause; you can also have concatenated columns or manipulate the contents through STRING, DATE, or any other function. The update will be successful as long as the result's left-hand side and right-hand side both have the same data type. As a result, you cannot place a character value into a numeric data-type field without converting the character to a numeric value.

If you are updating a column with a value from another column, the only value that it is possible to use is the value from the same row of information in that other column, provided this column has an appropriate data type. When I say "same row," remember that when tables are joined together, this means that values from these joined tables can also be used, as long as they are within the same row of information. Also, the expression could be the result of a subquery.

■ **Note** A *subquery* is a query that sits inside another query. You look at subqueries in Chapter 16.

The FROM table source clause will define the table(s) being used to find the data with which you will perform the update on the table that is defined next to the UPDATE statement. Like SELECT statements, it is possible to create JOIN statements; however, you must define the table you are updating within the FROM clause.

Finally, the WHERE condition is exactly as it is in the SELECT statement, and can be used in exactly the same way. Note that omitting the WHERE clause will mean the UPDATE statement will affect every row in the table.

Updating Data within Query Editor

To demonstrate the UPDATE statement, the first update to the data will be to change the name of a customer, replicating when someone changes his or her name due to marriage, for example. This uses the UPDATE statement in its simplest form, by locating a single record and updating a single column.

TRY IT OUT: UPDATING A ROW OF DATA

1. Ensure that Query Editor is running and that you are logged in with an account that can perform updates. In the Query Editor pane, enter the following UPDATE statement:

```
USE ApressFinancial
GO
UPDATE CustomerDetails.Customers
SET LastName = 'Mather'
WHERE CustomerId = 7
```

2. It is as simple as that! Now that the code is entered, execute it, and you should then see a message like this:

```
(1 row(s) affected)
```

3. Now enter a SELECT statement to check that Customer Id 7 is now Anne Mather. For your convenience, here's the statement, and the results are shown in Figure 11-24.

```
SELECT FirstName + ' ' + LastName
FROM CustomerDetails.Customers
WHERE CustomerId = 7
```

Figure 11-24. *Updating the surname of one customer*

4. Now here's a little trick that you should know, if you haven't stumbled across it already. If you check out Figure 11-25, you will see that the UPDATE code is still in the Query Editor pane, as is the SELECT statement. No, you aren't going to perform the UPDATE again! If you highlight the line with the SELECT statement by holding down the left mouse button and dragging the mouse, then only the highlighted code will run when you execute the code again.

```
  USE ApressFinancial
  GO
⊟UPDATE CustomerDetails.Customers
  SET LastName = 'Mather'
  WHERE CustomerId = 7

⊟SELECT FirstName + ' ' + LastName
  FROM CustomerDetails.Customers
  WHERE CustomerId = 7
```

Figure 11-25. *How to execute only specific code*

5. Upon executing the highlighted code, you should see only the values returned for the SELECT statement, as you saw previously, and no results saying that an update has been performed.

Updating Data from a Variable or Another Column

It is also possible to update data using information from another column within the table, or with the value from a variable. This next example will demonstrate how to update a row of information using the value within a variable, as well as a column from the same table. Notice how although the row will be found using the LastName column, the UPDATE statement will also update that column with a new value. To define a variable, you have to use the DECLARE statement, and any variable name needs to start with one @ sign for local variables and two @@ signs for global variables. A local variable is a variable that has a lifetime of the query that contains it; a global variable has a lifetime of the query that contains it, as well as any other query while the declaration query is active. You will see more on these in Chapter 16. Enter the following code and then execute it:

```
SELECT FirstName,LastName,ClearedBalance,UnclearedBalance
FROM CustomerDetails.Customers
WHERE lastname = 'Booth'

DECLARE @ValueToUpdate VARCHAR(30)
SET @ValueToUpdate = 'Prentice'
UPDATE CustomerDetails.Customers
   SET LastName = @ValueToUpdate,
       ClearedBalance = ClearedBalance + UnclearedBalance ,
       UnclearedBalance = 0
 WHERE LastName = 'Booth'

SELECT FirstName,LastName,ClearedBalance,UnclearedBalance
FROM CustomerDetails.Customers
WHERE lastname = 'Prentice'
```

You should then see the output shown in Figure 11-26.

	First Name	Last Name	ClearedBalance	UnclearedBalance
1	Misty	Booth	789.5141	NULL

	First Name	Last Name	ClearedBalance	UnclearedBalance
1	Misty	Prentice	NULL	0.00

Figure 11-26. *Showing the values of the customer before and after the update*

Updating a Column with Different Data Types

Now let's move on to updating columns in which the data types don't match. SQL Server does a pretty good job when it can to ensure the update occurs, and these following examples will demonstrate how well SQL Server copes with updating an integer data type with a value in a varchar data type.

1. The first example will demonstrate an instance in which a varchar value will successfully update a column defined as int. Enter the following code:

```
SELECT FirstName,LastName,ClearedBalance,UnclearedBalance
FROM CustomerDetails.Customers
WHERE lastname = 'Prentice'

DECLARE @ValueToUpdate VARCHAR(30)
SET @ValueToUpdate = '1422.26'
UPDATE CustomerDetails.Customers
   SET ClearedBalance = @ValueToUpdate
 WHERE LastName = 'Prentice'

SELECT FirstName,LastName,ClearedBalance,UnclearedBalance
FROM CustomerDetails.Customers
WHERE lastname = 'Prentice'
```

2. Execute the code; you should see the output shown in Figure 11-27, where the ClearedBalance becomes 1422.26. SQL Server has performed an internal data conversion (known as an implicit data type conversion) and has come up with a money data type from the value within varchar, as this is what the column expects, and therefore SQL Server can successfully update the column.

	First Name	Last Name	ClearedBalance	UnclearedBalance
1	Misty	Prentice	NULL	0.00

	First Name	Last Name	ClearedBalance	UnclearedBalance
1	Misty	Prentice	1422.26	0.00

Figure 11-27. *Showing the values of the customer before and after the update*

3. However, in this next example, the data type that SQL Server will come up with is a numeric data type. When you try to update an integer-based data type, `bigint`, with this value, which you can find in the `AddressId` column, the UPDATE does not take place. Enter the following code:

```
SELECT FirstName,LastName,ClearedBalance,UnclearedBalance
FROM CustomerDetails.Customers
WHERE lastname = 'Prentice'

DECLARE @ValueToUpdate VARCHAR(30)
SET @ValueToUpdate = 'Invalid'
UPDATE CustomerDetails.Customers
    SET ClearedBalance = @ValueToUpdate
 WHERE LastName = 'Prentice'

SELECT FirstName,LastName,ClearedBalance,UnclearedBalance
FROM CustomerDetails.Customers
WHERE lastname = 'Prentice'
```

4. Now execute the code. Notice when you do that SQL Server generates an error message informing you of the problem. Hence, never leave data conversions to SQL Server to perform; convert the data explicitly. Try to get the same data type updating the same data type. You can look at how to convert data further with the CAST statement in Chapter 16.

```
(1 row(s) affected)
Msg 235, Level 16, State 0, Line 7
Cannot convert a char value to money. The char value has incorrect syntax.
```

Updating data can be very straightforward, as the preceding examples have demonstrated. Where at all possible, use a unique identifier—for example, the `CustomerId`—when trying to find a customer, rather than a name. There can be multiple rows for the same name or other type of criteria, but by using a unique identifier, you can be sure of using the right record every time. To place this in a production scenario, say you had a Windows-based graphical system that allowed you to find details of customers by their name, address, or account number. Once you found the right customer, instead of keeping those details in order to find other related rows, you would keep a record of the unique identifier value instead.

Let us now return to the UPDATE statement and how it works. First of all, SQL Server will filter out from the table the first row that meets the criteria of the WHERE statement. The data modifications are then made, and SQL Server moves on to try to find the second row that matches the WHERE statement. This process is repeated until all the rows that meet the WHERE condition are modified. Therefore, if using a unique identifier, SQL Server will update only one row, but if the WHERE statement looks for rows that have a LastName of Dewson, multiple rows could be updated (Robin and Julie). Thus, choose your row selection criteria for updates carefully.

But what if you didn't want the update to occur immediately? There will be times when you will want to perform an update and then check that the update is correct before finally committing the changes to the table. Or when doing the update, you'll want to check for errors or unexpected data updates. This is where transactions come in, and these are covered next.

Updating Data: Using Transactions

Now, what if, in the first update query of this chapter, you made a mistake or an error occurred? For example, say you chose the wrong customer or, even worse, omitted the WHERE statement, and therefore all the rows were updated. These are unusual but not uncommon errors. More common errors could result when more than one data modification has to take place successfully, and the first one succeeds but a subsequent modification fails. By using a transaction, you would have had the chance to easily correct any mistakes, and could then revert to a consistent state. Of course, this next example is nice and simple, but by working through it, the subject of transactions will hopefully become a little easier to understand and appreciate.

TRY IT OUT: USING A TRANSACTION

1. Make sure Query Editor is running for this first example, which will demonstrate COMMIT TRAN in action. There should be no difference from an UPDATE without any transaction processing, as it will execute and update the data successfully. However, this should prove to be a valuable exercise, as it will also demonstrate how to name a transaction. Enter the following code:

    ```
    SELECT 'Before',ShareId, Description,CurrentPrice
      FROM ShareDetails.Shares
     WHERE ShareId = 3
    BEGIN TRAN ShareUpd
    UPDATE ShareDetails.Shares
        SET CurrentPrice = CurrentPrice * 1.1
     WHERE ShareId = 3
    SELECT 'During',ShareId, Description,CurrentPrice
      FROM ShareDetails.Shares
     WHERE ShareId = 3
    ROLLBACK TRAN
    SELECT 'After',ShareId, Description,CurrentPrice
      FROM ShareDetails.Shares
     WHERE ShareId = 3
    ```

2. Notice in the preceding code that ROLLBACK TRAN does not use the name associated with BEGIN TRAN. The label after BEGIN TRAN is simply that, a label, and it performs no function. It is therefore not necessary to then link up with a similarly labeled ROLLBACK TRAN.

3. Execute the code. Figure 11-28 shows the results, which list out the Shares table before and after the update within the transaction, as well as the value after the rollback, to show that the data change has not been committed to the table. This is a straightforward test of your code before update.

Figure 11-28. Updating with a transaction label and a ROLLBACK TRAN

4. However, if instead your code was as shown below, where within the UPDATE statement you forgot the ShareId filter in the WHERE expression, commented out with two dashes (–), you can see how building your code in a transaction with a ROLLBACK becomes important and would help you to avoid a potentially catastrophic error.

```
SELECT 'Before',ShareId,Description,CurrentPrice
  FROM ShareDetails.Shares
 WHERE ShareId = 3
BEGIN TRAN ShareUpd
UPDATE ShareDetails.Shares
   SET CurrentPrice = CurrentPrice * 1.1
-- WHERE ShareId = 3
SELECT 'Within the transaction',ShareId,Description,CurrentPrice
  FROM ShareDetails.Shares
ROLLBACK TRAN
SELECT 'After',ShareId,Description,CurrentPrice
  FROM ShareDetails.Shares
 WHERE ShareId = 3
```

One final point to note: In Chapter 10, I said, "In reality, minimal data are logged about what data pages have been deallocated and therefore removed from the database." This was followed by the cautionary note that there was no going back on a TRUNCATE outside of a transaction. However, there is the ability to roll back a TRUNCATE within a transaction. A TRUNCATE indicates within the transaction log the data pages that are to be deallocated within SQL Server. However, the deallocation has not happened and will not happen until the end of the transaction. Therefore, if you have a TRUNCATE TABLE command within a transaction, by issuing a ROLLBACK you can roll back a table truncation.

Nested Transactions

Let's look at one last example before moving on. It is possible to nest transactions inside one another. I touch on this enough for you to have a good understanding of nested transactions, but this is not complete coverage, as it can get very complex and messy if you involve save points, stored procedures, triggers, and so on. However, I believe that you have now covered a good amount of the T-SQL syntax, and it is at this point in the book that nested transactions become relevant. As a developer, you will find that you will have to work with nested transactions, but always keep in mind that, whether it is a nested transaction or a single transaction, you should keep the amount of time that the transaction is active to as short a period as possible, and you should update tables in the same order in all transactions. The aim of this section is to give you an understanding of the basic but crucial points of how nesting transactions work.

Nested transactions can occur in a number of different scenarios. For example, you could have a transaction in one set of code in a stored procedure, which calls a second stored procedure that also has a transaction. You will look at a simpler scenario in which you keep the transactions in just one set of code.

What you need to be clear about is how the ROLLBACK and COMMIT TRAN statements work in a nested transaction. First of all, let's see what I mean by nesting a simple transaction. The syntax is shown here, and you can see that two BEGIN TRAN statements occur before you get to a COMMIT or a ROLLBACK:

```
BEGIN TRAN
    Statements
    BEGIN TRAN
        Statements
    COMMIT|ROLLBACK TRAN
COMMIT|ROLLBACK TRAN
```

As each transaction commences, SQL Server increments a running count of transactions it holds in a system variable called @@TRANCOUNT. Therefore, as each BEGIN TRAN is executed, @@TRANCOUNT increases by 1. As each COMMIT TRAN is executed, @@TRANCOUNT decreases by 1. It is not until @@TRANCOUNT is at a value of 1 that you can actually commit the data to the database. The code that follows might help you to understand this a bit more.

Enter and execute this code, and take a look at the output, which should resemble Figure 11-29. The first BEGIN TRAN increases @@TRANCOUNT by 1, as does the second BEGIN TRAN. The first COMMIT TRAN marks the changes to be committed, but does not actually perform the changes because @@TRANCOUNT is 2. It simply creates the correct BEGIN/COMMIT TRAN nesting and reduces @@TRANCOUNT by 1. The second COMMIT TRAN will succeed and will commit the data, as @@TRANCOUNT is now 1.

```
BEGIN TRAN ShareUpd
    SELECT '1st TranCount',@@TRANCOUNT
    BEGIN TRAN ShareUpd2
        SELECT '2nd TranCount',@@TRANCOUNT
        COMMIT TRAN ShareUpd2
    SELECT '3rd TranCount',@@TRANCOUNT
COMMIT TRAN -- It is at this point that data modifications will be committed
SELECT 'Last TranCount',@@TRANCOUNT
```

	(No column name)	(No column name)
1	1st TranCount	1

	(No column name)	(No column name)
1	2nd TranCount	2

	(No column name)	(No column name)
1	3rd TranCount	1

	(No column name)	(No column name)
1	Last TranCount	0

Figure 11-29. Showing the @@TRANCOUNT

■ **Note** After the last COMMIT TRAN, @@TRANCOUNT is at 0. Any further instances of COMMIT TRAN or ROLLBACK TRAN will generate an error.

If within the code there is a ROLLBACK TRAN, then the data will immediately be rolled back no matter where you are within the nesting, and @@TRANCOUNT will be set to 0. Therefore, any further ROLLBACK TRAN or COMMIT TRAN instances will fail, so you do need to have error handling, which you will look at in Chapter 16

Try to avoid nesting transactions where possible, especially when one stored procedure calls another stored procedure within a transaction. It is not "wrong," but it does require a great deal of care.

Now that updating data has been completed, the only area of data manipulation left is row deletion, which you will look at now.

Using More Than One Table

The SELECT, UPDATE, and DELETE statements have dealt with and covered only the retrieval of data from one table. However, it is possible to have more than one table being used to retrieve data; you must keep in mind that the more tables included in the query, the more detrimental the effect on the query's performance. However, it is sometimes faster to build one query that joins to more than one table than to have several "one table" statements. If you are joining tables using an index, you will usually be fine as long as you do not have too many joins. A good rule of thumb is that as long as you are joining tables together using an index, until you start to have many joins, you should be okay. At all times, though, you should review your T-SQL. There is an aid called a query plan that you saw in Chapter 6 and will see in Chapter 17. I would like to cover a bit more about other areas before I take you through a couple of basic query plans.

When you include subsequent tables, there must be a link of some sort between the two tables, known as a *join*. A join will take place between at least one column in one table and a column from the joining table. The columns involved in the join do not have to be included in any key within the tables involved in the join. However, this is quite uncommon, and if you do find you are joining tables, then there is a high chance that a relationship exists between them, which would mean you do require a primary key and a foreign key. This was covered in Chapter 3.

It is possible that one of the columns on one side of the join is actually a concatenation of two or more columns. As long as the end result is one column, this is acceptable. Also, the two columns that are being joined do not have to have the same name, as long as they both have similar data types. For example, you can join a char with a varchar. What is not acceptable is that one side of the JOIN names a column and the other side names a variable or a literal that is really a filter that would be found in a WHERE statement. For example, you would not join LastName to Dewson.

Joining two tables together can be relatively straightforward, but it can also become quite complicated. Let's consider the various types of joins:

- INNER JOIN: The most basic join condition is a straight join between two tables, which is called an INNER JOIN. An INNER JOIN joins the two tables, and where there is a join of data using the columns from each of the two tables, then the data are returned. For example, if you are joining two tables on the share ID, and there is a share in the shares table that has no price, then you would see output only where there is a share with a share price. The share without a price would not be returned. You will see this in action in this chapter.

- OUTER JOIN: It is possible to return all the rows from one table where there is no join. This is known as an OUTER JOIN. Depending on which table you want the rows always to be returned from, this will be either a LEFT OUTER JOIN or a RIGHT OUTER JOIN. Taking the shares example, you could use an OUTER JOIN so that even when there is no share price, you can still list the share. This example will also be demonstrated later in this chapter.

- CROSS JOIN: The final type of join is the scariest and most dangerous join. If you wish for every row in one table to be joined with every row in the joining table, then you would use a CROSS JOIN. So, if you had 10 rows in one table and 12 rows in the other table, you would see returned 120 rows of data (10×12). As you can imagine, this type of join just needs two small tables to produce even a large amount of output.

You might hear of one further join called a self join. This uses one of the foregoing techniques, but the join would be between two elements of the same table. This occurs when there is some reference identifier in a table that can be used to find another row in the same table, such as an ID called a parent ID.

Although not the most helpful of syntax demonstrated within the book, the syntax for joining two tables is as follows:

```
FROM tablea
 [FULL[INNER|OUTER|CROSS]] JOIN tableb
{ON tableb.column1 = tablea.column2 {AND|OR tableb.column...}}
```

The best way to look at the syntax is within a described example. I will use two tables to demonstrate the inner join in this example: ShareDetails.Shares and ShareDetails.SharePrices.

Joining two tables could not be simpler. All the columns in both tables are available to be returned through the query, so I can list the columns desired as normal. However, if there are two columns of the same name, they must be prefixed with the name, or the alias name, of the table from which the information is derived.

■ **Note** It is recommended that whenever a join does take place, regardless of whether the column name is unique, all columns be prefixed with the table or alias name. This saves time if the query is expanded to include other tables, but it also clarifies exactly where the information is coming from.

TRY IT OUT: JOINING TWO TABLES

1. The first join you will look at is the INNER JOIN. This is where you have two tables and want to list all the values where there is a join. In this case, you want to list all the shares where there is a share price, and you want to see every share price for that share. Notice that you don't need to define the word INNER. This is presumed if nothing else is specified. Also take note that, like with columns, you have defined aliases for the table names. This makes prefixing columns easier. You are joining the two tables on ShareId, as this is the linking column between the two tables. Enter the following code:

    ```
    SELECT s.ShareId, s.Description,sp.Price,sp.PriceDate
      FROM ShareDetails.Shares s
      JOIN ShareDetails.SharePrices sp ON sp.ShareId = s.ShareId
     WHERE s.ShareId < 8
       AND sp.PriceDate BETWEEN '1 Jan 2012' AND '3 Jan 2012'
    ```

2. Once you have executed the code, you should see the output that appears in Figure 11-30. There is no output for ShareIds 4 and 6 as they have no share price between the dates specified in the WHERE.

	ShareId	Description	Price	PriceDate
1	1	ACME'S HOMEBAKE COOKIES INC	1.14767	2012-01-02 17:16:40.410
2	1	ACME'S HOMEBAKE COOKIES INC	9.60484	2012-01-02 15:34:03.350
3	1	ACME'S HOMEBAKE COOKIES INC	0.58554	2012-01-01 17:10:12.260
4	2	ACME'S HOMEBAKE COOKIES INC	23.55766	2012-01-01 15:28:26.960
5	3	Lomas Ambulances	3.30950	2012-01-01 19:54:22.810
6	3	Lomas Ambulances	9.07787	2012-01-01 03:08:12.810
7	5	Brownies	6.27370	2012-01-02 08:07:50.240
8	7	Rolling Maulers	13.66410	2012-01-01 16:53:56.970

Figure 11-30. *First inner join*

3. You can take this a stage further and filter the rows to list only the share price row that matches the `CurrentPrice` in the `ShareDetails.Shares` table. This could be done by filtering the data on a `WHERE` statement, and from a performance perspective it would be better, as neither of these columns are within an index and there could be a large number of rows for `ShareDetails.SharePrices` for each share as time goes on; for this example, it demonstrates how to add a second column for the join.

```
SELECT s.Description,sp.Price,sp.PriceDate
  FROM ShareDetails.Shares s
  JOIN ShareDetails.SharePrices sp ON sp.ShareId = s.ShareId
    AND sp.Price < s.CurrentPrice
WHERE s.ShareId < 8
    AND sp.PriceDate BETWEEN '1 Jan 2012' AND '3 Jan 2012'
```

4. Execute the preceding code, which returns the rows shown in Figure 11-31. As you can see, an `INNER JOIN` is very straightforward.

	Description	Price	PriceDate
1	ACME'S HOMEBAKE COOKIES INC	1.14767	2012-01-02 17:16:40.410
2	ACME'S HOMEBAKE COOKIES INC	0.58554	2012-01-01 17:10:12.260
3	Lomas Ambulances	3.30950	2012-01-01 19:54:22.810
4	Lomas Ambulances	9.07787	2012-01-01 03:08:12.810
5	Brownies	6.27370	2012-01-02 08:07:50.240
6	Rolling Maulers	13.66410	2012-01-01 16:53:56.970

Figure 11-31. *Inner join with multiple join columns*

5. You can combine more than one table using multiple joins and with a mixture of join types. In the next example, a request has been made where, for each customer, all transactions that involved a share and the current price for that share are returned. This involves joining the `CustomerDetails.Customers` table to the `TransactionDetails.Transactions` table, and then joining with the `ShareDetails.Shares` table. From the customer table, you will retrieve the first and last names of the customer; you will retrieve the transaction ID and the transaction total amount from the transaction details table, and finally the share description and the current share price from the shares table. Enter the query details here, execute, and you should see the results, as shown in Figure 11-32.

```
SELECT c.FirstName,c.LastName,t.TransactionId,t.Amount,
  s.ShareId,s.Description, s.CurrentPrice
  FROM CustomerDetails.Customers c
  JOIN TransactionDetails.Transactions t ON t.CustomerId = c.CustomerId
  JOIN ShareDetails.Shares s ON s.ShareId = t.RelatedShareId
  JOIN ShareDetails.SharePrices sp ON sp.ShareId = s.ShareId
WHERE s.ShareId < 8
    AND sp.PriceDate BETWEEN '1 Jan 2012' AND '3 Jan 2012'
```

Results | Messages

	FirstName	LastName	TransactionId	Amount	ShareId	Description	CurrentPrice
1	Noel	Morgala	836	48033.07880	7	Rolling Maulers	16.66973
2	Jane	Harper	6	41124.61950	1	ACME'S HOMEBAKE COOKIES INC	2.34125
3	Jane	Harper	6	41124.61950	1	ACME'S HOMEBAKE COOKIES INC	2.34125
4	Jane	Harper	6	41124.61950	1	ACME'S HOMEBAKE COOKIES INC	2.34125
5	Anne	Mather	529	98415.51520	3	Lomas Ambulances	31.26386
6	Anne	Mather	529	98415.51520	3	Lomas Ambulances	31.26386
7	Keri	Steele	566	589.75340	5	Brownies	28.75828
8	Kristie	Baker	312	52038.03670	1	ACME'S HOMEBAKE COOKIES INC	2.34125
9	Kristie	Baker	312	52038.03670	1	ACME'S HOMEBAKE COOKIES INC	2.34125
10	Kristie	Baker	312	52038.03670	1	ACME'S HOMEBAKE COOKIES INC	2.34125
11	Alfred	Bright	354	78310.32720	7	Rolling Maulers	16.66973
12	Kisha	Strong	896	90673.21310	3	Lomas Ambulances	31.26386
13	Kisha	Strong	896	90673.21310	3	Lomas Ambulances	31.26386

Figure 11-32. *Multiple table join*

Joining Tables with an Outer Join

The next join to look at is an OUTER JOIN—more specifically, a LEFT OUTER JOIN. In this instance, I want to return all the rows in the left table, regardless of whether there is any data in the right table. The left table in this case is the ShareDetails.Shares table, as it is the left named table of the two I am concerned with.

1. Enter the following code:

```
SELECT s.ShareId,s.Description,sp.Price,sp.PriceDate
  FROM ShareDetails.Shares s
  LEFT OUTER JOIN ShareDetails.SharePrices sp ON sp.ShareId = s.ShareId
WHERE  sp.PriceDate IS NULL
```

2. Once you execute this code, you should see the "missing share," as shown in Figure 11-33. Where no data exist in the ShareDetails.SharePrices table, the values are displayed as NULL.

Results | Messages

	ShareId	Description	Price	PriceDate
1	20	Mackrel Fisheries	NULL	NULL

Figure 11-33. *Left outer join*

3. Similar to the earlier multiple table join, you can mix in another type of join. In the code here, you will see the code from the INNER JOIN example, but you also need to know where the share price is *not* being updated. This can be found by completing a LEFT OUTER JOIN on the ShareDetails.SharePrices, but listing only where the SharePrice was NULL. A NULL value from the LEFT OUTER JOIN will show that there is no SharePrice row, and therefore it will be evident that the system is possibly not collecting share prices. This is something that, as a business owner, you would need to be rectified so that you could provide the customers with an up-to-date valuation. Enter the following code:

```
SELECT c.FirstName,c.LastName,t.TransactionId,t.Amount,
 s.ShareId,s.Description, s.CurrentPrice,
 sp.Price
  FROM CustomerDetails.Customers c
  JOIN TransactionDetails.Transactions t
              ON t.CustomerId = c.CustomerId
  JOIN ShareDetails.Shares s
              ON s.ShareId = t.RelatedShareId
  LEFT OUTER JOIN ShareDetails.SharePrices sp
              ON sp.ShareId = s.ShareId
  WHERE sp.Price IS NULL
```

4. Execute the code, and you will see that there are only 13 rows returned, as shown in Figure 11-34.

	FirstName	LastName	TransactionId	Amount	ShareId	Description	CurrentPrice	Price
1	Kristie	Baker	37	49223.90500	20	Mackrel Fisheries	15.88709	NULL
2	Ruth	Mckinney	506	55396.69940	20	Mackrel Fisheries	15.88709	NULL
3	Salvatore	Duran	677	7528.76480	20	Mackrel Fisheries	15.88709	NULL
4	Alex	Drake	387	94025.65070	20	Mackrel Fisheries	15.88709	NULL
5	Pamela	Houston	799	99829.93290	20	Mackrel Fisheries	15.88709	NULL
6	Cheri	Stout	33	78037.58340	20	Mackrel Fisheries	15.88709	NULL
7	Shauna	Lyons	95	33887.67310	20	Mackrel Fisheries	15.88709	NULL
8	Alvin	Rice	349	51239.62120	20	Mackrel Fisheries	15.88709	NULL
9	Gerard	Hoffman	661	19938.09020	20	Mackrel Fisheries	15.88709	NULL
10	Rachelle	Rios	518	92322.03890	20	Mackrel Fisheries	15.88709	NULL
11	Cassie	Levine	54	38466.51640	20	Mackrel Fisheries	15.88709	NULL
12	Gustavo	Morales	689	36249.70190	20	Mackrel Fisheries	15.88709	NULL
13	Tabitha	Tyler	272	64409.98370	20	Mackrel Fisheries	15.88709	NULL

Figure 11-34. *Multiple joins with a left outer showing a NULL price*

The next example is a RIGHT OUTER JOIN. Here I expect the table on the right to return rows where there are no entries on the table in the left. In the example, such a scenario does not exist, as it would break referential integrity; however, I can swap the tables around, which shows the same results as the first LEFT OUTER JOIN example. Take note that you don't have to alter the column order after the ON, as it is the table definition that defines the left and right tables.

5. Enter the following code:

```
SELECT s.Description,sp.Price,sp.PriceDate
  FROM ShareDetails.SharePrices sp
  RIGHT OUTER JOIN ShareDetails.Shares s ON sp.ShareId = s.ShareId
WHERE sp.PriceDate BETWEEN '1 Jan 2012' and '3 Jan 2012'
```

6. Executing this code gives you the results shown in Figure 11-35.

	Description	Price	PriceDate
1	ACME'S HOMEBAKE COOKIES INC	1.14767	2012-01-02 17:16:40.410
2	ACME'S HOMEBAKE COOKIES INC	9.60484	2012-01-02 15:34:03.350
3	ACME'S HOMEBAKE COOKIES INC	0.58554	2012-01-01 17:10:12.260
4	ACME'S HOMEBAKE COOKIES INC	23.55766	2012-01-01 15:28:26.960
5	Lomas Ambulances	3.30950	2012-01-01 19:54:22.810
6	Lomas Ambulances	9.07787	2012-01-01 03:08:12.810
7	Brownies	6.27370	2012-01-02 08:07:50.240
8	Rolling Maulers	13.66410	2012-01-01 16:53:56.970
9	Julies Pantry	19.61463	2012-01-02 23:50:51.910
10	Julies Pantry	10.32724	2012-01-02 16:38:53.240
11	Julies Pantry	19.97779	2012-01-02 07:56:55.450
12	Julies Pantry	8.28476	2012-01-01 06:47:49.800
13	Airing Cadets	2.83170	2012-01-02 06:48:25.770
14	Apress	31.08431	2012-01-02 15:14:56.490
15	Apress	19.54028	2012-01-02 01:28:33.860
16	Frying Tonight	10.33017	2012-01-01 11:15:06.630
17	Squirrels Servers	5.82124	2012-01-01 22:24:47.400
18	Squirrels Servers	13.80892	2012-01-01 07:05:26.880
19	Fishy Friars	18.80808	2012-01-01 05:36:00.460

Figure 11-35. *Right outer join*

If you want a LEFT OUTER JOIN and a RIGHT OUTER JOIN to be available at the same time, then you need to choose the FULL OUTER JOIN. This returns rows from both the left and right tables if there are no matching rows in the other table. So, to clarify, if there is a row in the left table but no match in the right table, the row from the left table will be returned with NULL values in the columns from the right table, and vice versa. This time you are going to break referential integrity and insert a share price with no share. You will then delete the row to keep referential integrity intact.

7. Enter the following code:

```
SELECT s.Description,sp.Price,sp.PriceDate
  FROM ShareDetails.SharePrices sp
  FULL OUTER JOIN ShareDetails.Shares s ON sp.ShareId = s.ShareId
 WHERE s.Description IS NULL
    OR sp.Price IS NULL
```

8. Once the preceding code has been executed, you will see the results that appear in Figure 11-36. Notice that you have a row from the ShareDetails.Shares table when there is no share price, and vice versa.

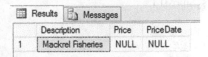

Figure 11-36. *Full outer join*

Working with a CROSS JOIN

The final demonstration is with a CROSS JOIN. This is a Cartesian join between the ShareDetails.Shares and ShareDetails.SharePrices tables. A CROSS JOIN cannot have any filtering on it; therefore, it cannot include a WHERE statement. As you are joining every row with every row, there is no need to provide an ON statement, because there is no specific row-on-row join. Due to the vast amount of data, to make it easier for you to scroll through I have put a TOP 4000 clause in the query and ordered the results by ShareId and SharePriceId. This will then allow you to see that for every SharePrice there are 1,000 share rows.

1. Enter the following code:

```
SELECT TOP 100 s.ShareId,sp.SharePriceId,
s.Description,sp.Price,sp.PriceDate
  FROM ShareDetails.SharePrices sp
  CROSS JOIN ShareDetails.Shares s
WHERE sp.PriceDate BETWEEN '1 Jan 2012' and '3 Jan 2012'
ORDER BY ShareId,SharePriceId
```

	ShareId	SharePriceId	Description	Price	PriceDate
1	1	35	Macrohard	1.14767	2012-01-02 17:16:40.410
2	1	36	Macrohard	9.60484	2012-01-02 15:34:03.350
3	1	37	Macrohard	0.58554	2012-01-01 17:10:12.260
4	1	91	Macrohard	23.55766	2012-01-01 15:28:26.960
5	1	133	Macrohard	3.30950	2012-01-01 19:54:22.810
6	1	134	Macrohard	9.07787	2012-01-01 03:08:12.810
7	1	236	Macrohard	6.27370	2012-01-02 08:07:50.240
8	1	339	Macrohard	13.66410	2012-01-01 16:53:56.970
9	1	479	Macrohard	19.61463	2012-01-02 23:50:51.910
10	1	480	Macrohard	10.32724	2012-01-02 16:38:53.240
11	1	481	Macrohard	19.97779	2012-01-02 07:56:55.450

Figure 11-37. *Cross join*

2. The preceding code, when executed, generates a large amount of output. Figure 11-37 shows only a snippet of the output.

It will be rare that you write a CROSS JOIN, and, given the dangerous nature of these joins, you should restrict the number of rows returned where possible. You should also ensure testing of any CROSS JOIN is completed on a test database prior to running against a production database instance.

Summary

This chapter has taken a look at how to retrieve data on a set of tables in the simplest form. Later in this book you will return to retrieving data with more complex language as well as work with data from more than one table within the single query. You should also be comfortable with getting information from tables using different searching, filtering, and ordering criteria.

Updating data can go wrong, and does, especially when you are working in a live environment and you wish to update data that is in flux. In such a scenario, getting the correct rows of information to update and then actually updating them is akin to a fine art.

Therefore, surrounding any of your work with a transaction will prevent any costly and potentially irreversible mistakes from taking place, so always surround data modifications or deletions with a transaction. With data inserts, it is not quite so critical that you surround your work with a transaction, although it is still recommended. For example, if you are inserting data within a test environment and the data insertion is easily removed if you have part of the insertion wrong, then perhaps it's not overly critical to use a transaction. However, to be safe, really and truly, I still recommend that you use a transaction.

Updating columns within a table is very straightforward. As long as the data type defined for the column being updated is the same as, or is compatible with, the data type of the column, variable, or static value that is being used to update this column, then you will have no problem. For example, you can update a varchar column with char data type values. However, it is not possible to update an integer column with a varchar value that has a noninteger value without converting the varchar value to an integer. But don't be fooled, you can update a varchar with an integer or numeric data type.

Finally you saw how to join two or more tables and the different methods you can use to achieve the desired results. Joining tables will become a staple of your coding diet, and, although only SELECT statements were demonstrated with joins, you can use the same techniques for DELETE and UPDATE. For these statements, you would use the joins to either create the ability to filter the data or to return values for updating the data. You will see more about joins throughout this book.

So, where can you go from here? The next chapter will look at views of data.

■ ■ ■

Working with In-Memory Tables

In Chapter 7 you were introduced to how to build an in-memory table and the choice of either using schema-only storage or also storing the data on disk. The aim of this chapter is to move forward and look at how to work with that data outside of stored procedures, as well as at the performance improvements in-memory-based data can provide. You will also see how in-memory tables use a concurrency model that tries to ensure that processes work as quickly as possible. You'll look at the overheads this model provides and compare it to a model that locks data so that only one process can work with a row of data. You will also look at how to merge data from a source location to a target location.

In this chapter you will be looking at

- The INSERT, UPDATE, DELETE, and SELECT statements

- Locking of data within tables for disk-based and in-memory-based tables

- What happens when two processes try to modify the same row of data

- The five different types of isolation levels and how data being modified is read in each type

- Speed comparison between disk-based, SCHEMA_AND_DATA, and SCHEMA_ONLY tables

- How to merge data from a source table in to a target table

- Unsupported functionality

Now it's time to get started and look at DML-based statements.

INSERT, UPDATE, DELETE, and SELECT Statements

The most efficient way to work with in-memory tables is to execute natively compiled code. Natively compiled code is found in stored procedures that only access in-memory tables, and you will see this in action in Chapter 15. However, you can still access in-memory tables using ad-hoc T-SQL statements, which will have the benefits that come from holding the data within memory along with other in-memory table benefits. Ad-hoc T-SQL statements are INSERT, UPDATE, DELETE, and SELECT DML statements executed within a query editor within SSMS; DML statements executed from code within a program such as .NET, Java, or Excel; or any DML statements executed within tools such as SQL Server Integration Services, to name a few examples of where DML can reside.

It is possible to execute T-SQL statements that are defined to execute against both in-memory and disk-based tables in just one statement, although performance will be impacted to match that of the slowest component. In other words, if the data from the disk-based table has to be read from disk, as it is not being read for data retained in memory, then performance will be impacted while reading the data from disk. Similarly, when writing data, if the data is disk based, this will be the slowest component. There is a caveat for in-memory tables though. If you have a SCHEMA_AND_DATA-based in-memory table that is being modified, then any data modification will have a performance gain resulting from the difference in locking from a disk-based table. However, there will still be disk I/O involved, as the data will be saved to disk. SCHEMA_ONLY-based tables will be the fastest tables for data modifications, as there is no disk element for writing to disk, although there would be transaction-log I/O for both types of in-memory tables.

I will come back to this subject shortly, but before I can demonstrate any speed differences and more on how you interact with in-memory tables, it is necessary to discuss locking and isolation levels.

Locking and Isolation Levels

It is necessary for a developer to know how their code interacts with data and the database when other code that is also interacting is executing. You need to know what will happen when one process is writing data while another is reading or writing data within the same table. It is also necessary to know if one process is going to wait for another process to complete some or all of its task. For example, if you have a process reading from the CustomerDetails. Customers table and another process altering rows within that table, you need to know what your process is going to do. Will it read the updated data? Will it wait until the process altering the data completes? These questions can be answered based on the isolation level used. One question that cannot be answered is whether a locked transaction will time out and fail, as that will come from a parameter called querytimeout.

By default SQL Server adopts a pessimistic locking model for disk-based tables. What this means is that processes writing data will stop (block) processes reading data, and processes reading data will block processes writing data. This may sound very restrictive, and you are probably wondering how you can have many processes running at the same time against data, but it works well and has advantages over optimistic locking, which will be discussed in a moment. Pessimistic locks should be held by your code for a very short period of time for several reasons, from fast and efficient processes acquiring and releasing locks through to processes waiting for that lock to be released. To put this sentence into practice, when working with data you need to make your code as efficient as possible while working with the data in as minimal and speed-efficient a manner as you can. You achieve this by writing queries that identify the rows of data to work with as quickly as possible through joins and WHERE clauses and through the use of indexes. Achieving efficient code comes through knowledge and practice.

Pessimistic locking does mean that the data you start your process with can be guaranteed to be what is expected at the end; you know that another process has not altered the expected result while your process is running (unless you specifically tell your query or session that you wish to work with modified data, which you can do and will see within the chapter). While locks are acquired and released and other processes wait on the locks being released, delays and performance issues result.

In-memory tables take a different approach and adopt an optimistic locking model, which means that locks are almost non-existent and really only exist when writing to the transaction log. An optimistic locking model achieves the ACID consistency via a technique called row versioning, which I mentioned in Chapter 7. This technique is where every modification creates a new version of a row, and the previous versions are also kept as part of the table data. This allows for reads to happen to a row of data even if another transaction is modifying the same row, as the read operation will be able to take the data from the correctly timestamped committed version of the row. So, by using optimistic locking, also known as optimistic concurrency, read operations will be faster.

Writing operations are also not required to wait for an exclusive (X) lock on the row, page, or table of data as the writing operation is simply creating a new row version. However, if you have two transactions trying to modify the same row, SQL Server will roll back all but one of transactions so that one update succeeds. Figure 12-1 demonstrates a flow update of a table's row versioning and adds perspective to the discussion. Table A starts with 1 row and therefore is known as version 1. An UPDATE then occurs, generating row version 2. Three simultaneous transactions try to access Row 1 at the same time. All three transactions will read Row 1 and retrieve that data. However, only one will succeed with its update. Although the figure demonstrates the first transaction as being the successful transaction and generating row version 3, it could be any of the transactions. SQL Server decides which are the best processes to kill based on information about the transactions.

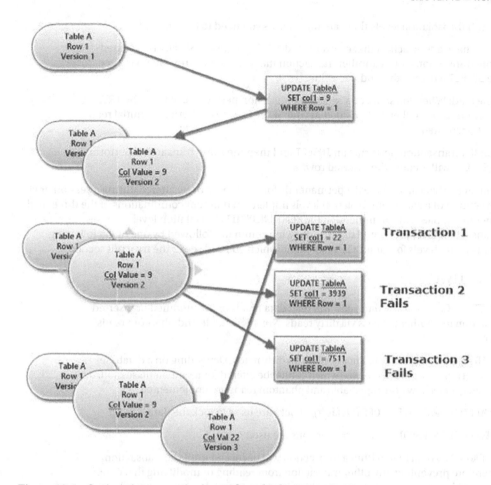

Figure 12-1. *Optimistic row versioning with multiple transactions*

You are therefore wondering why optimistic concurrency is not used in all scenarios with the locking benefits. The overhead with optimistic concurrency is the requirement to hold the row versions, as well as a higher risk—albeit that risk could be rare—of modification failures. If you have highly modified data through UPDATEs to the same row then there will be a number of versions held. Each version not only requires storage in either disk or within memory but there is also an overhead when reading optimistic data, as searches will also include looking at the row versions.

■ **Note** For in-memory tables, when there are 16 row versions (known as deltas), and when the 17th delta is to be added, data is consolidated and to reduce the number of deltas, therefore reducing the required space.

Before I take you through the isolation levels there are three terms you need to understand:

- Dirty read: If you have a transaction that executes an UPDATE and then a SELECT is executed within the same transaction—or in another transaction that will read the row that has been updated—the SELECT will read the updated value.

- Non-repeatable read: When the same or a separate transaction performs a DELETE, INSERT, or UPDATE that alters a row to then be included in your SELECT's WHERE criteria, the initial read cannot be exactly repeated.

- Phantom read: If a transaction performs an INSERT and then the same transaction performs a SELECT, the SELECT will include the inserted row.

There are five isolation levels that can either exist permanently for a database or be altered during a session or via locking hints during the execution of a statement. Isolation levels implement different combinations of the three read levels just described. In-memory tables cannot implement the READ UNCOMMITTED isolation level.

To define a session transaction level you would use the following command followed by one of the following options. You can define transaction levels for tables via a table hint, which you will see in the try it out section:

SET TRANSACTION ISOLATION LEVEL

- READ UNCOMMITTED – Can read any data, and will read data that is being modified or inserted within a transaction in another process via dirty reads. Non-repeatable and phantom reads will also occur.

- READ COMMITTED – SQL Server default. There will be no dirty reads. Depending on a database-level setting concerning snapshot isolation (which cannot be altered for a statement, session, or locking hint), determines how non-repeatable and phantom reads are implemented.

 - READ_COMMITTED_SNAPSHOT – OFF (Default) – Locks are used to lock the data

 - READ_COMMITTED_SNAPSHOT – ON – Row versions are used

- REPEATABLE READ – Any data read within a transaction will be locked until the transaction completes, therefore preventing any other transaction from reading or modifying that data. Data can be inserted by other transactions, resulting in phantom reads. Non-repeatable reads will not occur.

- SNAPSHOT – No dirty, non-repeatable, or phantom reads. Data modified within a transaction will be read as it was stored prior to the transaction committing. This isolation level, in essence, takes a logical snapshot of the tables prior to execution at the start of each transaction.

- SERIALIZABLE – Rarely used. No dirty, non-repeatable, or phantom reads are allowed. Within a transaction, at the start, the data that will be used within the transaction will be locked so that no other transaction can access or modify the data until it completes.

In-memory tables can have only three of these transaction levels due to optimistic concurrency—repeatable read, snapshot, and serializable—although all three will guarantee the read committed snapshot isolation level. This means that when working with in-memory tables only the rows that existed at the time the transaction started will be available to be read. If you only require when working with in-memory tables that you don't need repeatable reads or phantom reads, then when available use SNAPSHOT isolation. SNAPSHOT isolation is less resource intensive and therefore will aid performance.

Taking you back for a moment to the first section in this chapter concerning DML statements and in-memory tables, it is necessary when working with in-memory tables to define a table-locking hint within the query. This requirement means that when defining a table L you have to suffix the definition with a WITH (*locking_hint*), such as WITH (SNAPSHOT).

Now that you have an overview of how concurrency works with transaction levels in SQL Server, it's time to see them in action with the TransactionDetails.Transactions in-memory table.

TRY IT OUT: ISOLATION LEVELS

1. Open up two Query Editor windows and ensure they are connected to the ApressFinancial database. Each query window will have a transaction, and when executing the following code you will be running part of the transaction.

2. In the first query window enter the following code and execute. *This will keep an open transaction and should NOT be done except in controlled circumstances, and definitely should not be done in production.*

```
SET TRANSACTION ISOLATION LEVEL READ COMMITTED
GO
begin tran
-- will return 48033.07880
SELECT CustomerId, TransactionId, Amount
  FROM TransactionDetails.Transactions
  WITH (SNAPSHOT)
  WHERE CustomerId = 1
    AND TransactionId = 836

UPDATE TransactionDetails.Transactions WITH (SNAPSHOT)
  SET Amount = 234.56
  WHERE CustomerId = 1
    AND TransactionId = 836

-- will return 234.56
SELECT CustomerId, TransactionId, Amount
  FROM TransactionDetails.Transactions
  WITH (SNAPSHOT)
  WHERE CustomerId = 1
    AND TransactionId = 836
```

3. You should see an output of two results as shown in Figure 12-2. Within this transaction the value has been altered.

Figure 12-2. *Transaction 1 showing the update in-flight*

4. In the second query window enter the following code. This will return the non-dirty, repeatable, non-phantom row.

```
-- will return 48033.07880
SELECT CustomerId, TransactionId, Amount
  FROM TransactionDetails.Transactions
  WITH (SNAPSHOT)
 WHERE CustomerId = 1
   AND TransactionId = 836
```

5. Once the code is executed, you should see the original value, as shown in Figure 12-3.

	CustomerId	TransactionId	Amount
1	1	836	48033.07880

Figure 12-3. *The original row-version value*

6. Now complete the first transaction and perform a rollback, checking that the value is back as it was.

```
rollback tran
-- will return 48033.07880
SELECT CustomerId, TransactionId, Amount
  FROM TransactionDetails.Transactions
  WITH (SNAPSHOT)
 WHERE CustomerId = 1
   AND TransactionId = 836
```

7. Now, to demonstrate that SNAPSHOT will not read any phantom rows, alter the UPDATE query to be an INSERT. Enter all the code but don't execute any at this point. You will need two query windows.

8. The first query will look for the inserted row.

9. The second query will insert the row and demonstrate its existence.

10. In the first query, execute up to the comment STOP HERE.

```
SET TRANSACTION ISOLATION LEVEL READ COMMITTED
GO
begin tran
-- will return no row
SELECT CustomerId, TransactionId, Amount
  FROM TransactionDetails.Transactions
  WITH (SNAPSHOT)
 WHERE CustomerId = 1
   AND Amount = 101.32

-- STOP HERE
-- STOP HERE
```

11. Now execute the second query up to the comment STOP HERE. This will show that the row doesn't exist; it will then INSERT the row and show that the row now exists. The output will be shown in Figure 12-4.

```
SET TRANSACTION ISOLATION LEVEL READ COMMITTED
GO
begin tran

INSERT INTO TransactionDetails.Transactions
(CustomerId, TransactionType, DateEntered, Amount,RelatedProductId)
VALUES(1,1,GETDATE(),101.32,1)

SELECT CustomerId, TransactionId, Amount
  FROM TransactionDetails.Transactions
  WITH (SNAPSHOT)
 WHERE CustomerId = 1
   AND Amount = 101.32

-- STOP HERE
-- STOP HERE
```

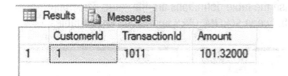

	CustomerId	TransactionId	Amount
1	1	1011	101.32000

Figure 12-4. The row has been inserted and is showing in transaction 2

12. Now return to the first query and run the SELECT statement again. Because the transaction has started, and because for in-memory tables READ COMMITTED means READ COMMITTED SNAPSHOT (and therefore there is no locking), the row will still not be showing.

```
-- will return no row
SELECT CustomerId, TransactionId, Amount
  FROM TransactionDetails.Transactions
  WITH (SNAPSHOT)
 WHERE CustomerId = 1
   AND Amount = 101.32

ROLLBACK TRAN
```

13. Finally, in the second transaction complete the code with a ROLLBACK TRAN.

```
rollback tran
```

You can change the example to execute against the disk-based TransactionDetails.Transactions_old table. What you will find is that in the first query with the UPDATE statement, the query performs the SELECT when the UPDATE transaction is still in flight. When you reach step 4, this query will hang until you receive a query timeout, until you cancel the query, or until you perform a ROLLBACK TRAN or COMMIT TRAN in the first query. This demonstrates the difference between optimistic and pessimistic locking, as the database for disk based will be defined as a default of READ COMMITTED SNAPSHOT OFF.

You will see more on isolation levels in Chapter 15, when you will see in-memory stored procedures demonstrated. I mentioned that I would take a look at performance differences between in-memory and disk-based tables. In the following example, it is an unscientific but useful method that demonstrates the speed differences between disk-based and in-memory operations. I say *unscientific* as this is a very clean situation with only one process running on very small amounts of data and no contention.

The example takes the in-memory and disk-based tables TransactionDetails.Transactions and TransactionDetails.Transactions_old and creates three new clean and empty tables. One is in-memory SCHEMA_ONLY, one is in-memory SCHEMA_AND_DATA, and one is disk based. The indexes differ for this example from the original table definitions because of the speed of inserts; due to the speed that row inserts will occur you cannot get uniqueness on the date and time easily. Otherwise the table definitions are the same. The main point to note in the following example is the speed differences between SCHEMA_ONLY and the other two tables. I would like to demonstrate before I discuss the results.

TRY IT OUT: SPEED TEST OF TABLES

1. First of all, create the three tables and indexes. Enter the code and execute.

```
CREATE TABLE [TransactionDetails].[Transactions_SCHEMAONLY]
(
    [TransactionId] [int] IDENTITY(1,1) NOT NULL,
    [CustomerId] [int] NOT NULL,
    [TransactionType] [smallint] NOT NULL,
    [DateEntered] [datetime] NOT NULL,
    [Amount] [numeric](18, 5) NOT NULL,
    [ReferenceDetails] [nvarchar](50)
        COLLATE Latin1_General_CI_AS NULL,
    [Notes] [varchar](4000) COLLATE Latin1_General_CI_AS NULL,
    [RelatedShareId] [int] NULL,
    [RelatedProductId] [int] NOT NULL,
        CONSTRAINT [TransactionsSCHEMAONLY_primaryKey]
            PRIMARY KEY NONCLUSTERED
(
    [TransactionId] ASC
)
```

```
) WITH ( MEMORY_OPTIMIZED = ON , DURABILITY = SCHEMA_ONLY )
GO
CREATE TABLE [TransactionDetails].[Transactions_SCHEMADATA]
(
    [TransactionId] [int] IDENTITY(1,1) NOT NULL,
    [CustomerId] [int] NOT NULL,
    [TransactionType] [smallint] NOT NULL,
    [DateEntered] [datetime] NOT NULL,
    [Amount] [numeric](18, 5) NOT NULL,
    [ReferenceDetails] [nvarchar](50)
        COLLATE Latin1_General_CI_AS NULL,
    [Notes] [varchar](4000) COLLATE Latin1_General_CI_AS NULL,
    [RelatedShareId] [int] NULL,
    [RelatedProductId] [int] NOT NULL,
      CONSTRAINT [TransactionsSCHEMADATA_primaryKey]
      PRIMARY KEY NONCLUSTERED
(
    [TransactionId] ASC
)
) WITH ( MEMORY_OPTIMIZED = ON , DURABILITY = SCHEMA_AND_DATA )
GO
CREATE TABLE [TransactionDetails].[Transactions_DiskBased](
    [TransactionId] [int] IDENTITY(1,1) NOT NULL,
    [CustomerId] [int] NOT NULL,
    [TransactionType] [smallint] NOT NULL,
    [DateEntered] [datetime] NOT NULL,
    [Amount] [numeric](18, 5) NOT NULL,
    [ReferenceDetails] [nvarchar](50) NULL,
    [Notes] [varchar](4000) NULL,
    [RelatedShareId] [int] NULL,
    [RelatedProductId] [int] NOT NULL)
GO
CREATE NONCLUSTERED INDEX IX_Transactions_DiskBased
ON TransactionDetails.Transactions_DiskBased
    (
    TransactionId
    ) WITH( STATISTICS_NORECOMPUTE = OFF, IGNORE_DUP_KEY = OFF,
     ALLOW_ROW_LOCKS = ON, ALLOW_PAGE_LOCKS = ON) ON [PRIMARY]
GO
```

2. The next step is to speed test all three tables as an INSERT. There will be 100,000 rows of data with the same values entered. This is achieved by placing a number after the GO statement.

3. The first run will be to insert data into the disk-based tables using INSERT. Once the code is entered, execute it. It will display two rows of two times.

■ **Note** The example inserts 100,000 rows. Whether you should reduce this down to a smaller number (like 10,000) will depend on several factors. I have a fast computer, hence the large number.

```
SELECT GETDATE()
GO
INSERT INTO TransactionDetails.Transactions_DiskBased
(CustomerId, TransactionType, DateEntered, Amount,
    RelatedProductId)
VALUES (1,1,'2014-11-05 23:22:11',100,1)
GO 100000
SELECT GETDATE()
GO
```

4. Figure 12-5 shows the times required for disk-based inserts, which in my system was 2 minutes 16 seconds.

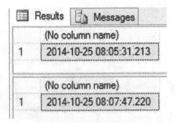

Figure 12-5. *Disk-based timings*

5. The next test I ran was the SCHEMA_AND_DATA INSERT. In this instance it took 50 seconds.

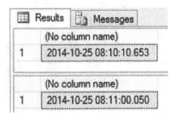

Figure 12-6. *SCHEMA_AND_DATA-based timings*

6. The final test is for SCHEMA_ONLY. This final test flew and only took 21 seconds.

Figure 12-7. *SCHEMA_ONLY-based timings*

7. The next test is to use SELECT on the data to check speeds of data retrievals. These results are from my machine, and of course your timings may differ. This test will return multiple results sets, so to see the data you will have to scroll the results-set grids' scrollbar rather than the inner results' scroll bar. The code is below; once entered, execute it.

```
SELECT 'Disk Based',GETDATE()
GO
SELECT * FROM TransactionDetails.Transactions_DiskBased
order by dateentered
GO
SELECT 'SCHEMA_AND_DATA',GETDATE()
GO
SELECT * FROM TransactionDetails.Transactions_SCHEMADATA
order by dateentered
GO
SELECT 'SCHEMA_ONLY Based',GETDATE()
GO
SELECT * FROM TransactionDetails.Transactions_SCHEMAONLY
order by dateentered
GO
SELECT 'Final',GETDATE()
GO
```

8. The results from the SELECT statement on my machine are below in Figure 11-8.

	(No column name)	(No column name)		
1	Disk Based	2014-10-25 12:34:06.193		

	TransactionId	CustomerId	TransactionType	DateEntered
1	10945	1	1	2014-11-05 23:22:11.000
2	10946	1	1	2014-11-05 23:22:11.000

	(No column name)	(No column name)		
1	SCHEMA_AND_DATA	2014-10-25 12:34:10.103		

	TransactionId	CustomerId	TransactionType	DateEntered
1	1	1	1	2014-11-05 23:22:11.000
2	2	1	1	2014-11-05 23:22:11.000

	(No column name)	(No column name)		
1	SCHEMA_ONLY Based	2014-10-25 12:34:13.277		

	TransactionId	CustomerId	TransactionType	DateEntered
1	1	1	1	2014-10-25 08:38:37.697
2	2	1	1	2014-10-25 08:38:37.700

	(No column name)	(No column name)		
1	Final	2014-10-25 12:34:15.900		

Figure 12-8. *SELECT statement timing*

The timings you see will be different and will be based on a number of factors, just as they will be in production. However, they do prove the point that disk based Is slower, followed by the faster SCHEMA_AND_DATA, with the fastest being SCHEMA_ONLY. You may find in some of your tests that disk-based and SCHEMA_AND_DATA have similar timings, especially on small amounts of data and on a system that has only one process running. As mentioned within this chapter, the concurrency model will define larger differences in speed as well as other factors, such as the pressures on the database system as a whole and its resources. Another thing to note is that the SQL is interpreted rather than natively compiled, which also has a speed-performance impact. Natively compiled code will be discussed in Chapter 15.

The final area that I want to look at in this chapter is the MERGE statement and disk- and in-memory-based tables.

MERGE Statement

When you have a table that could have an INSERT, UPDATE, or DELETE statement based on data from a source table, you can combine them into one statement called a MERGE rather than having three different statements—one statement dealing with each scenario. The MERGE allows you to join the data from the source table with the target table and, based on whether there is a match or not, allows you to perform an INSERT, UPDATE, or a DELETE. You can further refine the action based on more filtering, if required. The basics of a MERGE statement are:

```
MERGE [INTO] target_table [[AS] alias]
USING <source_table>
ON <matching_search_criteria>
[WHEN MATCHED [AND <clause_search>] THEN <statement_actions>]
[WHEN NOT MATCHED [AND TARGET] [AND <clause_search>] THEN <statement_actions>]
[WHEN NOT MATCHED [AND SOURCE] [AND <clause_search>] THEN <statement_actions>]
```

■ **Note** The MERGE statement has to end with a semicolon ;

The target table can be any disk-based table; however, the source table can be disk or in-memory based. It is not possible to use a MERGE statement to add data to in-memory tables. The ON criteria is the same as when performing a JOIN between two tables, as that is what is happening within the MERGE. There is no concept of INNER or OUTER JOIN, as MERGE exists with the WHEN MATCHED and WHEN NOT MATCHED conditions, and MATCHED is similar to an INNER JOIN and WHEN NOT MATCHED is similar to an OUTER JOIN. The statement actions are where you indicate what happens when the matching conditions are met. This will be an INSERT, UPDATE, or DELETE. A MERGE is best understood within an example, and the following one will create a row that is a known row that doesn't exist within the TranactionDetails.Transactions_old table. This will be within a transaction that is rolled back so that you can try other scenarios.

TRY IT OUT: MERGE STATEMENT

1. The code in this example is defined over several steps and is explained at each logical point. Step 9 will execute the code. First of all, start the transaction and insert the row that will be merged into the source table. This will demonstrate the MERGE WHEN NOT MATCHED.

    ```
    BEGIN TRAN

    INSERT INTO TransactionDetails.Transactions
    (CustomerId, TransactionType, DateEntered, Amount, RelatedShareId,RelatedProductId)
    values (1,1,GETDATE(),1876.11,1,1)
    ```

2. Now do a SELECT on the table that will be the target table to show the transactions that currently exist; therefore, the results will be without the new row. Your data may differ from the data below, but in essence the row above won't exist.

    ```
    SELECT TransactionId, CustomerId, Amount
      FROM TransactionDetails.Transactions_old
     WHERE CustomerId = 1
    ```

3. Once the code is executed, one sees the rows found in Figure 12-9. There is no transaction with an amount for 1876.11.

	TransactionId	CustomerId	Amount
1	509	1	62521.51010
2	836	1	48033.07880
3	1014	1	100.00000
4	1015	1	75.67000
5	1016	1	35.20000
6	1017	1	20.00000

Figure 12-9. *The existing transactions in the table*

4. The next step is the MERGE statement. First, define the table you are merging into. I have given it an alias of target for ease of identification.

    ```
    MERGE INTO TransactionDetails.Transactions_old target
    ```

5. Then define the source table. This is the in-memory table, which has to have the isolation level defined. The code also defines the join to get unique rows.

    ```
    USING TransactionDetails.Transactions source WITH (SNAPSHOT)
      ON (target.CustomerId = source.CustomerId
     AND target.TransactionId = source.TransactionId)
    ```

6. If the row is matched, update the amount value. In this exercise there will be no row found, and so the statement won't be executed; however, you can alter the example so that the source table does give a match.

```
WHEN MATCHED THEN
    UPDATE
        SET target.Amount = source.Amount
```

7. When not matched, insert the new row from the source table to the target table. This is the statement that will be executed:

```
WHEN NOT MATCHED THEN
        INSERT (CustomerId, TransactionType,
                DateEntered,Amount,
                        RelatedShareId,
                        RelatedProductId)
        VALUES (source.CustomerId, source.TransactionType,
                source.DateEntered, source.Amount,
                source.RelatedShareId,
                        COALESCE(source.RelatedProductId,1))
```

8. Finally, SELECT from the target table to show the new row inserted:

```
SELECT TransactionId, CustomerId, Amount
  FROM TransactionDetails.Transactions_old
 WHERE CustomerId = 1

ROLLBACK TRAN
```

9. Now execute the whole code and you will see that the new row did not exist in Figure 12-9 earlier, and that after the MERGE it does exist, as you can see in Figure 12-10 with transaction id 1047. As mentioned, your data may differ from the figure, but the main point is that the new row exists.

	TransactionId	CustomerId	Amount
1	509	1	62521.51010
2	836	1	48033.07880
3	1047	1	1876.11000
4	1014	1	100.00000
5	1015	1	75.67000
6	1016	1	35.20000
7	1017	1	20.00000

Figure 12-10. The row has been inserted and is showing in the SELECT

In-Memory Table Unsupported Functionality

Not all T-SQL statements and commands are supported within interpreted SQL against an in-memory table. As mentioned in Chapter 7 and discussed further in this chapter, how data is stored within an in-memory table differs from how it is done in a disk-based table, and the data is not replaced but rather a new version of a row is created. When a TRUNCATE TABLE statement is executed, SQL Server marks pages of data for deletion as a fast method of removing the data. In-memory tables don't hold data within pages and therefore this is not possible. If you require a transient table then you could use a SCHEMA_ONLY defined table, which instead of having a TRUNCATE TABLE statement executed, is dropped and recreated.

In Chapter 17 you will look at functionality where, instead of working with data in a set-based fashion, you will work a row at a time using functionality called *cursors*. Cursors can hold their data staticly in such a way that when the cursor is opened the data held within the cursor will not alter even if the underlying data in the tables alter. Cursors can have a dynamic set of data, however, where, when the underlying data alters, the data in the cursor will also change. Yet, dynamic or keyset cursors (a *keyset cursor* is where non-key data within the cursor can change, but not the data within the defined key) are not available, and if a dynamic or keyset cursor is defined where an in-memory table is part of the cursor, then the cursor will become a static cursor. This is an important note when migrating a disk-based table to an in-memory table and you have cursors, as you may find a functionality change to your system.

T-SQL is developed to work with data, and the commands and statements are designed as such. Sometimes, though, you need to extend that functionality by building specific functions or procedures that perform a lot more complex tasks than T-SQL allows. To achieve this you can write .NET-based functionality known as CLR (common language runtime) Modules; this functionality is available to in-memory tables, but you can not use the context connection. A context connection is when the .NET CLR module executes in the same connection as the SQL Server function that calls it.

Finally, in Chapter 13 you will be introduced to a concept of a view. A *view* is where an object is created that accesses one or more underlying tables to generate a set of columns from the table objects. Views can be indexed, but if you have an indexed view then the tables included in the view definition cannot be in-memory optimized.

Summary

In this chapter you have seen how you can write ad-hoc DML statements against in-memory tables. These are interpreted at run time and are therefore not as efficient as natively compiled code; however, there are still performance gains to be had with in-memory. Performance gains come from the type of concurrency model that in-memory uses, and although optimistic can give performance gains, it also has performance considerations.

A simple test demonstrated the speed differences between disk-based and in-memory-based tables and also how SCHEMA_ONLY can provide quick, significant gains. The final example demonstrated how to merge data from a source table into a target table and how you can insert, update, or delete data based on whether there was a match between the data in the source table and that in the target table.

CHAPTER 13

■ ■ ■

Building a View

A *view* is a virtual table that, in itself, doesn't contain any data or information. All it contains is the query that the user defines when creating the view. A view is a named query that can be used against one or more tables. Views are used as a security measure by restricting users to accessing only certain columns or rows from an underlying table, as a method of joining data from multiple tables and presenting it as if that data resided in one table, and as a method of returning summary data instead of detailed data.

Views can also be used to provide a method of accessing the underlying data in a manner that provides the end user with a business-ready layout. For example, you will see within this chapter the building of a view that shows customer details along with enriched transaction details, thus making it easier for anyone interrogating your data, even someone who has no knowledge of the underlying data model, to access useful information.

Building a simple view is a straightforward process and can be completed in SQL Server Management Studio or in a Query Editor pane using T-SQL within SQL Server. Each of these tools has two options to build a view, and this chapter covers all four options so that you will become comfortable with building a view, no matter which tool is currently at hand.

To give things a bit more bite in this chapter, I'll also demonstrate a query within a query, known as a subquery, along with how to create a subquery that will create a column in a result set.

Finally, having an index on a view can speed up data retrieval, but it can also create performance problems, just as indexes on tables can create performance problems. Building an index on a view is not quite as straightforward as building an index on a table.

The aim of this chapter is to:

- Make you aware of what a view is

- Inform you as to how views can improve a database's security

- Show how to encrypt your view so that the source tables accessed cannot be seen

- Demonstrate building a view using

 - Management Studio View Designer

 - An existing view

 - A Query Editor pane and T-SQL

- Show how to join two tables within a view

- Demonstrate subqueries within a view

- Build an index on a view and give the reasons you would or would not do this

Why a View?

There will be times when you'll want to group together data from more than one table, or perhaps allow users to see only specific information from a particular table, where some of the columns may contain sensitive or even irrelevant data. A view can take one or more columns from one or more tables and present this information to a user, without the user accessing the actual underlying tables. A view protects the data layer while allowing access to the necessary data. All of these scenarios can be seen as the basis and reason for building a view rather than using another method of data extraction. Views are similar to queries in Microsoft Access. Because a view represents data as if it were another table—a virtual table, in fact—it is also possible to create a view of a view.

Let's take a look at how a view works. In our example, there is a customer table that holds information about your customers, such as their first names, last names, account numbers, and balances. There will be times when you'll want your users to have access to only the first and last names, but not to the other sensitive data. This is where a view comes into play. You would create a view that returns only a customer's first and last name but no other information, hiding from sight his or her financially sensitive data.

Creating a view can give a user enough information to satisfy a query he or she may have about data within a database without that user having to know any T-SQL commands. A view actually stores the query that creates it, and when you execute the view, the underlying query is the code that is being executed. The underlying code can be as complex as required, but the view leaves the end user with a simple SELECT * statement to run with perhaps a small amount of filtering via a simple WHERE clause. Similar to retrieving data from a table, you should name your columns as you would like to see them to be returned from the view and not use the SELECT * format to return all columns.

Using a view, in addition to retrieving data, you can also modify the data that are being displayed, delete data, and in some situations, insert new data. There are several rules and limitations for deleting, modifying, and inserting data from multitable views, some of which will be covered in the "Indexing a View" section later in this chapter.

However, a view is not a tool for processing data like a stored procedure is. A view is able to hold only one query at a time. Therefore, a view is more like a query than a stored procedure. With views, you can include tables from databases that are running on different servers just as you can with stored procedures or queries within Query Editor. Providing the user ID has the necessary security credentials, it is possible to include tables from several databases.

So to summarize, a view is a virtual table created by a stored SQL statement that can span multiple tables. Views can be used as a method of security within your database, and they provide a simpler front end to a user querying the data.

Later in the chapter, you will see how to build a view and how all of these ideas are put into practice. Before we get to that, let's look in more depth at how a view can be used as a security vehicle

■ **Note** When there is frequently more than one table to retrieve data from, creating a view is quite often a sensible solution, even more so when you want to use views as a method of simplifying the database schema and abstracting the database data into a presentation layer for users.

Using Views for Security

Security is always an issue when building your database. So far, this book has covered the different database-provided roles, when to use them, how to set up different types of roles, and how useful they are. By restricting all users from accessing or modifying the data directly in the tables, you will then force everyone to use views and stored procedures to complete any data task. (There will be more on stored procedures in the next chapter.)

However, by taking a view on the data and assigning which role can have select access, update access, and so on, you are protecting not only the underlying tables, but also particular columns of data. This is all covered in the discussions involving security in this chapter, along with how to lock down direct access to the tables.

Security encompasses not only the protection of data, but also the protection of your system. At some point as a developer, you will build a view and then someone else will come along and remove or alter a column from an underlying table that was used in the view. This causes problems; however, this chapter will show you how to get around this problem and secure the build of a view so that this sort of thing doesn't happen.

Imagine that you have a table holding specific security-sensitive information alongside general information—an example would be where you perhaps work for the licensing agency for driver's licenses, and alongside the name and address, there is a column to define the number of fines that have had to be paid. As you can see, this is information that should not be viewed by all employees within the organization. So, what do you do?

The simplest answer is to create a view on the data where you exclude the columns holding the sensitive data. In this way, you can restrict access on the table to the bare minimum of roles or logins, and leave either a view or a stored procedure as the only method of data retrieval allowed. Thus, the information returned is restricted to only those columns that a general user is allowed to see.

It is also possible to place a WHERE clause within a view to restrict the rows returned. This could be useful when you don't wish all employee salaries to be listed; perhaps excluding the salaries of the top executives would be advised!

All of these methods give you, as a developer, a way of protecting the physical data in the base tables behind the views. Combine this with what you learned about roles and restricting table access, and you can really tighten the security surrounding your data. With more and more companies embracing initiatives like Sarbanes-Oxley, where security should be so tight a company can be defined as having secure data, views are a great method of moving toward this goal.

Another method of securing views is to encrypt the view definition, which we will explore next.

Encrypting View Definitions

As well as restricting access to certain tables or columns within a database, views also give you the option of encrypting the SQL query that is used to retrieve the data. Once a view is built and you are sure that it is functioning correctly, you would release that view to production; it is at this point that you would add the final area of security— you would encrypt the view.

The most common situation in which you will find views encrypted is when the information returned by the view is of a privileged nature. To expand further, not only are you using a view to return specific information, but also you don't wish anyone to see how that information was returned, for whatever reason. You would therefore encrypt the SQL code that makes up the view, which would mean that how the information was being returned would not be visible.

There is a downside to encrypting a view: once the process of encryption is completed, it is difficult to get back the details of the view. There are tools on the Internet that can decrypt an encrypted view. When you encrypt a view, the view definition is not processed via encryption algorithms, but is merely obfuscated—in other words, changed so that prying eyes cannot see the code. These tools can return the obfuscation back to the original code. Therefore, if you need to modify the view, you will find that it is awkward. Not only will you have to use a tool, but you will also have to delete the view and recreate it, as it will not be editable. So, if you build a view and encrypt it, you should make sure that you keep a copy of the source somewhere. This is why it is recommended that encrypted views be used with care and really should be utilized only in production, or, at worst, in user testing.

Always keep a copy of the original view, before encryption, in the company's source-control system—for example, Visual SourceSafe—and make sure that regular backups are available

Now that I have touched upon the security issues behind views, it is time to start creating views for the database solution that you are building.

Views and In-memory Tables

Views can be built against an in-memory table in the same way that views can be built against disk-based tables. However, views are not natively compiled, which means that you cannot place a view into a natively compiled stored procedure. A view against an in-memory table can be used by other views, by standard stored procedures, and by ad-hoc SQL, but not by natively compiled code.

Creating a View: SQL Server Management Studio

The first task for you is to create a view using SQL Server Management Studio. This is perhaps the simplest solution, as it allows you to use drag-and-drop to build the view. This may be the slowest method for creating a new view, but it does give you the greatest visual flexibility for building the view and setting up its presentation, and this may also be the best method for dealing with views that already exist and require only minor modifications.

View Designer can aid you in the design of a view or the modification of any view already built. For example, it can assist if you are trying to build a complex view from a simple view, or it can even be used as a trial-and-error tool while you are gaining your T-SQL knowledge. When you open View Designer, you are initially presented with a modal dialog where you can select the tables and/or views that you want to use within the view you are creating. You can add further tables or views at any point, so a base set of tables or views is a good place to start. Once a table is added, the beginnings of a SELECT statement are created. At any point, you can build a view using either SQL or tables.

There are four separate parts to View Designer, each of which can be switched on or off for viewing via the toolbar buttons on top. Take a look at these toolbar buttons, shown in Figure 13-1.

Figure 13-1. *View toolbar buttons*

An overview of the buttons, working left to right, is as follows:

- The first button brings up the top pane—the diagram pane—where you can see the tables involved and their relationship to each other in the view.

- The next button accesses the criteria pane, where you can filter the information you want to display.

- The third button accesses the SQL pane, where you will see the SELECT statement, the columns involved, the JOINs, and finally the WHERE filter critera.

- The fourth button accesses the Results pane. If you execute the view, the data returned will be displayed.

- The fifth button will execute the query in the view.

- The sixth button verifies the SQL, ideal if you are building a view via the SQL designer rather than the other panes in View Designer as you can check that the SQL you are entering is valid.

- The seventh button will add a new column to the column selector where data can be "grouped by." You will see GROUP BY in Chapter 16.

- The penultimate button allows further tables to be added via a table modal dialog selector.

- Finally, the last button is the same as Query Editor, where a derived table can be added.

However, enough of the background—let's take a look at how View Designer works. In this example, you will be making a view of ShareDetails.Shares.

TRY IT OUT: CREATING A VIEW IN SQL SERVER MANAGEMENT STUDIO

1. Ensure that SQL Server Management Studio is running and that the ApressFinancial database is expanded.

2. Find the Views node and right-click it—this displays the pop-up menu shown in Figure 13-2. From there, select New View.

Figure 13-2. Creating a new view

3. The next screen you will see is View Designer, with a modal dialog box on top presenting a list of tables that you can add to make the view. The background is pretty empty at the moment (move the dialog box around if you need to). It is within View Designer that you will see all of the information required to build a view. There are no tables in the view at this time, so View Designer has nothing to show. For those of you who are familiar with Access, you will see that View Designer is similar to the Access Query Designer, only a bit more sophisticated!

4. You want to add your table, so move back to the modal dialog box, shown in Figure 13-3, select ShareDetails.Shares, shown as Shares (ShareDetails) on the screen, click Add, and then click Close to remove the dialog box.

Figure 13-3. Selecting the tables for your view

5. Take a moment to see how View Designer has changed, as illustrated in Figure 13-4. Notice that the background Query Designer area has been altered, the ShareDetails.Shares table has been added, and the beginnings of a SELECT statement now appear about two-thirds of the way down the screen. You will see the ShareDetails.Shares table listed in the top part of Query Designer (the diagram pane) with no check marks against any of the column names, indicating that there are not yet any columns within the view.

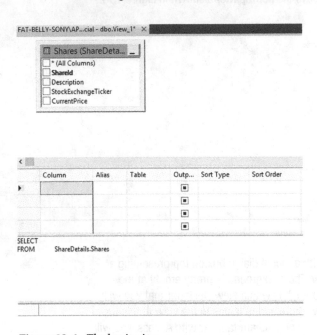

Figure 13-4. The basic view

6. What you want is a view that will display the share description, the stock market ticker ID, and the current price. You will also need the ShareId for the next exercise. If you wanted all the columns displayed, you would click the check box next to * (All Columns), but for this example, just place checks against all four columns, as shown in Figure 13-5. Notice as you check the boxes how the two areas below the table pane alter. The middle grid pane lists all the columns selected and gives you options for sorting and giving the column an alias name. The bottom part is the underlying query of the columns selected. The finished designer will look as shown in Figure 13-5.

Figure 13-5. *The view with the columns selected*

7. You are going to change the details in the column grid now to enforce default sorting criteria and to give the columns aliases. This means that if a user does just SELECT * from the view, then he or she will receive the data in the order defined by the view's query by default. (Of course they can change the order of the sort when defining the query used from the view). It also means that some of the column names will have been altered from those of the underlying table when the output is returned. You want to ensure that the shares come out from the view in ascending name order. Move to the Sort Type column and click in the row that corresponds to Description. Select Ascending, as shown in Figure 13-6.

Column	Alias	Table	Outp...	Sort Type	Sort Order
ShareId		Shares (Sh...	✓		
Description		Shares (Sh...	✓		
StockExchang...		Shares (Sh...	✓	Ascending	
CurrentPrice		Shares (Sh...	✓	Descending	
				Unsorted	

Figure 13-6. *Placing an order on the data*

8. In the next column, Sort Order, if you were defining more than one column to sort, you would define the order to sort the columns in. The value 1 is likely to have been automatically entered when you selected the Description to be sorted in ascending sequence. If you have more than one column, you can alter the sort order, as it is not enforced by the order in which you select your columns.

9. You still need to add aliases to give the column names more meaning, similar to using the AS clause you saw in Chapter 11; aliases can be found in the second column of the grid. Notice the fourth column name listed (fourth row down), CurrentPrice. To make this column more user-friendly, you make the name Latest Price, with a space. Be aware that having a column alias include a space is acceptable, but if you give a column an alias with a space and that column is then specifically named when displaying the data, the column name will require square brackets around it. You will see this in a moment. When you type this and tab out of the column, it becomes [Latest Price], as you see in Figure 13-7; SQL Server places the square brackets around the name because of the space.

	Column	Alias	Table	Outp...	Sort Type	Sort Order
	ShareId		Shares (ShareDetails)	✔		
	Description		Shares (ShareDetails)	✔	Ascending	1
	StockExchang...		Shares (ShareDetails)	✔		
▶	CurrentPrice	[Latest Price]	Shares (ShareDetails)	✔		

```
SELECT    TOP (100) PERCENT ShareId, Description, StockExchangeTicker, CurrentPrice AS [Latest Price]
FROM      ShareDetails.Shares
ORDER BY Description
```

Figure 13-7. *Alias with identifier*

10. To the right of the Sort Order is the column that allows you to define a filter for the view so that you can restrict what a user can see. Although sort orders can be changed by the T-SQL that calls the view, filters placed within the view cannot return more data than the view allows. So, for example, if you had a view that returned salaries, you could place a filter so that salaries of those people that should not be returned, such as a doctor, could be restricted within the view. In this example, you will list only those shares that have a current price—in other words, where CurrentPrice is greater than 0, as shown in Figure 13-8.

	Column	Alias	Table	Outp...	Sort Type	Sort Order	Filter
	ShareId		Shares (ShareDetails)	✔			
	Description		Shares (ShareDetails)	✔	Ascending	1	
	StockExchang...		Shares (ShareDetails)	✔			
▶	CurrentPrice	[Latest Price]	Shares (ShareDetails)	✔			> 0

```
SELECT    TOP (100) PERCENT ShareId, Description, StockExchangeTicker, CurrentPrice AS [Latest Price]
FROM      ShareDetails.Shares
ORDER BY Description
```

Figure 13-8. *Filtering the data*

11. Notice the SQL pane, which now has the filter within it as well as the sorting order. Also take a look at the diagram pane and how the table display has been altered, as you can see in Figure 13-9. The diagram pane indicates the columns that are defined in an ORDER BY and the columns that are filtered.

Figure 13-9. The table with the view options applied

12. Moving back to the T-SQL in the SQL pane, what about the TOP (100) PERCENT clause? Where did that come from? First of all, if you specify an order in a view, then by default SQL Server will place the TOP (100) PERCENT clause within the SQL, just as you saw in Chapter 11. It can be used if the table is very large and you don't want to allow users to return all the data on a production system, as it would tie up resources. You can also remove that clause from the SQL pane if you want; this will unlink your query from the designer and the Properties window, but you would also need to remove the ORDER BY. The ORDER BY is here only because of the TOP clause.

 Once SQL Server determines which rows are in the top N percent of rows to return, SQL Server is free to return those N percent rows in a random order. If the user of the view required a specific order, then an ORDER BY would be required when using the view (if the view did not already contain an ORDER BY clause). A final point to notice is how the column aliases are defined. The physical column is named, followed by AS and then the alias.

■ **Note** The AS when defining aliases is optional.

```
SELECT TOP (100) PERCENT ShareId, Description,
StockExchangeTicker, CurrentPrice AS [Latest Price]
FROM ShareDetails.Shares
WHERE (CurrentPrice > 0)
ORDER BY Description
```

13. If you wish to remove the TOP clause, it is better to do this within the Properties window, shown in Figure 13-10 and usually found on the right of SQL Server Management Studio. However, you also need to remove the sorting as mentioned a moment ago. (If the Properties window is not there, it can be found by selecting View ➤ Properties Window from the menu or by pressing F4). Within the Properties window, you can remove the TOP clause by setting Top Specification to No. You can also define whether this view is read-only by setting Update Specification to No.

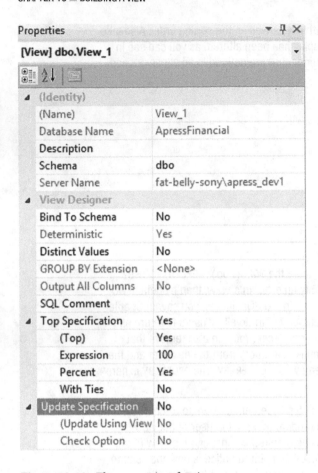

Properties ▾ �џ ✕

[View] dbo.View_1 ▾

▲ (Identity)	
(Name)	View_1
Database Name	ApressFinancial
Description	
Schema	dbo
Server Name	fat-belly-sony\apress_dev1
▲ View Designer	
Bind To Schema	No
Deterministic	Yes
Distinct Values	No
GROUP BY Extension	<None>
Output All Columns	No
SQL Comment	
▲ **Top Specification**	Yes
(Top)	Yes
Expression	100
Percent	Yes
With Ties	No
▲ Update Specification	No
(Update Using View	No
Check Option	No

Figure 13-10. The properties of a view

14. You do need to change some of the properties in the view definition, as shown in Figure 13-11.

- Description: It is very useful to give the view a description.

- Schema: Like a table, a view should belong to a schema. This can be an existing schema, or, if you have a view traversing more than one table, you may need a schema to cater to that scenario. In our example, it fits into the ShareDetails schema.

⊿	(Identity)	
	(Name)	View_1
	Database Name	ApressFinancial
	Description	
	Schema	ShareDetails
	Server Name	fat-belly-sony\apress_dev1
⊿	**View Designer**	
	Bind To Schema	No
	Deterministic	Yes
	Distinct Values	No
	GROUP BY Extension	<None>
	Output All Columns	No
	SQL Comment	
▷	Top Specification	Yes
▷	Update Specification	No

Figure 13-11. *Populated properties of a view*

15. Although the definition for the view is complete, you need to test it out. First, close the Properties window. By executing the query with the Execute button (the one sporting the red exclamation point), you will see the results in the Results pane.

16. Now that the view is complete, it is time to save it to the database. Clicking the Close button will bring up a dialog box asking whether you want to save the view, just as you saw in Chapter 5 when building a table. Click Yes to bring up the Choose Name dialog box, in which you give the view a name. You may find while starting out that there is a benefit to prefixing the name of the view with something like vw_ so that you know when looking at the object that it's a view. Many organizations do use this naming standard; however, it is not compulsory, and SQL Server Management Studio makes it clear what each object is, but it can be useful when looking at the T-SQL. The naming standard comes from a time when tools did not make it clear what object belonged to which group of object types. Once you have the name you wish, as shown in Figure 13-12, click OK.

Figure 13-12. *Naming the view*

17. You will be presented with a warning dialog box, as shown in Figure 13-13, that is the same information as in step 8. Click OK to save the view. This will bring you back to SQL Server Management Studio, where you will see the view saved.

Figure 13-13. ORDER BY *warning when saving a view*

You have now created your first view on the database. However, this method of building a view is a bit slow and cumbersome for something so simple. What if you wanted to combine two tables, or a view and another table?

Creating a View by Using a View

Creating a view that uses another view is as straightforward as building a view based on a table. The downside of building a view using another view is that it cannot be indexed for faster execution. Therefore, depending on what the T-SQL of the final view is, data retrieval may not be as fast as it could be with an index. Also, by having a view within a view, you are adding increased complexity when debugging or profiling its performance. Therefore, consider including the T-SQL from the selected view within this new view.

In this example, you will build a view of share prices using the vw_CurrentShares view created previously. In reality, you would use the ShareDetails.Shares table along with ShareDetails.SharesPrices for the reasons just discussed.

TRY IT OUT: CREATING A VIEW USING A VIEW

1. From SQL Server Management Studio Object Explorer, find Views, right-click, and select New View. The Add Table dialog box comes up as before.

2. From the Tables tab, select SharePrices(ShareDetails) and click Add.

3. Move to the Views tab; there should be only one view, shown in Figure 13-14, as that is all you have created. Select the view, click Add, and then click Close.

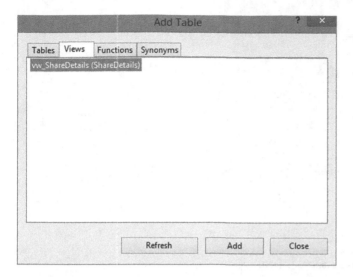

Figure 13-14. *Adding a view*

4. View Designer will now look similar to Figure 13-15, with one table and one view.

Figure 13-15. *With more than one object, how the basic view looks*

5. An INNER JOIN is required between the table and the view to provide the link, so that for each share you get only the share prices. It is very easy to link the two tables together by dragging a column from one table to a column in another table. This is very similar to how the relationships are built in Database Diagram Designer, as you saw earlier in this book.

First of all, click the ShareId column in the vw_CurrentShares view. Keeping the mouse button pressed, drag the mouse pointer from the vw_CurrentShares view over to the ShareId column in the ShareDetails.SharePrices table and then release it. View Designer should now look like Figure 13-16. You have not really created a relationship in the truest sense of the word—this is simply the relationship between the columns for the purpose of this query. You can see one gray line, which shows which fields are used for the join. You can also achieve the same result by entering the T-SQL in the SQL pane in View Designer.

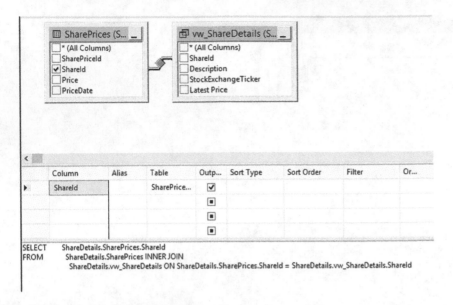

Figure 13-16. *The view with the JOIN completed*

6. Select `Price` and `PriceDate` from the `ShareDetails.SharePrices` table and `Description` from the `vw_ShareDetails` view, as shown in Figure 13-17. `ShareId` should already be selected in the `SharePrices` table from the drag-and-drop join in the previous step. If it is not selected, then select it now.

Figure 13-17. *How the view with a JOIN looks*

7. The final step to this view creation is to build the sort orders. You want the result to be in the order of ascending description, but you want the most recent price first and the first price last. Figure 13-18 shows the criteria pane with these options.

Column	Alias	Table	Outp...	Sort Type	Sort Order	Filter
ShareId		SharePrice...	✓			
PriceDate		SharePrice...	✓			
Price		SharePrice...	✓	Descending	2	
Description		vw_Share...	✓	Ascending	1	

Figure 13-18. *Sorting with ascending and descending columns*

8. Moving to the SQL pane, note that the code shows the columns, as well as the INNER JOIN of the two ShareId columns, and finally the ordering of the data for the TOP clause.

```
SELECT TOP (100) PERCENT ShareDetails.SharePrices.ShareId,
ShareDetails.SharePrices.PriceDate, ShareDetails.SharePrices.Price,
ShareDetails.vw_ShareDetails.Description
FROM ShareDetails.SharePrices
INNER JOIN ShareDetails.vw_ShareDetails
    ON ShareDetails.SharePrices.ShareId =
                ShareDetails.vw_ShareDetails.ShareId
ORDER BY ShareDetails.vw_ShareDetails.Description,
ShareDetails.SharePrices.Price DESC
```

9. Execute the code within the view's code window by pressing the Execute button, and you should then see the results, part of which are displayed in Figure 13-19.

ShareId	PriceDate	Price	Description
2	2012-03-07 09:49:33.890	36.07171	ACME'S HOMEBAKE COOKIES INC
1	2012-03-04 09:54:17.870	35.63776	ACME'S HOMEBAKE COOKIES INC
1	2011-12-27 17:01:59.650	35.16881	ACME'S HOMEBAKE COOKIES INC
2	2012-03-08 11:01:03.030	34.28388	ACME'S HOMEBAKE COOKIES INC
1	2012-03-28 10:12:42.740	34.25148	ACME'S HOMEBAKE COOKIES INC
2	2011-12-24 00:22:54.980	33.30250	ACME'S HOMEBAKE COOKIES INC
2	2012-03-04 11:37:29.870	32.83378	ACME'S HOMEBAKE COOKIES INC
1	2012-01-28 04:38:50.320	32.71544	ACME'S HOMEBAKE COOKIES INC
2	2011-12-15 08:42:59.690	32.35564	ACME'S HOMEBAKE COOKIES INC

Figure 13-19. *View test results*

10. Assign the view to the ShareDetails schema in the view's Properties window and supply a description, as shown in Figure 13-20; then click the Close button and save the view as vw_SharePrices.

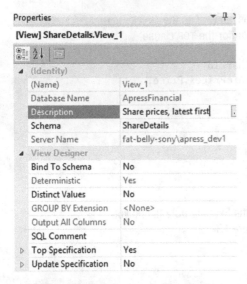

Figure 13-20. *Setting the view schema*

Now that you have built views using the designer, it's time to build one with T-SQL.

Creating a View Using T-SQL Syntax

Very quickly, you will find that creating a view using T-SQL is the better way forward. It is just as fast as building a view using the designer. To reiterate a point that I have made a few times, as a developer, knowing the T-SQL syntax is very useful for migrating changes from your development server to your production server, as well as for having the flexibility to build objects within your code in .NET and so on.

As with previous chapters, the next section will look at the full syntax and then the more usual syntax you will use when building a view.

The CREATE VIEW Syntax

The CREATE VIEW syntax is very simple and straightforward. The syntax for a view is very similar to the syntax for a table, although there are three interesting options that can also be attributed to the view. Here is the syntax for building a view:

```
CREATE VIEW [schema_name.]view_name
WITH {ENCRYPTION | SCHEMABINDING | VIEW_METADATA}
AS
SELECT_statement
[WITH CHECK OPTION]
```

Taking a look at the first section of the syntax, you will notice that the name of the view can be prefixed with the name of the schema; however, the schema name is optional. Provided that you are in the correct database and are logged in with the ID you want to create the view for, the schema_name option is not required, especially if the logon has the desired schema as its default, because the options will be assumed from the connection details. However, it may not be a similar login that executes the scripts later in your application's life, and the login used might not have the same default schema. It is best to define the view with the schema name for clarity. For production views, rather

than for views used purely by a single SQL Server user, it is recommended that they be built by the database owner. If the view is built by another, then when someone tries to execute the view, that user will need to prefix the name of the view with the login of the person who created it.

Following on from these options, you build the query, typically formed with a SELECT statement that makes up the view itself. As you saw in the previous example, the SELECT statement can cover one or many tables or views, many columns, and as many filtering options using the WHERE statement as you need. You cannot reference any temporary variable or temporary table within a view, or create a new table from a view by using the INTO clause. To clarify, it is not possible to have SELECT column INTO new_table.

The ENCRYPTION option will take the view created and encrypt the schema contained so that the view is secure and no one can see the underlying code or modify the contents of the SELECT statement within. However (I know I keep repeating this, but it is so important), do keep a backup of the contents of the view in a safe place in development in case any modifications are required.

■ **Tip** Encrypting views may seem like a good idea so as to hide even further the schema of your database from potential users; however, use encrypted views with caution, and always keep a backup of the source in a safe and secure environment. People have been known to keep a printout of the view just in case the source became corrupt. Use encrypted views sparsely, and only when really required.

The SCHEMABINDING option ensures that any column referenced within the view cannot be dropped from the underlying table without dropping the view built with SCHEMABINDING first. This, therefore, keeps the view secure with the knowledge that there will be no runtime errors when columns have been altered or dropped from the underlying table, and ensures the view is not altered in line with those changes. If you try to remove a column from the table that is contained within a schema-bound view, for example, then you will receive an error. There is one knock-on effect when using SCHEMABINDING: all tables or other views named within the SELECT statement must be prefixed with the name of the schema of the table or view, even if the owner of these objects is the same as the schema of the view. There is a section on this later in this chapter.

The final option for the view is VIEW_METADATA. When working with views using C#, Java, Excel, and so on, you can request for the metadata of the view to be returned. Without this option, the metadata will be that of the base tables within the view. To hide this information and display the column names from the view instead, build your view with the VIEW_METADATA option.

Let's go back to the two options that will be used less often, the first being the WITH CHECK option. If the view is being used as the basis of completing insertions or updates, then any modification should fit within the criteria of the view. To clarify this, if you have a view with a WHERE filter where the share price is greater than 0 and you try to alter a share price to a negative amount using the view rather than the base tables, the modification will fail. However, a change in price to a positive amount would be allowed. You will see this option in use in the next example.

■ **Note** Even with WITH CHECK OPTION defined, if the data are modified directly in the table, it won't be verified against any views defined with the underlying tables, although, of course, the data will be added to the table. Also, if the view uses TOP, then WITH CHECK OPTION cannot be used.

The final possible option, VIEW_METADATA, exposes the view's metadata if you are calling the view via ODBC, OLE DB, and so on—in other words, from a program that is external to SQL Server.

Now that you are aware of the basic syntax for creating a view, the next example will take this knowledge and build a new view for the database.

Creating a View with CREATE VIEW and SELECT

Creating views by using T-SQL code in a Query Editor pane is, in my experience, the fastest and best option. This can be a faster method for building views than using SQL Server Management Studio, especially as you become more experienced with T-SQL commands. This section will demonstrate the T-SQL syntax required to create a view.

The SELECT statement forms the basis for most views, so this is where most of the emphasis is placed when developing a view. By getting the SELECT statement correct and retrieving the required data, it can then be easily transformed into a view. This is how the view in the following example is created, so let's look at building a view using T-SQL and a Query Editor pane. In the following example, you will create a view that returns a list of transactions for each customer, along with some customer information.

TRY IT OUT: CREATING A VIEW IN A QUERY EDITOR PANE

1. Open Query Editor. First of all, let's get the T-SQL correct. You need to link two tables: the CustomerDetails.Customers table to get the name and address, and the TransactionDetails.Transactions table so you can get a list of transactions for the customer. As the view will be used as an updateable view, it is not possible to have a TOP clause, and because there is no TOP clause, you cannot have an ORDER BY. The code is as follows:

    ```
    SELECT c.CustomerId,c.FirstName,c.OtherInitials,
    t.DateEntered,t.Amount,t.ReferenceDetails
    FROM CustomerDetails.Customers c
    JOIN TransactionDetails.Transactions t
      ON t.CustomerId = c.CustomerId
    WHERE DateEntered >= '1 Jan 2012'
    ```

2. Once done, execute the code and check that the results are returned.

3. You can now wrap the CREATE VIEW statement around your code, and, because you want to ensure that the view will update only data that match the WHERE filter, you will also add the WITH CHECK OPTION at the end. Execute the following code to store the view in the ApressFinancial database:

    ```
    CREATE VIEW CustomerDetails.vw_CustTrans
    AS
    SELECT c.CustomerId,c.FirstName,c.OtherInitials,
    tt.Description,t.DateEntered,t.Amount,t.ReferenceDetails
    FROM CustomerDetails.Customers c
    JOIN TransactionDetails.Transactions t ON t.CustomerId = c.CustomerId
    JOIN TransactionDetails.TransactionTypes tt ON
      tt.TransactionTypeId = t.TransactionType
    WHERE DateEntered >= '1 Jan 2012'
    WITH CHECK OPTION
    ```

4. It is now possible to test the view to ensure that updates will occur only on data returned via the WHERE filter. The first test is to use the view to attempt to update a row where the DateEntered for a transaction is altered to be prior to January 1, 2012. For safety I have surrounded the code within a transaction.

```
BEGIN TRAN
UPDATE CustomerDetails.vw_CustTrans
    SET DateEntered = '1 Dec 1900'
 WHERE CustomerId = 1
ROLLBACK TRAN
```

5. Execute the foregoing code, and you should receive an error similar to the following, indicating that you are amending data that break the WITH CHECK option.

```
Msg 550, Level 16, State 1, Line 2
The attempted insert or update failed because the target view
either specifies WITH CHECK OPTION or spans a view that specifies
WITH CHECK OPTION and one or more rows resulting from the operation
did not qualify under the CHECK OPTION constraint.
The statement has been terminated.
```

6. A simple change to the code would be to alter the date entered to equal to or later than January 1, 2012, in which case the update will run. Do surround the code with a transaction and rollback so that the data remain the same for the remainder of the book.

```
BEGIN TRAN
UPDATE CustomerDetails.vw_CustTrans
    SET DateEntered = '1 Feb 2013'
 WHERE CustomerId = 1
ROLLBACK TRAN
```

7. Execute the foregoing code, and you should receive a message indicating that a number of rows have been updated. I have 1 rows updated.

```
(1 row(s) affected)
```

This view is a straightforward view with no ENCRYPTION or SCHEMABINDING options. The remainder of the SELECT statement syntax is very easy to follow.

Now that you have created a basic view using T-SQL, let's go a little deeper with an example incorporating SCHEMABINDING.

Binding Columns in a View with SCHEMABINDING

The following example will bind the columns used in the view to the actual tables that lie behind the view, so that if any column contained within the view is modified, an error message will be displayed and the changes will be canceled. The error received will be shown so that you can see for yourself what happens.

First of all, you need to build the view before going on to discuss the background. This view is going to list products for customers, therefore linking the Customers.CustomerProducts and CustomerDetails. FinancialProducts tables.

TRY IT OUT: CREATING A VIEW WITH SCHEMABINDING

1. Open a new Query Editor pane and connect it to the ApressFinancial database. You can then create the T-SQL that will form the basis of your view.

```
SELECT c.FirstName + ' ' + c.LastName AS CustomerName,
c.CustomerId, fp.ProductName, cp.AmountToCollect, cp.Frequency,
cp.LastCollected
FROM CustomerDetails.Customers c
JOIN CustomerDetails.CustomerProducts cp ON cp.CustomerId = c.CustomerId
JOIN CustomerDetails.FinancialProducts fp ON
    fp.ProductId = cp.FinancialProductId
```

2. Test out that the SELECT T-SQL works as required by executing it. The results you get returned should look similar to Figure 13-21.

	CustomerName	CustomerId	ProductName	AmountToCollect	Frequency	LastCollected
1	Noel Morgala	1	Doperex	78.36	0	2012-03-29 19:23:15.540
2	Aubrey Lomas	2	Monzapower	3428.0419	0	2011-12-01 07:24:58.560
3	Bernie McGee	3	Doptumilax	2194.2976	1	2012-03-15 20:08:49.090
4	Jane Harper	4	Varvenedgan	883.2759	0	2012-03-15 10:13:34.210
5	Mark Vernon-Smith	5	Empebex	3115.1158	2	2012-03-12 01:14:23.240
6	Terence Madden	6	Tipmunommax	809.8044	5	2011-12-15 04:41:51.310
7	Anne Mather	7	Hapvenor	3024.6817	3	2011-11-25 17:41:00.980
8	Mickey Ferguson	8	Grodimin	3169.5453	5	2012-01-16 17:09:37.350
9	Deanna Palmer	9	Kliwerpefax	1177.4662	6	2011-12-10 20:01:24.090
10	Anne Mann	10	Kliwerpefax	3103.9758	5	2012-02-13 03:40:55.010
11	Carlos Liu	11	Embanar	710.9484	4	2011-11-08 02:00:05.290
12	Hector Ramirez	12	Monzapower	3871.3496	1	2012-01-16 21:59:16.470
13	Keri Steele	13	Embanar	25.0247	2	2012-01-23 19:15:20.330

Figure 13-21. Testing schema binding in T-SQL

3. You now need to create the CREATE VIEW. First of all, you are completing a test to see whether the view already exists within the system catalogs. If it does, then you DROP it. Then you define the view using the WITH SCHEMABINDING clause. The other change to the T-SQL is to prefix the tables you are using with the name of the schema that the tables come from. This is to ensure that the schema binding is successful and can regulate when a column is dropped.

```
IF EXISTS(SELECT TABLE_NAME FROM   INFORMATION_SCHEMA.VIEWS
      WHERE  TABLE_NAME = N'vw_CustFinProducts'
         AND  TABLE_SCHEMA = N'CustomerDetails')
    DROP VIEW CustomerDetails.vw_CustFinProducts
GO
CREATE VIEW CustomerDetails.vw_CustFinProducts
WITH SCHEMABINDING
AS
SELECT c.FirstName + ' ' + c.LastName AS CustomerName,
c.CustomerId, fp.ProductName, cp.AmountToCollect, cp.Frequency,
cp.LastCollected
FROM CustomerDetails.Customers c
JOIN CustomerDetails.CustomerProducts cp ON
  cp.CustomerId = c.CustomerId
JOIN CustomerDetails.FinancialProducts fp ON
  fp.ProductId = cp.FinancialProductId
```

4. Once done, execute the code. You should then see the following message:

```
The command(s) completed successfully.
```

5. Now that your vw_CustFinProducts view is created, which you can check by looking in SQL Server Management Studio Object Explorer, it is possible to demonstrate what happens if you try to alter a column used in the view so as to affect one of the underlying tables. Enter the following code and then execute it:

```
ALTER TABLE CustomerDetails.Customers
ALTER COLUMN FirstName nvarchar(100)
```

6. You will then see in the Results pane two error messages: the first shows that an alteration has been attempted on the CustomerDetails.Customers table, has been disallowed, and names the view stopping this, and the second shows that the alteration failed.

```
Msg 5074, Level 16, State 1, Line 1
The object 'vw_CustFinProducts' is dependent on column 'FirstName'.
Msg 4922, Level 16, State 9, Line 1
ALTER TABLE ALTER COLUMN FirstName failed because one or more objects access this column.
```

> **■ Caution** You will find that in most cases when building views the SCHEMABINDING option is a good option to have on a view, ensuring that a view that works today will always work. Otherwise, it would be only when someone deliberately removed your view from the system to complete table changes and then didn't correctly put it back that you would find that a view had stopped working. Herein lies yet another scenario for keeping the code of encrypted views at hand: if you have encrypted views, along with SCHEMABINDING, and someone wants to alter an underlying table, you had better have the code available!

Indexing a View

Views can be indexed just as tables can be indexed. Rules in choosing columns to make indexes on a view are similar to those for a table. There are also some major requirements you need to meet before you can index a view. I will show you these first so that you are aware of which views can be indexed and what you have to do with your view.

When building indexes on views, the first index to be created must be a unique clustered index. Once such an index has been built, additional nonclustered indexes on this view can then be created. This can also be taken further, in that if you have a view with subsequent indexes on it, and you drop the unique clustered index, then all of the other indexes will automatically be dropped. Also, if you drop the view, as you would expect, the indexes are also dropped.

The view that the index is to build on must contain only tables and cannot contain views. The tables must all come from one database, and the view must also reside in that database and have been built with the SCHEMABINDING option.

As you saw when creating your database, certain options can be switched on or off. The following options must be set to ON while creating an index. These options need to be set to ON only for that session and would therefore precede the CREATE INDEX statement.

```
SET ANSI_NULLS ON
SET ANSI_PADDING ON
SET ANSI_WARNINGS ON
SET CONCAT_NULL_YIELDS_NULL ON
SET ARITHABORT ON
SET QUOTED_IDENTIFIER ON
```

On top of this, the NUMERIC_ROUNDABORT option must be set to OFF.

```
SET NUMERIC_ROUNDABORT OFF
```

Finally, the view itself cannot have text, ntext, or image columns defined in it (don't forget, though, that these three data types are being deprecated, so you should be avoiding creating tables with these contained within them anyway). In Chapter 16, you'll learn how to group data through a clause called GROUP BY. If you have grouping within your view, the columns used to group data are the only columns that can be in the first index.

Although these requirements seem like they could be quite restrictive, the upside is that indexing views also comes with major speed implications. If a view has no index, every time that the view is executed the data behind the view, including any joins, are rebuilt and executed. However, as the first index is a clustered index, this is similar to a clustered table index, and the data will be retrieved at index-creation time and stored in that order. Also, like table indexes, when the data are modified, then the index will receive the updates as well. Therefore, if SQL Server can use the clustered index, there will be no need to run the query again.

SQL Server will use any indexes that you have on the tables when building the views. Indexing a view is most beneficial when the data in the underlying tables are not changing frequently and when the view is executed often. Keep in mind that a view is taking information from other tables and is not a table itself, and therefore any updates to the underlying tables will not be reflected in the view until the view is rerun.

By placing an index on a view, the columns named within the index are stored within the database, as are all of the columns defined for the view, along with the data rows. Therefore, any changes to the raw data within the native tables will also be reflected in the data stored for the view. Keep in mind the performance issues with this. Every data change in the tables used in the views requires SQL Server to evaluate the effect the change has on the view. This requires more processing by SQL Server, causing a slowdown in performance. Temper this perceived gain of using an index with the downside of the extra processing required to keep the data up to date in two places for the table and two places for the index for those columns involved in the view.

Now that you are aware of the pros and cons of building indexes on views, and how they differ from indexes for tables, it is time to build an index on your view.

The aim of this index is to locate a row in the view quickly. You want to be able to find all the products for a customer based on his or her customer ID. Building the index is very quick and very simple, especially since you already know the basics from building indexes earlier in the book.

TRY IT OUT: INDEXING A VIEW

1. The view you want to index is vw_CustFinProducts, which was created with SCHEMABINDING. The unique clustered index will be on the CustomerId and ProductName, as you know that this will be unique. In a Query Editor pane, enter the following code:

```
CREATE UNIQUE CLUSTERED INDEX ix_CustFinProds
ON CustomerDetails.vw_CustFinProducts (CustomerId,ProductName)
```

2. Execute this code. When you do, you might get an error as follows; however, as long as no options have been altered for your SSMS and you have followed the book, this error should not be seen:

```
Msg 1935, Level 16, State 1, Line 1
Cannot create index. Object 'vw_CustFinProducts' was created with the
following SET options off: 'ANSI_NULLS, QUOTED_IDENTIFIER'.
```

3. As was mentioned when discussing the options required to index a view, you may not have these two options set to ON. You would therefore have to recreate the view. From Object Explorer, right-click vw_CustFinProducts and select Script View As ➤ DROP AND CREATE To ➤ New Query Editor Window, as shown in Figure 13-22.

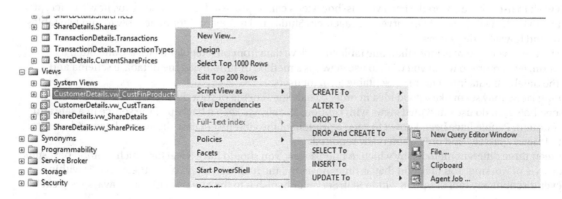

Figure 13-22. Scripting the view

4. This brings up the code in a new Query Editor pane. Modify the two SET options. Executing
the code should be successful.

```
USE [ApressFinancial]
GO
DROP VIEW [CustomerDetails].[vw_CustFinProducts]
GO
SET ANSI_NULLS ON
GO
SET QUOTED_IDENTIFIER ON
GO
CREATE VIEW [CustomerDetails].[vw_CustFinProducts]
    WITH SCHEMABINDING
AS
CREATE VIEW [CustomerDetails].[vw_CustFinProducts]
WITH SCHEMABINDING
AS
SELECT c.FirstName + ' ' + c.LastName AS CustomerName,
c.CustomerId, fp.ProductName, cp.AmountToCollect, cp.Frequency,
cp.LastCollected
FROM CustomerDetails.Customers c
JOIN CustomerDetails.CustomerProducts cp ON cp.CustomerId = c.CustomerId
JOIN CustomerDetails.FinancialProducts fp ON
    fp.ProductId = cp.FinancialProductIdGO
```

5. You can then move back to your pane with the CREATE INDEX statement and execute it.
Executing that code should be successful now even if you had the error before.

The index on a view has now been successfully created. As you can see, there are a number of restrictions, but
not to the point that no index can exist. You just have to think about what you are doing, and if you have a query in
your view that contains an item from the preceding list and you wish to create an index, you'll just have to find a
way around it.

Summary

This chapter should give you the confidence, when building your own view, of knowing which options and features
of views you wish to use. I have covered what a view is, how views can improve a database's security, how to encrypt
your view, how to build a view using SQL Server Management Studio and a Query Editor pane, how to join two tables
within a view, and how to index a view.

Creating a view, when there is more than one table to retrieve data from on a regular basis, is quite often a
sensible solution, even more so when you wish to use views as a method of simplifying the database schema and
abstracting the database data into a more presentable form for users.

Encrypting views may seem like a good idea in order to hide the schema of your database even further from
potential users; however, do use encrypted views with caution, and always keep a backup of the source in a safe and
secure environment. People have been known to keep a printout of the view just in case the source becomes corrupt.
Use encrypted views sparsely, and only when really required.

Having seen three different methods by which to build a view, you should have a feel for which method best suits
you and your style of working. You may find that as time moves on, the tool used alters, as do the methods within
that tool. Never discount any tool or option within SQL Server or banish it to the annals of history: always keep each

option and tool in mind, for one day that area may be your savior. When starting out, switch between each method for building a view so that you are fully conversant with each method.

You will find that in most cases when building views, the SCHEMABINDING option will be good to have on a view, ensuring that a view that works today will always work. It would be only when someone deliberately removes your view from the system to complete table changes, and then doesn't correctly put it back, that you would find that a view has stopped working. Herein lies yet another scenario for keeping the code of encrypted views at hand: if you have encrypted views, along with SCHEMABINDING, and someone wishes to alter an underlying table, then you had better have the code available!

Finally, being aware of the differences between indexes on tables and indexes in views is crucial to a successful and well-performing view. If you are unsure, then try out the view with and then without an index within your development environment.

■ ■ ■

Stored Procedures, Functions, and Security

Now that you know how to build queries written as single executable lines of T-SQL statements, it is time to look at how to place these into a *stored procedure* or a *function* within SQL Server, allowing them to be run as often as they are required without the need to be retyped every time. This also allows code to be written that can accept input parameters, return a status, return rows of data, and, most important, allow you to improve the security of your database. You will see all of this and more in this chapter.

■ **Note** Chapter 15 will look at specifics of natively compiled stored procedures and working with in-memory tables. This chapter will look at working with disk-based tables, although much of the chapter is relevant to both types of tables.

Stored procedures and functions are two different types of objects that provide different, yet similar, functionality. You will see these differences within the examples, but the main point is that a stored procedure is a set of code that runs as its own unit of work, while a function, which also runs as its own unit of work, is executed within the context of another unit of work. When I discuss functions later in this chapter, you will learn more about both the similarities and differences between these two types of objects.

Although you may save queries on a disk drive somewhere, you have not stored them within SQL Server itself up to this point, nor have you saved them as multiple units of work. Often, however, you need to execute multiple queries in series from SQL Server. To do this, you must employ stored procedures or functions. SQL Server assumes that a stored procedure or a function will be run more than once. Therefore, when it is executed for the first time, a query plan is created for it detailing how best to execute the query. It is also possible, just like with any other database object, to assign security to a stored procedure or a function so that only specific users can run it, lending added security as compared to a one-time-only query saved to a hard drive.

The aim of this chapter is to build a simple stored procedure for disk-based tables that will insert a single row into a table. I will then cover error handling and controlling the flow of execution within the procedure. Once a stored procedure that has several steps has been built, you will see how you can use tools within SQL Server to debug your code. You will then move on to building a user-defined function and invoking it. You will look at some system functions later, in a later chapter.

Therefore, this chapter will do the following:

- Describe what a stored procedure is

- Explain the advantages of a stored procedure over a view

- Cover the basic syntax for creating a stored procedure

- Show how to set values within variables

- Control the flow through a stored procedure

- Look at the differences between a function and a stored procedure

- Cover the basic syntax for creating a T-SQL user-defined function

First, let's take a look at what a stored procedure is.

What Is a Stored Procedure?

In simplest terms, a stored procedure is a collection of compiled T-SQL statements and commands that are directly accessible by SQL Server. The code placed within a stored procedure is executed as one single unit, or *batch*, of work. The benefit of this is that network traffic is greatly reduced, because multiple T-SQL statements are not forced to travel over the network individually. Only the name of the stored procedure to execute and the parameters to it need to be transmitted. In addition to executing SELECT, UPDATE, INSERT, or DELETE statements, stored procedures are able to call other stored procedures, use statements that control the flow of execution, create temporary tables using different commands, and perform aggregate functions or other calculations.

Any developer with access rights to create objects within SQL Server can build a stored procedure. There are also hundreds of system stored procedures, all of which start with a prefix of sp_, within SQL Server.

■ **Caution** Under no circumstances should you attempt to modify any system stored procedure that belongs to SQL Server, as this could corrupt not only your database, but also other databases, requiring you to perform a full restore.

There is little point in building a stored procedure just to run a set of T-SQL statements only once; conversely, a stored procedure is ideal for when you want to run a set of T-SQL statements many times. The reasons for choosing a stored procedure are similar to those that would persuade you to choose a view rather than letting users directly access table data. Stored procedures also supply benefits; for example, SQL Server will always cache a stored procedure plan in memory, and it is likely to remain in cache for reuse, whereas ad hoc SQL plans created when running ad hoc T-SQL may or may not be stored in the procedure cache. The latter may lead to the bloating of the procedure cache with lots of very similar plans for similar batches, as SQL Server won't match plans that use the same basic code but have different parameter values, for example.

Stored procedures give your application a single proven interface for accessing or manipulating your data. This means that you retain data integrity, make the correct modifications or selections to the data, and ensure that users of the database do not need to know structures, layouts, relationships, or related processes required to perform a specific function. You can also validate any data input and ensure that the data brought into the stored procedure are correct.

Just like with views and tables, you can grant very specific execute permission for users of stored procedures (the only permission available on a stored procedure is EXECUTE). Once you have worked with stored procedures a bit, I will go through the security of each object from a list of tables, views, and stored procedures and review how secure or insecure each can be.

To prevent access to the source code, you can encrypt stored procedures, although this really ought to be used only sparingly. The code itself isn't actually encrypted; it is only obfuscated, which means it is possible to decrypt the code if required. Therefore, it doesn't provide total prevention of viewing the code, but it does stop stray eyes. It also limits what can be seen when using a tool called SQL Server Profiler, which can profile the performance of stored procedures, code, and so on; thus, encryption can cause difficulty when checking out the source of any problems. Therefore, to reiterate, you need to carefully justify any encryption you want to do.

Creating a Stored Procedure

Now that you know what a stored procedure is, it is time to create your own. Once the syntax has been covered, you will build a stored procedure in Management Studio that will return a set of rows and multiple sets of rows, and then you will move on to look at controling the flow through your stored procedure.

The first task, though, is to take a look at the syntax.

CREATE PROCEDURE Syntax

You must begin a stored procedure with a CREATE PROCEDURE statement. The CREATE PROCEDURE syntax offers a great many flexible options and extends T-SQL with some additional commands. The syntax generally appears as follows:

```
CREATE PROCEDURE procedure_name
[ { @parameter_name} datatype [= default_value] [OUTPUT]] , [ ,...n ]
[ { WITH [RECOMPILE | ENCRYPTION | RECOMPILE, ENCRYPTION |EXECUTE AS clause] }
AS
[BEGIN]
   statements
[END]
```

Now let's break it down. First of all, it is necessary to inform SQL Server which action you want to perform. Obviously, you want to create a stored procedure, so you need to supply a CREATE PROCEDURE statement.

The next part of the syntax is to give the procedure a name. It would be advisable, just as it is with any SQL Server object, to adhere to a naming standard. Everyone has their own standard within their installation, but if you prefix the name with sp_, a very common naming convention, then you will know what that object is. However, this is not something I recommend, for two reasons. The first is that stored procedures prefixed by sp_ are seen as system stored procedures, and, therefore, if you name your stored procedures similarly, confusion will occur. For example, if you create a stored procedure with sp_ as the prefix and then Microsoft releases a system stored procedure with that same name, even more confusion will occur. I have seen user-created stored procedures with a double underscore in their name, such as sp__, which is where a developer has expanded the functionality of a system stored procedure, in this case sp_who. This is valid. The second reason I do not recommend using sp_ is that you can hit some unnecessary compile locks because of system stored procedure lookups. If you name your stored procedure with a prefix of sp_, then SQL Server checks the master database for the stored procedure first. Therefore, do avoid this naming convention.

Many people adopt a different naming convention whereby the prefix defines what the stored procedure will do; for example, an update would have a prefix of up, a deletion dt, and a selection sl. There are many different prefixes you could use, including prefixing the name of the stored procedure with the system name. Some large systems are split into subsystems but share the same database. One example is when you have one database for your whole company but there are subsystems for purchasing, sales, and so on. Once you have decided on your standard, you should stick with it.

Some procedures may require information to be provided in order for them to do their work; this is achieved by passing in a parameter. For example, passing in a customer number to a stored procedure would provide the necessary information to allow creation of a list of transactions for a statement. More than one parameter can be passed in—all you do is separate them with a comma.

Any parameter defined must be prefixed with an @ sign. Not all procedures will require parameters, so this is optional; however, if you do want to pass in parameters to a stored procedure, name the parameters and follow them with the data type and, where required, the length of the data to pass in. For example, the following specifies a parameter of name L_Name, with a data type of varchar of length 50:

```
@L_Name varchar(50)
```

You can also specify a default parameter value in the event that a user does not provide one at execution time. The value specified must be a constant value, like 'DEFAULT' or 24031964, or it can be NULL. It is not possible to define a variable as a default value, since the procedure cannot resolve this when the procedure is built. For example, if your application is commonly, but not exclusively, used by the marketing department, you could make the department parameter variable optional by setting a default of 'marketing':

```
@department varchar(50) = 'marketing'
```

Thus, in this example, if you were from marketing, you would not need to provide the department input. If you were from information services, however, you could simply provide a value for a department that would override the default.

It is also possible to return a value, a number of values, or even a table of data from a stored procedure by using a parameter to pass the information out. The parameter would still be defined as if it were for input, with one exception and one extra option. First of all, the exception: It is not possible to define a default value for this parameter. If you try to do so, no errors will be generated, but the definition will be ignored. The extra syntax option that is required is to suffix the parameter with the keyword OUTPUT. This must follow the data type definition:

```
@calc_result varchar(50) OUTPUT
```

You are not required to place OUTPUT parameters after the input parameters; they can be intermixed. Conventionally, however, try to keep the OUTPUT parameters until last, as it will make the stored procedure easier to understand.

■ **Tip** Output parameters can also be used as input parameters, and therefore they can be used to pass a value in as well as return a value.

Before continuing, one last thing about parameters needs to be discussed having to do with executing the procedure and working with the defined parameters. When it comes to executing a stored procedure that has input parameters, there are two ways to run it.

The first method is to name the stored procedure and then pass the input values for the parameters in the same order that they are defined. SQL Server will then take each comma-delimited value set and assign it to the defined variable. However, this makes an assumption that the order of the parameters does not change, and that any default value-defined parameters are also set with a value.

The second, and preferred, method of executing a stored procedure is to name the parameter and follow this with the value to pass in. You are then ensuring that, at execution time, it doesn't matter what order in which the stored procedure has named the parameters, because SQL Server will be able to match the parameter defined with the parameter defined within the stored procedure. You then don't need to define a value for parameters that already have default values. Also, if the stored procedure needs to be expanded, for backward compatibility, for instance, any new parameters can be defined with default values, therefore removing the need to change every calling code. Finally, when you call a stored procedure from code, such as .NET, Excel, and so forth, each parameter has to be named.

There will be examples of each of the two different methods of passing in values to parameters within this chapter.

Next come two options that define how the stored procedure is built. First of all, just as a reminder, a stored procedure, when first run without an existing plan in the procedure cache, is compiled into an execution plan, which is an internal data structure in SQL Server that describes how it should go about performing the operations requested within the stored procedure. SQL Server stores the compiled code for subsequent executions, which saves time and resources. If there is an existing plan in the procedure cache, then SQL Server will use this.

However, the RECOMPILE option in a stored procedure dictates to SQL Server that every time the stored procedure is run, the whole procedure is recompiled. Typically, when a parameter can greatly affect the number of rows returned, you may want to add the RECOMPILE option to the stored procedure to force the optimizer to produce the best plan every time (i.e., you want to avoid reusing a plan that may not be very good for certain parameter values).

The second of the two options is the ENCRYPTION keyword. It is possible to encrypt—well, obfuscate at least—a stored procedure so that the contents of the stored procedure cannot be viewed easily. Keep in mind that ENCRYPTION does not secure the data, but rather protects the source code from inspection and modification. Both ENCRYPTION and RECOMPILE are preceded by the WITH keyword and can be employed together when separated by a comma:

```
CREATE PROCEDURE sp_do_nothing
    @nothing int
    WITH ENCRYPTION, RECOMPILE
AS
    SELECT something FROM nothing
```

The keyword AS defines the start of the T-SQL code, which will be the body of the stored procedure. AS has no other function, but is mandatory within the CREATE PROCEDURE command as it defines the end of all variable definitions and procedure creation options. Once the keyword AS is defined, you can then start creating your T-SQL code.

It is then possible to surround your code with a BEGIN...END block. I tend to do this as a matter of course so that there is no doubt where the start and end of the procedure lie.

There is one option not covered, and that is EXECUTE AS, which I will cover later in the chapter.

Returning a Set of Rows

One method of achieving output from a stored procedure is to return a set of rows, also known as a *result set*. This result set may contain zero, one, or many rows as a single batch of output. It is also possible to return more than one result set and then process them one result set at a time. This is not common but does happen, and there can be some small performance gains from doing this. Returning a result set is achieved through the use of the SELECT statement within a stored procedure—what is selected is returned as the output of the stored procedure.

In this chapter, you will see both single and multiple result sets of data returned and how these look within Query Editor.

Creating a Stored Procedure: Management Studio

Now that you have seen some of the merits of a stored procedure over other methods of working with data, it is time to create the first stored procedure in this chapter. This stored procedure will be built within SQL Server Management Studio and will insert a customer into the CustomerDetails.Customers table from the information passed to it. This is also the first part in the overall security solution. By using a stored procedure to enter the data into the underlying table, you will be in control of what data are entered, as the data can be validated and verified. You can also remove all access to the table and leave the stored procedure to serve as the only method of inserting data (you would also have stored procedures that update, delete, and retrieve data). You will look at this toward the end of the chapter.

The first exercise uses a template of a stored procedure as the basis of the code. Templates are either "out of the box" templates of code that exist as part of the SQL Server installation or are code templates that can be built either in-house or externally and provide the basis of functionality within SQL Server. There are templates for many areas of SQL Server that can be accessed within SQL Server Management Studio from View ➤ Template Explorer. Templates are ideal for reminding you of syntax or as a starting point for building a SQL Server object to a company standard. I personally find templates to be not as flexible as I would like, but this is a personal choice and many people do find them useful, especially for infrequent or complex tasks.

TRY IT OUT: CREATING A STORED PROCEDURE USING SQL SERVER MANAGEMENT STUDIO

1. Navigate to the ApressFinancial database, expand the Programmability node, and right-click Stored Procedures. From the pop-up menu, select New Stored Procedure.

2. This opens a Query Editor pane with code from a basic stored procedure template—the template called Create Stored Procedure (New Menu), to be exact. You can alter the procedure by changing the template options, by selecting from the Query toolbar the Specify Values for Template Parameters button (the rightmost button), by pressing Ctr+Shift+M, or by just writing the code from scratch. As you have chosen to create a stored procedure via the Object Explorer menu option, you will use the template this time. Figure 14-1 shows the template options that can be changed.

Figure 14-1. *A stored procedure's blank template*

3. The first three options, shown in Figure 14-2, are not part of the stored procedure syntax; they are extra options used within the comments of the stored procedure. The first option, Author, is very useful because it will probably be a dbo account that adds the stored procedure to the database, and therefore it will be hard to track who the actual creator of the stored procedure was. It may be that only one account "releases" all the code to production for deployment. The second option, Create Date, is not quite as relevant, as this can be found by interrogating system views. The Description option is excellent and should form part of

every stored procedure, as it will allow a short description of what the stored procedure is trying to achieve. Never go into too much detail in a description, because not everyone has good discipline in updating the comments when the stored procedure changes. However, a short "you are trying to achieve" set of text is perfect.

Parameter	Type	Value
Author		Robin Dewson
Create Date		20th Sept 2014
Description		This is to insert a customer

Figure 14-2. *First set of template options filled in*

4. You can now move to the template options that form part of the CREATE PROCEDURE syntax. The first option is the name. I have called this apf_insCustomer to define that it's a stored procedure in the ApressFinancial system and that the stored procedure is inserting a row in the CustomerDetails.Customers table. Then you can insert two parameters, as this is what the template is set up for. The first two parameters will be used to populate FirstName and LastName. You will look at the rest in a moment. The parameter values do not have to be the same name as the columns they will be working with, but it is best to have similar names. The data type and data length should be defined with the same type and length as the columns they will be used for. Failure to do this could lead to problems with data truncation if you make the parameter columns' length too long, for example. Also remove the values in the default options. Your template options should now look similar to what you see in Figure 14-3.

Figure 14-3. *The remaining parameters*

5. Click OK. The code will now look like the following:

```
-- ===================================================
-- Template generated from Template Explorer using:
-- Create Procedure (New Menu).SQL
--
-- Use the Specify Values for Template Parameters
-- command (Ctrl-Shift-M) to fill in the parameter
-- values below.
--
-- This block of comments will not be included in
-- the definition of the procedure.
-- ===================================================
SET ANSI_NULLS ON
GO
SET QUOTED_IDENTIFIER ON
GO
-- =================================================
-- Author:          Robin Dewson
-- Create date: 20th Sept 2014
-- Description:     This is to insert a customer
-- =================================================
CREATE PROCEDURE apf_insCustomer
    -- Add the parameters for the stored procedure here
    @FirstName varchar(5) = ,
    @LastName varchar(50) =
AS
BEGIN
    -- SET NOCOUNT ON added to prevent extra result sets from
    -- interfering with SELECT statements.
    SET NOCOUNT ON;

    -- Insert statements for procedure here
    SELECT @FirstName, @LastName
END
GO
```

6. You can now define the remaining parameters and fix up the two parameters already defined, as they currently have an equal sign and no value. The equal sign should be removed from the parameters. The code with the remaining parameters is shown here:

```
CREATE PROCEDURE CustomerDetails.apf_InsertCustomer
    -- Add the parameters for the procedure here
    @CustTitle int,
    @FirstName varchar(50) ,
    @CustInitials varchar(10),
    @LastName varchar(50),
    @AddressLine1 varchar(50),
    @AddressLine2 varchar(50),
    @AddressLine3 varchar(50),
    @TownOrCity int,
    @ZipCode varchar(20),
```

```
@USState tinyint,
@AccountTypeId int,
@ClearedBalance money
```

7. There are a couple of points to make before you progress. First of all, the parameters can be in any order, although it is best to group parameters together. Put all the input parameters first, and then specify the output parameters. You will see output parameters later in this chapter. You could also group together parameters used for table modification and then parameters used within the stored procedure that are discarded once you are finished with them within your stored procedure. Finally, within the "discarded group," group together parameters that are optional and have a default value assigned if no value is passed to the stored procedure. Personally, I group the parameters in a logical order. This can mean that the main key parameters are first, such as CustomerId, or that I group them in order, such as first name, surname, address, as you would see within a screen. Optional parameters tend to be toward the end, and finally the output parameters are last. The second point is that parameters like @CustTitle, @TownOrCity, @USState, and @AccountTypeId in this example are showing the numerical reference values that would come from values defined in a graphical front end. You may be wondering why the stored procedure is not generating these values from other information passed. For example, why is the stored procedure not producing the title ID from Mr., Miss, etc.? It is likely that the operator using the front end had a combobox with a list of possible values to choose from, with IDs corresponding to titles. The combobox would have been generated using the Title key value and display value. In the case of the town or city, the ID would link back to an external address database, so rather than holding the whole town or city, you could receive just the ID selected when the operator used the address lookup.

8. Moving on to the remaining section of the stored procedure, it will take the values of the parameters and use these values for the relevant columns. The remaining code for the stored procedure is as follows:

```
AS
BEGIN

    INSERT INTO CustomerDetails.Customers (Title, FirstName,
    OtherInitials,LastName,AddressLine1,AddressLine2,
    AddressLine3, TownOrCity,ZipCode,USState,AccountType,ClearedBalance)
    VALUES (@CustTitle, @FirstName, @CustInitials, @LastName,
    @AddressLine1,@AddressLine2,@AddressLine3,@TownOrCity,
    @ZipCode, @USState, @AccountTypeId,@ClearedBalance)

END
GO
```

9. When you execute the preceding code, provided you have made no typing mistakes, you should see the following output:

```
Command(s) completed successfully.
```

10. This will have added the stored procedure to the database. You can check this. Move back to Object Explorer, right-click Stored Procedures, and select Refresh. After the refresh, expand the Stored Procedures node, and you should see the stored procedure in Object Explorer, as shown in Figure 14-4.

- ⊟ 🗄 ApressFinancial
 - ⊞ 📁 Database Diagrams
 - ⊞ 📁 Tables
 - ⊞ 📁 Views
 - ⊞ 📁 Synonyms
 - ⊟ 📁 Programmability
 - ⊟ 📁 Stored Procedures
 - ⊞ 📁 System Stored Procedures
 - ⊞ 🗐 CustomerDetails.apf_InsertCustomer

Figure 14-4. Object Explorer with the stored procedure listed

11. You have completed your first developer-built stored procedure within the system. Inserting data using the stored procedure will now be demonstrated so you can see the procedure in action. To execute this stored procedure, you need to specify its name and pass the data in with parameters. There are two ways you can progress, as mentioned earlier. The first method is to pass the data across in the same order as the parameters defined within the stored procedure, as follows:

```
CustomerDetails.apf_InsertCustomer 1,'Steve',NULL,'Nicklin',
'645 Hyde Park',NULL,NULL,7545,'W1A 1AA',0,1,0
```

12. If you execute this, you should see the following output:

```
(1 row(s) affected)
```

13. However, as mentioned earlier, there is a downside to this method: if someone alters the stored procedure and places a new parameter in the middle of the existing list or changes the order of the parameters, or perhaps you don't know the order of the parameters, then you are at risk for errors. The preferred method is to name the parameters and the values as shown in the next example. Notice as well that the order has changed:

```
CustomerDetails.apf_InsertCustomer @CustTitle=1,@FirstName='James',
@CustInitials='A',@LastName='McVey',
@AddressLine1='127 Rothsbury Avenue',@AddressLine2='Teguise Coast',
@AddressLine3=NULL,@TownOrCity=94511,@ZipCode='121100',
@USState=0,@AccountTypeId=2,@ClearedBalance=0
```

14. Again, if you execute this, you should see the same results:

```
(1 row(s) affected)
```

You can check that the two customers have been entered correctly if you want. Let's take a look at two different methods for executing procedures next.

Different Methods of Execution

There are two different methods of executing a stored procedure. The first is to just call the stored procedure, as you saw in the preceding example. The second method is to use the EXEC(UTE) command. Both have the end result of invoking the stored procedure, but which is better for you to use depends on the particular situation.

- *No* EXEC: It is possible to call a stored procedure without prefixing the stored procedure name with the EXEC(UTE) statement. However, the stored procedure call must be the first statement within a batch of statements if you want to execute this statement.

- *With* EXEC: As I have just indicated, if the stored procedure call is the second or subsequent statement within a batch, then you must prefix the stored procedure with the EXEC(UTE) statement. On top of this, if you are calling a stored procedure within another stored procedure, then you will need to prefix that call with the EXEC(UTE) statement.

Returning Results

A stored procedure is built for more than inserting, updating, or deleting data. It is also used to return data from a return value, a value in a parameter, a value within a single column of a single row, known as a scalar value, or finally in one or more record sets. In the following sections, you will see each of these types of stored procedures.

The first area you will look at is returning a value. This value could be an error code or a specific value denoting a piece of information.

Using RETURN

One reason for returning a value from a stored procedure is to indicate an error; this is done with the RETURN statement. This statement immediately stops a stored procedure and passes control back out of it. Therefore, any statements after the RETURN statement will not be executed.

It is not compulsory to have a RETURN statement within your code; it is necessary only when you want to either return an error code or exit from a stored procedure without running any further code from that point. A logical RETURN is performed at the end of a stored procedure, returning a value of 0.

By default, 0 is returned if no value is specified after the RETURN statement, which means that the stored procedure was successful. Any other integer value could mean that an unexpected result occurred and that you should check the return code. It is also possible to return the number of rows affected by the stored procedure. Notice that the word "error" wasn't mentioned, as it may be valid for a nonzero return code from a stored procedure.

In this example, you will create a stored procedure that will return two output parameters back to the calling procedure or code, indicating both the cleared and uncleared balances of a specific customer.

The stored procedure will also use RETURN to indicate whether the customer ID passed to the stored procedure finds no rows. Note that this is not an error, as the stored procedure code will be working as expected.

You are probably wondering when to use output parameters and when to use RETURN. Output parameters are used to return information to a calling set of code and can handle any data type. On the other hand, a RETURN can return only an integer numeric value and is used more often for indicating success or failure.

TRY IT OUT: USING RETURN AND OUTPUT PARAMETERS

1. Template Explorer contains a template set up for output parameters. Navigate to this template, shown in Figure 14-5, and double-click it. The Template Explorer can be found from the View ➤ Template Explorer menu option and then under the Stored Procedure node.

- Stored Procedure
 - Alter Stored Procedure
 - Create Natively Compiled Stored Procedure
 - Create Procedure Basic Template
 - Create Procedure with CURSOR OUTPUT Parameter
 - Create Procedure with OUTPUT Parameter
 - Create Stored Procedure (New Menu)
 - Drop Stored Procedure

Figure 14-5. Template Explorer with the OUTPUT stored procedure

2. This will open up a new Query Editor pane with the basics of the relevant stored procedure, which is shown, reformatted, in the following code block. Take a moment to peruse this code. First of all, the first batch within the template sets up checks to see whether the stored procedure already exists by checking the system tables, and if it does exist, the code deletes the procedure through the DROP PROCEDURE command. After running DROP PROCEDURE, just like after dropping any object, all of the permissions associated with that object are lost when you recreate it, as discussed earlier. The template then demonstrates the building of the stored procedure with an example of how to execute the stored procedure at the end.

```
-- =================================================
-- Create stored procedure with OUTPUT parameters
-- =================================================
-- Drop stored procedure if it already exists
IF EXISTS (
  SELECT *
    FROM INFORMATION_SCHEMA.ROUTINES
   WHERE SPECIFIC_SCHEMA = N'<Schema_Name, sysname, Schema_Name>'
     AND SPECIFIC_NAME = N'<Procedure_Name, sysname, Procedure_Name>'
)
   DROP PROCEDURE <Schema_Name, sysname, Schema_Name>.<Procedure_Name,
   sysname, Procedure_Name>
GO

CREATE PROCEDURE <Schema_Name, sysname, Schema_Name>.
<Procedure_Name, sysname, Procedure_Name>
     <@param1, sysname, @p1> <datatype_for_param1, , int> =
     <default_value_for_param1, , 0>,
     <@param2, sysname, @p2> <datatype_for_param2, , int>  OUTPUT
AS
     SELECT @p2 = @p2 + @p1
GO
```

```
-- =================================================
-- Example to execute the stored procedure
-- =================================================
DECLARE <@variable_for_output_parameter, sysname, @p2_output>
<datatype_for_output_parameter, , int>

EXECUTE <Schema_Name, sysname, Schema_Name>.
<Procedure_Name, sysname, Procedure_Name> <value_for_param1, , 1>,
<@variable_for_output_parameter, sysname, @p2_output> OUTPUT

SELECT <@variable_for_output_parameter, sysname, @p2_output>
GO
```

3. Now that you have seen the code, it is time to update the template parameters. Again, you will find that the template is not ideal for the final solution, as you have only one input parameter and two output parameters. This stored procedure will belong to the CustomerDetails schema. The input parameter is a single-integer input parameter for the customer ID, followed by the first of the two output parameters, which will be used for cleared balances. Once you have entered these settings, as shown in Figure 14-6, click OK.

Figure 14-6. *Template values for the OUTPUT stored procedure*

■ **Note** You have to enter the output parameter twice in Template Explorer.

4. Let's look at the code that was generated. The first section of code checks whether the stored procedure exists. If it does, then at execution it is deleted by using the DROP PROCEDURE statement.

```
-- =================================================
-- Create stored procedure with OUTPUT parameters
-- =================================================
-- Drop stored procedure if it already exists
IF EXISTS (
  SELECT *
    FROM INFORMATION_SCHEMA.ROUTINES
   WHERE SPECIFIC_SCHEMA = N'CustomerDetails'
     AND SPECIFIC_NAME = N'apf_CustBalance'
)
    DROP PROCEDURE CustomerDetails.apf_CustBalance
GO
```

5. Move on to the second section, which creates the contents of the stored procedure; I will go through each part of it in turn. This stored procedure takes three parameters: an input parameter of @CustomerId and two output parameters that will be passed back to either another stored procedure or a program, perhaps written in C#, for example. Don't worry—it is possible to use Query Editor to see the value of the output parameter, but retrieving the values in a development language will be demonstrated in Chapter 19. When defining parameters in a stored procedure, there is no need to specify that a parameter is set for input, as this is the default; however, if you do need to define a parameter as an output parameter, you will have to insert OUTPUT as a suffix to each parameter. You will need to tidy up the code built by the template.

■ **Tip** If you define an OUTPUT parameter but do not define a value within the stored procedure, it will have a value of NULL.

```
CREATE PROCEDURE CustomerDetails.apf_CustBalance
    @CustomerId int,
    @ClearedBalance money OUTPUT, @UnclearedBalance money OUTPUT
AS
```

6. Take a look at the next section of code, which is very similar to what I have covered several times earlier in the book in that variables have values assigned to them:

```
BEGIN
SELECT @ClearedBalance = ClearedBalance, @UnclearedBalance = UnclearedBalance
  FROM CustomerDetails.Customers
 WHERE CustomerId = @CustomerId
```

7. The final section of the stored procedure returns a value from a system global variable, @@ ROWCOUNT. You'll look at this variable in the next chapter; it returns the number of rows returned in the previous T-SQL statement. From this, the calling code can tell whether there have been problems and can then decide whether to ignore any values in the OUTPUT parameter.

```
    RETURN @@ROWCOUNT
END
GO
```

8. This completes the stored procedure definition. The template continues defining how to execute the stored procedure. The first part of this section defines the variables that hold the output values and the return value. Then the code moves to the EXECUTE section of code. When a value is returned from a stored procedure, it is set on the left-hand side of the stored procedure call and is not a parameter value. Then the stored procedure is defined with the three parameters. Note that each output parameter has to have the OUTPUT keyword after it. The final section of the code is a SELECT statement that displays the values returned and the output parameter.

```
-- ================================================
-- Example to execute the stored procedure
-- ================================================
DECLARE @ClearedBalance Money, @UnclearedBalance Money
DECLARE @RetVal int

EXECUTE @RetVal=CustomerDetails.apf_CustBalance 2,
@ClearedBalance OUTPUT,
@UnclearedBalance OUTPUT

SELECT @RetVal AS ReturnValue, @ClearedBalance AS ClearedBalance,
@UnclearedBalance AS UnclearedBalance
GO
```

9. Now that the template has been altered with the changes that are required, execute the whole template code. This will create the stored procedure and run the example at the end to demonstrate the procedure. Of course, you can run this section of code as many times as you want because the whole scenario, from dropping and losing the stored procedure through to recreating the stored procedure, is all there, ready for you. The stored procedure will pass back output parameter values to the @ClearedBalance and @UnclearedBalance variables defined within the execution batch and will send the return value to the @RetVal variable. From there, once the variables are set, the values can be printed out using a SELECT statement. This will produce the output shown in Figure 14-7 in the Results pane.

	ReturnValue	ClearedBalance	UnclearedBalance
1	1	337.97	-10.56

Figure 14-7. Results after running the OUTPUT stored procedure

10. If you run the stored procedure with a customer number that is not in the database, you will see NULL values in the two output parameters and a return value of 0. The code to see this is here:

```
DECLARE @ClearedBalance Money, @UnclearedBalance Money
DECLARE @RetVal int

EXECUTE @RetVal=CustomerDetails.apf_CustBalance 8653568,
@ClearedBalance OUTPUT,
@UnclearedBalance OUTPUT

SELECT @RetVal AS ReturnValue, @ClearedBalance AS ClearedBalance,
@UnclearedBalance AS UnclearedBalance
GO
```

You have now built two very basic stored procedures in which you are performing an INSERT and a SELECT. Next you will look at returning multiple result sets.

Returning Multiple Result Sets

As mentioned earlier, although it is not common, it is possible to return multiple result sets to your calling program. You will see how to handle this in Chapter 19. In the ApressFinancial database, you may want to return every share with the share details and the price movement of each share price for analysis. You could call two stored procedures, one for each set of data, or you could call one stored procedure that completes both actions. There is nothing new from a SQL Server viewpoint, but here you will create a stored procedure to be used when you call the stored procedure from an example in Chapter 19.

```
┌─────────────────────────────────────────────────────────────┐
│      TRY IT OUT: RETURNING MULTIPLE RESULT SETS               │
└─────────────────────────────────────────────────────────────┘
```

1. From an empty Query Editor, create the following stored procedure. Notice that there are two SELECT statements. Once you have entered the code, execute it so that the stored procedure is created.

```
CREATE PROCEDURE ShareDetails.AllShareDetails @ShareId int
AS
BEGIN

SELECT ShareId, Description, StockExchangeTicker
  FROM ShareDetails.Shares
 WHERE ShareId = @ShareId

SELECT SharePriceId, ShareId, Price, PriceDate
  FROM ShareDetails.SharePrices
 WHERE ShareId = @ShareId
 ORDER BY PriceDate DESC
END
```

2. Test the stored procedure by entering and executing the following code:

```
ShareDetails.AllShareDetails 1
```

3. Your results should be similar to those in Figure 14-8.

	ShareId	Description	StockExchangeTicker
1	1	ACME'S HOMEBAKE COOKIES INC	AHCI

	SharePriceId	ShareId	Price	PriceDate
1	1	1	34.25148	2012-03-28 10:12:42.740
2	2	1	6.62765	2012-03-27 06:47:46.900
3	3	1	6.44350	2012-03-25 21:51:29.910
4	4	1	32.04574	2012-03-12 19:57:07.630
5	5	1	32.00452	2012-03-06 16:59:24.430
6	6	1	30.16576	2012-03-06 01:09:36.260
7	7	1	7.12997	2012-03-05 05:29:29.280
8	8	1	35.63776	2012-03-04 09:54:17.870

Figure 14-8. *Results after running the OUTPUT stored procedure*

Controlling the Flow

When working on a stored procedure, there will be times when it is necessary to control the flow of execution through it. The main control of flow is handled with an IF...ELSE statement. You can also control the flow with a WHILE...BREAK statement.

■ **Note** The GOTO statement can also control the flow of a stored procedure. You can use this statement to jump to a label within a stored procedure, but this can be a dangerous practice and really is something that should be avoided. For example, it might be better to nest the stored procedure calls.

Controlling the flow through a stored procedure will probably be required when a procedure does anything more than work with one T-SQL statement. The flow will depend on your procedure taking an expression and making a true or false decision, and then taking one of two separate actions depending on the answer from the decision.

IF . . . ELSE

At times, a logical expression will need to be evaluated that results in either a true or false answer. This is where an IF...ELSE statement is needed. You have come across this statement a few times within this chapter. There are many ways of making a true or false condition, and most of the possibilities involve relational operators such as <, >, =, and NOT; however, these can be combined with string functions, other mathematical equations, comparisons between values in local variables, or even system-wide variables. It is also possible to place a SELECT statement within an IF...ELSE block, as long as a single value is returned.

A basic IF...ELSE statement block would perhaps look like the following:

```
IF A=B
   Statement when True
ELSE
   Statement when False
```

`IF...ELSE` statements can also be nested and would look like the following. This example also shows you how to include a `SELECT` statement within an `IF` decision:

```
IF A=B
    IF (SELECT ClearedBalance FROM Customers WHERE CustomerId = 1) > $20000
        Statement2 when True
    ELSE
        Statement2 when False
ELSE
    Statement when False
```

As you can see, there is only one statement within each of the `IF...ELSE` blocks. If you want to have more than one line of executable code after the `IF` or the `ELSE`, you must include another control-of-flow statement, the `BEGIN...END` block.

BEGIN...END

If you want to execute more than one statement in the `IF` or `ELSE` code block, you need to batch the statements up. To batch statements together within an `IF...ELSE` block, you must surround them with a `BEGIN` and `END` block. If you try to have more than one statement after the `IF`, the second and subsequent statements will run no matter what the setting of the `IF` statement is.

So if you have the following code, then the `SELECT 2` statement would run no matter what value you have for `@VarTest`. See the following:

```
DECLARE @VarTest
SET @VarTest = 2
IF @VarTest=1
SELECT 1
SELECT 2
```

If you want `SELECT 2` to run only when `@VarTest` is 1, then you would use the following code, thus placing the code you want to run within the `BEGIN...END` block:

```
DECLARE @VarTest
SET @VarTest = 2
IF @VarTest=1
BEGIN
    SELECT 1
    SELECT 2
END
```

If you use an `ELSE` statement after a second or subsequent statement after an `IF` that has no `BEGIN...END` block, you would get an error message. Therefore, the only way around this is to use `BEGIN...END`.

WHILE...BREAK Statement

The WHILE...BREAK statement is a method of looping around the same section of code from zero to multiple times based on the answer from a Boolean test condition, or until explicitly instructed to exit by the BREAK statement. The syntax for this command is as follows:

```
WHILE Boolean_expression
    { sql_statement | statement_block }
    [ BREAK ]
    { sql_statement | statement_block }
    [ CONTINUE ]
    { sql_statement | statement_block }
```

The code defined for the WHILE statement will execute as long as the Boolean expression returns a value of True. You can have other control-of-flow statements such as an IF...ELSE block within your WHILE block. This is where BREAK and CONTINUE could be used if required. You may want to test a condition and, if it returns a particular result, BREAK the loop and exit the WHILE block. The other option that can be used is the CONTINUE statement. This moves processing straight to the WHILE statement again and will stop any execution of code that is defined after it. The best way to illustrate these concepts is to show a simple example of these three options in action.

TRY IT OUT: WHILE...BREAK

1. The first option demonstrates how to build a WHILE loop and then test the value of a variable. If the test returns True, you will break out of the loop; if it returns False, you will continue processing. Within the example, there are two SELECT statements, one before and one after an IF...ELSE statement. In this example, the first SELECT will show the values of the variables, but the IF test will either stop the loop via BREAK or move the code back to the WHILE statement via the CONTINUE statement. Either of these actions will mean that the second SELECT will not execute.

   ```
   DECLARE @LoopCount int, @TestCount int
   SET @LoopCount = 0
   SET @TestCount = 0
   WHILE @LoopCount < 20
   BEGIN
       SET @LoopCount = @LoopCount + 1
       SET @TestCount = @TestCount + 1
       SELECT @LoopCount, @TestCount
       IF @TestCount > 10
          BREAK
       ELSE
          CONTINUE
       SELECT @LoopCount, @TestCount
   END
   ```

2. When the code is executed, you don't actually make it around the 20 loops due to the value of @TestCount causing the break. Also, the CONTINUE statement causes the execution to move to the END statement and therefore it skips the SELECT statement and continue with the next iteration of the loop. The output is partially shown in Figure 14-9.

	(No column name)	(No column name)
1	8	8

	(No column name)	(No column name)
1	9	9

	(No column name)	(No column name)
1	10	10

	(No column name)	(No column name)
1	11	11

Figure 14-9. WHILE with BREAK and CONTINUE

3. If you change the code to remove the ELSE CONTINUE statement, the second SELECT statement will be executed. The two rows changed have been highlighted. You are not going to execute the two lines because they have been commented out by prefixing the code with two hyphens (--).

```
DECLARE @LoopCount int, @TestCount int
SET @LoopCount = 0
SET @TestCount = 0
WHILE @LoopCount < 20
BEGIN
    SET @LoopCount = @LoopCount + 1
    SET @TestCount = @TestCount + 1
    SELECT @LoopCount, @TestCount
    IF @TestCount > 10
        BREAK
--    ELSE
--        CONTINUE
    SELECT @LoopCount, @TestCount
END
```

A snapshot of some of the output from this is shown in Figure 14-10.

⊞ Results	🗎 Messages

	(No column name)	(No column name)
1	1	1

	(No column name)	(No column name)
1	1	1

	(No column name)	(No column name)
1	2	2

	(No column name)	(No column name)
1	2	2

Figure 14-10. WHILE with BREAK only

The third statement you will look at in this section is the CASE statement. While not a control-of-flow statement used in your stored procedure, it also can be used to control the execution flow.

CASE Statement

When a query has more than a plain true or false answer—in other words, when there are several potential answers—you should use the CASE statement.

A CASE statement forms a decision-making process within a SELECT or an UPDATE statement. It is possible to set a value for a column within a result set based on a CASE statement and the resultant value. Obviously, with this knowledge, you realize that a CASE statement cannot form part of a DELETE statement.

Several parts of a CASE statement can be placed within a stored procedure to control the statement executed, depending on each scenario. Two different syntaxes exist for the CASE statement depending on how you want to test a condition or what you want to test. Let's take a look at all the parts of the first CASE statement syntax:

```
CASE expression
WHEN value_matched THEN
    statement
[[WHEN value_matched2 THEN]
   [Statement2]]
...
...
...
[[ELSE]
   [catch_all_code]
END
```

First, you need to define the expression that is to be tested. This could be the value of a variable, a column value from within the T-SQL statement, or any valid expression within SQL Server. This expression is then used to determine the values to be matched in each WHEN clause.

You can have as many WHEN clauses as you want within the CASE condition, and you do not need to cover every condition or possible value that could occur. Once a condition is matched, only the statements within the appropriate WHEN block will be executed. Of course, only the WHEN conditions that are defined will be tested. However, you can cover yourself for any value within the expression that has not been defined within a WHEN statement by using an ELSE condition. This is used as a catch-all statement. Any value not matched would drop into the ELSE condition, and from there you could deal with it.

The second syntax is used for computing a value depending on the condition. See the following:

```
CASE
    WHEN Boolean_expression THEN result_expression
    [ ...n ]
    [
    ELSE else_result_expression
    ]
END
```

As just indicated, CASE statements can be part of SELECT, UPDATE, or INSERT statements, therefore possibly working on multiple rows of data. As each row is retrieved from the table, the CASE statement kicks in, and instead of the column value being returned, it is the value from the decision-making process that is inserted instead. This happens after the data have been retrieved and just before the rows returned are displayed in the results pane. The actual value is initially returned from the table and is then validated through the CASE statement; once this is done, the value is discarded if no longer required.

Now that you are familiar with CASE statements, you can look at them in action.

TRY IT OUT: USING THE CASE STATEMENT

1. The first example will demonstrate the first CASE syntax, where you will take a column and
 test for a specific value. The results of this test will determine which action will be performed.

    ```
    SELECT Description,
    CASE CreditType
    WHEN 0 THEN 'Debiting the account'
    WHEN 1 THEN 'Crediting the account'
    END
    FROM TransactionDetails.TransactionTypes
    ```

2. Execute this code, and you should see the output shown in Figure 14-11.

	Description	(No column name)
1	Buy	Debiting the account
2	Sell	Crediting the account
3	Cash Deposit	Crediting the account
4	Cash Withdrawal	Debiting the account
5	Rights Issue	Crediting the account
6	Warrants	Debiting the account

Figure 14-11. Simple CASE statement output

3. A customer can have a positive or a negative ClearedBalance. The CASE statement that
 follows will demonstrate this by showing either In Credit or Overdrawn. In this case, you
 want to use the second CASE syntax. You cannot use the first syntax, as you have an operator
 included within the test and you are not looking for a specific value. The code is defined as
 follows:

    ```
    SELECT CustomerId,
    CASE
    WHEN ClearedBalance < 0 THEN 'OverDrawn'
    WHEN ClearedBalance > 0 THEN 'In Credit'
    ELSE 'Flat'
    END, ClearedBalance
    FROM CustomerDetails.Customers
    ```

4. Execute the code. This produces output similar to what you see in Figure 14-12.

3	918	In Credit	279.6371
4	664	In Credit	181.2152
5	52	Flat	0.00
6	211	In Credit	85.4319
7	860	In Credit	463.7111
8	421	Flat	0.00
9	609	In Credit	13.8752

Figure 14-12. Searched CASE statement output

Bringing It All Together

Now that you have seen the control-of-flow statements, you can bring all of this together in the most complex set of code so far. The aim of this stored procedure is to take a "from" and "to" date, which can be over any period, and return the movement of a particular customer's transactions that have affected the cash balance. This mimics your bank statement when it says whether you have spent more than you have deposited.

In the following example, you will be returning a value that will later be used as a "scalar" value within Chapter 19.

■ **Note** In this example, you are performing a loop around rows of data within a table. This example demonstrates some of the functionality just covered with decisions and control of flow. SQL Server works best with sets of data, rather than with a row at a time. However, there will be times that row-by-row processing like this happens. In SQL Server, you have the option to write .NET-based stored procedures, and this example would certainly be considered a candidate for this treatment. This example works with one row at a time, and you would have a running total of a customer's balance so that you could calculate interest to charge or to pay.

TRY IT OUT: BRINGING IT ALL TOGETHER

1. First of all, let's create the stored procedure. Enter the CREATE PROCEDURE statement in an empty Query Editor pane, and then name the procedure with the three input parameters.

```
CREATE PROCEDURE CustomerDetails.apf_CustMovement @CustId bigint,
@FromDate datetime, @ToDate datetime
AS
BEGIN
```

2. You then need three internal variables. This stored procedure will return one row of transactions at a time while you are still within the date range. As you move through each row, you need to keep a running balance of the amounts for each transaction. You know that the data in the TransactionDetails.Transactions_old table have an ascending TransactionId as each transaction is entered, so the next transaction from the one returned

443

must have a higher value. Therefore, you can store the transaction ID in a variable called @LastTran and use that in filtering. Once the variables are declared, you then set them to an initial value. You use @StillCalc as a test for the WHILE loop. This could be any variable, as you are using the CONTINUE and BREAK statements to determine when you should exit the loop.

```
DECLARE @RunningBal money, @StillCalc Bit, @LastTran bigint

SELECT @StillCalc = 1, @LastTran = 0, @RunningBal = 0
```

3. Tell the loop to continue until you get no rows back from the SELECT statement. Once you get no rows, you will know that there are no more transactions in the date range.

```
WHILE @StillCalc = 1
BEGIN
```

4. A more complex SELECT statement will return one row where the TransactionId is greater than the previous TransactionId returned; the transaction would affect the customer's cash balance, and the transaction occurred between the two dates passed in. If there is a transaction, then you add or subtract the value from the @RunningBal variable. Use a CASE statement to decide whether you need to make the value a negative value for adding to the variable.

```
    SELECT TOP 1 @RunningBal = @RunningBal + CASE
                 WHEN tt.CreditType = 1 THEN t.Amount
                 ELSE t.Amount * -1 END,
                 @LastTran = t.TransactionId
      FROM CustomerDetails.Customers c
      JOIN TransactionDetails.Transactions_old t ON
        t.CustomerId = c.CustomerId
      JOIN TransactionDetails.TransactionTypes tt ON
        tt.TransactionTypeId = t.TransactionType
     WHERE t.TransactionId > @LastTran
       AND tt.AffectCashBalance = 1
       AND DateEntered BETWEEN @FromDate AND @ToDate
     ORDER BY DateEntered
```

5. If you get a row returned, then you continue the loop. Once you get no rows returned, you know that there are no further transactions in the date range.

```
    IF @@ROWCOUNT > 0
      -- Perform some interest calculation here...
      CONTINUE
    ELSE
      BREAK
    END

    SELECT @RunningBal AS 'End Balance'
END
GO
```

6. You can now create the stored procedure and test it. The example is going to check whether customer ID 1 has had a positive or a negative movement on his or her cash balance in the month of August 2011. The code to find this out follows. First of all, you insert some TransactionDetails.Transactions records to test it out. You also prefix the stored procedure with an EXEC(UTE) statement, as this is part of a batch of statements.

```
INSERT INTO TransactionDetails.Transactions_old
(CustomerId,TransactionType,DateEntered,Amount,RelatedProductId)
 VALUES (1,1,'1 Aug 2015',100.00,1),
 (1,1,'3 Aug 2015',75.67,1),
 (1,2,'5 Aug 2015',35.20,1),
 (1,2,'6 Aug 2015',20.00,1)
EXEC  CustomerDetails.apf_CustMovement 1,'1 Aug 2015','31 Aug 2015'
```

7. Execute the preceding code, which should return a value that you expect, as shown in Figure 14-13.

Figure 14-13. Complex stored procedure output

Security

Now that you have tables, views, and stored procedures established, the current system is so secure that nobody has access to any data once a login has been granted to ApressFinancial. The only people that have access are database owners. This is very restrictive, and you need to be able to give the right database users the correct access. In the following section, I will discuss further areas of security, building on the foundations laid in Chapter 4.

Security Gains

The two worst-case scenarios from a security standpoint are that all database users are database owners or that all database users are granted full access rights to all objects. In this section of the chapter, I will cover security, what is best practice, and how to implement this.

Here is a quick reminder of some terminology before you proceed:

- *Windows user id/account*: An account used to log on to a Windows computer

- *Windows group*: A group of users that can be created in some Windows editions and on networks that allow Windows accounts to be grouped for simplifying tasks

- *Server login*: Allows you to connect to the server

- *Database user account*: Allows a server login to connect to a database

- *Principal*: A name given to a collection of security-based items; examples of a principal are application roles, database users, a Windows login, and a Windows group.

First of all, here is a quick summary of the current security settings from earlier in the book. In Chapter 4, you created two Windows accounts, MSmith and NMorgala, as well as two Windows groups, Apress_Product_Controllers and Apress_Client_Information. MSmith was then added to Windows group Apress_Product_Controllers. The Windows group was added as a server login to SQL Server, which allows anyone in that Windows group to log on to SQL Server. This same process was completed for the MSmith Windows account as part of the examples in that chapter. Both Apress_Product_Controllers and MSmith were added as database users to the ApressFinancial database, although MSmith was added as a database owner. So at the moment, MSmith as a database owner has full access to the ApressFinancial database. At present, only your account and MSmith have any access to the data, stored procedures, views, and so on, as no further access has been granted at any point throughout the book.

To prove MSmith has full access, log on to Windows as MSmith, then start SQL Server Management Studio, open a Query Editor window, and, within a transaction, update a table. The example code I used to prove MSmith's access was as follows:

```
BEGIN TRAN
UPDATE CustomerDetails.CustomerProducts
SET AmountToCollect = 300
WHERE CustomerFinancialProductId = 1
ROLLBACK TRAN
```

You can see the Windows groups and MSmith in Figure 14-14 in the Permissions page of the Database Properties screen.

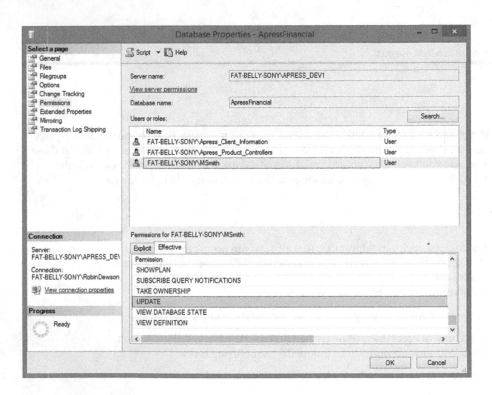

Figure 14-14. *ApressFinancial database users and effective permissions*

So now you know how the security is currently defined within the database. You can now correct any errors and implement the correct security model. MSmith should not be a database owner, as it is not a developer- or database administrator–based account.

The first security consideration is to define who can create, modify, or drop objects in your database. Objects are tables, views, stored procedures, and so on as well as database users, roles, and so forth. This is the most dangerous area of a database, as users can accidently or maliciously perform these actions and potentially destroy your database. Hackers look for ways to access a SQL Server database to complete these actions. This can occur by users in the database owner role giving all database users the database owner role. Under no circumstances should you implement this. Only developers (or, in larger corporations, those who release code to production) should be given the database owner role.

The next security consideration is data access and how this should be implemented. There are two schools of thought on how to achieve this. The first school of thought is that all data access, regardless of whether it is to insert, update, delete, or view data, should be done through stored procedures or views. This means that there is no direct table access. A stored procedure should be written for each action on each table or tables. Some advantages of having all-encompassing stored procedures are as follows:

- Data integrity is strictly controlled via the stored procedures. The stored procedures will enforce referential data integrity on top of any relationships you have between tables by ensuring that data in columns fit into the overall database design, and that all data returned either internally in the stored procedure or externally to the executing connection are valid, in a defined format, and contain only the required information.

- User accounts less familiar with your data model can work with your data in a safe manner. If someone new joins a team or if you have a separate team of people who maintain your database data, allowing you and your team to develop further enhancements, the maintenance team doesn't need to know the underlying data structures or design. Correcting any issues or enhancing the data can all be controlled via stored procedure access.

- It is a lot harder for hackers to see the database design and structure and, therefore, to maliciously alter your database.

However, some of the downsides include the following:

- Ad hoc data corrections may not have a stored procedure available at the time the correction is required.

- Changes to the database design, as you enhance your system, can mean changing a large number of related stored procedures.

- You may find that you build a system in which one stored procedure calls another stored procedure, which in turn calls another stored procedure, and so on. This is known as nested procedures, and it could be that within the nesting you find it difficult to follow and perform the right actions in the right order.

- Stored procedures may have a large number of optional parameters with default values so as to fit every access path.

The second school of thought is that the application knows its data the best and thus all data access should be via direct T-SQL. The GUI would build up T-SQL statements and send them to SQL Server for action and the results would be sent back to the GUI to take further. Some advantages of this school of thought include the following:

- The GUI can build the specific code required to perform the necessary action. Optional data requirements can be included or omitted in the T-SQL statement as required.

- The development code, if built well, can implement object-oriented techniques, and this can help build solid T-SQL based on the data held.

- Modifications to the data structure in the database could mean that one alteration in the development code that would permeate all database changes.

- All data validation and business rules are held outside of the database, and this can aid development time.

And some of the disadvantages include the following:

- Extra code has to be written to stop SQL injection attacks. An SQL injection is where a hacker builds T-SQL statements, which can then be passed to the database and reveal data or schema to the hacker, who can then hack your database further. This can happen from a text box where a hacker can insert a code terminator that would terminate the code you are building and then execute the hacker's code.

- A larger amount of code is being passed over the network, and this will result in some performance reduction, depending on the network.

Changes to the database schema can also mean a deployment of the application to reflect those changes.

These lists are not exhaustive, and different developers will have different views and reasons for each method of proceeding. I just wanted to present to you that there is no right or wrong answer. What you have to decide is what is right for you and what is right for the development you are working on. I tend to adopt a mixed-approach strategy in most of my development, where I will have stored procedures and direct T-SQL. I use T-SQL where the code required can alter on each request, such as the columns to return or the tables to work with, and I use stored procedures wherever else I can. If I do have to use T-SQL, I will also try to use views as much as possible before I use direct table access.

However, at this point, non-database owners can do nothing, so it is time to take a look at how you can grant and revoke access to database users.

Granting and Revoking Permissions

It is possible to give or bar a specific principal access rights to specific objects. Within the following section, you will see how you can grant and revoke rights to an object and how these actions can secure access to specific objects.

■ **Note** Granting and revoking extends beyond database objects to many other areas. You would then replace the term *objects* with the term *securables*, as you saw in Chapter 4, when adding Windows groups to SQL Server and giving them access rights to the ApressFinancial database.

GRANT

To give a principal a specific permission on an object requires a GRANT statement, and removing permission necessitates a REVOKE statement. The first statement you will use will be the GRANT statement. This gives specifically defined permissions on a specific object to a specific principal. The generic format of the GRANT statement is as follows:

```
GRANT { [ PRIVILEGES ] }
    | permission [ ( column [ ,...n ] ) ] [ ,...n ]
    [ ON [ class :: ] securable ] TO principal [ ,...n ]
    [ WITH GRANT OPTION ] [ AS principal ]
```

This statement alters depending on the object you are applying the GRANT to. However, let's take a moment to look at the options:

- PRIVILEGES: This keyword is optional and exists due to ISO compliance and is non-functional on permissions.

- permission: The permission you will be granting; permissions include EXECUTE, SELECT, INSERT, DELETE, and UPDATE.

- column: The name or list of the column(s) that you will be granting privileges on; the list has to be surrounded by parentheses.

- ON securable: Optional; the securable object you are granting privileges on; this could be the table, stored procedure, or view.

- TO principal: The security principal that is receiving the privilege; this could be a database user or an application role.

- WITH GRANT OPTION: Optional; you can allow the principal defined in the statement to grant this permission to other principals. This is something you need to take care with as you could allow that principal to grant the privilege to another principal that you have no control over.

- AS principal: Optional; it is possible to grant an object permission to a specific principal, but that principal derives its permissions from a different principal.

The GRANT statement covers a large range of objects, from granting a principal the ability to create a database through to the ability to insert data into tables, execute stored procedures, and even deal with specific columns within a table. One example: You give access to the CustomerDetails.Customers table to several principals but grant to only one principal the ability to see the customer balance amounts within that table. You will see this in action in the example shortly.

REVOKE

Of course, you need the ability to revoke any privileges. Revoking privileges is ideal when you no longer wish a user/principal to have access to a specific securable/object. This can happen when you have given an object too much access. Revoking privileges tends to be used less than granting privileges once a system is live, as part of the go-live would be to have the right privileges granted at that time.

The format for this statement is as follows:

```
REVOKE [ GRANT OPTION FOR ]
    {
      [PRIVILEGES ]
      |
            permission [ ( column [ ,...n ] ) ] [ ,...n ]
    }
    [ ON [ class :: ] securable ]
    { TO | FROM } principal [ ,...n ]
    [ CASCADE] [ AS principal ]
```

The options are as follows:

- GRANT OPTION FOR: If you have granted permission and included the WITH GRANT option, you can revoke the ability to pass on privileges.

- PRIVILEGES: The keyword is included for ISO compliance and has no effect on permissions.

- permission: The permission you wish to revoke

- ON securable: The securable object that you are revoking the permission on

- TO | FROM principal: The security principal that you are revoking the privilege from

- CASCADE: If you granted permission on an object to a principal using the WITH GRANT option, and this principal granted permission to another principal and so on, then by using the CASCADE option, the privilege will be revoked for the principal mentioned plus all the principals down the chain.

- AS principal: Optional; it works for REVOKE much as it does for GRANT, but revokes instead of grants.

In the following example, you will allow the Apress_Product_Controllers database user access to execute two procedures and return data from one table, but the user will be unable to see the value from a column.

TRY IT OUT: SECURING YOUR DATABASE

1. First of all, you should remove the MSmith database user from the database. If you recall in Chapter 4, MSmith was added and then given the db_owner server role. This allowed MSmith to create tables and to insert, update, and delete data, among several other database actions.

   ```
   DROP USER [FAT-BELLY-SONY\MSmith]
   ```

2. If you switch the user to MSmith within Windows, you can still connect to SQL Server. MSmith still has a server login. However, if you try to expand the ApressFinancial database and see what tables exist they will still be displayed, but you are unable to expand a specific table to see the columns contained. If MSmith tries to run a query against the ApressFinancial database, you will find that the user cannot do this. Figure 14-15 shows that no columns can be seen and shows the error message you will receive when MSmith tries to execute some T-SQL.

Figure 14-15. MSmith has lost all ability to work within the ApressFinancial database

3. The next step is to give the database user `Apress_Product_Controllers` access to the objects in the `ApressFinancial` database that is required for the user to complete the work. The first action will be to give access to execute permissions on securable stored procedure `CustomerDetails.apf_CustMovement` using the Properties screen. Find the stored procedure, right-click, and select Properties from the menu. From the screen that appears, select the Permissions page from the menu on the left. This should display Figure 14-16, where no explicit permissions have been granted.

Figure 14-16. *Permissions page for the stored procedure*

4. To add `Apress_Product_Controllers`, click the Search button on the right side of the page. This will bring up the search dialog box as shown in Figure 14-17, where you can select the user or role you wish to give the privilege to.

Figure 14-17. Searching for a user or a role

5. Click the Browse button. This will display the possible objects that meet the search criteria, which should be similar to Figure 14-18. You will see the two user groups of `Apress_Client_Information` and `Apress_Product_Controllers`. You will also see the application role Banking Transactions, as well as the database role `public` and the user "guest." Select `Apress_Product_Controllers` and click OK. This will add this user to the search dialog. Click OK twice to return you to the Properties page.

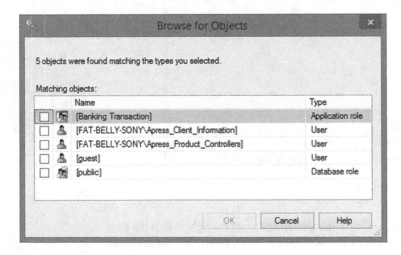

Figure 14-18. The roles and users that can be chosen

6. The Permissions page will now resemble Figure 14-19. The user has been added in the top half of the page, and the potential permissions for the principal to be given for this object are listed at the bottom of the page.

Figure 14-19. *The user added and the potential permissions that can be granted*

7. There are five possible options, but the option required is Execute. This will then give this user the ability to execute the stored procedure. Select Execute under the Grant column, as shown in Figure 14-20, and click OK to apply the changes. The other options are as follows:

 - *Alter*: Selecting this option would allow the principal to alter the code.

 - *Control*: Similar to owning a securable/object, by granting this the principal would have similar permissions. However, you can then deny specific actions.

 - *Take ownership*: At present this object is owned by the account that created it. It is possible to take ownership of the object. This option is more likely to be set on schemas than on stored procedures.

 - *View definition*: Allows the user to see the metadata of the object; in this case, you would be able to see the contents of the stored procedure.

Figure 14-20. Execute permission selected

8. The permission is now applied, which you can check by switching to MSmith and executing the following code:

```
EXEC  CustomerDetails.apf_CustMovement 1,'1 Aug 2015','31 Aug 2015'
```

9. You can achieve the same permissions via T-SQL using the GRANT statement:

```
GRANT EXECUTE ON CustomerDetails.apf_CustMovement
TO [FAT-BELLY-SONY\Apress_Product_Controllers]
```

10. The final demonstration will be to grant Apress_Product_Controllers the ability to perform a SELECT on the CustomerDetails.Customers table, but without being able to retrieve data from the ClearedBalance column. First of all, highlight the CustomerDetails.Customers table, right-click, and select Properties. Choose the Permissions option. Then add the Apress_Product_Controllers user using the same steps as in the previous parts of this exercise. Your Permissions page should now look like Figure 14-21.

Figure 14-21. *Adding the Windows group to the table properties*

11. If you now click the Select permission within the Grant column, it will enable the Column Properties button on the right-hand side. If you click this button, you will see the Column Permissions screen, as shown in Figure 14-22.

Figure 14-22. *Columns that could be granted or denied permissions*

12. Find the ClearedBalance column and click Deny. For all other columns in the list, you need to click the Grant column. This will then deny this principal from accessing the ClearedBalance column but will allow it to SELECT from all the others. You should see something like Figure 14-23. Click OK, which will return you to the Permissions page. You can click OK, or click Cancel and then execute the following T-SQL statement instead:

```
GRANT SELECT ON CustomerDetails.Customers (CustomerId,
Title, FirstName, OtherInitials, LastName,AddressLine1,
AddressLine2,AddressLine3,TownOrCity,ZipCode,USState,
AccountType, UnclearedBalance, DateOpened,DateClosed)
TO [FAT-BELLY-SONY\Apress_Product_Controllers]
```

Figure 14-23. *Access to* ClearedBalance *denied, but all other columns granted*

13. You can test out this permission by switching to MSmith one last time and executing the following code examples. The first is to perform a SELECT against CustomerDetails. Customers and return the FirstName and LastName, as follows:

```
SELECT FirstName, LastName
FROM CustomerDetails.Customers
```

14. The next example will try to retrieve the ClearedBalance. This will give an error. See the following:

```
SELECT FirstName, LastName, ClearedBalance
FROM CustomerDetails.Customers
```

15. The final example is to demonstrate that it is not possible for MSmith to delete a row from the table:

```
DELETE FROM CustomerDetails.Customers WHERE CustomerId = 2
```

User-Defined Functions

As you have seen, a stored procedure takes a set of data, completes the work as required, and then finishes. It is not possible to take a stored procedure and execute it within, for example, a SELECT statement. This is where *user-defined functions* (UDFs) come into play. There are two methods of creating UDFs: through T-SQL and through .NET. However you create them, stored functions take a set of inputs and produce output that a query invoking a particular function can further use. UDFs are similar to stored procedures, but it is their ability to be used within a query that provides their power. You have already seen a few system-defined functions within this book, including GETDATE(), which gets today's date and time and returns it within a query, such as SELECT GETDATE().

Functions come in two types, scalar and table-valued, and you will see both of these demonstrated in the final sections of this chapter.

Scalar Functions

The first function that is covered is a scalar function. A scalar function can return only a single value. The GETDATE() function that you are familiar with, shown in Chapter 5 when giving a column a default value, is a scalar function. The following shows the basic syntax to define a scalar function:

```
CREATE FUNCTION [ schema_name. ] function_name
( [ { @parameter_name data_type [ = default ] [ READONLY ] } [ ,...n ] ] )
RETURNS return_data_type
    [ WITH <function_option> [ ,...n ] ]
    [ AS ]
    BEGIN
                function_body
        RETURN scalar_expression
    END
```

Note that zero, one, or more parameters can be passed into the function. Prefix each parameter in the definition with the local variable definition @ sign and define the data type. Every parameter can be modified within the function as part of the function's execution, unless you place the keyword READONLY after the data type when defining the function. As with stored procedures, it is possible to call a function and omit specifying one or more of that function's parameters. Any parameters that you omit must have been previously defined with default values. In that case, you can call the function with the keyword DEFAULT in the location that such a parameter is expected. The use of default values is demonstrated within the example that follows in the upcoming "Try It Out" section.

The RETURNS clause in a function definition defines the type of data that will be returned. All data types, with the exception of the timestamp data type, can be returned.

The contents of a function are similar to a stored procedure, with the exceptions already discussed. You must place a RETURN statement when you want the function to complete and return control to the calling code.

Table-Valued Functions

A table-valued function lets you return a table of data rather than a single value. You can use a table-valued function to replace the list of tables in the FROM clause of a SELECT statement. The basic syntax for a table-valued function follows. Most of the syntax is similar to that of scalar functions; however, this time you're returning a TABLE data type, and the data to return is defined in terms of a SELECT statement.

```
CREATE FUNCTION [ schema_name. ] function_name
( [ { @parameter_name parameter_datatype [ = default ] [ READONLY ] } [ ,...n ]    ]
RETURNS TABLE
    [ WITH <function_option> [ ,...n ] ]
    [ AS ]
    RETURN [ ( ] select_stmt [ ) ]
```

A table function is not built in this chapter, but will be completed in Chapter 19, as I want to show more advanced T-SQL with this functionality, and you need to read Chapter 16 before I can do that.

■ **Note** It is also possible to define a stored procedure so as to receive a TABLE data type as an input-only parameter.

Considerations When Building Functions

Functions must be robust. If an error is generated within a function, whether it is from invalid data being passed in or from errors in the logic, then the function will stop executing at that point, and the T-SQL calling the function will cancel. A function must also not alter any external resource such as a table, and it must not execute a system function that alters resources, such as a function that sends an e-mail. Finally, you need to know whether a function can be used in computed columns.

Once a column is added to a table, it is possible to apply a function to it in order to get a computed column. For example, you may have a table that is holding customer orders. Within that table, there are two columns called NetValue and LocalTax. You could then have a third column called GrossValue, which is a computation of NetValue + Tax + LocalTax. The value of Tax would come from a user-defined function that computes the gross tax for where the order originated. Either the GrossValue column would have an expression of the gross value of the order using the data from the two columns and the function, or the function would complete all the work. Either way, the value is computed within the column directly and is not set by the user.

The computed column would then have a property called IsComputed (set by SQL Server) defined for it. An important point to note is that by default, if a column is a computed column, it won't physically exist within the table, but rather is recalculated each time it is used. If you need the value to be defined once and not be recalculated when any other column value is altered that is used in the computation, then you need to set the Is Persisted option to Yes within the T-SQL you write. When building your table using the designer, you have to set the Is Persisted property to Yes within the Table Designer and then set the value within your INSERT or UPDATE statement. There are, of course, valid scenarios for having the column computed each time, but you have to be aware that there will be a small performance overhead with this. By defining the column with the PERSISTED keyword, the value will be stored in the table and will change only when a value in one of the columns used to perform the calculation alters. So, there is a trade-off with space and speed.

However, not all functions can be assigned to a column to make it computed. Once a function has been built, you can check its suitability by using the OBJECTPROPERTY function to check whether it is deterministic. If a function is deterministic (defined shortly), then it is a candidate for being used to generate a computed column.

The syntax is as follows:

```
SELECT OBJECTPROPERTY(OBJECT_ID('schema.object'), 'property')
```

■ **Note** The property value to check whether a function is deterministic is IsDeterministic. If you call the function and it returns the same value every time, then you can define the function as being deterministic. GETDATE() is not deterministic, because it returns a different value each time.

Similar to checking your function properties, there are properties assigned to a column when it is created that are useful when the column is a computed column. The values of the properties can be checked by using the COLUMNPROPERTY function once the function has been added to a column, thus making it a computed column.

If you want to use COLUMNPROPERTY, the function call syntax is as follows:

```
SELECT COLUMNPROPERTY (OBJECT_ID('schema.table'),
```

```
'columnname', 'property')
```

Here are five properties of interest that you can determine the value of when inspecting a computed column:

- IsDeterministic: If the column will have the same value every time you call the associated function with the same values, it is deterministic.

- IsPrecise: The column can be either precise or imprecise. For example, an exact number is precise, but a floating-point number is imprecise.

- IsSystemVerified: If SQL Server can determine the values of the first two properties, this property will be set to true; otherwise, it will be set to false.

- SystemDataAccess: This is true if any system information is accessed, such as information from system catalogs or views.

- UserDataAccess: This is true if any user data from the local instance of SQL Server are used.

In the following exercise, you will build a scalar function to calculate an amount of interest either gained or lost based on an amount, an interest rate, and two dates. Once the function is built, you will then see a simple usage of the function and check its deterministic value. In Chapter 18, when your T-SQL knowledge is advanced, you will then use this function against the TransactionDetails.Transactions_old table to calculate interest for every transaction entered.

TRY IT OUT: A SCALAR FUNCTION TO CALCULATE INTEREST

1. The first part of creating a function is to define its name, including the schema it will belong to, and then the parameter values that will be coming into it. The following function will calculate the amount of interest from a defined rate, and will use two dates for the number of days the interest shall be for. The first parameter (the interest rate) has a default value of 10, meaning 10%.

```
CREATE FUNCTION TransactionDetails.fn_IntCalc
(@InterestRate numeric(6,3)=10,@Amount numeric(18,5),
 @FromDate Date, @ToDate Date)
```

2. Next, you need to define what data type is to be returned. In this instance, it is a numeric data type with up to five decimal places. This granularity may not be required for your purposes, but it is defined here so that in an audit situation, accurate global summation of interest can be accrued (recall the earlier example about interest). The following is the return type definition:

```
RETURNS numeric(18,5)
```

3. Include the following EXECUTE AS clause to specify that the function will execute in the same security context as the calling code does. This security context is determined by the AS CALLER clause. It is possible to alter the security context of EXECUTE AS to another account. Doing so is ideal when you want to ensure that no matter what the account is that is connected, the function can be called. Conversely, you can set up a function so that only specific accounts can execute the code:

```
WITH EXECUTE AS CALLER
```

4. Now that the preliminaries have been dealt with, you can move on to building the remainder of the function. A local variable that will hold the interest is defined using the same data type and size as the RETURNS definition. Then the variable is set using the calculation required for calculating the interest. Here is the resulting code:

```
AS
BEGIN
    DECLARE @IntCalculated numeric(18,5)
    SELECT @IntCalculated = @Amount *
            ((@InterestRate/100.00) * (DATEDIFF(d,@FromDate, @ToDate) / 365.00))
```

5. Finally, the RETURN statement returns the calculated value, taking into account whether a NULL value is being returned.

```
    RETURN(ISNULL(@IntCalculated,0))
END
GO
```

6. You can now test the function by executing it against a set of values. The interest rate default value demonstrates how to specify default parameter values when invoking a function. The results are shown in Figure 14-24.

```
SELECT TransactionDetails.fn_IntCalc(DEFAULT,2000,'Mar 1 2015','Mar 10 2015')
```

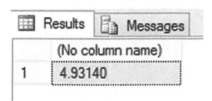

Figure 14-24. *Inline function results for interest*

7. It is now possible to check if the function is deterministic using the OBJECTPROPERTY function. This returns a value of 0, or FALSE, because this function returns a different value each time. Therefore, this function could not be used as a computed column.

```
SELECT OBJECTPROPERTY(OBJECT_ID('TransactionDetails.fn_IntCalc'),
 'IsDeterministic')
GO
```

In Chapter 18, where you'll see more advanced T-SQL, this function will be updated to calculate interest for customer transactions. In that chapter you will also see how to build an inline table-valued function.

Summary

In this chapter, you have encountered stored procedures and functions, which are collections of T-SQL statements compiled and ready to be executed by SQL Server. You have learned the advantages of a stored procedure over an ad hoc query, encountered the basic `CREATE PROCEDURE` and `CREATE FUNCTION` syntaxes, and created some simple stored procedures and functions.

The basics of building a stored procedure are very simple and straightforward. Therefore, building a stored procedure within Query Editor may be as attractive as using a template. As stored procedures are sets of T-SQL statements combined together, you will tend to find that you first build up your query and then at the end surround it with a `CREATE PROCEDURE` statement.

You have also seen an inline T-SQL-based function. To reiterate, it is possible to also have functions that are written using .NET code, which provides you with more possibilities regarding functionality and other processing abilities.

Probably the largest area of code creation outside of data manipulation and searching will be through control-of-flow statements. You will look at other areas, such as error handling, in later chapters.

CHAPTER 15

■ ■ ■

Natively Compiled Stored Procedures

Now that disk-based stored procedures have been covered it's time to look at natively compiled stored procedures. These procedures are built to execute against in-memory tables as quickly and as efficiently as possible. For the most part, the functionality available in standard stored procedures exists within natively compiled stored procedures, but there are important differences that this chapter will go through.

The aim of the chapter is to cover the differences that exist between creating a natively compiled stored procedure and creating a standard stored procedure, as well as to show the speed differences between natively compiled code found within a stored procedure and natively compiled code found outside of a stored procedure.

In this chapter you will see discussed:

- What a natively compiled stored procedure is

- How a natively compiled stored procedure differs from a standard stored procedure

- The syntax of a natively compiled stored procedure

- What options and mandatory arguments need to be used when creating a stored procedure

- A demonstration of creating a stored procedure

- The performance of a natively compiled stored procedure compared to interpreted SQL

- How to ensure optimum performance from a natively compiled stored procedure

What Is a Natively Compiled Stored Procedure?

A natively compiled stored procedure is similar to the standard SQL procedure that you saw in Chapter 14 in that it is a set of instructions grouped together in a program that executes against tables. It can be executed once or many times and can accept parameter inputs and return values or sets of data. However, natively compiled stored procedures are built, are stored, and work differently than standard procedures.

First of all, a natively compiled procedure is natively compiled. What this means is that when the stored procedure is created or when the database or SQL Server is started, SQL Server compiles natively compiled procedures to native computer code and generates a DLL, similar to compiling a .NET class library. When the compilation occurs as part of the compilation process, SQL Server generates the query plan, which is held alongside the C code DLL. Therefore, the query execution plan is based on the data within the tables at that time. Although the code is C based, this is not of a concern to you as you will not be required to look at the DLL code. By becoming a DLL, the code is executed outside of the SQL Server engine in its own OLTP in-memory engine. As in-memory tables are also compiled as DLL's, all in-memory interaction is done at the machine-level code base and will execute in its own engine, thus giving the fastest interactions.

Standard SQL Server stored procedures allow for the ability to be recompiled (using RECOMPILE) if a developer feels that the underlying data profile alters between executions. This is not possible with natively compiled stored procedures, and if the profile of the data does change then you will need to drop and recreate the natively compiled stored procedure. This isn't ideal, and you may find that creating a standard stored procedure that you can RECOMPILE is the better option. You will be sacrificing performance, however, and therefore you should try to keep natively compiled stored procedures.

Many of the standard T-SQL statements and functions are available within natively compiled stored procedures. However, you cannot access disk-based tables, and to achieve this access you would need to create a standard procedure. You also cannot have an EXISTS if you want to test whether a row exists; you also cannot have CASE statements, which are similar to inline IF statements. You will see CASE and EXISTS in Chapters 16 and 17. You also cannot have an OUTER JOIN, and an INNER JOIN and CROSS JOIN are only supported on SELECT statements. It is not possible to access temporary tables (local or global), and you need to put the data into a table data type. The table data type is also covered in Chapter 17. Finally, you cannot have an OR or a NOT within a search predicate. This means you cannot have WHERE a=2 OR b=4, for example.

You *can* get around some of these limitations; however they are not included here as they do slow down processing, and you may find that the extra work required to achieve this functionality and the complexities it brings may not be justifiable over a standard stored procedure. Keep in mind that the aim of natively compiled stored procedures is speed.

There are a number of other restrictions not covered in this chapter but that are mentioned in later chapters. For example, some further restrictions are that you cannot have subqueries, and you cannot have a TOP clause over 8192 rows if you use a constant (however, if the TOP clause uses a variable, that value can be greater than 8192). This number of 8192 does reduce when there are joins.

Some restrictions are due to reasons of speed, and others I would hope will be included in future releases. Let's now take a look at the syntax for a natively compiled stored procedure.

CREATE PROCEDURE and Syntax

The CREATE PROCEDURE statement for natively compiled stored procedures has a number of similarities to a standard stored procedure, but there is some extra functionality, as well as different mandatory arguments to be used. Let's first take a look at the syntax:

```
CREATE PROCEDURE [schema_name.] procedure_name
[ { @parameter_name} datatype [ NULL | NOT NULL ]
[= default_value] [OUTPUT] [READONLY] ] , [ ,...n ]
WITH NATIVE_COMPILATION, SCHEMA_BINDING, EXECUTE AS clause
AS
BEGIN ATOMIC WITH (set_option [,...n])
    statements
[END]
```

As with standard SQL procedures, you create the stored procedure with an optional schema name and then a procedure name. If no schema name is defined then the procedure will be created with the user's default schema name.

With standard stored procedures parameters can, by default, accept NULL and non-null values. With natively compiled stored procedures the parameters can be defined so that a value must always be passed with a non-null value by using the NOT NULL option. If neither option is defined, the default is that the parameter will be defined as NULL. When executing a natively compiled stored procedure avoid using named parameters and use position parameters, as this will provide a performance gain. Also avoid implicit casting of data types. If a stored procedure expects a VARCHAR as the data type, then pass in a VARCHAR rather than an INT, which is then cast.

The arguments that are the most crucial though are WITH NATIVE_COMPILATION, SCHEMA_BINDING, and EXECUTE AS. All three of these are mandatory for natively compiled stored procedures. WITH NATIVE_COMPILATION tells SQL Server that this is not a standard stored procedure and is required to be compiled as a DLL. Every natively compiled stored procedure is required to be bound to the schema of the tables accessed. This ensures that if the underlying table schema cannot be altered as that would affect the stored procedure. Finally, you must define the execution context of the stored procedure, although it has to be one of EXECUTE AS OWNER, EXECUTE AS SELF, or EXECUTE AS user. It is not possible to define a natively compiled procedure as EXECUTE AS CALLER.

As opposed to the option BEGIN keyword used with standard SQL procedures, there is a mandatory BEGIN ATOMIC WITH (set options) for a natively compiled stored procedure. This keyword states that the code in the block will either succeed as a complete transaction or will fail and roll back as a complete transaction. In Chapter 10 there was a discussion about a transaction being ACID and atomic, and that's what this keyword is ensuring. The main difference between an atomic block and a transaction is that this is a complete transaction within either an explicit or implicit transaction. To give clarity on this, if you have a transaction that calls an atomic block of code, then when the atomic block of code starts, a transaction savepoint is created. The atomic block of code executes, and as long as that succeeds then the savepoint is committed. A *savepoint* is when, within a transaction, a point in time is saved for the transaction to allow for a rollback if a problem arises, in which case the rollback rolls the changes back to where they stood at the savepoint. You must still COMMIT TRAN or ROLLBACK TRAN the main transaction though, otherwise the transaction count will be greater than 0. Keep in mind that if the natively compiled stored procedure is the only code executed, this will become the complete transaction, and you won't need to surround a call to a natively compiled stored procedure with a transaction.

When defining an atomic block you also have to define the session settings, including the TRANSACTION ISOLATION LEVEL and the LANGUAGE. Isolation levels were discussed in Chapter 12. The language setting is required because the natively compiled stored procedure is executed as C code externally to SQL Server and is not aware of whether date and formatting options have been changed since compilation. Therefore, it has to make its own determination of how to deal with these changes. There are three other natively compiled- specific optional settings to be aware of, although any session setting is available to be defined, such as NOCOUNT, ANSI_NULLS, and IDENTITY_INSERT. Those three settings are as follows:

- DATEFIRST – This is a language override where you can say which numerical definition is the first day of the week, starting with 1 as Monday. So if the language default is that 7, Sunday, is the first day of the week, you can use this to indicate that 2, Tuesday, is the first day of the week instead.

- DATEFORMAT - Allows you to override the LANGUAGE format for dates. If a language format default is YYYY/MM/DD, then you can use this setting to alter the format to YYYY/DD/MM, for example.

- DELAYED_DURABILITY – ON (default) or OFF.

DELAYED_DURABILITY is how SQL Server deals with committed transactions and the data modified in them. By default, how a transaction commits follows a set of steps. The transaction starts, rows are modified, the transaction is committed, the transaction log records are written to disk, the transaction is signaled as complete, control is returned to the client issuing the implicit or explicit transaction, and processing continues. This process can be sped up by passing control back to the client when the transaction issues a COMMIT TRAN statement by setting DELAYED_DURABILITY to ON. The transaction is still written to the transaction log; however, if there is a failure and the transaction log rows are not written, the client will assume that the data has been successfully written. Having a delay in the durability not only returns processing back to the client and therefore reduces the time the client is waiting, especially if there are transaction log waits, but also how the transaction log is flushed to disk alters so that larger blocks of data can be written, therefore potentially increasing the amount of data throughput. In addition, as the transaction is complete, any locks on the rows of data will be released earlier, which means there will be less blocking. Any data waiting on a lock will read the modified version of the committed transaction whether the data has been written to the transaction log or not. Of course the downside of delayed durability, as indicated, is that you can suffer data loss. In most systems this can be a problem; however, there may be situations in which data loss is not a major issue. For example, in the ApressFinancial system, recoding share price movements so that you can see the latest share price may not need to be recorded for posterity. As long as the next transaction can read the data, that's all that matters. In this instance a natively compiled stored procedure could set the DELAYED_DURABILITY to ON.

> ■ **Note** DELAYED_DURABILITY is not solely for natively compiled stored procedures, but can also be set via the ALTER DATABASE command and set for the database.

There has been a fair amount of discussion, so let's now take a look at our first natively compiled procedures. In Chapter 12 you saw three INSERT timed examples, one against disk based, one against SCHEMA_AND_DATA, and one against SCHEMA_ONLY. The two stored procedures within the following example will show timings for natively compiled stored procedures against in-memory tables. Just to remind you, disk-based tables took 2 minutes 16 seconds, SCHEMA_AND_DATA took 50 seconds, and SCHEMA_ONLY took just 21 seconds.

TRY IT OUT: CREATE NATIVELY COMPILED STORED PROCEDURE

1. First of all, define the CREATE PROCEDURE with the execution context of owner.

   ```
   CREATE PROCEDURE dbo.apf_InsertDataSpeedTest
     WITH NATIVE_COMPILATION, SCHEMABINDING, EXECUTE AS OWNER
     AS
   ```

2. Now define the atomic block of code. The isolation level will at the SNAPSHOT isolation level, and the language will be US_ENGLISH.

   ```
   BEGIN ATOMIC
   WITH (TRANSACTION ISOLATION LEVEL = SNAPSHOT, LANGUAGE = N'us_english')
   ```

3. The code within the stored procedure will be the same as the interpreted T-SQL defined in Chapter 12 for the SCHEMA_AND_DATA table.

   ```
   SELECT GETDATE()

   DECLARE @i INT = 1;

   WHILE @i <= 100000
   BEGIN;
       INSERT INTO TransactionDetails.Transactions_SCHEMADATA
       (CustomerId, TransactionType, DateEntered, Amount,
           RelatedProductId)
       VALUES (1,1,GETDATE(),100,1);
       SET @i += 1;
   END;
   SELECT GETDATE()
   END
   ```

4. Once the code is entered, execute it to create the procedure in the database. Now that the stored procedure is defined, it can be executed.

   ```
   EXEC apf_InsertDataSpeedTest
   ```

5. Once it is executed you will see start and end times for inserting 100,000 rows. Figure 15-1 shows the times on my computer. Recall that this took 50 seconds when the SQL was run as interpreted. In this instance it took just over 2 seconds.

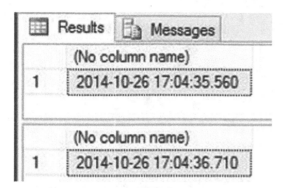

Figure 15-1. *SCHEMA_AND_DATA-based timings*

6. The second stored procedure will be very similar to the stored procedure just defined, but will point to the SCHEMA_ONLY table. Enter and execute the following code to create the stored procedure:

```
CREATE PROCEDURE dbo.apf_InsertDataSpeedTest2
  WITH NATIVE_COMPILATION, SCHEMABINDING, EXECUTE AS OWNER
  AS
  BEGIN ATOMIC
  WITH (TRANSACTION ISOLATION LEVEL = SNAPSHOT, LANGUAGE = N'us_english')
  SELECT GETDATE()

  DECLARE @i INT = 1;

  WHILE @i <= 100000
  BEGIN;
      INSERT INTO TransactionDetails.Transactions_SCHEMAONLY
      (CustomerId, TransactionType, DateEntered, Amount,
          RelatedProductId)
      VALUES (1,1,GETDATE(),100,1);
      SET @i += 1;
  END;
  SELECT GETDATE()
END
```

7. Once the procedure is created it can be executed.

```
EXEC apf_InsertDataSpeedTest2
```

467

8. In this instance it was almost instantaneous, with it taking only a couple of hundredths of a second, as you can see in Figure 15-2.

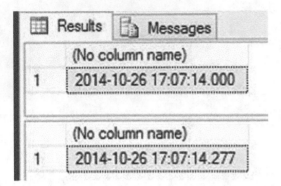

Figure 15-2. SCHEMA_ONLY-based timings

As expected, using natively compiled code is significantly faster for inserting data. You will see similar gains for other scenarios.

Natively compiled stored procedures are best for dealing with larger data sets rather than for using very small sets of data. The more data to be dealt with, the bigger the performance gain you are likely to see. You have seen this yourself with the exercise just performed. To recap the points within the chapter, to get the best performance gains from natively compiled procedures:

- Work with larger sets of data and avoid small sets of data

- Use positional parameters rather than named parameters

- Avoid implicit casting

- Execute frequently

Summary

Although this is a short chapter, there are some major points that have been covered. You have seen the differences between natively compiled and standard stored procedures, not just in syntax but also in that a natively compiled stored procedure generates a DLL. You have also seen the performance differences in the two types of in-memory tables, as well as against interpreted SQL. Natively compiled stored procedures are perfect in situations where there are a reasonable number of rows and where the profile of the data doesn't change.

CHAPTER 16

■ ■ ■

Essentials for Effective Coding

Now that you know how to build and work with SQL Server objects, and how to insert, update, and delete data as well as retrieve it, you can move on to more of the T-SQL essentials required to complete your programming knowledge.

The most important area covered by this chapter is probably error handling. After all, no matter how good your code is, if it cannot cope when an error occurs then it will be hard to keep the code stable and reliable. There will always be times that the unexpected happens, from strange input data to something going wrong on the server. However, error handling is not the only area of interest to us. You will be looking at methods to perform aggregations of data and to group data together. Finally, there will be times that you want to hold data either in a variable or in a table and have it exist for only a short period of time. This is quite a great deal to cover, but this chapter and the next will be the stepping stones that move you from novice to professional developer.

This chapter will therefore look at the following:

- Having a method of storing information temporarily using variables

- Storing rows of information in a nonpermanent table

- Aggregating values

- Organizing output data into groups of relevant information

- Returning unique and distinct values

- Looking at and using system functions

- Handling errors, e.g., creating your own errors, trapping errors, and making code secure

Variables

Sometimes you'll need to hold a value or work with a value that does not come directly from a column. Or perhaps you'll need to retrieve a value from a single row of data and a single column that you want to use in a different part of a query. It is possible to do this via a variable.

You can declare a `variable` at any time within a set of T-SQL instructions, whether it is ad hoc or a stored procedure or a trigger. However, a variable has a finite lifetime. To inform SQL Server that you want to use a variable, use the following syntax:

```
DECLARE @variable_name datatype[, @variable_name2 datatype]
```

All variables have to be preceded with an @ sign, and as you can see from the syntax, more than one variable can be declared, although multiple variables must be separated by a comma or be placed on a new line with a new `DECLARE` statement. Code can be held on more than one line within the editor, just like all other T-SQL syntax, such as having `DECLARE` on line 1 and then the variables on line 2. All variables can hold a `NULL` value, and there is not an

option to say that the variable cannot hold a NULL value. By default, then, when a variable is declared, it will have an initial value of NULL. It is also possible to assign a value at the time of declaration. You'll see this in the first set of the following code. To assign a value to a variable, you can use a SET statement or a SELECT statement. It is standard to use SET to set a variable value when you are not working with any tables. This is useful when you want to set the values of multiple variables at the same time. It is also useful when you want to check the system variables @@ERROR or @@ROWCOUNT following some other DML statements. You will see these system variables later within this chapter. Let's take a look at some examples to see more of how to work with variables and their finite lifetime.

TRY IT OUT: DECLARING AND WORKING WITH VARIABLES

1. In this example, you will define two variables; in the first, you will place the current date and time using the system function GETDATE(), and in the second, you will set the value of the variable @CurrPriceInCents to the value from a column within a table, with a mathematical function tagged on. Once these two have been set using SET and SELECT, you will then list them out, which can be done only via a SELECT statement.

```
DECLARE @MyDate datetime=GETDATE(), @CurrPriceInCents money
SELECT @CurrPriceInCents = CurrentPrice * 100
   FROM ShareDetails.Shares
 WHERE ShareId = 2
SELECT @MyDate,@CurrPriceInCents
```

2. Execute the code, and you will see something like the results shown in Figure 16-1. The first column shows your current date and time.

| Results | Messages | |
|---|---|
| (No column name) | (No column name) |
| 1 | 2014-09-12 06:18:04.227 | 234.125 |

Figure 16-1. *Working with a local variable*

3. If you change the query into two batches, the variables in the second batch will not exist, and when you try to execute all of the code at once, you will get an error. Enter the code as it appears here:

```
DECLARE @MyDate datetime= GETDATE(), @CurrPriceInCents money
SELECT @CurrPriceInCents = CurrentPrice * 100
   FROM ShareDetails.Shares
 WHERE ShareId = 2GO
SELECT @MyDate,@CurrPriceInCents
```

4. The error returned when this code is executed is shown here. You are being informed that SQL Server doesn't know about the first variable in the last statement. This is because SQL Server is parsing the whole set of T-SQL before executing, rather than one batch at a time.

```
Msg 137, Level 15, State 2, Line 6
Must declare the scalar variable "@MyDate".
```

5. Remove the GO statement so that you can see one more example of how variables work. You also need to remove the WHERE statement in the example so that you return all rows from the ShareDetails.Shares table. The value that will be assigned to the variable @CurrPriceInCents will be the last value returned from the query of data. The code you want to execute is as follows. The two lines have been retained in the query, but they have now been prefixed with two dashes: --. This indicates to SQL Server that the lines of code have been commented out and should be ignored.

```
DECLARE @MyDate datetime= GETDATE(), @CurrPriceInCents money
SELECT @CurrPriceInCents = CurrentPrice * 100
  FROM ShareDetails.Shares
--WHERE ShareId = 2
--GO
SELECT @MyDate,@CurrPriceInCents
```

6. If you look at the results that this produces, as shown in Figure 16-2, you can see that the value in the second column is from the last row in the set of data returned from the ShareDetails.Shares table.

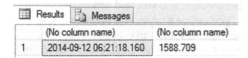

Figure 16-2. *Variables and batches*

■ **Note** Recall from previous chapters that the query as detailed in step 4 will retrieve a value in any order; it will not necessarily be the last row inserted into the physical table, but rather it will be the last row built in the set of data.

Temporary Tables

There are two types of temporary tables: local and global. These temporary tables are created in tempdb and not within the database you are connected to. They also have a finite lifetime. Unlike with a variable, the length of time such a table can "survive" can vary.

1. A local temporary table survives until the connection it was created within is dropped. This can happen when the stored procedure that created the temporary table completes, or when the Query Editor window is closed. A local temporary table is defined by prefixing the table name by a single hash mark: #. The scope of a local temporary table is the connection that created it only.

2. A global temporary table is defined by prefixing the table name by a double hash mark: ##. The scope of a global temporary table differs significantly. When a connection creates the table, it is then available to be used by any user and any connection, just like a permanent table. A global temporary table will be "deleted" only when all connections to it have been closed.

Recall that SELECT...INTO allows a permanent table to be built from data from either another table or tables, or from a list of variables. You could make this table more transient by defining the INTO table so as to reside within tempdb. However, it will continue to exist within tempdb until either it is dropped or SQL Server is stopped and restarted. This is slightly better, but not perfect for when you just want to build an interim table between two sets of T-SQL statements.

The need for a temporary table could arise for a number of reasons. Building a single T-SQL statement that returns information from a number of tables can get complex, and perhaps could not even be ideally optimized for returning the data quickly. Splitting the query into two may make the code easier to maintain and perform better. To give an example, as your customers "age," they will have more and more transactions against their account IDs. It may be that when working out any interest to accrue, the query will take a long time to run, as there are more and more transactions. It might be better to create a temporary table of just the transactions you are interested in, and then use this temporary table in code that then calculates the interest, rather than trying to complete all the work in one pass of the data.

When it comes time to work with a temporary table, such a table can be built either by using the CREATE TABLE statement or by using the SELECT...INTO command. From a performance perspective, you will find defining a temporary table and then populating it faster than using a SELECT...INTO. If you define a table, SQL Server will know each column's data type from the definition; however, with a SELECT...INTO, SQL Server has to calculate what data each column holds from the data itself and then decide on the data type. Let's take a look at temporary tables in action.

TRY IT OUT: TEMPORARY TABLES

The first example will create a local temporary table based on the CREATE TABLE statement. You will populate the table with some data and then retrieve the data. You will next open up a different Query Editor pane and try to retrieve data from the table to show that it is local. Also of interest here is how you can use a SELECT statement in conjunction with an INSERT statement to add the values. Provided that the number of columns returned in the SELECT statement matches either the number of columns within the table or the number of columns in the INSERT column list, using a SELECT statement is a great way of populating tables, especially temporary tables.

1. First, create the temporary table. For the moment, just enter the code; don't execute it.

```
CREATE TABLE #SharesTmp
(ShareDesc varchar(50),
Price numeric(18,5),
PriceDate datetime)
```

2. Next, you want to populate the temporary table with information from the ShareDetails.Shares and the ShareDetails.SharePrices tables. Because you are populating every column within the local temp table, you don't need to list the columns within the local temp table in the INSERT INTO table part of the query. Then, use the results from a SELECT statement to populate many rows in one set of T-SQL. You can execute the code now if you want, but when you get to the third part in a moment, run the SELECT * from the same Query Editor window.

```
INSERT INTO #SharesTmp
SELECT s.Description,sp.Price,sp.PriceDate
  FROM ShareDetails.Shares s
  JOIN ShareDetails.SharePrices sp ON sp.ShareId = s.ShareId
```

3. The final part is to prove that there are data in the table.

```
SELECT * FROM #SharesTmp
```

4. When the code is executed, you should see the output that appears in Figure 16-3.

	ShareDesc	Price	PriceDate
1	ACME'S HOMEBAKE COOKIES INC	34.25148	2012-03-28 10:12:42.740
2	ACME'S HOMEBAKE COOKIES INC	6.62765	2012-03-27 06:47:46.900
3	ACME'S HOMEBAKE COOKIES INC	6.44350	2012-03-25 21:51:29.910
4	ACME'S HOMEBAKE COOKIES INC	32.04574	2012-03-12 19:57:07.630
5	ACME'S HOMEBAKE COOKIES INC	32.00452	2012-03-06 16:59:24.430
6	ACME'S HOMEBAKE COOKIES INC	30.16576	2012-03-06 01:09:36.260
7	ACME'S HOMEBAKE COOKIES INC	7.12997	2012-03-05 05:29:29.280

Figure 16-3. A local temporary table

5. Open up a fresh Query Editor, keeping the current connection and Query Editor open, and then try to execute the following code:

```
SELECT * FROM #SharesTmp
```

6. Now instead of returning a set of results like those shown in Figure 16-3, you will get an error message similar to that here. This is because the temporary table is a local temporary table and is available only from the connection that created it.

```
Msg 208, Level 16, State 0, Line 1
Invalid object name '#SharesTmp'.
```

7. If you change the whole query to now work with a global temporary table, you will see a different end result. To ensure you are starting afresh, clear all the Query Editors or execute the following DROP TABLE command in the first Query Editor:

```
DROP TABLE #SharesTmp
```

■ **Note** It is good practice to DROP a temporary table when you have finished using it rather than letting SQL Server drop the table when the connection closes. If you leave Query Editor open, then the temporary table will continue to exist in tempdb. If you generate one or more large temporary tables, you can find that you have no tempdb database space left and your database will stop processing when it requires space in tempdb to perform some other work.

8. Enter the following code, taking note of the double hash marks, in one of the Query Editors:

```
CREATE TABLE ##SharesTmp
(ShareDesc varchar(50),
Price numeric(18,5),
PriceDate datetime)
INSERT INTO ##SharesTmp
SELECT s.Description,sp.Price,sp.PriceDate
  FROM ShareDetails.Shares s
  JOIN ShareDetails.SharePrices sp ON sp.ShareId = s.ShareId
SELECT * FROM ##SharesTmp
```

9. When you execute the code, you should see the same results as you did with the first query (refer back to Figure 16-3).

10. Move to a new Query Editor pane, ensuring that you leave the previous Query Editor pane open. Then enter the following SELECT statement:

```
SELECT * FROM ##SharesTmp
```

11. When this is executed, you will see the same results again, as shown originally in Figure 16-3.

It is not until the first Query Editor pane that defined the global table is closed or until a DROP TABLE ##SharesTmp is executed that the table will disappear.

Aggregations

An *aggregation* is where SQL Server performs a function on a set of data to return one aggregated value per grouping of data. This will vary from counting the number of rows returned from a SELECT statement through to figuring out maximum and minimum values. Combining some of these functions with the DISTINCT function, discussed later in the "Distinct Values" section, can provide some useful functionality. An example might be when you want to show the highest value for each distinct share to demonstrate when the share was worth the greatest amount.

Let's dive straight in by looking at different aggregation types and working through examples of each.

COUNT/COUNT_BIG

COUNT/COUNT_BIG is probably the most commonly used aggregation, and it finds out the number of rows returned from a query. You use this for checking the total number of rows in a table, or more likely the number of rows returned from a particular set of filtering criteria. Quite often this is used to cross-check the number of rows from a query in SQL Server with the number of rows an application is showing to a user.

The syntax is COUNT(*) or COUNT_BIG(*). There are no columns defined, as it is rows that are being counted.

■ **Note** The difference between these two functions is that COUNT returns an integer data type and COUNT_BIG returns a bigint data type.

TRY IT OUT: COUNTING ROWS

1. This example will count the number of rows in the ShareDetails.Shares table. In the example, you will see an asterisk between the brackets. This is the normal method, although you could have a number or a column; however, I find these confusing. There is no performance difference. You will likely find that you use COUNT either to ensure a table has the number of rows you expect or to populate a variable. If you find you are returning the count as a result set outside of a stored procedure, you should name the column with an alias, as demonstrated in the example:

    ```
    SELECT COUNT(*) AS 'Number of Rows'
    FROM ShareDetails.Shares
    ```

2. Execute the code, and you will see the results shown in Figure 16-4.

Figure 16-4. Using COUNT()

3. Of course, you could add a filter, such as the following, which counts the number of customers who do not have an uncleared balance pending to clear.

    ```
    SELECT COUNT_BIG(*) AS 'Number of Rows'
    FROM CustomerDetails.Customers
    WHERE UnclearedBalance IS NULL
    ```

4. Execute the code, and you will now see a count of 710, shown in Figure 16-5, as expected.

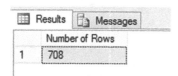

Figure 16-5. COUNT_BIG with a filter

SUM

If you have numeric values in a column, it is possible to aggregate them into a sum. One scenario for this is to add the transaction amounts in a bank account to see how much the balance has changed. This could be daily, weekly, monthly, or over any time period required. For example, a negative amount would show that more has been taken out of the account than has been put in.

The syntax can be shown as SUM(column1|@variable|Mathematical function). The summation does not have to be of a column, but could include a math function. One example would be to sum up the cost of purchasing shares, in which case you would multiply the number of shares bought by the cost paid.

TRY IT OUT: SUMMING VALUES

1. You can do a simple SUM to add up the amount of money that has passed through the account as a deposit. The transaction type for this from the TransactionDetails.Transactions table is those instances where the column TransactionType has a value of 1.

    ```
    SELECT SUM(Amount) AS 'Amount Deposited'
      FROM TransactionDetails.Transactions
     WHERE CustomerId = 1
       AND TransactionType = 1
    ```

2. Executing this code adds up two rows you inserted for customer 1. The result is 175.67, as shown in Figure 16-6.

Figure 16-6. SUMming values

MAX/MIN

Within a set of data, it is possible to get the minimum and maximum values of a specific column of data. This is useful if you want to see values such as the smallest share price or the greatest portfolio value. In other scenarios outside of the example, you might want to find the maximum number of sales of each product in a period of time, or the minimum sold, so that you can see if some days are quieter than others.

TRY IT OUT: MAX AND MIN

1. In this example, you will see how to find the maximum and minimum values for a share with one statement. Enter the following code:

```
SELECT MAX(Price) MaxPrice,MIN(Price) MinPrice
FROM ShareDetails.SharePrices
WHERE ShareId = 1
```

2. Executing the code produces the results shown in Figure 16-7.

	MaxPrice	MinPrice
1	35.63776	0.58554

Figure 16-7. Find the maximum and minimum

AVG

As you might expect, the AVG aggregation returns the average value of a column of data for the filtered rows. All of the values are added and then divided by the number of rows that formed the underlying result set.

TRY IT OUT: AVERAGING IT OUT

1. This last aggregation example will produce an average value for the share prices found for share ID 1. Enter the following code:

```
SELECT AVG(Price) AvgPrice
FROM ShareDetails.SharePrices
WHERE ShareId = 1
```

2. Once you have executed the code, you should see the results shown in Figure 16-8.

	AvgPrice
1	18.119669

Figure 16-8. Finding the average

Now that you have taken a look at aggregations, you can move on to looking at grouping data. Aggregations, as you have seen, are useful but limited. In the next section, I will show you how you can expand these aggregations so that they are used with groups of data.

Grouping Data

Using aggregations works well when you want just a single row of results for a specific filtered item. If you want to find the average price of several shares, you may be thinking you need to provide a SELECT AVG() for each share. This section will demonstrate that this is not the case. By using GROUP BY, you can instruct SQL Server to group the data to return and provide a summary value for each grouping of data. To clarify, as you will see in the upcoming examples, you could remove the WHERE ShareId=1 statement, which would then allow you to group the results by each different ShareId.

The basic syntax for grouping follows. (

```
GROUP BY [ALL] (column1[,column2,...])
```

The option ALL is a bit like an OUTER JOIN. If you have a WHERE statement as part of your SELECT statement, any grouping filtered out will still return a row in the results, but instead of aggregating the column, a value of NULL will be returned. I tend to use this as a checking mechanism. I can see the rows with values and the rows without values, and visually this will tell me that my filtering is correct.

When working with GROUP BY, the main point that you have to be aware of is that any column defined in the SELECT statement that does not form part of the aggregation *must* be contained within the GROUP BY clause and be in the same order as the SELECT statement. Failure to do this will mean that the query will give erroneous results, and in many cases, will use a lot of resources in giving these results.

TRY IT OUT: GROUP BY

1. This first example will demonstrate how to find maximum and minimum values for every share that has a row in the ShareDetails.SharePrices table where the share Description is greater than Julies Pantry. The code is as follows:

```
SELECT sp.ShareId, s.Description,MIN(Price) MinPrice, Max(Price) MaxPrice
  FROM ShareDetails.SharePrices sp
  LEFT JOIN ShareDetails.Shares s ON s.ShareId = sp.ShareId
 WHERE s.Description > 'Julies Pantry'
 GROUP BY sp.ShareId, s.Description
```

2. When the code is executed, you will see the nine shares listed with their corresponding minimum and maximum values, as shown in Figure 16-9.

	ShareId	Description	MinPrice	MaxPrice
1	3	Lomas Ambulances	0.48568	35.81974
2	6	Nicklins Nickle Ore	0.09746	36.88668
3	7	Rolling Maulers	1.46478	36.72606
4	4	Toland's Irish Whisky	2.94299	35.99788
5	13	Old Time Movies	1.29242	36.69624
6	17	Squirrels Servers	0.16252	36.37206
7	11	Shiny Shoes Shone	0.20641	36.52747
8	14	Kinga Roys	0.08732	34.51412
9	8	MVS Inc	0.65863	36.85264

Figure 16-9. Max and min of a group

3. If you want to include all rows where there is no `Price`, as it has been removed by the `WHERE` clause, then you would use the `ALL` option with `GROUP BY`:

```
SELECT sp.ShareId, s.Description,MIN(Price) MinPrice, Max(Price) MaxPrice
  FROM ShareDetails.SharePrices sp
  LEFT JOIN ShareDetails.Shares s ON s.ShareId = sp.ShareId
 WHERE s.Description > 'Julies Pantry'
 GROUP BY ALL sp.ShareId, s.Description
```

4. When you execute the code, the `Price` row that is outside of the filtering returns a `NULL` value. The other rows return details as shown in Figure 16-10.

	ShareId	Description	MinPrice	MaxPrice
1	1	ACME'S HOMEBAKE COOKIES INC	NULL	NULL
2	2	ACME'S HOMEBAKE COOKIES INC	NULL	NULL
3	12	Airing Cadets	NULL	NULL
4	15	Apress	NULL	NULL
5	5	Brownies	NULL	NULL
6	9	Ding Dong Bells	NULL	NULL
7	18	Downtown Donuts	NULL	NULL
8	19	Fishy Friars	NULL	NULL
9	16	Frying Tonight	NULL	NULL
10	10	Julies Pantry	NULL	NULL
11	14	Kinga Roys	0.08732	34.51412
12	3	Lomas Ambulances	0.48568	35.81974
13	8	MVS Inc	0.65863	36.85264
14	6	Nicklins Nickle Ore	0.09746	36.88668
15	13	Old Time Movies	1.29242	36.69624
16	7	Rolling Maulers	1.46478	36.72606
17	11	Shiny Shoes Shone	0.20641	36.52747
18	17	Squirrels Servers	0.16252	36.37206
19	4	Toland's Irish Whisky	2.94299	35.99788

Figure 16-10. A JOIN with a max and min and group by all

HAVING

When using the GROUP BY clause, it is possible to supplement your query with a HAVING clause. The HAVING clause is like a filter, but it works on aggregations of the data rather than on the rows of data prior to the aggregation. Hence, it has to be included with a GROUP BY clause. It will also include the aggregation you want to check. The code would therefore look as follows:

```
GROUP BY column1[,column2...]
HAVING [aggregation_condition]
```

The aggregation_condition would be where you place the aggregation and the test you want to perform. For example, my bank charges me if I have more than 20 nonregular items pass through my account in a month. In this case, the query would group by customer ID, counting the number of nonregular transactions for each calendar month. If the count were less than or equal to 20 items, then you would like this list to not include the customer in question. To clarify this, the query code would look something like the following if you were running this in August 2014:

```
SELECT CustomerId,COUNT(*)
FROM CustomerBankTransactions
WHERE TransactionDate BETWEEN '1 Aug 2014' AND '31 Aug 2014'
GROUP BY CustomerId
HAVING COUNT(*) > 20
```

TRY IT OUT: HAVING

1. In the following example, you will use the MIN aggregate function to remove rows where the minimum share price is less than $10. This query is taken from the GROUP BY ALL example shown earlier. Although you have kept the ALL option within the GROUP BY statement, it is ignored, as it is followed by the HAVING clause, which supercedes it.

```
SELECT sp.ShareId, s.Description,MIN(Price) MinPrice, Max(Price) MaxPrice
  FROM ShareDetails.SharePrices sp
  LEFT JOIN ShareDetails.Shares s ON s.ShareId = sp.ShareId
WHERE s.Description > 'Julies Pantry'
 GROUP BY ALL sp.ShareId, s.Description
HAVING MIN(Price) < 10
```

2. The results of the executed code will return 11 values, as you see in Figure 16-11, and will ignore the shares that have a MinPrice value of NULL that would be returned by the ALL statement.

	ShareId	Description	MinPrice	MaxPrice
1	14	Kinga Roys	0.08732	34.51412
2	3	Lomas Ambulances	0.48568	35.81974
3	8	MVS Inc	0.65863	36.85264
4	6	Nicklins Nickle Ore	0.09746	36.88668
5	13	Old Time Movies	1.29242	36.69624
6	7	Rolling Maulers	1.46478	36.72606
7	11	Shiny Shoes Shone	0.20641	36.52747
8	17	Squirrels Servers	0.16252	36.37206
9	4	Toland's Irish Whisky	2.94299	35.99788

Figure 16-11. When you want to have only certain aggregated rows

Even if you changed the HAVING scenario to including amounts greater than $10, the shares with a Description of less than or equal to Julies Pantry would still be ignored due to HAVING overriding the GROUP BY ALL. Not only that, but NULL, as you know, is a "special" value and is neither less than nor greater than any value.

Distinct Values

With some of the tables in these examples, multiple entries will exist for the same value. To clarify, in the ShareDetails.SharePrices table, there can be multiple entries for each share as each new price is stored. There may be some shares with no price, of course. But what if you want to see a listing of shares that do have prices, but you want to see each share listed only once? This is a simple example, and you will see more complex examples later on when I cover how to use aggregations within SQL Server. That aside, the example that follows serves its purpose well.

The syntax is to place the keyword DISTINCT after the SELECT statement and before the list of columns. The following list of columns is then tested for all the rows returned, and for each set of unique distinct values, one row will be listed.

TRY IT OUT: DISTINCT VALUES

1. You have to join the ShareDetails.Shares and ShareDetails.SharePrices tables again so that you know you are returning only rows that have a share price. You had that code in the JOIN section earlier in the chapter, in step 2 of the "Temporary Tables" exercise. It is replicated here, and you can execute it if you want:

```
SELECT s.Description,sp.Price,sp.PriceDate
  FROM ShareDetails.Shares s
  JOIN ShareDetails.SharePrices sp ON sp.ShareId = s.ShareId
```

2. As you know, this returns multiple rows for each share. Placing DISTINCT at the start of the column list doesn't make any difference, because there are different prices and different price dates.

```
SELECT DISTINCT s.Description,sp.Price,sp.PriceDate
  FROM ShareDetails.Shares s
  JOIN ShareDetails.SharePrices sp ON sp.ShareId = s.ShareId
```

3. To get a list of shares that have a value, it is necessary to remove the last two columns and list only the ShareDesc column.

```
SELECT DISTINCT s.Description
  FROM ShareDetails.Shares s
  JOIN ShareDetails.SharePrices sp ON sp.ShareId = s.ShareId
```

4. When you execute this code, you will see the desired results, as partly shown in Figure 16-12.

	Description
1	ACME'S HOMEBAKE COOKIES INC
2	Airing Cadets
3	Apress
4	Brownies
5	Ding Dong Bells
6	Downtown Donuts
7	Fishy Friars
8	Frying Tonight
9	Julies Pantry
10	Kinga Roys
11	Lomas Ambulances

Figure 16-12. *Finding unique values*

Functions

To bring more flexibility to your T-SQL code, you can use a number of functions with the data from variables and columns. This section does not include a comprehensive list, but it does contain the most commonly used functions and the functions you will come across early in your development career. They have been split into three categories: date and time, string, and system functions. There is a short explanation for each, with some code demonstrating each function in an example with results.

Date and Time

The functions in the first set involve either working with a variable that holds a date and time value or using a system function to retrieve the current date and time.

DATEADD()

If you want to add or subtract an amount of time to a column or a variable, then display a new value in a rowset or set a variable with that new value, use DATEADD(). The syntax for DATEADD() is as follows:

```
DATEADD(datepart, number, date)
```

The datepart option applies to all of the date functions and details what you want to add, from milliseconds to years. These are defined as reserved words and therefore are not surrounded by quotation marks. There are a number of possible values, as listed in Table 16-1.

Table 16-1. *Potential values for datepart*

datepart Definition	Meaning
isowk, isoww	ISO week is a numbering system used to give every week in the calendar a unique, ascending number. An ISO week starts on a Monday, and Week 1 is the week containing the first Thursday of that year. For example, in 2008, the first Thursday occurred on January 3, so Week 1 ran from December 31, 2007 through January 6, 2008.
tz	Timezone offset
ns	Nanosecond
mcs	Microsecond
ms	Millisecond
ss, s	Second
mi, n	Minute
hh	Hour
dw, w	Weekday
wk, ww	Week
dd, d	Day
dy, y	Day of year
mm, n	Month
qq, q	Quarter
yy, yyyy	Year

For the second parameter of the datepart function, to add, use a positive value, and to subtract, use a negative value. The final parameter can be a value, a variable, or a date-type column holding the date and time you want to change.

TRY IT OUT: DATEADD()

1. In this example, you will set a local variable to a date and time. Once the variable is set, you will add four hours to the value and display the results. Enter the code here and then execute it, which should return results as shown in Figure 16-13.

```
DECLARE @OldTime datetime
SET @OldTime = '24 March 2015 3:00 PM'
SELECT DATEADD(hh,4,@OldTime)
```

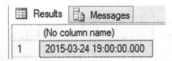

Figure 16-13. Adding hours to a date

2. To do the reverse, you will take the same variable and subtract six hours. The results should appear as shown in Figure 16-14.

```
DECLARE @OldTime datetime
SET @OldTime = '24 March 2015 3:00 PM'
SELECT DATEADD(hh,-6,@OldTime)
```

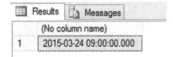

Figure 16-14. Subtracting hours from a date

DATEDIFF()

To find the difference between two dates, use the function DATEDIFF(). The syntax for this function is as follows:

DATEDIFF(datepart, startdate, enddate)

The first option contains the same options as for DATEADD(), and startdate and enddate are the two days you want to compare. A negative number shows that the enddate is before the startdate.

TRY IT OUT: DATEDIFF()

You will set two local variables to a date and time. Then, by using the DATEDIFF() function, you will find the difference in milliseconds. Enter the following code:

```
DECLARE @FirstTime datetime, @SecondTime datetime
SET @FirstTime = '24 March 2015 3:00 PM'
SET @SecondTime = '24 March 2015 3:33PM'
SELECT DATEDIFF(ms,@FirstTime,@SecondTime)
```

Figure 16-15 shows the results after executing this code.

Figure 16-15. The difference between two dates in milliseconds

DATENAME()

Returning the name of the part of the date is great for using with things such as customer statements. Changing the number 6 to the word *June* makes for more pleasant reading.

The syntax is as follows:

```
DATENAME(datepart, datetoinspect)
```

You will also see this in action in DATEPART().

TRY IT OUT: DATENAME()

In this example, you will set one date and time and then return the day of the week. You know this to be a Thursday by checking a calendar. Enter the following code:

```
DECLARE @StatementDate datetime
SET @StatementDate = '24 March 2015 3:00 PM'
SELECT DATENAME(dw,@StatementDate)
```

Figure 16-16 shows the results after executing this code.

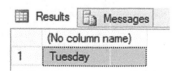

Figure 16-16. The day name of a date

DATEPART()

If you want to achieve returning part of a date from a date variable, column, or value, you can use DATEPART() within a SELECT statement.

As you may be expecting by now, the syntax has datepart as the first option, and then datetoinspect as the second option, which returns the numerical day of the week from the date inspected.

```
DATEPART(datepart, datetoinspect)
```

TRY IT OUT: DATEPART()

1. In this example, you need to set only one local variable to a date and time. After that, you will find the day of the month. In this instance, the variable will have the value set at the time of the definition. Enter the following code:

   ```
   DECLARE @WhatsTheDay datetime = '24 March 2015 3:00 PM'
   SELECT DATEPART(dd, @WhatsTheDay)
   ```

 Figure 16-17 shows the results after executing this code.

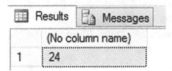

Figure 16-17. *Finding part of a date*

2. To produce a more pleasing date and time for a statement, you can combine DATEPART() and DATENAME() to have a meaningful output. The function CAST(), which you will look at in detail shortly, is needed here, as it is a data type conversion function.

   ```
   DECLARE @WhatsTheDay datetime = '24 March 2015 3:00 PM'
   SELECT DATENAME(dw, @WhatsTheDay) + ', ' +
   CAST(DATEPART(dd,@WhatsTheDay) AS varchar(2)) + ' ' +
   DATENAME(mm,@WhatsTheDay) + ' ' +
   CAST(DATEPART(yyyy,@WhatsTheDay) AS char(4))
   ```

3. When this is executed, it will produce the more meaningful date shown in Figure 16-18.

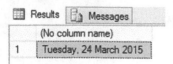

Figure 16-18. *Finding and concatenating to provide a useful date*

FORMAT()

The next example in this section on dates demonstrates a function that allows you to format locale-aware dates and numbers. Be aware that this function will not be available on SQL Server installations that do not have the .NET CLR installed. It does not have to be enabled, just installed. The FORMAT() function in SQL Server is similar to the function found in Excel and .NET.

TRY IT OUT: FORMAT()

1. This example will return a date that is in the US format and reformat it to display as it should in the UK. Enter the following code:

```
DECLARE @MyDate DATETIME
SELECT @MyDate = 'Jun 1 2015'
SELECT FORMAT(@MyDate, 'dd MMM yyyy', 'en-GB' ) AS UKDate
```

2. Execute the code, and you will see the date alter its format to display in the UK format, as shown in Figure 16-19.

Figure 16-19. *Format with a locale*

DATEFROMPARTS() / SMALLDATETIMEFROMPARTS()

There may be times when you have either a date or a part of a date in three variables or columns holding the year, month, and day, or a combination in which one or more of these are derived and the others are supplied. It is possible to convert these three values into a valid date using DATEFROMPARTS(). You can then expand this with other functions if required.

If you want to build a time as well as a date, then you can use the SMALLDATETIMEFROMPARTS() function to achieve this.

TRY IT OUT: DATEFROMPARTS() AND SMALLDATETIMEFROMPARTS()

1. This example will create five variables and define a value for each. The variable names in the example denote what each will be used for. The first SELECT statement will change the integers into a valid date and then format the value to show the day, the full month name, and the year. The second example appends to this the time based on the 24-hour clock. Begin the first example by using this code:

```
DECLARE @Year int=2015, @Month int=12, @Day int=30

DECLARE @Hour int=14, @Minute int=45

SELECT FORMAT(DATEFROMPARTS(@Year,@Month,@Day),
'dd MMMM yyyy','en-GB')

SELECT FORMAT(SMALLDATETIMEFROMPARTS(@Year,@Month,@Day,
@Hour,@Minute),'dd MMMM yyyy hh:mm tt','en-GB')
```

2. When you execute this code, you will see two results, as shown in Figure 16-20.

Figure 16-20. Showing dates from parts with formatting

3. If you enter an invalid value—for example, if you set the day to a value of 40—an error would be thrown that would be the same as that here.

```
Msg 289, Level 16, State 1, Line 4
Cannot construct data type date, some of the arguments have values which are not valid.
```

TIMEFROMPARTS()

Similar to DATEFROMPARTS(), there is a TIMEFROMPARTS() function that will return a time up to fractions of a second from separate variables or values. The function takes five parameters, with the first four being hour, minute, seconds, and fractions of a second. The fifth parameter determines the precision of the fraction portion of the time. If you had a precision of 2, then the fraction number would be defined in 1/100ths.

TRY IT OUT: TIMEFROMPARTS()

1. This example will create five variables and define a value for each. The variable names in the example denote what each will be used for. The precision in this example is set to 1/100ths, and therefore a value of 5 is 5/100ths.

```
DECLARE @Hour int=14, @Minute int=45, @Seconds int=22
DECLARE @Fractions int=2

SELECT FORMAT(CONVERT(datetime,TIMEFROMPARTS
(@Hour,@Minute,@Seconds,@Fractions,2)),
'hh:mm:ss:ffff tt','en-GB')
```

2. When you execute this code, you will see the result shown in Figure 16-21.

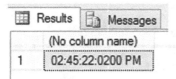

Figure 16-21. Showing times with fractions and precision from parts, with formatting

DATETIME2FROMPARTS()

It is possible to combine the previous two functions to take a date and time set of values and return a datetime2 data type.

TRY IT OUT: DATETIME2FROMPARTS()

1. This example will create seven variables and set a value for each. The variable names should denote what each will be used for. In this example, you will see what happens when the precision is less than the fractions of a second. A precision of zero denotes that there are no fractions to be displayed. Enter the following code:

```
DECLARE @Year int=2015, @Month int=6, @Day int=22
DECLARE @Hour int=23, @Minute int=45, @Seconds int=22
DECLARE @Fractions int=231

SELECT FORMAT(DATETIME2FROMPARTS(@Year,@Month,@Day,@Hour,
@Minute,@Seconds,@Fractions,0),
'hh:mm:ss:ffff tt','en-GB')
```

2. When you execute this code, an error is generated. The precision parameter defined in the function must be able to cope with the precision value presented in the fractions parameter. Truncation, which you might expect in this example, does not occur. The error you would see follows:

```
Msg 289, Level 16, State 5, Line 5
Cannot construct data type datetime2, some of the arguments have
values which are not valid.
```

3. Correct the code by altering the @Precision variable to 3, and when the code is executed with the correction, you should see the output as shown in Figure 16-22.

Figure 16-22. *Showing datetime2 data type from date and time parts, with formatting*

DATETIMEOFFSETFROMPARTS()

There will be times when you have a date and a time and you have to apply an offset to it. One example would be when you are working with different time zones, or when you want to add to a date and time a length of time for a response queue estimate before a response to a query is sent. Adding an hour and minute offset to a date and time will provide you with this functionality. The DATETIMEOFFSETFROMPARTS() function still has the ability to work in fractions and precision, keeping it in alignment with the other "from parts" functions.

TRY IT OUT: DATETIMEOFFSETFROMPARTS()

1. This example will create nine variables and define a value for each. The variable names in the example denote what each will be used for. In this example, you are adding 3 hours and 12 minutes to the time. This will cause the day portion to move to the next day. Enter the following code:

```
DECLARE @Year int=2015, @Month int=6, @Day int=22
DECLARE @Hour int=23, @Minute int=45, @Seconds int=22
DECLARE @HourOffset int=3, @MinuteOffset int=12
DECLARE @Fractions int=0

SELECT DATETIMEOFFSETFROMPARTS(@Year,@Month,@Day,
@Hour,@Minute,@Seconds,@Fractions,@HourOffset, @MinuteOffset,0)
```

2. When you execute this code, you will see the result shown in Figure 16-23.

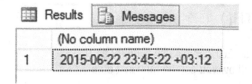

Figure 16-23. *Showing a date and time moved for an offset*

3. You can also move the offset backward by having negative hour and minute offsets. In the following example, you are moving the date and time back in time. You could use this functionality to check the date and time of a delivery, represented by the values in the variables, against a date and time retrieved from variables or columns, so as to check if you have met your target.

```
DECLARE @Year int=2015, @Month int=6, @Day int=22
DECLARE @Hour int=23, @Minute int=45, @Seconds int=22
DECLARE @HourOffset int=-6, @MinuteOffset int=-50
DECLARE @Fractions int=0

SELECT DATETIMEOFFSETFROMPARTS(@Year,@Month,@Day,
@Hour,@Minute,@Seconds,@Fractions,
@HourOffset, @MinuteOffset,0)
```

4. If you execute the foregoing code, you should see a result as shown in Figure 16-24.

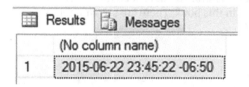

Figure 16-24. *Showing a time offset that is in the past*

EOMONTH()

Knowing the last day of the month can be more important than knowing the first day of the month, as months vary in the number of days they have. By knowing the last day of the month, you can work backward or even add one day to get the first day of the next month. This is achieved in SQL Server using EOMONTH(), which can also have a date offset option.

TRY IT OUT: EOMONTH()

1. This example will use EOMONTH() to find the last day of February 2012. It will use January as the month and then add one month to this date, demonstrating how you can find the last date of the next month. Enter the following code.

    ```
    SELECT EOMONTH('Jan 12 2016',1)
    ```

2. When you execute this code, you will see the result shown in Figure 16-25, showing the end of the month of February 2016 to be the 29th, as it is a leap year.

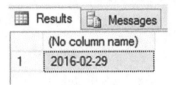

Figure 16-25. *Determine the end of the month from a date*

GETDATE()/SYSDATETIME()

GETDATE() is a great function for returning the exact date and time from the system. You have seen this in action when setting up a table with a default value, as well as at a couple of other points in this book. There are no parameters. If you need accuracy to nanoseconds and further, then use SYSDATETIME().

String

This next section will look at some functions that can act on character-based types, such as varchar and char.

ASCII()

ASCII() converts a single character to the equivalent ASCII code.

TRY IT OUT: ASCII()

1. This example will return the ASCII code of the first character within a string. If the string has more than one character, then only the first will be taken.

    ```
    DECLARE @StringTest char(10)
    SET @StringTest = ASCII('Robin     ')
    SELECT @StringTest
    ```

2. Executing the code, you will see the ASCII value of the letter "R" returned, as shown in Figure 16-26.

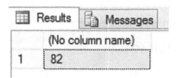

Figure 16-26. *An ASCII value*

CHAR()

The reverse of ASCII() is the CHAR() function, which takes a numeric value within the ASCII character range and turns it into an alphanumeric character.

TRY IT OUT: CHAR()

1. In this example, you will define a local variable. Notice that the variable is a character-based data type. You will then place the ASCII() value of "R" into this variable. From there, you will convert back to a CHAR(). There is an implicit conversion from a character to a numeric. If the conversion results in a value greater than 255—the last value for an ASCII character—then NULL is returned. Enter the following code:

    ```
    DECLARE @StringTest char(10)
    SET @StringTest = ASCII('Robin     ')
    SELECT CHAR(@StringTest)
    ```

2. Executing the code, you will see an "R," as shown in Figure 16-27.

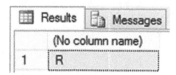

Figure 16-27. *Changing a number to a character*

3. The same result could be derived using a data type that is expected that is numeric-based.

```
DECLARE @StringTest int
SET @StringTest = ASCII('Robin    ')
SELECT CHAR(@StringTest)
```

LEFT()

When it is necessary to return the first *n* left characters from a string-based variable, you can achieve this through the use of LEFT(), replacing *n* with the number of characters you want to return.

TRY IT OUT: LEFT()

1. In this example, you will take the first three characters from a local variable. Here you are taking the first three characters from Robin, to return Rob:

```
DECLARE @StringTest char(10)
SET @StringTest = 'Robin     '
SELECT LEFT(@StringTest,3)
```

2. As expected, you should get the results shown in Figure 16-28 when you execute the code.

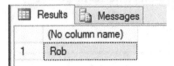

Figure 16-28. *The first LEFT characters*

LOWER()

To change alphabetic characters within a string to ensure that all characters are in lowercase, you can use the LOWER() function.

TRY IT OUT: LOWER()

1. The LOWER() example will combine this function along with another string function, LEFT(). Like all these functions, they can be combined together to perform several functions at once.

```
DECLARE @StringTest char(10)
SET @StringTest = 'Robin      '
SELECT LOWER(LEFT(@StringTest,3))
```

2. As you can see, this results in displaying *rob* in lowercase, as shown in Figure 16-29.

Figure 16-29. *Changing letters to lowercase*

LTRIM()

There will be times when leading spaces will occur in a string and you'll want to remove them. LTRIM() will trim these spaces on the left.

TRY IT OUT: LTRIM()

1. To prove that leading spaces are removed by the LTRIM() function, you have to change the value within the local variable. On top of that, you have to put a string prefixing the variable to show that the variable has had the spaces removed.

```
DECLARE @StringTest char(10)
SET @StringTest = '      Robin'
SELECT 'Start-'+LTRIM(@StringTest),'Start-'+@StringTest
```

2. This produces two columns of output, as shown in Figure 16-30: the first with the variable trimmed and the second showing that the variable did have the leading spaces.

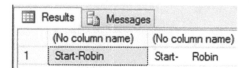

Figure 16-30. *Removing spaces from the left*

RIGHT()

The opposite of LEFT() is, of course, RIGHT(), and this function returns the characters from the right-hand side.

TRY IT OUT: RIGHT()

1. Keep the variable used in LTRIM(), as it will allow you to return bin, which are the three characters on the right-hand side of the variable.

```
DECLARE @StringTest char(10)
SET @StringTest = '    Robin'
SELECT RIGHT(@StringTest,3)
```

2. The results should appear as shown in Figure 16-31.

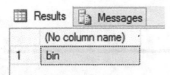

Figure 16-31. *Returning a number of characters starting from the right*

RTRIM()

When you have a CHAR() data type, no matter how many characters you enter, the variable will be filled with spaces on the right, known as being right-padded,. To remove these, use RTRIM. This changes the data from a fixed-length CHAR() to a variable-length value.

TRY IT OUT: RTRIM()

1. This example wants no spaces after Robin; you will remove the space padding within the first column returned using the following code. The second column has the spaces trimmed.

```
DECLARE @StringTest char(10)
SET @StringTest = 'Robin'
SELECT @StringTest+'-End',RTRIM(@StringTest)+'-End'
```

2. The results are as expected, as shown in Figure 16-32.

Figure 16-32. *Removing spaces from the right*

STR()/CONCAT()

Some data types have implicit conversions. You will see later how to do explicit conversions, but a simple conversion that will take any numeric value and convert it to a variable-length string can be done with STR(), which you will look at next. However, SQL Server sometimes has to decide which way the conversion has to go. You will see this problem in the first example in the "Try It Out" exercise. If you want to concatenate two values into a string, then, as you will see in the second example, you will invoke the STR() function. However, you will see that this also causes a little bit more work to be done within the code in order to achieve the desired results. To concatenate two values, you can use the CONCAT() function, similar to the function found in Excel.

TRY IT OUT: STR()

1. The first example demonstrates that you cannot add a number, 82, to a string.

   ```
   SELECT 'A'+82
   ```

2. When the preceding code is executed, you will see the following error:

```
Msg 245, Level 16, State 1, Line 1
Conversion failed when converting the varchar value 'A' to data type int.
```

3. Changing the example to include the STR() function will convert this numeric to a string of varying length, such as varchar().

   ```
   SELECT 'A'+STR(82)
   ```

4. Instead of an error, you now see the desired result, which appears in Figure 16-33. However, it isn't really desirable, as there are spaces between the letter and the number. Leading zeros are translated to spaces.

Figure 16-33. *Changing a number to a string*

5. By including an LTRIM() invocation, you can remove those spaces.

   ```
   SELECT 'A'+LTRIM(STR(82))
   ```

6. This code now produces the correct results, as you see in Figure 16-34.

Figure 16-34. Changing a number to a string and removing leading spaces

7. A cleaner set of code that removes the need for the LTRIM and STR functions would be to use the CONCAT function. The code here demonstrates how simple the code can be:

```
SELECT CONCAT('A',82)
```

8. This will produce the results in Figure 16-35.

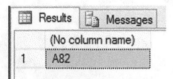

Figure 16-35. Using CONCAT to concatenate mixed data types

SUBSTRING()

As you have seen, you can take a number of characters from the left and from the right of a string. To retrieve a number of characters that do not start with the first or last character, you need to use the function SUBSTRING(). This has three parameters: the variable or column, which character to start the retrieval from, and the number of characters to return.

TRY IT OUT: SUBSTRING()

1. Define the variable you want to return a substring from. Once complete, you can then take the variable, inform SQL Server you want to start the substring at character position 3, and return the next 2 characters.

```
DECLARE @StringTest char(10)
SET @StringTest = 'Robin      '
SELECT SUBSTRING(@StringTest,3,2)
```

2. And you have the desired result, as shown in Figure 16-36.

Figure 16-36. Returning part of a string from within a string

UPPER()

The final string example is the reverse of the LOWER() function; it changes all characters to uppercase.

TRY IT OUT: UPPER()

1. After the declared variable has been set, you then use the UPPER() function to change the value to uppercase.

    ```
    DECLARE @StringTest char(10)
    SET @StringTest = 'Robin      '
    SELECT UPPER(@StringTest)
    ```

2. Execute the foregoing code and, as you can see from Figure 16-37, Robin becomes ROBIN.

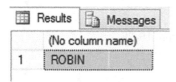

Figure 16-37. *Changing the case of a string to uppercase*

System Functions

System functions are functions that provide extra functionality outside of the boundaries that can be defined as string-, numeric-, or date-related. Three of these functions will be used extensively throughout your code, and therefore you should pay special attention to CASE, CAST, and ISNULL.

CASE WHEN...THEN...ELSE...END

The first function is for when you want to test a condition. WHEN that condition is true, THEN you can do further processing; ELSE if it is false, then you can do something else. What happens in the WHEN section and the THEN section can range from another CASE statement to providing a value that sets a column or a variable.

The CASE WHEN statement can be used to return a value or, if on the right-hand side of an equality statement, to set a value. Both of these scenarios are covered in the following examples.

TRY IT OUT: CASE

1. This example will use a CASE statement to add up customers' TransactionDetails.
 Transactions for the month of August. If the TransactionType is 0, then this is a Debit;
 if it is a 1, then it is a Credit. By using the SUM aggregation, you can add up the amounts.
 Combine this with a GROUP BY where the TransactionDetails.Transactions are split
 between Credit and Debit, and you will get two rows in the results set: one for debits and one
 for credits.

   ```
   SELECT CustomerId,
   CASE WHEN CreditType = 0 THEN 'Debits' ELSE 'Credits' END
   AS TranType,SUM(Amount)
     FROM TransactionDetails.Transactions t
     JOIN TransactionDetails.TransactionTypes tt ON
           tt.TransactionTypeId = t.TransactionType
     WHERE t.DateEntered BETWEEN '1 Jan 2012' AND '4 Jan 2012'
     GROUP BY CustomerId,CreditType
   ```

2. When the code is run, you should see the results that are partly shown in Figure 16-38.

	CustomerId	TranType	(No column name)
1	107	Debits	47296.25990
2	606	Debits	297.16180
3	683	Debits	98459.89340
4	711	Debits	62343.61300
5	722	Debits	52348.63240
6	743	Debits	71865.45530
7	756	Debits	59905.47910
8	879	Debits	68026.30720
9	18	Credits	89817.46120
10	74	Credits	91477.41120
11	271	Credits	78234.35140

Figure 16-38. Using a CASE decision with an aggregation

IIF()

If you have used Excel or Access, among some other tools, you have quite possibly met IIF() when coding. IIF(),
also known as an inline IF, is very similar to the CASE statement demonstrated in the previous example. Where CASE
can have many choices, IIF() has only two choices. The syntax is as follows:

```
IIF(boolean_test_condition, true_value, false_value)
```

TRY IT OUT: IIF()

1. To demonstrate the similarity, but also the reduction in the amount you have to code, I will take the example from the CASE statement and alter that to become an IIF() statement.

```
SELECT CustomerId,
IIF(CreditType = 0,'Debits','Credits') 'Debit/Credit',SUM(Amount)
  FROM TransactionDetails.Transactions t
  JOIN TransactionDetails.TransactionTypes tt ON
        tt.TransactionTypeId = t.TransactionType
  WHERE t.DateEntered BETWEEN '1 Jan 2012' AND '4 Jan 2012'
  GROUP BY CustomerId,CreditType
```

2. Figure 16-39 will have similar output as that in Figure 16-38; the alias for the Debit/Credit column has been altered to show that a different set of code has been run.

8	879	Debits	68026.30720
9	18	Credits	89817.46120
10	74	Credits	91477.41120
11	271	Credits	78234.35140
12	455	Credits	33003.62760
13	506	Credits	17915.43430
14	549	Credits	34792.16110

Figure 16-39. CASE statement converted to an IIF()

CHOOSE()

The ability to return a value based on a separate value can be useful. A good explanation example would be that a number with a range of one through seven could be used as the basis of determining the day name of the week. There is a function that already does this, as demonstrated earlier in the chapter with DATENAME(). In the ApressFinancial database, it might have been possible to use CHOOSE() for the transaction types to denote a debit or a credit type. However, for only two choices, IIF() is a better option. CHOOSE() is good for cases in which there are three or more possible options for the testing value and you need to translate it to a new value.

There is a large caveat here, and that is that you should not necessarily replace tables that have a few rows using a CHOOSE() statement. Having the data in a table gives a number of advantages, including a single point for the data and the ability to join the data; if you have to add any new data, you can simply add it to the table rather than having to alter one or more stored procedures and functions.

I have yet to be convinced of using CHOOSE() instead of a cross-reference table, unless you have the CHOOSE() choices within a user-defined function. So, for example, you would place the following example as a user-defined function to return the choice value rather than using the TransactionDetails.TransactionTypes table.

TRY IT OUT: CHOOSE()

1. This example demonstrates how you could move the TransactionDetails.
 TransactionTypes table functionality into a CHOOSE() statement. Although this works and
 demonstrates the use of the CHOOSE() statement, it should also demonstrate that it is not
 always appropriate to take data from a table and replace the logic and functionality that
 having said data in a table provides.

```
SELECT CustomerId,
CHOOSE(TransactionType,'DEBIT','CREDIT','Share Purchase',
'Dividend','Share Transfer','Interest') as 'Types',
SUM(Amount)
  FROM TransactionDetails.Transactions t
 WHERE t.DateEntered BETWEEN '1 Jan 2012' AND '4 Jan 2012'
 GROUP BY CustomerId,TransactionType
```

2. When you execute the code, you will see the results shown in Figure 16-40, which are similar
 to the results in Figures 16-38 and 16-39.

12	778	Share Purchase	17149.04210
13	606	Dividend	297.16180
14	683	Dividend	98459.89340
15	711	Dividend	62343.61300
16	722	Dividend	52348.63240

Figure 16-40. CHOOSE returning transaction types instead of your using a table

CAST()/CONVERT()

These are two functions used to convert from one data type to another. The main difference between them is that
CAST() is ANSI SQL-92 compliant, but CONVERT() has more functionality.

The syntax for CAST() is as follows:

```
CAST(variable_or_column AS datatype)
```

This is different than the syntax for CONVERT(), which is as follows:

```
CONVERT(datatype,variable_or_column)
```

Not all data types can be converted between each other, such as converting a datetime to a text data type,
and some conversions need neither a CAST() nor a CONVERT(). There is a grid in "Books Online" that provides the
necessary information.

If you want to CAST() from numeric to decimal or vice versa, you need to use CAST(); otherwise, you will
lose precision.

TRY IT OUT: CAST()/CONVERT()

1. The first example will use CAST to move a number to a char(10).

```
DECLARE @Cast int
SET @Cast = 1234
SELECT CAST(@Cast as char(10)) + '-End'
```

2. Executing this code results in a left-filled character variable, as shown in Figure 16-41.

Figure 16-41. *Changing the data type of a value*

3. The second example completes the same conversion, but this time you use the CONVERT() function.

```
DECLARE @Convert int
SET @Convert = 5678
SELECT CONVERT(char(10),@Convert) + '-End'
```

4. As you can see from Figure 16-42, the only change is in the value output.

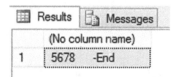

Figure 16-42. *Changing the data type of a value using the non-ANSI standard*

ISDATE()

Although ISDATE() is a function that works with dates and times, this system function takes a value in a column or a variable and confirms whether it contains a valid date or time. The value returned is 0, or false, for an invalid date, or 1 for true if the date is okay. The formatting of the date for testing within the ISDATE() function has to be in the same regional format as you have set previously with SET DATEFORMAT or SET LANGUAGE. If you are testing in a European format but have your database set to the US format, you will get a false value returned.

TRY IT OUT: ISDATE()

1. The first example demonstrates where a date is invalid. There are only 30 days in September.

```
DECLARE @IsDate char(15)
SET @IsDate = '31 Sep 2015'
SELECT ISDATE(@IsDate)
```

2. Execute the code, and you should get the results shown in Figure 16-43.

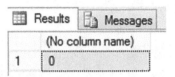

Figure 16-43. *Testing whether a value is a valid date and showing it is invalid*

3. The second example is a valid date.

```
DECLARE @IsDate char(15)
SET @IsDate = '30 Sep 2015'
SELECT ISDATE(@IsDate)
```

4. This time when you run the code, you will see a value of 1, as shown in Figure 16-44, denoting a valid entry.

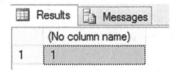

Figure 16-44. *Showing that a value is a valid date*

5. You can then combine this code with a CASE statement to test whether a variable is a valid date; if it is, you can then format the date as you wish. You could also display something if the date is invalid. In the following exercise, a char() data type is tested as to whether it is a date. If it is, it is then converted from a char() to a date data type and formatted.

```
DECLARE @IsDate char(15)
SET @IsDate = '30 Sep 2015'
SELECT CASE WHEN ISDATE(@IsDate) = 1
    THEN FORMAT(CONVERT(DATE,@IsDate),'MMM dd yyyy', 'en-GB' )
    ELSE 'Invalid Date'
    END AS 'DateOutput'
```

6. The code checks if the value is a date. When it is, the value will be converted and formatted. You should see the date in the month, day, year format, as shown in Figure 16-45.

Figure 16-45. Checking whether the value is a valid date and formatting it

ISNULL()

Many times thus far, you have seen NULL values within a column of returned data. As a value, NULL is very useful. However, you may want to test whether a column contains a NULL value. If there were a value, you would retain it, but if there were a NULL, you would convert it to a value. This function could be used to convert a NULL value in an aggregation, for example. The syntax is as follows, where the first parameter is the column or variable to test for a NULL value, and the second option defines what to change the value to if there is indeed a NULL value:

```
ISNULL(value_to_test,new_value)
```

This change occurs only in the results and doesn't change the underlying data that the value came from.

TRY IT OUT: ISNULL()

1. In this example, you will define a char() variable of ten characters in length and then set the value explicitly to NULL. The example will also work without the second line of code, which is simply there for clarity. The third line tests the variable, and as it is NULL, it changes it to a date. Note, though, that a date is more than ten characters, so the value is truncated.

    ```
    DECLARE @IsNull char(10)
    SET @IsNull = NULL
    SELECT ISNULL(@IsNull,GETDATE())
    ```

2. As expected, when you execute the code, you get the first ten characters of the relevant date, as shown in Figure 16-46.

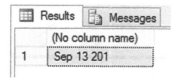

Figure 16-46. Changing a NULL value to a different value in the results

ISNUMERIC()

This system function tests the value within a column or variable and ascertains whether it is numeric. The value returned is 0, or false, for an invalid number, or 1 for true if the value can be converted to a numeric value.

■ **Note** Currency symbols such as £ and $ will also return 1 for a valid numeric value.

TRY IT OUT: ISNUMERIC()

1. The first example to demonstrate ISNUMERIC() defines a character variable and contains alphabetic values. This test fails, as shown in Figure 16-47.

    ```
    DECLARE @IsNum char(10)
    SET @IsNum = 'Robin     '
    SELECT ISNUMERIC(@IsNum)
    ```

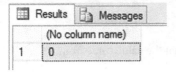

Figure 16-47. *Checking whether a value is a number and finding out it is not*

2. This second example places numbers and spaces into a char field. The ISNUMERIC() test ignores the spaces, provided that there are no further alphanumeric characters.

    ```
    DECLARE @IsNum char(10)
    SET @IsNum = '1234     '
    SELECT ISNUMERIC(@IsNum)
    ```

3. Figure 16-48 shows the results of running this code.

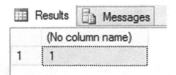

Figure 16-48. *Finding out if a value is numeric*

TRY_CONVERT()

As you have seen in the last few examples, you can test whether data fit certain data types; you can also cast from one data type to another. However, it is possible to be in a situation where you cannot cast the data to the relevant data type. In the previous example, an error would be received if you tried to convert the data to a data type where the data would not be valid. Using TRY...CONVERT(), you can attempt to cast the data, and if the conversion is not possible, a NULL value is returned.

One example of where TRY...CONVERT() would be better than a straight conversion is where data that are valid in one system are transferred and not valid in another; for instance, where one system for a date can hold a specific date, a date range, or a date length such as three months while another system cannot. Another example is where mnemonics are stored for a number, like M for million. The receiving system could then use TRY_CONVERT() to place the data in one of three columns depending on the scenario. By using TRY...CONVERT() and the CASE statement, you could fulfill the three tests on the date and populate the relevant column in your system. The example you will see will demonstrate this.

TRY IT OUT: TRY_CONVERT()

1. This first example will try to convert "3 months" to a date. This will fail and therefore will return a NULL value.

    ```
    DECLARE @InputDate char(15)
    SET @InputDate = '3 Months'
    SELECT TRY_CONVERT(DATE,@InputDate) AS OutputDate
    ```

2. Executing this code results in a NULL value, as this is not a valid date, as shown in Figure 16-49.

Figure 16-49. *Trying to convert an invalid date to a valid date*

3. It is possible to extend the code so that it attempts to convert the data to a valid data type, and if it is unable to convert, to use a default data value. The code here shows one method of combining IIF() with TRY_CONVERT. I have placed the three different settings that can be used to test the code.

    ```
    DECLARE @InputDate char(15), @DateValue date, @DateRange date
    DECLARE @Default varchar(15)
    -- SET @InputDate = '3 Sep 2015'
    -- SET @InputDate = '
    0
    3'
    SET @InputDate = 'Rubbish'
    ```

```
SELECT @DateValue  = TRY_CONVERT(DATE,@InputDate),
    @DateRange = IIF(TRY_CONVERT(int,@InputDate) IS NULL,NULL,
        DATEADD(d,CONVERT(int,@InputDate),'30 Dec 2016')),
    @Default = IIF(TRY_CONVERT(DATE,@InputDate) IS NULL,
        IIF(TRY_CONVERT(int,@InputDate) IS NULL,@InputDate,
            NULL),NULL)
SELECT @DateValue, @DateRange, @Default
```

4. Executing the three different tests will give the results shown in Figure 16-50.

	(No column name)	(No column name)	(No column name)
1	2015-09-03	NULL	NULL

	(No column name)	(No column name)	(No column name)
1	NULL	2017-01-02	NULL

	(No column name)	(No column name)	(No column name)
1	NULL	NULL	Rubbish

Figure 16-50. *A test result for each of the TRY_CONVERT tests*

PARSE/TRY_PARSE()

CAST and CONVERT are ideal for general conversion, but for specific conversions from string to a number or a datetime, PARSE is the preferred option. From other data types, you should use CONVERT/TRY_CONVERT. PARSE is similar to CONVERT, and, as you might expect, TRY_PARSE is similar to TRY_CONVERT, in that you can test the variable, and if the cast fails, then a NULL value is returned. It is possible to include culture information as part of the parsing so that the conversion takes the defined locale into consideration.

TRY IT OUT: PARSE() AND TRY_PARSE()

1. The first example will try to parse "KJ" to an integer. This will fail and return an error, as it assumes that the incoming value is of a valid data type.

    ```
    DECLARE @InputNumber char(2)
    SET @InputNumber = 'KJ'
    SELECT PARSE(@InputNumber as int) AS OutputNumeric
    ```

2. Execute the code and you should see the following:

```
Msg 9819, Level 16, State 1, Line 3
Error converting string value 'KJ' into data type int using culture ''.
```

3. The next example will try to parse "KJ" to an integer, which would be the better solution if there is a chance that data type is involved. This will fail, but this time it will return a NULL value.

```
DECLARE @InputNumber char(2)
SET @InputNumber = 'KJ'
SELECT TRY_PARSE(@InputNumber as int) AS OutputNumeric
```

4. Execute the code, and you should see a better result, as shown in Figure 16-51.

Figure 16-51. Trying to parse a string variable to a number

Even though the many system functions have been demonstrated, several of which allow you to test data to try to avoid an unexpected error, you can never plan for every eventuality. In the following section, you will see how to work with errors when they *do* occur.

RAISERROR

Before you learn about handling errors, you need to be aware of what an error is, how it is generated, the information it generates, and how to generate your own errors when something is wrong. The T-SQL command RAISERROR allows you as a developer to have the ability to produce your own SQL Server error messages when running queries or stored procedures. You are not tied to using just the error messages that come with SQL Server; you can set up your own messages and your own level of severity for those messages. It is also possible to determine whether the message is recorded in the Windows error log.

However, whether you want to use your own error message or a system error message, you can still generate an error message from SQL Server as if SQL Server itself raised it. Enterprise environments typically experience the same errors on repeated occasions, since they employ SQL Server in very specific ways depending on their business model. With this in mind, attention to employing RAISERROR can have big benefits by providing more meaningful feedback as well as suggested solutions for users. You will see a second method for generating an error later in this chapter.

By using RAISERROR, SQL Server acts as if SQL Server raised the error, as you have seen within this book. RAISERROR can be used in one of two ways; looking at the syntax will make this clear:

```
RAISERROR ({msg_id|msg_str} {,severity,state}
          [,argument [ ,...n ] ])
          [WITH option [ ,...n ]]
```

You can either use a specific msg_id or provide an actual output string, msg_str, either as a literal or as a local variable defined as string-based, containing the error message that will be recorded. The msg_id references system- and user-defined messages that already exist within the SQL Server error messages table.

When specifying a text message in the first parameter of the RAISERROR function instead of a message ID, you may find that the following is easier to write than creating a new message:

```
RAISERROR('You made an error', 10, 1)
```

The next two parameters in the RAISERROR syntax are numerical and relate to how severe the error is and provide information about how the error was invoked. Severity levels range from 1 at the innocuous end to 25 at the fatal end. Severity levels of 2 to 14 are generally informational. Severity level 15 is for warnings, and levels 16 or higher represent errors. Severity levels from 20 to 25 are considered fatal and require the WITH LOG option, which means that the error is logged in the Windows Application Event Log and in the SQL error log and the connection is terminated; quite simply, the stored procedure stops executing. The connection referred to here is the connection within Query Editor, or the connection made by an application using a data access method like ADO.NET. Only for a most extreme error would you set the severity to this level; in most cases, you would use a number between 1 and 19.

The last parameter of the function specifies state. Use a 1 here for most implementations, although the legitimate range is from 1 to 127. You may use this to indicate which error was thrown by providing a different state for each RAISERROR invocation in your stored procedure. SQL Server does not act on any legitimate state value, but the parameter is required.

A msg_str can define parameters within the text. By placing the value, either statically or via a variable, after the last parameter that you define, msg_str replaces the message parameter with that value. This is demonstrated in an upcoming example. If you do want to add a parameter to a message string, you have to define a conversion specification. The format is as follows:

```
% [[flag] [width] [. precision] [{h | l}]] type
```

The options are as follows:

- flag: A code that determines justification and spacing of the value entered:
 - - (minus): Left-justify the value
 - + (plus): The value shows a + or a – sign.
 - 0: Prefix the output with zeros
 - #: Preface any nonzero with a 0, 0x, or 0X, depending on the formatting
 - (blank): Prefix with blanks
- width: The minimum width of the output
- precision: The maximum number of characters to be used from the argument
- h: Character types:
 - d or i: Signed integer
 - o: Unsigned octal
 - s: String
 - u: Unsigned integer
 - x or X: Unsigned hex
- To place a parameter within a message string where the parameter needs to be inserted, put a % sign followed by one of the following options: d or i for a signed integer, p for a pointer, s for a string, u for an unsigned integer, x or X for an unsigned hexadecimal, and o for an unsigned octal. Note that float, double, and single are not supported as parameter types for messages. You will see this in the upcoming examples.

Finally, there are three options that could be placed at the end of the RAISERROR message. These are the WITH options:

- LOG places the error message within the Windows error log.

- NOWAIT sends the error directly to the client.

- SETERROR resets the error number to 50000 within the message string only.

When using any of these last WITH options, do take the greatest of care, as their misuse can create more problems than they solve. For example, you may unnecessarily use LOG a great deal, filling up the Windows Application Event Log and the SQL error log, which can lead to further problems.

There is a system stored procedure, sp_addmessage, that can create a new global error message for use by RAISERROR by defining the @msgnum to be added. The syntax for adding such a message is as follows:

```
sp_addmessage [@msgnum =]msg_id,
[@severity = ] severity , [ @msgtext = ] 'msg'
   [ , [ @lang = ] 'language' ]
   [ , [ @with_log = ] 'with_log' ]
   [ , [ @replace = ] 'replace' ]
```

The parameters in this system stored procedure are as follows:

- @msgnum: The number of the message is typically greater than 50000.

- @severity: A number in the range of 1 to 25

- @lang: Use this if you need to define the language of the error message. Normally, this is left empty.

- @with_log: Set to TRUE if you want to write a message to the Windows error log.

- @replace: Set to 'replace' if you are replacing an existing message and updating any of the preceding values with new settings.

■ **Note** Any message added will be specific for that database rather than for the server.

It is time to move to an example that will set up an error message to be used when a customer is overdrawn.

TRY IT OUT: RAISERROR

1. First of all, you will want to add a new user-defined error message. To do this, you will use sp_addmessage. You can now add any new SQL Server message that you want. Any user-defined error message number must be greater than 50000, so the first error message would normally be 50001.

   ```
   sp_addmessage @msgnum=50001,@severity=1,
   @msgtext='Customer is overdrawn'
   ```

2. You can then perform a RAISERROR to see the message displayed. Notice that you have to define the severity again. This is mandatory, but it would be better if it were optional so you could always default to the severity defined.

   ```
   RAISERROR (50001,1,1)
   ```

3. When this is executed, you will see the following output:

```
Customer is overdrawn
Msg 50001, Level 1, State 1
```

4. This is not the friendliest of messages, as it would be better to perhaps give out the customer number as well. You can do this via a parameter. In the code that follows, you will replace the message just added so as to include a parameter where you are formatting with flag 0, which means you are prefixing the output with zeros. Then you will include the number 10, which is the degree of precision, which means the number will be ten digits; and finally you will indicate that the message will be unsigned by using the option u.

```
sp_addmessage @msgnum =50001,@severity=1,
@msgtext='Customer is overdrawn. CustomerId= %010u',@replace='replace'
```

5. You can then change the RAISERROR so that you add on another parameter. You are hard-coding the customer number as customer number 243, but you could use a local variable.

```
RAISERROR (50001,1,1,243)
```

6. Executing the code now produces output that is much better and more informative for debugging, if required.

```
Customer is overdrawn. CustomerId= 0000000243
Msg 50001, Level 1, State 1
```

Now that you know how you can raise your own errors if scenarios crop up that need them, you can take a look at how SQL Server deals with errors. You do come back to RAISERROR when looking at these two next options.

Error Handling

When working with T-SQL, it is important to have some sort of error handling to cater to those times when something goes wrong. Errors can be of different varieties; for example, you might expect at least one row of data to be returned from a query, but you receive no rows. However, what I am discussing here is when SQL Server informs you there is something more drastically wrong. You have seen some errors throughout this book, and even in this chapter. There are two methods of error catching you can employ in such cases. The first uses a system variable, @@ERROR.

@@ERROR

This is the most basic method of error handling. It has served SQL Server developers well over the years, but it can be cumbersome. When an error occurs, such as you have seen as you have gone through this book creating and manipulating objects, a global variable, @@ERROR, is set with the SQL Server error message number. Similarly, if you try to do something with a set of data that is invalid, such as dividing a number by zero or exceeding the number of digits allowed in a numeric data type, then SQL Server will set this variable for you to inspect.

The downside is that the @@ERROR variable setting lasts only for the duration of the next statement following the line of code that has been executed; therefore, when you think there might be problems, you need to either pass the data to a local variable or inspect it straightaway. The first example demonstrates this.

TRY IT OUT: USING @@ERROR

1. This example tries to divide 100 by zero, which results in an error. You then list out the error number, and then again list out the error number. Enter the following code and execute it:

   ```
   SELECT 100/0
   SELECT @@ERROR
   SELECT @@ERROR
   ```

2. It is necessary in this instance to check both the Results and the Messages tabs. The first tab is the Messages tab, which shows you the error encountered. As expected, you see the "Divide by zero error encountered" message.

```
Msg 8134, Level 16, State 1, Line 1
Divide by zero error encountered.
(1 row(s) affected)
(1 row(s) affected)
```

3. Moving to the Results tab, you should see three result sets, as shown in Figure 16-52. The first, showing no information, would be where SQL Server would have put the division results had it succeeded. The second result set is the number from the first SELECT @@ERROR. Notice the number corresponds to the msg number found in the Messages tab. The third result set shows a value of 0. This is because the first SELECT @@ERROR worked successfully and therefore set the system variable to 0. This demonstrates the lifetime of the value within @@ERROR.

Figure 16-52. Showing @@ERROR in multiple statements

4. When you use the `RAISERROR` function, it also sets the `@@ERROR` variable, as you can see in the following code. However, the value will be set to 0 using the preceding example. This is because the severity level was below 11.

```
RAISERROR (50001,1,1,243)
SELECT @@ERROR
```

5. When the code is executed, you can see that `@@ERROR` is set to 0, as shown in Figure 16-53.

Figure 16-53. *When severity is too low to set @@ERROR*

6. By changing the severity to 11 or above, the `@@ERROR` setting will now be set to the message number within the `RAISERROR`.

```
RAISERROR (50001,11,1,243)
SELECT @@ERROR
```

7. The preceding code produces the same message as shown within the `RAISERROR` example, but as you can see in Figure 16-54, the error number setting now reflects the value placed in the `msgnum` parameter.

Figure 16-54. *With a higher severity, the message number is set*

Although `@@ERROR` is a useful tool, it would be better to use the next error-handling routine to be demonstrated, `TRY...CATCH` with `THROW`.

TRY...CATCH and THROW

It can be said that, no matter what, any piece of code has the ability to fail and generate some sort of error. For the vast majority of this code, you will want to trap any error that occurs, check what the error is, and deal with it as best you can. As you saw previously, this could be done one statement at a time using `@@ERROR` to test for any error codes. Improved functionality exists whereby a set of statements can try to execute, and if any statement has a runtime error, it will be caught. This is known as a `TRY...CATCH` block. If you find an error within your code where you were expecting something—such as a specific value or a range of values, for example—then it is possible to generate an

error with a THROW statement. In essence, TRY...CATCH and THROW are greatly improved and more flexible versions of RAISERROR and @@ERROR. There is one slight catch, and that is that a THROW statement must be preceded with a line of code that is terminated with a semicolon.

Surrounding a single batch of code with the ability to execute that code and to then catch any errors and try to deal with them has been around for quite a number of years in languages such as C++. Thankfully, you see this within SQL Server as well. You can use TRY...CATCH with a transaction; however, you have to take care where to place the BEGIN TRANSACTION along with the ROLLBACK and COMMIT TRANSACTION statements. You will see an instance of this within the examples.

The syntax for TRY...CATCH is pretty straightforward. There are two "blocks" of code. The first block, BEGIN TRY, is where there is one or more T-SQL statements that you want to try to run. If any of the statements has an error, then no further processing within that block will be done, and processing will switch to the second block, BEGIN CATCH.

```
BEGIN TRY
     { sql_statement | statement_block }
END TRY
BEGIN CATCH
     { sql_statement | statement_block }
END CATCH
```

It is possible to generate your own error via a RAISERROR, as you saw earlier, or you can execute a THROW statement either within or outside a TRY or CATCH block. A RAISERROR within a TRY...CATCH will work as it would outside a TRY...CATCH; that is to say that it will set the error details, and then if the severity is 10 or lower, processing will continue. If the severity is in the range of 11 to 19, then the RAISERROR would pass execution to the CATCH block. A severity of 20 or above would stop execution immediately and close the connection, and processing would not pass to the CATCH block. Rather than using RAISERROR, you can THROW an error that will always move the execution of the code to the CATCH block of code. This allows you as a developer to do cleanup actions when an error has occurred, such as to roll back a transaction or do any other actions you want to perform to help you with any investigation.

TRY...CATCH blocks can be nested. This gives you several advantages. The first is that you can pass any error up through the nested levels with a rethrow. This is achieved by issuing the THROW statement with no parameters in each CATCH block in the nesting. You will sometimes hear this called "bubbling up the error." There are advantages to bubbling, as it allows a controlled way of getting out of a difficult situation; however, it can also lead to confusion if you rethrow every exception. So when you rethrow an error, ensure that this is the action you want to do.

Nesting allows you to surround a stored procedure call with a TRY...CATCH. This will then allow for any error that is thrown in the called stored procedure to be caught in the calling stored procedure.

Within the TRY...CATCH block, it is possible to retrieve error information. The system functions that can be used to find useful debugging information are detailed here:

- ERROR_LINE(): The line number that caused the error or performed the RAISERROR or the THROW statement; this is physical rather than relative (i.e., you don't have to remove blank lines within the T-SQL to get the correct line number, unlike in some software that does require this).

- ERROR_MESSAGE(): The text message

- ERROR_NUMBER(): The number associated with the message

- ERROR_PROCEDURE(): If you are retrieving this within a stored procedure or trigger, the name of it will be contained here. If you are running ad hoc T-SQL code, then the value will be NULL.

- ERROR_SEVERITY(): The numeric severity value for the error

- ERROR_STATE(): The numeric state value for the error

Not all errors are caught within a TRY...CATCH block, unfortunately. Those that aren't caught are compile errors or errors that occur when deferred name resolution takes place and the name created doesn't exist. To clarify these two points, when T-SQL code is either ad hoc or within a stored procedure, SQL Server compiles the code, looking for syntax errors. However, not all code can be fully compiled, and often is not compiled until the statement is about to be executed. If there is an error, then this will terminate the batch immediately. The second error that will not be caught is one resulting when you have code that references a temporary table, for example, in which case the table won't exist at runtime and column names won't be able to be checked. This is known as *deferred name resolution*, and if you try to use a column that doesn't exist, this will also generate an error, thus terminating the batch.

There is a great deal more to TRY...CATCH blocks in areas that are quite advanced, but now that you know the basics, let's look at some examples demonstrating what I have just discussed.

TRY IT OUT: TRY...CATCH...THROW

1. Your first example is a simple error where you have defined an integer local variable. Within your error-handling block, after outputting a statement to demonstrate that you are within that block, you try to set a string to the variable. This is a standard error and immediately moves the execution to the CATCH block; the last SELECT is not executed.

```
DECLARE @Probs int
BEGIN TRY
    SELECT 'This will work'
    SELECT @Probs='Not Right'
    SELECT 10+5,
     'This will also work, however the error means it will not run'
END TRY
BEGIN CATCH
    SELECT 'An error has occurred at line ' +
        LTRIM(STR(ERROR_LINE())) +
        ' with error ' + LTRIM(STR(ERROR_NUMBER())) + ' ' + ERROR_MESSAGE()
END CATCH
```

2. When you run the code, you will see the first statement and then the SELECT statement that executes when the error is caught. System functions are used to display relevant information, which appears in Figure 16-55.

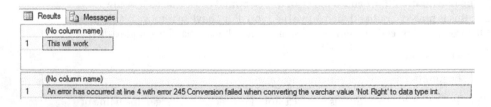

Figure 16-55. An error is caught

3. The second example demonstrates nesting TRY...CATCH blocks and how execution can continue within the outer block when an error arises within the second block. Keep the same error and see the error message in the second catch block. Once this is executed, processing continues, and this code will now work.

```
DECLARE @Probs int
BEGIN TRY
    SELECT 'This will work'
    BEGIN TRY
      SELECT @Probs='Not Right'
       SELECT 10+5,
       'This will also work, however the error means it will not run'
    END TRY
    BEGIN CATCH
        SELECT 'The second catch block'
    END CATCH
    SELECT 'And then this will now work'
END TRY
BEGIN CATCH
    SELECT 'An error has occurred at line ' +
        LTRIM(STR(ERROR_LINE())) +
        ' with error ' + LTRIM(STR(ERROR_NUMBER())) + ' ' + ERROR_MESSAGE()
END CATCH
```

4. As expected, you see three lines of output, as shown in Figure 16-56. The code in the outer CATCH block doesn't run, as the error is handled within the inner block.

Figure 16-56. *An error is caught in a nested batch*

5. The foregoing example could be modified so that in the inner CATCH block the error is thrown to the outer catch block. The outer catch block would then hold all the rollback processing, error logging, and so on.

```
DECLARE @Probs int
BEGIN TRY
   SELECT 'This will work'
   BEGIN TRY
     SELECT @Probs='Not Right'
      SELECT 10+5,
      'This will also work, however the error means it will not run'
   END TRY
   BEGIN CATCH
      THROW
   END CATCH
   SELECT 'The THROW means this is skipped'
END TRY
BEGIN CATCH
   SELECT 'An error has occurred at line ' +
      LTRIM(STR(ERROR_LINE())) +
      ' with error ' + LTRIM(STR(ERROR_NUMBER())) + ' ' + ERROR_MESSAGE()
      IF @@TRANCOUNT > 0
         ROLLBACK TRAN
END CATCH
```

6. After you execute the foregoing code and the error occurs, control will be passed to the inner catch block, which will then THROW the error to the next nesting level. In this example, control is passed to the outer block of code, where the error is listed. A test is then performed to roll back any open transactions as part of the cleanup exercise. You can see the output in Figure 16-57.

Figure 16-57. *An error is thrown to the outer catch*

7. This time, you can see how your T-SQL code can be successfully precompiled and execution begun. Then when you try to display results from a temporary table that doesn't exist, the CATCH block does not fire, as execution terminates immediately.

```
DECLARE @Probs int
BEGIN TRY
   SELECT 'This will work'
   BEGIN TRY
      SELECT * FROM #Temp
   END TRY
```

```
BEGIN CATCH
    SELECT 'The second catch block'
END CATCH
SELECT 'And then this will now work'
END TRY
BEGIN CATCH
    SELECT 'An error has occurred at line ' +
        LTRIM(STR(ERROR_LINE())) +
        ' with error ' + LTRIM(STR(ERROR_NUMBER())) + ' ' + ERROR_MESSAGE()
END CATCH
```

8. When the code is run, you see the following output in the Messages tab, detailing how one row has been returned, which comes from the first SELECT statement. You then see the SQL Server error. Looking at Figure 16-58, you see just the first SELECT statement output.

```
(1 row(s) affected)
Msg 208, Level 16, State 0, Line 5
Invalid object name '#Temp'.
```

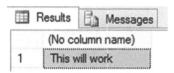

Figure 16-58. *What happens when SQL Server terminates execution*

9. The next example demonstrates how to throw an error from an inner exception handler to an outer handler. You would normally see this in nested stored procedures, but for simplicity it will be demonstrated in the following simplified example.

```
BEGIN TRY
    SELECT 'Outer level'
    BEGIN TRY
        SELECT 'Inner level';
        THROW 51200, 'Inner level throw', 1
    END TRY
    BEGIN CATCH
        SELECT 'Inner Catch with re-throw';
        THROW
    END CATCH
END TRY
BEGIN CATCH
    SELECT 'Outer Catch';
    THROW
END CATCH
```

■ **Note** Remember that the statement previous to a THROW must be terminated by a semicolon.

10. The inner throw will be passed to the inner catch, which will rethrow the error to the outer catch, which in turn throws the error to the outermost calling code, which in this instance is the end of the code, which finally lists the error. You can see this tracked in the output from the foregoing executed code in the results in Figure 16-59.

Figure 16-59. *What happens when SQL Server terminates execution*

11. The error itself is placed in the Messages tab, which is shown here.

```
(1 row(s) affected)
(1 row(s) affected)
(1 row(s) affected)
(1 row(s) affected)
Msg 51200, Level 16, State 1, Line 5
Inner level throw
```

Error handling and having the ability to control errors will lead to code that is more robust, and when an error occurs it can be tracked in a more constructive fashion and handled in a controlled manner. Remembering to use a semicolon in the statement prior to a THROW may seem odd; however, this is simply Microsoft trying to take you down the route of statement termination via a delimiter.

Summary

The text for this chapter is not the most fluid, but the information will be very useful as you start using SQL Server. The functions demonstrated here are the most common and most likely ones you will use, and this is why they have been demonstrated. Each section you have read contains a great deal of useful and pertinent information, and rereading the chapter and maybe even trying out different ideas based on the basics demonstrated here will give you a stronger understanding of what is happening. The main areas of focus were error handling and joining tables to return results. In addition, looking at some of the system predefined functions and how useful they can be is important, as you will use some of these functions many number of times when coding. Take time to fully understand what is happening and how you can use these two features.

CHAPTER 17

■ ■ ■

Advanced T-SQL and Debugging

By now, you really are becoming proficient in SQL Server and writing code to work with the data and the objects within the database. Already you have seen some T-SQL code and encountered some scenarios that have advanced your skills as a T-SQL developer. You can now look at more advanced areas of T-SQL programming to round out your knowledge and really get you going with queries that do more than the basics.

This chapter will cover the occasions when you need a query within a query, known as a subquery. This is ideal for producing a list of values to search for, or for producing a value from another table to set a column or a variable with. It is also possible to create a transient table of data to use within a query, known as a common table expression. You will look at both subqueries and common table expressions in this chapter.

From there, you will explore how to take a set of data and pivot the results, just as you can do within Excel. You will also take a look at different types of ranking functions, where you can take your set of data and attach rankings to rows or groups of rows of data.

Finally, you will see how to deal with varchar(max) and varbinary(max) data types when loading large text, images, movies, and so on.

Creating a SEQUENCE

Chapter 5 introduced sequences as an alternative to IDENTITY columns. Now in this section, sequences will be discussed in more detail. A sequence is held in its own object with a separate node under Programmability within SSMS. This helps to logically break the link between a sequence and its assignment to a specific table. Creating a sequence is more in tune with programming functions, such as a stored procedure, as you will see when looking at the syntax.

The syntax for the SEQUENCE object is very basic, with a number of options that can be attached to the sequence creation. The syntax is as follows:

```
CREATE SEQUENCE [schema_name . ] sequence_name
    [ AS [ built_in_integer_type | user-defined_integer_type ] ]
    [ START WITH <constant> ]
    [ INCREMENT BY <constant> ]
    [ { MINVALUE [ <constant> ] } | { NO MINVALUE } ]
    [ { MAXVALUE [ <constant> ] } | { NO MAXVALUE } ]
    [ CYCLE | { NO CYCLE } ]
    [ { CACHE [ <constant> ] } | { NO CACHE } ]
```

The CREATE SEQUENCE has a number of options; the only mandatory option is the sequence_name. The options are as follows

- schema_name: The schema that the sequence belongs to

- sequence_name: The name you want to call the sequence

- AS: Although optional, I would recommend defining the data type to avoid confusion. If not defined, though, the data type will be bigint. Valid base data types are tinyint, smallint, int, bigint, decimal, and numeric. Any user-defined type based on one of these base data types could also be assigned.

- START WITH: The number the sequence starts with; 1 is the default.

- INCREMENT BY: Each time a sequence number is requested, this defines the increment from the previous number. This can be a negative (for descending numbers) or positive, and the default increment is 1.

- MINVALUE value|NO MINVALUE: This is used in conjunction with the CYCLE option. This will define the minimum value if the sequence numbers exceed the MAXVALUE if defined, and the CYCLE option is defined. The default is the minimum value for the data range for the data type of the sequence.

- MAXVALUE value|NO MAXVALUE: This is used to define the maximum value of the sequence. The default is the maximum value for the data type. If the sequence reaches the maximum value, the next request for a number will generate an error if you have NOCYCLE defined or will put the sequence to the MINVALUE if CYCLE is defined.

- CYCLE|NO CYCLE: When the maximum value for a sequence is reached, it can generate an error if NO CYCLE is defined, or will set the sequence to MINVALUE if CYCLE is defined.

- CACHE|NO CACHE: Every time you want the next number in the sequence, SQL Server will perform disk I/O to retrieve the value when using NO CACHE. It is possible to cache a range of numbers in memory so that you retrieve the next value from memory, which is a great deal faster. SQL Server will generate the numbers and write the last number to disk, holding the numbers in memory for use. To achieve this, you would create the sequence with the CACHE option, which is the default. The downside to CACHE is that if you need to restart the server or the SQL Server windows process, then that range of numbers in memory will be lost and a gap will exist. If that is not an issue and you are inserting a large number of rows, then CACHE would be a good choice.

Once a sequence is created, you then retrieve the next value using the following:

```
NEXT VALUE FOR [schema_name.]sequence_name
```

Now that you know what a sequence is and the options available, it is time to build and alter a sequence. A sequence will be built for the CustomerDetails.FinancialProducts table that already has data within it. You will see valid insertions to the table, and then you will see what happens when a maximum is reached and how to progress from that point.

TRY IT OUT: BUILDING AND USING A SEQUENCE

1. First of all, it is useful to know what number the sequence will start at based on the maximum value of ProductIds within the CustomerDetails.FinancialProducts table.

   ```
   SELECT MAX(ProductId) + 1
     FROM CustomerDetails.FinancialProducts
   ```

2. Next, the sequence is created within the CustomerDetails schema with a unique name. The return value will be an integer and will start at 42, as product ID 41 is my last financial product ID. For the moment, I am setting a max value of 44 and that each sequence will be retrieved one at a time, no caching. Execute the following code.

   ```
   CREATE SEQUENCE CustomerDetails.SeqFinancialProducts
   AS int
   START WITH 42
   MAXVALUE 44
   NO CACHE
   ```

■ **Note** You cannot use a local variable to define any values for options. It has to be a constant.

3. You should then see the sequence under the Programmability node within Object Explorer for SQL Server, as shown in Figure 17-1.

Figure 17-1. *The new sequence created and showing in Object Explorer*

4. You can now test the sequence by inserting three rows of data. This will keep the sequence number within the bounds of the max value. When you execute the code, all three rows should insert successfully.

```
INSERT CustomerDetails.FinancialProducts(ProductId, ProductName)
    VALUES (NEXT VALUE FOR CustomerDetails.SeqFinancialProducts,
            'Life Insurance') ,
        (NEXT VALUE FOR CustomerDetails.SeqFinancialProducts,
            'Unit Trusts'),
        (NEXT VALUE FOR CustomerDetails.SeqFinancialProducts,
            'Investment Trusts')
```

5. The next insertion will fail. Enter the following code for the next insertion.

```
INSERT CustomerDetails.FinancialProducts(ProductId, ProductName)
    VALUES (NEXT VALUE FOR CustomerDetails.SeqFinancialProducts,
            'Repurchase Agreements')
```

6. When you execute the code, you will see an error, as shown here:

```
Msg 11728, Level 16, State 1, Line 1
The sequence object 'SeqFinancialProducts' has reached its
minimum or maximum value. Restart the sequence object to allow
new values to be generated.
```

At this point, all further insertions will fail, which may be a valid scenario for your system; however, if it is not, then you need to build your sequence with an alternative strategy in mind.

In the next section, you will see how to alter the sequence so that insertions can be successfully completed going forward. This is achieved via the ALTER SEQUENCE command.

Altering the Sequence

Before you dive into altering the sequence, you need to know what the syntax is. It is very similar to the CREATE SEQUENCE as it has the same options; however, there is a further option called RESTART. RESTART on its own, which is the default, would reseed the sequence to the lowest value for the data type, which would be -2,147,483,648 for the int data type. To restart with a specific value, you add WITH and a constant value. You will see this in the following exercise. The syntax follows, and then the exercise will use this syntax to alter the sequence:

```
ALTER SEQUENCE [schema_name. ] sequence_name
    [ RESTART [ WITH <constant> ] ]
```

7. The first example will demonstrate cycling the sequence only. This will cause the sequence to loop around to the beginning, and as there is no RESTART option you will see the data type's minimum value added for the new row.

```
ALTER SEQUENCE CustomerDetails.SeqFinancialProducts
CYCLE
```

8. Insert the row of data that in the CREATE SEQUENCE example failed as the maximum was reached. When you execute the code this time, it will succeed.

```
INSERT CustomerDetails.FinancialProducts(ProductId, ProductName)
    VALUES (NEXT VALUE FOR CustomerDetails.SeqFinancialProducts, 'Repurchase
    Agreements')
```

9. You can check the value given to the row from the sequence via the following code.

```
SELECT ProductId,ProductName
FROM CustomerDetails.FinancialProducts
ORDER BY ProductId
```

10. When you execute the code, you will see the row as shown in Figure 17-2.

	ProductId	ProductName
1	-2147483648	Repurchase Agreements
2	1	Thrubanower
3	2	Doperex
4	3	Hapvenor
5	4	Barripedgar
6	5	Emdimicator
7	6	Lomhupistor
8	7	Froquestefax
9	8	Qwieronor
10	9	Lomhupax
11	10	Empebex

Figure 17-2. *New row inserted with the minimum value*

11. As this was generated in error, you could modify the ProductId with an UPDATE; however, for this example, let's delete the row so it can be inserted correctly.

```
DELETE FROM CustomerDetails.FinancialProducts
WHERE ProductId < 0
```

12. You now need to alter the sequence to indicate the restart value of 1. You will also need to CYCLE the sequence.

```
ALTER SEQUENCE CustomerDetails.SeqFinancialProducts
CYCLE
RESTART WITH 1
```

13. It is now possible to insert the row with the correct sequence value of 1 and then inspect the table to see if the ProductId is 1.

```
INSERT CustomerDetails.FinancialProducts(ProductId, ProductName)
    VALUES (NEXT VALUE FOR CustomerDetails.SeqFinancialProducts,
                'Repurchase Agreements')

SELECT ProductId,ProductName
FROM CustomerDetails.FinancialProducts
ORDER BY ProductId
```

14. This time the correct sequence has been generated, but notice in Figure 17-3 that you now have two rows with a ProductId of 1, which is what was desired with the alter sequence in step 6.

	ProductId	ProductName
1	1	Thrubanower
2	1	Repurchase Agreements
3	2	Doperex
4	3	Hapvenor
5	4	Barnipedgar
6	5	Emdimicator
7	6	Lomhupistor
8	7	Froquestefax
9	8	Qwieronor
10	9	Lomhupax
11	10	Empebex

Figure 17-3. *Row now inserted with the restarted value*

If you wanted the sequence to carry on, then you would have, in step 6, set a new maximum value and set the RESTART WITH value to the max value in the ProductId column and not CYCLEd the sequence. You can delete one of the ProductId ones by executing the following code. I have deleted one of the rows.

```
DELETE TOP (1) FROM CustomerDetails.FinancialProducts where ProductId = 1
```

Subqueries

A *subquery* is a query embedded within another query or statement and can be used anywhere an expression is allowed. It can be used to check or set a value of a variable or column, or used to test whether a row of data exists in a WHERE clause.

Using Subqueries

Sometimes, you may want to set a column value based on data from another query. One example you have is the ShareDetails.Shares table. .Imagine you have a column defined for MaximumSharePrice that holds the highest price the share price had reached for that year. Rather than doing a test every time the share price moved, you could

use the MAX function to get the highest share price, put that value into a variable, and then set the column via that variable. Without the use of a subquery, with the exception of the ALTER TABLE, the code would be similar to that defined here:

```
ALTER TABLE ShareDetails.Shares
ADD MaximumSharePrice money
GO
DECLARE @MaxPrice money
SELECT @MaxPrice = MAX(Price)
    FROM ShareDetails.SharePrices
  WHERE ShareId = 1
SELECT @MaxPrice
UPDATE ShareDetails.Shares
SET MaximumSharePrice = @MaxPrice
WHERE ShareId = 1
```

In the preceding code, if you wanted to work with more than one share, you would need to implement a loop and process each share one at a time. However, you could also perform a subquery, which implements the same functionality as shown in the code that follows. The subquery still finds the maximum price for a given share and sets the column. Notice that this time you can update all shares with one statement. The subquery joins with the main query via a WHERE clause so that as each share is dealt with, the subquery can take that ShareId and still get the maximum value. If you want to run the following code, then you still need the ALTER TABLE statement used previously, even if you did not run the preceding code.

■ **Note** This type of subquery is called a *correlated subquery*.

```
SELECT ShareId,MaximumSharePrice
FROM ShareDetails.Shares
UPDATE ShareDetails.Shares
SET MaximumSharePrice =
    (SELECT MAX(Price)
        FROM ShareDetails.SharePrices sp
      WHERE sp.ShareId = s.ShareId)
FROM ShareDetails.Shares s
SELECT ShareId,MaximumSharePrice
FROM ShareDetails.Shares
```

You also came across a subquery way back in Chapter 8 when you were testing whether a backup had successfully completed. The code is replicated here, with the subquery section highlighted in bold. In this instance, instead of setting a value in a column, you are looking for a value to be used as part of a filtering criterion. Recall from Chapter 8 that you know the last backup will have the greatest backup_set_id. You use the subquery to find this value (as there is no system function or variable that can return this at the time of creating the backup). Once you have this value, you can use it to reinterrogate the same table, filtering out everything but the last row for the backup just created.

■ **Note** Don't forget that for the FROM DISK option, you will have a different file name than the one in the following code.

```
declare @backupSetId as int
select @backupSetId = position
from msdb..backupset
where database_name=N'ApressFinancial'
and backup_set_id=(select max(backup_set_id)
                    from msdb..backupset
                    where database_name=N'ApressFinancial')
if @backupSetId is null
begin
    raiserror(N'Verify failed. Backup information for
    database ''ApressFinancial'' not found.', 16, 1)
end
RESTORE VERIFYONLY
FROM DISK = N'C:\Program Files\Microsoft SQL Server\
MSSQL11.APRESS_DEV1\MSSQL\Backup\ApressFinancial.bak'
WITH FILE = @backupSetId,
NOUNLOAD,
NOREWIND
GO
```

In both of these cases, you are returning a single value within the subquery, but this need not always be the case. You can also return more than one value. One value must be returned when you are trying to set a value. This is because you are using an equals (=) sign. It is possible in a WHERE clause to look for a number of values using the IN clause.

IN

If you want to look for a number of values in your WHERE clause, such as a list of values from the ShareDetails.Shares table where the ShareId is 1, 11, or 15, then you can use an IN clause. The code to complete this example would be as follows:

```
SELECT *
  FROM ShareDetails.Shares
 WHERE ShareId IN (1,11,15)
```

Using a subquery, it would be possible to replace these numbers with the results from the subquery. The preceding query could also be written using the code that follows. This example shows how it is possible to combine a subquery and an aggregation to produce the list of ShareIds that form the IN:

```
SELECT *
  FROM ShareDetails.Shares
 WHERE ShareId IN (SELECT ShareId
                     FROM ShareDetails.Shares
                    WHERE CurrentPrice > (SELECT MIN(CurrentPrice)
                                            FROM ShareDetails.Shares)
                      AND CurrentPrice < (SELECT MAX(CurrentPrice) / 3
                                            FROM ShareDetails.Shares))
```

■ **Note** If a query starts becoming very complex, you may find that it starts performing badly. This book doesn't look at the performance of queries, although it has discussed indexes and how they can help your query perform better. Always take a step back and think, "Would this work better as two queries where the first query creates a subset of data?" Writing a very complex query that processes all the data in one pass may not always be the best answer. Consider also that a complex query can be difficult to figure out should you need to revise later.

Both of these examples replace what would require a number of OR clauses within the WHERE filter, such as you see in this code:

```
SELECT *
  FROM ShareDetails.Shares
 WHERE ShareId = 1
    OR ShareId = 11
    OR ShareId = 15
```

These are just three different ways a subquery can work. The fourth way involves using a subquery to check whether a row of data exists, which you will look at next.

EXISTS

EXISTS is a clause that is very similar to IN, in that it tests a column value against a subset of data from a subquery. The difference is that EXISTS uses a join to join values from a column to a column within the subquery, as opposed to IN, which compares against a comma-delimited set of values and requires no join.

Over time, your ShareDetails.Shares and ShareDetails.SharePrice tables will grow to quite large sizes. If you wanted to shrink them, you could use cascading deletes so that when you delete from the ShareDetails.Shares table, you would also delete all the SharePrice records. But how would you know which shares to delete? One way would be to see what shares are still held within your TransactionDetails.Transactions table. You would do this via EXISTS, but instead of looking for ShareIds that exist, you would use NOT EXISTS.

At present, you have no shares listed within the TransactionDetails.Transactions table, so you would see all of the ShareDetails.Shares listed. You can make life easier with EXISTS by giving tables an alias, but you also have to use the WHERE statement to make the join between the tables. However, you aren't really joining the tables as such; a better way of looking at it is to say you are filtering rows from the subquery table.

The final point to note is that you can return whatever you want after the SELECT statement in the subquery, but it should be only one column or a value; it cannot be more than this. The subquery can be in the columns returned and the single value returned, displayed along with the other columns. However, if subquery is in the WHERE condition, then the value cannot be displayed.

■ **Note** When using EXISTS, it is most common in SQL Server to use * rather than a constant like 1, as it simply returns a true or false setting.

The following code shows EXISTS in action prefixed with a NOT:

```
SELECT *
  FROM ShareDetails.Shares s
 WHERE NOT EXISTS (SELECT *
                   FROM TransactionDetails.Transactions t
                  WHERE t.RelatedShareId = s.ShareId)
```

■ **Note** Both EXISTS and IN can be prefixed with NOT.

Tidying Up the Loose End

You have a loose end from a previous chapter that you need to tidy up. In Chapter 14, you built a scalar function to calculate interest between two dates using a rate. It was called TransactionDetails.fn_IntCalc. When I demonstrated this, you had to pass in the specific information; however, by using a subquery, it is possible to use this function to calculate interest for customers based on their transactions. The following "Try it Out" exercise shows you how to invoke the function with a subquery result as one of the arguments. The subquery computes the "to date" for each transaction returned by the outermost SELECT statement.

TRY IT OUT: USING A SCALAR FUNCTION WITH SUBQUERIES

1. In the first part of the query, you are returning some data from the TransactionDetails. Transactions table:

   ```
   SELECT t1.TransactionId, t1.DateEntered,t1.Amount,
   ```

2. The second part of the query is where it is necessary to compute the "to date" for calculating the interest, as DateEntered will be used as the "from date." To do this, it is necessary to find the next transaction in the TransactionDetails.Transactions table. To do that, you need to find the minimum DateEntered—using the minimum function—where that minimum DateEntered is greater than that for the transaction you are on in the main query. However, you also need to ensure you are doing this for the same customer as the SELECT used previously. You need to make a join from the main table to the subquery joining on the customer ID. Without this, you could be selecting any minimum date entered from any customer.

   ```
   SELECT MIN(DateEntered)
     FROM TransactionDetails.Transactions t2
          WHERE t2.CustomerId = t1.CustomerId
             AND t2.DateEntered> t1.DateEntered) as 'To Date',
   ```

3. Finally, you can put the same query into the call to the interest calculation function. The final part is where you are just looking for the transactions for customer ID 1. The following is the entire query. The outer query invokes the function. One of the arguments to the function is the result of the subquery that computes each transaction's "to date."

```
SELECT t1.TransactionId, t1.DateEntered,t1.Amount,
TransactionDetails.fn_IntCalc(3,t1.Amount,t1.DateEntered,
(SELECT MIN(DateEntered)
FROM TransactionDetails.Transactions t2
WHERE t2.CustomerId = t1.CustomerId
AND t2.DateEntered> t1.DateEntered)) AS 'Interest Earned'
FROM TransactionDetails.Transactions t1
WHERE CustomerId = 1
```

4. Once you have the code together, you can then execute the query, which should produce output as shown in Figure 17-4.

	TransactionId	DateEntered	Amount	Interest Earned
1	836	2012-03-10 16:38:08.960	48033.07880	0.00000
2	509	2011-12-05 13:54:54.880	62521.51010	493.31910

Figure 17-4. *Using a subquery to call a function*

The APPLY Operator

It is possible to return a table as the data type from a function. The table data type can hold multiple columns and multiple rows of data as you would expect, and this is one of the main ways it differs from other data types, such as varchar, int, and so on. Returning a table of data from a function gives the code invoking the function the flexibility to work with returned data as if the table permanently existed or was built as a temporary table.

To supply extensibility to this type of function, SQL Server provides you with an operator called APPLY, which works with a table-valued function and joins data from the calling table(s) to the data returned from the function. The function will sit on the right-hand side of the query expression, and, through the use of APPLY, can return data as if you had a RIGHT OUTER JOIN or a LEFT OUTER JOIN on a "permanent" table. Before you see an example, you need to be aware that there are two types of APPLY: a CROSS APPLY and an OUTER APPLY.

- CROSS APPLY: Returns only the rows that are contained within the outer table where the row produces a result set from the table-valued function

- OUTER APPLY: Returns the rows from the outer table and the table-valued function regardless of whether a join exists; this is similar to an OUTER JOIN, which you saw in Chapter 11. If no row exists in the table-valued function, then you will see a NULL in the columns from that function.

CROSS APPLY

In your example, you will build a table-valued function that accepts a `CustomerId` as an input parameter and returns a table of `TransactionDetails.Transactions` rows.

TRY IT OUT: TABLE FUNCTION AND CROSS APPLY

1. Similar to what you did in Chapter 14, you will create a function with input and output parameters, followed by a query detailing the data to return. The difference in this example is that a table of data will be returned rather than a single value. Therefore, you need to name the table using a local variable followed by the TABLE clause. You then need to define the table layout for every column and data type. Enter the following code, and then execute it to create the function.

```
CREATE FUNCTION TransactionDetails.ReturnTransactions
(@CustId bigint) RETURNS @Trans TABLE
(TransactionId bigint,
CustomerId bigint,
TransactionDescription nvarchar(30),
DateEntered datetime,
Amount money)
AS
BEGIN
 INSERT INTO @Trans
 SELECT t.TransactionId, t.CustomerId, tt.Description,
         t.DateEntered, t.Amount
   FROM TransactionDetails.Transactions t
   JOIN TransactionDetails.TransactionTypes tt ON
          tt.TransactionTypeId = t.TransactionType
  WHERE CustomerId = @CustId
    RETURN
END
GO
```

2. Now that you have the table-valued function built, you can call it and use CROSS APPLY to return only the `CustomerDetails.Customers` rows where there is a customer number within the table from the table-valued function. To clarify what is happening, for every row found in the SELECT command that is retrieving customers from the `CustomerDetails.Customers` table, the `CustomerId` is passed to the function created in the first step, the function returns a table of data that has a name alias of `Trans`, and the table of data is then joined using the CROSS APPLY clause to the `CustomerDetails.Customers` table to give the results. The following code demonstrates this:

```
SELECT c. FirstName, LastName,
Trans.TransactionId,TransactionDescription,
DateEntered,Amount
FROM CustomerDetails.Customers AS c
  CROSS APPLY
   TransactionDetails.ReturnTransactions(c.CustomerId)
   AS Trans
```

3. The results from the preceding code are shown in Figure 17-5, where you can see that only rows from the `CustomerDetails.Customers` table are displayed where there is a corresponding row in the `TransactionDetails.Transactions` table.

	FirstName	LastName	TransactionId	TransactionDescription	DateEntered	Amount
1	Noel	Morgala	836	Cash Deposit	2012-03-10 16:38:08.960	48033.0788
2	Noel	Morgala	509	Buy	2011-12-05 13:54:54.880	62521.5101
3	Aubrey	Lomas	1007	Buy	2014-09-06 10:19:50.283	200.00
4	Aubrey	Lomas	244	Buy	2012-03-22 22:04:05.440	14149.7153
5	Aubrey	Lomas	607	Sell	2012-03-06 14:20:18.770	34215.274
6	Bernie	McGee	926	Sell	2011-11-10 02:01:26.640	75316.5828
7	Jane	Harper	6	Sell	2012-01-21 16:14:49.450	41124.6195
8	Terence	Madden	121	Cash Withdrawal	2012-01-29 09:22:33.250	52477.0824
9	Terence	Madden	511	Buy	2012-01-11 22:57:02.670	1037.0005
10	Anne	Mather	529	Cash Withdrawal	2012-03-23 05:47:13.830	98415.5152
11	Mickey	Ferguson	786	Sell	2012-03-19 09:42:09.840	73237.3412

Figure 17-5. *Partial results of the* CROSS APPLY *from a table-valued function*

OUTER APPLY

As mentioned previously, OUTER APPLY is very much like a RIGHT OUTER JOIN on a table, but you need to use OUTER APPLY when working with a table-valued function.

For your example, you can still use the function you built for the CROSS APPLY. With the code that follows, you are expecting those customers that have no rows returned from the table-valued function to be listed with NULL values.

TRY IT OUT: TABLE FUNCTION AND OUTER APPLY

1. Enter the following code, which will perform an OUTER APPLY on the user-defined function created in the previous example.

```
SELECT c. FirstName, LastName,
Trans.TransactionId,TransactionDescription,
DateEntered,Amount
FROM CustomerDetails.Customers AS c
  OUTER APPLY
    TransactionDetails.ReturnTransactions(c.CustomerId)
    AS Trans
```

2. When this is executed, you will see the output shown in Figure 17-6. Only part of the output is shown.

	FirstName	LastName	TransactionId	TransactionDescription	DateEntered	Amount
1	Noel	Morgala	836	Cash Deposit	2012-03-10 16:38:08.960	48033.0788
2	Noel	Morgala	509	Buy	2011-12-05 13:54:54.880	62521.5101
3	Aubrey	Lomas	1007	Buy	2014-09-06 10:19:50.283	200.00
4	Aubrey	Lomas	244	Buy	2012-03-22 22:04:05.440	14149.7153
5	Aubrey	Lomas	607	Sell	2012-03-06 14:20:18.770	34215.274
6	Bernie	McGee	926	Sell	2011-11-10 02:01:26.640	75316.5828
7	Jane	Harper	6	Sell	2012-01-21 16:14:49.450	41124.6195
8	Mark	Vernon-Smith	NULL	NULL	NULL	NULL
9	Terence	Madden	121	Cash Withdrawal	2012-01-29 09:22:33.250	52477.0824
10	Terence	Madden	511	Buy	2012-01-11 22:57:02.670	1037.0005

Figure 17-6. OUTER APPLY from a table-valued function

Common Table Expressions

A *common table expression* (CTE) is a bit like a temporary table. It's transient, lasting only as long as the query requires it. Temporary tables are available for use during the lifetime of the session of the query running the code or until they are explicitly dropped. The creation and use of temporary tables are a two- or three-part process: table creation, population, and use. A CTE is built in the same code line as the SELECT, INSERT, UPDATE, or DELETE statements that use it.

Using Common Table Expressions

As mentioned a CTE lasts only as long as the query that uses it. If you need a set of data to exist for this amount of time only, then a CTE can be better in performance terms than a temporary table. Earlier in the book, you had a look at temporary tables by defining a table in code and prefixing the name with a hash mark (#). The best way to understand a CTE is to demonstrate an example with some code.

The first example code will build a temporary table and then use this within a query. The second example will demonstrate how to complete the same task but by using a CTE and will show how simple the code can be. First of all, it is necessary to download the Microsoft sample database AdventureWorks and install it on your system. The code and installation instructions can be found on the CodePlex site, www.codeplex.com. I am using this database as it has a good set of mixed and related data. This is also possible to achieve within the Red Gate SQL Data Generator software but takes time, and as a developer, unless there is good reason to reinvent the wheel, don't.

Within the AdventureWorks sample database, there are a number of products held in the Production.Product table. For this example, let's say you want to know the maximum list price of stock you're holding over all the product categories. Using a temporary table, this would be a two-part process, as follows:

```
USE AdventureWorks2014
GO
SELECT p.ProductSubcategoryID, s.Name,SUM(ListPrice) AS ListPrice
  INTO #Temp1
  FROM Production.Product p
```

```
JOIN Production.ProductSubcategory s ON s.ProductSubcategoryID =
  p.ProductSubcategoryID
WHERE p.ProductSubcategoryID IS NOT NULL
GROUP BY p.ProductSubcategoryID, s.Name

SELECT ProductSubcategoryID,Name,MAX(ListPrice)
  FROM #Temp1
  GROUP BY ProductSubcategoryID, Name
HAVING MAX(ListPrice) = (SELECT MAX(ListPrice) FROM #Temp1)

DROP TABLE #Temp1
```

However, with CTEs, this becomes a bit simpler and more efficient. In the preceding code snippet, I have created a temporary table. This table has no index on it, and therefore SQL Server will complete a table scan operation on it when executing the second part. In contrast, the upcoming code snippet uses the raw AdventureWorks tables. There is no creation of a temporary table, which would have used up processing time, and also existing indexes could be used in building up the query, rather than a table scan.

The CTE is built up using the WITH keyword, which defines the name of the CTE you'll be returning—in this case, ProdList—and the columns contained within it. The columns returned within the CTE will take the data types placed into it from the SELECT statement within the parentheses. Of course, the number of columns within the CTE has to be the same as the table defined within the brackets. This table is built up, returned, and passed immediately into the following SELECT statement outside of the WITH block, where the rows of data can then be processed as required. Therefore, the rows returned between the brackets could be seen as a temporary table that is used by the statement outside of the brackets.

```
WITH ProdList (ProductSubcategoryID,Name,ListPrice) AS
(
SELECT p.ProductSubcategoryID, s.Name,SUM(ListPrice) AS ListPrice
  FROM Production.Product p
  JOIN Production.ProductSubcategory s ON s.ProductSubcategoryID =
    p.ProductSubcategoryID
  WHERE p.ProductSubcategoryID IS NOT NULL
  GROUP BY p.ProductSubcategoryID, s.Name
)
SELECT ProductSubcategoryID,Name,MAX(ListPrice)
  FROM ProdList
  GROUP BY ProductSubcategoryID, Name
  HAVING MAX(ListPrice) = (SELECT MAX(ListPrice) FROM ProdList)
```

When the code is executed, the results should resemble the output shown in Figure 17-7.

	ProductSubcategoryID	Name	(No column name)
1	2	Road Bikes	68690.35

Figure 17-7. CTE output

Recursive CTE

A *recursive CTE* is where an initial CTE is built and then the results from that are called recursively in a UNION statement, returning subsets of data until all the data are returned. This gives you the ability to create data in a hierarchical fashion, as you will see in the next example. An example of a recursive CTE would be where you have a row of data that is linked to another row of data, such as a table that holds employee details (which is the example you will build shortly). You would have the owner at the top, followed by the CEO, the board of directors, the people who report to the board, and all the way down to the graduate intern. A recursive CTE would look at the results at each level of the organization.

The basis of building a recursive CTE is to build your initial query just as you saw earlier, but then append to that a UNION ALL statement with a join on the cte_name. This works so that in the "normal" CTE, data are created and built with the cte_name, which can then be referenced within the CTE from the UNION ALL. The syntax that you can see here demonstrates how this looks in its simplest form:

```
WITH cte_name ( column_name [,...n] )
AS
(
CTE_query_definition
UNION ALL
CTE_query_definition with a join on cte_name
)
```

As with all UNION statements, the number of columns must be the same in all queries that make up the recursive CTE. The data types must also match up.

■ **Caution**　Care *must* be taken when creating a recursive CTE. It is possible to create a recursive CTE that goes into an infinite loop. While testing the recursive CTE, you can use the MAXRECURSION option, as you will see in the next example.

The following example demonstrates a recursive query that will list every employee, their job titles, and the names of their managers. This example has a number of complexities, which are needed to get that reporting functionality to work because of the design of the AdventureWorks2014 schema. However, in many ways, this complexity is a positive development, because you should be becoming very competent in understanding the complexities required to use SQL Server. Where the AdventureWorks2014 database becomes quite complex is in how it structures the hierarchy of employees and managers within the organization. To get the hierarchy, you need to use a system function, GetAncestor. The GetAncestor function works alongside the hierarchyid data type to retrieve the parent node of a hierarchical set of data. You'll use GetAncestor in the following example to return the parent—in this case, the manager—of the employee within the organization that you are inspecting. GetAncestor has a positive number as the input parameter that determines how many nodes to move within the hierarchy. A parameter of 1 would mean that you want to return the parent of the hierarchy identifier you are inspecting; a parameter value of 2 would be the grandparent, and so on.

Each employee in the HumanResources.Employee table has a hierarchyid data type in a column called OrganizationNode. The example can use the data in OrganizationNode with the GetAncestor function as I have just described. The GetAncestor function will be passed with the parameter value of 1, indicating that we want the parent of the employee, and by combining this returned value with a JOIN clause, the example can perform a join to find that parent row. This then allows you to use this knowledge to build your recursive CTE to build up the organizational hierarchy.

```
USE AdventureWorks2014
GO
WITH [EMP_cte]([BusinessEntityID], [OrganizationNode], [FirstName],
[LastName], [RecursionLevel]) -- CTE name and columns
AS (
SELECT e.[BusinessEntityID], e.[OrganizationNode], p.[FirstName],
p.[LastName], 0
FROM [HumanResources].[Employee] e
INNER JOIN [Person].[Person] p
ON p.[BusinessEntityID] = e.[BusinessEntityID]
WHERE e.[BusinessEntityID] = 2
UNION ALL
SELECT e.[BusinessEntityID], e.[OrganizationNode], p.[FirstName],
p.[LastName], [RecursionLevel] + 1 -- Join recursive member to anchor
FROM [HumanResources].[Employee] e
INNER JOIN [EMP_cte]
ON e.[OrganizationNode].GetAncestor(1) = [EMP_cte].[OrganizationNode]
INNER JOIN [Person].[Person] p
ON p.[BusinessEntityID] = e.[BusinessEntityID]
)
SELECT [EMP_cte].[RecursionLevel], [EMP_cte].[OrganizationNode].ToString() as
[OrganizationNode], p.[FirstName] AS 'ManagerFirstName', p.[LastName] AS
'ManagerLastName',
[EMP_cte].[BusinessEntityID], [EMP_cte].[FirstName], [EMP_cte].[LastName]
-- Outer select from the CTE
FROM [EMP_cte]
INNER JOIN [HumanResources].[Employee] e
ON [EMP_cte].[OrganizationNode].GetAncestor(1) = e.[OrganizationNode]
INNER JOIN [Person].[Person] p
ON p.[BusinessEntityID] = e.[BusinessEntityID]
ORDER BY [EMP_cte].[BusinessEntityID],[RecursionLevel],
[EMP_cte].[OrganizationNode].ToString()
OPTION (MAXRECURSION 25)
```

First, it is necessary to define the layout of the columns to return from the CTE, and you will find that layout defined in the WITH expression. Moving to the first SELECT, this provides you with the top level of the CTE, which in this case is the manager. You can check this by just running the SELECT on its own and looking at the single row.

You then need to use this data to move to the next level of the hierarchy. By completing an inner join on the CTE, you take the data populated from the first SELECT that has the manager ID to get the next level of employees. The data returned will then be populated in the CTE so that the recursive CTE can then use the level-two employees to find the level-three employees. This process continues either until the whole structure is completed or until the maximum recursion is reached. Now all the data are within the CTE, and the data in the CTE can be used just like any other table to join against, which is what the SELECT after the recursive CTE does. A join is made to the necessary tables to return the data until all the data are returned or until the number of recursions defined is exceeded. In the following example, the number of recursions is defined as 25. CTEs are used not only as stand-alone expressions but also within other functions, such as those used to pivot data. You'll see pivot functions in action next. You can see a sample of the output in Figure 17-8.

	RecursionLevel	OrganizationNode	ManagerFirstName	ManagerLastName	BusinessEntityID	FirstName	LastName
1	1	/1/1/	Terri	Duffy	3	Roberto	Tamburello
2	2	/1/1/1/	Roberto	Tamburello	4	Rob	Walters
3	2	/1/1/2/	Roberto	Tamburello	5	Gail	Erickson
4	2	/1/1/3/	Roberto	Tamburello	6	Jossef	Goldberg
5	2	/1/1/4/	Roberto	Tamburello	7	Dylan	Miller
6	3	/1/1/4/1/	Dylan	Miller	8	Diane	Margheim
7	3	/1/1/4/2/	Dylan	Miller	9	Gigi	Matthew
8	3	/1/1/4/3/	Dylan	Miller	10	Michael	Raheem
9	2	/1/1/5/	Roberto	Tamburello	11	Ovidiu	Cracium
10	3	/1/1/5/1/	Ovidiu	Cracium	12	Thierry	D'Hers
11	3	/1/1/5/2/	Ovidiu	Cracium	13	Janice	Galvin

Figure 17-8. Recursive CTE output demonstrating hierarchical employees

Pivoting Data

If you have ever used Excel, then you have probably had to pivot data results so that rows of information are pivoted into columns of information. It is now possible to perform this kind of operation within SQL Server via a PIVOT operator. Pivoted data can also be changed back using the UNPIVOT operator, where columns of data can be changed into rows of data. In this section, you will see both of these in action. You will be using the AdventureWorks example in this section. The table involved in this example is the SalesOrderDetail table belonging to the Sales schema. This holds details of products ordered, the quantity requested, the price they are at, and the discount on the order received.T–SQL code.

PIVOT

Before you see PIVOT in action, you need to look at the information that you will pivot. The following code lists three products, and for each product, you will sum up the amount sold, taking the discount into account:

```
SELECT ProductID,UnitPriceDiscount,SUM(LineTotal)
  FROM Sales.SalesOrderDetail
  WHERE ProductID IN (776,711,747)
  GROUP BY ProductID,UnitPriceDiscount
  ORDER BY ProductID,UnitPriceDiscount
```

This produces one line of output for each product/discount combination, as you can see in the following results:

```
711    0.00    143788.908000
711    0.02    11421.237324
711    0.05    4384.931245
711    0.10    2679.760530
711    0.15    3131.779950
747    0.00    501788.197700
776    0.00    1198796.448000
776    0.02    23020.131792
776    0.35    32906.152500
```

By using PIVOT, you can alter this data so that you can create columns for each of the products. Each row is defined for the discount, giving a cross-reference of products to discount.

```
SELECT pt.Discount,ISNULL([711],0.00) As Product711,
    ISNULL([747],0.00) As Product747,ISNULL([776],0.00) As Product776
FROM
(SELECT sod.LineTotal, sod.ProductID, sod.UnitPriceDiscount as Discount
   FROM Sales.SalesOrderDetail sod) so
PIVOT
(
SUM(so.LineTotal)
FOR so.ProductID IN ([776], [711], [747])
) AS pt
ORDER BY pt.Discount
```

Before you execute this code, let's take a look at what is happening. First of all, you need to create a subquery that contains the columns of data that the PIVOT operator can use for its aggregation (it will also be used later for displaying in the output). No filtering has been completed at this point—any columns not used in the aggregation will be ignored. The code generates a table-valued expression with an alias of so. From this table, you then instruct SQL Server to PIVOT the columns while completing an aggregation on a specific column—in your case, a SUM of the LineTotal column from the table-valued expression. It is also at this point you define the columns to create via the FOR clause—in your case, a column for each product of the three products. This is the equivalent to using GROUP BY for the aggregation, and it's also the equivalent of filtering data from the so table-valued expression. However, within the so table-valued expression, there's also a third column, UnitPriceDiscount. Without this, the output from the PIVOT would produce one row with three columns—one for each product. So this table-valued expression with the PIVOT operation produces a temporary result set, which you name pt. You can then use this temporary result set to produce your output.

When you run the code, you should see output similar to what is shown in Figure 17-9.

	Discount	Product711	Product747	Product776
1	0.00	143788.908000	501788.197700	1198796.448000
2	0.02	11421.237324	0.000000	23020.131792
3	0.05	4384.931245	0.000000	0.000000
4	0.10	2679.760530	0.000000	0.000000
5	0.15	3131.779950	0.000000	0.000000
6	0.20	0.000000	0.000000	0.000000
7	0.30	0.000000	0.000000	0.000000
8	0.35	0.000000	0.000000	32906.152500
9	0.40	0.000000	0.000000	0.000000

Figure 17-9. *Pivot data results*

UNPIVOT

The reverse of PIVOT is, of course, UNPIVOT, which will unpivot data by placing column data into rows. You can prove this by unpivoting the data just pivoted using the preceding query. The code that follows will rebuild the pivot and place the data into a temporary table. From that temporary table, you can unpivot the data.

> ■ **Note** Although PIVOT aggregates multiple rows into a single row in the output, UNPIVOT does not reproduce the original table-valued expression result because the rows have been aggregated. Besides, NULL values in the input of UNPIVOT disappear in the output, whereas there may have been original NULL values in the input before the PIVOT operation and the original structure has been lost.

```
SELECT pt.Discount,ISNULL([711],0.00) As Product711,
    ISNULL([747],0.00) As Product747,ISNULL([776],0.00) As Product776
INTO #Temp1
FROM
(SELECT sod.LineTotal, sod.ProductID, sod.UnitPriceDiscount as Discount
   FROM Sales.SalesOrderDetail sod) so
PIVOT
(
SUM(so.LineTotal)
FOR so.ProductID IN ([776], [711], [747])
) AS pt
ORDER BY pt.Discount
```

UNPIVOT has similarities to PIVOT in that you build a table-valued expression—in this case, calling it up1—which you then use as the basis of unpivoting. Once the table-valued expression is defined, you use UNPIVOT with the column definitions of the columns to create, DiscountAppl and ProductID. Using IN defines the rows that will be produced back from the UNPIVOT.

```
SELECT ProductID,Discount, DiscountAppl
  FROM (SELECT Discount, Product711, Product747, Product776
          FROM #Temp1) up1
UNPIVOT ( DiscountAppl FOR ProductID
    IN (Product711, Product747, Product776)) As upv2
WHERE DiscountAppl <> 0
ORDER BY ProductID
```

When the preceding code (both sections) is executed, the data are unpivoted, as shown in Figure 17-10.

	ProductID	Discount	DiscountAppl
1	Product711	0.00	143788.908000
2	Product711	0.15	3131.779950
3	Product711	0.10	2679.760530
4	Product711	0.05	4384.931245
5	Product711	0.02	11421.237324
6	Product747	0.00	501788.197700
7	Product776	0.00	1198796.448000
8	Product776	0.35	32906.152500
9	Product776	0.02	23020.131792

Figure 17-10. *Unpivoted data results*

Now that you have pivoted data, you can take a look at how you can rank output.

Table Variables

It is possible to define a variable as a table, and such a variable known as a *table variable*. Table variables have a local scope and therefore can only be used in a similar fashion to a locally defined temporary table. The main benefit of a table variable over a temporary table is in the lack of a need for recompiling. A temporary table can cause your stored procedure of function to be recompiled at each execution, therefore slowing down the process of execution. A table variable can still cause compilations, however they should occur less often.

Table variables are designed to be used for small data sets on the order of 10's of rows. When SQL Server compiles a function or stored procedure that contains a table variable, SQL Server will assume that the table variable has zero rows. If you then put thousands of rows in the variable, then the procedure may be marked for re-compilation. You can help this process along by using the RECOMPILE option on the query that uses the table variable.

Table variables can also be defined as in-memory table variables. Do this by using the WITH (MEMORY_OPTIMIZED = ON) argument when declaring the table variable type, as well as when defining the indexes and bucket counts as you would with an in-memory table. In-memory table variables should also have an index defined as part of the complete table variable definition, whereas standard table variables cannot have an index defined.

You should still look at how large an in-memory table variable will become, as it will take up memory resources like any other table that is held in memory. Another area to be aware of is that an in-memory table variable will be compiled when the variable is defined within your code. If you have a stored procedure that uses an in-memory table variable, and that procedure is executed frequently, then you may find that the recompilation at each variable declaration outweighs the gains from the table's being in-memory to begin with.

TRY IT OUT: TABLE VARIABLES

Let's take a look at table value variables using a derivative of the #Shares temporary table example earlier. Follow these steps:

1. Create the temporary table variable. Write a DECLARE statement and give the variable a type of TABLE. You then define the table variable as you would a table. For example:

```
DECLARE @SharesTmp
TABLE(ShareDesc varchar(50),
Price numeric(18,5),
PriceDate datetime)
```

2. Then use the table variable like any other table. Reference it from INSERT, UPDATE, and DELETE, SELECT statements. In this instance an INSERT will be used to populate the table:

```
INSERT INTO @SharesTmp
SELECT s.Description,sp.Price,sp.PriceDate
  FROM ShareDetails.Shares s
  JOIN ShareDetails.SharePrices sp ON sp.ShareId = s.ShareId
 WHERE s.ShareId = 1
```

3. You can then inspect the data using a SELECT. For example:

```
SELECT ShareDesc, Price, PriceDate
  FROM @SharesTmp
```

4. Execute all three code statements and you will see the following output:

```
ShareDesc                        Price     PriceDate
-----------------------------    --------  -----------------------
ACME'S HOMEBAKE COOKIES INC      34.25148  2012-03-28 10:12:42.740
ACME'S HOMEBAKE COOKIES INC      6.62765   2012-03-27 06:47:46.900
ACME'S HOMEBAKE COOKIES INC      6.44350   2012-03-25 21:51:29.910
ACME'S HOMEBAKE COOKIES INC      32.04574  2012-03-12 19:57:07.630
ACME'S HOMEBAKE COOKIES INC      32.00452  2012-03-06 16:59:24.430
ACME'S HOMEBAKE COOKIES INC      30.16576  2012-03-06 01:09:36.260
ACME'S HOMEBAKE COOKIES INC      7.12997   2012-03-05 05:29:29.280
```

5. If you find that the profile of the data is sufficiently different from a table with zero rows that a RECOMPILE would benefit the execution, you can add the RECOMPILE query hint to the SELECT statement as in the following procedure example:

```
CREATE PROCEDURE ShareDetails.TableVariable
AS
BEGIN
      DECLARE @SharesTmp
      TABLE(ShareDesc varchar(50),
      Price numeric(18,5),
      PriceDate datetime)

      INSERT INTO @SharesTmp
      SELECT s.Description,sp.Price,sp.PriceDate
        FROM ShareDetails.Shares s
        JOIN ShareDetails.SharePrices sp ON sp.ShareId = s.ShareId
       WHERE s.ShareId = 1

      SELECT ShareDesc, Price, PriceDate
        FROM @SharesTmp RECOMPILE
END
GO
EXEC ShareDetails.TableVariable
```

6. Next, convert the example to use in-memory tables. You know the number of rows that will be in the table variable, 50 rows, from the previous output. This knowledge will aid the decision on the hash bucket count definition. Also, an in-memory table variable requires a CREATE TYPE statement, and the resulting type defines the in-memory table. Execute the following code to add the type:

```
CREATE TYPE ShareDetails.SharesTmp
AS TABLE(ShareId int NOT NULL,
ShareDesc varchar(50),
Price numeric(18,5),
PriceDate datetime,

INDEX [IX_ShareId] HASH ([ShareId]) WITH ( BUCKET_COUNT = 1)

)
WITH ( MEMORY_OPTIMIZED = ON )
```

7. Now that the type has been defined, the variable can be defined using the in-memory table type. Following is an example, but don't execute the code just yet.

```
DECLARE @SharesTmp ShareDetails.SharesTmp
```

8. Insert data in to the variable and then list out the rows. You can now execute the variable declaration and the code below. You should see the same results as from the disk-based table variable.

```
INSERT INTO @SharesTmp
SELECT s.ShareId,s.Description,sp.Price,sp.PriceDate
    FROM ShareDetails.Shares s
    JOIN ShareDetails.SharePrices sp ON sp.ShareId = s.ShareId
    WHERE s.ShareId = 1

SELECT ShareId,ShareDesc, Price, PriceDate

    FROM @SharesTmp
```

Ranking Functions

With SQL Server, it's possible to rank rows of data in your T-SQL code. *Ranking functions* give you the ability to rank each row of data to provide a method of organizing the output in an ascending sequence. You can give each row a unique number or each group of similar rows the same number. You may be wondering what is wrong with other methods of ranking data, which might include IDENTITY columns. These types of columns do provide unique numbers, but gaps can form. You are also tied into each row having its own number, when you may want to group rows together.

So then, why not use GROUP BY? Well, yes, you can use GROUP BY, but what if the grouping was over more than one column? In this case, processing the data further would require knowledge about those columns. Ranking functions make it possible to provide a value that allows data to be ranked in the order required, and then that value can be used for splitting the data into further groupings.

There are four ranking functions, which I'll discuss in detail in upcoming sections:

- ROW_NUMBER: Allows you to provide sequential integer values to the result rows of a query

- RANK: Provides an ascending, nonunique ranking number to a set of rows, giving the same number to a row of the same value as another; numbers are skipped for the number of rows that have the same value.

- DENSE_RANK: This is similar to RANK, but each row number returned will be one greater than the previous setting, no matter how many rows are the same.

- NTILE: This takes the rows from the query and places them into an equal (or as close to equal as possible) number of specified numbered groups, where NTILE returns the group number the row belongs to.

■ **Note** These ranking functions can be used only with the SELECT and ORDER BY statements. Sadly, they can't be used directly in a WHERE or GROUP BY clause, but you can use them in a CTE or derived table.

The following code demonstrates a CTE with the ranking function ROW_NUMBER():

```
WITH OrderedOrders AS
(SELECT SalesOrderID, OrderDate,
ROW_NUMBER() OVER (order by OrderDate)as RowNumber
FROM Sales.SalesOrderHeader )
SELECT *
FROM OrderedOrders
WHERE RowNumber between 50 and 60
```

The syntax for ranking functions is shown as follows:

```
<function_name>() OVER([PARTITION BY <partition_by_list>]
ORDER BY <order_by_list>)
```

Taking each option as it comes, you can see how this can be placed within a SELECT statement—for example:

- function_name: Can be one of ROW_NUMBER, RANK, DENSE_RANK, and NTILE

- OVER: Defines the details of how the ranking should order or split the data

- PARTITION BY: Details which data the column should use as the basis of the splits

- ORDER BY: Details the ordering of the data

ROW_NUMBER

Your first ranking function, ROW_NUMBER, allows your code to guarantee an ascending sequence of numbers to give each row a unique number. Until now, it has not been possible to guarantee sequencing of numbers, although an IDENTITY-based column could potentially give a sequence, providing all INSERTs succeeded and no DELETEs took place.

This function is ideal for giving your output a reference point—for example, "Please take a look at row 10 and you'll see. . ." Another use for this function is to break the data into exact chunks for scrolling purposes in GUI systems. For example, if five rows of data are returned, row 1 could be displayed, and then Next would allow the application to move to row 2 easily rather than using some other method.

The following is an example that shows how the ROW_NUMBER() function can provide an ascending number for each row returned when inspecting. The ROW_NUMBER() function is nondeterministic, and since the ORDER BY within the OVER function doesn't produce a unique sequence of data (because there might be several people with the same last name, for example), then you would need to find some other way to achieve uniqueness, if getting the same order with each execution were mandatory.

■ **Note** The following code and all code from this point is from the ApressFinancial database.

```
USE ApressFinancial
GO
SELECT ROW_NUMBER() OVER (ORDER BY LastName) AS RowNum,
       CONCAT(FirstName,' ',LastName) AS CustomerName,
          UnclearedBalance
  FROM CustomerDetails.Customers
 WHERE UnclearedBalance is not null
```

When you execute the code, you see the names in last name order, as shown in Figure 17-11.

	RowNum	CustomerName	UnclearedBalance
1	1	Floyd Aguilar	745.0109
2	2	Katie Ali	683.4624
3	3	Janice Ali	287.1872
4	4	Jayson Allen	459.7421
5	5	Lawrence Allison	987.1718
6	6	Omar Alvarado	418.8572
7	7	Gina Andersen	97.5126
8	8	Lawanda Andrews	312.2116
9	9	Ricky Arnold	64.9729
10	10	Doris Arroyo	954.1533
11	11	Rickey Atkins	961.2129

Figure 17-11. Rows with row numbering

It's also possible to reset the sequence to give a unique ascending number within a section, or partition of data, using the PARTITION BY option. This would be ideal if, for example, in the same marathon you had different races, such as male, female, disabled male, disabled female, over 60, and so on. Using the category the runner is competing within as the basis of the partition, no matter in which order the runners cross the line, you would still have the correct order of finishing for each category.

The following example will reset the sequential number at each change of first letter in the last name of the employees and will order the results in LastName descending order:

```
SELECT ROW_NUMBER() OVER (PARTITION BY SUBSTRING(LastName,1,1)
       ORDER BY LastName) AS RowNum,
       CONCAT(FirstName,' ',LastName) AS CustomerName,
           UnclearedBalance
  FROM CustomerDetails.Customers
 WHERE UnclearedBalance is not null
 ORDER BY LastName DESC
```

When you execute the code, as the first letter of the last name alters, you see the RowNum column, which contains the value for ROW_NUMBER(), alter, as shown in Figure 17-12. However, you will also see a side effect that can happen when you include an ORDER BY statement within the code, which is the row numbering can become random. This occurs because the ordering of the results occurs after the data have been returned from the underlying table and the sequencing has been applied.

	RowNum	CustomerName	UnclearedBalance
1	1	Kenya Zamora	830.2807
2	1	Marissa Young	833.074
3	20	Ann Wood	249.2369
4	18	Orlando Winters	243.5694
5	19	Angie Winters	110.6261
6	16	Gary Williamson	854.302
7	17	Tyson Williamson	786.5303
8	15	Joseph Wilkinson	455.2015
9	13	Wanda Wiley	136.5265
10	14	Brock Wiley	669.4325

Figure 17-12. Rows with row numbering resetting on change of last name, first letter

It is possible to see how SQL Server processes your query by inspecting the query plan diagram. If you click the Include Actual Execution Plan button on your toolbar, this will display the query plan for the foregoing code once it is executed. After clicking the button, if you execute the previous code, there will be a new tab called Execution Plan. By selecting this tab, you will see something similar to Figure 17-13. A query plan works right to left; therefore the final result is the icon that is known as the step on the far left. There are two Sort steps within the plan. The Sort on the right is used to sort the data ready to be passed to the Segment and Sequence Project steps, and the Sort on the left is used to order the data.

Figure 17-13. Query plan demonstrating ROW_NUMBER and ORDER BY DESC out of sequence

You can add the RowNum alias to specify the first column to the ORDER BY statement to be descending, as this will correct the sequencing if this is required.

RANK

If a row of data is returned that contains the same values as another row as defined in the ORDER BY clause of your statement, the keyword RANK will give these rows the same numerical value. An internal count is kept so that on a change of value, you will see a jump in the value. For example, say you watch a sport like golf, and in a golf tournament you're following Tiger Woods, who wins the tournament on a score of 4 under par, but Lee Westwood, Luke Donald, and Phil Mickelson are tied for second at 3 under par. Finally, Bubba Watson finishes his round at 2 under par. Tiger would have the value 1; Lee, Luke, and Phil would have the value 2; and Bubba would have the value 5. This is exactly what RANK does. This function would also be useful in applications that wanted to return different rankings of data but show only the data from one rank at any one time on each page.

In the following example, the ROW_NUMBER() function is also used as it was in the previous example, enabling a cross-check where the RANK function skips to the right number. The SUBSTRING has also been altered from the previous example to look at the first two characters to enable a good demonstration of RANK. When you run the query, you'll find that there is one row with a LastName that starts Ab. RANK will assign this row the number 1. When the LastName changes to Ac, the RANK will change to the value 2. After these two rows, you will see the RANK change to 4.

```
SELECT ROW_NUMBER() OVER (PARTITION BY SUBSTRING(LastName,1,2)
        ORDER BY LastName) AS RowNum,
            RANK() OVER(ORDER BY SUBSTRING(LastName,1,2) ) AS Ranking,
        CONCAT(FirstName,' ',LastName) AS CustomerName,
            UnclearedBalance
  FROM CustomerDetails.Customers
 WHERE UnclearedBalance is not null
 ORDER BY Ranking
```

Partial results are shown in Figure 17-14, where you can see in the Ranking column that the values remain static when the values are the same, and then skip to the correct number on a change of value.

	RowNum	Ranking	CustomerName	UnclearedBalance
1	1	1	Floyd Aguilar	745.0109
2	1	2	Katie Ali	683.4624
3	2	2	Janice Ali	287.1872
4	3	2	Jayson Allen	459.7421
5	4	2	Lawrence Allison	987.1718
6	5	2	Omar Alvarado	418.8572
7	1	7	Gina Andersen	97.5126
8	2	7	Lawanda Andrews	312.2116
9	1	9	Ricky Arnold	64.9729
10	2	9	Doris Arroyo	954.1533
11	1	11	Rickey Atkins	961.2129

Figure 17-14. *Ranking and row numbering*

DENSE_RANK

DENSE_RANK gives each group the next number in the sequence and does not jump forward if there is more than one item in a group. In the golf example from the previous section, for example, Bubba Watson would have a value of 3 instead of a value of 5 because his score is the third highest. The following code demonstrates DENSE_RANK:

```
SELECT ROW_NUMBER() OVER (PARTITION BY SUBSTRING(LastName,1,2)
        ORDER BY LastName) AS RowNum,
            DENSE_RANK() OVER(ORDER BY SUBSTRING(LastName,1,2) ) AS Ranking,
        CONCAT(FirstName,' ',LastName) AS CustomerName,
            UnclearedBalance
  FROM CustomerDetails.Customers
 WHERE UnclearedBalance is not null
 ORDER BY Ranking
```

The results can be seen in Figure 17-15. Notice that this time, on change of the first two characters of the column LastName, the Ranking becomes 3 when Ac becomes Ad, instead of moving to 4.

	RowNum	Ranking	CustomerName	UnclearedBalance
1	1	1	Floyd Aguilar	745.0109
2	1	2	Katie Ali	683.4624
3	2	2	Janice Ali	287.1872
4	3	2	Jayson Allen	459.7421
5	4	2	Lawrence Allison	987.1718
6	5	2	Omar Alvarado	418.8572
7	1	3	Gina Andersen	97.5126
8	2	3	Lawanda Andrews	312.2116
9	1	4	Ricky Arnold	64.9729
10	2	4	Doris Arroyo	954.1533
11	1	5	Rickey Atkins	961.2129

Figure 17-15. Dense ranking and row numbering

NTILE

Batching output into manageable groups has always been tricky. For example, if you have a batch of work that needs cross-checking among a number of people, then GROUP BY has to be used, though this wouldn't give an even split. NTILE is used to give the split a more even, although approximated, grouping. The value in parentheses after NTILE defines the number of groups to produce, so NTILE(25) would produce 25 groups of as close a split as possible of even numbers

```
SELECT NTILE(10) OVER (ORDER BY LastName) AS BatchNumber,
        CONCAT(FirstName,' ',LastName) AS CustomerName,
            UnclearedBalance
  FROM CustomerDetails.Customers
 WHERE UnclearedBalance is not null
 ORDER BY BatchNumber
```

This produces 10 groups of 99 rows each. In Figure 17-16, you will see where the first batch ends and the second batch commences.

	BatchNumber	CustomerName	UnclearedBalance
1	1	Floyd Aguilar	745.0109
2	1	Katie Ali	683.4624
3	1	Janice Ali	287.1872
4	1	Jayson Allen	459.7421
5	1	Lawrence Allison	987.1718
6	1	Omar Alvarado	418.8572
7	1	Gina Andersen	97.5126
8	1	Lawanda Andrews	312.2116
9	1	Ricky Arnold	64.9729
10	1	Doris Arroyo	954.1533
11	1	Rickey Atkins	961.2129

Figure 17-16. Batching output into groups of data

Cursors

SQL Server works best with sets of data. So far in the book, this is what you have seen demonstrated. However, there will be occasions when you need to work with a set of data a row at a time, and this is when you will need to work with cursors. A cursor builds a set of data based on a SELECT statement, which can then be read a row at a time.

Cursors are quite powerful and avoid passing a large set of data across a network, to then be processed with a development language such as .NET a row at a time, and then the resulting information passed back to SQL Server. Cursors can also update the underlying table data a row at a time if this is required. They can also be navigated to relative and specific positions within the set of data within the cursor. This can lead a SQL Server developer to think that they are the answer to all problems, but there are downsides. Cursors can and almost always are slower than using sets of data, and although they should not be avoided, they should not be approached lightly.

Let's take a look at the syntax.

There are a number of options when declaring a cursor, and in this section you will see what each option will do. The cursor declaration is as follows:

```
DECLARE cursor_name CURSOR [ LOCAL | GLOBAL ]
    [ FORWARD_ONLY | SCROLL ]
    [ STATIC | KEYSET | DYNAMIC | FAST_FORWARD ]
    [ READ_ONLY | SCROLL_LOCKS | OPTIMISTIC ]
    [ TYPE_WARNING ]
    FOR select_statement
    [ FOR UPDATE [ OF column_name [ ,...n ] ] ]
```

The options are as follows:

- cursor_name: The name of the cursor that will then be referenced with the other cursor statements

- LOCAL|GLOBAL: Similar to temporary tables, there are two scopes for cursors, the local connection or the global connection. Local is the default.

- FORWARD_ONLY|SCROLL: Forward indicates only that you are scrolling a row at a time from the start of the cursor to the end. This is the default. The SCROLL option indicates that you can move forward, backward, first, last, and to a specific position.

- STATIC|KEYSET|DYNAMIC|FAST FORWARD: If any of these options are defined, then the default on the foregoing option is SCROLL.

 - STATIC: A temporary copy of the data is placed into tempdb. Therefore within your cursor or in an external process any updates to the base tables will be outside of the cursor. This is ideal if you are running a cursor when modifications to the underlying tables could occur and you don't want to process the updates. STATIC is the default.

 - KEYSET: All tables defined within a cursor that has the KEYSET option must have a unique key. The unique key values are copied to tempdb. Data altered in nonkey value columns are visible provided the changes are within the cursor. Changes made outside the cursor are not visible. Changes to key values can result in a -2 @@FETCH_STATUS, row not found.

 - DYNAMIC: While you are scrolling through a cursor fetching rows, the data within the cursor are not static and any updates to the underlying tables would be reflected within the cursor. You have to be aware that more rows could be added while you are scrolling through, and you may also retrieve a row that you retrieved earlier if the values have been altered so that they would be refound. For example, if you ordered the cursor to be in an order of last updated and you updated the column with GETDATE(), you would retrieve the row again as it would be placed at the end of the cursor.

 - FAST FORWARD: A performance-enhanced, forward-only, read-only cursor

- READ_ONLY|SCROLL LOCKS|OPTIMISTIC

 - READ ONLY: The cursor is read-only and cannot be updated.

 - SCROLL LOCKS: For update cursors, a lock is placed on the rows within the cursor to ensure that updates succeed. This will block any other process that wants access to the underlying data until the cursor lock is released with the DEALLOCATE command. This can mean just the row being locked, but it can also mean that the whole table or multiple tables are locked.

 - OPTIMISTIC: If you believe that any rows that you update within the cursor will succeed, you can select optimistic locking. What this means is that when the cursor is opened, rows are not locked at this point, but when updated, the row is checked against the base table. If the row has not been updated since the cursor was opened, then the update will succeed. If the row has been updated, then the update will fail.

- TYPE WARNING: A warning message will be sent when a cursor is implicitly converted from one type to another. Sometimes SQL Server will convert a cursor to another type of cursor. This isn't an error but a warning. An example would be where you define a cursor as KEYSET but one of the tables does not have a unique index, the cursor would change to STATIC.

- FOR select_statement: The SELECT statement used to return the rows to build the cursor

- FOR UPDATE: If you want your cursor to be able to update the underlying tables, then you would define the cursor with this option.

- OF column_name: If you want only some columns updated, then you would list them with the OF option. Without this option defined, all columns within the cursor can be modified.

Once the cursor is declared, there are a number of steps that should be followed to work with your cursor effectively. The steps in order are as follows:

1. OPEN cursor_name: Once a cursor is declared, you do need to open it. If you don't open it, an error will occur when you try to read from it. The OPEN populates the cursor, not the DECLARE.

2. FETCH NEXT FROM cursor_name [INTO @variables]: Once the cursor is opened, you then need to fetch each row from the cursor. If you want to work with the data, you would retrieve from the cursor into local variables. To display the data only rather than work with the values in variables, you can omit the variables and each row will be output. This is useful if you are wishing to append information like a SELECT can output column values for each row rather than working with the values. Note that you must fetch for the first time before processing a row. The first row will not be automatically read.

3. @@FETCH_STATUS: The SQL Server status of the cursor. This is used as the test while looping around each cursor row until you reach the end. A value of 0 means that the row was returned successfully; a value of -1 indicates you are at the end of the cursor; and a value of -2 means that the cursor row was missing. You would see this value in an updatable cursor and if the row expected was no longer there in the cursor.

4. CLOSE cursor_name: Once you have finished with the cursor, close it to release locks. The cursor remains and could be reopened and the data refetched if you wished.

5. DEALLOCATE cursor_name: Releases the data structures and therefore the cursor allocation and the used resources back to SQL Server

Now that you have the syntax for a cursor and the constituent parts of building code for a cursor, the next exercise will see these parts brought together to create a forward-only cursor. The code will be broken out in steps and then once complete will be executed. Finally, at the end, do keep the code handy as it will be used in the next section on debugging.

TRY IT OUT: BUILDING AND RUNNING A CURSOR

The first cursor option that you will see is a read-only, forward-only cursor. This will be modified in the subsequent examples for other options.

1. The first section of code will define the variables to hold the data from each of the columns of the cursor. There is also a local variable required to keep a running total of the amount collected. The variable used for this is @TotalCollected and is initialized to 0.

```
DECLARE @FirstName varchar(50), @LastName varchar(50),
        @ProductName nvarchar(50), @Amount money,
        @LastCollect datetime

DECLARE @TotalCollected money = 0
```

2. The next step is to declare the cursor name and the SELECT statement to return the rows of data for the cursor. The aim of the cursor is to return rows where there is a monthly amount to collect from a customer, and the last amount collected was in March. Hard-coded dates are being used for simplicity, as a GETDATE() will differ depending on when you are reading this exercise.

```
      DECLARE FinProductsColl CURSOR
           FOR SELECT c.FirstName, c.LastName, f.ProductName,
                   cp.AmountToCollect, cp.LastCollected
             FROM CustomerDetails.Customers c
             JOIN CustomerDetails.CustomerProducts cp
                ON cp.CustomerId = c.CustomerId
             JOIN CustomerDetails.FinancialProducts f
                ON f.ProductId = cp.FinancialProductId
            WHERE cp.Frequency = 2
              AND cp.LastCollected BETWEEN '1 Mar 2012' AND '31 Mar 2012'
```

3. Once the cursor is declared, it can be opened, ready for processing.

```
OPEN FinProductsColl
```

4. The first action against the cursor is to retrieve the first row and place the data from the columns into local variables.

```
FETCH NEXT FROM FinProductsColl
INTO @FirstName, @LastName, @ProductName, @Amount, @LastCollect
```

5. You should then check the status of the FETCH to ensure that a row has been returned. While a row is returned, loop around, and the loop is defined with the WHILE and BEGIN statements.

```
WHILE @@FETCH_STATUS = 0
BEGIN
```

6. Now that you are confident you have a row, you can work with the data in the local variables from the row of data from the cursor. In this instance, the cursor is totaling the amount collected.

```
SELECT @TotalCollected = @TotalCollected + @Amount
```

7. The local variable values are listed for display. A conversion from the money data type is required so that it can be concatenated with the other information.

```
SELECT @FirstName, @LastName, @ProductName, @Amount,
  'Running total is ' + CONVERT(varchar(20),@TotalCollected)
```

8. At the end of the loop, the next row from the cursor set is retrieved and the values placed into the local variables. The loop is closed with the END statement.

```
    FETCH NEXT FROM FinProductsColl
    INTO @FirstName, @LastName, @ProductName, @Amount, @LastCollect
END
```

9. Once the loop completes, when @@FETCH_STATUS is not zero, then you have finished processing the cursor, you can list out how much has been collected. The cursor is then closed and deallocated. This is the end of the code.

```
SELECT 'Total collected is ' + CONVERT(varchar(20),@TotalCollected)
CLOSE FinProductsColl
DEALLOCATE FinProductsColl
```

10. You can now execute the code, and the results that can be found at the end showing the total collected are shown in Figure 17-17.

	(No column name)	(No column name)	(No column name)	(No column name)	(No column name)
1	Joel	Hicks	Lomhupistor	2953.9633	Running total is 46567.55

	(No column name)	(No column name)	(No column name)	(No column name)	(No column name)
1	Brian	Mendoza	Lomhupistor	2975.0959	Running total is 49542.65

	(No column name)	(No column name)	(No column name)	(No column name)	(No column name)
1	Tim	Cervantes	Froquestefax	2926.7631	Running total is 52469.41

	(No column name)
1	Total collected is 52469.41

Figure 17-17. *The end results showing the grand total*

You can extend cursors to updatable cursors and other functionality, but you will mainly work with forward-only, read-only cursors. Just to clarify, some developers are quite scathing of cursors. Where possible, you should work with sets of data as this is how SQL Server performs best, but there will be times when you will have to work on a row at a time. As long as you are clear that set-based processing is not possible, then you should consider using a cursor. However, it is worth looking at updatable cursors, which you will see next.

Working with an Updatable Cursor

This exercise will take the customer products that require money to be collected, total the amount, and then update the underlying CustomerDetails.CustomerProducts table to indicate that the money has been collected by updating the LastCollected column. The code is surrounded by a transaction around the cursor and the updates, and the transaction is rolled back so that the underlying data remain static, so that you can run this test multiple times in case of a coding error. You can run it with a COMMIT if you want to complete a full check; however, the code will prove that an update to the underlying data has taken place and completed. The code is very close to that built in the read-only cursor, and I will break where there is a change for you to note.

11. Start your code with the BEGIN TRAN and then the variable declarations. There is a new variable that will hold the date and time the collection was made, which is called @DateCollection and will hold a static value.

```
BEGIN TRAN

DECLARE @FirstName varchar(50), @LastName varchar(50),
        @ProductName nvarchar(50), @Amount money,
        @LastCollect datetime

DECLARE @TotalCollected money = 0, @DateCollected datetime = '1 Apr 2012'
```

12. This SELECT statement will use the same joins and filters as the cursor to ensure that the same data are returned as the cursor. It will show the date and time defined for the @DateCollected variable and a count of the number of rows. You could also use the @@CURSOR_ROWS variable after the cursor is open; however, this SELECT is defined to demonstrate that there are no smoke-and-mirrors in the example.

```
SELECT @DateCollected, COUNT(*)
        FROM CustomerDetails.Customers c
        JOIN CustomerDetails.CustomerProducts cp
            ON cp.CustomerId = c.CustomerId
        JOIN CustomerDetails.FinancialProducts f
            ON f.ProductId = cp.FinancialProductId
      WHERE cp.Frequency = 2
        AND cp.LastCollected BETWEEN '1 Mar 2012' AND '31 Mar 2012'
        AND cp.LastCollection > '1 Apr 2012'
```

13. The cursor has two new options at the end. FOR UPDATE shows that the underlying data can be modified, but the cursor allows only one column, LastCollected, to be modified. The code then moves on to open and work with the cursor. To reduce output, the SELECT statement that outputs the variables from the cursor is commented out. I have put this in bold for ease.

```
DECLARE FinProductsColl CURSOR
    FOR SELECT c.FirstName, c.LastName, f.ProductName,
                cp.AmountToCollect, cp.LastCollected
          FROM CustomerDetails.Customers c
          JOIN CustomerDetails.CustomerProducts cp
              ON cp.CustomerId = c.CustomerId
          JOIN CustomerDetails.FinancialProducts f
              ON f.ProductId = cp.FinancialProductId
        WHERE cp.Frequency = 2
          AND cp.LastCollected BETWEEN '1 Mar 2012' AND '31 Mar 2012'
          AND cp.LastCollection > '1 Apr 2012'
      FOR UPDATE
      OF LastCollected

OPEN FinProductsColl

FETCH NEXT FROM FinProductsColl
INTO @FirstName, @LastName, @ProductName, @Amount, @LastCollect

WHILE @@FETCH_STATUS = 0
BEGIN

    SELECT @TotalCollected = @TotalCollected + @Amount

--    SELECT @FirstName, @LastName, @ProductName, @Amount,
--        'Running total is ' + CONVERT(varchar(20),@TotalCollected)
```

14. Moving to the next new section of code, you will find the update to one of the underlying tables. To update within a cursor, you still define the table to modify but instead of finding the row with a WHERE column = value, the faster method—and one that will update the same row as you are at within the cursor—is to use CURRENT OF and then the name of the cursor. The code then continues as the read-only cursor.

```
UPDATE CustomerDetails.CustomerProducts
    SET LastCollected = @DateCollected
    WHERE CURRENT OF FinProductsColl

FETCH NEXT FROM FinProductsColl
INTO @FirstName, @LastName, @ProductName, @Amount, @LastCollect

END
```

15. Before completing the code, do a quick test to see if the same number of rows now has the @DateCollected date and time as there was at the start of the example.

```
SELECT COUNT(*)
  FROM CustomerDetails.Customers c
  JOIN CustomerDetails.CustomerProducts cp
    ON cp.CustomerId = c.CustomerId
  JOIN CustomerDetails.FinancialProducts f
    ON f.ProductId = cp.FinancialProductId
 WHERE cp.Frequency = 2
   AND cp.LastCollected = @DateCollected
```

16. The transaction is rolled back.

```
ROLLBACK TRAN

SELECT 'Total collected is ' + CONVERT(varchar(20),@TotalCollected)
CLOSE FinProductsColl
DEALLOCATE FinProductsColl
```

17. When you execute the foregoing code, you should see something similar to Figure 17-18, where the number of rows should match in the first two result sets.

Figure 17-18. *The test results from the updatable cursor*

Let's be clear: cursors are usually not the best way to work with your data, but there are times that you have to work a row at a time, and although slower than working with sets, it may be the best option for what is required. Never disregard cursors outright as some developers do.

Debugging Your Code

Now that you are at the point where you have the knowledge to build advanced T-SQL, you will be entering a stage of development where you will need to debug your code. So why and when do you need to debug code?

Debugging code can occur during development, testing, and even post-release. When you are developing your code, you may build a stored procedure a section at a time, checking that you have the information you expect at a specific point in time. It may be that you want to check that variables have the correct information before, during, or after execution. Or you may want to check that your CASE statements, loops, WHERE statements, etc. are all performing as expected. This can always be achieved by displaying information via a SELECT or PRINT statement, but these statements can be left behind in the stored procedure and inadvertently released to production. If you have the ability to step through your code a line or a block at a time, and when the code is paused to have the ability to inspect values in a transient way among many other features, this would eliminate code being released in error.

SQL Server has greatly improved the ability to debug your code over the years and is very close to how code is debugged in Visual Studio. There are a number of options and windows that help you debug your code, which I will go through before displaying an example of how to debug your code.

There are a number of requirements to make a good debugger. You need to see your code and at what point of execution you are; be able to pause, or breakpoint, your code; be able to display and alter values of variables; and be able to step your code so you can execute a line of code at a time. All of these tasks should be simple to perform.

You can debug database code within Visual Studio, but the ability to debug code within SQL Server using Management Studio can help you to debug code in an easier fashion, because all of the work is being completed on SQL Server. A number of options are available from several areas of SSMS, giving you, as a developer, a good level of flexibility. The first area that is available is from the menu in SSMS when a code window is open. You can see the options in Figure 17-19.

Figure 17-19. *The Debug menu within SSMS*

There are only three windows defined in the menu, but as you debug, then more windows become available, which I will cover in the next section.

Debugging Windows

Debug windows are ideal for viewing information or performing actions against code being debugged. Each window provides useful but specific information. The windows that are available (some only once debugging starts) are as follows:

- *Call Stack*: If you have nested stored procedures or you call functions, then the Call Stack window will show each object in a hierarchy. It will allow you to see via which route you reach the point in code that you have breakpointed at. The Call Stack window is not available until debugging starts, and can be found in tabs at the bottom of SSMS. You will see the tab in Figure 17-20.

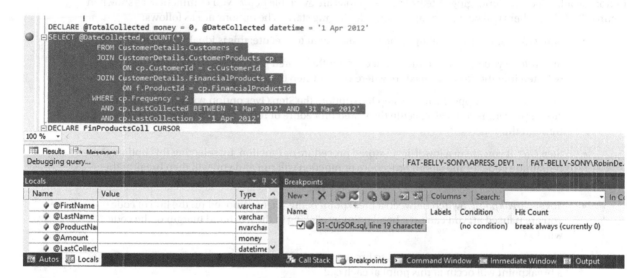

Figure 17-20. *The Breakpoints window*

- *Breakpoints*: A breakpoint is an indicator in your code where you want SQL Server to pause execution. You can have one or more breakpoints within your code, and these are ideal for pausing your execution to inspect variables, check information, and generally decide how you want to procede. Figure 17-20 shows the details of one breakpoint that you will set in the forthcoming example. The columns Labels, Condition, and Hit Count are covered in a few moments

- Command: Allows for commands to be executed; these are explicit commands, such as Debug.AddWatch and Debug.StepInto.

- Output: When setting a breakpoint, it is also possible to write out information at that time. You will see this in the forthcoming example, and output from the breakpoint will be placed in the output window.

- Immediate: Like the Command window, you can execute commands immediately, and you can also run stored procedures and other code immediately.

- Autos: This will show the variables like the local window but only variables in the current statement and the previous statement.

- Locals: This will automatically display any locally defined variables and their current values.

- Watch: If you have variables that you want to watch the values of as you process your code, then you would add these to the Watch window so that they are available. You can also alter the value of a variable within a Watch window if required to aid testing. You will see this in the example.

Now that the windows have been covered, you can take a look at the options available to you to debug your code.

Debugging Options

The ability to be in control of code execution is a cornerstone of debugging code. In this section, you will see the options available when debugging. A few of these options are available before you commence, as shown in Figure 17-19, but others will become enabled once debugging starts. The options are as follows:

- *Show Next Statement*: Highlight the next statement to execute; this is ideal when looping.

- *Step Into*: If you have a statement that calls another stored procedure or function, this option will step into the stored procedure where you can step through each line.

- *Step Over*: As an opposite to the Step Into option, the Step Over option will not step into the stored procedure and will execute the stored procedure or function, but you will not step through the code.

- *Step Out*: If you are in a lower-level stored procedure or function, by selecting this option, the remaining code for the stored procedure or function will run and you will then break at the line of code that called the stored procedure, ready to proceed to the next line.

- *Toggle Breakpoint*: Switch between a breakpoint being set, or removed on the line of code you are paused at; you can set a breakpoint by clicking in the left-hand margin of the code window.

- *New Breakpoint*: Define a function to breakpoint at; if you call the same function several times, a breakpoint will occur at this point at each call.

- *Delete All Breakpoints*: Remove all the breakpoints in your code

- *Clear All DataTips*: A datatip is where you highlight a variable within code and pin it within the code. This will then add a watch to the variable, but instead of being in a Watch window, it will be inline within the code. Clear All DataTips will remove from your code any tips that you have. A datatip is shown in Figure 17-21.

```
SELECT @TotalCollected = @TotalCollected + @Amount    @TotalCollected  5198.1525
```

Figure 17-21. *A datatip in code showing a value*

- *Export DataTips*: Once at least one datatip has been set, it can be exported so that any other developers can take those tips and import them for their own debugging. Also you can export the tips and store them in a source control system for debugging in the future.

- *Import DataTips*: Any exported datatips can be imported and used for debugging.

So you are now well on the way to starting to debug your code.

Debugging Pop-Up Window

Once debugging starts, within the Query Editor window, a pop-up dialog becomes available. If you right-click in the query window, a pop-up, as shown in Figure 17-22, will be displayed. This gives you a number of further options for debugging based on the line of code the cursor is on. So although you may be breakpointed at one line of code, you can move the cursor to a different line of code and right-click, and you will be acting on that line of code instead of the breakpoint.

Figure 17-22. *Debug options within Query Editor*

The options are as follows:

- *Delete Breakpoint:* Remove the breakpoint so that the code will continue when that line of code is reached

- *Disable Breakpoint:* Keep the breakpoint for future debugging but disable the breakpoint

- *Location...:* Define a breakpoint by file, line, and character

- *Condition...:* Break when a condition is met or has altered; this is useful for when you want to track a variable, but you are not sure where it is changed.

- *Hit Count...:* Break your code when the line highlighted is "hit" the number of times defined when you click Hit Count; this can be useful for testing how a loop behaves in the middle of its iterations.

- *Filter...:* It is possible to breakpoint on a different process and thread. This is good for when you are calling code outside of your process.

- *When Hit...:* When the breakpoint is hit, output some information to the output window; you will see this demonstrated in the following example.

- *Edit Labels...:* It is possible to label your breakpoint. By default, breakpoints have no label, but by having the ability to label, you can have multiple breakpoints grouped and therefore make tracking of the breaks easier to follow. This is a bit like labeling nested transactions.

- *Export...:* Breakpoints can be exported and stored with your stored procedures or code so that they can exist for future debugging or as some sort of test evidence. Breakpoints are exported as an XML file.

Now that the options available for debugging your code have been covered, it is time to see debugging in action and put some of this information into an example. This exercise will show only a small amount of what is possible with debugging, as it would require a whole chapter to show everything in detail. You will see the fundamentals and enough for many situations.

TRY IT OUT: DEBUGGING CODE

If you have closed the query window containing the forward-only, read-only cursor, then re-open the window as it is going to be used in the upcoming steps to demonstrate debugging.

1. Scroll to the OPEN cursor command and ensure the cursor is on that line of code. Click in the left-hand margin, and you should see a red dot, as shown in Figure 17-23. You should do the same at the line of code that updates the @TotalCollected variable.

```
OPEN FinProductsColl

FETCH NEXT FROM FinProductsColl
INTO @FirstName, @LastName, @ProductName, @Amount, @LastCollect

WHILE @@FETCH_STATUS = 0
BEGIN

    SELECT @TotalCollected = @TotalCollected + @Amount
```

Figure 17-23. The two breakpoints within the code

2. Click Debug from the toolbar at the top of Management Studio. It is to the right of the Execute button, as shown in Figure 17-24. You can also press Alt+F5.

Figure 17-24. The Debug toolbar option before debugging starts

3. The Query Editor window should now change and look like Figure 17-25. A yellow line will be on the first line of code that is to be executed, and a yellow cursor appears in the left-hand margin. You will also see the windows described earlier appear at the foot of the screen.

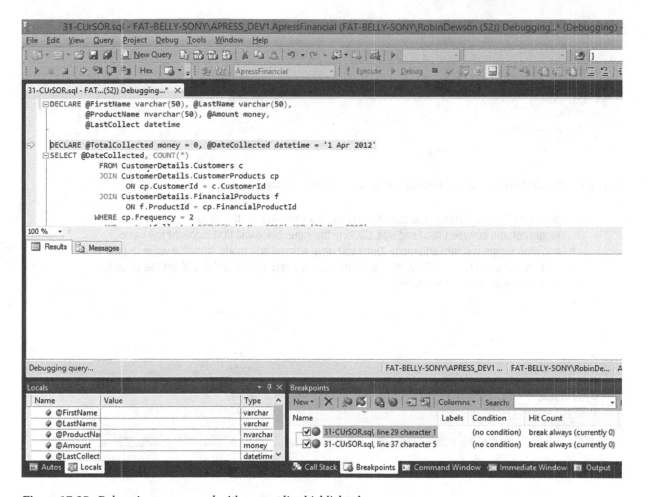

Figure 17-25. *Debugging commenced with current line highlighted*

4. The first DECLARE is not highlighted, as that is just defining variables and has no code that can be debugged. However, with the @TotalCollected variable, it is assigned a value and so SQL Server will breakpoint here.

5. If you move to the Locals screen, as shown in Figure 17-26, you will see the variables defined and each current value. Special attention is on @TotalCollected, as you will see in the next step.

Locals			▾ ⏸
Name	**Value**	**Type**	
@FirstName		varchar	
@LastName		varchar	
@ProductName		nvarchar	
@Amount		money	
@LastCollect		datetime	
@TotalCollected		money	
@DateCollected		datetime	

Figure 17-26. *The Locals window showing the variables and their values*

6. Within the Locals window, you can alter the value a variable has; the Value column is a toggle column between read and edit. Clicking the value twice will first highlight the value, and then toggle you into edit mode. Once you have entered edit mode, alter the value to be 100, as shown in Figure 17-27. (Be aware that the line you are paused at will set the value to zero once you resume execution).

Locals			▾ ⏸
Name	**Value**	**Type**	
@FirstName		varchar	
@LastName		varchar	
@ProductName		nvarchar	
@Amount		money	
@LastCollect		datetime	
@TotalCollected	100	money	
@DateCollected		datetime	

Figure 17-27. *The Locals window with a value defined*

7. Now that you have the debugger started, and for your testing a value has been defined for a local variable, it is time to run to the first breakpoint, as shown in Figure 17-28. There are three ways to get to this point: either step a line at a time via F10, or press Alt+F5, or click the green arrow on the toolbar. Thelatter two options will run every line up to the first breakpoint, or to the end of execution if no breakpoint has been defined.

Figure 17-28. *Hitting the first breakpoint*

8. Perform the same action (green button, ALT+F5, or F10) to reach the second breakpoint, as shown in Figure 17-29.

Figure 17-29. *The second breakpoint where a row from the cursor is being processed*

9. Notice in Figures 18-28 and 18-29 that the Locals window has values for the local variables taken from the cursor row and that the @TotalCollected variable has increased by the @Amount variable.

10. Before moving on, rather than breakpointing each time you loop around the cursor to check the value in the variable, you can output information to the Output window when this line of code is hit. Move to the left-hand margin and right-click. This will display the pop-up window as shown in Figure 17-30 and discussed earlier. Select the When Hit... option.

Figure 17-30. *Debug pop-up window*

■ **Note** The link of When Hit... does not need to be a breakpoint line.

11. From the window that is displayed, you can enter relevant text. Within the window, you will see some predefined variable options that you can put in the text, as shown in Figure 17-31. Enter the following text into the "Print a message" text box. The "Continue execution" check box will automatically select.

```
Function: $FUNCTION, Breakpoint hit - TotalCollected is {@TotalCollected}
```

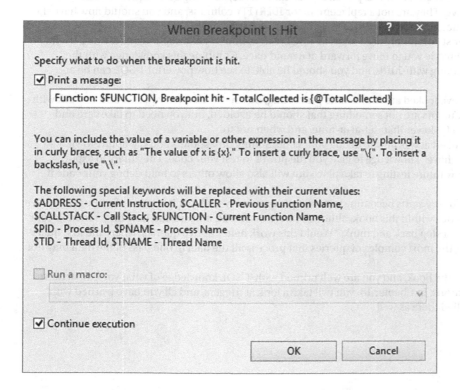

Figure 17-31. *When Breakpoint Is Hit window with the required text to output*

12. This will remove the breakpoint so that the code will not break each time it is hit.

13. Press Alt+F5 or click the green arrow. This will instruct the debugger to continue processing, and as there are no more breakpoints, execution will complete.

14. If you look at the output window, you will see the information from the When Hit... Only part of the output is displayed here.

```
Function: 9781ch1415_ForwardReadonlyCursor.sql, Breakpoint hit -
TotalCollected is 2625.6224
Function: 9781ch1415_ForwardReadonlyCursor.sql, Breakpoint hit - TotalCollected is 5298.1525
Function: 9781ch1415_ForwardReadonlyCursor.sql, Breakpoint hit -
TotalCollected is 8372.6048
Function: 9781ch1415_ForwardReadonlyCursor.sql, Breakpoint hit -
TotalCollected is 10658.8615
```

This concludes the introduction and details about debugging and completes the chapter. Debugging is detective work, so exactly what debugging statements you need will depend on the specific circumstances. It is a crucial tool for a developer, and you can expect to use a debugger as much as any other area of SQL Server that you have seen.

Summary

The comparison of sequences with IDENTITY was explored and demonstrated, showing how sequences can be a better and more flexible alternative. They are not a replacement for IDENTITY columns, and you should now have the knowledge of when to use sequences instead of IDENTITY.

Subqueries are one of the most commonly used areas of T-SQL, but common table expressions are also useful, so knowing these areas well will enable you to move forward at a rapid pace. Combine this knowledge with the functionality especially when working with JOINs, and you should be able to see how powerful T-SQL can be at working with time-based data.

Throughout the book, you have looked at set-at-a-time processing, but in this chapter, you saw how to work with data a row at a time via cursors. Cursors are not something that should be avoided, but you need to take care and know when to use a cursor, which is slower than set-at-a-time, and when not to.

One of the final areas you looked at was how to debug your code. Setting breakpoints and the ability to view values within variables are "must-have" knowledge to give you the power to test your code. The ability to export breakpoints and datatips will allow future testing to take place but will also allow others to help debug your code if help is required.

One last piece of advice: If a query starts becoming very complex, you may find that it starts performing badly. We won't look at performance of queries within this book, although I have discussed indexes and how they can help your query perform better. Always take a step back and think, "Would this work better as two queries, where the first query creates a subset of data?" Writing the most complex of queries that process all the data in one pass of the data may not always be the best answer.

You are coming to the end of the book, and you are well primed with T-SQL knowledge of what you can achieve with stored procedures and functions. In Chapter 18, you will take a look at triggers, and all you have learned with programming T-SQL can be applied there as well.

■ ■ ■

Triggers

At times a modification to data somewhere within your database will require an automatic action on data elsewhere, either in your database, another database, or elsewhere within SQL Server; a trigger is the object that will do this for you. When a modification to your data occurs, SQL Server will fire a trigger, which is a specialized stored procedure that will run, performing the actions that you desire. Triggers are most commonly used to perform business rules validation, carry out cascading data modifications (changes on one table causing changes to be made on other tables), and keep track of changes for each record (audit trail). You can also do any other processing that you require when data on a specific table are modified, such as auditing. You actually have come across triggers when looking at Declarative Management Framework earlier in the book. These specialized system triggers are built to ensure the system's integrity. You will see how these work by building your own DDL trigger later in this chapter.

The aim of this chapter is as follows:

- Describe what a trigger is

- Detail potential problems surrounding triggers

- Show the CREATE TRIGGER T-SQL syntax

- Discuss when to use a constraint and when to use a trigger

- Show the system tables and functions specific to triggers

- Demonstrate the creation of a trigger through a template and straight T-SQL statements

- Discuss image data types and the problems that surround updating these columns and firing a trigger

First of all, let's see just what constitutes a trigger.

What Is a Trigger?

A *trigger* is a specialized database object similar to a stored procedure that will be executed either on a data modification, known as a Data Manipulation Language (DML) trigger, or on a data model action, such as CREATE TABLE, known as a Data Definition Language (DDL) trigger. DML triggers are pieces of code attached to a specific table that are set to automatically run in response to an INSERT, DELETE, or UPDATE command. However, a DDL trigger is attached to an action that occurs either within a database or within a server. The first part of the chapter will look at DML triggers, followed by an investigation of DDL triggers. As a developer, you will use DML triggers mainly, and you will find DDL triggers used mainly by database administrators to ensure that certain actions cannot happen or are reported.

SQL Server does not allow for a trigger to be defined for an in-memory table, although a trigger definition can access an in-memory table and issue commands against it. One use for accessing in-memory tables could be in a scenario where you have an in-memory table defined that holds key information from a wider, disk-based table.

567

For example, you might have a table that holds all the details of a share of stock, such as dividend date, last dividend amount paid, listed stock exchange, share price, and and so forth. Then you might have an in-memory table that only holds the internal share id, stock exchange ticker code, and the current share price. The in-memory table data is updated when the share price alters, but the data can be read extremely fast if you want to just see the current share price.

■ **Note** Unlike stored procedures, you cannot manually make a trigger run, you cannot use parameters with triggers, and you cannot use return values with triggers.

The DML Trigger

Triggers have many uses. Perhaps the most common for a DML trigger is to enforce a business rule. For example, when a customer places an order, a trigger would check that they have sufficient funds or that you have enough stock; if any of these checks fail, you can complete further actions or return error messages and roll back the update.

DML triggers can be used as a form of extra validation—for example, to perform complex checks on data that a constraint could not achieve. Keep in mind that using constraints instead of triggers gives you better performance, but triggers are the better choice when dealing with complex data validation. Another use for a DML trigger is to make changes in another table based on what is about to happen within the original triggered table. For example, when you add an order, you would create a DML trigger that would reduce the quantity of items in stock. Finally, DML triggers can be used to create an automated audit trail that generates a change history for each record. Since the Sarbanes-Oxley Act (SOX) of 2002, DML triggers for the purpose of logging changes over time are created more and more often. Although triggers have a performance impact, they do ensure that auditing is completed automatically.

You can create separate triggers for any table modification action, or triggers that will fire on any combination of table actions. This means that you cannot create a trigger for SELECT. Obviously, as no table modifications occur on a SELECT statement, it is impossible to create such a trigger. There are three actions that can invoke triggers:

- INSERT trigger
- DELETE trigger
- UPDATE trigger

You can also have a combination of the three types of trigger actions, and you will find one trigger for each action and a trigger for multiple actions within database developments. I prefer to have one trigger per action as this keeps the code within the trigger optimized without my having to write code to figure out which of the actions have invoked the trigger, and thus which code path to take.

Triggers can update tables within other databases if desired, and it is also possible for triggers to span servers as well, so don't think the scope of triggers is limited to the current database or server.

It is possible for a trigger to fire a data modification, which in turn will execute another trigger, which is known as a *nested trigger*. For example, imagine you have Table A, which has a trigger on it to fire a modification within Table B, which in turn has a trigger on it that fires a modification within Table C. If a modification is made to Table A, then Table A's trigger will fire, modifying the data in Table B, which will fire the trigger in Table B, thus modifying data in Table C. This nesting of triggers can go up to 32 triggers deep before you reach the limit set within SQL Server; however, if you start getting close to that sort of level, either you have a very complex system, or perhaps you have been overly zealous with your creation of triggers!

It is also possible to switch off any nesting of triggers so that when one trigger fires, no other trigger can fire; however, this is not usually the norm. Be aware that your performance will suffer greatly when you start using nested triggers; use them only when necessary.

■ **Note** There is one statement that will not fire a DELETE trigger while still removing rows. If you issue a TRUNCATE TABLE statement, it is as if the table had been wiped without any data logging, and no DELETE triggers will fire.

As with stored procedures, do take care when building triggers: you don't want to create a potentially endless loop in which a trigger causes an update, which fires a trigger already fired earlier within the loop, thereby repeating the process.

CREATE TRIGGER Syntax for DML Triggers

The creation of a trigger through T-SQL code can be quite complex if you use the full trigger syntax. However, the reduced version that I cover here is much more manageable and easier to demonstrate. When building a trigger, you can create it for a single action or for multiple actions. To expand on this, a trigger can be for the insertion of a record only, or it can cover inserting and updating the record. Any combination is possible.

■ **Note** Although this chapter will demonstrate DML triggers on tables, a trigger can also be placed on a view as well, so that when data is modified through a view, it too can fire a trigger if required. Any underlying triggers will also fire, of course.

Here is the syntax for creating a basic trigger:

```
CREATE TRIGGER [schema_name.]trigger_name
ON {table|view}
[WITH ENCRYPTION]
{
{{FOR {AFTER|INSTEAD OF} {[INSERT] [,] [UPDATE] [,] [DELETE]}
AS
[{IF [UPDATE (column)
[{AND|OR} UPDATE (column)]] ]
COLUMNS_UPDATE()]
sql_statements}}
```

Let's explore the options in this syntax more closely:

- CREATE TRIGGER schema_name.trigger_name: As ever, you need to inform SQL Server what you are attempting to do, and in this instance, you want to create a trigger. The name for the trigger must also follow the SQL Server standards for naming objects within a database, and a trigger should also belong to a schema just like other objects.

- ON {table|view}: It is then necessary to give the name of the single table or view that the trigger relates to, which is named after the ON keyword. Each trigger is attached to one table only.

- [WITH ENCRYPTION]: As with views and stored procedures, you can encrypt the trigger using the WITH ENCRYPTION options so that the code cannot be viewed by prying eyes.

- {FOR|AFTER|INSTEAD OF}:

 - The FOR|AFTER trigger will run the code within the trigger after the underlying data is modified. Therefore, if you have any constraints on the table for cascading changes, then the table changes and these cascade changes will complete successfully before the trigger fires. You specify either FOR or AFTER.

 - INSTEAD OF: This is the most complex of the three options to understand as a trigger defined with this option will run the T-SQL within the trigger rather than allow the data modification to run. One example would be where you capture a DELETE action on the data with an INSTEAD OF trigger, and that trigger in turn executes some code that updates the target rows to indicate to your application that they are to be considered as deleted, but they are not actually deleted.

- {[INSERT] [,] [UPDATE] [,] [DELETE]}: This section of the syntax determines on what action(s) the trigger will execute. This can be an INSERT, an UPDATE, or a DELETE T-SQL command. As mentioned earlier, the trigger can fire on one, two, or three of these commands, depending on what you want the trigger to do. Therefore, at this point, you need to mention which combination of commands, separated by a comma, you want to work with.

- AS: The keyword AS defines that the trigger code has commenced, just as the AS keyword defines the start of a stored procedure. After all, a trigger is just a specialized stored procedure.

- [{IF UPDATE (column) [{AND|OR} UPDATE (column)]}]: This option is a test to check whether a specific column has been modified. This happens through the use of the UPDATE() keyword. By placing the name of the column to test between the parentheses, a logical TRUE or FALSE will be returned depending on whether the column has been updated. The deletion of a record will not set the UPDATE test to TRUE or FALSE, as you are removing an item and not updating it. An INSERT or an UPDATE will set the UPDATE test to the necessary value. This function is demonstrated later in the chapter.

- COLUMNS_UPDATE(): This has functionality similar to UPDATE(), but instead of testing a specific named column, it tests multiple columns in one test.

- sql_statements: At this point, you code the trigger just like any other stored procedure.

The main thought you must keep in mind when building a trigger is that a trigger fires after each statement that modifies data is executed, but before the modification is made to rows in the table. Therefore, if you have an UPDATE statement that updates many rows, the trigger will fire after all the UPDATE statement has completed, not when each of the rows has been dealt with.

■ **Note** Keep in mind that the FOR trigger executes before the underlying data is modified; therefore, a trigger can issue a ROLLBACK for that particular action if so desired.

Now that you know how to create a trigger, you will learn which situations they best apply to, as opposed to constraints.

Why Not Use a Constraint?

There is nothing stopping you from using a constraint to enforce a business rule, and in fact, constraints should be used to enforce data integrity. Constraints also give you better performance than triggers. However, they are limited in what they can achieve and what information is available to them to complete their job.

Triggers are more commonly used for the validation of business rules, or for more complex data validation, which may or may not then go on to complete further updates of data elsewhere within SQL Server.

A constraint is able to validate only data that are within the table the constraint is being built for or a specified value entered at design time. This is in contrast to a trigger, which can span databases, or even servers, and check against any data set at design time or a data set built from data collected from other actions against any table. This can happen if the necessary access rights are given to all objects involved.

However, constraints are the objects to use when you want to ensure that data forming a key are correct, or when you need to enforce referential integrity through a foreign key constraint.

At times a fine line will exist between building a constraint and a trigger, when the trigger is meant to perform a very simple validation task. In this case, if the decision deals with any form of data integrity, then use a constraint, which will give you better performance than using a trigger. If the object to be built is for business rules and requires complex validation, needs to handle multiple databases or servers, or requires advanced error handling, then build a trigger. For example, a trigger must be used if you need a change on one table to result in an action (update, delete, etc.) on a table that is located in another database. You might have this situation if you keep an audit trail (change history) database separate from your production database. It is doubtful that you would want to use a trigger if you are doing something simple, such as verifying that a date field contains only values within a certain range.

Deleted and Inserted Logical Tables

When a table is modified, whether this is by an insertion, an update, or deletion, any associated trigger to that action will run. The trigger will take an exact copy of the row of data that is held in two system logical tables called DELETED and INSERTED. When a record is inserted into a table within a database, a full copy of the insertion of the record is placed into the INSERTED table. Every item of information placed into each column for the insertion is then available for checking. If a deletion is performed, a full copy of the row of data is placed in the DELETED table. Finally, when an update occurs on a row of data, a full copy of the row before the modification is placed in the DELETED table, and then a copy of the row of data after the modification is placed in the INSERTED table.

The INSERTED and DELETED tables will hold one record from each table for each modification. Therefore, if you perform an UPDATE that updates 100 rows, the DELETED logical table is populated with the 100 rows prior to the UPDATE. The modification then takes place, and then the INSERTED table is populated with 100 rows. Finally, the trigger will fire. Once the trigger has completed, the data for that table are removed from the relevant logical tables.

These tables are held within the tempdb temporary database, and therefore triggers will affect the performance of the tempdb and will be affected by any other process utilizing tempdb. However, it is not possible to complete any further processing on these tables, such as creating an index, as they are held in a version store, and the data can be interrogated only via a SELECT statement and cannot be modified. You can access these tables only within a trigger to find out which records have been inserted, updated, or deleted.

■ **Note** There are two version stores within each instance of SQL Server. This is an advanced topic, but in essence, one version store holds versions of each row of data where you have online index build operations on them, and the other index store is for rows of data where you don't have online index build operations. These exist to reduce the amount of I/O on the transaction log.

To check what columns have been modified, it would be possible to compare each and every column value between the two tables to see what information had been altered. Luckily, as was discussed when you examined the syntax, there is a function, UPDATE(), that can test whether a column has been modified.

Now that you are fully up to date as to what a DML trigger is and how it works, it is time to create and test the first trigger within the database.

Creating a DML FOR/AFTER Trigger

The first trigger you will be looking at is a DML trigger to work with a customer record when a transaction occurs. The following example will demonstrate how to create a trigger on a data insertion, but also what happens to that INSERT when there is a problem in the trigger itself. As you are near the end of the book, the T-SQL within the trigger will be more advanced than some of the code so far.

TRY IT OUT: CREATING A TRIGGER IN QUERY EDITOR

The purpose of this example is to change a customer's account balance when a financial transaction occurs as defined by an INSERT in the TransactionDetails.Transactions_old table, the table originally created in Chapter 5 prior to migration to an in-memory. You want to change the balance AFTER the row has been inserted into the TransactionDetails.Transactions_old table. This is so you do not change the customer's account balance if later in the INSERT of the row a problem occurs and the INSERT does not complete.

1. First of all, it is necessary to give the trigger a meaningful name. Then you define the table that the trigger will be attached to, which in this case is the TransactionDetails. Transactions_old table. The final part of the start of the trigger will then define the type of trigger and on what actions the trigger will execute. This will be a FOR AFTER trigger on an INSERT on the TransactionDetails.Transactions_old table. The first part of the code looks as follows:

```
USE ApressFinancial
GO
CREATE TRIGGER TransactionDetails.trgInsTransactions
ON TransactionDetails.Transactions_old
AFTER INSERT
AS
BEGIN
```

2. It is now time to enter the remainder of the code for the trigger. You need to retrieve the Amount and TransactionType from the INSERTED table to be able to use these in the update of the CustomerDetails.Customers table. You can JOIN from the INSERTED table to the TransactionDetails.TransactionTypes table to find out whether you are dealing with a credit or a debit transaction. If it is a debit, then through the use of a subquery and a CASE statement you can alter the Amount by multiplying it by -1 so that you are reducing a customer's balance. Notice the subquery includes a WHERE statement so that if you are entering a transaction type that does not affect the cash balance, such as recording a share movement, then the ClearedBalance will not be altered. The final action is to update the customer's balance, which you will do via an UPDATE statement. There is a great deal to take in, so take time over the code. Also, the two examples of running this trigger should clear up any queries you might have.

```
UPDATE CustomerDetails.Customers
   SET ClearedBalance = ClearedBalance +
      (SELECT CASE WHEN CreditType = 0
                   THEN i.Amount * -1
                   ELSE i.Amount
                   END
```

```
        FROM INSERTED i
        JOIN TransactionDetails.TransactionTypes tt
          ON tt.TransactionTypeId = i.TransactionType
        WHERE AffectCashBalance = 1)
    FROM CustomerDetails.Customers c
    JOIN INSERTED i ON i.CustomerId = c.CustomerId
END
```

3. Execute the code to create the trigger in the database. You can test the trigger now
 by inserting a cash withdrawal or deposit relating to the two transaction types you
 currently have. You will list the customer balance before executing the INSERT into the
 TransactionDetails.Transactions_old table, and then you will add the row and look
 at the balance again to show that it has changed. Enter the following code, which inserts a
 withdrawal of $200 from CustomerId 1's account:

```
SELECT ClearedBalance
  FROM CustomerDetails.Customers
 WHERE customerId=2

INSERT INTO TransactionDetails.Transactions_old (CustomerId,TransactionType,
Amount,RelatedProductId, DateEntered)
VALUES (2,4,200,1,GETDATE())

SELECT ClearedBalance
  FROM CustomerDetails.Customers
 WHERE customerId=2
```

4. Execute the code. As you see in Figure 18-1, the results should show that the balance has
 dropped by $200 as expected. You could also double-check that the transaction exists in the
 TransactionDetails.Transactions_old table.

Figure 18-1. *Balance reduction after trigger action*

5. The next test simulates a noncash transaction that has been recorded. For example, if you bought some shares, there would be the cash transaction removing the funds from your bank account, `TransactionType=4`, which was executed in the previous step, and then a second row entered on `TransactionType=6`, which is the equities product showing the addition of shares and is shown in the code next. This is a simple accounting procedure of one debit of cash and one credit of shares, and the credit of shares doesn't affect the cash balance. I want to demonstrate, though, what happens when a trigger fails, and to achieve this, the `CustomerDetails.Customers` table needs to have its structure altered.

6. Enter and execute the following code:

```
UPDATE CustomerDetails.Customers
SET ClearedBalance = 0
WHERE ClearedBalance IS NULL
GO
DROP INDEX IX_Customers_LastNameZip ON CustomerDetails.Customers
GO
ALTER TABLE CustomerDetails.Customers
ALTER COLUMN ClearedBalance money NOT NULL
GO
CREATE NONCLUSTERED INDEX IX_Customers_LastNameZip ON CustomerDetails.Customers
(
        LastName ASC,
        ZipCode ASC
)
INCLUDE (        ClearedBalance) WITH (PAD_INDEX = ON,
STATISTICS_NORECOMPUTE = OFF, SORT_IN_TEMPDB = OFF,
DROP_EXISTING = OFF, ONLINE = OFF, ALLOW_ROW_LOCKS = ON,
ALLOW_PAGE_LOCKS = ON, FILLFACTOR = 90)
GO
```

7. Enter the following code, which will simulate a noncash transaction:

```
SELECT ClearedBalance
  FROM CustomerDetails.Customers
 WHERE customerId=2

INSERT INTO TransactionDetails.Transactions_old (CustomerId,TransactionType,
Amount,RelatedProductId, DateEntered)
VALUES (2,6,200,1,GETDATE())

SELECT ClearedBalance
  FROM CustomerDetails.Customers
 WHERE customerId=2
```

8. Now execute the code. You will be presented with an error indicating that you cannot enter a NULL value in the ClearedBalance column. This has occurred because the CASE statement in the trigger will generate a NULL. Move to the Results tab, where only the opening balance is displayed, as shown in Figure 18-2. The trigger has a bug in that the subquery will attempt to update a balance even when there is a NULL cash value to update, and the trigger has not accounted for that scenario.

```
(1 row(s) affected)
Msg 515, Level 16, State 2, Procedure trgInsTransactions, Line 6
Cannot insert the value NULL into column 'ClearedBalance',
table 'ApressFinancial.CustomerDetails.Customers'; column does not
allow nulls. UPDATE fails.
The statement has been terminated.
```

Figure 18-2. *Balance not updated*

9. To reiterate, the INSERT statement into the TransactionDetails.Transactions_old table is correct and would normally work. However, the trigger has a bug, so the transaction did not insert the data and was rolled back. You can see this by inspecting the TransactionDetails.Transactions_old table with the following code and the results shown in Figure 18-3.

```
SELECT *
  FROM TransactionDetails.Transactions
 WHERE CustomerId=2
ORDER BY DateEntered DESC
```

	TransactionId	CustomerId	TransactionType	DateEntered	Amount	ReferenceDetails
1	1007	2	1	2014-09-06 10:19:50.283	200.00000	NULL
2	244	2	1	2012-03-22 22:04:05.440	14149.71530	NULL
3	607	2	2	2012-03-06 14:20:18.770	34215.27400	1NOVTZGPX1NES3PIK001IYYVRSTLW2W

Figure 18-3. *Transaction table listing*

10. You can change a trigger using the ALTER TRIGGER command. The changes to the code occur in the subquery: you surround the single column you will have returned with an ISNULL() test. If the result is NULL, then you transpose this with the value of 0 as the cash balance is not to alter. The code you need to change is in bold.

```
ALTER TRIGGER TransactionDetails.trgInsTransactions
ON TransactionDetails.Transactions_old
AFTER INSERT
AS
UPDATE CustomerDetails.Customers
    SET ClearedBalance = ClearedBalance +
        ISNULL((SELECT CASE WHEN CreditType = 0
                        THEN i.Amount * -1
                        ELSE i.Amount
                        END
            FROM INSERTED i
            JOIN TransactionDetails.TransactionTypes tt
              ON tt.TransactionTypeId = i.TransactionType
            WHERE AffectCashBalance = 1),0)
    FROM CustomerDetails.Customers c
    JOIN INSERTED i ON i.CustomerId = c.CustomerId
```

11. Once the changes have been completed, you can then execute the code to alter the trigger. You can now rerun the test, which will add a row to the TransactionDetails. Transactions_old table without altering the balance. If you want, you could also list the TransactionDetails.Transactions_old table to prove that the INSERT succeeded this time, as Figure 18-4 demonstrates.

```
SELECT ClearedBalance
  FROM CustomerDetails.Customers
 WHERE customerId=2

INSERT INTO TransactionDetails.Transactions_old (CustomerId,TransactionType,
Amount,RelatedProductId, DateEntered)
VALUES (2,6,200,1,GETDATE())

SELECT ClearedBalance
  FROM CustomerDetails.Customers
 WHERE customerId=2
```

Figure 18-4. *Transactions table with no balance change*

Checking Specific Columns

It is possible to check whether a specific column or set of columns has been updated via the UPDATE() or COLUMNS_UPDATED() functions available within a trigger. This can reduce the amount of processing within the trigger and therefore speed up your batch and transactions. Keep in mind that a trigger should be as quick and as short as possible. Checking columns and performing specific T-SQL code only if a column is altered will reduce trigger overheads. As you will see, only when an amount or type of transaction has altered do you really need to perform an UPDATE on the CustomerDetails.Customers table.

The first statement you will look at is UPDATE().

Using UPDATE()

The UPDATE() function is a very simple yet powerful tool to a developer who is building a trigger. It is possible to check against a specific column, or a list of columns, to see whether a value has been inserted or updated within that column. It is not possible to check whether a value has been deleted from a column, because, quite simply, you cannot delete columns; you can delete only whole rows of data. If you want to check more than one column at the same time, place the columns one after another with either an AND or an OR depending on what you want to happen. Each individual UPDATE() will return TRUE if a value has been updated. If there are a number of columns, each column will have to be defined separately—for example:

IF UPDATE(column1) [AND|OR UPDATE(column2)]

You can use this function to deal with updates to the TransactionDetails.Transactions_old table. For example, there will be times that a transaction record has been incorrectly inserted. The trigger you created previously would have to be modified to deal with an UPDATE to alter the CustomerDetails.Customers ClearedBalance. The UPDATE would remove the value within the DELETED table and then apply the value within the INSERTED table. However, what if the alteration has nothing to do with any transaction that would alter the cash balance? For example, you were changing the date entered. By simply checking each column as necessary, it is possible to see whether an update is required to the CustomerDetails.Customers table. The two columns that are of interest within the trigger are Amount and TransactionType.

TRY IT OUT: UPDATE() FUNCTION

1. Within Query Editor, let's alter the trigger to deal with an UPDATE first of all before moving to the UPDATE() function. This will let you see a demonstration of the saving. The first part of the alteration is to tag an UPDATE to the AFTER statement.

```
ALTER TRIGGER TransactionDetails.trgInsTransactions
ON TransactionDetails.Transactions_old
AFTER INSERT,UPDATE
AS
```

2. Then you need to deal with the undoing of the amount in the DELETED table row from the CustomerDetails.Customers table. The actions on the ClearedBalance need to be the opposite of the addition.

```
UPDATE CustomerDetails.Customers
    SET ClearedBalance = ClearedBalance -
        ISNULL((SELECT CASE WHEN CreditType = 0
                        THEN d.Amount * -1
                        ELSE d.Amount
                        END
```

```
        FROM DELETED d
        JOIN TransactionDetails.TransactionTypes tt
          ON tt.TransactionTypeId = d.TransactionType
       WHERE AffectCashBalance = 1),0)
    FROM CustomerDetails.Customers c
    JOIN DELETED d ON d.CustomerId = c.CustomerId
```

3. The remainder of the trigger is the same. Once you have added in the following code, execute it so that the trigger is altered:

```
UPDATE CustomerDetails.Customers
   SET ClearedBalance = ClearedBalance +
       ISNULL((SELECT CASE WHEN CreditType = 0
                   THEN i.Amount * -1
                   ELSE i.Amount
                   END
           FROM INSERTED i
           JOIN TransactionDetails.TransactionTypes tt
             ON tt.TransactionTypeId = i.TransactionType
          WHERE AffectCashBalance = 1),0)
    FROM CustomerDetails.Customers c
    JOIN INSERTED i ON i.CustomerId = c.CustomerId
```

4. You can test that the trigger works by reducing the amount of a withdrawal—for me the `TransactionId` number is 1002—which currently sits at a value of $200. The following code will list the transactions for `CustomerId=2` and the current cleared balance. You then alter the amount of withdrawal from $200 down to $100. The final actions will list the tables to prove the update to the `TransactionDetails.Transactions_old` and `CustomerDetails.Customers` tables has succeeded.

```
SELECT *
  FROM TransactionDetails.Transactions_old
 WHERE CustomerId = 2
SELECT ClearedBalance
  FROM CustomerDetails.Customers
 WHERE CustomerId = 2
UPDATE TransactionDetails.Transactions_old
   SET Amount = 100
 WHERE TransactionId = 1002 -- Alter as required
SELECT *
  FROM TransactionDetails.Transactions_old
 WHERE CustomerId = 2
SELECT ClearedBalance
  FROM CustomerDetails.Customers
 WHERE CustomerId = 2
```

5. Once you execute the code, the transactions amount and cleared balances are altered, as shown in Figure 18-5. So now you know the trigger has worked and will do these actions no matter what happens to the `TransactionDetails.Transactions_old` table.

	TransactionId	CustomerId	TransactionType	DateEntered	Amount	ReferenceDetails
1	607	2	2	2012-03-06 14:20:18.770	34215.27400	1NOVTZGPX1NES
2	244	2	1	2012-03-22 22:04:05.440	14149.71530	NULL
3	1002	2	4	2014-09-06 10:17:35.590	200.00000	NULL
4	1013	2	6	2014-09-07 07:54:56.923	200.00000	NULL

	ClearedBalance
1	237.97

	TransactionId	CustomerId	TransactionType	DateEntered	Amount	ReferenceDetails
1	607	2	2	2012-03-06 14:20:18.770	34215.27400	1NOVTZGPX1NES
2	244	2	1	2012-03-22 22:04:05.440	14149.71530	NULL
3	1002	2	4	2014-09-06 10:17:35.590	100.00000	NULL
4	1013	2	6	2014-09-07 07:54:56.923	200.00000	NULL

	ClearedBalance
1	337.97

Figure 18-5. *Transactions and balances*

6. You are now going to alter the trigger to test the Amount and TransactionType columns. If there is an update, you will complete the actions described previously; if not, then you will skip this processing. You will prove which path the trigger takes by using the system function RAISERROR, which you saw in the discussion of error handling in Chapter 16. Each section of the IF statement will have an appropriate RAISERROR.

7. To alter the trigger to update only the CustomerDetails.Customers table if Amount or TransactionType is altered, you will need to add or alter the lines of code in bold here. If you execute this code, you will have a RAISERROR saying this is what you have done. Similarly, if you don't update the table, you will have an appropriate but different RAISERROR. The trigger is defined in the following code with the alterations shown in bold. Once you have made the same changes, execute the code to alter the trigger.

```
ALTER TRIGGER TransactionDetails.trgInsTransactions
ON TransactionDetails.Transactions_old
AFTER INSERT,UPDATE
AS
IF UPDATE(Amount) OR Update(TransactionType)
BEGIN
UPDATE CustomerDetails.Customers
   SET ClearedBalance = ClearedBalance -
      ISNULL((SELECT CASE WHEN CreditType = 0
                  THEN d.Amount * -1
                  ELSE d.Amount
                  END
         FROM DELETED d
         JOIN TransactionDetails.TransactionTypes tt
           ON tt.TransactionTypeId = d.TransactionType
        WHERE AffectCashBalance = 1),0)
```

```
    FROM CustomerDetails.Customers c
    JOIN DELETED d ON d.CustomerId = c.CustomerId

UPDATE CustomerDetails.Customers
    SET ClearedBalance = ClearedBalance +
        ISNULL((SELECT CASE WHEN CreditType = 0
                    THEN i.Amount * -1
                    ELSE i.Amount
                    END
            FROM INSERTED i
            JOIN TransactionDetails.TransactionTypes tt
              ON tt.TransactionTypeId = i.TransactionType
            WHERE AffectCashBalance = 1),0)
    FROM CustomerDetails.Customers c
    JOIN INSERTED i ON i.CustomerId = c.CustomerId
RAISERROR ('You have completed an update',10,1)
END
ELSE
RAISERROR ('Updates have been skipped',10,1)
```

8. You can now test out the example, which will not update the Amount or TransactionType but will alter the DateEntered.

```
SELECT *
  FROM TransactionDetails.Transactions_old
 WHERE TransactionId=1002 -- Alter as required
SELECT ClearedBalance
  FROM CustomerDetails.Customers
 WHERE CustomerId = 2
UPDATE TransactionDetails.Transactions_old
   SET DateEntered = DATEADD(dd,-1,DateEntered)
 WHERE TransactionId = 1002 -- Alter as required
SELECT *
  FROM TransactionDetails.Transactions_old
 WHERE TransactionId=1002 -- Alter as required
SELECT ClearedBalance
  FROM CustomerDetails.Customers
 WHERE CustomerId = 2
```

9. Once you have run this code, you will see the Results tab showing the DateEntered being altered but the ClearedBalance not, as Figure 18-6 illustrates. However, at this point, you don't know if this is because you have removed and then readded the amount, giving a null effect.

	TransactionId	CustomerId	TransactionType	DateEntered	Amount	ReferenceDetails	Notes
1	1002	2	4	2014-09-06 10:17:35.590	100.00000	NULL	NULL

	ClearedBalance
1	337.97

	TransactionId	CustomerId	TransactionType	DateEntered	Amount	ReferenceDetails	Notes
1	1002	2	4	2014-09-05 10:17:35.590	100.00000	NULL	NULL

	ClearedBalance
1	337.97

Figure 18-6. *Details where updates have been skipped*

10. Moving to the Messages tab, you can see the RAISERROR that occurred when you skipped updating the CustomerDetails.Customers table. There are also fewer "row(s) affected" messages.

```
(1 row(s) affected)
(1 row(s) affected)
Updates have been skipped
(1 row(s) affected)
(1 row(s) affected)
(1 row(s) affected)
```

This brings us to the end of looking at the UPDATE() function. Let's move on to COLUMNS_UPDATED().

Using COLUMNS_UPDATED()

Instead of working with a named single column, the COLUMNS_UPDATED() function can work with multiple columns. It does this through the use of bit flags rather than naming columns, and therefore if you change the order of columns, you can get into trouble. There are eight bits in a byte, and a bit can be either off (a value of 0) or on (a value of 1).

COLUMNS_UPDATED() checks the bits of a single byte, which is provided by SQL Server, to see whether a column has been updated. It can do this by correlating a bit with a column in the underlying table. So to clarify, the TransactionDetails.Transactions_old table has nine columns. The first column, TransactionId, would relate to the first bit within the byte. The Amount column is the fifth column and therefore would relate to the fifth bit within the byte. If the first bit is on (a value of 1), the TransactionId column has been updated. Similarly, if the fourth bit is on, the Amount column has been updated.

■ **Note** Confusingly, when talking about bits, the first bit is known as bit 0, the second bit is known as bit 1, and the byte is made up of bits 0 through 7. Therefore, the TransactionId column is bit 0, and the Amount column is bit 4. You will use this convention from this point onward.

The bit flag settings are based on the column order of the table definition. To test for a bit value, you use the ampersand (&) operator to test a specific bit or multiple set of bits. Before you discuss how this works, inspect Table 18-1. A bit value increases by the power of 2 as you progress down the bit settings, as you can see.

Table 18-1. Bit Settings and the Equivalent Decimal Value

Bit	Value
0	1
1	2
2	4
3	8
4	16
5	32
6	64
7	128

■ **Note** Another point about bits is that they work from right to left. For example, 00000010 shows bit 1 is set and therefore a value of 2.

Now if bits 2 and 4 are switched on within a byte—in other words, if they have a setting of true (00010100)—then the value is 4 + 16, which equates to 20. Therefore, to test whether the third and fifth columns of the table have *both* been altered, you would use the following syntax:

```
IF COLUMNS_UPDATE() & 20 = 20
```

This is a great deal to take in and understand, so I have included the following code to help you to understand this further. Here you have a byte data type variable. You then set the variable to a value; in this case, you believe that bits 0 and 1 will be set. By using the & operator, you can check this. To reiterate, slightly confusingly, it's not the bit position you have to test, but the corresponding bit value, so bit 0 has a value of 1.

```
DECLARE @BitTest varbinary
SET @BitTest = 3
SELECT @BitTest & 1,@BitTest & 2,@BitTest & 4,@BitTest & 8,@BitTest & 16
```

As a byte contains eight bits, COLUMNS_UPDATED() can test only the first eight columns on this basis. Obviously, tables will contain more than eight columns, as you have seen with the TransactionDetails.Transaction table you have just been using.

Once a table has more than eight columns, things change. Instead of being able to test COLUMNS_UPDATED() & 20 > 0 to check whether columns 3 or 5 have updated, it is necessary to SUBSTRING() the value first. Therefore, to test columns 3 or 5, the code needs to read as follows:

```
IF (SUBSTRING(COLUMNS_UPDATED(),1,1) & 20) > 0
```

However, even this is not the correct solution, although you are almost there. It is necessary to substring the COLUMNS_UPDATED() into eight-bit chunks for each set of eight columns. However, you need to involve the power() function to get the correct value to test for. The syntax for the power() section of the test is as follows:

```
power(2,(column_to_test - 1))
```

Therefore, if you want to test whether column 9 has been updated, the statement would be as follows, where you take the second set of eight columns using the SUBSTRING character 2, and then test the first column of the second set of eight—in other words, column 8 + 1 = 9.

```
IF (SUBSTRING(COLUMNS_UPDATED(),2,1)=power(2,(1-1)))
```

The following tests columns 1, 4, and 10 to see whether any of them has changed:

```
IF (SUBSTRING(COLUMNS_UPDATED(),1,1)=power(2,(1-1))
OR SUBSTRING(COLUMNS_UPDATED(),1,1)=power(2,(4-1))
OR SUBSTRING(COLUMNS_UPDATED(),2,1)=power(2,(2-1)))
```

You can use this function to deal with updates to the TransactionDetails.Transactions_old table. For example, there will be times that a transaction record has been incorrectly inserted. The trigger you created previously would have to be modified to deal with an UPDATE that alters the customer's ClearedBalance. The UPDATE would remove the value within the DELETED table and then apply the value within the INSERTED table. However, what if the alteration has nothing to do with any transaction that would alter the cash balance? For example, say you were changing the date entered. By simply checking each column as necessary, it is possible to see whether an update is required to the CustomerDetails.Customers table. The two columns that would interest the trigger are Amount and TransactionType.

TRY IT OUT: COLUMNS_UPDATED()

The code here takes the same example as UPDATE() and converts it to use COLUMNS_UPDATED(). It is a two-line change. The following test will see whether either the TransactionType *or* the Amount has altered by checking the two column settings using the power() function.

1. Alter the trigger, and then the example will follow the previous example to ensure you get the same results. The changes are in bold. Execute the code when you have made the changes.

```
ALTER TRIGGER TransactionDetails.trgInsTransactions
ON TransactionDetails.Transactions_old
AFTER UPDATE,INSERT
AS
    IF (SUBSTRING(COLUMNS_UPDATED(),1,1) = power(2,(3-1))
    OR SUBSTRING(COLUMNS_UPDATED(),1,1) = power(2,(5-1)))
BEGIN
UPDATE CustomerDetails.Customers
    SET ClearedBalance = ClearedBalance -
        ISNULL((SELECT CASE WHEN CreditType = 0
                    THEN d.Amount * -1
                    ELSE d.Amount
                    END
```

```
                            FROM DELETED d
                            JOIN TransactionDetails.TransactionTypes tt
                                ON tt.TransactionTypeId = d.TransactionType
                            WHERE AffectCashBalance = 1),0)
                    FROM CustomerDetails.Customers c
                    JOIN DELETED d ON d.CustomerId = c.CustomerId

                UPDATE CustomerDetails.Customers
                    SET ClearedBalance = ClearedBalance +
                        ISNULL((SELECT CASE WHEN CreditType = 0
                                    THEN i.Amount * -1
                                    ELSE i.Amount
                                    END
                            FROM INSERTED i
                            JOIN TransactionDetails.TransactionTypes tt
                                ON tt.TransactionTypeId = i.TransactionType
                            WHERE AffectCashBalance = 1),0)
                    FROM CustomerDetails.Customers c
                    JOIN INSERTED i ON i.CustomerId = c.CustomerId
                RAISERROR ('You have completed an update ',10,1)
                END
                ELSE
                RAISERROR ('Updates have been skipped',10,1)
```

2. Now test the change by entering the following to test the trigger.

```
SELECT *
  FROM TransactionDetails.Transactions_old
 WHERE TransactionId=1002
SELECT ClearedBalance
  FROM CustomerDetails.Customers
 WHERE CustomerId = 2
UPDATE TransactionDetails.Transactions_old
   SET DateEntered = DATEADD(dd,-1,DateEntered)
 WHERE TransactionId = 1002
SELECT *
  FROM TransactionDetails.Transactions_old
 WHERE TransactionId=1002
SELECT ClearedBalance
  FROM CustomerDetails.Customers
 WHERE CustomerId = 2
```

3. When the foregoing code is executed, you should have results similar to Figure 18-7, where the balance of the customer remains constant but the DateEntered is reduced by a day.

	TransactionId	CustomerId	TransactionType	DateEntered	Amount
1	1002	2	4	2014-09-06 10:17:35.590	100.00000

	ClearedBalance
1	337.97

	TransactionId	CustomerId	TransactionType	DateEntered	Amount
1	1002	2	4	2014-09-05 10:17:35.590	100.00000

	ClearedBalance
1	337.97

Figure 18-7. *Using COLUMNS_UPDATED() within a trigger test results*

Now that you have covered DML triggers, you can take a look at DDL triggers.

DDL Triggers

Checking whether an action has happened on an object within SQL Server either on a database or within the server is not code that you will write every day. As more and more audit requirements are enforced on companies to ensure that their data are safe and have not been amended, auditors are now also turning their attention to areas that may cause that data to be altered. A DDL trigger is like a data trigger, as it can execute on the creation, deletion, or modification of rows within system tables rather than on user tables. So how does this help you?

I am sure you can recall specific stories involving major institutions having a program running that removed funds or stock. My favorite is one in which a developer wrote a program that calculated interest on clients' accounts. Obviously, there needed to be roundings, so the bank always rounded down to the nearest cent. However, all the "down roundings" added up each month to a fairly substantial amount of money. Of course, auditors saw that the data updates were correct, as the amount on the transaction table matched the amount in the client's account. The interest calculation stored procedure also passed QA at the time. However, once it was live, the developer altered the stored procedure so that all the down roundings were added up in a local variable, and at the end of the process, the amount was added to a "hidden" account. It was a simple stored procedure that never went wrong, and of course it was obfuscated, so nobody by chance could see what the developer had done. They could, of course, see the code as it is only obfuscated, but as it never went wrong, they had no need to. If the stored procedure needed an update, it was the "old" correct code that went live, and the developer simply waited until the time was right and reapplied his code. Auditors could not figure out why at a global level thousands of dollars could not be accounted for over time. Of course, eventually they did, but if they had a DDL trigger so that they received an e-mail or some other notification whenever a stored procedure was released, they could have immediately seen two releases of the stored procedure and asked "Why?" within minutes. Our example will demonstrate this in action.

You have also seen some system DDL triggers as I mentioned at the start of the chapter with the Declarative Management Framework. They are a great deal more complex than the trigger that will be demonstrated and also interact with Management Studio to show what is happening, but in essence they are the same.

First of all, let's look at database-scoped events, and then toward the end of the section, you will pull the information together in a working example.

DDL Database-Level Events

This section covers events that can force a DDL trigger to execute. Similar to DML triggers that can execute on one or more actions, a DDL trigger can also be linked to one or more actions. However, a DDL trigger is not linked to a specific user table and type of action. Therefore, one trigger could execute on any number of unrelated actions. For example, the same trigger could fire on a stored procedure being created, a user login being dropped, and a table being altered. I doubt if you will create many, if any, triggers like this, but it is possible. A DDL trigger that accepts multiple events that occur can decide what to do with each event, from ignoring upward. However, catching every event results in an overhead on every action.

There are two ways that you can create a trap for events that fire. It is possible to either trap these events individually (or as a comma-separated list) or as a catchall. You will see how to do this once you have looked at what events are available.

Database-Scoped Events

Table 18-2 lists some of the DDL database actions that can be trapped. The full list is comprehensive and covers every database event there is. Many of the actions you will recognize from previous chapters, although the commands have spaces between words rather than underscores.

Table 18-2. *Possible Database-Scoped Events to Listen For*

CREATE_TABLE	ALTER_TABLE	DROP_TABLE
CREATE_VIEW	ALTER_VIEW	DROP_VIEW
CREATE_FUNCTION	ALTER_FUNCTION	DROP_FUNCTION
CREATE_PROCEDURE	ALTER_PROCEDURE	DROP_PROCEDURE
CREATE_TRIGGER	ALTER_TRIGGER	DROP_TRIGGER
CREATE_EVENT_NOTIFICATION		DROP_EVENT_NOTIFICATION
CREATE_INDEX	ALTER_INDEX	DROP_INDEX
CREATE_STATISTICS	UPDATE_STATISTICS	DROP_STATISTICS
CREATE_USER	ALTER_USER	DROP_USER
CREATE_ROLE	ALTER_ROLE	DROP_ROLE
CREATE_APPLICATION_ROLE	ALTER_APPLICATION_ROLE	DROP_APPLICATION_ROLE
CREATE_SCHEMA	ALTER_SCHEMA	DROP_SCHEMA
GRANT_DATABASE	DENY_DATABASE	REVOKE_DATABASE

DDL Statements with Server Scope

Database-level events are not the only events that can be trapped within a trigger; server events can also be caught.

Table 18-3 shows some of the DDL statements that have the scope of the whole server. Many of these you may not come across for a while, if at all, so you will concentrate on database-scoped events.

Table 18-3. *DDL Server-Scoped Statements You Can Listen For*

CREATE_LOGIN	ALTER_LOGIN	DROP_LOGIN
CREATE_HTTP_ENDPOINT		DROP_HTTP_ENDPOINT
CREATE_CERT	ALTER_CERT	DROP_CERT
GRANT_SERVER_ACCESS	DENY_SERVER_ACCESS	REVOKE_SERVER_ACCESS

■ **Note** It is not possible to have a trigger that fires on both server and database events; it's one or the other.

The syntax for a DDL trigger is very similar to that for a DML trigger:

```
CREATE TRIGGER trigger_name
ON {ALL SERVER|DATABASE}
[WITH ENCRYPTION]
{
{{FOR |AFTER } {event_type,...}
AS
sql_statements}}
```

The main options that are different are as follows:

- ALL SERVER|DATABASE: The trigger fires either for the server or the database you are attached to when creating the trigger.

- Event_type: This is a comma-separated list from either the database or server list of DDL actions that can be trapped.

■ **Note** You can also catch events that can be grouped together. For example, all table and view events can be defined with a group, or this group can be refined down to just table events or view events. The only grouping you will look at is how to catch every database-level event.

Dropping a DDL Trigger

Removing a DDL trigger from the system is not like removing other objects where you simply say DROP object_type object_name. With a DDL trigger, you have to suffix this with the scope of the trigger.

```
DROP TRIGGER trigger_name ON {DATABASE|ALL SERVER}
```

EVENTDATA()

As an event fires, although there are no INSERTED and DELETED tables to inspect what has changed, you can use a function called EVENTDATA(). This function returns an XML data type containing information about the event that fired the trigger. The basic syntax of the XML data is as follows, although the contents of the function will be altered depending on what event fired:

```
<SQLInstance>
    <PostTime>date-time</PostTime>
    <SPID>spid</SPID>
    <ComputerName>name</ComputerName>
</SQLInstance>
```

I won't detail what each event will return in XML format; otherwise, you will be here for many pages. However, in one of the examples that follow, you will create a trigger that will fire on every database event, trap the event data, and display the details.

Database-level events have the following base syntax, different from the previously shown base syntax:

```
<SQLInstance>
    <PostTime>date-time</PostTime>
    <SPID>spid</SPID>
    <ComputerName>name</ComputerName>
    <DatabaseName>name</DatabaseName>
    <UserName>name</UserName>
    <LoginName>name</LoginName>
</SQLInstance>
```

The XML elements can be described as follows:

- PostTime: The date and time of the event firing

- SPID: The SQL Server process ID that was assigned to the code that caused the trigger to fire

- ComputerName: The name of the computer that caused the event to fire

- DatabaseName: The name of the database that caused the event to fire

- UserName: The name of the user who caused the event to fire

- LoginName: The login name of the user who caused the event to fire

It's time to see a DDL trigger in action.

TRY IT OUT: DDL TRIGGER

This first example will create a trigger that will execute when a stored procedure is created, altered, or dropped. When it finds this action, it will check the time of day, and if the time is during the working day, then the action will be disallowed and be rolled back. On top of this, you will raise an error listing the stored procedure. This will allow you to see how to retrieve information from the EVENTDATA() function. The final action is to roll back the changes if an action is happening during the working day and send an e-mail.

■ **Note** If you are using SQL Server Express, then it is not possible to send e-mails as this is not available in this edition.

1. Enter and execute the following trigger, which will fire when a stored procedure is created, modified, or dropped. Of course, enter your own e-mail address for the @recipients. Also alter the @profile_name if you used a different profile name in earlier in the book. Finally, the @subject is split here for reading and should be either two strings or on one line.

```
CREATE TRIGGER trgSprocs
ON DATABASE
FOR CREATE_PROCEDURE, ALTER_PROCEDURE, DROP_PROCEDURE
AS
IF DATEPART(hh,GETDATE()) > 8 AND DATEPART(hh,GETDATE()) < 18
BEGIN
    DECLARE @Message nvarchar(max)
    SELECT @Message =
      'Completing work during core hours. Trying to release - '
      + EVENTDATA().value
        ('(/EVENT_INSTANCE/TSQLCommand/CommandText)[1]','nvarchar(max)')
    RAISERROR (@Message, 16, 1)
    ROLLBACK
EXEC msdb.dbo.sp_send_dbmail
    @profile_name = 'ApressFinancialDBMA',
    @recipients = 'robin@fat-belly.com',
    @body = 'A stored procedure change',
    @subject = 'A stored procedure change has been initiated and rolled back
during core hours'

END
```

2. You can now test the trigger. Depending on what time of day you run the code, the following will either succeed or fail:

```
CREATE PROCEDURE Test1
AS
SELECT 'Hello all'
```

3. Try running the preceding code between 9 a.m. and 5 p.m. so that it is possible to see the creation fail. Running the code in the afternoon provided me with the following error:

```
Msg 50000, Level 16, State 1, Procedure trgSprocs, Line 12
Completing work during core hours. Trying to release -
CREATE PROCEDURE Test1
AS
SELECT 'Hello all'
Mail (Id: 2) queued.
Msg 3609, Level 16, State 2, Procedure Test1, Line 1
The transaction ended in the trigger.
The batch has been aborted.
```

4. It is necessary to drop the preceding trigger so you can move on, unless of course you are now outside of the prohibited hours and you want the trigger to remain.

```
DROP TRIGGER trgSprocs ON DATABASE
```

5. This next DDL trigger will not look for any specific event but instead this trigger will execute on any action that occurs at the database. This will allow you to see the XML data generated on any event you want to.

```
CREATE TRIGGER trgDBDump
ON DATABASE
FOR DDL_DATABASE_LEVEL_EVENTS
AS
    SELECT EVENTDATA()
```

6. This trigger can be tested by successfully creating the stored procedure you couldn't in the first example.

```
CREATE PROCEDURE Test1
AS
SELECT 'Hello all'
```

7. Check the results window. You should see results that you have not seen before. What is returned is XML data, and the results window displays the data as partly shown in Figure 18-8.

Figure 18-8. Event data XML

8. If you click the row, a new Query Editor pane opens after a few moments, and the XML data are transposed into an XML document layout. Each of the nodes can be inspected just like the CommandText node was earlier.

```xml
<EVENT_INSTANCE>
  <EventType>CREATE_PROCEDURE</EventType>
  <PostTime>2014-09-07T18:53:00.623</PostTime>
  <SPID>55</SPID>
  <ServerName>FAT-BELLY-SONY\APRESS_DEV1</ServerName>
  <LoginName>FAT-BELLY-SONY\RobinDewson</LoginName>
  <UserName>dbo</UserName>
  <DatabaseName>ApressFinancial</DatabaseName>
  <SchemaName>dbo</SchemaName>
  <ObjectName>Test1</ObjectName>
  <ObjectType>PROCEDURE</ObjectType>
  <TSQLCommand>
    <SetOptions ANSI_NULLS="ON" ANSI_NULL_DEFAULT="ON"
    ANSI_PADDING="ON" QUOTED_IDENTIFIER="ON" ENCRYPTED="FALSE" />
    <CommandText>CREATE PROCEDURE Test1
AS
SELECT 'Hello all'
</CommandText>
  </TSQLCommand>
</EVENT_INSTANCE>
```

Summary

DML triggers should be seen as specialized and specific stored procedures set up to help your system with maintaining data integrity, cascading updates throughout a system, or enforcing business rules. If you take out the fact that there are two system tables, INSERTED and DELETED, and that you can check what columns have been modified, then the whole essence of a trigger is that it is a stored procedure that runs automatically when a set data-modification condition arises on a specific table.

DDL triggers will be built mainly for security or reporting of system changes to compliance departments and the like. With the EventData() XML information available to a trigger, a great deal of useful information can be inspected and used further.

Coding a trigger is just like coding a stored procedure with the full control of flow, error handling, and processing that is available to you within a stored procedure object.

The aim of this chapter was to demonstrate how a trigger is fired and how to use the information that is available to you within the system to update subsequent tables or to stop processing and roll back the changes.

The DML triggers built within this chapter have demonstrated how to use the logical tables, as well as how to determine whether a column has been modified. The DDL triggers built have demonstrated how you can trap events and determine what has been changed within either a database or a server.

CHAPTER 19

■ ■ ■

Connecting via Code

If you defined yourself as a pure database developer, you would only be writing T-SQL code building on your knowledge gained within this book. However, some DBAs write code outside of the database to access data and execute stored procedures, as well as many other tasks. This can be accomplished in many different programming languages and tools. The aim of this chapter is to demonstrate how you can connect to SQL Server and accomplish working with your data using Excel VBA, .NET, and Java, as these are the most common coding platforms that you are likely to use. To be clear, the aim of this chapter is not to make you an expert or even quite proficient in these languages or tools but to demonstrate basic code that provides you with a good start to expand on via Apress books or other media.

Each development tool has its own section, allowing you to jump straight to the relevant code you want to see an example of and where you will see the ApressFinancial database accessed and data displayed in console output. It will be assumed that each tool has been installed on your computer, although there will be links on my web site, www.fat-belly.com, to the software used within the book, or if there is a later relevant version of the software that should be used, post-publication of this book. Although there will be one example of working with the data in each language within this chapter, every example demonstrated will be available in every language from my web site and with the source code for this book.

Connecting to SQL Server can be achieved using the techniques and methods that have been described throughout the book so far. SQL Server Management Studio is a tool written using a development language and provides the techniques of connecting via Windows authentication or SQL Server authentication, which then uses role techniques to allow and restrict what you can do. To this end, you could conceivably rewrite SSMS in one of many languages that you will see demonstrated.

Before you get started in this chapter, there is one point I want to make clear. In each of the tools, there are different ways you can achieve the same goal that is being demonstrated. From Excel through to Java, there is more than one method to connect and work with SQL Server. However, what I demonstrate in each section is what I have personally found to be the best and the most common method that is used for that technology and a good basis to start your development from. If you use or find a different method that suits you better, I am happy to hear from you, and I can investigate putting alternatives on my web site. However, these examples will be perfect for getting any developer up and running but also provide a good base to progress. In this chapter, you will learn the following:

- General application security

- Working with Excel using the Data ribbon and then using VBA

- Using Visual Studio to build a VB.NET and C# console application

- Developing a solution using Eclipse, Java, and the SQL Java JDBC driver

The first step is to look at general application security.

General Application Security

Throughout the book, you have worked through examples of security and how you should consider and implement different security measures, ensuring that your database is secured from inadvertent or rogue access. Measures include authentication, roles, object permissions, and schemas. It is useful to summarize a few of the points again so that they are fresh in your mind while developing an application and so that any areas missed can be addressed.

The first area would be to ensure that a Windows group exists purely for accessing the server and database. You can then use this group for application-specific access to the correct objects. Bear in mind that your database solution may have more than one application connecting to it. This could include a GUI-based solution for administrative tasks and an Excel solution built to retrieve data for ad hoc reporting by some users. Having two Windows groups allows permissions to be defined specifically for each application's needs, one for modification access and one for read-only reporting access.

You should also consider having and using an application role within the database, as discussed in Chapter 4.

Building stored procedures or views to retrieve and update the data that will retrieved by the application and grant execute permissions to these objects only to the Windows group or specific individuals if you are using SQL Server authentication will protect the data. If a report is built from data of a highly sensitive nature, then you may wish to give permission for the stored procedure or view to a specific individual to give the necessary granularity.

Whether some applications will build ad hoc T-SQL may be dependent on options selected in a GUI. The T-SQL-built code is then verified within the application to ensure that it does not contain an SQL injection, and is passed to the database for execution. This does not fit into the stored procedures or views model, and you therefore need to ensure that the most granular level of access is defined to give this login the minimum rights required to achieve its goal. Although the easiest and quickest way to provision SQL server is to allow all levels of permissions to all users, this is actually the biggest mistake you can make.

An SQL injection is where ad hoc SQL is built within an application legitimately, but someone has appended or replaced their own SQL via some area that allows user-entered information. This can happen via several methods, but one method is where an application has a user-entry field and a value from that field is used as part of the query, quite often used as part of the WHERE clause. If someone entered T-SQL code that would complete the WHERE clause in the user-entry field that performed an UPDATE or DELETE, then this is where an SQL injection has occurred; someone has injected destructive SQL into your SQL. You need to ensure that this sort of injection is blocked.

All of these security areas are database-based, but one area of security that is important is to hide the connection details of the application's connection to your database. This can be achieved via basic or complex encryption of the details. Windows authentication does reduce the need to encrypt details, as this is quite a secure method, but if you offer mixed-mode authentication, then you must encrypt any database user and password you use.

Never store a clear text user and password. There is example code on my web site, which you can use to encrypt and decrypt a password, along with instructions on what you should change to ensure that the encryption values are secure for you. The main point is that you should *never* store connection details anywhere as clear text. The details within the book are clear text for ease of reading, although they are invalid outside the scope of this book.

■ **Caution** Do as I say, not as I do.

Now that the main security items have been refreshed and new application security issues addressed that need to be considered when developing an application, it's time to look at connecting to your data via different methods.

Connecting with Excel or Excel Visual Basic for Applications (VBA)

The simplest and quickest tool in this chapter to access your data is Excel. By completing a handful of clicks, you can connect to your database, choose a specific table, or execute a stored procedure, and the data will be returned and placed within an Excel workbook and data displayed ready to send out. This is why Excel is a quick and easy tool and used by so many users and developers for reporting purposes.

You can connect to SQL Server using several methods, but the two that this chapter will concentrate on are through the Data ribbon and Visual Basic for Applications, commonly known as VBA. Using the Data ribbon, there are also a number of different methods to connect to SQL Server from different options on the ribbon. These will be demonstrated within the example shortly, but these first few statements show the flexibility of Excel and the security dangers that can exist.

When saving the Excel workbook, the credentials used to access SQL Server are stored, allowing you or anyone with the right tool on their computers the potential to refresh their data almost instantly if required. But keep in mind the security implications: if you are using mixed-mode authentication, you could have someone who you don't want refreshing the data. In this instance, you would remove the data connection details.

By storing the connection details within the workbook, anyone who gains access to the Excel file could run the code or even execute their own code by editing what was stored, as I just mentioned. If you have Windows authentication, then you may have already locked down the tables so that the user trying to access your SQL Server can't. This is standard developer practice. With SQL Server/mixed-mode authentication, security becomes more open, and anyone in the world could end up with your Excel sheet and potentially access your server and database. If you must use authentication that is not Windows authentication, then you must lock down your database objects tightly and, if possible, remove the connection details from the Excel sheet and get them provided either by a prompt or some other external method. I realize that this is the third or fourth time I have mentioned this point in very quick succession, but it can be the largest hole in your security if you don't get it right.

It is now time to look at using Excel to connect to your database and work with your data. The exercise is split into two parts, with the first part of the example using the Data ribbon and the second part using Excel VBA.

Using Excel with the Data Ribbon

The first example will use the Data ribbon. This is a ribbon that exists within Excel for connecting to external data sources, and in the example you will be connecting to the ApressFinancial database. It's time to dive into the next "Try It Out" exercise.

TRY IT OUT: CONNECTING VIA EXCEL 2013

1. Start Excel 2013, create a new blank workbook, select the Data ribbon, and then from the options in the ribbon select Connections, as shown in Figure 19-1.

Figure 19-1. *Selecting the Excel Connections option within the workbook*

2. This then displays a dialog that details all the connections that this Excel workbook has contained within it. At present there are no connections, and so the list is empty, as shown in Figure 19-2. Click Add.

Figure 19-2. Displaying any existing connections

3. You will now see a new dialog that lists connections that exist on your computer, as well as connections that are known on the network. At this point, I have no known connections, as shown in Figure 19-3. If a connection existed, you could highlight it and click Add, or you click "Browse for more..." to search for it. This scenario will exist after the end of the exercise, when you will have created a connection for the workbook, and therefore you could add this connection in a subsequent worksheet in which you were working with the data. You also need to click "Browse for more..." to create a new connection.

Figure 19-3. *Displaying the known local and network connections*

4. The next screen you will see is shown in Figure 19-4, where you can select a data source that Excel doesn't know about, or in this instance you can click the New Source... button. This is what is required, so click that button now.

Figure 19-4. *Searching for other connections or creating a new source*

5. From the dialog that is displayed, you can select Microsoft SQL Server from the options, as shown in Figure 19-5. Once selected, click Next.

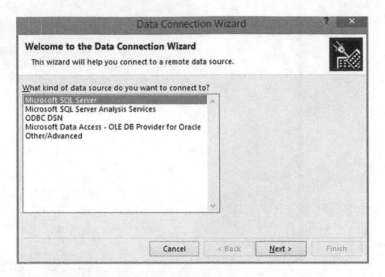

Figure 19-5. Microsoft SQL Server data connection selected

6. The next dialog allows you to enter the database server and instance name. In Figure 19-6, you will see I have entered my server and the APRESS_DEV1 instance name. I have also selected Windows Authentication. Enter your details, and click Next.

Figure 19-6. Defining your SQL Server server and instance and connection method

■ **Note** The main connection issues surround the server name being incorrectly typed. This should be the same value as the connection dialog in SSMS.

7. If your connection is successful, the next dialog in the wizard lists the databases that are found on the server. Select ApressFinancial, as shown in Figure 19-7.

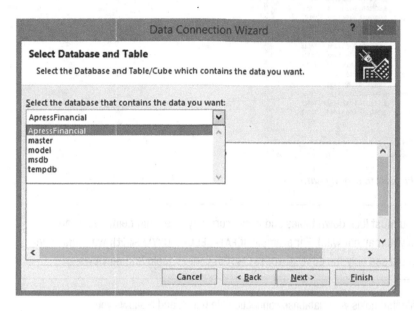

Figure 19-7. Choosing the correct database

8. Once the database is selected, you see a list of the tables and views that the account has access to, as shown in Figure 19-8. As you are connecting to the database with your login, which is a sysadmin server role, you will see all the objects. For this example, you will display the data from the view vw_SharePrices. Once you have chosen your table or view, click Next.

Figure 19-8. *Tables and views that can be used to display data*

■ **Tip** Figure 19-8 demonstrates why you must lock down tables and views correctly. The login being used can access tables directly, which is something you may not want. For example, if `FAT-BELLY-SONY\MSmith` was connecting to `ApressFinancial` via Excel, then he would see only the `CustomerDetails.Customers` table and no views.

9. Figure 19-9 shows the `.odc` file that holds your database connection file name, and it allows you to place a description against that file. This is the final dialog in the wizard; therefore, click Finish.

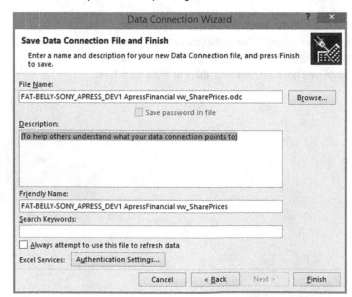

Figure 19-9. *The file name and description for the connection*

10. The wizard will close, and the connection will be added to the Workbook Connections window, as shown in Figure 19-10. It is possible to have more than one connection in a workbook, and therefore any further connections would also be listed here. Highlight the connection, and click Properties.

Figure 19-10. *All the connections defined for the Excel workbook*

11. You should now see the screen as shown in Figure 19-11. The bottom half of the properties concerns OLAP (Analysis Services systems). The default options on the Usage tab are acceptable as you will not be refreshing the data on a timed basis or when the workbook is opened.

Figure 19-11. *Usage options for the connection*

12. The three options of interest are as follows:

- *Enable background refresh*: The Excel screen will retrieve the data in the background. You will see a spinning world while the data is being brought back. The Excel workbook can accept input while the refresh is occurring.

- *Refresh every ...*: The data can be refreshed while the workbook is open at specific periods of time. If you enable this option, then you need to ensure that you are not putting an unnecessary strain on SQL Server resources with a complex, long-running query.

- *Refresh data when opening the file*: When the workbook is opened, then a refresh of the data is performed. This is ideal for the start of the day to retrieve any changes completed overnight.

13. Moving to the Definition tab as shown in Figure 19-12, there is some useful information and some warnings that I discussed prior to the exercise with the name of the connection and "Command text" text box. Click OK, and then click Close to close the Connection window.

Figure 19-12. *Definition details allowing new command text to be entered*

14. The options on the Definition tab are as follows:

- *Connection type*: The type of connection Excel will use to connect itself with SQL Server; this is a specific type for Office applications. You will see different types in other sections within the chapter.

- *Connection file*: The file name and location storing the connection details

- *Connection string*: The file connection string used by Excel to connect to SQL Server

- *Command type*: How you are accessing the data; if you were executing a T-SQL command, you would alter this option to Text. You will see these different command types within the .NET try-it-outs.

- *Command text*: The command text you will be executing

■ **Tip** The connection string will be useful to be aware of in the remaining examples as a reference point.

15. You should now be back at the Excel workbook. It is possible to get back to the connection dialog shown in Figure 19-3 by clicking the Existing Connections icon, shown in Figure 19-13. Click the icon.

Existing
Connections

Figure 19-13. *The Existing Connections icon*

16. Figure 19-14 shows the connections I have and the existing connection. Highlight the top connection, and click Open.

Figure 19-14. *Selecting the new connection for use*

17. You are now presented with the Import Data screen as shown in Figure 19-15, where you can define how the data is imported and where it is placed. Clicking Properties would take you back to Figure 19-11. Leave the options as they are, and click OK.

Figure 19-15. *How to retrieve the data and where to place it*

18. Excel will now execute the code in the "Command text" text box from Figure 19-12, and display the information based on the options in Figure 19-15. Excel also adds a filter row and coloring, as shown in Figure 19-16. There are options in the Design ribbon that allow you to modify the look and feel of the data. You can also move to the Data ribbon for further options such as removing duplicates.

Figure 19-16. *Displaying some of the returned data within Excel*

You can now save the Excel sheet and send it to your users, and as long as they have Windows authentication logins to your server and they are users within your database, then they should be able to refresh your data.

Using Excel with the steps demonstrated in the previous exercise is in my opinion the simplest method to retrieve data for your users. However, it is possible to take this a stage further so that Excel retrieves the data programmatically and you have the ability to work with the information before placing it in Excel, and this is where VBA can be used.

Using Excel with VBA

In the following exercise you will see how to build Excel VBA code in a module within a workbook. You will extract data from the worksheet that will be used to insert a row in the database. By having the code in a module rather than a specific sheet, code is available from all sheets, and this is what you will tend to find most often. You will also find that VBA code is quite often initiated from an action, whether it is the Excel sheet opening, a value in a cell changing, or a button placed on a sheet and being pressed. Within the following example, you will step through the code initially within VBA to insert a customer, and then you will place a button on the sheet and call the routine to insert a second customer.

TRY IT OUT: CONNECTING VIA EXCEL VBA

1. First of all, start Microsoft Excel and enter data in to the first sheet within the workbook, as shown in Figure 19-17. Column A details the parameters that the stored procedure will use. This information is within the sheet for your reference only. Column B holds the values that will be used for the insertion.

⊿	A	B
1	CustTitle	1
2	FirstName	John
3	CustInitials	
4	LastName	Doe
5	AddressLine1	9833 DingDong Dell
6	AddressLine2	Rickmansworth
7	AddressLine3	
8	TownOrCity	213431
9	ZipCode	
10	USState	12
11	AccountTypeId	1

Figure 19-17. *The values in the Excel sheet to insert a new customer*

■ **Note** Don't forget that this is downloadable from Apress or from my web site, www.fat-belly.com.

2. You can get to the Visual Basic Editor (VB Editor) by pressing Alt+F11; however, there is a Developer ribbon within Excel that would be better to have displayed. From Excel click File and then Options, which opens up a dialog. Select Customize Ribbon, and from the list box on the right select Developer, as shown in Figure 19-18. Once complete, click OK.

Figure 19-18. *Selecting the Developer ribbon from the Excel options*

3. Navigate to the Developer ribbon so that it is the active ribbon. On the left, there is an icon labeled Visual Basic, as shown in Figure 19-19. Click this icon.

Figure 19-19. *Visual Basic icon in the Developer ribbon*

4. Excel will open up a new application, the VB Editor, and you will see a new application on your Windows toolbar. The editor should look like Figure 19-20.

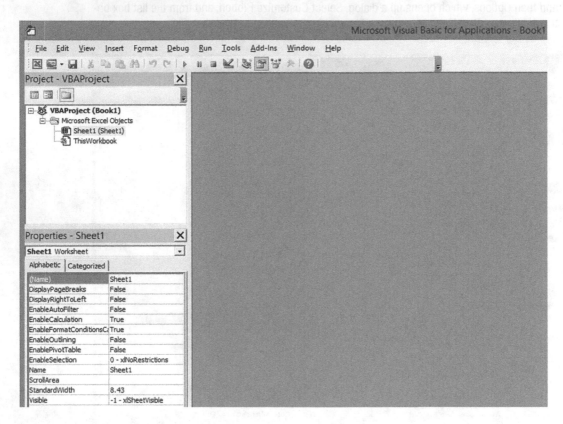

Figure 19-20. *The VB Editor IDE*

5. If you have ever used Visual Basic, then the editor is very much like it. On the left in the Project Explorer, you will see the three sheets that exist within the workbook and the workbook itself. These are macro areas for those specific areas. If you have code that is specific to a sheet, then you would place the code in that sheet. This is not what is wanted in the example, as the code you will be creating could come from any sheet.

6. A basic Excel VBA project will have the basic functionality enabled. Connecting to SQL Server is extended functionality and is required to be added. From the menu within the VB Editor, select Tools ➤ References.

7. A dialog is displayed with a very long list of references. The references listed are extensions that can be added to a VBA project. Scroll through the list until you find the reference Microsoft ActiveX Data Objects Library, and find the latest version. On my system, this is version 6.1. Select this as shown in Figure 19-21.

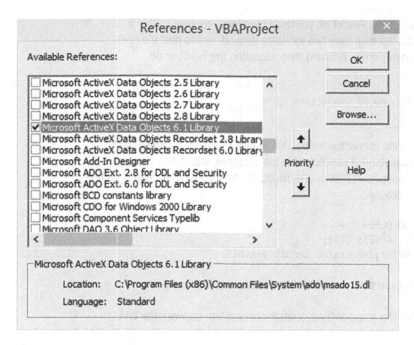

Figure 19-21. Microsoft ActiveX Data Objects 6.0 Library

8. There is one last action to perform before you start writing code, and that is to add a module to the VB Editor to write the code into. From the Project Explorer, ensure that it has the focus, right-click, and from the pop-up menu select Insert ➤ Module, as shown in Figure 19-22.

Figure 19-22. Inserting a new module into your VBA project

9. Finally you can now enter some code. First of all, you need to define a routine, as it is a routine that will hold your code. You then have two variables defined, one to hold the ADO connection and one for holding any errors returned from executing the T-SQL code:

```
Sub InsertData()
    Dim dbConnection As New ADODB.Connection
    Dim anError As ADODB.error
```

10. The next statement is to define the connection string. One of two nonobvious parameters is the Provider, which defines the method of connection to the database, and in this instance you are using the SQL Server–specific OLEDB data provider. The final parameter defines that you are using Windows authentication.

```
sConnString = "Provider=SQLOLEDB;" + _
    "server=FAT-BELLY-Sony\APRESS_DEV1;" + _
    "database=ApressFinancial;Integrated Security=sspi"
```

11. The default for VBA code is that you don't need to define a variable before using it.

12. Now that you have your connection string defined, open the connection between the VBA code and SQL Server.

```
dbConnection.Open (sConnString)
```

13. The next step builds up the SQL to execute. This is achieved by building up a string containing the stored procedure and each parameter.

```
sSQL = "CustomerDetails.apf_InsertCustomer "
sSQL = sSQL + "@CustTitle=" + IIf(Len(Trim(Str(Range("B1").Value)) > 0) _
    And Range("B1").Value <> Empty, Str(Range("B1").Value), "NULL")
sSQL = sSQL + ", @FirstName=" + IIf(Len(Trim(Range("B2").Value) > 0) _
    And Range("B2").Value <> Empty, "'" + Range("B2").Value + "'", "NULL")
sSQL = sSQL + ", @CustInitials=" + IIf(Len(Trim(Range("B3").Value) > 0) _
    And Range("B3").Value <> Empty, "'" + Range("B3").Value + "'", "NULL")
sSQL = sSQL + ", @LastName=" + IIf(Len(Trim(Range("B4").Value) > 0) _
    And Range("B4").Value <> Empty, "'" + Range("B4").Value + "'", "NULL")
sSQL = sSQL + ", @AddressLine1=" + IIf(Len(Trim(Range("B5").Value) > 0) _
    And Range("B5").Value <> Empty, "'" + Range("B5").Value + "'", "NULL")
sSQL = sSQL + ", @AddressLine2=" + IIf(Len(Trim(Range("B6").Value) > 0) _
    And Range("B6").Value <> Empty, "'" + Range("B6").Value + "'", "NULL")
sSQL = sSQL + ", @AddressLine3=" + IIf(Len(Trim(Range("B7").Value) > 0) _
    And Range("B7").Value <> Empty, "'" + Range("B7").Value + "'", "NULL")
sSQL = sSQL + ", @TownOrCity=" + IIf(Len(Trim(Str(Range("B8").Value)) > 0) _
    And Range("B8").Value <> Empty, Str(Range("B8").Value), "NULL")
sSQL = sSQL + ", @ZipCode=" + IIf(Len(Trim(Range("B9").Value) > 0) _
    And Range("B9").Value <> Empty, "'" + Range("B9").Value + "'", "NULL")
sSQL = sSQL + ", @USState=" + IIf(Len(Trim(Str(Range("B10").Value)) > 0) _
    And Range("B10").Value <> Empty, Str(Range("B10").Value), "NULL")
sSQL = sSQL + ", @AccountTypeId=" + IIf(Len(Trim(Str(Range("B11").Value)) > 0) _
    And Range("B11").Value <> Empty, Str(Range("B11").Value), "NULL")
sSQL = sSQL + ", @ClearedBalance=0"
```

14. A new line in VB/VBA is generated by the use of an underscore.

15. It is now possible to execute the SQL to insert the new customer:

```
dbConnection.Execute (sSQL)
```

16. Once the code has been executed, it will either succeed or fail. A failure could be that a parameter is incorrectly named, the stored procedure doesn't exist, or the account running the query does not have the permissions. If an error has occurred, then the Errors collection will be populated and you can inspect the collection count.

```
If dbConnection.Errors.Count > 0 Then
```

17. Any errors come in a collection, and to navigate a collection, you need to use a For Each. Any errors found will be printed out to the Immediate window for you to inspect. Close the loop, close the If, and close the subroutine.

```
        For Each anError In dbConnection.Errors
            Debug.Print ("An error has occurred executing the following ")
            Debug.Print (sSQL)
            Debug.Print ("The error is...")
            Debug.Print (anError.Description)
        Next
    Else
        Debug.Print ("Record inserted")
    End If
End Sub
```

18. To see any output from the routine, whether it is the errors or that the record has been successfully entered, you need to have the Immediate window displayed, which is not displayed by default. This is remedied by selecting from the menu in the VB Editor, View ➤ Immediate Window, as shown in Figure 19-23.

Figure 19-23. *Displaying the Immediate window within the VB Editor*

19. Finally it's time to run the code. The two requirements that enable you to avoid problems with the code used here are to ensure that the Excel sheet that has the data to insert has the focus and that the routine in the VB Editor has focus. Within the VB Editor, you should have the standard toolbar, and there is a Run icon that looks the same as the Execute button in SSMS. It is highlighted in Figure 19-24. Click Run or press F5.

Run Sub/UserForm (F5)

Figure 19-24. *Run button*

20. Providing you have no errors, you should see that the record is inserted, as shown in Figure 19-25. Any errors would be displayed in the same window.

Immediate

```
Record inserted
```

Figure 19-25. *A successful insertion of a new customer*

21. One area where you may have problems is a typing error within the data in Figure 19-17 causing a Type Mismatch error.

These are two of the most common methods of working with data in Excel. You will find many jobs that look for Excel VBA, and some of these will look for SQL Server access. My experience is that this is a good set of skills to have under your belt, and using Excel via the Developer ribbon is a quick method as a developer to get data out to your users that they can then pivot.

■ **Caution** Always keep in mind that, although there is a link between the VBA code and Excel sheet, the VB Editor is a different IDE to Excel and therefore all code needs to be saved in the VB Editor. Saving the Excel sheet will *not* save your VBA code.

Excel is a good tool, and you have seen how simple it is to work with SQL Server. All other development tools are just as straightforward to connect to SQL Server. The next tool you will look at is Visual Studio using VB.NET and C#.

Visual Studio

Although you can use Notepad or a third-party tool, the best way to develop a .NET solution is by using Visual Studio or Visual Studio Express. Visual Studio full version (Professional and upward) comes with extra functionality over the Express edition, as you would expect, but the Express edition is more than ample to get you started. Before working with the examples, you can either download the relevant Express edition language of choice or follow the examples, or if you have the full paid edition, you can set up the environment to replicate the development language you will use most.

You can follow and work the examples using any edition. However, if you have the full edition, then when you install you will be asked which language you wish to set Visual Studio to. I have the full edition, and this is what is demonstrated within the examples; my language of choice is C#. This means that when Visual Studio starts and you use it for new projects, the templates shown by default will be for Visual C#, as shown in Figure 19-26. If you download the Express Edition, then you will want the Express Edition for Windows Desktop.

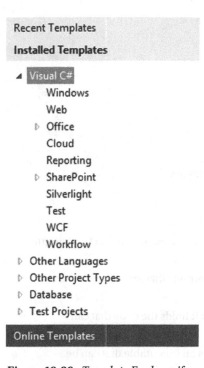

Figure 19-26. *Template Explorer if you have chosen the Visual C# setup at install time*

■ **Note** At the time of writing the book, Visual Studio 2010 Professional was used.

If you have the Express edition, then things are a bit simpler. The number of templates is fewer, and the number of default project types that can be built is fewer as the Express Editions are built for specific areas of development to make them lightweight. Figure 19-27 shows the page that will be displayed when using Visual C# and you are creating a new project (as you will see within the examples).

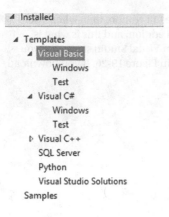

Figure 19-27. *Visual C# Express new project template options*

Before I take you through some code, there is some terminology to go through first.

Terminology

This section has some of the basic terminology and what it means for .NET. This isn't a full list, and in fact it is quite limited, but these are terms that are good to know for the following examples.

- *Class*: A construct that allows you to create an object or reference methods that are logically linked

- *Module*: An object similar to a class but more restricted than a class; it holds the code that can be executed to achieve a goal.

- *.NET libraries*: A combination of one or more classes that are built as an executable that can be used to extend functionality of another executable

- *Imports (VB.NET)/using (C#)*: Statements commonly known as a namespace; they are directives used in VB.NET or C# programs, respectively, to import a .NET reference library to be used in that class. It works as a "code shortcut" so that you don't have to qualify it each time you want to use something from it.

■ **Note** As readers may read just the section on the technology they want to use, you may see some information repeated in each section.

VB.NET

The first language within Visual Studio that you will explore is VB.NET. In this example, you will build a console application that will execute a stored procedure with a parameter as input. A console application is one that runs and outputs information in a command prompt.

```
┌─────────────────────────────────────────────────────────────────────┐
│         TRY IT OUT: RUNNING A PARAMETERIZED STORED PROCEDURE         │
│                            USING VB.NET                              │
└─────────────────────────────────────────────────────────────────────┘
```

1. Start Visual Studio, and from the menu select File ➤ New ➤ Project, or from Visual Basic Express select New Project from the Start page.

2. From the New Project dialog, ensure the Visual Basic templates node in the Installed Templates explorer is expanded, and select Windows if you are using Visual Studio. From the list of templates in any Visual Studio version, select Console Application, as shown in Figure 19-28 (taken from Visual Studio Professional). You may find your Installed Templates slightly differ depending on the language chosen while installing Visual Studio, and they will differ in the Express edition, but the Console Application will be there.

Figure 19-28. *Selecting Visual Basic Console Application*

3. Give the solution a name, in this instance `ReturnAValue`, and navigate to a location that you want to hold your code. The solution name will prepopulate with the value in the Name text box; leave it as it is. You should have at the bottom of your New Project dialog the values as shown in Figure 19-29. Click OK.

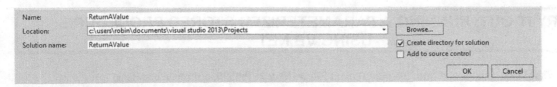

Figure 19-29. *Naming the Visual Basic Application*

4. After a moment, Visual Studio should look like Figure 19-30 no matter what edition you use. The large screen on the left is the code window, and the explorer on the right is Solution Explorer, detailing the contents of your Visual Studio solution.

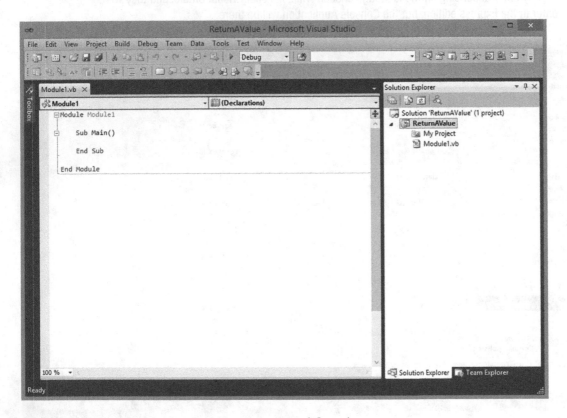

Figure 19-30. *Visual Studio detailing the code for the* `Module1.vb`

5. It is time to add the directives, mentioned earlier, to the code to qualify code used for the access. Add the `System.Data` and `System.Data.SqlClient` namespaces into the code in the `Module1.vb`. Both of these namespaces live in the `System.Data` library. The code at the start of `Module1.vb` should now look like Figure 19-31.

Figure 19-31. *Importing the SqlClient*

6. After the SqlClient is imported, within the main subroutine you will test that one and only one parameter is passed to your application. If this is not the case, then an error will be printed to the console.

```
Imports System.Data.SqlClient
Module Module1
    Sub Main(ByVal args() As String)
        If args.Length <> 1 Then
            Console.WriteLine("Invalid arguments. You only need 1 argument")
            Return
        End If
```

7. The Sub statement defines a subroutine, which is a set of commands and statements that perform a set of actions. The information between the curved brackets is known as parameters. The Sub Main() in the following code is defined as the entry point for your program and is the first line of code that will be executed. Using args() as the parameter indicates that parameters can be passed into your program.

8. The next line of code will define a variable as a string, and the string will be the connection details to SQL Server. The connection string will contain the name of the server, instance, database, and that you are using Windows authentication.

```
Dim connectionString As String = _
        "Server=FAT-BELLY-Sony\APRESS_DEV1;" + _
        "Database=ApressFinancial;Trusted_Connection=True;"
```

9. If you want to use SQL Server authentication, then the connection string would be something like the following with your own User and Pwd:

```
Dim connectionString As String = __
        "Server=FAT-BELLY-Sony\APRESS_DEV1;" + _
        "Database=ApressFinancial;Trusted_Connection=False;" + _
        "User=MySQLServerLogin;Pwd=T3st!t;"
```

10. You now need to define a variable that will create and hold the connection object that has the connection details within it. The connection is created but has not been opened at this point.

```
Dim databaseConnection As SqlConnection =
        New SqlConnection(connectionString)
```

11. It is now possible to open the connection between your code and the database so that you can execute some T-SQL.

```
databaseConnection.Open()
```

12. To execute code, you need to create a variable that will hold an SQL command object. The command object will hold the text to execute, which in this case is the parameter passed into your program. The SQL command object also needs to know which connection object to use as you could have multiple connections to different servers open.

```
Dim tsqlCommand = New _
        SqlCommand(args(0), databaseConnection)
```

13. A command object could be one of three different types: plain text, the name of a table, or a stored procedure. In this instance, although you are executing a stored procedure, it could also be plain text that is passed in.

```
tsqlCommand.CommandType = CommandType.Text
```

14. The SQL code can now be executed and the value returned. By using the ExecuteScalar method, you are indicating to the SqlClient ADO.NET driver that you are interested only in the first value returned. If the stored procedure returned more than one column of information, all other columns would be ignored. The returned value is placed into a variable. As you don't know the type of data returned, even a NULL value, place it into an Object data type, which can be tested and transposed as required.

```
Dim returnedValue As Object = tsqlCommand.ExecuteScalar()
```

15. The first test is to see if the value returned is a NULL value. If it is, then convert the value to a string so that it can be displayed.

```
If IsDBNull(returnedValue) Then
    returnedValue = "NULL"
End If
```

16. You can now output the value to the command prompt console with instructions on how to finish execution by pressing the Enter key.

```
Console.WriteLine("The returned value is " + returnedValue.ToString())
Console.WriteLine("Press <ENTER> to continue")
Console.ReadLine()
```

17. Once you are finished, you close the connection. For efficiency, you can move the following code to be placed immediately after the code in point 12.

```
databaseConnection.Close()
```

18. The final lines of code close the subroutine and the module. The code is now complete.

```
    End Sub
End Module
```

19. While testing and debugging the code within Visual Studio, it is possible to define parameters to be passed in at the time of execution. This is achieved by selecting the Project menu and then the name of the project, which in this case is ReturnAValue Properties…, as shown in Figure 19-32.

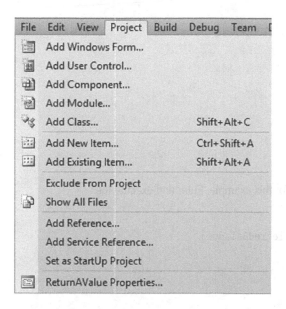

Figure 19-32. *Navigate to the project properties*

20. You are now presented with a screen with all of the properties of the project. You need to move to the Debug tab, as shown in Figure 19-33. You will also see in the figure a stored procedure and value, which is the parameter to the stored procedure, in the Command Line Arguments text box. This is the value that will be passed in to the args() parameter in the main subroutine. As there is only one parameter, you need to surround the information with double quotation marks. Once you are happy, click OK.

Application	Configuration:	Active (Debug)	⌄	Platform:	Active (x86)	⌄
Compile						
Debug*	**Start Action**					
References	⦿ Start project					
Resources	○ Start external program:					...
Services	○ Start browser with URL:					
Settings	**Start Options**					
Signing	Command line arguments:	"CustomerDetails.apf_CustClearedBalance 2"				
My Extensions						
Security						
Publish	Working directory:					...
	☐ Use remote machine					

Figure 19-33. *Project properties with the command line entered*

21. The command-line arguments would be as follows:

    ```
    "CustomerDetails.apf_CustClearedBalance 2"
    ```

22. There is a stored procedure to add to ApressFinancial for this example. Enter and execute the following code:

    ```
    CREATE PROCEDURE [CustomerDetails].[apf_CustClearedBalance]
        @CustomerId int
    AS

    BEGIN

    SELECT ClearedBalance
      FROM CustomerDetails.Customers
     WHERE CustomerId = @CustomerId

    END
    ```

23. You can now execute your code by pressing F5. A command prompt should be displayed, the stored procedure executed, and the cleared balance returned, as shown in Figure 19-34.

Figure 19-34. Running the code and displaying the returned value

24. What has happened is that Visual Studio has executed your program, and because you are outputting information to the console via the `Console.WriteLine` statement, Visual Studio will create a command-line console and output the information you have requested. What follows is an alternative execution method.

25. You can also execute your code outside of Visual Studio. You can do with this one of several methods, but I will show you how to run the code from a command prompt. Within Windows 7, click the Windows Start button. Then in the text box that is displayed above the Start button, type **cmd** and press Enter as shown in Figure 19-35, or in Windows 8 find the Command Prompt app.

Figure 19-35. Starting the command prompt

26. From the command prompt, you can either run the code or navigate to where the code was compiled by Visual Studio. When building the solution, I gave you the name of the solution, and then the project. The compiled code is then placed in the `bin` subfolder and then either the `Release` or `Debug` subfolder. The following code will change the directory to my `Debug` folder location.

```
Cd C:\Users\Robin\Documents\Visual Studio 2010\Projects\ReturnAValue\ReturnAValue\bin\Debug
```

27. You can now run the executable with the parameter as before, as shown in the following code.

```
ReturnAValue.exe "CustomerDetails.apf_CustClearedBalance 2"
```

28. Figure 19-36 shows the change of directory, then the code being executed, and finally the result displayed.

```
Microsoft Windows [Version 6.3.9600]
(c) 2013 Microsoft Corporation. All rights reserved.

C:\Users\Robin>cd C:\Users\Robin\Documents\Visual Studio 2010\Projects\ReturnAValue\ReturnAValue\bin\Debug

C:\Users\Robin\Documents\Visual Studio 2010\Projects\ReturnAValue\ReturnAValue\bin\Debug>ReturnAValue.exe "CustomerDetai
ls.apf_CustClearedBalance 2"
The returned value is 337.9700
Press <ENTER> to continue
```

Figure 19-36. *Running the code external to Visual Studio*

29. Press the Enter key to complete the execution.

And that's your first VB.NET application complete.

You may still be a little daunted by the foregoing code, but I hope that is not the case. The main points to take away are how to connect to SQL Server and to execute a stored procedure and return a value. If you have found this interesting, then take a look at C#, which is next.

C#

Working with C# has similarities with working with VB.NET, in that you are using Visual Studio, and the logic for achieving the results is the same. It is purely the syntax that differs, at least in the case of our example. Don't be fooled, though, into thinking that for more complex development this statement is true for all code, as it is not. There are differences between the two languages when you are developing more intricate code, but I have avoided this by keeping the examples simple.

Many VB.NET developers are those that have come from VBA or Visual Basic 6, but with C#, developers will have many different backgrounds such as Java, C++, and Delphi, as well as any of the foregoing.

In the following example, you will use Visual Studio to build a C# console application that will run a parameterized stored procedure called CustomerDetails.apf_CustBalance.

TRY IT OUT: RUNNING A PARAMETERIZED QUERY USING C#

1. Start Visual Studio, and from the menu select File ➤ New ➤ Project.

2. From the New Project dialog, ensure the Visual C# templates node in the Installed Templates explorer is expanded, and select Windows. From the list of Templates, select Console Application, as shown in Figure 19-37. You may find your Installed Templates slightly differ depending on the language chosen while installing Visual Studio.

Figure 19-37. *Selecting Visual C# Console Application*

3. Give the solution a name, in this instance `RunAParameterizedStoredProcedure`, and navigate to a location that you want to hold your code. The solution name will prepopulate with the value in the Name text box; leave it as it is. You should have at the bottom of your New Project dialog the values similar to those as shown in Figure 19-38. Click OK.

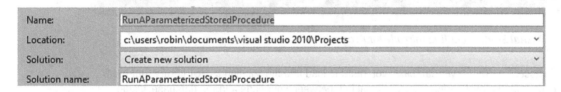

Figure 19-38. *Giving the application a name*

4. After a moment, Visual Studio should look like Figure 19-39. You will have an explorer on the left, called Toolbox, which is unpinned and therefore minimized. The middle screen is the code window, and the explorer on the right is Solution Explorer, detailing the contents of your Visual Studio solution.

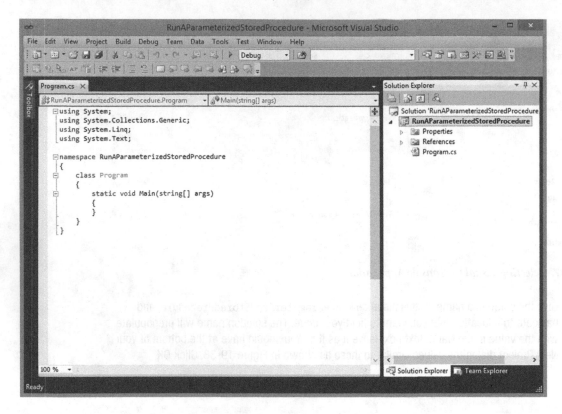

Figure 19-39. *Visual Studio detailing the code for* `Program.cs`

5. To access a SQL Server database, you need to load into the solution a .NET library that has code built that will perform the low-level link between your code and the database. Visual Studio will have completed this automatically with the type of project, and you can check this in the References node in Solution Explorer, which you can expand as shown in Figure 19-40.

Figure 19-40. Visual Studio detailing the code for `Program.cs`

6. It is time to bring in the directives to the code to qualify code used for the access. Add the `System.Data` and `System.Data.SqlClient` namespaces into the code in `Program.cs`. Both of these namespaces live in the `System.Data` library. The code at the start of `Program.cs` should now look like Figure 19-41.

```
Program.cs ×
RunAParameterizedStoredProcedure.Program
using System;
using System.Collections.Generic;
using System.Linq;
using System.Text;
using System.Data;
using System.Data.SqlClient;

namespace RunAParameterizedStoredProcedure
{
    class Program
    {
        static void Main(string[] args)
        {
```

Figure 19-41. The full set of namespaces imported

7. There are three variables that will be used to hold the returned values from the stored procedure. Good practice is to define them at the top of your code. In this instance, they are required only within the `Main` method, and so they will be defined there. The code will now look like the following:

```
using System;
using System.Collections.Generic;
using System.Linq;
using System.Text;
using System.Data;
using System.Data.SqlClient;

namespace RunAParameterizedStoredProcedure
{
    class Program
    {
        static void Main(string[] args)
        {
            string clearedBalance = "";
            string unClearedBalance = "";
            string returnValue = "";
```

8. The next stage is to define a variable with the connection details to the SQL Server database. The following connection details are for a Windows authentication. For the `Server` parameter, you have to define the server and the instance.

```
try
{
    string connectionString = @"Server=FAT-BELLY-Sony\APRESS_DEV1;" +
                    "Database=ApressFinancial;Trusted_Connection=True;";
```

9. The @ sign is a C# indicator that allows \ to be included in the string. A \ in C# is an escape character, and without the @ sign then you would need to place double \\ for a single \ to exist in the string.

10. Now that you have the connection string, you can create a new database connection that will link your application to SQL Server using the connection settings. Like VB.NET, the connection is not yet open at this point.

```
SqlConnection databaseConnection = new SqlConnection(connectionString);
```

11. You can now open the connection between the two.

```
databaseConnection.Open();
```

12. Once the connection is open, you can execute the T-SQL code. In this instance, it will be the
CustomerDetails.apf_CustBalance stored procedure.

```
            SqlCommand tsqlCommand = new
SqlCommand("CustomerDetails.apf_CustBalance",databaseConnection);
```

13. This time, unlike the VB.NET example, you will explicitly define the command as a stored
procedure, as you want to inspect the return value parameter, which is the first parameter.

```
tsqlCommand.CommandType = CommandType.StoredProcedure;
tsqlCommand.Parameters.Add("ReturnValue", SqlDbType.Int);
tsqlCommand.Parameters[0].Direction = ParameterDirection.ReturnValue;
```

14. The second parameter is the customer ID, which is an input parameter.

```
tsqlCommand.Parameters.Add("@CustomerId", SqlDbType.Int);
tsqlCommand.Parameters[1].Direction = ParameterDirection.Input;
tsqlCommand.Parameters[1].Value = 2;
```

15. The stored procedure has two output parameters, one for the cleared balance and one for the
uncleared balance. These are defined next.

```
tsqlCommand.Parameters.Add("@ClearedBalance", SqlDbType.Money);
tsqlCommand.Parameters[2].Direction = ParameterDirection.Output;
tsqlCommand.Parameters.Add("@UnclearedBalance", SqlDbType.Money);
tsqlCommand.Parameters[3].Direction = ParameterDirection.Output;
```

16. As no data that form a result set are returned from the query, only parameter values, you
would execute the stored procedure as a nonquery.

```
tsqlCommand.ExecuteNonQuery();
```

17. Once the code is executed, you can inspect the relevant parameters to retrieve the returned
values.

```
            clearedBalance = tsqlCommand.Parameters[2].Value ==
DBNull.Value ? "NULL" : tsqlCommand.Parameters[2].Value.ToString();
            unClearedBalance = tsqlCommand.Parameters[3].Value ==
DBNull.Value ? "NULL" : tsqlCommand.Parameters[3].Value.ToString();
            returnValue = tsqlCommand.Parameters[0].Value ==
DBNull.Value ? "NULL" : tsqlCommand.Parameters[0].Value.ToString();
```

18. It is now possible to close the connection as the values are held in local variables.

```
databaseConnection.Close();
```

19. You then have some error handling code but also the ability to display the returned values.

```
}
catch (Exception exc)
{
    Console.WriteLine("Problems running the T-SQL" + exc.Message);
}
Console.WriteLine("The return values are " +
    "Cleared Balance = " + clearedBalance +
    " Uncleared Balance = " + unClearedBalance +
    " Returned Value = " + returnValue);
```

20. The final lines of code will hold the command prompt screen open until the Enter key is pressed.

```
Console.WriteLine("Press <ENTER> to finish....");
Console.ReadLine();
```

21. If you now press F5, this will execute the code. A command prompt should be displayed with the results from Customer ID 2, as shown in Figure 19-42.

Figure 19-42. *The code executed and a command prompt displayed*

22. You can achieve the same by executing the compiled exe. The location is based on the folder location, the solution, and the project name when you created the project at the start of the exercise.

```
C:\Users\Robin\Documents\Visual Studio 2010\Projects\RunAParameterizedStoredProcedure\
RunAParameterizedStoredProcedure\bin\Debug\RunAParameterizedStoredProcedure.exe
```

So that's Visual Studio with VB.NET and C# examples completed. Visual Studio and the .NET languages are the best tools and environments to work with SQL Server as you might expect, as they are Microsoft technologies. However, you can use non-Microsoft technologies, and in the next section you will see how another extremely popular development language can be used via Java.

Java

Java was one of the languages used as a base when Microsoft came to develop C# and is used quite widely for server-side development within firms, especially financial firms. However, Java is more commonly connected to Oracle and Sybase rather than SQL Server in my experience, but the combination of Java to SQL Server does exist. Part of the reason was that connecting to SQL Server from Java had no specific driver and had to use a general ODBC driver. This led to several issues, and therefore the take-up was low.

Connecting to a SQL Server database can be achieved through a Java ODBC connection, which over time has been improved, or you can connect through the Microsoft driver known as SQLJDBC. = This will need to be downloaded from Microsoft and extracted for this section of the chapter. If you are connecting via Windows authentication, as demonstrated in the example, you will also require an authorization library. This will also be part of the demonstration in the following example.

■ **Tip** I will have on my web site links to the locations to download the latest software.

Java and C# have a number of similarities, such as the use of the semicolon as an end-of-line delimiter, the use of namespaces known as packages in Java, the syntax, and statement structures, allowing the learning curve between C# and Java to be less than if you switched to other languages. However, one difference between these two languages surrounds accessing and retrieving data. Sadly all data retrieved is returned as a record set, and therefore you have to read around the record set even to retrieve a scalar value.

Like .NET you can use an integrated development environment to build your solutions, or you can use Notepad and a command-line prompt to compile and run your code. There are several IDEs around, such as NetBeans, but in this book I will use Eclipse.

The following example will connect to the ApressFinancial database, call a new stored procedure called CustomerDetails.apf_CustClearedBalance, which accepts the customer ID as an input parameter, and return the cleared balance as a scalar value. To run this example, you need to have done the following:

- Downloaded and installed a Java runtime

- Downloaded and extracted Eclipse

- Downloaded and extracted the SQLJDBC driver

TRY IT OUT: RETURNING A SCALAR VALUE USING JAVA WITH ECLIPSE

1. First of all, the stored procedure to return a scalar value needs to be built, if you have not already built the stored procedure when looking at the examples for other development languages in this chapter. Enter and execute the following code in SQL Server Management Studio.

```
CREATE PROCEDURE CustomerDetails.apf_CustClearedBalance
    @CustomerId int
AS
BEGIN
    SELECT ClearedBalance
      FROM CustomerDetails.Customers
     WHERE CustomerId = @CustomerId
END
```

2. Eclipse should have been downloaded and extracted somewhere on your computer. The location doesn't really matter as it is self-contained. I have a specific folder for my downloads, and within this I have my Eclipse installation, as shown in the code here. Find your location and start Eclipse.

```
C:\Users\Robin\Downloads\eclipse-standard-luna-R-win32-x86_64\eclipse\eclipse.exe
```

3. Eclipse should start and ask for the name of a workspace. This is just somewhere for the projects in your solution to be stored. The location doesn't matter, but the final folder I have called ReturnAScalarValue. The full path I used follows, and you can see in Figure 19-43 how this looks. Click OK.

```
C:\Users\Robin\Workspace\ReturnAScalarValue
```

Figure 19-43. *Defining the workspace for the Java project*

4. You are now presented with Eclipse opened and a Welcome tab, as shown in Figure 19-44. Close this tab by clicking the cross next to Welcome.

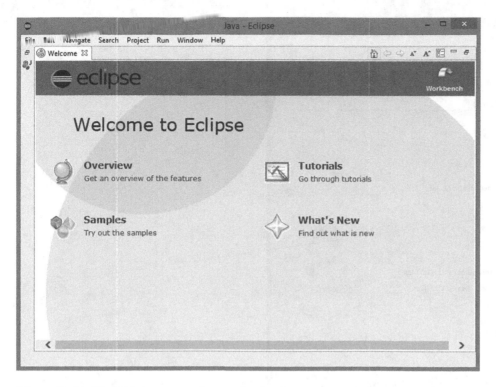

Figure 19-44. *The Welcome screen that can be closed*

5. You are now presented with an empty development environment not too dissimilar to Visual Studio and SQL Server Management Studio. At the moment, you have an empty workspace and therefore you need to create a Java project to build the example. From the menu, select File ➤ New ➤ Java Project, as demonstrated in Figure 19-45.

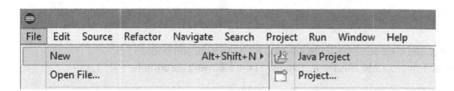

Figure 19-45. *Creating a new Java project*

6. This will start a new Java project wizard, where you need to enter a project name and select the Java Runtime Engine (JRE) to use. I have used the same name as the workspace, but this is not mandatory. The example also uses the 1.7 JRE version. The name and the default options, which are the options you should use, are shown in Figure 19-46. Click Next.

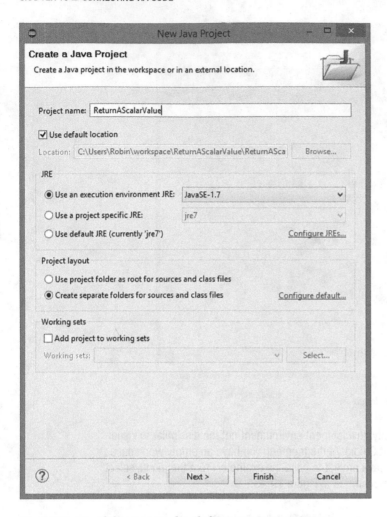

Figure 19-46. *Ability to enter details for a new Java project*

7. You can develop for earlier and later versions. If you develop for a Java version prior to 1.5, be sure you use the version-appropriate JAR file mentioned in the following paragraph. Click Next.

8. The next stage of the wizard is to inform Eclipse of other projects you want to use and the order of how those projects would be built, but for this example you need to let Eclipse know of any external libraries to use when compiling the code. If you are using a JRE of 1.5 or above, then you would need to add `sqljdbc4.jar` in the next step, otherwise it will be `sqljdbc.jar`. You will have downloaded and extracted these earlier.

9. To add the relevant jar, select the Libraries tab and click Add External JARs..., navigate to where `sqljdbc4.jar` exists, select it, and click OK. It should now be loaded and visible, as shown in Figure 19-47. Click Finish.

Figure 19-47. *Adding the SQL JDBC library*

10. You now have an Eclipse IDE with a few items in Package Explorer, which is similar to Visual Studio Solution Explorer. You now need to add a class for your program code. From the project ReturnAScalarValue in Package Explorer, right-click, select New, and then Select Class, as shown in Figure 19-48.

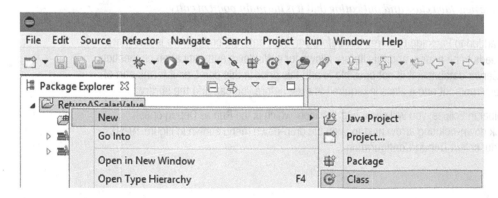

Figure 19-48. *Selecting the option to create a new class*

11. You are now presented with the New Java Class window. The source folder will remain the same, and the package will remain blank. In the Name field, name the class "main" as this is the main program. You can call it by a different name if you wish, but you should select the first option from the check boxes within "Which method stubs would you like to create?". The third option should already be selected. Figure 19-49 shows the class I generated. When you are happy, click Finish.

Figure 19-49. *Detailing the new Java class and indicating that it is the main point of entry*

12. A new file is added to Package Explorer, but before you start entering code, there is one more library that needs to be added, and this library allows for a Windows authentication connection to your SQL Server database. It is not possible to add this prior to this point, as it forms part of the runtime environment and a class is required to exist before you can add the library.

13. From the toolbar in Eclipse, you will see a bug-like icon, which is the Run as Debug option. Click the black down-pointing arrow next to open the drop-down menu shown in Figure 19-50. From the menu, select Debug Configuration...

Figure 19-50. *Creating the debug configuration*

14. You will now see a screen where you can define configuration details for your package. As you are building a Java application, either highlight Java Application from the options on the left and click the New Icon from the toolbar above the options, as shown in Figure 19-51, or just double-click the Java Application option. You will now have a debug configuration for your package.

Figure 19-51. *Defining that the debug configuration is a Java application*

15. Within the configuration, you can define runtime arguments. You can also define a runtime change to your CLASSPATH within Windows if you need Eclipse at runtime to find libraries external to Eclipse. For this package, you need to select the Arguments tab and add the following path to the virtual machine (VM) arguments, as shown in Figure 19-52, which is the path where sql_auth.dll resides. This .dll is part of the SQLJDBC download. Click Apply and then click Close.

```
-Djava.library.path=C:\Users\Robin\Downloads\JDBCDriver\sqljdbc_4.0\enu\auth\x64
```

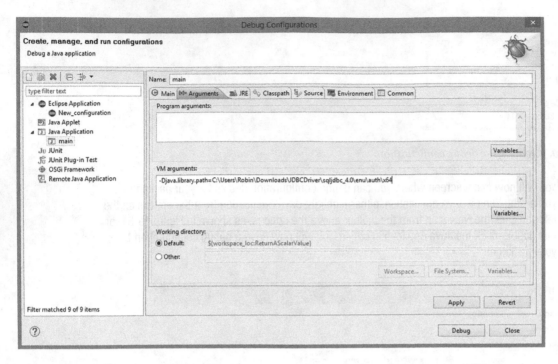

Figure 19-52. *Detailing the virtual machine arguments for the Windows authentication* .dll

■ **Note** A virtual machine (VM) is a platform-independent execution environment that is used to run your Java code.

16. You are now ready to start entering the code for the application. Eclipse should look something like Figure 19-53, with the main.java class open, ready for coding.

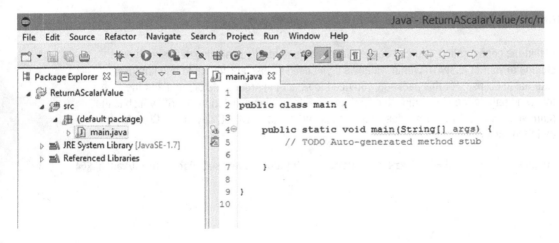

Figure 19-53. *The start of your Java code*

17. The first line of code will be inserted as the first line prior to the public class main line. The import statement is used to import a Java package into your class, similar to using an import in .NET. This will import the SQL package that is used to build the SQL code statements.

```
import java.sql.*;
```

18. Within the main class, you will define three variables for the returned data, the database connection, and the SQL to execute. These variables are added to the main Java class and the main() method.

```
public class main {
    /**
     * @param args
     */
    public static void main(String[] args) {
        // TODO Auto-generated method stub

        ResultSet returnedData = null;
        Connection databaseConnection = null;
        PreparedStatement prepStatement = null;
```

19. The main() method is the default way to start a Java application.

20. The code used to access and work with SQL Server is surrounded with a try...catch block. After this is defined, you define your connection string to your SQL Server, the instance, the database, and that you are using Windows authentication. The first option defines that JRE should use the SQL Server JDBC driver.

```
try {
String connString = "jdbc:sqlserver://FAT-BELLY-Sony\\" +
    "APRESS_DEV1;databaseName=ApressFinancial;" +
    "integratedSecurity=true";
```

21. Moving to the next line, you are required to inform the JRE to dynamically load the JDBC driver at runtime. This is the sqljdbc4.jar.

```
Class.forName("com.microsoft.sqlserver.jdbc.SQLServerDriver");
```

22. The dot notation name is the full package name for the driver. Once you start building larger Java applications, you will develop a package hierarchy, which traditionally but not mandatorily will start with com, then your organization, the top-level package, and then down through the project hierarchy.

23. The next step is to create a database connection using the connection string defined in step 15.

```
databaseConnection = DriverManager.getConnection(connString);
```

24. You now define the stored procedure to execute with a ? at the end for the input parameter. If you had more than one parameter, you would separate each parameter with a comma.

```
String sqlToExecute = "CustomerDetails.apf_CustClearedBalance ?";
```

25. It is possible to execute code against a database using one of two methods. For this example, I will use the prepareStatement method against the connection, which takes the SQL and prepares it for parameters and then to execute against SQL Server.

```
prepStatement = databaseConnection.prepareStatement(sqlToExecute);
```

26. Now that you have the prepared statement built, you can define the values for the parameters. You would use one of several methods, depending on the data type to pass across. As CustomerId is an integer, you need to use setInt and then define the parameter number, in this case 1, and then the value. I have chosen to output the value from CustomerId 2.

```
prepStatement.setInt(1, 2);
```

27. Once the parameters are defined, you can execute the query against the database.

```
returnedData = prepStatement.executeQuery();
```

28. If you recall, Java returns either no data or a data record set of data. The next steps are to loop around the data, output the returned value, and print the result to the console. Any errors will be caught in the catch. The final actions are to clean up and to remove the memory used for the record set, the prepared SQL, and finally the connection.

```
while (returnedData.next()) {
    System.out.println("The return value was " + returnedData.getString(1));
}
}
catch (Exception e) {
    e.printStackTrace();
}
finally {
    if (returnedData != null)
    try {
        returnedData.close();
    }
    catch(Exception e) {}

    if (prepStatement != null)
    try {
        prepStatement.close();
    }
```

```
        catch(Exception e) {}
        if (databaseConnection != null)
        try {
            databaseConnection.close();
        }
        catch(Exception e) {}
    }
    }
    }
```

29. Your code is now complete, and all the options to execute the code have been defined. You can now step through your code by clicking the Debug icon you saw earlier at the start of the exercise, which will start the main class. A dialog will appear saying you will be switching modes. Click OK. Your code should now run through, and you will see Eclipse now looking like Figure 19-54, with the result of the stored procedure call in the Console window.

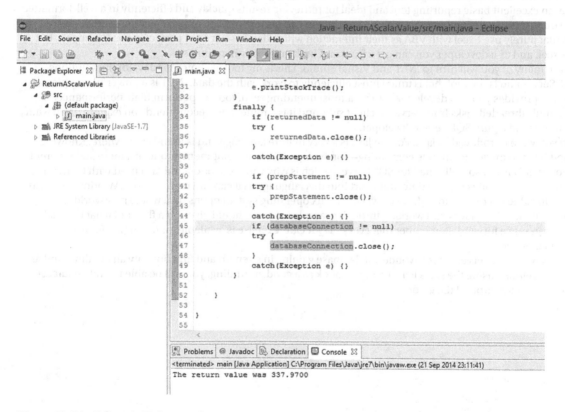

Figure 19-54. Eclipse in Debug mode

Eclipse is now in Debug mode, as indicated in the top right of the screenshot, where the Debug toolbar button is highlighted. You can switch back to Java mode by clicking the toolbar button next to Debug. You can also put breakpoints in the bar to the left of the code and step through the code as you can with Visual Studio.

As you will have noticed, there is a great deal of similarity between Java with Eclipse and either VB.NET or C# with Visual Studio. There are differences, of course, but there are a lot of similarities, and therefore if you know one technology, picking up the other from a "server side" of development is not difficult.

■ **Note** Client-side development differs greatly between Java and .NET, and I believe .NET is by far the superior tool to use.

Summary

So you are now at the end of the book and should be feeling confident in working with SQL Server from installation through developing for it. This chapter saw the final piece of the jigsaw, where you could now connect and execute code against a SQL Server database from one of several different languages and tools.

Excel is an excellent basic reporting tool and ideal for retrieving results quickly and efficiently in a well-formatted manner to your users. If you combine this with VBA code, you can perform a huge range of actions, and there are companies that purely use Excel with VBA as their interaction with a database. It's not perfect in some respects, but users love Excel, and as a developer you can get a front end built and ready in minutes.

However, many of you will turn to .NET and Visual Studio. This is my tool of choice for developing solutions against SQL Server and is the tool that is tuned most efficiently to work with the data. .NET is a powerful complex framework that provides you as a developer with an almost unending set of tools to perform high-performance, low-latency, multithreaded tasks from server to client side, and it is a route that I recommend you explore if you want to become more than a pure SQL Server developer.

Finally you were introduced to Java. For me Java is a very mature language and is found everywhere. Knowing Java is a good basis to move into mobile computing—for example, game development or one of a thousand different avenues. However, it is not so well tuned for SQL Server, which is why you more often find Java used with Oracle or Sybase. However, Microsoft is putting time and effort into this language as it can run on more than Windows, such as Linux, and being able to connect to SQL Server via the Linux operating system opens up a whole new world.

Taking all of these languages and working through examples of each should give you a flavor of what is possible and how you can move forward. Remember that every "Try It Out" exercise is available for download for each development language.

Good luck with SQL Server—it is a wonderful database gaining in strength and functionality all the time, and as a SQL Server developer, using the skills learned in this book as a good grounding, you will be able to build database solutions that can reach around the globe.

Index